T0203560

Autonomous Driving and Advanced Driver-Assistance Systems (ADAS)

Chapman & Hall/CRC Artificial Intelligence and Robotics Series

Series Editor: Roman V. Yampolskiy

Artificial Intelligence Safety and Security
Roman V. Yampolskiy

Artificial Intelligence for Autonomous Networks
Mazin Gilbert

Virtual Humans
David Burden, Maggi Savin-Baden

Deep Neural Networks
WASD Neuronet Models, Algorithms, and Applications
Yunong Zhang, Dechao Chen, Chengxu Ye

Introduction to Self-Driving Vehicle Technology
Hanky Sjafrie

Digital Afterlife
Death Matters in a Digital Age
Maggi Savin-Baden, Victoria Mason-Robbie

Multi-UAV Planning and Task Allocation
Yasmina Bestaoui Sebbane

Cunning Machines
Your Pocket Guide to the World of Artificial Intelligence
Jędrzej Osiński

Autonomous Driving and Advanced Driver-Assistance Systems
Applications, Development, Legal Issues, and Testing
Edited by Lentin Joseph, Amit Kumar Mondal

Digital Afterlife and the Spiritual Realm
Maggi Savin-Baden

For more information about this series please visit: https://www.routledge.com/
Chapman--HallCRC-Artificial-Intelligence-and-Robotics-Series/book-series/ARTILRO

Autonomous Driving and Advanced Driver-Assistance Systems (ADAS)

Applications, Development, Legal Issues, and Testing

Edited by

Lentin Joseph

Amit Kumar Mondal

CRC Press
Taylor & Francis Group
Boca Raton London New York

CRC Press is an imprint of the
Taylor & Francis Group, an **informa** business

A CHAPMAN & HALL BOOK

First edition published 2022
by CRC Press
6000 Broken Sound Parkway NW, Suite 300, Boca Raton, FL 33487-2742

and by CRC Press
2 Park Square, Milton Park, Abingdon, Oxon, OX14 4RN

© 2022 selection and editorial matter, Lentin Joseph and Amit Mondal; individual chapters, the contributors

CRC Press is an imprint of Taylor & Francis Group, LLC

Library of Congress Cataloging-in-Publication Data

Names: Joseph, Lentin, editor. | Mondal, Amit Kumar, editor.
Title: Autonomous driving and advanced driver-assistance systems (ADAS) :
applications, development, legal issues, and testing / edited by Lentin
Joseph, Amit Kumar Mondal.
Description: First edition. | Boca Raton : CRC Press, [2022] | Series:
Chapman & Hall/CRC artificial intelligence and robotics series |
Includes bibliographical references and index.
Identifiers: LCCN 2021030233 | ISBN 9780367499747 (hbk) | ISBN
9780367495367 (pbk) | ISBN 9781003048381 (ebk)
Subjects: LCSH: Automated vehicles. | Driver assistance systems.
Classification: LCC TL152.8 .A868 2022 | DDC 629.2--dc23
LC record available at https://lccn.loc.gov/2021030233

ISBN: 978-0-367-49974-7 (hbk)
ISBN: 978-0-367-49536-7 (pbk)
ISBN: 978-1-003-04838-1 (ebk)

DOI: 10.1201/9781003048381

Typeset in Minion Pro
by KnowledgeWorks Global Ltd.

Contents

Preface

Advanced driver-assistance systems (ADASs) are systems in a vehicle that assist the driver in a variety of ways. The ADASs can provide important information about road traffic like signals, blockage, and closures and can suggest better routes to avoid the same. These systems can also detect any fatigue or distraction from the human driver and can alert him or her and can even take control of the vehicle from the human driver automatically. It can also perform functions like cruise control, parking, etc., without human intervention.

The objective of this book is to provide the reader with ongoing research that is relevant to the development and testing of sensor fusion, sensor placement, control algorithms, computer vision, etc., for ADASs. It describes how the current research on ADASs is developed, tested, and verified for real-time situations. With an infinite number of real-time possibilities that need to be addressed, this book provides new methods to solve the complexity of an ADAS.

There are 24 chapters organized into three parts: Section I, "Autonomous Vehicle Test and Development"; Section II, "ADAS and AV Legal Issues and Liabilities"; and Section III, "Autonomous Vehicle Applications."

- **Chapter 1** by Rick Voßwinkel et al. discusses rule-based and artificial intelligence (AI)-based decision making and (model-based and model-free) motion planning.

- **Chapter 2** by Chinmay Vilas Samak et al. focuses on self-driving technology from a control perspective and investigates the control strategies used in autonomous vehicles and advanced driver-assistance systems (ADASs) from both theoretical and practical viewpoints. The chapter provides a comparative study on bang-bang, PID, geometry, model predictive, imitation learning-based, and reinforcement learning-based control strategies.

- **Chapter 3** by Pranjal Paul and Abhishek Sharma presents SLAM with recognition and tracing of moving objects, in the context of dynamic outdoor environments. The objective of this chapter is to provide a comprehensive overview of the contemporary developments related to the navigation system, design, and safety issues for autonomous vehicle systems.

- **Chapter 4** by Sridevi M et al. focuses on the problem of unified vehicle detection, tracking, and trajectory prediction of objects around the ego vehicle, and subsequent sections explain individual tasks in detail.

- **Chapter 5** by Mrunmayee V. Daithankar et al. focuses on the vision system and video super-resolution. This chapter is a systematic look at the basics, recent developments, challenges, and scope of the vision system with video resolution as the key parameter. The motive behind exploring this area is related to image or video processing, which will benefit through from provided information and will be motivated to contribute in the same rising area.

- **Chapter 6** by Any Gupta and Ayesha Choudhary proposes a spatiotemporal incremental clustering algorithm that detects and tracks traffic lanes accurately under real-time scenarios.

- **Chapter 7** by Kishorjit Nongmeikapam et al. proposes a fast and efficient stereo vision-based simultaneous localization and mapping (SLAM) system. The major point of this chapter is the significant reduction in the computational cost and the error in the resulting trajectory, which is realized via a new scheme of feature extraction along with matching technique between any two successive frames.

- **Chapter 8** by Gayathri R et al. discusses in detail the ontology-based model for representing an indoor environment. The chapter also proposes a planning domain and definition language (PDDL) and sampling-based algorithm to improve the perception ability of mobile robots during semantic navigation.

- **Chapter 9** by Anubha Parashar et al. mentions a project in which steering control is achieved by pixel mapping using a single-front camera.

- **Chapter 10** by Mallika et al. discusses various deep learning solutions available for obstacle detection and their adapted version to improve performance.

- **Chapter 11** by Wahengbam Kanan Kumar et al. proposes a way to replace standard RGB images with a multiple channel type feature vector called the "array of processed channels (AOPC)" for improving the time in determining objects from image frames.

- **Chapter 12** by Syama R et al. proposes a game-theoretic approach of behavior prediction based on the Stackelberg game and Gaussian mixture model (GMM)-hidden Markov model (HMM) to improve behavior prediction performance in a mixed vehicle scenario.

- **Chapter 13** by Franz Wotawa et al. focuses on system testing for advanced driver-assistance systems and discusses recent testing approaches as well as challenges faced when applying these approaches to an ADAS.

- **Chapter 14** by Stefan Brandenburg discusses the state-of-the-art human factors studies in the field of vehicle automation and sorts them into four stages of human factor research challenges in automated driving.

- **Chapter 15** by Sunil Kr. Sharma et al. discusses the conceptual description of vehicle automation in the rail and road transport sector and elaborates on the role of human factors in the interaction of autonomous vehicles, human drivers, and system users.

- **Chapter 16** by Rakesh Kumar Chopra and Abhijeet Srivastava advocates the idea for strengthening cyber security laws for ADAS technology and then analyzes the existing framework under Indian laws. The chapter also provides a glimpse of the global legal scenario on this subject, mainly in the United States and India.

- **Chapter 17** by Neeta Maitre and Neeraj Hanumante discusses the criticality of the human-centric nature of ADS during its usage.

- **Chapter 18** by Sujata Bali and Shamneesh Sharma focuses on the critical analysis of crimes associated with automated driving vehicles and the priorities and the interests of the occupant of the vehicle in situations with conflicts of interest.

- **Chapter 19** by Madhusmita Mishra and Abhishek Kumar discusses cooperative ADAS challenges and legal risks.

- **Chapter 20** by Sridevi M et al. discusses various techniques available for SLAM using different sensors.

- **Chapter 21** by Ashwani Kumar Aggarwal discusses the use of wireless sensor networks and inertial navigation systems with GPS in urban environments.

- **Chapter 22** by Earnest Paul Ijjina proposes a video-based accident recognition system for cars, where dashboard cameras and deep learning techniques are used to recognize if the vehicle had an accident.

- **Chapter 23** by Ravishankar C V and Kavitha K S discusses the legal perspective of autonomous car accidents from a global perspective.

- **Chapter 24** by Apoorva Parashar et al. discusses the working of a robot in an open-pit mine condition using ADAS.

We believe that this book will be a valuable asset for ADAS developers to learn more about ADAS capabilities and features.

Lentin Joseph
Kochi, Kerala, India

Amit Kumar Mondal
Dubai, UAE

May 13, 2021

MATLAB® is a registered trademark of The MathWorks, Inc. For product information, please contact:
The MathWorks, Inc.
3 Apple Hill Drive
Natick, MA, 01760-2098 USA
Tel: 508-647-7000
Fax: 508-647-7001
E-mail: info@mathworks.com
Web: www.mathworks.com

Acknowledgments

The editors thank Neelu Jyoti Ahuja, Pankaj Badoni, Simone Baldi, Tarun Bharani, Akashdeep Bhardwaj, Shouvik Chakraborty, Vinay Chowdary, Amiya Das, Vindhya Devalla, Prashant Dwivedi, Ravishankar Dudhe, Shival Dubey, Hanumat Sastry G, Rajib Ghosh, Arpit Jain, Vivek Kaundal, Anupam Kumar, Nitin Kumar, Amrit Mukherjee, Jawid Nazir, Shamik Palit, Shunmuga Perumal P, Thomas Plocher, Ramesh C. Poonia, Sophia Rahman, Ragesh Kumar Ramachandran, Deepak Rao, Abhinav Sharma, Paawan Sharma, Vijay Bhaskar Semwal, and Syed Mohammad Tauseef for helping in reviewing the chapters.

Editors

Lentin Joseph is an author, roboticist, and robotics entrepreneur from India. He is the CEO of Qbotics Labs, a robotics software company in Kochi/Kerala. His experience in the robotics domain is primarily in the Robot Operating System (ROS), OpenCV, and PCL. He has an M.Tech in Robotics and Automation from Amrita Vishwa Vidyapeetham, India and has worked at the Robotics Institute at Carnegie Mellon University, Pittsburgh, PA. He is a TEDx speaker and has authored several books on ROS.

Amit Kumar Mondal, PhD, is an assistant professor in the Department of Mechatronics Engineering, Manipal Academy of Higher Education, Dubai, UAE. His areas of research interest are mobile robotics, autonomous systems, and industrial automation. He has published more than 30 papers in national and international journals and conferences. He has filed three patents and successfully worked on three externally funded projects from Science and Engineering Research Board (SERB), Indo-US Science and Technology Forum (IUSSTF).

Contributors

Ashwani Kumar Aggarwal
Electrical and Instrumentation
    Engineering Department
Sant Longowal Institute of Engineering
    and Technology
Longowal, India

Vidyadhar Aski
Department of Computer and
    Communication Engineering
Manipal University
Jaipur, India

Sujata Bali
School of Law
University of Petroleum and Energy Studies
Dehradun, India

Stefan Brandenburg
Institute for Psychology and Ergonomics
Department of Ergonomics, Technische
    Universität
Berlin, Germany

Rakesh Kumar Chopra
School of Law
University of Petroleum and Energy
    Studies (UPES)
Dehradun, India

Ayesha Choudhary
School of Computer and Systems Sciences
Jawaharlal Nehru University
New Delhi, India

Mrunmayee V. Daithankar
Department of Electronics
    Engineering
Walchand College of
    Engineering
Sangli, India

Hermann Felbinger
AVL List GmbH
Graz, Austria

Gayathri R
Department of Computer Science
    Engineering
Pondicherry University
Kalapet, Puducherry, India

Mallika Garg
Department of Electronics and
    Communication Engineering
Indian Institute of Technology
    Roorkee
Roorkee, India

Maximilian Gerwien
IAV GmbH
Chemnitz, Germany

Any Gupta
School of Computer and Systems
    Sciences
Jawaharlal Nehru University
New Delhi, India

Neeraj Hanumante
Department of Chemical
    Engineering
Indian Institute of Technology
    Bombay
Mumbai, India

Alexander Jungmann
IAV GmbH
Chemnitz, Germany

Sivanathan Kandhasamy
Department of Mechatronics
    Engineering
SRM Institute of Science and
    Technology
Kattankulathur, India

Kavitha K S
Department of Computer Science and
    Engineering
Dayananda Sagar College of Engineering
Bengaluru, India

Wahengbam Kanan Kumar
Department of ECE
North Eastern Regional Institute
    of Science and Technology
Doimukh, India

B Ravi Kiran
Navya
Paris, France

Florian Klück
Institute of Software Technology
Graz University of Technology
Graz, Austria

Abhishek Kumar
ECE Department
IIT Jodhpur
Rajasthan, India

Earnest Paul Ijjina
Department of Computer Science
    and Engineering
National Institute of Technology Warangal
Telangana, India

Yihao Li
School of Information and Electrical
    Engineering
Ludong University
Shandong, China

Neeta Maitre
Department of Computer Science
    Engineering
Cummins College of Engineering for Women
Pune, India

C Mala
Department of Computer Science and
    Engineering
National Institute of Technology
Tiruchirappalli, India

Madhusmita Mishra
ECE Department
NIT Rourkela
Odisha, India

Mihai Nica
AVL List GmbH
Graz, Austria

Kishorjit Nongmeikapam
Department of CSE
Indian Institute of Information Technology
Manipur, India

Bettina O'Brien
Department of Computer Science and
    Engineering
Pondicherry University, India
Kalapet, Puducherry, India

Subhash Panja
Department of Mechanical Engineering
Jadavpur University
Kolkata, India

Anubha Parashar
Department of Computer Science and
    Engineering
School of Computing and Information
    Technology
Manipal University
Jaipur, India

Apoorva Parashar
Department of Computer Science
    Engineering
Maharshi Dayanand University
Rohtak, India

Pranjal Paul
Department of Research and
    Development
University of Petroleum and Energy
    Studies (UPES)
Dehradun, India

Hazem Rashed
Valeo R&D
Cairo, Egypt

Sachin D. Ruikar
Department of Electronics
    Engineering
Walchand College of Engineering
Sangli, India

Chinmay Vilas Samak
Department of Mechatronics
    Engineering
SRM Institute of Science and
    Technology
Kattankulathur, India

Tanmay Vilas Samak
Department of Mechatronics
    Engineering
SRM Institute of Science and Technology
Kattankulathur, India

Frank Schrödel
Automation Technology and Robotics
Schmalkalden University of Applied
    Sciences
Schmalkalden, Germany

Abhishek Sharma
Department of Research and Development
University of Petroleum and Energy
    Studies
Dehradun, India

Shamneesh Sharma
School of Computer Science and
    Engineering
Poornima University
Jaipur, India

Sunil Kr. Sharma
Indian Railway
Kolkata, India

Aheibam Dinamani Singh
Department of ECE
National Institute of Technology
Manipur, India

Sunil Kr. Singh
CCET
Punjab University
Chandigarh, India

Sridevi M
Department of Computer Science and
    Engineering
National Institute of Technology
Tiruchirappalli, India

Abhijeet Srivastava
School of Law
University of Petroleum and Energy Studies
Dehradun, India

Syama R
Department of Computer Science and
    Engineering
National Institute of Technology
Tiruchirappalli, India

Sugirtha T
National Institute of Technology
Tiruchirappalli, India

Jianbo Tao
AVL List GmbH
Graz, Austria

Jagpal Singh Ubhi
Electronics and Communication
    Engineering Department
Sant Longowal Institute of Engineering
    and Technology
Longowal, India

Ravishankar C V
Department of Electronics and
    Communication Engineering
Sambhram Institute of Technology
Bengaluru, India

Uma V
Department of Computer Science
    Engineering
Pondicherry University, India
Kalapet, Puducherry, India

Rick Voßwinkel
IAV GmbH
Chemnitz, Germany

Franz Wotawa
Institute for Software
    Technology
Technische Universität
Graz, Austria

Senthil Yogamani
Valeo Vision Systems
Tuam, Ireland

Martin Zimmermann
Institute for Software Technology
Technische Universität
Graz, Austria

I

Autonomous Vehicle Testing and Development

CHAPTER 1

Intelligent Decision-Making and Motion Planning for Automated Vehicles

Rick Voßwinkel, Maximilian Gerwien, and Alexander Jungmann
IAV GmbH
Chemnitz, Germany

Frank Schrödel
Schmalkalden University of Applied Sciences
Schmalkalden, Germany

CONTENTS

DOI: 10.1201/9781003048381-2

Futuristic and autonomous vehicles are currently a trendy topic with a strong, growing market; see, e.g., [1]. Their systems promise a high level of automation. Through the last three decades, this topic has been drawing great attention from both academia and industry. Current assistance systems on the automotive market primarily support the driver through monitoring and warning functions or simple vehicle guidance tasks in well-defined areas such as parking lots or highways. This chapter focuses on rule-based and artificial intelligence–based decision-making and on model-based and model-free motion planning. Perception tasks like object fusion and lane and free-space detection are not covered.

1.1 INTRODUCTION

A fundamental component for realizing automated driving (AD), in addition to the underlying vehicle platform and the sensors for environmental perception, is the automated driving system (AD system), which enables a vehicle to automatically perform dynamic driving tasks (DDTs) in the prevailing operational design domain (ODD). In this context, an ODD is defined by environmental conditions and restrictions, roadway characteristics, and traffic situations [2]. A DDT, in turn, refers to the maneuvers to be performed by a vehicle, such as keeping the lane, changing between lanes, or stopping at a red traffic light.

Generally speaking, AD systems have to be extended in two ways in order to increase the level of automation. On the one hand, to achieve continuous automation without human intervention, high-level decision-making means have to be incorporated. High-level decision-making enables a vehicle to select, plan, and perform driving maneuvers in order to fulfill the parent mission according to the concrete situation currently prevailing. On the other hand, in order to be able to perform a driving task under a broader range of environmental conditions, the scope of the each ODD has to be expanded step by step.

The core functionality of an AD system can usually be divided into perception, planning, and acting [3]. Perception refers to sensing and understanding the environment, e.g., by detecting and classifying objects such as other traffic participants or traffic signs. The planning part implements the high-level driving behavior of the vehicle and chooses the actual course of action based on the perceived environment. Planning is typically divided into three different decision-making and planning levels: strategic planning for navigation and anticipatory driving tasks, tactical planning for orchestrating appropriate maneuvers given concrete situations, and operational planning for computing the actual path as well as trajectories. The acting part is responsible for performing the previously chosen actions based on control strategies. As a result, inputs for the on-board vehicle control are obtained.

Let us consider a lane change as a concrete maneuver. Assuming that all required information such as objects and lanes can be robustly perceived, the planning part has to decide when a lane change might be the right course of action (e.g., when a vehicle in front is driving too slowly). Furthermore, the planning part has to validate if a lane change is feasible (e.g., by checking that no other vehicles are blocking the target lane or will not be blocking it soon). And finally, the planning part has to decide how to perform the lane change (e.g., by computing a path with a velocity profile that can be subsequently translated into a trajectory as input for a low-level control algorithm).

Since a lane change is a rather fundamental maneuver, it has to be performed for different reasons, in different situations, and under different environmental conditions. When we switch from the well-structured highway ODD to a far more complex urban ODD with more complex traffic rules, additional traffic participants, crossings, traffic lights, etc., the AD system still has to be able to decide when, if, and how to perform a maneuver. Figure 1.1 shows lane change maneuvers of an ego vehicle (blue) in different situations. While the reason for performing a lane change differs from situation to situation, the overall goal is always the same: the ego vehicle has to follow a route (green lanes) to reach its final destination. Let us have a closer look at the different situations:

- In Figure 1.1a, the ego vehicle has to change lanes due to an obstacle (red) in the current lane. The adjacent lane might be completely or partially blocked by other vehicles (gray).

- In Figure 1.1b, the ego vehicle wants to change lanes due to a slowly driving vehicle in front. Changing lanes, however, would result in a critical situation, since the adjacent lane ends in x meters. As a consequence, performing a lane change—although desired—might not be a good choice.

- In Figure 1.1c, the ego vehicle wants to change lanes due to a slowly driving vehicle in front. After passing the first vehicle, the ego vehicle should usually change back to the right lane. However, to avoid unsettling human drivers by odd driving behavior and to keep a constant overall traffic flow, the ego vehicle might choose to stay in the left lane and pass other slow-moving vehicles before changing back to the right lane.

- In Figure 1.1d, the ego vehicle has to change lanes because the current lane ends in x meters. The adjacent lane might be completely or partially blocked by other vehicles. This situation usually—but not exclusively—occurs when driving on a highway.

- In Figure 1.1e, the ego vehicle has to perform multiple successive lane changes to leave the current road in x meters. Adjacent lanes, however, might be completely or partially blocked by other vehicles.

- In Figure 1.1f, the ego vehicle has to change lanes in order to turn right in x meters. The traffic light at the point of the turn, however, is currently red. As a consequence,

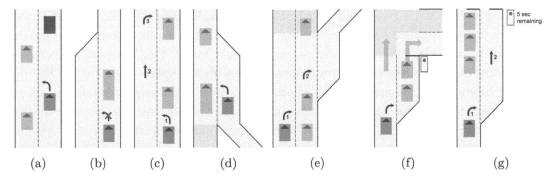

(a)   (b)   (c)   (d)   (e)   (f)   (g)

FIGURE 1.1   Lane change maneuvers for different reasons in different situations. Where the reason in (a) blocked adjacent lane. (b) Slowly driving vehicle in front. (c) Several slow vehicles in front. (d) Lane change because of a merge in ramp on the scenario. (e) Lane change because of a ramp off scenario. (f) and (g) Lane change scenario with traffic lights to keep the course or a better traffic flow. Scenario (f) and (g) are generally found in urban settings whereas scenarios (a) to (e) are neither restricted to highway nor urban environments.

the right lane is blocked by vehicles that are waiting for the traffic light to turn green. The ego vehicle has to wait until the right lane is not completely blocked anymore.

- In Figure 1.1g, the ego vehicle is approaching a crossroad controlled by traffic lights. Both lanes are valid for staying on the route. The current lane, however, is blocked in x meters due to vehicles waiting for the traffic light to turn green. Since that traffic light is still red for another 5 seconds, the ego vehicle might change lanes to avoid coming to a complete stop before the traffic light turns green and to keep a smooth traffic flow.

The first five scenarios are not restricted to highway or urban environments but can occur in different environments with different environmental conditions. The last two scenarios, however, can usually be found in urban settings.

The described situations were not arbitrarily defined by us to simply support the necessity for intelligent decision-making and planning approaches. The situations represent challenges that we already partially tackled in past projects and that we especially face in our latest projects. Two of our recently completed projects are SYNCAR [4] and HarmonizeDD [5]. In SYNCAR, we constructed an experimental vehicle by equipping a series vehicle with additional sensors, computing hardware, and communication capabilities. Furthermore, we successfully designed, implemented, and tested innovative driving functions for cooperative automated driving in an urban environment. The same experimental vehicle was used in HarmonizeDD to successfully test the connected, automated driving functions we designed and implemented for mixed traffic scenarios. In this context, mixed traffic refers to the interaction between both automated and nonautomated vehicles in the same scenario. For more details, please refer to [6]. In the current project AutoAkzept [7, 8], we are focusing on gaining driver acceptance and minimizing uncertainty. Besides new human-machine interface concepts, we are examining driving behaviors for automated vehicles. The objective of the project OPA³L [9] is to automate recurrent maneuvers in known areas and, in particular, to present possible solutions for cooperative maneuvers in such areas.

While SYNCAR, HarmonizeDD, AutoAkzept, and OPA³L address automated driving solutions for private transport, two of our latest and still running projects focus on public transport: ABSOLUT [10] and HEAT [11]. The overall vision of both projects is the development of so-called people movers—i.e., shuttles that drive autonomously on public roads to transport limited numbers of passengers. In ABSOLUT, IAV is in charge of creating planning and acting algorithms that can cope with low-speed scenarios for driving in an exhibition environment with lots of people around (the Leipzig trade fair) as well as medium-speed scenarios for driving on public roads. For HEAT, IAV is responsible for the entire shuttle development, including vehicle platform and architecture, exterior design, sensor concept, and, of course, software components for AD. The HEAT shuttle will drive in the harbor city of Hamburg at the ITS World Congress in 2021.

While each project—in its own right—poses a great challenge, we make huge efforts to follow a holistic development policy that allows us to gradually extend and improve the capabilities of our AD system with each project. One very essential part is the development of intelligent decision-making and planning (cf. Section 1.4) as well as motion planning (cf. Section 1.5) approaches for coping with the significantly increasing complexity across all past and current projects while simultaneously keeping future expandability in mind.

Without an all-encompassing functional architecture (cf. Section 1.3), however, this long-term strategy would not be feasible at all.

1.2 OPTIMIZATION—A KEY INGREDIENT FOR AUTOMATED DRIVING

The purpose of this section is to introduce optimization as a fundamental aspect of AD. We present some optimization basics and argue that optimization is used and sometimes necessary in nearly all parts of an AD system, such as sensor fusion, data acquisition, maneuver planning, and control optimization.

To achieve robust and comfortable performance, we need optimal behavior in the individual steps of the AD system. The question now is: What is meant by the term *optimization*? Different people might have different understandings of what optimization means. Neither considering different designs or configurations and choosing the best one nor following some suggestions or rules to improve overall behavior is the way we understand optimization. In fact, we use the term *optimization* from a mathematical point of view: optimization describes a systematical procedure to find an optimal solution (or at least a local one) to a given problem.

The initial point of every optimization is a proper problem formulation, as in Equation 1.1:

$$\min J = F(\ldots) \text{ s.t.}$$
$$\sum_i g_i(\ldots) = 0$$
$$\sum_j h_j(\ldots) > 0, \tag{1.1}$$

with the cost functional $J = F(\ldots)$. This cost functional defines the main optimization goal. The arguments of the function F depend on the particular problem. Often, arguments like time and system states (velocity, acceleration, jerk, etc.), and more abstract ones like comfort, are considered. In other words, we define with the cost functional what is important for us: Do we want to drive sportive or defensive? Do we have to follow the shortest or the fastest route? Do we prefer a comfortable driving behavior over a strict and precise driving behavior? The functions g_i and h_i define inequality and equality constraints. Such constraints are used to describe physical limitations or other saturations and conditions resulting from law or comfort considerations. The method or algorithm we choose to solve a given optimization problem is determined by their properties. While linear and convex problems are generally very effectively solved with gradient-based methods [12], we need more sophisticated algorithms to find global optima of nonlinear problems. Furthermore, we need to distinguish between a parameter optimization, where we want to find an optimal set of parameters solving the optimization problem, and an optimal control problem (e.g., [13]), where we are looking for an optimal input function for a given problem.

The first real systematic technique for optimization was proposed by Fermat [14]. Nowadays, setting the first derivatives to zero to compute extrema is one of the basics of every textbook on calculus and a frequent application of differentiation. After Fermat, the iterative approaches of Newton [15] and Gauss were the next steps in searching for an optimum [16]. This iterative idea is picked up several times, like in the steepest gradient method, which can be traced back to Riemann and Cauchy [17]; the celebrated simplex method of Dantzig [18]; and quasi-Newton methods [19]. At the beginning of the 1980s, metaheuristic approaches, like genetic algorithms [20], simulated annealing [21], and particle swarm optimization [22], became popular. These algorithms are inspired by nature or other heuristics and have some benefits, such as global optimization and a gradient-free computation. Nevertheless, they need a lot of sample points to converge to the optimum, which creates a computational barrier for applications, even as they generally support parallel computing.

Today, machine learning (ML) approaches have become more and more relevant. These data-driven methods construct a metamodel based on sample points and are able to learn how to solve detection, classification, planning, control, and prediction problems. In the ML domain, three types of learning have prevailed [23–25]:

- *Supervised learning:* Supervised learning considers input and desired output data to minimize the error between the predicted outcome and the labeled output data.

- *Unsupervised Learning:* Unsupervised learning approaches consider only the input data and try to find structure and patterns in the provided data set.

- *Reinforcement learning:* Reinforcement learning (RL) techniques learn the desired behavior by interacting with the environment; put simply, they learn by doing) [26]. Reward functions evaluate the outcome of each action.

ML techniques are mostly inspired by human learning behavior and psychological models.

Optimization can be found in nearly every part of the AD structure. It begins with modeling the vehicle dynamics, which is generally based on minimizing the cumulated modeling errors (e.g., [27]). The part of the introduced AD system that is nearest to the vehicle is the control. Optimization, either direct for the control strategy [28] or indirectly with regard to the control quality (e.g., [29]), is important for successful implementation. The next layer is the operational planning, which mainly consists of a trajectory planning module or a model predictive control (MPC). Since optimization is the key feature of these layers, they will be described in more detail later on. The decision-making levels are the levels that decide which action to choose based on the presented environment and the interpreted situational context with a long-term prediction horizon. The optimization goal here is to maximize the expected reward or value function to get the most beneficial policy for all actions [30, 31]. The whole structure is closed via sensor fusion and perception. In this part, we can optimize as well, using, e.g., Kalman filters [32, 33].

1.3 FUNCTIONAL ARCHITECTURES FOR AUTOMATED DRIVING

Choosing an appropriate functional architecture for AD is fundamental for if the system is to make the right decisions in line with requirements regarding the intended driving behavior. Mastering the complexity of AD, especially in urban traffic scenarios, while simultaneously adhering to functional safety requirements, is a challenging task that has to be considered from scratch when developing the architecture and the methods of decision-making.

Two classical architecture approaches can be pointed out in automated systems [34–36]. The first one is referred to as function-based, top-down, or knowledge-driven architecture. It uses an explicit world model for decision-making and planning as well as coupling deliberative agents with explicit knowledge. An overall mission for each agent is decomposed into subgoals within a hierarchical control structure. That is, higher layers in the hierarchy create subgoals for the lower layers. This includes the sense-model-plan-act paradigm, as found in the standard NASRAM architecture [37]. In consequence, the high-level side has long planning cycles and no fast reactions to dynamic environment changes. Deliberative agents are well suited for structured and highly foreseeable environments. This approach provides also the benefits of mission-oriented planning and high-level intelligence. However, top-down architectures require a general world model that is hard to represent and also computationally expensive. Therefore, the world representation is often reduced to topological and semantic maps. Furthermore, purely deliberative agents are not sufficient to realize intelligent behavior because of oversimplification [38, 39]. The problem of static world representation is caused by the absence of intuitive interpretation and solutions in dynamic environments.

The second architecture approach focuses on reactive agents. Reactive agents implement decision-making and planning functionality by bottom-up or data-driven models that react to their sensory input directly without high-level planning and overall missions [34, 38–40]. The aim is a timely robotic response in dynamic and unstructured worlds. The main advantage is the robustness of the directly coupled approach of perception and action (behavior). For a purely reactive approach to be applicable, however, actions (or driving functions, in our case) have to be explicitly defined and made available in advance, leading to a deficiency of flexibility in the architecture. For an example of this approach, see also the subsumption architecture [41].

Different hybrid architectures were developed to combine the benefits of both deliberative and reacting agents and to eliminate or at least minimize the drawbacks of each approach. In AD, hybrid models are in fact the most common approach and gain a lot of attention in research [35, 42–45]. Reactive and deliberative functions are typically combined within a three-layered architecture [46, 47]: the deliberative layer, the sequencing layer, and the reactive layer. The deliberative layer is responsible for long-term strategic mission planning, including mission adaption. The sequencing layer, in turn, coordinates the interaction between the deliberative and the reactive layers to execute appropriate maneuvers using context-dependent rules. The term *tactic* in this context refers to a predefined, ordered, and structured set of actions. The reactive layer acts with metric information and numerical control. The difficulty lies in the interface of these different layers because they work asynchronously, with different time scales and data representations.

Choosing the most appropriate functional architecture for AD usually depends on the application and the corresponding requirements. Early work in this context was inspired by the real-time control system domain and might be interpreted as active seeing (AS) [48–51]. These architectures were the breakthrough for developing functional hybrid architectures

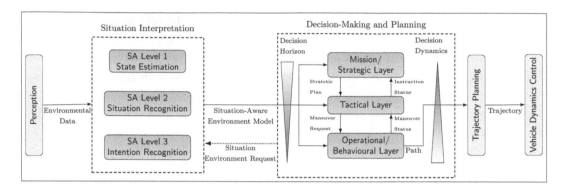

FIGURE 1.2   Functional architecture for our AD system.

for AD and are particularly characterized by their hierarchical planning. Furthermore, the well-known DARPA challenge gave rise to various hybrid architectures [52–55], where each architecture was specialized for solving the course defined by the challenge. Urban scenarios, however, were only partially considered. Later architectures focused more on urban environments. The first experience was collected with projects like Stadtpilot by TU Braunschweig [56] and the PRORETA 3 project by TU Darmstadt [57]. Further research in functional architectures for AD finally led to a three-layered decision-making approach consisting of a strategical, a tactical, and an operational layer [58–60].

In our work, we gradually adapt and refine this three-layer approach to serve as holistic architecture that incorporates any AD functionality that is already available, is currently in development, or might be developed in the future. By doing so, we ensure that the performance and consequently the level of automation of our AD system increase systematically over time. Figure 1.2 gives a rough overview of our functional architecture. The perception cluster is responsible for perceiving the environment and will not be further discussed in this chapter. The situation interpretation cluster translates the environmental data into an environmental model (or situation model) according to the decision-making and planning level that requires the respective information. Information maximization and reduction (e.g., by selection or abstraction) and information representation are key aspects. Both clusters are indeed tightly coupled and allow for situation-aware decision-making and planning. Section 1.4 gives a detailed overview of the two function clusters and the respective layers of hierarchy within the clusters, while Section 1.5 introduces concrete algorithms for motion planning on the operational layer. The trajectory planning cluster translates geometric paths with velocity annotations into trajectories or even alternative representations (cf. Section 1.5). Finally, the vehicle dynamics control cluster is responsible for generating control variables such as steering angle and acceleration.

1.4   SITUATION INTERPRETATION AND DECISION-MAKING

The decision-making process for intelligent high-level planning vehicles requires a hierarchical and situation-aware representation of the world. The focus of this section is presenting methods that handle, in a safe manner, decisions based on uncertain and incomplete information. Therefore, we present the underlying optimization problem in information and decision theory and give a short overview of different applications and tasks in automated driving.

1.4.1 Environment Presentation and Situation Interpretation

Situation interpretation is the elaboration of the situational context, whereby not only the current situation but also past conditions are considered to create awareness of a certain situation. Awareness of a situation thus involves a focus on possible resources and possible future events. This time-dependent and uncertain process is also called situation awareness (SA). The concept of SA has its origins in psychology [61–63] and serves as the basis for any situation-related decision and risk assessment. The model [61] originally had three levels, which can be subdivided with regard to the decision-making process:

- *SA Level 1:* Estimation and representation of the current environment and entities.

- *SA Level 2:* Comprehension, classification, and combination with the mission-related goal for the current situation.

- *SA Level 3:* Prediction and intention detection of future situations and status.

Figure 1.2 shows the adapted concept of SA included in the functional architecture of our AD system. Thus, the situation interpretation and the different levels serve as a service for the various decision-making processes.

The difficulty in SA Level 1, which must represent the current environment, lies in adequately combining data in one consistent comprehensive environment model (CEM) [64] that acts as a generic abstraction layer for the decision-making process. Since the environment representation can be metric, topological, static, dynamic, and semantic, a lot of effort is required to combine those representations to provide each functionality the corresponding information and requirements [65]. Each decision layer subsumes a solid situation interpretation of the scenario and situation depending on the task and the goals of each decision-making layer. But the whole CEM is not necessary for each decision layer to consider the hierarchically structured information.

SA Level 2 generally conveys an understanding of the specific scenario and can recognize the situation in that scenario. The main task is to classify and recognize, based on SA Level 1, different scenarios and situations. To achieve this goal, three different approaches are conceivable. First, information from static data like road maps provides the situation or the scenario. Second, expert systems with predefined rules divide situations [66–68]. As a third point, SA Level 2 learns in a supervised manner to classify [69] predefined scenarios.

SA Level 3 will estimate and predict future states in special situations [65, 70–73]. The tasks at this level go beyond predicting the future trajectories and movements of an object in the situation and include predicting maneuvers, interactions, and indicators like collision risk or time-to-x values.

1.4.1.1 Problem Formulation of Situation-Aware Interpretation

There are five main factors of uncertainty in robotics and thus also in AD systems [74]. The inherently unpredictable environment, the perception by sensors, the inaccuracy of actuators, every system model, and each calculation with the computer system come with uncertainties. In consequence, uncertainties have to be considered and could be also modeled. Therefore, we have to define a stochastic process. Based on the stochastic process, the focus is on information-based cost functions from which the underlying optimization task can be derived.

A stochastic process is characterized by the fact that the random variable X depends on a parameter t. In most cases, the parameter t represents the time. A stochastic process $X = \{X_t, t \in T\}$ is thus a family of random variables. In the following, it is always assumed that T is the index set for the time. The realization of X_t for all points of time $t \in T$ results in a real function $x = x(t)$, which is also called the trajectory or time sequence process. The trajectories can be discrete or continuous, where the state space contains measurable metric or symbolic states [75].

Important for the perception and measurement of a stochastic process is the information that each measurement receives for a realization of $P(X = x)$. With the assumption that not every realization receives the same amount of information, the Shannon information can be expressed as in Equation 1.2:

$$H(X = x) = \log \frac{1}{P(X = x)} = -\log P(X = x) \tag{1.2}$$

If the information measure were zero, the process would be fully predictable from the information a priori available from $P(X)$. Thus, the variable x would also be deterministic and no longer stochastic.

Two main tasks can be pointed out in situation-aware interpretation. At first, the well-known problem is to model a dynamic system, dynamic situation, or just situation aspects from the observed data set Y_t. The aim is to estimate X_t from the previous values Y_s, where at any time t only $\{Y_s; s < t\}$ previous values can be observed. A solution for the so-called filter problem is a modeling task that calculates the system dynamics and the observation dynamics explicitly or implicitly. This can be expressed with the state space system, as in Equations 1.3 and 1.4:

$$x_t = f(x_{t-1}, u_{t-1}, \varepsilon \mid \theta) \tag{1.3}$$

$$y_t = g(x_t, \sigma \mid \theta). \tag{1.4}$$

A parametrization of the function f and the observation dynamics g is necessary. The solution to the filter problem and the modeling of the stochastic system can be very different depending on the methodology. The following aspects have to be considered:

- Are probability distributions known from the process or subprocesses?

- What properties are subordinated to the process (Markov property, Bayesian process, etc.)?

- What parameter estimation techniques are used?

The second main task that can be pointed out is the selection of good data. Especially data-driven classifiers and planning algorithms need more quality in the data instead of huge data amounts to find the optimal solution. An observer that is actively involved in the perception of actions when these are performed by a demonstrator is called active seeing (AS) [51, 76]. Besides the integration of active seeing in the functional architecture in AD, which has to be organized in a hierarchical and distributed manner, a measure of information gain is needed to find the right queries for each decision level and a suitable information-based cost function. The process of maximizing the information gain and minimizing the amount of data needed in the sense of a priori knowledge and posterior data is also called active learning (AL) [77].

The information gain (IG) indicates how much information a feature gives us about the class. This is normally expressed by calculating the entropy of a stochastic process X, as in Equation 1.5:

$$H(X) = -\sum_i f(x_i) \log_2 f(x_i) \tag{1.5}$$

Calculating the minimum of entropy is maximizing the IG.

An information-based cost function can be described with similar information measures and will also model the notions of IG. In the case of modeling the distribution with the parameter-set θ, the expected value of the IG is also known as the Kullback-Leibler (KL) divergence and describes the mutual information between an a priori distribution $P(x)$ and the posterior distribution $Q(X|\theta)$. The expression measures how different the distributions are, where D_{KL} is zero if and only if both distributions are equal. The optimization criterion has to be minimized to find the optimal model, as in Equations 1.6 and 1.7:

$$D_{KL}(Q \| P) = \sum_i Q(x_i|\theta) \log_2 \frac{Q(x_i|\theta)}{P(x_i)} \tag{1.6}$$

$$\min J = D_{KL}(Q \| P) \tag{1.7}$$

This leads to a modeling problem, where not only uncertainty is considered but also the nonlinearity and the dependency of different states are considered. A lot of applications in AD research use this approach directly or indirectly to predict future states to observe intention or maneuver symbolically [65] as well as in a metric manner to predict future trajectories and interactions of surrounding participants [70–73].

In the sense of AL and choosing unseen data, we also can use the KL divergence. To measure the amount of IG expected from the available but unused data (x'), the KL divergence of the posterior is modeled, as in Equation 1.8:

$$\max J = D_{KL}(Q(\theta|x, x') \| Q(\theta|x)) \tag{1.8}$$

Here the goal is to choose data x' that maximizes the KL divergence between posterior and prior data such that the largest KL divergence between the updated posterior probability and the current posterior probability represents the largest gain.

In the model for the solution of the filter problem and the active learning part, the KL divergence is usually chosen because there the posterior and the prior have to be compared.

1.4.2 Intelligent Decision-Making for Maneuver Selection

Decision-making is essential for planning, selecting, and finally performing maneuvers. In Figure 1.2, the decision-making and planning cluster is hierarchically structured into multiple layers:

- *Mission layer:* The mission layer provides all long-term goals and tasks that come with the intention of the human driver. It encompasses the global graph search algorithm to find the route in the road network given constraints like the fastest way or the most resource-saving way.

- *Strategic layer:* The strategic layer includes the graph search algorithms to find the optimal route in a lane-specific manner and in a predefined horizon to reach the driving destination. Vehicle-to-everything (V2X) information can be used to avoid construction sites or very busy roads or to adapt the driving behavior due to critical weather forecasts. The strategical layer and the mission layer mainly incorporate global sensor information for decision-making.

- *Tactical layer:* The tactical layer can be considered as the interface between the high-level planning side and the low-level behavioral planning side, where the data structure between these layers may vary. This layer uses global and internal sensor information as the foundation for decision-making. The tactical layer modifies the strategic lane-specific commands into an available maneuver, while other road users are also observed. The abstract lane change advisory from the strategic layer becomes a concrete collision-free lane change at a spatial location and point in time. Therefore, the different possible spatial points have to be observed and selected for the optimal gap depending on constraints like driving style, alternative navigation routes, and V2X communication. Also, this layer generates a sequence of predefined operational functions for achieving more complex maneuvers such as overtaking maneuvers, or it may generate acceleration and deceleration recommendations for the operational layer. Depending on the operational layer and the implemented behaviors, the tasks of the tactical layer can be very different and include symbolic (e.g., a maneuver selection) and also metric (e.g., an acceleration advisory) decisions. In any case, these decisions always have to take prevailing and emerging situations into account.

- *Operational layer:* The operational layer subsumes everything necessary to translate maneuvers selected on the tactical decision-making layer into valid paths and trajectories. The corresponding driving functionality may also receive parameter sets from the tactical layer to realize the same maneuver in different scenarios and to adapt optimization functions. More details regarding the operational layer can be found in Section 1.5.

1.4.2.1 Top-Down Decomposition

To better understand the interaction between the different layers, let us consider the situation depicted in Figure 1.1e. First and foremost, the ego vehicle has one overall mission: to follow a given route (indicated by green lanes) to reach a final destination. While the decision and planning horizon usually comprises the entire area between the current position and the final position, the decision dynamics (i.e., the frequency of adjusting the route due to unforeseen events) are generally rather low.

To complete a mission (i.e., to follow a dynamically changing route), the strategic layer decomposes the route into a sequence of so-called complex maneuvers such as "follow the course of the road" and "turn left." In Figure 1.1e, we have a transition between two complex maneuvers: while the ego vehicle is still performing the complex maneuver "follow the course of the road," it has to prepare for the next complex maneuver, "take exit." Formally speaking, while performing the current complex maneuver, the ego vehicle has to make sure that the preconditions for the subsequent complex maneuver are fulfilled in time. In this concrete situation, the ego vehicle has a very restricted time frame for the first lane change to meet the precondition (drive in right lane) for taking the exit.

The tactical layer is responsible for decomposing complex maneuvers into sequences of basic maneuvers (or simply maneuvers). A lane change is a basic maneuver that serves as one of many building blocks for realizing complex maneuvers. In Figure 1.1e, we have two explicitly indicated basic maneuvers in terms of the two lane changes. However, we can see a complete chain of basic maneuvers. The ego vehicle is currently performing the maneuver "follow lane" while waiting until the preconditions for performing the lane change are met—either by passively observing how the situation evolves or by actively trying to change the current situation. After performing the first lane change, the ego vehicle follows the new lane. In either case, the ego vehicle is continuously performing the complex maneuver "follow the course of the road" on the strategic layer.

To execute a basic maneuver, the tactical layer interacts with the operational layer, which provides driving behaviors or actions as the most atomic building blocks in this hierarchy. The maneuver "follow lane" in Figure 1.1e, e.g., can be further decomposed into at least two parallel actions: one for longitudinal driving behavior such as adaptive cruise control (ACC) and one for lateral driving behavior for staying in the lane. In the past, there have been different approaches to making decisions about the choice of behavior or the execution of the planning maneuver, and currently, there are no uniform solutions or an optimal solution. The tactical layer in particular plays a special role, as the interface to the operational layer has to be defined and this is where difficulties are usually encountered. This is due to the fact that planning and decision-making depend on the functional architecture and also work asynchronously, with different time scales and data representations. According to Arkin [34], there are four main interface strategies for the different hybrid architectures (selection, consultation, adaptation, and shifting). In automated driving, selection and adaptation can be observed. The selection strategy is basically the sequential generation of various predefined behavioral functions. Consequently, the predefined set is atomic functions that are selected and combined at the tactical layer to fully meet the mission objectives. The adaptation is regarded as an adaptation system, in which the tactical layer continuously changes the behavioral function in the light of changing conditions, scenarios, and situations. This can be achieved by parameterizing or consulting for scenario-dependent constraints.

1.4.2.2 Composition Strategies and Methods

By using building blocks to compose complex functionality on higher hierarchy layers, we can flexibly apply different composition methods on different layers, while taking decision dynamics and horizons into account. Composition, in this context, refers to coming up with a plan to achieve the goal on the next-higher hierarchy layer. Since automated vehicles have to deal with a nondeterministic, highly dynamic environment, planning, executing a plan, and revising a plan might also be tightly interwoven—especially on the lower hierarchy layers.

A very common and straightforward approach to composing high-level functionality is to encode all possible plans in state machines when the AD system is designed. Roughly speaking, depending on a current state (or situation) and according to predefined transitions with transition conditions between the states, a state machine clearly defines in which situation and under which condition an action (e.g., a complex or basic maneuver) may be selected. Although this approach is indeed very intuitive, it is also very restricted: knowledge that was not encoded into the state machines during design time is not available when the AD system is online and running. That is, the developers and domain experts have to consider all situations that may occur in the desired application and precisely define all relevant transitions and corresponding conditions in advance. For a very restricted ODD and a limited set of DDTs, this approach usually works pretty well, since a thorough investigation of possible situations and necessary maneuvers is still manageable, while state machines that encode the result of the investigation are still maintainable. With increasing AD functionality, however, this approach is not feasible anymore and should be replaced by artificial intelligence (AI) approaches in terms of automated planning and ML techniques.

Purely symbolic AI planning approaches can be used to separate domain knowledge from the actual planning process in order to facilitate online planning [30]. This strategy is quite similar to that for solving the service composition problem in the service-oriented computing domain. For example, image-processing services are interpreted as building blocks to automatically generate more complex image-processing software solutions, where the functionality of building blocks is described based on ontologies [78]. In our context, the functionality of maneuvers can be described to define (1) the condition under which a maneuver may be performed and (2) the effects performing a maneuver may have. Having functional specifications of maneuvers available, an online search algorithm can identify a valid sequence of maneuvers that transforms the current situation into the desired situation. In any case, identifying whether performing a maneuver in a situation at hand is valid or not is no longer explicitly defined in terms of static transitions between predefined states but can be flexibly computed online.

Purely symbolic approaches, however, have multiple drawbacks. While they indeed facilitate the flexible and automated composition of high-level functionality, they do not work well on lower layers where less abstract environmental models are required, e.g., to cope with uncertainty and higher dynamics. Furthermore, symbolic approaches usually allow only for identifying valid maneuvers. Whether one valid maneuver is more appropriate than another valid maneuver in a specific situation cannot be evaluated. That is, purely symbolic planning algorithms do not rate or rank alternative solutions to decide which is the best one.

The normative decision problem can be described mathematically [30] such that there is a choice of various actions and the environment is presented with the set of states. The actions to the environment may influence the states such that states have a conditional probability distribution. For the rating of each action, there is a utility function that specifies the payoff if the state is located and an action is chosen. So the task of normative decision theory is to select the action that maximizes the expected utility.

A straightforward solution for this decision-making problem is to incorporate hand-crafted, domain-specific heuristics to determine the value of a maneuver given the current situation. Yet again, we face the challenge that developers and domain experts have to define such heuristics in advance. Alternatively, symbolic planning approaches can be extended [79] or replaced by reward-based RL techniques based on Markov decision processes (MDPs) [80], which comprise a mathematical framework for modeling sequential decision-making problems. Formally, a classical MDP $\mathcal{M}$ is a quintuple:

$$\mathcal{M} = (\mathbb{T}, \mathbb{S}, \mathbb{A}, p_t(\cdot \mid x, a), r_t(x, a))$$

where

- $\mathbb{T} = \{1, 2, ..., N\}, N \in \mathbb{N}$, is a discrete finite set of decision epochs with $t \in \mathbb{T}$ representing a point in time when a decision is made.

- $\mathbb{S}$ is a discrete finite set of states with $x_t \in \mathbb{S}$ being the state occupied at decision epoch $t \in \mathbb{T}$.

- $\mathbb{A} = \bigcup_{x \in \mathbb{S}} \mathbb{A}_x$ is a discrete finite set of actions with $\mathbb{A}_x$ being the set of possible actions in state $x \in \mathbb{S}$.

- $p_t(x' \mid x, a) \in [0, 1]$ is the transition probability at decision epoch $t \in \mathbb{T}$ for transitioning from state $x \in \mathbb{S}$ into state $x' \in \mathbb{S}$ when performing action $a \in \mathbb{A}_x$.

- The expected reward at decision epoch $t \in \mathbb{T}$ for being in state $x \in \mathbb{S}$ and performing action $a \in \mathbb{A}_x$ is defined by

$$r_t(x, a) = \sum_{x' \in \mathbb{S}} r_I(x, a, x') \cdot p_t(x' \mid x, a)$$

with $r_I(x, a, x')$ being the immediate reward for transitioning to a successor state, $x' \in \mathbb{S}$.

A policy $\pi = (\pi_1, ..., \pi_t, ..., \pi_{N-1})$ specifies for each decision epoch $1 \le t < N$ a decision rule π_t in a deterministic ($\pi_t : \mathbb{S} \to \mathbb{A}$) or in a stochastic ($\pi_t : \mathbb{S} \to P(\mathbb{A})$) manner. Solving an MDP is equivalent to finding an optimal policy π^* that maximizes the discounted cumulative reward

$$R_t = \sum_{k=0}^{\infty} \gamma^k r_{t+k+1}$$

with the discount factor $\gamma, 0 \le \gamma \le 1$.

The expected cumulative reward of a policy π is usually defined as a value function, where a distinction is made between *state-value* and *state-action-value* functions. The state-value function in Equation 1.9:

$$V^\pi(x) = E_\pi \{ R_t | x_t = x, \pi \} \tag{1.9}$$

represents how good it is to be in state x. It depends on the policy that performs the actions. The state-action-value function in Equation 1.10:

$$Q^\pi(x, a) = E_\pi \{ R_t | x_t = x, a_t = a \} \tag{1.10}$$

is an indication for how good it is to choose an action a while being in state x. Regarding the state-value function (Equation 1.9), the optimal policy π^* for an MDP is defined in Equations 1.11 as

$$\pi^* \in \arg\max_{\pi \in \Pi} V^\pi(x), \tag{1.11}$$

where Π is the set of all possible policies. The optimal policy for the state-action-value function (Equation 1.10) is achieved by Equation 1.12:

$$\pi^* \in \arg\max_{a \in \mathbb{A}_x} Q^\pi(x, a). \tag{1.12}$$

If the environment is completely known—i.e., if all elements of an MDP are known in advance—dynamic programming algorithms such as value iteration and policy iteration can be applied to compute π^* [26]. Otherwise, model-free RL techniques such as Q-learning [81] can be applied in order to maximize the cumulative reward over time. In this case, the algorithm has to actively learn through the experience of interactions with the environment, and only the current possible states and actions can be observed.

MDPs are indeed a sound mathematical framework for sequential decision-making. Classical MDPs consider discrete state and action spaces as well as discrete time intervals for performing actions. Furthermore, classical MDPs incorporate transition probabilities to model uncertainty when performing actions (e.g., when a maneuver does not bring about the desired result). However, classical MDPs assume that the environment is always completely observable. For that reason, partially observable Markov decision processes (POMDPs) additionally incorporate observation probabilities to model the uncertainty not only when acting but also when perceiving and trying to interpret the situation [82]. Another relevant extension of classical MDPs is semi-Markov decision processes (SMDPs). SMDPs consider the duration of actions to be randomly distributed. This is essential for AD, in particular for the lowest hierarchy layers, since performing the same maneuver usually takes different times on different layers.

1.5 ANYWHERE, ANYTIME, ANYWISE: MOTION-PLANNING PROBLEM

1.5.1 Path Representation and Trajectory Generation Problem

As a result of the decision-making process illustrated in Section 1.4, we know what needs to be done. This section focuses on the realization of these maneuvers. In order to compute proper driving trajectories, we have to place ourselves in the environment and determine the situation around us—especially the road conditions, including lanes, roadside units, other road users, and many others. For that purpose, AD vehicles are equipped with many sensors, like LIDAR, cameras, and ultrasonic sensors. The data from these sources is fused and offers us a good idea of the situation around us. With that in hand, a suitable path can be computed for the requested maneuver.

A common method for path calculation is the potential field method. The potential field method is inspired by the physical phenomena of magnetic fields and was described by Khatib [83] for the first time. Initialized with a starting point and an endpoint, repulsive forces and attractive forces are introduced to create a potential field by forming the negative gradient of a potential function. In a general potential field, algorithms can fulfill real-time requirements, but they lead often to local minima. Thus, a nonoptimal path is computed, or the algorithm cannot find a proper solution. Beyond that, potential field algorithms are not able to handle kinematic constraints.

In the context of graph search–based algorithms, the congruence space of the vehicle is approximated as a grid or lattice. In [84] is the Dijkstra algorithm, used to adaptively determine the waypoints according to the road situation. The A* algorithm is a grabbing heuristic search algorithm. In practical applications, the performance is restricted to the resolution of the map. In 2008, Hybrid-A* was introduced in the Stanford self-driving Junior vehicle used in the DARPA Urban Challenge [85]. Taking into consideration curvature and kinematic constraints, the state lattice algorithms were developed and successfully applied in unstructured environments [86]. However, the incremental properties of the search algorithm led to an exponential growth of the computing complexity.

In our case, the path is determined based on the earlier chosen maneuvers. Thus, if we want to stay in the lane, the path is the middle of the lane. If a lane change is necessary, a smooth function is fitted from one lane to the other, etc. This piecewise and maneuver-based path computation makes it possible to set up a smart interface between the different planning layers and adjust the path quickly due to new environment data.

The path consists of four parts. The first one is the reference, which is located in the middle of the drivable corridor. The left and right boundaries of this corridor give the second and the third parts (see Figure 1.3). The last part is a velocity profile, which represents the maximum permitted velocity in a step-function like representation. The path consists of points based on the arc length containing these four pieces of information.

Now let us consider a lane change scenario (cf. Figure 1.1) to illustrate the path concept. While we are staying in the lane, the reference is the middle of that lane, and the left and right boundaries are the boundaries, including some safety distances. The velocity profile is determined by the traffic rules or other limitations (e.g., driver input). If a lane change is requested, a new drivable corridor is generated. Thus, the reference is planned from the

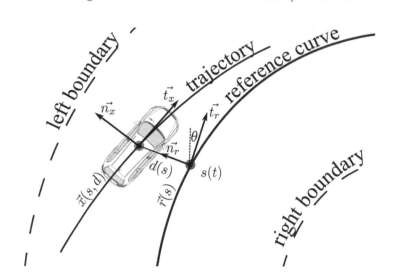

FIGURE 1.3   Frenét space: trajectory and reference.

center of the actual lane to the center of the desired lane, and the boundaries are appropriately adjusted. The velocity profile is a priori not modified, but it might be necessary, a situation addressed in the following.

To ensure safety, comfort, and something often called "human-like driving," we need to adapt the planned driving path. Thus, the path is subsequently adjusted based on different factors of influence. One of these factors is the green light optimal speed advisory (GLOSA) vehicle guidance concept, which explicitly considers the current and predicted states of multiple traffic lights ahead, including lane-use recommendations. This information can be used to adapt the vehicle's dynamics. Consequently, the vehicle can drive in urban situations with high driving comfort and much more energy efficiency, which can be used to enlarge the range of electric vehicles or to save fuel while additionally improving travel time. Predictive velocity adaption (PREVA) represents a predictive longitudinal vehicle guidance concept. Here adaptations of the reference velocity are realized based on road curvature or width and weather and road conditions as well as driver-related impacts like mood or uncertainty. A safety layer is used to ensure collision-free driving. For this purpose, the actual path is compared to aggregated clearance information (i.e., low-level sensor data). In a crucial situation, this layer leads to a full stop. An obstacle avoidance algorithm realizes the need to avoid small objects in the lane without needing to do a full lane change.

For the subsequent calculation, it is necessary to determine an analytical description of the point-cloud describing the path. Based on Beziér-Splines, a piecewise polynomial description of the path called a reference trajectory is computed. These polynomials are represented as functions of the arc length covered along the reference trajectory.

1.5.2 Proven Planning Approach

In this section, a model-free trajectory planning algorithm is introduced, which calculates an optimal longitudinal and lateral trajectory for vehicle guidance based on the previously discussed reference path. A number of approaches exist for tackling trajectory computation. In [87] and [88], trajectories are generated by searching in a discrete state lattice. The principle is that the state space is discretized, generating a large number of target states. In combination with optimization control strategies, this can generate jerk-optimal trajectories [89]. However, the high number of different combinations results in a suboptimal solution with considerable computational effort.

Another possibility gives the optimization of kinematic variables. This procedure is based on the mass point model and minimizes kinematic or geometric quantities [90]. Various functions such as polynomials, sigmoids, and splines are used for trajectory planning, followed by optimization. In [91] and [92], a trajectory is planned using continuous curvature polynomials. This algorithm first discretizes points on the road and connects them with curvature polynomials. By numerical optimization, an optimal trajectory is generated. However, the curvature is dependent on the speed and acceleration of the vehicle, and the polynomials used and the cost functional are not matched, so that stability cannot be guaranteed [93].

MPC allows us to solve an optimal control problem cyclically by using the feedback of the current system state and to predict the behavior of road users. This basic idea can be applied to the motion planning of vehicles. In the work of [94] and [95], the planning is implemented with the MPC, which determines an optimal trajectory including a quality functional. In the work of [96], an approach for longitudinal and lateral guidance based on the MPC is developed. Due to the special formulation for trajectory optimization, a follow-up driving behavior on curved scenes can be realized. This planning is based on the Frenét coordinates and results in an efficient calculation for longitudinal and lateral guidance. The model-predictive method uses system models to calculate not only the optimal trajectory but also the optimal manipulated variables. The advantage of the MPC is its ability to integrate the constraints of the system. The disadvantage, however, is the computational effort that increases with the prediction horizon. In order to reduce the computational effort, an explicit MPC can be used, which provides an efficient calculation.

Due to the practical relevance, we will describe a model-free approach based on [89] and an MPC approach [97] in more detail.

In the case of the model-free approach and due to the Frenét coordinate system (see Figure 1.3), we can individually solve the lateral and the longitudinal problems. Thus, optimal longitudinal ($s(t)$) and lateral ($d(s)$) trajectories are computed and merged afterward. Using this Frenét system, a position $\vec{x}(s(t), d(s))$ at a specific time t is described by Equation 1.13:

$$\vec{x}(s(t),d(s)) = \vec{r}(s(t)) + d(s)\vec{n}_r(s(t)) \tag{1.13}$$

where $s(t)$ is the arc length, $d(s)$ is the lateral offset on the respective path length, $\vec{n}_r(s(t)) = [-\sin\theta_r(s), \cos\theta_r(s)]^T$ is the normal vector on the path at the point $\vec{r}(s(t)) = [r_1(s(t)), r_2(s(t))]^T$, and $\theta_r(s)$ is the orientation of the path [98]. Based on Pontryagin's minimum principle, the unconstrained lateral and longitudinal optimization problems are analytically solved [99].

1.5.3 Optimal Trajectory Computation—The Longitudinal Case

The calculation of valid longitudinal trajectories is of significant importance for safety and comfort. Thus, the velocity profile is determined by solving an optimal control problem (OCP), considering the traffic situation as well as road infrastructure. Such an OCP is a special case of the general optimization problem. For that purpose, the longitudinal OCP is formulated using the kinematic relations in Equations 1.14a–1.14c:

$$\min_{u} J_s = k_{t_f} t_f + \int_0^{t_f} \frac{\alpha_s}{2} u_s^2(t) + \frac{\gamma_s}{2} s_3^2(t) dt \tag{1.14a}$$

$$\text{s.t. } \dot{s}(t) = \begin{bmatrix} 0 & 1 & 0 \\ 0 & 0 & 1 \\ 0 & 0 & 0 \end{bmatrix} s(t) + \begin{bmatrix} 0 \\ 0 \\ 1 \end{bmatrix} u_s(t) \tag{1.14b}$$

$$s(0) = s_0 \quad \text{and} \quad s(t_f) = s_{t_f} \tag{1.14c}$$

where the state $s \in \mathbb{R}^3$ represents the arc length and its first (velocity) and second (acceleration) derivatives of the ego vehicle. The control input $u_s(t)$ represents the jerk and t_f the final time, which gives the optimization horizon. The three terms of the cost functional J_s contain the jerk, the acceleration, and the final time. These terms are weighted with the parameters k_{tf}, α_s, and $\gamma_s \in \mathbb{R}^+$. The resulting OCP is solved using the Hamiltonian (Equation 1.15):

$$\mathcal{H}(t, s^*, u_s^*, \lambda) = \lambda_1 s_2 + \lambda_2 s_3 + \lambda_3 u_s + \frac{\alpha_s}{2} u_s^2 + \frac{\gamma_s}{2} s_3^2 \tag{1.15}$$

with the Lagrange multipliers $\lambda = [\lambda_1, \lambda_2, \lambda_3]$. Following the ideas of the calculus of variations, the analytical solution of the optimization problem can be computed as in Equation 1.16:

$$s_1(t) = \sigma_0 + \sigma_1 t + \sigma_2 t^2 + \sigma_3 t^3 + \sigma_4 e^{k_s t} + \sigma_5 e^{-k_s t} \tag{1.16}$$

where $K_s = \sqrt{\gamma_s / \alpha_s}$. The coefficients $\sigma_0 \ldots \sigma_5$ will now be determined using the initial and final conditions in Equation 1.17:

$$\begin{pmatrix} 1 & 0 & 0 & 0 & 1 & 1 \\ 0 & 1 & 0 & 0 & k_s & -k_s \\ 0 & 0 & 2 & 0 & k_s^2 & k_s^2 \\ 1 & t_{f,j}^i & t_{f,j}^{i2} & t_{f,j}^{i3} & e^{k_s t_{f,j}^i} & e^{-k_s t_{f,j}^i} \\ 0 & 1 & 2t_{f,j}^i & 3t_{f,j}^{i2} & k_s e^{k_s t_{f,j}^i} & -k_s e^{-k_s t_{f,j}^i} \\ 0 & 0 & 2 & 6t_{f,j}^i & k_s^2 e^{k_s t_{f,j}^i} & k_s^2 e^{-k_s t_{f,j}^i} \end{pmatrix} \begin{pmatrix} \sigma_0^i \\ \sigma_1^i \\ \sigma_2^i \\ \sigma_3^i \\ \sigma_4^i \\ \sigma_5^i \end{pmatrix} \tag{1.17}$$

$$= \begin{pmatrix} s_0 & \dot{s}_0 & \ddot{s}_0 & s^i & \dot{s}^i & \ddot{s}^i \end{pmatrix}^T.$$

While the initial conditions are determined based on the actual position, velocity, and acceleration or on the previous trajectory, the final conditions are not a priori clear. Since no constraints are considered in the OCP (Equations 1.14a–1.14c), theoretically all values can arbitrarily increase. To tackle that issue the final conditions are varied, and the resulting trajectories are filtered due to constraints and sorted based on the cost functional. Beside the indicated degree of freedom, the reference contains for the velocity such that the final value for the velocity is clear, but when we will reach it is fittable. For more details, see [100].

Since there is no velocity term in the optimization problem (see Equation 1.14a), it becomes hard to track the velocity request at every time instant. Thus, the incoming velocity profile is artificially partitioned [100]. This leads to a trackable velocity request.

1.5.4 The Lateral Optimal Control Problem

As in the longitudinal case, a special form of Equation 1.1 and the kinematic relations of the lateral behavior are used to formulate an OCP in Equations 1.18a–1.18c:

$$\min_{u} J_d = k_{t_f} t_f + \int_0^{t_f} \frac{\alpha_d}{2} u_d^2(t) + \frac{\gamma_d}{2} d_d^2(t) dt \tag{1.18a}$$

$$\text{s.t.} \quad \dot{d}(s(t)) = \begin{bmatrix} 0 & 1 & 0 \\ 0 & 0 & 1 \\ 0 & 0 & 0 \end{bmatrix} d(s(t)) + \begin{bmatrix} 0 \\ 0 \\ 1 \end{bmatrix} u_d(t) \tag{1.18b}$$

$$d(0) = d_0 \quad \text{and} \quad d(s(t_f)) = d_{s(t_f)} \tag{1.18c}$$

As above, the analytical solution can be reached using Pontryagin's minimum principle, as seen in Equation 1.19:

$$d_1(s(t)) = \delta_0 + \delta_1 s + e^{k_d s} \left(\delta_2 \cos(k_d s) + \delta_3 \sin(k_d s) \right)$$
$$+ e^{-k_d s} \left(\delta_4 \cos(k_d s) + \delta_5 \sin(k_d s) \right) \tag{1.19}$$

where $k_d = \sqrt[4]{\dfrac{\gamma_d}{4\alpha_d}}$. Following the same argumentation as in longitudinal calculations, a linear set of equations is formulated and solved several times. The control references consist of the path information introduced in Section 1.5.1. As a result, we get a number of lateral trajectories of the form in Equation 1.19 that are specified via different values for $\delta_0, \ldots, \delta_5$. With these two sets of trajectories (one for lateral and one for longitudinal) in hand, all combinations are determined. These combinations are trajectories in the plane and can be used as input for the underlying following control. Now the question arises as to which trajectory should be chosen. For that purpose, the resulting 2-D trajectories are filtered due to inherent requirements like physical or comfort limits—e.g., the maximum acceleration or the path boundaries. As a result, a list of possible drivable trajectories is achieved.

This list containing the lateral and longitudinal trajectories is sorted according to the overall cost functional in Equation 1.20:

$$J(s(t), d(s)) = k_s J_s(s(t)) + k_d J_d(d(s)) \tag{1.20}$$

The best trajectory is then transferred to control.

At first glance, it looks a little bit intricate to compute numerous trajectories and filter them afterward. Nevertheless, it is computationally very efficient to solve the underlying linear set of equations using the analytical solution such that no online optimization and thus no extensive online optimization solver are needed. An alternative approach is given in the next section.

1.5.5 The MPC-Based Approach

In this section, we will show how path following is realized by utilizing an MPC-based approach. Here we consider explicitly a vehicle dynamic and kinematic model. Consequently, the resulting trajectories are more preferable, especially in challenging urban situations (heavy traffic and narrow roads). However, the MPC-based approach is less computationally efficient in comparison to the model-free approach previously discussed.

In the case of the MPC, optimization is a central tool with which to achieve comfortable and even derivable trajectories. Thus, we will come back to the basic definitions of Section 1.2. With the reference path in hand, we could directly control the vehicle using the path information as input. Nevertheless, this might lead to uncomfortable driving behavior as well as controller inconsistency. To smooth the path and directly consider comfort requirements, optimization techniques are used again. In contrast to the previous section, here we address an MPC approach that directly takes the vehicle model into account.

As mentioned before, a vehicle model is needed in order to set up the MPC. Accordingly, the longitudinal and lateral dynamics of the vehicle are modeled as a continuous-time nonlinear system in the form in Equations 1.21a and 1.21b:

$$\dot{x}(t) = f(x(t), u(t)), \quad x(t_0) = x_0 \tag{1.21a}$$

$$y(t) = h(x(t)) \tag{1.21b}$$

with the maps $f : \mathbb{R}^9 \times \mathbb{R}^2 \to \mathbb{R}^9$ and $h : \mathbb{R}^9 \to \mathbb{R}^3$. The state vector $x = [x, y, \psi, \dot{\psi}, \beta, v, v_{ref}, \delta_s, \delta_{s,ref}]^T$ consists of the vehicle states, like the coordinates of the center of gravity (CG) in an inertial frame x and y, the yaw angle ψ, the yaw rate $\dot{\psi}$, the side slip angle β, the velocity v, the target velocity v_{ref}, the steering wheel angle δ_s, and the steering wheel target angle $\delta_{s,ref}$. The control input $u = [a_{ref}, \omega_{s,ref}]^T$ contains the target acceleration a_{ref} and the steering wheel target angular velocity $\omega_{s,ref}$ of the vehicle. Furthermore, the output vector $y = [x_f, y_f, \psi]^T$ includes the coordinates of the middle of the front axle x_f and y_f as well as the vehicle orientation ψ.

More specifically, we are using a single-track model according to [27] in order to describe the lateral vehicle behavior. By assuming a steerable front wheel, we receive the model equation set in Equations 1.22a–1.22d:

$$\dot{x}(t) = v(t)\cos(\psi(t) + \beta(t)) \tag{1.22a}$$

$$\dot{y}(t) = v(t)\sin(\psi(t) + \beta(t)) \tag{1.22b}$$

$$\ddot{\psi}(t) = -\frac{c_{sf}l_f^2 + c_{sr}l_r^2}{J_z v(t)}\dot{\psi}(t) - \frac{c_{sf}l_f - c_{sr}l_r}{J_z}\beta(t)$$
$$+ \frac{c_{sf}l_f}{J_z}\delta_a(t) \tag{1.22c}$$

$$\dot{\beta}(t) = \left(-1 - \frac{c_{sf}l_f - c_{sr}l_r}{mv(t)^2}\right)\dot{\psi}(t) - \frac{c_{sf} + c_{sr}}{mv(t)}\beta(t)$$
$$+ \frac{c_{sf}}{mv(t)}\delta_a(t). \tag{1.22d}$$

The parameters l_f and l_r denote the distance from CG to the front and rear wheels, respectively. Furthermore, the parameters c_{sf} and c_{sr} represent the cornering stiffnesses of the two wheels. The total mass and the yaw moment of inertia of the whole system are denoted by m and J_z.

The lateral vehicle dynamics are represented by an model consisting of an integrator and PT_1 model (Equations 1.23a–1.23b).

$$\dot{v}(t) = \frac{1}{T_v}(v_{ref}(t) - v(t)) \tag{1.23a}$$

$$\dot{v}_{ref}(t) = a_{ref}(t) \tag{1.23b}$$

with the target acceleration a_{ref} and the time constant T_v. This model represents the dynamics of the engine and braking system as well as the utilized low-level controller of the vehicle. For more details on the utilized dynamic single-track model, refer to [97].

To finalize the model description, we also have to consider the sets of state and input constraints, which are due to the physical limitations of the vehicle. These sets of constraints are given by $x \in \mathcal{X} \subseteq \mathbb{R}^9$ and $u \in \mathcal{U} \subseteq \mathbb{R}^2$.

The primary goal of the MPC vehicle guidance approach is to create an output sequence of the system (Equation 1.21) that realizes a proper tracking of the geometric reference path. To realize a path tracking, we have to define the tracking error. Therefore, we utilize the deviation from the path as in Equation 1.24:

$$e(t) := h(x(t)) - p(s(t)) \tag{1.24}$$

This gives us the opportunity to formulate the path-following problem. For the given system (Equation 1.21) and the reference path, we want to design a control algorithm that calculates an optimal $u(\cdot)$ as well as $s(\cdot)$ and ensures the following three criteria are met:

1. *Path convergence*: The system output y converges to the reference path such that $\lim_{t\to\infty}\|e(t)\| = 0$.

2. *Velocity convergence*: The path velocity $\dot{s}(t)$ converges to a predefined evolution $\dot{s}_{ref}(t) \geq 0$ such that $\lim_{t\to\infty}\|\dot{s}(t) - \dot{s}_{ref}(t)\| = 0$.

3. *Constraint satisfaction*: The state and input constraints $\mathcal{X}$ and $\mathcal{U}$ are satisfied $\forall t \in [t_0, \infty)$.

A common procedure for the definition of a path-following MPC is to use a path parameter s in the form of a virtual state. In the current case, the time evolution of these virtual states is described by a differential equation called a timing law. We defined a timing law as a single integrator (Equation 1.25)

$$\dot{s}(t): = \vartheta(t) \tag{1.25}$$

where $\vartheta \in \mathcal{V} \subset \mathbb{R}$ is an additional (virtual) control input of the MPC.

We are formulating the path-following problem in the form of a standard optimization problem, as initially sketched in Equation 1.1 and formulated in Equation 1.14a. In order to solve these problems, a sampled-data MPC approach is used, similar to [101–103]. That is, we obtain the system input via the repeated solution of an OCP at each discrete sampling time instance $t_k = kT_s$ in a decreasing horizon manner. In what follows, the predicted system states and inputs are denoted by $\bar{x}(\cdot)$ and $\bar{u}(\cdot)$. The cost functional to be minimized for the prediction horizon T_p is given by Equation 1.26:

$$J(x(t_k), s(t_k), \bar{u}(\cdot), \bar{\vartheta}(\cdot)) =$$

$$\int_{t_k}^{t_k+T_p} \left\| \begin{matrix} \bar{e} \\ a_{lat}(\bar{x}) \end{matrix} \right\|_Q^2 + \left\| \begin{matrix} \bar{u} \\ \bar{\vartheta} - \vartheta_{ref} \end{matrix} \right\|_R^2 d\tau + \left\| \begin{matrix} \bar{e} \\ a_{lat}(\bar{x}) \end{matrix} \right\|_P^2 \tag{1.26}$$

where $Q = \mathrm{diag}(q_x, q_y, q_\psi, q_a)$, $P = \mathrm{diag}(p_x, p_y, p_\psi, p_a)$, and $R = \mathrm{diag}(r_a, r_\omega, r_\vartheta)$ are positive definite weighting matrices. Furthermore, $a_{lat}(x) = v(t)\,\dot{\psi}(t)$ is an approximation of the lateral acceleration of the vehicle. The resulting OCP solved at every sampling time instance is shown in Equation 1.27a:

$$\min_{\bar{u}(\cdot), \bar{\vartheta}(\cdot)} J(x(t_k), s(t_k), \bar{u}(\cdot), \bar{\vartheta}(\cdot)) \tag{1.27a}$$

subject to the constraints in Equations 1.27b–1.27g:

$$\dot{\overline{x}}(\tau) = f(\overline{x}(\tau), \overline{u}(\tau)), \quad \overline{x}(t_k) = x(t_k) \tag{1.27b}$$

$$\dot{\overline{s}}(\tau) = \overline{\vartheta}(\tau), \quad \overline{s}(t_k) = s(t_k) \tag{1.27c}$$

$$\overline{e}(\tau) = h(\overline{x}(\tau)) - p(\overline{s}(\tau)) \tag{1.27d}$$

$$\overline{u}(\tau) \in \mathcal{U}, \quad \overline{x}(\tau) \in \mathcal{X} \tag{1.27e}$$

$$\overline{s}(\tau) \in [0, s_{max}], \quad \overline{\vartheta}(\tau) \in \mathcal{V} \tag{1.27f}$$

$$h_c(\overline{x}(\tau), \overline{u}(\tau)) \leq 0 \tag{1.27g}$$

which have to hold for all $\tau \in [t_k, t_k + T_p]$. The constraints in Equations 1.27b and 1.27c represent the dynamics of the system (Equation 1.21) and the time law (Equation 1.25) with their respective initial conditions. Due to the fact that we want to realize a proper path-following behavior, we try to minimize the deviation of the system output from the path. Therefore, the path deviation (Equation 1.24) is stated by Equation 1.27d. Equations 1.27e and 1.27f represent the state and input constraints, including the virtual state $\overline{s}$ and the virtual input $\overline{\vartheta}$. Finally, Equation 1.27g defines further constraints with the constraint function h_c. The optimal input trajectory $\overline{u}_k^\star(\cdot)$ that results from the OCP is applied to the system (Equation 1.21) in Equation 1.28:

$$\forall t \in [t_k, t_k + T_s) : u(t) = \overline{u}_k^\star(t) \tag{1.28}$$

More in detail, the input trajectory $\overline{u}_k^\star(\cdot)$ is transmitted to the follow-up controller. The follow-up controller is realized as a classical PID-based cascade controller, which handles the longitudinal and lateral tracking control problems independently of each other. The main objective of the follow-up controller is the transformation of the trajectory $\overline{u}_k^\star(\cdot)$ into a suitable control variable for the vehicle interface (vehicle CAN) as well as the elimination of disturbance effects.

At each new time instance $t_k + T_s$, the optimization horizon is shifted forward, and the OCP from Equation 1.27 is solved again for new initial conditions, and then the whole process is repeated.

After introducing the two approaches for the calculation of suitable driving trajectories, the question arises as to which is better or which should be used in which situation. While this question is generally hard to answer, we illustrate how the algorithms act on the following use case.

To briefly illustrate the differences between the two approaches introduced in Sections 1.5.2–1.5.4 and 1.5.5, a small case study is introduced. Thus, real test data is presented, and the influences of the two different planning strategies (the MPC and trajectory-planning approaches) on the driven velocity are considered. For that purpose, we drove the path shown in Figure 1.4a at a velocity of $v = 30\,\mathrm{km\,h^{-1}} \approx 8,3\,\mathrm{m\,s^{-1}}$. The lateral and the longitudinal problems are solved, but the achieved differences on the lateral behavior are not so descriptive. Thus, the longitudinal tracking is investigated more in detail. Figure 1.4b shows that the velocity tracking of the trajectory-planning approach is quite good. There is just some noise on the velocity, which is a result of the measurement disturbances coming from the ground as well as the environment. At first glance, we see that the velocity tracking of the MPC is much worse. There are two sections (gray shaded) where the velocity significantly decreased, while the set value remains fixed. Certainly, this is a feature and no bug. Based on the gray shaded areas in Figure 1.4, we see that the break in the velocity occurs in the curves of the path. In the cost functional (Equation 1.26) the lateral acceleration (a_{lat}) is weighted and thus influences the requested velocity of the MPC. Driving in the curves leads to an increase in the lateral acceleration. In order to limit this increase, the velocity is decreased. In other words, the minimum of the cost functional (Equation 1.26) is affected by the velocity error as well as the lateral acceleration. Thus, a compromise results.

To tackle the previously teased question, let us sum up some properties of the two approaches. The MPC approach has the advantage that it takes the dynamic model of the vehicle into account. In a nutshell, this leads to a more comfortable and more easily trackable trajectory. However, online optimization is needed, which results in a high computational load and might lead to suboptimal or nonvalid solutions. The trajectory-planning approach is undemanding in terms of the resources needed, since the optimization problem is solved analytically and transformed into the solving of a linear set of equations. However, we need to calculate a lot of trajectories. Due to the considered kinematic model, all dynamic effects need to be addressed in the underlying controller.

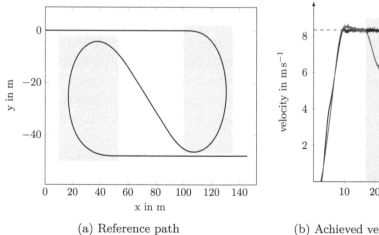

(a) Reference path

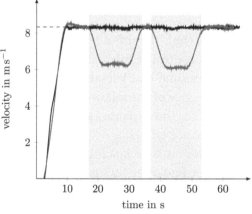

(b) Achieved velocity for the kinematic trajectory planning approach (—) as well as the MPC(—)

FIGURE 1.4 Test drive data for the trajectory-planning approach and MPC. (a) Reference path. (b) Achieved velocity for the kinematic trajectory planning approach (—) as well as the MPC(—).

Thus, the concrete choice for one of the algorithms significantly depends on the hardware available, the ODD, and the DDT as well as the requirements regarding comfort and tracking quality.

1.6 CONCLUSION

Futuristic and autonomous vehicles are currently a trendy topic with great attention from both academia and industry. We were presenting a survey that offers an overview of automated driving architectures and functionalities. As an introduction to the topic, we started with a detailed analysis of one concrete automated driving task (lane change). The task of realizing a lane change serves as a running example. Following this, we showed that mathematical optimization is a key technology with which to realize automated driving functionalities. Therefore, we formulated a generalized optimization problem and discussed which automated driving functions are using such optimizing methods. Following this, we discussed concrete functional architectures for automated driving applications realized by different companies and universities.

After these discussions, we went more in detail and focused on environment representation, situation-aware interpretation, and rule-based and AI-based intelligent decision-making subfunctions. Here, we started with the formal problem statements and discussed realization aspects. Finally, we presented one model-free and one model-based motion planning approach. Also here, we started with the formal problem statements and discussed thereafter concrete realization aspects. All the automated driving subfunctions discussed were already implemented and tested in IAV's test vehicles in open traffic situations in Germany.

In our future work, we will gradually realize and expand our situation-aware maneuver-planning approach by adopting a two-pronged strategy. On the one hand, from the short-term application and project perspective, respectively, we will focus on more straightforward decision-making approaches (e.g., in terms of hierarchical state machines) but extend the number of available basic maneuvers and improve the existing maneuvers and driving behaviors to be applicable in more complex situations. For our shuttle project ABSOLUT, e.g., the lane change maneuver has to be revised to be applicable for both highway and more complex urban scenarios. On the other hand, while extending the number of maneuvers and driving behaviors with each project, we will step by step replace the straightforward decision-making and planning approaches with more intelligent approaches that, among other things, can cope with uncertainties, allow for online planning on different levels of abstraction, and can even adapt to new and unforeseen situations.

The urban scenarios considered in the project OPA³L guide this progress in decision-making and planning techniques. Furthermore, the MPC is a significant topic in sequel development such that intelligent velocity preprocessing and path adjustments to realize an obstacle avoidance functionality within the MPC, as well as object-based control, are essential parts of our actual and future work.

ACRONYMS

ACC	adaptive cruise control
AD	Automated driving
AD system	automated driving system
AI	artificial intelligence
AL	active learning
AS	active seeing
CEM	comprehensive environment model
DDT	dynamic driving task
GLOSA	green light optimal speed advisory
IG	information gain
KL	Kullback-Leibler
MDP	Markov decision process
ML	machine learning
MPC	model predictive control
OCP	optimal control problem
ODD	operational design domain
POMDP	partially observable Markov decision process
PREVA	predictive velocity adaption
RL	reinforcement learning
SA	situation awareness
SMDP	semi-Markov decision process
V2X	vehicle-to-everything

ACKNOWLEDGMENT

We gratefully acknowledge the financial support of this work by the Federal Ministry for Economic Affairs and Energy under the grant 50NA1912.

REFERENCES

1. Zongwei Liu, Hao Jiang, Hong Tan, and Fuquan Zhou. An overview of the latest progress and core challenge of autonomous vehicle technologies. *MATEC Web of Conference*, 308:06002, 2020.
2. SAE International. Taxonomy and Definitions for Terms Related to Driving Automation Systems for On-Road Motor Vehicles, June 2018.
3. Alexander Jungmann, Christian Lang, Florian Pinsker, Roland Kallweit, Mirko Taubenreuther, and Matthias Butenuth. Artificial intelligence for automated driving—Quo vadis? In *Automatisiertes Fahren 2019*, pp. 117–134. Springer Fachmedien Wiesbaden, Wiesbaden, 2020.
4. SYNCAR—Synchronized Automated Driving in Urban Areas. https://www.synchrone-mobilitaet.de/en/projects/syncar.html, 2020. Accessed: 2020–08–04.
5. HarmonizeDD—Continuous Support of Connected and Automated Driving for Mixed Traffic with Heterogeneously Equipped Vehicles. https://www.synchrone-mobilitaet.de/en/projects/harmonizedd.html, 2020. Accessed: 2020–08–04.
6. Rico Auerswald, Roman Busse, Markus Dod, Richard Fritzsche, Alexander Jungmann, Michael Klöppel-Gersdorf, Josef F. Krems, Sven Lorenz, Franziska Schmalfuß, Sabine Springer, and Severin Strobl. Cooperative driving in mixed traffic with heterogeneous

communications and cloud infrastructure. In *Proceedings of the 5th International Conference on Vehicle Technology and Intelligent Transport Systems*, pp. 95–105, 2019.

7. Automation ohne Unsicherheit zur Erhöhung der Akzeptanz automatisierten und vernetzten Fahrens—AutoAkzept. https://www.bmvi.de/SharedDocs/DE/Artikel/DG/AVF-projekte/autoakzept.html, 2020. Accessed: 2020-08-17.

8. Uwe Drewitz, Klas Ihme, Michael Oehl, Frank Schrödel, Rick Voßwinkel, Franziska Hartwich, Cornelia Hollander, Anna-Antonia Pape, Tobias Fleischer, Sonja Cornelsen, Andreas Lüdtke, Daniela Gräfing, and Alexander Trende. Automation ohne Unsicherheit: Vorstellung des Förderprojekts AutoAkzept zur Erhöhung der Akzeptanz automatisierten Fahrens. *VDI Fachtagung Mensch-Maschine-Mobilität*, 10:1–19, November 2019.

9. OPA³L—Optimal Assistierte, hoch Automatisierte, Autonome und kooperative Fahrzeugnavigation und Lokalisation. http://www.math.uni-bremen.de/zetem/cms/detail.php?id=19184, 2020. Accessed: 2020-08-17.

10. ABSOLUT—Anspruchsvoll, Ganzheitlich, Intelligent. https://absolut-projekt.de/, 2020. Accessed: 2020-08-04.

11. HEAT—Hamburg Electric Autonomous Transportation. https://bit.ly/2BXUUkR, 2020. Accessed: 2020-08-04.

12. Elijah Polak. *Optimization: Algorithms and Consistent Approximations*. Springer, New York, 1997.

13. Leonid T. Aschepkov, Dmitriy V. Dolgy, Taekyun Kim, and Ravi P. Agarwal. *Optimization: Algorithms and Consistent Approximations*. Springer International Publishing, New York, 2016.

14. Pierre de Fermat. *Pierre de Fermats Abhandlungen über Maxima und Minima (1629)*. Akademische Verlagsgesellschaft m.b.h., Leipzig, 1934.

15. John Wallis. A treatise of algebra, both historical and practical. *Philosophical Transactions of the Royal Society of London*, 15(173):1095–1106, 1685.

16. Ding-Zhu Du, Panos M. Pardalos, and Weili Wu. History of optimization. In *Encyclopedia of Optimization*, pp. 1538–1542. Springer, Boston, 2009.

17. Svetlana S. Petrova and Alexander D. Solov'ev. The origin of the method of steepest descent. *Historia Mathematica*, 24(4):361–375, 1997.

18. George B. Dantzig and Mukund N. Thapa. *Linear Programming 1: Introduction*. Springer, New York, 1997.

19. Charles G. Broyden. Quasi-Newton methods. In *Numerical Methods for Unconstrained Optimization*, pp. 87–106. Academic Press, London, 1972.

20. John H. Holland. *Adaptation in Natural and Artificial Systems: An Introductory Analysis with Applications to Biology, Control and Artificial Intelligence*. MIT Press, Cambridge, MA, 1992.

21. Scott Kirkpatrick, Danial Gelatt, and Mario P. Vecchi. Optimization by simulated annealing. *Science*, 220(4598):671–680, 1983.

22. James Kennedy, Russel C. Eberhart, and Yuhui Shi. *Swarm Intelligence*. Morgan Kaufmann/Academic Press, San Francisco/San Diego, 2001.

23. Christopher M. Bishop. *Pattern Recognition and Machine Learning*. Springer, New York, 2006.

24. Kevin P. Murphy. *Machine Learning: A Probabilistic Perspective*. MIT Press, Cambridge, MA, 2012.

25. Ian Goodfellow, Yoshua Bengio, and Aaron Courville. *Deep Learning*. MIT Press, Cambridge, MA, 2016.

26. Richard S. Sutton and Andrew G. Barto. *Reinforcement Learning: An Introduction*. MIT Press, Cambridge, MA, 1998.

27. Rajesh Rajamani. *Vehicle Dynamics and Control*. Springer, New York, 2012.

28. Ali Boyali, Seiichi Mita, and Vijay John. A tutorial on autonomous vehicle steering controller design, simulation and implementation. *ArXiv*, abs/1803.03758, 2018.

29. Pan Zhao, Jiajia Chen, Yan Song, Xiang Tao, Tiejuan Xu, and Tao Mei. Design of a control system for an autonomous vehicle based on adaptive-PID. *International Journal of Advanced Robotic Systems*, 9(2):44, 2012.

30. Malik Ghallab, Dana Nau, and Paolo Traverso. *Automated Planning: Theory & Practice.* Morgan Kaufmann, San Francisco, 2004.

31. Wilko Schwarting, Javier Alonso-Mora, and Daniela Rus. Planning and decision-making for autonomous vehicles. *Annual Review of Control, Robotics, and Autonomous Systems*, 1: 187–210 2018.

32. Christopher V. Rao, James B. Rawlings, and Jay H. Lee. Constrained linear state estimation— A moving horizon approach. *Automatica*, 37(10):1619–1628, 2001.

33. Afnan Alofi, Anwaar A. Alghamdi, Razan Faisal Alahmadi, Najla Aljuaid, and M Hemalatha. A review of data fusion techniques. *International Journal of Computer Applications*, 167:37–41, 2017.

34. Ronald C. Arkin. *Behavior-Based Robotics.* MIT Press, Cambridge, MA, 1998.

35. Mohamed Salah Hamdi. *Entwurf adaptiver lernender Roboter.* PhD thesis, UniversitÄt Hamburg, 1999.

36. Robin R. Murphy. *Introduction to AI Robotics.* MIT Press, Cambridge, MA, 2019.

37. James S. Albus, Harry McCain, and Ronald Lumia. NASA/NBS Standard Reference Model for Telerobot Control System Architecture (NASREM). Technical report, 1989.

38. Rodney Brooks. Achieving Artificial Intelligence through Building Robots. Technical report, 1986.

39. Rodney Brooks. Intelligence without representation. *Artificial Intelligence*, 47(1–3):139–159, 1991.

40. Tucker Balch and Ronald C. Arkin. Behavior-based formation control for multirobot teams. *IEEE Transactions on Robotics and Automation*, 14(6):926–939, 1998.

41. Rodney Brooks. A robust layered control system for a mobile robot. *IEEE Journal on Robotics and Automation*, 2(1):14–23, 1986.

42. James S. Albus. The NIST real-time control system (RCS): An approach to intelligent systems research. *Journal of Experimental & Theoretical Artificial Intelligence*, 9(2–3): 157–174, 1997.

43. Malik Ghallab, Dana Nau, and Paolo Traverso. The actor's view of automated planning and acting: A position paper. *Artificial Intelligence*, 208:1–17, 2014.

44. Felix Lotz. *Eine Referenzarchitektur für die assistierte und automatisierte Fahrzeugführung mit Fahrereinbindung [A Reference Architecture for Assisted and Automated Vehicle Guidance with Driver Interaction].* PhD thesis, Technische Universität Darmstadt, 2017.

45. Félix Ingrand and Malik Ghallab. Deliberation for autonomous robots: A survey. *Artificial Intelligence*, 247:10–44, 2017.

46. Erann Gat. On three-layer architectures. *Artificial Intelligence and Mobile Robots*, 195:210, 1998.

47. Rachid Alami, Raja Chatila, Sara Fleury, Malik Ghallab, and Félix Ingrand. An architecture for autonomy. *International Journal of Robotics Research*, 17(4):315–337, 1998.

48. Ernst Dieter Dickmanns, Reinhold Behringer, Dirk Dickmanns, Thomas Hildebrandt, Markus Maurer, Frank Thomanek, and Joachim Schiehlen. The seeing passenger car "VaMoRs-P." In *Proceedings of the Intelligent Vehicles' 94 Symposium*, pp. 68–73. IEEE, 1994.

49. Ernst Dieter Dickmanns. *Dynamic Vision for Perception and Control of Motion.* Springer, London, 2007.

50. Markus Maurer. *Flexible Automatisierung von StraBenfahrzeugen mit Rechnersehen.* PhD thesis, Universität der Bundeswehr München, 2000.

51. Martin Pellkofer. *Verhaltensentscheidung für autonome Fahrzeuge mit Blickrichtungssteuerung.* PhD thesis, Universität der Bundeswehr Münche, 2003.

52. Sören Kammel, Julius Ziegler, Benjamin Pitzer, Moritz Werling, Tobias Gindele, Daniel Jagzent, Joachim Schröder, Michael Thuy, Matthias Goebl, Felix von Hundelshausen et al. Team AnnieWAY's autonomous system for the 2007 DARPA Urban Challenge. *Journal of Field Robotics*, 25(9):615–639, 2008.

53. Charles Reinholtz, Dennis Hong, Al Wicks, Andrew Bacha, Cheryl Bauman, Ruel Faruque, Michael Fleming, Chris Terwelp, Thomas Alberi, David Anderson et al. Odin: Team VictorTango's entry in the DARPA Urban Challenge. In *The DARPA Urban Challenge*, pp. 125–162. Springer, Berlin, Heidelberg, 2009.

54. Michael Montemerlo, Jan Becker, Suhrid Bhat, Hendrik Dahlkamp, Dmitri Dolgov, Scott Ettinger, Dirk Haehnel, Tim Hilden, Gabe Hoffmann, Burkhard Huhnke et al. Junior: The Stanford entry in the Urban Challenge. *Journal of Field Robotics*, 25(9):569–597, 2008.

55. Chris Urmson, Joshua Anhalt, Drew Bagnell, Christopher Baker, Robert Bittner, MN Clark, John Dolan, Dave Duggins, Tugrul Galatali, Chris Geyer et al. Autonomous driving in urban environments: Boss and the Urban Challenge. *Journal of Field Robotics*, 25(8):425–466, 2008.

56. Tobias Nothdurft, Peter Hecker, Sebastian Ohl, Falko Saust, Markus Maurer, Andreas Reschka, and Jürgen Rüdiger Böhmer. Stadtpilot: First fully autonomous test drives in urban traffic. In *2011 14th International IEEE Conference on Intelligent Transportation Systems (ITSC)*, pp. 919–924. IEEE, 2011.

57. Eric Bauer, Felix Lotz, Matthias Pfromm, Matthias Schreier, Stephan Cieler, Alfred Eckert, Andree Hohm, Stefan Lüke, Peter Rieth, Bettina Abendroth, Volker Willert, Jürgen Adamy, Ralph Bruder, Ulrich Konigorski, and Hermann Winner. Proreta 3: An integrated approach to collision avoidance and vehicle automation. *at-Automatisierungstechnik*, 60(12):755–765, 2012.

58. Tobias Nothdurft. *Ein Kontextmodell für sicherheitsrelevante Anwendungen in der autonomen Fahrzeugführung*. PhD thesis, Technische Universität Braunschweig, 2014.

59. Richard Matthaei and Markus Maurer. Autonomous driving—A top-down-approach. *at-Automatisierungstechnik*, 63(3):155–167, 2015.

60. Frank Schrödel and Matthias Freese. Concept and validation of a guidance approach for highly automated shuttles. *IFAC-PapersOnLine*, 52(5):359–365, 2019.

61. Mica Endsley. Toward a theory of situation awareness in dynamic systems. *Human Factors*, 37(1):32–64, 1995.

62. Mica Endsley. Situation awareness and human error: Designing to support human performance. In *Proceedings of the High Consequence Systems Surety Conference*, pp. 2–9, 1999.

63. Thanh Nguyen, Chee Peng Lim, Ngoc Duy Nguyen, Lee Gordon-Brown, and Saeid Nahavandi. A review of situation awareness assessment approaches in aviation environments. *IEEE Systems Journal*, 13(3):3590–3603, 2019.

64. Matthias Schreier. Environment representations for automated on-road vehicles. *at-Automatisierungstechnik*, 66(2):107–118, 2018.

65. Stéphanie Lefèvre, Dizan Vasquez, and Christian Laugier. A survey on motion prediction and risk assessment for intelligent vehicles. *ROBOMECH Journal*, 1(1):1, 2014.

66. Britta Hummel. *Description Logic for Scene Understanding: At the Example of Urban Road Intersections*. PhD thesis, Universität Karlsruhe, 2010.

67. Michael Huelsen. *Knowledge-Based Driver Assistance Systems: Traffic Situation Description and Situation Feature Relevance*. Springer Vieweg, Wiesbaden, 2014.

68. Stefan Brunner, Markus Kucera, and Thomas Waas. Ontologies used in robotics: A survey with an outlook for automated driving. In *IEEE International Conference on Vehicular Electronics and Safety*, pp. 81–84. IEEE, 2017.

69. Christian Roesener, Felix Fahrenkrog, Axel Uhlig, and Lutz Eckstein. A scenario-based assessment approach for automated driving by using time series classification of human-driving behaviour. In *IEEE 19th International Conference on Intelligent Transportation Systems*, pp. 1360–1365. IEEE, 2016.

70. ByeoungDo Kim, Chang Mook Kang, Jaekyum Kim, Seung Hi Lee, Chung Choo Chung, and Jun Won Choi. Probabilistic vehicle trajectory prediction over occupancy grid map via recurrent neural network. In *IEEE 20th International Conference on Intelligent Transportation Systems*, pp. 399–404. IEEE, 2017.

71. Florent Altché and Arnaud de La Fortelle. An LSTM network for highway trajectory prediction. In *IEEE 20th International Conference on Intelligent Transportation Systems*, pp. 353–359. IEEE, 2017.

72. Nachiket Deo and Mohan M. Trivedi. Convolutional social pooling for vehicle trajectory prediction. In *Proceedings of the IEEE Conference on Computer Vision and Pattern Recognition Workshops*, pp. 1468–1476, 2018.

73. Xin Li, Xiaowen Ying, and Mooi Choo Chuah. Grip++: Graph-based interaction-aware trajectory prediction. In *IEEE Intelligent Transportation Systems Conference*, pp. 3960–3966, IEEE, 2019.

74. Sebastian Thrun, Wolfram Burgard, and Dieter Fox. *Probabilistic Robotics*. MIT Press, Cambridge, MA, 2005.

75. Achim Klenke. *Wahrscheinlichkeitstheorie*. Springer, Berlin, Heidelberg, 2006.

76. Yiannis Demiris and Bassam Khadhouri. Hierarchical attentive multiple models for execution and recognition of actions. *Robotics and Autonomous Systems*, 54(5):361–369, 2006.

77. Mehdi Elahi, Francesco Ricci, and Neil Rubens. A survey of active learning in collaborative filtering recommender systems. *Computer Science Review*, 20:29–50, 2016.

78. Alexander Jungmann and Bernd Kleinjohann. Automatic composition of service-based image processing applications. In *Proceedings of the 13th IEEE International Conference on Services Computing*, pp. 106–113. IEEE, 2016.

79. Alexander Jungmann and Bernd Kleinjohann. A holistic and adaptive approach for automated prototyping of image processing functionality. In *Proceedings of the 21st IEEE International Conference on Emerging Technologies and Factory Automation*, pp. 1–8. IEEE, 2016.

80. Martin L. Puterman. *Markov Decision Processes: Discrete Stochastic Dynamic Programming*. Wiley-Interscience, Hoboken, NJ, 2005.

81. Christopher J. C. H. Watkins and Peter Dayan. Q-learning. *Machine Learning*, 8:279–292, 1992.

82. Leslie Pack Kaelbling, Michael L. Littman, and Anthony R. Cassandra. Planning and acting in partially observable stochastic domains. *Artificial Intelligence*, 101(1):99–134, 1998.

83. Oussama Khatib. Real-time obstacle avoidance for manipulators and mobile robots. In IEEE International Conference on Robotics and Automation, pp. 500–505. IEEE, 1985.

84. Jonathan Bohren, Tully Foote, Jim Keller, Alex Kushleyev, Daniel Lee, Alex Stewart, Paul Vernaza, Jason Derenick, John Spletzer, and Brian Satterfield. Little Ben: The Ben Franklin Racing Team's entry in the 2007 DARPA Urban Challenge. *Journal of Field Robotics*, 25(9):598–614, 2008.

85. Michael Montemerlo, Jan Becker, Suhrid Bhat, Hendrik Dahlkamp, Dmitri Dolgov, Scott Ettinger, Dirk Haehnel, Tim Hilden, Gabe Hoffmann, Burkhard Huhnke, Doug Johnston, Stefan Klumpp, Dirk Langer, Anthony Levandowski, Jesse Levinson, Julien Marcil, David Orenstein, Johannes Paefgen, Isaac Penny, Anna Petrovskaya, Mike Pflueger, Ganymed Stanek, David Stavens, Antone Vogt, and Sebastian Thrun. Junior: The Stanford entry in the Urban Challenge. In *The DARPA Urban Challenge*, pp. 91–123. Springer, Berlin, Heidelberg, 2009.

86. Thomas M. Howard and Alonzo Kelly. Optimal rough terrain trajectory generation for wheeled mobile robots. *International Journal of Robotics Research*, 26(2):141–166, 2007.

87. Julius Ziegler and Christoph Stiller. Spatiotemporal state lattices for fast trajectory planning in dynamic on-road driving scenarios. In *IEEE/RSJ International Conference on Intelligent Robots and Systems*, pp. 1879–1884, 2009.

88. John M. Dolan, Jin-Woo Lee, Matthew McNaughton, and Chris Urmson. Motion planning for autonomous driving with a conformal spatiotemporal lattice. In *IEEE International Conference on Robotics and Automation*, pp. 4889–4895, IEEE, 2011.

89. Moritz Werling, Julius Ziegler, Sören Kammel, and Sebastian Thrun. Optimal trajectory generation for dynamic street scenarios in a Frenet frame. *IEEE International Conference on Robotics and Automation*, pp. 987–993, IEEE, 2010.

90. Martin Keller. *Trajektorienplanung zur Kollisionsvermeidung im Straßenverkehr.* PhD thesis, Technische Universität Dortmund, 2017.
91. Alanzo Kelly and Bryan Nagy. Reactive nonholonomic trajectory generation via parametric optimal control. *International Journal of Robotics Research,* 22(7–8):583–601, 2003.
92. Wenda Xu, Junqing Wei, John M. Dolan, Huijing Zhao, and Hongbin Zha. A real-time motion planner with trajectory optimization for autonomous vehicles. In *IEEE International Conference on Robotics and Automation,* pp. 2061–2067. IEEE, 2012.
93. Christian Rathgeber. *Trajektorienplanung und -folgeregelung für assistiertes bis hochautomatisiertes Fahren.* PhD thesis, Technischen Universität Berlin, 2016.
94. Sterling Anderson, Steven Peters, Thomas Pilutti, and Karl Iagnemma. An optimal-control-based framework for trajectory planning, threat assessment, and semi-autonomous control of passenger vehicles in hazard avoidance scenarios. *International Journal of Vehicle Autonomous Systems,* 8:190–216, 2010.
95. Moritz Werling and Darren Liccardo. Automatic collision avoidance using model-predictive online optimization. In *51st IEEE Conference on Decision and Control,* pp. 6309–6314. IEEE, 2012.
96. Benjamin Gutjahr, Christian Pek, Lutz Gröll, and Moritz Werling. Recheneffiziente Trajektorienoptimierung für Fahrzeuge mittels quadratischem Programm. *at – Automatisierungstechnik,* 64:786–794, 2016.
97. Robert Ritschel, Frank Schrödel, Juliane Hädrich, and Jens Jäkel. Nonlinear model predictive path-following control for highly automated driving. *IFAC-PapersOnLine,* 52(8):350–355, 2019.
98. İlhan Mutlu, Matthias Freese, Khaled Alaa, and Frank Schrödel. Case study on model free determination of optimal trajectories in highly automated driving. In *9th Symposium on Advances in Automotive Control,* 2019.
99. Magnus R. Hestene. *Calculus of Variations and Optimal Control Theory.* Wiley, New York, 1966.
100. Rick Voßwinkel, İlhan Mutlu, Khaled Alaa, and Frank Schrödel. A modular and model-free trajectory planning strategy for automated driving. In *European Control Conference,* 2020.
101. Timm Faulwasser, Benjamin Kern, and Rolf Findeisen. Model predictive path-following for constrained nonlinear systems. In *Proceedings of the 48h IEEE Conference on Decision and Control Held Jointly with 28th Chinese Control Conference,* pp. 8642–8647. IEEE, 2009.
102. Timm Faulwasser, Tobias Weber, Pablo Zometa, and Rolf Findeisen. Implementation of nonlinear model predictive path-following control for an industrial robot. *IEEE Transactions on Control Systems Technology,* 25(4):1505–1511, 2017.
103. Martin Böck and Andreas Kugi. Real-time nonlinear model predictive path-following control of a laboratory tower crane. *IEEE Transactions on Control Systems Technology,* 22(4):1461–1473, 2014.

CHAPTER 2

Control Strategies for Autonomous Vehicles

Chinmay Vilas Samak, Tanmay Vilas Samak, and Sivanathan Kandhasamy

SRM Institute of Science and Technology
Kattankulathur, India

CONTENTS

DOI: 10.1201/9781003048381-3

This chapter focuses on self-driving technology from a control perspective and investigates the control strategies used in autonomous vehicles and advanced driver-assistance systems (ADASs) from both theoretical and practical viewpoints.

First, we introduce self-driving technology as a whole, including perception, planning, and control techniques required for accomplishing the challenging task of autonomous driving. We then dwell on each of these operations to explain their role in the autonomous system architecture, with a prime focus on control strategies.

The core portion of this chapter commences with detailed mathematical modeling of autonomous vehicles, followed by a comprehensive discussion on control strategies. This chapter covers longitudinal as well as lateral control strategies for autonomous vehicles with coupled and decoupled control schemes. We also discuss some of the machine learning techniques applied to autonomous vehicle control.

Finally, we provide a brief summary of some of the research work that our team has carried out at the Autonomous Systems Lab (SRMIST) and conclude with some thoughtful closing remarks.

2.1 INTRODUCTION

Autonomous vehicles, or self-driving cars as they are publicly referred to, have been the dream of humankind for decades. This is a rather complex problem statement to address, and it requires interdisciplinary expertise, especially when considering the safety, comfort, and convenience of the passengers, along with the variable environmental factors and highly stochastic fellow agents such as other vehicles and pedestrians. The complete realization of this technology will therefore mark a significant step in the field of engineering.

2.1.1 Autonomous Driving Technology

An autonomous vehicle perceives the environment using a comprehensive sensor suite and processes the raw data from the sensors in order to make informed decisions. The vehicle then plans the trajectory and executes controlled maneuvers in order to track the trajectory autonomously. This process is elucidated below.

The system architecture of an autonomous vehicle is fundamentally laid out as a stack that constitutes of the subsystems shown in Figure 2.1:

1. *Perception:* Autonomous vehicles employ various types of sensors such as cameras, LIDARs, RADARs, SONARs, IMUs, and GNSS receivers in order to perceive the environment (object and event detection and tracking) and monitor their own physical parameters (localization and state estimation) for making informed decisions. Suitable sensor fusion and filtering algorithms, including simpler ones such as the complementary filter and moving average filter and advanced ones such as Kalman filter (and its variants) and particle filter, are adopted in order to reduce measurement uncertainty due to noisy sensor data. In a nutshell, this subsystem is responsible for providing both intrinsic and extrinsic knowledge to the ego vehicle using various sensing modalities.

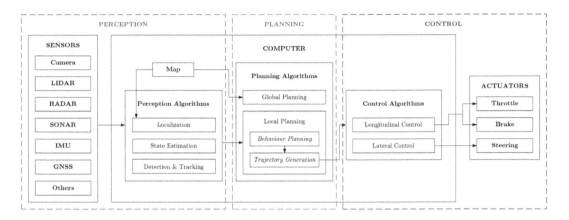

FIGURE 2.1   System architecture of an autonomous vehicle.

2. *Planning:* Using the data obtained from the perception subsystem, the ego vehicle performs behavior planning wherein the most optimal behavior to be adopted by the ego vehicle needs to be decided by predicting states of the ego vehicle as well as other dynamic objects in the environment into the future through a certain prediction horizon. Based on the planned behavior, the motion planning module generates an optimal trajectory, considering the global plan, passenger safety, comfort as well as hard and soft motion constraints. This entire process is termed as *motion planning*. Note that there is a subtle difference between path planning and motion planning in that the prior is responsible only for planning the reference "path" to a goal location (ultimate or intermediate goal), whereas the latter is responsible for planning the reference "trajectory" to a goal location (i.e., it considers not just the pose but also its higher derivatives such as velocity, acceleration, and jerk, thereby assigning a temporal component to the reference path).

3. *Control:* Finally, the control subsystem is responsible for accurately tracking the trajectory provided by the planning subsystem. It does so by appropriately adjusting the final control elements (throttle, brake, and steering) of the vehicle.

2.1.2 Significance of Control System

A control system is responsible for regulating or maintaining the process conditions of a plant at their respective desired values by manipulating certain process variables to adjust the variables of interest, which are generally the output variables.

From the perspective of autonomous vehicles, the control system is dedicated to generating appropriate commands for the throttle, brake, and steering (input variables) so that the vehicle (plant) tracks a prescribed trajectory by executing a controlled motion (where motion parameters such as position, orientation, velocity, acceleration, and jerk are the output variables). It is to be noted that the input and output variables (aka manipulated/process variables and controlled variables, respectively) are so designated with respect to the plant and not the controller, which is a common source of confusion.

Control system plays a very crucial role in the entire architecture of an autonomous vehicle, and being the last member of the pipeline, it is responsible for actually "driving" the vehicle. It is this subsystem that ultimately decides how the ego vehicle will behave and interact with the environment.

Although the control subsystem cannot function independently without the perception and planning subsystems, it is also a valid argument that the perception and planning subsystems are rendered useless if the controller is not able to track the prescribed trajectory accurately.

2.1.3 Control System Architecture for Autonomous Vehicles

The entire control system of an autonomous vehicle is fundamentally broken down into the following two components:

- *Longitudinal control:* This component controls the longitudinal motion of the ego vehicle, considering its longitudinal dynamics. The controlled variables in this case are the throttle and brake inputs to the ego vehicle, which govern its motion (velocity, acceleration, jerk, and higher derivatives) in the longitudinal direction.

- *Lateral control:* This component controls the lateral motion of the ego vehicle, considering its lateral dynamics. The controlled variable in this case is the steering input to the ego vehicle, which governs its steering angle and heading. Note that steering angle and heading are two different terminologies. While steering angle describes the orientation of the steerable wheels and hence the direction of motion of the ego vehicle, heading is concerned with the orientation of the ego vehicle.

2.2 MATHEMATICAL MODELING

Mathematical modeling of a system refers to the notion of describing the response of a system to the control inputs while accounting for the state of the system using mathematical equations. The following analogy of an autonomous vehicle better explains this notion.

When control inputs are applied to an autonomous vehicle, it moves in a very specific way depending on the control inputs. For example, the throttle increases acceleration, and the brake reduces it, while the steering alters heading of the vehicle by certain amount. A mathematical model of such an autonomous vehicle will represent the exact amount of linear and/or angular displacement, velocity, acceleration, etc. of the vehicle depending on the amount of applied throttle, brake, and/or steering input(s).

In order to actually develop mathematical model of an autonomous vehicle (or any system for that matter), there are two methods widely used in industry and academia:

1. *First principles modeling:* This approach is concerned with applying the fundamental principles and constituent laws to derive the system models. It is a theoretical way of dealing with mathematical modeling that does not necessarily require access to the actual system and is mostly adopted for deducing generalized mathematical models

of the concerned system. We will be using this approach in the upcoming section to formulate the kinematic and dynamic models of a front-wheel-steered nonholonomic (autonomous) vehicle.

2. *Modeling by system identification:* This approach is concerned with applying known inputs to the system, recording its responses to those inputs, and statistically analyzing the input-output relations to deduce the system models. This approach is a practical way of dealing with mathematical modeling that requires access to the actual system and is mostly adopted for modeling complex systems, especially where realistic system parameters are to be captured. It is to be noted that this approach is often helpful to estimate system parameters even though the models are derived using the first principles approach.

System models can vary from very simplistic linear models to highly detailed and complex nonlinear models. The complexity of the model being adopted depends on the problem at hand.

There is always a trade-off between model accuracy and the computational complexity that comes with it. Owing to their accuracy, complex motion models may seem attractive at first glance; however, they may consume a considerable amount of time for computation, rendering them far from being executable in real time. When it comes to safety-critical systems like autonomous vehicles, latency is considered a serious problem, as failing to perform actions in real time may lead to catastrophic consequences. Thus, in practice, for systems like autonomous vehicles, often approximate motion models are used to represent the system dynamics. Again, the level of approximation depends on factors like driving speed, computational capacity, and the quality of sensors and actuators.

It is to be noted here that the models describing vehicle motion are not only useful in control system design but also a very important tool for predicting future states of the ego vehicle or other objects in the scene (with associated uncertainty), which is extremely useful in the perception and planning phases of autonomous vehicles.

We make the following assumptions and consider the following motion constraints for modeling the vehicle.

- Assumptions

  - The road surface is perfectly planar; any elevations or depressions are disregarded. This is known as the *planar assumption.*

  - Front and rear wheels are connected by a rigid link of fixed length.

  - Front wheels are steerable and act together and can be effectively represented as a single wheel.

  - Rear wheels act together and can be effectively represented as a single wheel.

  - The vehicle is actually controllable like a bicycle.

- Motion Constraints

  - *Pure rolling constraint:* This constraint implies that each wheel follows a pure rolling motion with respect to the ground; there is no slipping or skidding of the wheels.

  - *Nonholonomic constraint:* This constraint implies that the vehicle can move only along the direction of its heading and cannot arbitrarily slide along the lateral direction.

2.2.1 Kinematic Model

Kinematics is the study of motion of a system disregarding the forces and torques that govern it. Kinematic models can be employed in situations wherein kinematic relations are able to sufficiently approximate the actual system dynamics. It is important to note, however, that this approximation holds true only for systems that perform nonaggressive maneuvers at lower speeds. As an example, kinematic models can provide a nearly accurate representation of a vehicle driving slowly and making smooth turns. However, if we consider something like a racing car, it is very likely that the kinematic model would fail to capture the actual system dynamics.

In this section, we present one of the most widely used kinematic models for autonomous vehicles, the *kinematic bicycle model*. This model performs well at capturing the actual vehicle dynamics under nominal driving conditions. In practice, this model tends to strike a good balance between simplicity and accuracy and is therefore widely adopted. That being said, one can always develop more detailed and complex models depending on the requirement.

The idea is to define the vehicle state and see how it evolves over time based on the previous state and current control inputs given to the vehicle.

Let the vehicle state constitute x and y components of position, heading angle or orientation θ, and velocity (in the heading direction) v. Summarizing, the ego vehicle state vector q is defined as follows:

$$q = \left[x, y, \theta, v \right]^{T} \qquad (2.1)$$

For control inputs, we need to consider both longitudinal (throttle and brake) and lateral (steering) commands. The brake and throttle commands contribute to longitudinal accelerations in the range of $\left[-a'_{max}, a_{max} \right]$, where negative values represent deceleration due to braking and positive values represent acceleration due to throttling (forward or reverse, depending on the transmission state). Note that the limits a'_{max} and a_{max} are intentionally denoted so as to distinctly illustrate the difference between the physical limits of acceleration due to throttling and those of deceleration due to braking. The steering command alters the steering angle δ of the vehicle, where $\delta \in \left[-\delta_{max}, \delta_{max} \right]$ such that negative steering angles dictate left turns and positive steering angles otherwise. Note that generally the control inputs are clamped in the range of $\left[-1, 1 \right]$ based on the actuators for proper scaling of control commands in terms of actuation limits. Summarizing, ego vehicle control vector u is defined as follows:

$$u = [a, \delta]^T \tag{2.2}$$

We will now derive the kinematic model of the ego vehicle. As shown in Figure 2.2, the local reference frame is located at the center of gravity of the ego vehicle.

Using the distance between the rear wheel axle and the vehicle's center of gravity, we can compute the slip angle β as follows:

$$tan(\beta) = \frac{l_r}{S} = \frac{l_r}{\left(\dfrac{L}{tan(\delta)}\right)} = \frac{l_r}{L} * tan(\delta) \tag{2.3}$$

$$\therefore \beta = tan^{-1}\left(\frac{l_r}{L} * tan(\delta)\right)$$

Ideally, $l_r = L/2 \Rightarrow \beta = tan^{-1}\left(\dfrac{tan(\delta)}{2}\right)$.

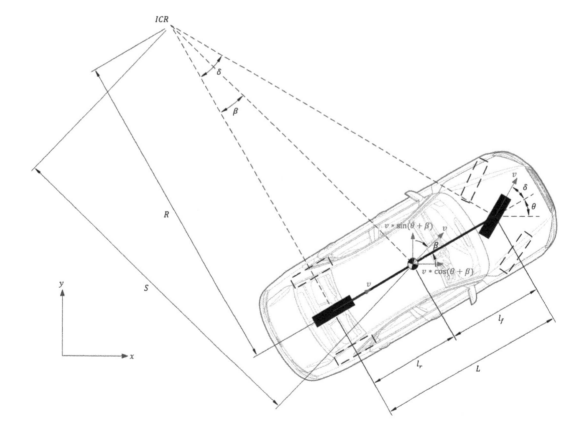

FIGURE 2.2   Vehicle kinematics.

Resolving the velocity vector v into x and y components using the laws of trigonometry, we get

$$\dot{x} = v * \cos(\theta + \beta) \tag{2.4}$$

$$\dot{y} = v * \sin(\theta + \beta) \tag{2.5}$$

In order to compute $\dot{\theta}$, we first need to calculate S using the following relation:

$$S = \frac{L}{\tan(\delta)} \tag{2.6}$$

Using S obtained from Equation 2.6, we can compute R as follows:

$$R = \frac{S}{\cos(\beta)} = \frac{L}{(\tan(\delta) * \cos(\beta))} \tag{2.7}$$

Using R obtained from Equation 2.7, we can deduce $\dot{\theta}$ as follows:

$$\dot{\theta} = \frac{v}{R} = \frac{v * \tan(\delta) * \cos(\beta)}{L} \tag{2.8}$$

Finally, we can compute $\dot{v}$ using the rudimentary differential relation:

$$\dot{v} = a \tag{2.9}$$

Using Equations 2.4, 2.5, 2.8, and 2.9, we can formulate the continuous-time kinematic model of an autonomous vehicle:

$$\dot{q} = \begin{bmatrix} \dot{x} \\ \dot{y} \\ \dot{\theta} \\ \dot{v} \end{bmatrix} = \begin{bmatrix} v * \cos(\theta + \beta) \\ v * \sin(\theta + \beta) \\ \dfrac{v * \tan(\delta) * \cos(\beta)}{L} \\ a \end{bmatrix} \tag{2.10}$$

Based on the formulation in Equation 2.10, we can formulate the discrete-time model of an autonomous vehicle:

$$\begin{cases} x_{t+1} = x_t + \dot{x}_t * \Delta t \\ y_{t+1} = y_t + \dot{y}_t * \Delta t \\ \theta_{t+1} = \theta_t + \dot{\theta}_t * \Delta t \\ v_{t+1} = v_t + \dot{v}_t * \Delta t \end{cases} \tag{2.11}$$

Note that Equation 2.11 is known as the *state transition equation* (generally represented as $q_{t+1} = q_t + \dot{q}_t * \Delta t$), where t in the subscript denotes current time instant and $t+1$ in the subscript denotes next time instant.

2.2.2 Dynamic Model

Dynamics is the study of motion of a system with regard to the forces and torques that govern it. In other words, dynamic models are motion models of a system that closely resemble the actual system dynamics. Such models tend to be more complex and inefficient to solve in real time (depending on computational hardware) but are required for high-performance scenarios such as racing, where driving at high speeds and with aggressive maneuvers is common.

There are two popular methodologies for formulating dynamic model of a system: the Newton-Euler method and the Lagrange method. In the Newton-Euler approach, one has to consider all the forces and torques acting on the system, whereas in the Lagrange approach, the forces and torques are represented in terms of potential and kinetic energies of the system. It is to be noted that both approaches are equally correct and result in equivalent formulations of dynamic models. In this section, we will present longitudinal and lateral dynamic models of an autonomous vehicle using Newton-Euler approach.

2.2.2.1 Longitudinal Vehicle Dynamics

The free-body diagram of an autonomous vehicle along the longitudinal direction (denoted as x) is depicted in Figure 2.3. The longitudinal forces considered include the vehicle inertial term $m * \ddot{x}$, front and rear tire forces F_{xf} and F_{xr}, aerodynamic resistance F_{aero}, front and rear rolling resistance R_{xf} and R_{xr}, and x component of the gravitational force $m * g * sin(\alpha)$ (since the y component of gravitational force $m * g * cos(\alpha)$ and the normal force F_N cancel each other). Note that the tire forces help the vehicle to move forward, whereas all other forces resist the forward vehicle motion.

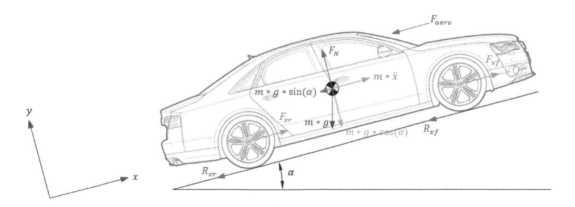

FIGURE 2.3   Longitudinal vehicle dynamics.

Thus, applying Newton's second law of motion to the free-body diagram, we get

$$m * \ddot{x} = F_{xf} + F_{xr} - F_{aero} - R_{xf} - R_{xr} - m * g * sin(\alpha)$$

The above dynamic equation can be simplified as follows. Let the front and rear tire forces collectively represent traction force F_x and the front and rear rolling resistances collectively represent net rolling resistance R_x. Also, making a small angle approximation for α, we can say that $sin(\alpha) \approx \alpha$. Therefore we have

$$m * \ddot{x} = F_x - F_{aero} - R_x - m * g * \alpha$$
$$\therefore \ddot{x} = \frac{F_x}{m} - \frac{F_{aero}}{m} - \frac{R_x}{m} - g * \alpha \tag{2.12}$$

The individual forces can be modeled as follows:

- *Traction force* F_x depends on vehicle mass m, wheel radius r_{wheel}, and angular acceleration of the wheel $\ddot{\theta}_{wheel}$. Since $F = m * a$ and $a = r * \ddot{\theta}$, we have

$$F_x = m * r_{wheel} * \ddot{\theta}_{wheel} \tag{2.13}$$

- *Aerodynamic resistance* F_{aero} depends on air density ρ, frontal surface area of the vehicle A, and velocity of the vehicle v. Using proportionality constant C_α, we have

$$F_{aero} = \frac{1}{2} * C_\alpha * \rho * A * v^2 \approx C_\alpha * v^2 \tag{2.14}$$

- *Rolling resistance* R_x depends on tire normal force N, tire pressure P, and velocity of the vehicle v. Note that tire pressure is a function of vehicle velocity.

$$R_x = N * P(v)$$

where $P(v) = \hat{C}_{r,0} + \hat{C}_{r,1} * |v| + \hat{C}_{r,2} * v^2$.

$$\therefore R_x = N * \left(\hat{C}_{r,0} + \hat{C}_{r,1} * |v| + \hat{C}_{r,2} * v^2 \right) \approx \hat{C}_{r,1} * |v| \tag{2.15}$$

Substituting Equations 2.13, 2.14, and 2.15 in Equation 2.12, we get

$$\ddot{x} = r_{wheel} * \ddot{\theta}_{wheel} - \frac{C_\alpha * v^2}{m} - \frac{\hat{C}_{r,1} * |v|}{m} - g * \alpha \tag{2.16}$$

We can represent the second time derivative of velocity as jerk (the rate of change of acceleration) as follows:

$$\ddot{v} = j \tag{2.17}$$

2.2.2.2 Lateral Vehicle Dynamics

The free-body diagram of an autonomous vehicle along the lateral direction (denoted as y) is depicted in Figure 2.4. The lateral forces considered include the inertial term $m*a_y$ and the front and rear tire forces F_{yf} and F_{yr}, respectively. The torques considered include vehicle torque about instantaneous center of rotation $I_z*\ddot{\theta}$ and moments of front and rear tire forces l_f*F_{yf} and l_r*F_{yr}, respectively (acting in opposite directions).

Thus, applying Newton's second law of motion to the free-body diagram, we get

$$m*a_y = F_{yf} + F_{yr} \tag{2.18}$$

$$I_z*\ddot{\theta} = l_f*F_{yf} - l_r*F_{yr} \tag{2.19}$$

The linear lateral acceleration $\ddot{y}$ and centripetal acceleration $R*\dot{\theta}^2$ collectively contribute to the total lateral acceleration a_y of the ego vehicle. Hence, we have

$$a_y = \ddot{y} + R*\dot{\theta}^2 = \ddot{y} + v*\dot{\theta} \tag{2.20}$$

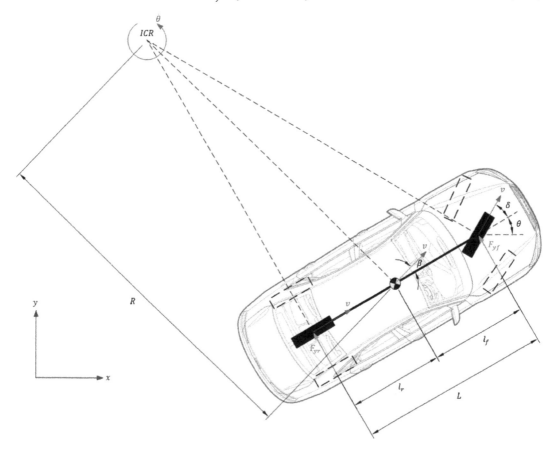

FIGURE 2.4   Lateral vehicle dynamics.

Substituting Equation 2.20 into Equation 2.18, we get

$$m*(\ddot{y}+v*\dot{\theta})= F_{yf} + F_{yr} \tag{2.21}$$

The linearized lateral tire forces F_{yf} and F_{yr}, also known as cornering forces, can be modeled using front and rear tire slip angles α_f and α_r and cornering stiffness of front and rear tires C_f and C_r as follows:

$$\begin{cases} F_{yf} = C_f*\alpha_f = C_f*\left(\delta-\beta-\dfrac{l_f*\dot{\theta}}{v}\right) \\ \\ F_{yr} = C_r*\alpha_r = C_r*\left(-\beta+\dfrac{l_r*\dot{\theta}}{v}\right) \end{cases} \tag{2.22}$$

Substituting the values of linearized lateral tire forces F_{yf} and F_{yr} from Equation 2.22 into Equations 2.21 and 2.19, respectively, and rearranging the terms, we get

$$\ddot{y}=-\frac{(C_f+C_r)}{m}*\beta+\left(\frac{C_r*l_r-C_f*l_f}{m*v}-v\right)*\dot{\theta}+\frac{C_f}{m}*\delta \tag{2.23}$$

$$\ddot{\theta}=\frac{C_r*l_r-C_f*l_f}{I_z}*\beta-\frac{C_r*l_r^2+C_f*l_f^2}{I_z*v}*\dot{\theta}+\frac{C_f*l_f}{I_z}*\delta \tag{2.24}$$

2.2.2.3 Consolidated Dynamic Model

Equations 2.16, 2.17, 2.23, and 2.24 represent the dynamic model of an autonomous vehicle. The consolidated continuous-time dynamic model of an autonomous vehicle can be therefore formulated as follows:

$$\ddot{q}=\begin{bmatrix}\ddot{x}\\\ddot{y}\\\ddot{\theta}\\\ddot{v}\end{bmatrix}=\begin{bmatrix}r_{wheel}*\ddot{\theta}_{wheel}-\dfrac{C_\alpha*v^2}{m}-\dfrac{\hat{C}_{r,1}*|v|}{m}-g*\alpha\\[3mm]-\dfrac{(C_f+C_r)}{m}*\beta+\left(\dfrac{C_r*l_r-C_f*l_f}{m*v}-v\right)*\dot{\theta}+\dfrac{C_f}{m}*\delta\\[3mm]\dfrac{C_r*l_r-C_f*l_f}{I_z}*\beta-\dfrac{C_r*l_r^2+C_f*l_f^2}{I_z*v}*\dot{\theta}+\dfrac{C_f*l_f}{I_z}*\delta\\[3mm]j\end{bmatrix} \tag{2.25}$$

Based on the formulation in Equations 2.25 and 2.10, we can formulate the discrete-time model of an autonomous vehicle as follows:

$$
\begin{cases}
x_{t+1} = x_t + \dot{x}_t * \Delta t + \ddot{x}_t * \dfrac{\Delta t^2}{2} \\[2ex]
y_{t+1} = y_t + \dot{y}_t * \Delta t + \ddot{y}_t * \dfrac{\Delta t^2}{2} \\[2ex]
\theta_{t+1} = \theta_t + \dot{\theta}_t * \Delta t + \ddot{\theta}_t * \dfrac{\Delta t^2}{2} \\[2ex]
v_{t+1} = v_t + \dot{v}_t * \Delta t + \ddot{v}_t * \dfrac{\Delta t^2}{2}
\end{cases}
\tag{2.26}
$$

Note that Equation 2.26 is known as the *state transition equation* (generally represented as $q_{t+1} = q_t + \dot{q}_t * \Delta t + \ddot{q}_t * \dfrac{\Delta t^2}{2}$), where t in the subscript denotes current time instant and $t+1$ in the subscript denotes next time instant.

2.3 CONTROL STRATEGIES

Thus far, we have discussed in detail all the background concepts related to control strategies for autonomous vehicles (or any other system, for that matter).

In this section, we present classical as well as some of the current state-of-the-art control strategies for autonomous vehicles. Some of these are pretty easy and intuitive, while others are not. We begin by discussing simpler ones and then introduce more complex strategies for vehicle control, but first let us see the different control schemes.

2.3.1 Control Schemes

As stated in Section 2.1.3, the control system of an autonomous vehicle is split into longitudinal and lateral components. Depending on whether or not these components influence each other, the control schemes can be referred to as *coupled* or *decoupled* control.

2.3.1.1 Coupled Control

Coupled control refers to a control scheme wherein the lateral and longitudinal controllers operate synergistically and have some form of influence over each other. Although this approach is very realistic, the major difficulty in practical implementation lies in accurately determining the "amount" of influence the controllers are supposed to have over one another, considering the motion model and the operational design domain (ODD) of the ego vehicle.

In a coupled-control scheme, the lateral controller may influence the longitudinal controller or vice versa, or both may have an influence over each other. Let us consider each case independently with an example.

2.3.1.1.1 Longitudinal Controller Influencing Lateral Controller   In this case, the longitudinal controller is dominant or has a higher preference over the lateral controller. As a result, the longitudinal control action is computed independently, and this influences the lateral control action with an inverse relation (i.e., inverse proportionality). Since it is not a good idea to have a large steering angle at high speed, the controller regulates the maximum steering limit inversely proportional to the vehicle speed.

2.3.1.1.2 Lateral Controller Influencing Longitudinal Controller   As opposed to the previous case, in this one, the lateral controller is dominant or has a higher preference over the longitudinal controller. As a result, the lateral control action is computed independently, and this influences the longitudinal control action with an inverse relation (i.e., inverse proportionality). Since it is a bad idea to have high speed with large steering angle, the controller regulates the maximum speed limit inversely proportional to the steering angle.

2.3.1.1.3 Longitudinal and Lateral Controllers Influencing Each Other   In this case, both controllers tend to influence each other depending on the operating conditions. If it is more important to maintain high speeds, the longitudinal controller has a greater (more dominant) influence over the lateral controller, and if the maneuver requires cornering at sharp turns, the lateral controller has a greater (more dominant) influence over the longitudinal controller. Generally, the operating conditions change over the course of duration, and "weights" need to be shifted in order to switch the dominance of lateral and longitudinal controllers.

2.3.1.2 Decoupled Control
Decoupled control refers to a control scheme wherein the lateral and longitudinal controllers do not have any influence on each other; i.e., both the controllers operate independently, disregarding the control actions generated by other.

Although this simplifies the control problem to a large extent, this type of control scheme does not seem very realistic, considering the fact that lateral and longitudinal vehicle dynamics inherently affect each other. In other words, this control scheme is applicable only to highly specific and uniform driving scenarios (i.e., limited ODD).

2.3.2 Traditional Control
Traditional control is one of the most widely used and reliable control strategies, especially when it comes to safety-critical systems such as autonomous vehicles.

There are primarily three objectives of a controller:

1. *Stability:* Stability refers to the fact that a system should always produce a bounded output (response) when excited with a bounded input signal. This criterion for stability is popularly known as the bounded-input, bounded-output (BIBO) criterion. This is especially significant for inherently unstable systems.

2. *Tracking:* Tracking refers to the fact that a control system should be able to track the desired reference value (aka set point). In other words, the system response should be

as close to the set point as possible, with minimal transient and/or steady-state error (zero in the ideal case).

3. *Robustness:* Robustness refers to the fact that a control system should be able to exhibit stability and tracking despite external disturbances. In other words, the system must remain stable (i.e., meet the BIBO criterion), and its response should be as close to the set point as possible even when it is disturbed by external factors.

Since traditional controllers can be tuned and analyzed to meet the objectives stated above, they become the primary choice among control strategies, especially for systems such as autonomous robots and vehicles.

Traditional control systems can be either open loop, which do not use any state feedback, or closed loop, which do. However, when it comes to motion control of autonomous vehicles, a control problem where operating conditions are continuously changing, open loop control is not a possibility. Thus, for control of autonomous vehicles, closed loop control systems are implemented with an assumption that the state is directly measurable or can be estimated by implementing state observers. Such traditional controllers can be classified as *model-free* and *model-based* controllers.

1. *Model-free controllers:* These types of controllers do not use any mathematical model of the system being controlled. They tend to take "corrective" action based on the "error" between set point and current state. These controllers are quite easy to implement, since they do not require in-depth knowledge of the behavior of the system; however, they are difficult to tune, do not guarantee optimal performance, and perform satisfactorily only under limited operating conditions. Common examples of these type of controllers include bang-bang controllers, proportional-integral-derivative (PID) controllers, and intelligent PID (iPID) controllers.

2. *Model-based controllers:* These types of controllers use some type of mathematical model of the system being controlled. Depending on the model complexity and the exact approach followed to generate the control commands, these can be further classified as follows:

   a. *Kinematic controllers:* These types of controllers use simplified motion models of the system and are based on the geometry and kinematics of the system (generally employing first-order approximation). They assume no slip, no skid and often ignore internal or external forces acting on the system. Therefore, these types of controllers are often restricted to low-speed applications (where system dynamics can be approximated), but they offer an advantage of low computational complexity (which is extremely significant in real-world implementation as opposed to theoretical formulation or simulation).

   b. *Dynamic controllers:* These types of controllers use detailed motion models of the system and are based on system dynamics. They consider forces and torques acting on the system as well as any disturbances (incorporated in the dynamic model). Therefore, these types of controllers have an upper hand when compared to kinematic controllers due to the unrestricted ODD, but they suffer from higher computational complexity owing to the complex computations involving detailed models at each time step.

c. *Model predictive controllers:* These types of controllers use linear or nonlinear motion models of the system to predict its future states (up to a finite receding horizon) and determine the optimal control action by numerically solving a bounded optimization problem at each time step (essentially treating the control problem as an optimization problem, a strategy known as optimal control). The optimization problem is bounded, since model predictive controllers explicitly handle motion constraints, which is another reason for their popularity. Although this sounds like the perfect control strategy, it is to be noted that since model predictive controllers use complex motion models and additionally solve an online optimization problem at each time step, they are computationally expensive and may cause undesirable control latency (sometimes even of the order of a few seconds) if not implemented wisely.

The upcoming sections discuss these traditional control strategies for autonomous vehicles in greater detail.

2.3.2.1 Bang-Bang Control

The bang-bang controller is a simple binary controller. It is extremely easy to implement, which is the most significant (and perhaps the only) reason for adopting it. The control action u is switched between two states, u_{max} and u_{min} (analogous to on/off, high/low, true/false, set/reset, 1/0, etc.), based on whether the input signal x is above or below the reference value x_{ref}.

$$u = \begin{cases} u_{max} & ; x < x_{ref} \\ u_{min} & ; x > x_{ref} \end{cases}$$

Note that a multistep controller may be adopted to switch the control action based on more than just two cases. For example, a third control action of 0 is also possible in case the error becomes exactly zero (i.e., $x = x_{ref}$); however, practically, this case will last only an instant, since even a small error value will overshoot the system response.

The bang-bang controller, in either of its two states, generates the same control action regardless of the error value. In other words, it does not account for the magnitude of error signal. It is therefore termed "unstable" due to its abrupt responses and is recommended for application only to *variable structure systems (VSS)* that allow *sliding motion control (SMC)*.

Considering the final control elements (throttle, brake, and steering) of an autonomous vehicle, it is safe to say that a bang-bang controller may not be applied to control the lateral vehicle dynamics; the vehicle would constantly oscillate about the mean position, trying to minimize the cross-track error e_Δ and/or heading error e_ψ by completely turning the steering wheel in one direction or the other, which would be not only uncomfortable but also dangerous and could even cause a rollover at higher velocities. Nonetheless, a bang-bang controller may be applied to control the longitudinal vehicle dynamics by fully actuating the throttle and brakes based on the velocity error e_v, and while this may be safe, it may still result in exceeding the nominal jerk values, causing a rather uncomfortable ride. It is important to note at this point that abrupt control actions generated by a bang-bang controller can possibly cause lifetime reduction, if not immediate breakdown, of actuators, which is highly undesirable.

2.3.2.1.1 Bang-Bang Control Implementation   Implementation of a bang-bang controller for lateral control of a simulated autonomous vehicle is illustrated in Figure 2.5 (although we noted that this is not a good idea). In order to have uniformity across all the implementations discussed in this chapter, a well-tuned PID controller was employed for longitudinal control of the ego vehicle.

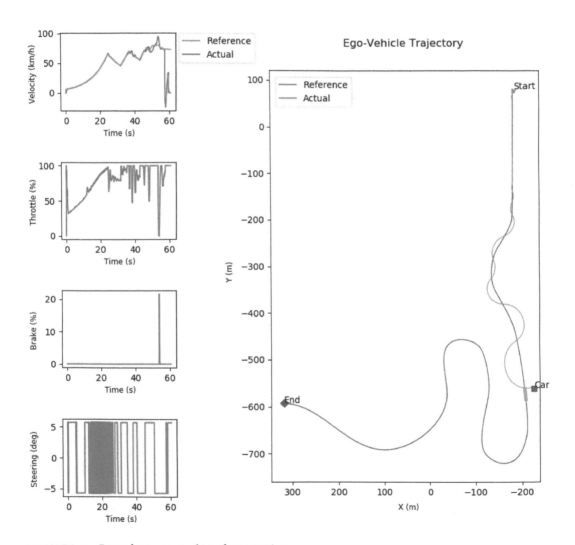

FIGURE 2.5   Bang-bang control implementation.

For the purpose of this implementation, the reference trajectory to be followed by the ego vehicle (shown in green in the trajectory plot) was discretized into waypoints to be tracked by the lateral controller, and each waypoint had an associated velocity set point to be tracked by the longitudinal controller.

The bang-bang controller response was alleviated by multiplying the control action by a limiting factor of 0.1, thereby restricting the steering actuation limit $\delta \in [-7°, 7°]$. This allowed the bang-bang controller to track the waypoints at least for awhile, after which the ego vehicle went out of control and crashed!

The steering commands generated by the bang-bang controller are worth noting. It can be clearly seen how the controller switches back and forth between the two extremities, and although it was programmed to produce no control action (i.e., zero) when the cross-track error was negligible, such an incident never occurred during the course of the simulation.

In reality, it is the abrupt control actions that quickly render the plant uncontrollable, which implies that the controller harms itself. Furthermore, it is to be noted that generating such abrupt control actions may not be possible practically, since the actuators have a finitely positive time-constant (especially for the steering actuation mechanism), and generating such abrupt actions could cause serious damage to the actuation elements (especially at high frequencies, such as those observed between time steps 15 and 25). This fact further adds to the controllability problem, rendering the bang-bang controller close to useless for controlling lateral vehicle dynamics.

2.3.2.2 PID Control

From the previous discussion, it is evident that a bang-bang controller is not a very promising option for vehicle control (especially not for lateral control but not so good for longitudinal control either), and better control strategies are required.

2.3.2.2.1 P Controller   The most intuitive upgrade from a bang-bang controller is the proportional (P) controller. The P controller generates a control action u proportional to the error signal e, and the proportionality constant that scales the control action is called the gain of the P controller (generally denoted as k_p).

In continuous time, the P controller is represented as follows:

$$u(t) = k_p * e(t)$$

In discrete time, the above equation takes the following form:

$$u_{t+1} = k_p * e_t$$

It is extremely important to tune the gain value so as to obtain a desired system response. A low gain value would increase the settling time of the system drastically, whereas a high gain value would overshoot the system in the opposite direction. A moderate proportional gain would try to minimize the error; however, being an error-driven controller, it would still leave behind a significantly large steady-state error.

2.3.2.2.2 PD Controller   The PD controller can be thought of as a compound controller constituted of the proportional (P) and derivative (D) controllers.

The P component of the PD controller, as stated earlier, produces a "surrogate" control action proportional to the error signal e. The proportional gain k_p is deliberately set slightly higher so that the system oscillates about the set point. The D component of the PD controller damps out the resulting oscillations by observing the temporal derivative (rate of change) of error and modifies the control action accordingly. The proportionality constant that scales the derivative control action is called the gain of the D controller and is generally denoted as k_D.

In continuous time, the PD controller is represented as follows:

$$u(t) = k_p * e(t) + k_D * \frac{\mathrm{d}}{\mathrm{d}t} e(t)$$

In discrete time, the above equation takes the following form:

$$u_{t+1} = k_p * e_t + k_D * \left[\frac{e_t - e_{t-1}}{\Delta t} \right]$$

The modified control action smooths the system response and reduces any overshoots. However, the system may still struggle in cases where its dynamics are disturbed due to physical interactions.

It is to be noted that the D controller is extremely susceptible to noise; even a small noise in the sensor readings can lead to miscalculation of the error values, resulting in larger or smaller derivatives and ultimately leading to instability. The gain k_D must therefore be tuned wisely. Another way to remedy this issue is to use a low-pass filter to reject the high-frequency components of the feedback signal, which are generally constituents of noise.

2.3.2.2.3 PI Controller   The PI controller can be thought of as a compound controller constituted of the proportional (P) and integral (I) controllers.

The P component of the PD controller, as stated earlier, produces a "surrogate" control action proportional to the error signal e. The proportional gain k_p is set to a moderate value so that the system tries really hard to converge to the set point. The I component of the PI controller modifies the control action based on the error accumulated over a certain time interval. The proportionality constant that scales the integral control action is called the gain of the I controller and is generally denoted as k_I.

In continuous time, the PI controller is represented as follows:

$$u(t) = k_p * e(t) + k_I * \int_{t_o}^{t} e(t)\,\mathrm{d}t$$

In discrete time, the above equation takes the following form:

$$u_{t+1} = k_p * e_t + k_I * \sum_{i=t_o}^{t} e_i$$

Here $t - t_o$ represents the temporal size of the history buffer over which the error is integrated.

The modified control action forces the overall system response to move much closer to the set point value with time. In other words, it helps the system better converge to the desired value. It is worth mentioning that the I component is effective in dealing with any systematic biases, such as inherent misalignments and disturbance forces. However, with a simple PI controller implemented, the system may tend to overshoot every time a control action is executed.

It is also to be noted that since the I controller acts on the accumulated error, which is a large value, its gain k_I is usually set very low.

2.3.2.2.4 PID Controller   The proportional (P), integral (I), and derivative (D) controllers work in tandem to give rise to a much more efficient PID controller. The PID controller takes advantage of all three primary controllers to generate a sophisticated control action that proportionally corrects the error, dampens the resulting overshoots, and reduces any steady-state error over time.

In continuous time, the PID controller is represented as follows:

$$u(t) = k_P * e(t) + k_I * \int_{t_o}^{t} e(t)\, dt + k_D * \frac{d}{dt} e(t)$$

In discrete time, the above equation takes the following form:

$$u_{t+1} = k_P * e_t + k_I * \sum_{i=t_o}^{t} e_i + k_D * \left[\frac{e_t - e_{t-1}}{\Delta t} \right]$$

As stated earlier, $t - t_o$ represents the temporal size of the history buffer over which the error is integrated.

The gains of the designed PID controller need to be tuned manually at first. A general rule of thumb is to start by initializing the k_I and k_D values to zero and tuning up the k_P value until the system starts oscillating about the set point. The k_D value is then tuned until the oscillations are damped out in most of the cases. Finally, the k_I value is tuned to reduce any steady-state error. An optimizer algorithm (such as twiddle or gradient descent) can then be adopted to fine-tune the gains through recursive updates.

Characteristics of the controller gains (i.e., the effects of gain amplification on the closed loop system response) for the proportional, integral, and derivative terms of the PID controller have been summarized in Table 2.1. This information is extremely useful for controller gain tuning in order to achieve the desired system response.

TABLE 2.1   Characteristics of PID Controller Gains

Controller Gain Amplification	Closed Loop System Response			
	Rise Time (t_r)	Overshoot (M_p)	Settling Time (t_s)	Steady-State Error (e_{ss})
k_P	Decrease	Increase	Small change	Decrease
k_I	Decrease	Increase	Increase	Eliminate
k_D	Small change	Decrease	Decrease	Small change

In general, the P controller can be thought of as correcting the present error by generating a control action proportional to it. The I controller can be thought of as correcting any past error by generating a control action proportional to the error accumulated over time. Finally, the D controller can be thought of as correcting any future error by generating a control action proportional to the rate of change of error.

Note that the integral and derivative controllers cannot be employed alone; they can only assist the proportional controller. The same is true for the ID controller.

2.3.2.2.5 PID Control Implementation   Implementation of the PID controller for lateral control of a simulated autonomous vehicle is illustrated in Figure 2.6.

The implementation also employs a secondary PID controller for controlling the longitudinal vehicle dynamics. It is to be noted that the two controllers are decoupled and

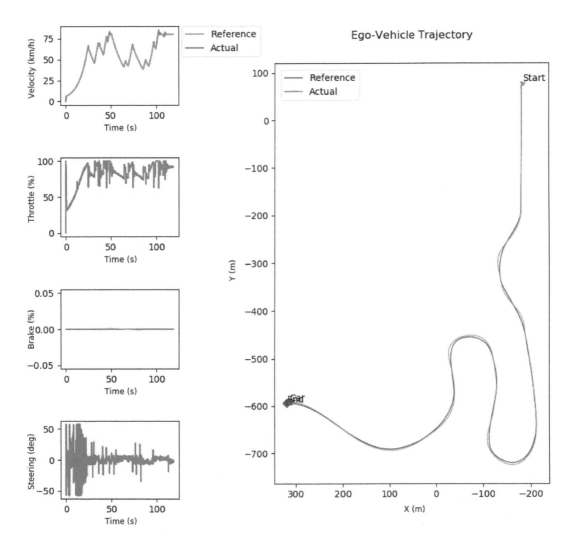

FIGURE 2.6   PID control implementation.

perform independently. In order to avoid confusion, the lateral controller shall be the point of interest for this topic unless specified otherwise.

For the purpose of this implementation, the reference trajectory to be followed by the ego vehicle (shown in green in the trajectory plot) was discretized into waypoints to be tracked by the lateral controller, and each waypoint had an associated velocity set point to be tracked by the longitudinal controller.

The PID controller was tuned in order to obtain the best possible results for tracking the entire reference trajectory (which included both straight and curved segments) at varying longitudinal velocities. It is to be noted that although the controller does not compromise with comfort or safety, the tracking accuracy is quite limited even after recursive gain tuning, especially at higher road curvatures.

It can therefore be concluded that a stand-alone PID controller is a "satisfactory" solution to the problem of controlling lateral vehicle dynamics and that advanced strategies (such as gain scheduling) and/or better controllers are a more attractive choice for this task.

2.3.2.3 Geometric Control

Geometric control refers to the notion of computing the control commands for the ego vehicle purely using the "geometry" of the vehicle kinematics and reference trajectory.

Although this type of control strategy is applicable to both lateral and longitudinal control, a PID controller is a better choice when it comes to longitudinal control as compared to geometric controllers, since it operates directly on the velocity error. For lateral control though, a geometric controller is a better choice, since PID controllers used for lateral vehicle control need to be tuned for specific velocity ranges, beyond which they are either too sluggish or too reactive.

There are two highly popular geometric path tracking controllers for lateral motion control of autonomous vehicles: pure pursuit and Stanley controllers.

2.3.2.3.1 Pure Pursuit Controller   A pure pursuit controller is a geometric trajectory tracking controller that uses a *lookahead point* on the reference trajectory at a fixed distance ahead of the ego vehicle in order to determine the cross-track error e_Δ. The controller then decides the steering angle command in order to minimize this cross-track error and ultimately to try to reach the lookahead point. However, since the lookahead point is a fixed distance ahead of the ego vehicle, the vehicle is constantly in pursuit of that point, and hence, this controller is called a pure pursuit controller.

If we consider the center of the rear axle of the ego vehicle as the frame of reference, we have the geometric relations shown in Figure 2.7. Here the ego vehicle wheelbase is L, the forward velocity of the ego vehicle is v_f, the steering angle of the ego vehicle is δ, the distance between the lookahead point on the reference trajectory and the center of the rear axle of the ego vehicle is the lookahead distance d_l, and the angle between the vehicle heading and the lookahead line is α. Since the vehicle is a rigid body with forward steerable wheels, for nonzero v_f and δ, the vehicle follows a circular path of radius R (corresponding to curvature κ) about the instantaneous center of rotation (ICR).

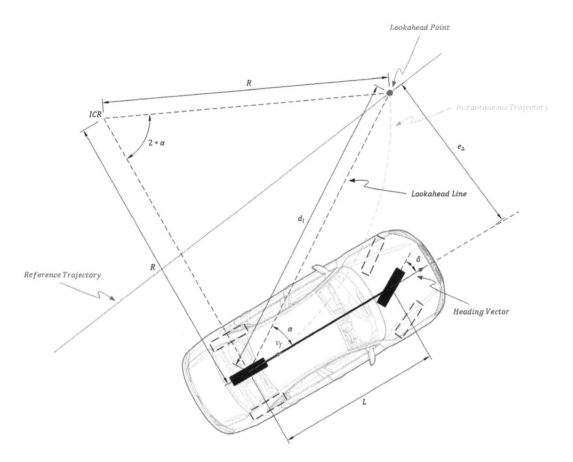

FIGURE 2.7   Pure pursuit control.

With reference to Figure 2.7, from the law of sines, we have

$$\frac{d_l}{sin(2*\alpha)} = \frac{R}{sin\left(\frac{\pi}{2}-\alpha\right)}$$

$$\therefore \frac{d_l}{2*sin(\alpha)*cos(\alpha)} = \frac{R}{cos(\alpha)}$$

$$\therefore \frac{d_l}{sin(\alpha)} = 2*R$$

$$\therefore \kappa = \frac{1}{R} = \frac{2*sin(\alpha)}{d_l} \tag{2.27}$$

$$\because sin(\alpha) = \frac{e_\Delta}{d_l} \Rightarrow \kappa = \frac{2}{d_l^2}*e_\Delta \Rightarrow \kappa \propto e_\Delta \tag{2.28}$$

It can be seen from Equation 2.28 that the curvature of the instantaneous trajectory κ is directly proportional to the cross-track error e_Δ. Thus, as the cross-track error increases, so does the trajectory curvature, thereby aggressively bringing the vehicle back toward the reference trajectory. Note that the term $\dfrac{2}{d_l^2}$ can be thought of as a proportionality gain, which can be tuned based on the lookahead distance parameter.

With reference to Figure 2.7, the steering angle command δ can be computed using the following relation:

$$tan(\delta) = \frac{L}{R} = L * \kappa \tag{2.29}$$

Substituting the value of κ from Equation 2.27 in Equation 2.29 and solving for δ, we get

$$\delta = tan^{-1}\left(\frac{2 * L * sin(\alpha)}{d_l}\right) \tag{2.30}$$

Equation 2.30 presents the decoupled scheme of a pure pursuit controller (i.e., the steering law is independent of vehicle velocity). As a result, if the controller is tuned for low speed, it will be dangerously aggressive at higher speeds, while if it is tuned for high speed, it will be too sluggish at lower speeds. One potentially simple improvement would be to vary the lookahead distance d_l proportional to the vehicle velocity v_f using k_v as the proportionality constant (this constant/gain will act as the tuning parameter for the pure pursuit controller).

$$d_l = k_v * v_f \tag{2.31}$$

Substituting the value of d_l from Equation 2.31 in Equation 2.30, we get the complete coupled pure pursuit control law formulation:

$$\delta = tan^{-1}\left(\frac{2 * L * sin(\alpha)}{k_v * v_f}\right) ; \delta \in \left[-\delta_{max}, \delta_{max}\right] \tag{2.32}$$

In summary, it can be seen that a pure pursuit controller acts as a geometric proportional controller of steering angle δ operating on the cross-track error e_Δ while observing the steering actuation limits.

2.3.2.3.2 Pure Pursuit Control Implementation   Implementation of a pure pursuit controller for lateral control of a simulated autonomous vehicle is illustrated in Figure 2.8. The implementation also employs a PID controller for controlling the longitudinal vehicle dynamics. It is to be noted that this implementation uses a coupled control scheme wherein the steering action is influenced by the vehicle velocity following an inverse relation.

For the purpose of this implementation, the reference trajectory to be followed by the ego vehicle (shown in green in the trajectory plot) was discretized into waypoints to be

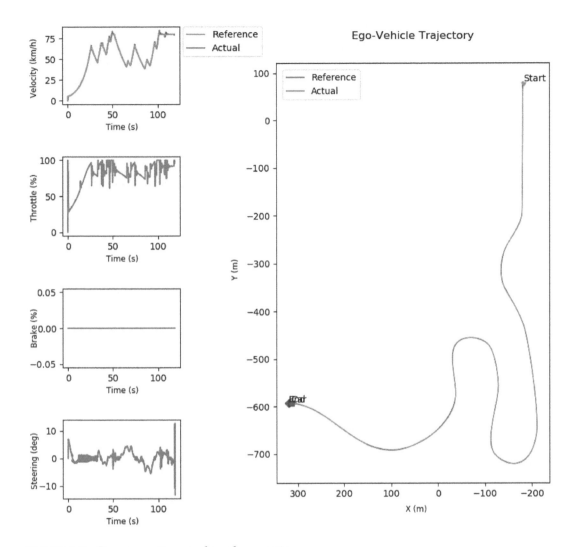

FIGURE 2.8 Pure pursuit control implementation.

tracked by the lateral controller, and each waypoint had an associated velocity set point to be tracked by the longitudinal controller.

The lateral controller parameter k_v was tuned in order to obtain the best possible results for tracking the entire reference trajectory (which included both straight and curved segments) at varying forward velocities. The controller was very well able to track the prescribed trajectory with a promising level of precision. Additionally, the control actions generated during the entire course of simulation fell within a short span, $\delta \in [-15°, 15°]$, which is an indication of the controller having good command over the system.

Nonetheless, the green line (representing the reference trajectory) can be seen in the neighborhood of the actual trajectory followed by the ego vehicle, which indicates that the tracking was not "perfect." This may be partially due to the fact that the pure pursuit control law has a single tunable parameter d_l having an approximated first-order relation with v_f. However, a more convincing reason for potential errors in trajectory tracking, when it comes to a pure pursuit controller, is that it generates steering action regardless of the heading error of the vehicle, making it difficult to actually align the vehicle precisely along the reference trajectory.

Furthermore, being a kinematic controller, a pure pursuit controller disregards actual system dynamics and, as a result, compromises trajectory tracking accuracy. Now, although this may not affect a vehicle driving under nominal conditions, a racing vehicle, for example, would experience serious trajectory deviations under rigorous driving conditions.

A pure pursuit controller also has a pretty nonintuitive issue associated with it, which is generally undiscovered during infinitely continuous or looped trajectory tracking. Particularly toward the end of a finite reference trajectory, the pure pursuit controller generates erratic steering actions owing to the fact that the lookahead point it uses in order to deduce the steering control action is no longer available, since the further waypoints are not really defined. This may lead to undesired stoppage of the vehicle or even cause the vehicle to wander off of the trajectory in the final few seconds of the mission.

In conclusion, a pure pursuit controller is really good for regulating the lateral dynamics of a vehicle operating under nominal driving conditions, although there is room for further improvement.

2.3.2.3.3 Stanley Controller   The Stanley controller is a geometric trajectory tracking controller developed by Stanford University's Stanford Racing Team for their autonomous vehicle "Stanley" at the DARPA Grand Challenge (2005). As opposed to the pure pursuit controller (discussed earlier), which uses only the cross-track error to determine the steering action, the Stanley controller uses both heading and cross-track errors to determine the same. The cross-track error e_Δ is defined with respect to the closest point on the reference trajectory (as opposed to the lookahead point used by the pure pursuit controller), whereas the heading error e_ψ is defined using the vehicle heading relative to the reference trajectory.

If we consider the center of the front axle of the ego vehicle as the frame of reference, we have the geometric relations shown in Figure 2.9. Here the ego vehicle wheelbase is L, the forward velocity of the ego vehicle is v_f, and the steering angle of the ego vehicle is δ.

The Stanley controller uses both heading and cross-track errors to determine the steering command. Furthermore, the steering angle generated by this (or any other) method must observe the steering actuation limits. The Stanley control law is therefore essentially defined to meet the following three requirements:

1. *Heading error correction:* To correct the heading error e_ψ by producing a steering control action δ proportional (or equal) to it such that the vehicle heading aligns with the desired heading.

$$\delta = e_\psi \qquad (2.33)$$

2. *Cross-track error correction:* To correct the cross-track error e_Δ by producing a steering control action δ directly proportional to it and inversely proportional to the

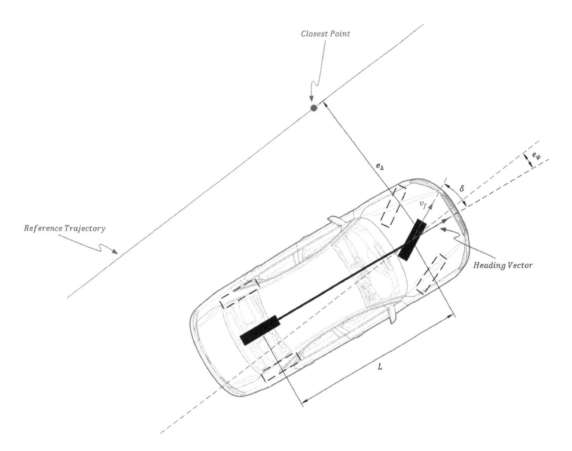

FIGURE 2.9   Stanley control.

vehicle velocity v_f in order to achieve coupled control. Moreover, the effect for large cross-track errors can be limited by using an inverse tangent function.

$$\delta = tan^{-1}\left(\frac{k_\Delta * e_\Delta}{v_f}\right) \qquad (2.34)$$

It is to be noted that at this stage of the formulation, the inverse relation between steering angle and vehicle speed can cause numerical instability in control actions.

At lower speeds, the denominator becomes small, thus causing the steering command to shoot to higher values, which is undesirable for human comfort. Hence, an extra softening coefficient k_s may be used in the denominator as an additive term in order to keep the steering commands smaller for smoother steering actions.

In contrast, at higher velocities, the denominator becomes large, making the steering commands small in order to avoid large lateral accelerations. However, even these small steering actions might be high in some cases, causing high lateral accelerations.

Hence, an extra damping coefficient k_d may be used in order to dampen the steering action proportional to vehicle velocity.

$$\delta = tan^{-1}\left(\frac{k_\Delta * e_\Delta}{k_s + k_d * v_f} \right) \tag{2.35}$$

3. *Clipping control action:* To continuously observe the steering actuation limits $[-\delta_{max}, \delta_{max}]$ and clip the steering command within these bounds.

$$\delta \in [-\delta_{max}, \delta_{max}] \tag{2.36}$$

Using Equations 2.33, 2.35, and 2.36, we can formulate the complete Stanley control law as follows:

$$\delta = e_\psi + tan^{-1}\left(\frac{k_\Delta * e_\Delta}{k_s + k_d * v_f} \right); \delta \in [-\delta_{max}, \delta_{max}] \tag{2.37}$$

In summary, it can be seen that the Stanley controller acts as a geometric proportional controller of steering angle δ operating on the heading error e_ψ as well as the cross-track error e_Δ while observing the steering actuation limits.

2.3.2.3.4 Stanley Control Implementation   Implementation of the Stanley controller for lateral control of a simulated autonomous vehicle is illustrated in Figure 2.10. The implementation also employs a PID controller for controlling the longitudinal vehicle dynamics. It is to be noted that this implementation uses a coupled control scheme wherein the steering action is influenced by the vehicle velocity following an inverse relation.

For the purpose of this implementation, the reference trajectory to be followed by the ego vehicle (shown in green in the trajectory plot) was discretized into waypoints to be tracked by the lateral controller, and each waypoint had an associated velocity set point to be tracked by the longitudinal controller.

The lateral controller parameters k_Δ, k_s, and k_d were tuned in order to obtain the best possible results for tracking the entire reference trajectory (which included both straight and curved segments) at varying forward velocities. The controller was able to track the prescribed trajectory with a promising level of precision.

Nonetheless, the green line (representing the reference trajectory) can be occasionally spotted in the neighborhood of the actual trajectory followed by the ego vehicle, which indicates that the tracking was suboptimal or only near perfect. This may be due to the first-order approximations involved in the formulation. Furthermore, being a kinematic geometric controller, the Stanley controller disregards actual system dynamics and, as a result, compromises trajectory tracking accuracy, especially under rigorous driving conditions.

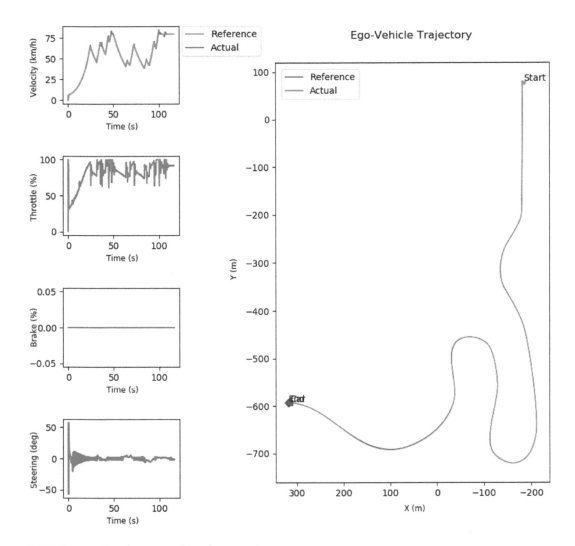

FIGURE 2.10   Stanley control implementation.

The Stanley controller uses the closest waypoint to compute the cross-track error and therefore may become highly reactive at times. Since this implementation assumed static waypoints defined along a racetrack (i.e., in the global frame) and the ego vehicle was spawned toward one side of the track, the initial cross-track error was quite high. This made the controller react erratically, thereby generating steering commands of over 50° in either direction. However, this is not a significant problem practically, since the local trajectory is recursively planned as a finite set of waypoints originating from the vehicle coordinate system, thereby ensuring that the immediately next waypoint is not too far from the vehicle.

In conclusion, the Stanley controller is one of the best for regulating the lateral dynamics of a vehicle operating under nominal driving conditions, especially considering the computational complexity at which it offers such accuracy and robustness.

2.3.2.4 Model Predictive Control

Model predictive control (MPC) is a type of optimal control strategy that basically treats the control task as a constrained or bounded optimization problem. As depicted in Figure 2.11, model predictive controller predicts the future states of the system (ego vehicle) up to a certain prediction horizon using the motion model and then solves an online optimization problem considering the constraints (or control bounds). From that, it selects the optimal set of control inputs by minimizing a cost function such that the future state(s) of the ego vehicle closely align with the goal state (as required for trajectory tracking).

In other words, given the current state and the reference trajectory to follow, MPC involves simulating different control inputs (without actually applying them to the system), predicting the resulting future states (in the form of a predicted trajectory) using a motion model up to a certain prediction horizon, selecting the optimal set of control inputs corresponding to the minimal cost trajectory (considering the constraints) at each step in time, and applying the very first set of optimal control inputs (up to a certain control horizon) to the ego vehicle while discarding the rest. With the updated state, we again repeat the same algorithm to compute a new optimal predicted trajectory up to the prediction horizon. In that sense, we are computing optimal control inputs over a constantly moving prediction horizon. Thus, this approach is also known as *receding horizon control*.

There are two main reasons for following the receding horizon approach in MPC:

1. The motion model is only an approximate representation of the actual vehicle dynamics, and despite our best efforts, it won't match the real world exactly. Hence, once we apply the optimal control input to the ego vehicle, our actual trajectory may not be exactly same as the trajectory we predicted. It is therefore extremely crucial that we constantly reevaluate our optimal control actions in a receding horizon manner so that we do not build up a large error between the predicted and actual vehicle states.

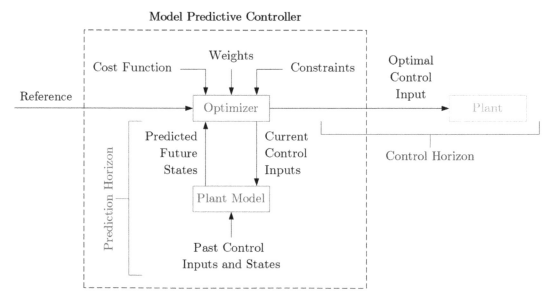

FIGURE 2.11   Model predictive control architecture.

2. Beyond a specific prediction horizon, the environment will change enough that it won't make sense to predict any further into the future. It is therefore a better idea to restrict the prediction horizon to a finite value and follow the receding horizon approach to predict, using the updated vehicle state at each time interval.

MPC is extremely popular in autonomous vehicles for the following reasons:

- It can handle multi-input, multi-output (MIMO) systems that have cross-interactions between the inputs and outputs, which is very well suited for the vehicle control problem.

- It can consider constraints or bounds to compute optimal control actions. The constraints are often imposed due to actuation limits, comfort bounds, and safety considerations, the violation of which may potentially lead to uncontrollable, uncomfortable, or unsafe scenarios, respectively.

- It has a future preview capability similar to feedforward control (i.e., it can incorporate future reference information into the control problem to improve controller performance for smoother state transitioning).

- It can handle control latency. Since MPC uses a system model for making an informed prediction, we can incorporate any control latency (the time difference between application of the control input and actual actuation) into the system model, thereby enabling the controller to adapt to the latency.

Following are some of the practical considerations for implementing MPC for motion control of autonomous vehicles:

- *Motion model:* For predicting the future states of the ego vehicle, we can use kinematic or dynamic motion models, as described in Section 2.2. Note that depending on the problem statement, one may choose simpler models, the exact same models, or even complex models. However, in most implementations (for nominal driving conditions), it is suggested to use kinematic models, since they offer a good balance between simplicity and accuracy.

- *MPC design parameters:*

  - *Sample time (T_s):* The sample time determines the rate at which the control loop is executed. If it is too large, the controller response will be sluggish and may not be able to correct the system fast enough, leading to accidents. Also, a large sample time makes it difficult to approximate a continuous reference trajectory by discrete paths. This is known as *discretization error.* On the other hand, if the sample time is too small, the controller might become highly reactive (sometimes overreactive) and might lead to a uncomfortable and/or unsafe ride. Also, the smaller the sample time, the more computational complexity there is, since an entire control loop is supposed to be executed within the time interval (including online optimization). Thus, a proper sample time must be chosen such that the controller is neither sluggish nor overreactive but can quickly respond to disturbances or set point changes. It is recommended to have a sample time T_s of 5 to 10% of the rise time t_r of the open-loop step response of the system.

$$0.05*t_r \leqslant T_s \leqslant 0.1*t_r$$

- *Prediction horizon (p)*: The prediction horizon is the number of time steps in the future over which state predictions are made by the model predictive controller. If it is too small, the controller may not be able to take the necessary control actions sufficiently in advance, making it "too late" in some situations. On the other hand, a large prediction horizon will make the controller predict too long into the future, making it a wasteful effort, since a major part (almost all) of the predicted trajectory will be discarded in each control loop. Thus, a proper prediction horizon must be chosen such that it covers significant dynamics of the system and at the same time is not excessively large. It is recommended to determine a prediction horizon p depending on the sample time T_s and the settling time t_s of the open-loop step response of the system (at a 2% steady-state error criterion).

$$\frac{t_s}{T_s} \leqslant p \leqslant 1.5*\frac{t_s}{T_s}$$

- *Control horizon (m)*: The control horizon is the number of time steps in the future for which the optimal control actions are computed by the optimizer. If it is too short, the optimizer may not return the best possible control action(s). On the other hand, if the control horizon is longer, the model predictive controller can make better predictions of future states, and thus, the optimizer can find the best possible solutions for control actions. One can also make the control horizon equal to the prediction horizon; however, note that usually only the first couple of control actions have a significant effect on the predicted states. Thus, an excessively large control horizon only increases the computational complexity without being much of a help. Therefore, a general rule of thumb is to have a control horizon m of 10 to 20% of the prediction horizon p.

$$0.1*p \leqslant m \leqslant 0.2*p$$

- *Constraints:* The model predictive controller can incorporate constraints on control inputs (and their derivatives) and the vehicle state (or predicted output). These can be either hard constraints (which cannot be violated under any circumstances) or soft constraints (which can be violated with a minimum necessary amount). It is recommended to have hard constraints for control inputs, thereby accounting for actuation limits. However, for the outputs and time derivatives (time rates of change) of control inputs, it is not a good idea to have hard constraints, as these constraints may conflict with each other (since none can be violated) and lead to an infeasible solution for the optimization problem. It is therefore recommended to have soft constraints for the outputs and time derivatives of control inputs, which may be occasionally violated (if required). Note that in order to keep the violation of soft constraints small, it is minimized by the optimizer.

- *Weights:* The model predictive controller has to achieve multiple goals simultaneously (which may compete/conflict with each other), such as minimizing the error between the current state and reference while limiting the rate of chance of control inputs (and obeying other constraints). In order to ensure a balanced performance between these competing goals, it is a good idea to weight the goals in order of importance or criticality. For example, since it is more important to track the ego vehicle's pose than its velocity (minor variations in velocity do not affect much), one may assign a higher weight to pose tracking as compared to velocity tracking. This will cause the optimizer to give more weight to the vehicle pose as compared to its velocity (similar to how hard constraints are weighted morer than soft constraints).

- *Cost function (J):* The exact choice of cost function depends very much on the specific problem statement requirements and is up to the control engineer. To state an example, for longitudinal control, one may use the velocity error e_v or distance to goal e_χ as a cost, while for lateral control, one may use the cross-track error e_Δ and/or heading error e_ψ as the cost. Practically, it is advised to use quadratic (or higher-degree) cost functions as opposed to linear ones, since they penalize more for deviations from reference and tend to converge the optimizer faster. Furthermore, it is a good idea to associate cost not only for the error from desired reference e but also for the amount of change in control inputs Δu between each time step so that comfort and safety are maintained. For that, one may choose a cost function that considers the weighted squared sums of predicted errors and control input increments as follows:

$$J = \sum_{i=1}^{p} w_e * e_{t+i}^2 + \sum_{i=0}^{p-1} w_{\Delta u} * \Delta u_{t+i}^2; \text{where} \begin{cases} t \rightarrow \text{present} \\ t+i \rightarrow \text{future} \end{cases}$$

- *Optimization:* The main purpose of optimization is to choose the optimal set of control inputs $u_{optimal}$ (from a set of all plausible controls u) corresponding to the predicted trajectory with the lowest cost (whilst considering current state x, reference state x_{ref}, and constraints). As a result, there is no restriction on the optimizer to be used for this purpose, and the choice is left to the control engineer, who should consider the cost function J as well as the time complexity required for solving the optimization problem. Practically, it is a good idea to set a tolerance up to which minimization optimization is to be carried out and beyond which optimization is to be terminated, and an optimal set of control inputs corresponding to the predicted trajectory with the lowest cost should be returned. A general optimization function might look something like the following:

$$u_{optimal} = argmin\big(J \mid u, x, x_{ref}, \langle\text{optimizer}\rangle, \langle\text{constraints}\rangle, \langle\text{tolerance}\rangle\big)$$

Following are some of the variants of MPC depending on the nature of the system (plant model), constraints, and cost function:

1. *Linear time-invariant MPC:* If the plant model and constraints are linear and the cost function is quadratic, it gives rise to a *convex optimization problem*, where there is a single global minima and a variety of numerical methods exist to solve such optimization problems. Thus, we can use a linear time-invariant model predictive controller to control such systems.

2. *Linear time-variant MPC:* If the plant model is nonlinear, we may need to linearize it at different operation points (varying in time), thereby calling for a linear time-variant model predictive controller.

   - *Adaptive MPC:* If the structure of the optimization problem remains the same across all operating conditions (i.e., states and constraints do not change with operating conditions), we can simply approximate the nonlinear plant model to a linear model (linearization) and use an adaptive model predictive controller, which updates the plant model recursively as the operating conditions change.

   - *Gain-scheduled MPC:* If the plant model is nonlinear and the states and/or constraints change with the operating conditions, we need to use gain-scheduled model predictive controller. In this approach, we perform off-line linearization at operating points of interest, and for each operating point, we design an independent linear model predictive controller, considering the states and constraints for that particular operating point. We then select the suitable linear model predictive controller for a specific range of operating conditions and switch between these linear model predictive controllers as operating conditions change.

3. *Nonlinear MPC:* If it is not possible/recommended to linearize the plant model, we need to use a nonlinear model predictive controller. Although this method is the most powerful one, since it uses the most accurate representation of the plant model, it is by far the most challenging one in terms of real time execution. Additionally, the nonlinear constraints and cost function give rise to a *nonconvex optimization problem* with multiple local optima. It is quite difficult to find the global optimum, and getting stuck in the local optima is possible. This approach is therefore highly complex in terms of computation, and its efficiency depends on the nonlinear solver used for optimization.

A general rule of thumb for selecting from the variants of MPC is to start simple and go complex if and only if it is necessary. Thus, linear time-invariant or traditional MPC and adaptive MPC are the two most commonly used approaches for autonomous vehicle control under nominal driving conditions.

2.3.2.4.1 Model Predictive Control Implementation   Implementation of a model predictive controller for lateral control of a simulated autonomous vehicle is illustrated in Figure 2.12. The implementation also employs a PID controller for controlling the longitudinal vehicle dynamics.

For the purpose of this implementation, the reference trajectory to be followed by the ego vehicle (shown in green in the trajectory plot) was discretized into waypoints to be tracked by the lateral controller, and each waypoint had an associated velocity set point to be tracked by the longitudinal controller.

A simple kinematic bicycle model also worked really well for tracking the entire reference trajectory (which included both straight and curved segments) at varying longitudinal

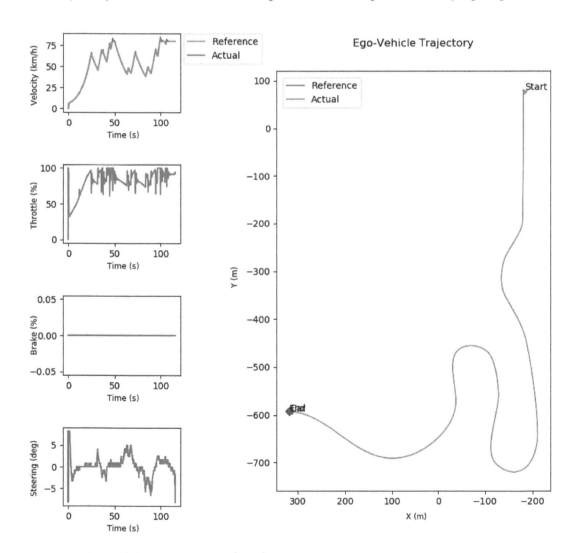

FIGURE 2.12   Model predictive control implementation.

velocities. The model predictive controller was able to track the prescribed trajectory with a promising level of precision and accuracy. Additionally, the steering control commands generated during the entire course of simulation lay well within the span $\delta \in [-10°, 10°]$, which is an indication of the controller being able to generate optimal control actions at the right times.

One of the most significant drawbacks of MPC is its heavy requirement of computational resources. However, this can be easily counteracted by limiting the prediction and control horizons to moderately small and small magnitudes respectively, formulating simpler cost functions, using less-detailed motion models or setting a higher tolerance for optimization convergence. Although this may lead to suboptimal solutions, it reduces computational overhead to a great extent, thereby ensuring real-time execution of the control algorithm.

In conclusion, MPC can be regarded as the best control strategy for both simplistic and rigorous driving behaviors, provided a sufficiently powerful computational resource is available online.

2.3.3 Learning-Based Control

As stated in Section 2.3.2, traditional controllers require in-depth knowledge of the process flow involved in designing and tuning them. Additionally, in the case of model-based controllers, the physical parameters of the system, along with its kinematic and/or dynamic models, need to be known before designing a suitable controller. To add to the problem, most traditional controllers are scenario-specific and do not adapt to varying operating conditions; they need to be retuned in case of a scenario change, which makes working with them quite inconvenient. Lastly, most of the advanced traditional controllers are computationally expensive, which causes a time lag-derived error in the processing pipeline.

Recently, the use of learning-based control strategies, especially end-to-end learning, has started growing. Such controllers hardly require any system-level knowledge and are much easier to implement. The system engineer may not need to implement the perception, planning, and control subsystems, since the artificially intelligent (AI) agent learns to perform these operations implicitly; it is rather difficult to tell exactly which part of the neural network acts as the perception subsystem, which acts as the planning subsystem, and which acts as the control subsystem. Although the "learning" process is computationally quite expensive, this step may be performed off-line once, after which the trained model may be incorporated into the system architecture of the autonomous vehicle for a real-time implementation. Another advantage of such controllers is their ability to generalize across a range of similar scenarios, which makes them fit for minor deviations in the driving conditions. All in all, learning-based control schemes seem to be a tempting alternative for the traditional ones. However, there is still a long way to go in achieving this goal, as learning-based controllers are somewhat unreliable; if presented with an unseen scenario, they can generate erratic control actions based on the learned features. Constant research is being carried out in this field to understand the way these controllers learn and how to guide them to learn the most appropriate features.

The learning-based control strategies can be broadly classified into two categories: *imitation learning* and *reinforcement learning*. While the former is a supervised learning strategy, the latter is more of a self-learning technique. The upcoming sections discuss these strategies in greater detail.

It is to be noted that apart from end-to-end control, hybrid control strategies are also possible, meaning that some aspects of traditional controllers (such as the gains of a PID controller or system model for MPC) can be "learned" through recursive training (using imitation/reinforcement learning), thereby improving the performance of the controller.

2.3.3.1 Imitation Learning-Based Control

Imitation learning is adopted to train an AI agent using a set of labeled data. The agent learns to map the features to the labels while minimizing the error in its predictions. This technique produces fairly good results even at an early stage of the training process. However, achieving perfection using this technique requires a larger data set, a sufficiently prolonged training duration, and a lot of hyperparameter tuning.

We shall consider *behavioral cloning*, an exemplar implementation of this technique, as a case study. Behavioral cloning is concerned with cloning the driving behavior of an agent (a human driver or a traditional controller) by learning specific features from the training data provided. Figure 2.13 illustrates the training and deployment phases of imitation learning, which are discussed in the following sections.

2.3.3.1.1 Training Phase   During the training phase, the ego vehicle is driven (either manually or using a traditional controller) in a scenario resembling one in the deployment phase, and time-stamped sensor readings (images, point cloud, etc.), along with the control input measurements (throttle, brake, and steering), are recorded in a driving log. The collected data set is then balanced to remove any inherent prejudice, after which it is augmented

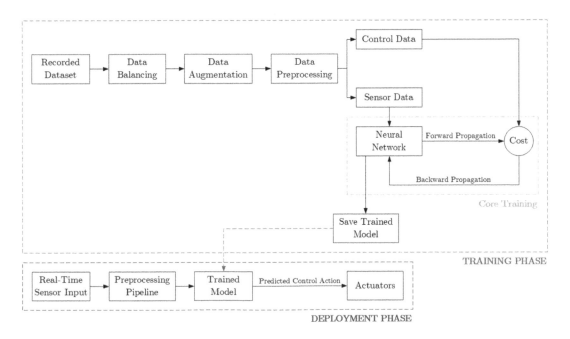

FIGURE 2.13   Imitation learning architecture.

and preprocessed, thereby imparting robustness to the model and helping it generalize to a range of similar scenarios. Practically, the augmentation and preprocessing steps are performed on the go during the training process using a *batch generator*. Finally, a deep neural network is "trained" to directly predict the control inputs based on sensor readings.

It is to be noted that practically the collected data set influences the training process more than anything else. Other important factors affecting the training, in order of importance, include neural network architecture (coarse-tuning is sufficient in most cases), augmentation and preprocessing techniques used, and hyperparameter values chosen (fine-tuning may be required based on the application). It is also completely possible that one training pipeline works well on one data set, while the other works well on a different one.

Training a neural network end to end in order to predict the control actions required to drive an autonomous vehicle based on the sensory inputs is essentially modeling the entire system as a non-linear approximationof input *features* to predict the output *labels*. The training process can be described as follows.

First, a suitable neural network architecture is defined; this architecture may be iteratively modified based on experimental results. The trainable parameters of the model include *weights* and *biases*. Generally, the weights are initialized to a small nonzero random value, whereas the biases are initialized to zero.

The network then performs what is called a *forward propagation* step. Here each neuron of every layer of the neural network calculates a weighted average of the activated input vector a it receives from the previous layer, based on its current weight vector w_i, and adds a bias term b_i to it. For the first layer, however, the input vector x is considered in place of $a^{[l-1]}$. The result of this operation, z_i, is then passed through a nonlinear activation function, $g(z)$, to produce an activated output a_i.

$$z_i^{[l]} = w_i^T \cdot a^{[l-1]} + b_i$$
$$a_i^{[l]} = g^{[l]}(z_i^{[l]})$$

Note that l here denotes the lth layer of the neural network and i denotes the ith neuron of that layer.

Practically, however, these operations are not performed sequentially for each and every neuron. Instead, *vectorization* is adopted, which groups the similar variables and vectors into distinct matrices and performs all the matrix manipulations at once, thereby reducing the computational complexity of the operation. The activated output vector of the last layer is termed as predicted output $\hat{y}$ of the neural network.

The predicted output $\hat{y}$ is then used to compute the loss L of the forward propagation, based on the loss function defined. Intuitively, loss is basically a measure of incorrectness (i.e., error) of the predicted output with respect to the labeled output.

Generally, for a regression problem like the one we are talking about, the most commonly adopted loss function is the *mean squared error (MSE)*. It is defined as follows:

$$L(\hat{y}, y) = \frac{1}{n} \sum_{i=1}^{n} \|y_i - \hat{y}_i\|^2$$

For classification problems though, the *cross-entropy loss function* is a favorable choice. For a data set with M different classes, it is defined as follows:

$$L(\hat{y}, y) = \begin{cases} -(y_i * log(\hat{y}_i) + (1 - y_i) * log(1 - \hat{y}_i)) & ; M = 2 \\ \\ -\displaystyle\sum_{i=1}^{M} y_i * log(\hat{y}_i) & ; M > 2 \end{cases}$$

The equations defined above are used to compute loss for each training example. These individual losses L over m training examples can be used to evaluate an overall cost J using the following relation:

$$J(w, b) = \frac{1}{m} \sum_{i=1}^{m} L(\hat{y}^{(i)}, y^{(i)})$$

Note that w and b in the above equation denote a vectorized form of weights and biases, respectively, across the entire training set (or a minibatch).

The cost is then minimized by recursively updating the weights and biases using an optimizer. This step is known as *back propagation*.

The most traditional optimizer is the *gradient descent algorithm*. In its very rudimentary form, the algorithm updates trainable parameters (i.e., weights and biases) by subtracting from them their respective gradients dw and db with respect to the cost function J, scaled by the *learning rate* hyperparameter α.

$$\begin{cases} w^{[l]} = w^{[l]} - \alpha * dw^{[l]} \\ b^{[l]} = b^{[l]} - \alpha * db^{[l]} \end{cases}$$

where dw and db are computed as follows:

$$\begin{cases} dw^{[l]} = \dfrac{\partial J}{\partial w^{[l]}} = dz^{[l']} \cdot a^{[l-1]} \\ \\ db^{[l]} = \dfrac{\partial J}{\partial b^{[l]}} = dz^{[l]} \end{cases}$$

Here dz and da, interdependent on each other, can be computed using the following relations:

$$\begin{cases} dz^{[l]} = da^{[l]} * g^{[l]}(z^{[l]}) \\ da^{[l-1]} = w^{[l]^T} \cdot dz^{[l]} \end{cases}$$

However, the current state-of-the-art optimizer adopted by most domain experts is the *Adam optimizer*. The algorithm commences by computing the gradients dw and db

using the gradient descent method and then computes the exponential moving averages of the gradients V and their squares S, similar to *Momentum* and *RMSprop algorithms*, respectively.

$$\begin{cases} V_{dw} = \beta_1 * V_{dw} + (1-\beta_1) * dw \\ V_{db} = \beta_1 * V_{db} + (1-\beta_1) * db \end{cases}$$

$$\begin{cases} S_{dw} = \beta_2 * S_{dw} + (1-\beta_2) * dw^2 \\ S_{db} = \beta_2 * S_{db} + (1-\beta_2) * db^2 \end{cases}$$

The bias correction equations for the exponential moving averages after t iterations are given as follows:

$$\begin{cases} \hat{V}_{dw} = \dfrac{V_{dw}}{(1-\beta_1^t)} \\[2ex] \hat{V}_{db} = \dfrac{V_{db}}{(1-\beta_1^t)} \\[3ex] \hat{S}_{dw} = \dfrac{S_{dw}}{(1-\beta_2^t)} \\[2ex] \hat{S}_{db} = \dfrac{S_{db}}{(1-\beta_2^t)} \end{cases}$$

The final update equations for the training parameters are therefore as follows:

$$\begin{cases} w = w - \alpha * \dfrac{\hat{V}_{dw}}{\sqrt{\hat{S}_{dw}} + \varepsilon} \\[3ex] b = b - \alpha * \dfrac{\hat{V}_{db}}{\sqrt{\hat{S}_{db}} + \varepsilon} \end{cases}$$

Note that ε in the above equations is a small factor that prevents division by zero. The authors of the Adam optimizer propose the default values of 0.9 for β_1, 0.999 for β_2, and 10^{-8} for ε. They show empirically that Adam works well in practice and compares favorably to other adaptive learning-based algorithms.

2.3.3.1.2 Deployment Phase   During the deployment phase, the trained model is incorporated into the control architecture of the ego vehicle to predict (forward propagation step alone), in real time, the same set of control inputs (throttle, brake, and steering) based on measurements (images, point cloud, etc.) from the same set of sensors as during the training phase.

It is worth mentioning that the pipeline adopted for the deployment phase should have minimum latency in order to ensure real-time performance.

2.3.3.1.3 Imitation Learning-Based Control Implementation   Implementation of an imitation learning strategy for lateral control of a simulated autonomous vehicle is illustrated in Figure 2.14. Specifically, the longitudinal vehicle dynamics are controlled using a pretuned PID controller, while the lateral vehicle dynamics are controlled using a neural network trained end to end.

The ego vehicle was manually driven for 20 laps, wherein a front-facing virtual camera mounted on the vehicle hood captured still frames of the road ahead. The steering angle corresponding to each frame was also recorded. This comprised the labeled data set for training a deep neural network to mimic the driving skills of the human driver in an end-to-end manner (aka behavioral cloning). The trained neural network model was saved at the end of training phase.

The trained model was then deployed onto the ego vehicle, which was allowed to drive autonomously on the same track so as to validate the autonomy. The AI agent was successful in cloning most of the human driving behavior and exhibited 100% autonomy, meaning it could complete several laps of the track autonomously. The lap time achieved by AI agent trained using imitation learning was 52.9 seconds, as compared to ~48.3 seconds (statistical average) achieved by human driver.

The greatest advantage of adopting imitation learning for the control of autonomous vehicles is its simplistic implementation and its ability to train fairly quickly (as compared to reinforcement learning). The neural network simply "learns" to drive using the data set provided, without the need of any complex formulations governing the input-output relations of the system. However, for the very same reason, this approach is highly susceptible

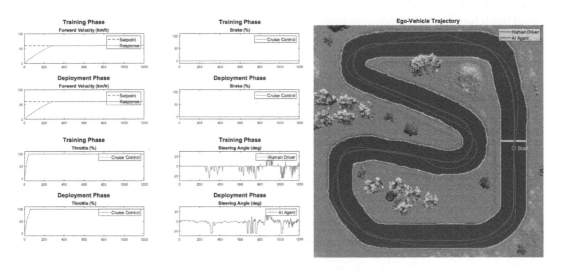

FIGURE 2.14   Imitation learning–based control implementation.

to mislabeled or biased data, in which case the neural network may learn incorrectly (this can be thought of as a bad teacher imparting erroneous knowledge to the students).

In conclusion, imitation learning is a convincing control strategy; however, advancements are required before achieving sufficient accuracy and reliability.

2.3.3.2 Reinforcement Learning-Based Control

Imitation learning simply teaches the learner to mimic the trainer's behavior, and the learner may never surpass the performance of its trainer. This is where reinforcement learning comes into the picture.

As depicted in Figure 2.15, an *agent* trained using reinforcement learning essentially learns through trial and error. This allows the agent to explore the *environment* and discover new strategies on its own, possibly some that may be even better than those of human beings!

Generally, the *policy* π to be trained for optimal behavior is a neural network, which acts as a function approximator governing the relationship between input *observations o* and output *actions a*.

$$\pi(a|o)$$

The agent is *rewarded* for performing a set of "good" actions and is *penalized* for performing any "bad" actions. The agent's goal is therefore to maximize the expected reward, given a specific policy.

$$argmax\ E[R|\pi(a|o)]$$

Note that the term *expected reward* is used instead of just *reward*. The expectation E here can be thought of as a simple average over a set of previous rewards based on a history of actions. While certain actions can produce exceedingly high/low reward points, it is a good habit to average them out in order to generalize rewarding in the right direction. This reinforces the policy by updating its parameters such that "generally good" actions are more likely to be performed in the future.

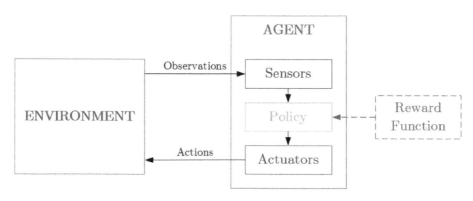

FIGURE 2.15   Reinforcement learning architecture.

The most critical portion of reinforcement learning is therefore defining a *reward function*. However, reward functions can be tricky to define. It is to be noted that the agent will perform any possible action(s) in order to maximize the reward, including cheating at times, essentially not learning the intended behavior at all. Defining a complex reward function, on the other hand, may limit the agent's creativity in terms of discovering novel strategies. Furthermore, rewarding the agent after performing good actions for a prolonged duration is also not a good idea, as the agent may wander randomly in the pursuit of maximizing its reward but may likely never achieve the training objective.

That being said, let us see how the agent actually learns. At its core, there are two approaches to "train" a policy: working in the action space and working in the parameter space. The former approach converges faster, while the latter provides a chance of better exploration.

2.3.3.2.1 Working in Action Space   As depicted in Figure 2.16, this approach deals with perturbing the action space and observing the reward being collected. The policy gradient can then be computed, which points toward the direction in which the policy parameters need to be updated.

One of the standard algorithms employing this approach is the *proximal policy optimization (PPO) algorithm*. Initially, the agent performs random actions in order to explore the environment. The policy is recursively updated toward the rewarding actions using the *gradient ascent* technique.

Instead of updating the policy regardless of how large its change was, PPO considers the probability ratio r of old and new policies.

$$r = \frac{\pi_{new}(a \mid o)}{\pi_{old}(a \mid o)}$$

In order to reduce variance, the reward function is replaced by a more general *advantage function A*. The "surrogate" objective function L for PPO can be therefore written as follows:

$$L = E\left[\frac{\pi_{new}(a \mid o)}{\pi_{old}(a \mid o)} * A\right] = E[r * A]$$

The PPO algorithm ensures that the updated policy π_{new} may not be far away from the old policy π_{old} by clamping the probability ratio r within a suitable interval $[1-\varepsilon, 1+\varepsilon]$, where

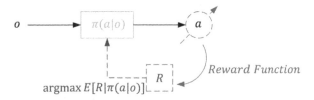

FIGURE 2.16   Reinforcement learning in action space.

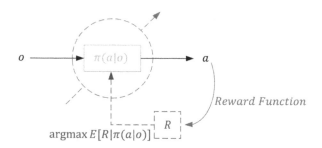

FIGURE 2.17   Reinforcement learning in parameter space.

ε is a hyperparameter, say, $\varepsilon = 0.2$. The main objective function L_{clip} for the PPO algorithm can be therefore written as follows:

$$L_{clip} = E\big[min(r*A, clip(r, 1-\varepsilon, 1+\varepsilon)*A)\big]$$

Finally, the gradient ascent update rule for updating the policy parameters $\theta \in \mathbb{R}^d$ (weights and biases), considering a *learning rate* hyperparameter α, is defined as follows:

$$\Delta\theta = \alpha * \nabla L_{clip}$$

While this approach increases stability and convergence rate, it reduces the agent's creativity, and the agent may therefore get stuck in a suboptimal solution.

2.3.3.2.2 Working in Parameter Space   As depicted in Figure 2.17, this approach deals with perturbing the parameter space directly and observing the reward being collected. This technique falls under the domain of *genetic algorithms (GA)* or *evolutionary strategies (ES)*.

Initially, a random population of policies is generated, which are all evaluated in order to analyze the reward obtained in each case. A new generation of policies is then populated in the direction with most promising results (maximum reward points) through the process of *natural selection*. Random *mutations* may also be introduced in order to take a chance of creating a "breakthrough" generation altogether. This process is repeated until an "optimal" policy is obtained.

Since the policy is already updated as a part of exploration, this approach does not involve any gradient computation or back propagation, which makes it extremely easy to implement and ensures faster execution. Furthermore, this approach almost guarantees better exploration behavior as compared to the algorithms working in action space. Mathematically, this translates to a reduced risk of getting stuck in local optima. However, algorithms working in the parameter space take a lot of time to converge. One has to therefore make a trade-off between convergence rate and exploration behavior or design a hybrid approach addressing the problem at hand.

2.3.3.2.3 Reinforcement Learning-Based Control Implementation   Implementation of a reinforcement learning strategy for lateral control of a simulated autonomous vehicle is illustrated in Figure 2.18. Specifically, the longitudinal vehicle dynamics are controlled using a

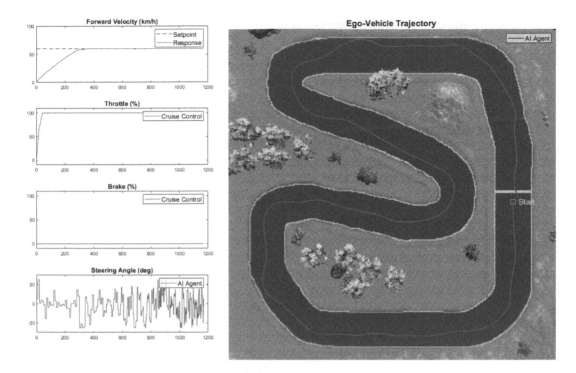

FIGURE 2.18   Reinforcement learning–based control implementation.

pretuned PID controller, while the lateral vehicle dynamics are controlled using a neural network trained end to end (using the PPO algorithm).

Initially, the training was weighted toward completing an entire lap. The agent (ego vehicle) was rewarded in proportion to its driving distance and was penalized for wandering off the road. The agent started off by performing random actions until it could get a sense of what was truly required in order to maximize its reward, and it was finally able to complete an entire lap autonomously. The training was then weighted more toward reducing the lap time, and the agent was rewarded in inverse proportion to the lap time achieved and was penalized in case the lap time was more than the average lap time achieved by human driver (~48.3 seconds). The final lap time achieved by AI agent trained using reinforcement learning was 47.2 seconds, which was better than the human driver!

Reinforcement learning has an upper hand when it comes to "learning" unknown behaviors from scratch through self-exploration. The policy adapts itself in order to maximize the expected reward, and explicit relations governing characteristics of the system are not necessary. Another peculiar advantage of this technique is its ability to discover novel strategies and even surpass human performance.

Nonetheless, owing to its exploratory nature, reinforcement learning requires a significantly large amount of training time, which might pose as a major issue in case of development-analysis cycles. Furthermore, this approach calls for a handcrafted reward function, which, if defined inefficiently, may cause unintended rewarding, thereby leading to erroneous learning.

In conclusion, reinforcement learning is a powerful strategy, especially in terms of achieving superhuman performance. However, it is generally better to have at least a basic pretrained model available to work on top of, in order to skip the initial (and most time-consuming) portion of the training phase, wherein the agent generates almost random actions with an aim of primary exploration.

2.4 OUR RESEARCH AT AUTONOMOUS SYSTEMS LAB (SRMIST)

The Autonomous Systems Lab at the Department of Mechatronics Engineering, SRM Institute of Science and Technology (SRMIST), is headed by Mr. Sivanathan Kandhasamy and is focused on research and development in various aspects of autonomous systems. Specifically focusing on autonomous vehicles, our team is constantly working on the three subsystems: perception, planning, and control. Although most of our past works are limited to simulation, we are currently working toward developing our own research platform for testing hardware implementations as well.

Further narrowing down to control of autonomous vehicles, our team has worked on most, if not all, of the aforementioned control strategies, and we are continuously studying and experimenting with them in order to analyze their performance and test their limits. We are also working on developing novel and hybrid control strategies with an aim of improving controller performance (i.e., improved stability, tracking, and robustness) and/ or reducing computational cost (allowing real-time execution).

It is to be noted that an exhaustive discussion of each and every research project carried out at Autonomous Systems Lab (SRMIST) is beyond the scope of this chapter. Nonetheless, some of our team's research project demonstrations pertaining to autonomous vehicles are available at www.youtube.com/playlist?list=PLdOCgvQ2Iny8g9OPmEJeVCas9tKr6auB3

2.5 CLOSING REMARKS

Throughout this chapter, we have discussed most of the current *state-of-the-art* control strategies employed for autonomous vehicles, from the basic ones such as bang-bang and PID control all the way up to advanced ones such as MPC and end-to-end learning, from theoretical, conceptual, and practical viewpoints. Now, as we come to the end of this chapter, we would like to add a few notes on some minute details pertaining to performance enhancement of control strategies for autonomous vehicles based on our knowledge and experience in the field.

- *Gain scheduling:* Most nonlinear systems exhibit varying dynamics under different operating conditions. In such cases, a controller with single set of gains may not be able to regulate the system effectively throughout the operational design domain as the operating conditions change. The gain scheduling technique overcomes this limitation by employing multiple sets of gains appropriately across the entire range of operating conditions.

- *Integral windup:* For PI and PID controllers, integrating the error over a prolonged duration may lead to very large values, resulting in loss of stability. It is therefore advised to limit the upper value of the accumulated error to a safe value. This can be achieved using a wide array of techniques, one of them being imposing upper and lower bounds on the accumulated error and clipping the value within that range. Another approach is limiting the size of the history buffer over which the error is integrated through the use of a *queue* data structure of limited size, using the first-in-first-out (FIFO) principle to discard error values that are too old.

- *Smoothing controller outputs:* Most of the controllers have a tendency to generate abrupt responses in case of a highly dynamic event, and while it may be appropriate in a few cases, it is generally undesirable. Such abrupt control actions may cause loss of stability or even affect the actuation elements adversely. It therefore becomes necessary to smoothen the controller outputs before applying them to the plant, and one way of achieving this is to clamp the controller outputs within a safe range (determined through rigorous testing) such that the controller is still able to track the set point under all the operating conditions. A secondary approach is to limit the rate of change of the control output, thereby enabling a smoother transition.

- *Introduction of dead-bands:* Most corrective controllers oscillate about the set point, trying really hard to converge, and while this might be desirable in the case of highly precise systems, it is generally not really necessary to achieve the set point exactly. The controller action may be nullified then in close proximity to the set point. This is known as a dead-band. It must be noted, however, that the width of the dead-band must be chosen wisely depending on the precision requirements of the system in question.

- *Safe reinforcement learning:* As discussed earlier, reinforcement learning involves discovery of novel strategies largely through a trial-and-error approach; as a result, it is seldom directly applied to a physical system (you don't want to take millions of episodes to learn by crashing the agent almost each time). However, there are a few techniques that can be employed to overcome this limitation, one of them being training a simulated agent under pseudorealistic operating conditions and then transferring the trained model onto the physical agent. Another way of approaching this problem is to penalize the policy prior to any catastrophic event by self-supervising the agent through an array of sensors. A third (and more elegant) approach is to train the agent for a "safe" behavior using imitation learning and then to improve its performance by training it further using reinforcement learning.

As a final note, we summarize the control strategies described in this chapter against a set of qualitative comparison metrics in Table 2.2.

Generally, when it comes to traditional control strategies, PI or PID controllers are the primary choice for longitudinal control, whereas MPC or geometric controllers are predominantly employed for lateral control. However, the exact choice depend on the specifics of the problem statement. Learning-based control strategies, on the other hand, do not have any "preferred" implementations, and it would be appropriate to say that these techniques are currently in their infant stage with a bright future ahead of them.

TABLE 2.2 Summary of Control Strategies for Autonomous Vehicles

Comparison Metric	Bang-Bang Control	PID Control	Geometric Control	Model Predictive Control	Imitation Learning-Based Control	Reinforcement Learning-Based Control
Principle of operation	Error driven (FSM)	Error driven (corrective)	Model based (corrective)	Model based (optimal)	Supervised learning	Reinforcement learning
Tracking	Poor	Good	Very good	Excellent	Good	–
Robustness	Poor	Very good	Very good	Excellent	Good	Good
Stability	Poor	Very good	Very good	Excellent	Good	Good
Reliability	Very low	Very high	Very high	Extremely high	Low	Low
Technical complexity	Very low	Low	Low	Very high	Low	High
Computational overhead	Very low	Low	Low	Very high	High	High
Constraint satisfaction	Poor	Good	Good	Excellent	–	–
Technical maturity	Very high	Very high	High	Moderate	Low	Very low

BIBLIOGRAPHY

Babu, M., Theerthala, R. R., Singh, A. K., Baladhurgesh, B. P., Gopalakrishnan, B., and Krishna, K. M. (2019). Model Predictive Control for Autonomous Driving Considering Actuator Dynamics. *American Control Conference (ACC)*, Philadelphia, pp. 1983–1989.

Bojarski, M., Testa, D. D., Dworakowski, D., Firner, B., Flepp, B., Goyal, P., Jackel, L. D., Monfort, M., Muller, U., Zhang, J., Zhang, X., Zhao, J., and Zieba, K. (2016). End to End Learning for Self-Driving Cars. *Preprint*, arXiv:1604.07316.

Coulter, R. C. (1992). Implementation of the Pure Pursuit Path Tracking Algorithm. *CMU-RI-TR-92-01*. [Online]. Available: http://ri.cmu.edu/pub_files/pub3/coulter_r_craig_1992_1/coulter_r_craig_1992_1.pdf

Drews, P., Williams, G., Goldfain, B., Theodorou, E. A., and Rehg, J. M. (2018). Vision-Based High Speed Driving with a Deep Dynamic Observer. *Preprint*, arXiv:1812.02071.

Emirler, M. T., Uygan, I. M. C., Guvenc, B. A., and Guvenc, L. (2014). Robust PID Steering Control in Parameter Space for Highly Automated Driving. *International Journal of Vehicular Technology*, vol. 2014.

Hoffmann, G. M., Tomlin, C. J., Montemerlo, M., and Thrun, S. (2007). Autonomous Automobile Trajectory Tracking for Off-Road Driving: Controller Design, Experimental Validation and Racing. *Proceedings of the American Control Conference*, New York, pp. 2296–2301.

Kabzan, J., Hewing, L., Liniger, A., and Zeilinger, M. N. (2019). Learning-Based Model Predictive Control for Autonomous Racing. *IEEE Robotics and Automation Letters*, vol. 4, no. 4, pp. 3363–3370.

Kendall, A., Hawke, J., Janz, D., Mazur, P., Reda, D., Allen, J. M., Lam, V. D., Bewley, A., and Shah, A. (2018). Learning to Drive in a Day. *Preprint*, arXiv:1807.00412.

Kong, J., Pfeiffer, M., Schildbach, G., and Borrelli, F. (2015). Kinematic and Dynamic Vehicle Models for Autonomous Driving Control Design. *IEEE Intelligent Vehicles Symposium (IV)*, Seoul, pp. 1094–1099.

LeCun, Y., Muller, U., Ben, J., Cosatto, E., and Flepp, B. (2005). Off-Road Obstacle Avoidance through End-to-End Learning. *Advances in Neural Information Processing Systems*, pp. 739–746.

Li, D., Zhao, D., Zhang, Q., and Chen, Y. (2019). Reinforcement Learning and Deep Learning Based Lateral Control for Autonomous Driving (Application Notes). *IEEE Computational Intelligence Magazine*, vol. 14, no. 2, pp. 83–98.

Obayashi, M., and Takano, G. (2018). Real-Time Autonomous Car Motion Planning Using NMPC with Approximated Problem Considering Traffic Environment. *6th IFAC Conference on Nonlinear Model Predictive Control NMPC*, IFAC-PapersOnLine, vol. 51, no. 20, pp. 279–286.

O'Brien, R. T. (2006). Bang-Bang Control for Type-2 Systems. *Proceeding of the Thirty-Eighth Southeastern Symposium on System Theory*, Cookeville, pp. 163–166.

Ogata, K. (2010). *Modern Control Engineering*. 5th ed. Prentice Hall, Upper Saddle River, NJ.

Polack, P., Altche, F., Novel, B. A., and de La Fortelle, A. (2017). The Kinematic Bicycle Model: A Consistent Model for Planning Feasible Trajectories for Autonomous Vehicles? *IEEE Intelligent Vehicles Symposium (IV)*, Redondo Beach, pp. 812–818.

Pomerleau, D. (1989). ALVINN: An Autonomous Land Vehicle in a Neural Network. *Proceedings of Advances in Neural Information Processing Systems*, 1, pp. 305–313.

Riedmiller, M., Montemerlo, M., and Dahlkamp, H. (2007). Learning to Drive a Real Car in 20 Minutes. Frontiers in the Convergence of Bioscience and Information Technologies, Jeju City, pp. 645–650.

Rosolia, U., and Borrelli, F. (2020). Learning How to Autonomously Race a Car: A Predictive Control Approach. *IEEE Transactions on Control Systems Technology*, vol. 28, no. 6, pp. 2713–2719.

Samak, T. V., Samak, C. V., and Kandhasamy, S. (2020). Robust Behavioral Cloning for Autonomous Vehicles Using End-to-End Imitation Learning. *Preprint*, arXiv:2010.04767.

Snider, J. M. (2009). Automatic Steering Methods for Autonomous Automobile Path Tracking. *CMU-RI-TR-09-08*. [Online]. Available: https://www.ri.cmu.edu/pub_files/2009/2/Automatic_Steering_Methods_for_Autonomous_Automobile_Path_Tracking.pdf

Tampuu, A., Semikin, M., Muhammad, N., Fishman, D., and Matiisen, T. (2020). A Survey of End-to-End Driving: Architectures and Training Methods. *Preprint*, arXiv:2003.06404.

Zanon, M., Frasch, J., Vukov, M., Sager, S., and Diehl, M. (2014). *Model Predictive Control of Autonomous Vehicles*. In H. Waschl, I. Kolmanovsky, M. Steinbuch, and L. del Re (eds.), *Optimization and Optimal Control in Automotive Systems: Lecture Notes in Control and Information Sciences*, vol. 455, Springer, Cham.

A Comprehensive Review of Navigation System, Design, and Safety Issues for Autonomous Vehicle Development

Pranjal Paul and Abhishek Sharma

University of Petroleum and Energy Studies
Dehradun, India

CONTENTS

DOI: 10.1201/9781003048381-4

3.1 INTRODUCTION

An autonomous vehicle (AV), or an unmanned vehicle, can drive itself, performing required complex functions without any human involvement by acknowledging its surrounding environment through sensors and actuators. AVs have immense potential to allow time to be spent on productive works rather than on driving while providing greater safety and reducing overcrowding, energy consumption, and pollution.

The Society of Automotive Engineers (SAE) has categorized six levels of automation with respect to decreased dependency on manual driving. At level 0, the vehicle is completely manual (i.e., the humans monitor the driving environment), and at level 5, the advanced driver-assistance system (ADAS) makes the car completely self-driving [1]. Even though ADAS improves safety, becoming aware of the procedure and continuously practicing helps the user to gain trust in the system. Sensors, collectively, help the vehicle to perceive its surrounding with increased accuracy, leading toward automated driving [2]. One of the phases of the vehicle machinery used in AVs is adaptive cruise control (ACC). It is intended to maintain consistent intervals between vehicles throughout their travel [3]. Also, with knowledge of the vehicle's position and localization, autonomous navigation, tracking, and obstacle avoidance can be achieved [4]. This requires the technique of odometry, with vision-based odometry being a well-known robust and economical technique. Additionally, a voice-controlled system can be integrated into the AV for its advancement like the one developed for unmanned aerial vehicles [5].

Table 3.1 summarizes SAE's J3016 guidelines for different levels of driving automation.

Acknowledgment of surroundings is obligatory for the design of ADAS, as it is responsible for dealing with controllers by providing information about the environment based on laser, radio detection and ranging (RADAR), and other crucial sensors. Lane and road marking detection and recognition is the initial task, enabling the location sensing of the AV and any cars around it. Even though it has been a recurring subject over recent years [6], researchers are developing new methodologies to improve the efficiency and robustness of the system, such as reducing the use of redundant sensors to avoid errors in measurement, mainly in intercity environments [7, 8]. Despite the progress made, existing sensor technologies needs further advancement to meet safety requirements at an acceptable price. The workflow of driver assistance system is shown in Figure 3.1.

However, the development of virtual simulation platforms like Unity, Nvidia Drive Constellation, and CARLA simulator provides an easy way to study the dynamic behavior of the vehicle with proper simulation results that enable analysis of the interaction of AVs with the various real-time elements involved during driving [9]. In the past few decades, much research work has been published with the aim of identifying and describing the most important variables to be considered for developing the more efficient systems that are required to operate in real-time conditions and to mimic the behavior of the car driver [10]. Besides this, the key idea of ADAS is path planning, which needs to be satisfied foremost. Due to its planning factor, it is usually done before the motion of the

TABLE 3.1   SAE's J3016 Guidelines for Automated Driving

Type of Automation	Level	Description	Remarks
No automation	0	The vehicle is completely human assisted and manually controlled.	Example: A base model vehicle with conventional cruise control.
Assisted driving	1	Abilities like adaptive cruise control (ACC) and/or parking sensors are available in the vehicle. They assist the driver in maneuvering the vehicle within the physical environment.	Many of the vehicles we see on the road today are considered SAE level 1 vehicles. Example: Honda Civic with ACC.
	2	The vehicle has two or more driving assistance features that work simultaneously: for example, acceleration adjustment according to traffic speed or highway steering. The vehicle is, in a sense, conditionally automated.	Example: 2018 Tesla Model S with autopilot, lane changing, ACC, and self-parking features.
Automated driving	3	The vehicle is partially intelligent, able to make decisions in certain situations. It takes full control of operation when certain conditions are met during a route, but the driver needs to be attentive in case something doesn't go as intended.	Example: 2019 Audi A8 with artificial intelligence and hybrid drive is the first level 3 vehicle available in the market.
	4	The vehicle can drive itself independently in most conditions. However, in situations where visibility is poor due to, for example, a windstorm or when the vehicle is driving on back roads, the driver can request control. The vehicle is in self-driving mode under the established conditions, and human input is not required when driving on the highway or maneuvering through a traffic jam.	Example: Hyundai's NEXO is currently being tested as a level 4 car; Google Waymo.
	5	A level 5 vehicle is considered to be completely autonomous, that is, no human driver will be required under any circumstances. The vehicle's ability to operate autonomously through elevated terrains or judge environmental conditions and behave accordingly could be envisioned in a fully autonomous car.	Nonexistent currently but with the integration of more V2X technology to alleviate risks, level 5 vehicle automation will evolve.

car. Hence, it can be renamed as path preplanning. Cumulation of actuators, processors and controllers, sensor fusion, and advanced algorithms is required for the execution of automated driving, and hence this chapter provides a comprehensive review of these key points.

This chapter provides a comprehensive review of navigation system, design architecture, and safety issues related to the self-driving car (SDC). The remainder of this chapter covers the following: Section 3.2 elaborates the features of autonomous vehicles. Section 3.3 explains various sensors consolidated in the system. Sections 3.4 and 3.5 report on design characteristics and safety matters related to SDC technology. This chapter concludes with Section 3.6.

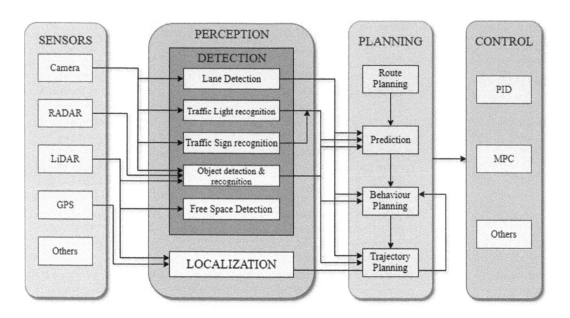

FIGURE 3.1   Workflow of advanced driver-assistance system [see Ref. 36].

3.2 FEATURES OF AUTONOMOUS VEHICLES

Over recent years, the abilities of cars have progressed to the point that there are level 4 AVs successfully running on the road. To achieve a completely driverless car, the prime concern is safety assurance. The most advanced successful AVs incorporate some or all the features that are discussed in subsequent text.

3.2.1 Lane Detection and Changing

An AV is able to remain inside the lanes safely by observing distant road ridges and traces and nearby hindrances or obstructions. In most cases, it utilizes the global positioning system (GPS), or even RADAR and LIDAR, to pinpoint locations. Lane detection [11] and lane changing features mainly depend on controlling the steering wheel actuator using odometrical relations. Odometry predicts the real location, direction, and alignment relative to a regarded set point if the wheel speed or contact-point displacement is known. The odometry equations are summarized as follows:

$$x_{i+1} = x_i + \Delta L \cos\left(\theta_i + \frac{\Delta \theta}{2}\right) \tag{3.1}$$

$$y_{i+1} = y_i + \Delta L \sin\left(\theta_i + \frac{\Delta \theta}{2}\right) \tag{3.2}$$

$$\theta_{i+1} = \theta_i + \frac{\delta_R - \delta_L}{2e} \tag{3.3}$$

where x and y represent the vehicle's center position, θ is the vehicle's orientation, ΔL stands for displacement, δ_R *and* δ_L represent the rotation of the wheel, and e represents half the axle length. The combination of vision and odometry helps to achieve the requirements of the lane-changing feature.

3.2.2 Adaptive Cruise Control

The adaptive cruise control (ACC) system was established for driving on highways where traffic congestion is comparatively less than in the city region. The system helps the driver to maintain a safe driving speed and longitudinal distance relative to any other vehicle in its surroundings. ACC has two operating modes: cruise mode, which maintains a reference speed, and follow mode, which maintains a safe distance from the surrounding automobiles.

The working principle of the control system depends on the Doppler effect, which measures speed by the shift in the frequency of the reflected beam. Accordingly, the brake and accelerator are controlled to keep the vehicle in a safe position. The high-pitched sound reaching the driver's ear means that a vehicle is coming close to the ACC-equipped vehicle, and a low-pitched sound means the vehicle has passed the car and is moving into the distance [12]. Figure 3.2 depicts the general block diagram of adaptive cruise control.

ACC will mechanically modify the rate of speed to maintain a correct distance between any obstacle and the vehicle. This can be achieved by employing a laser or RADAR beam to calculate the relative distance between the adjacent objects. Researchers are developing algorithms like vision-based pattern matching [14] to improve the functionality of ACC.

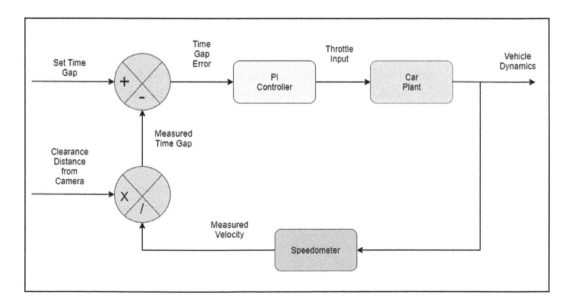

FIGURE 3.2   Block diagram of adaptive cruise control [see Ref. 13].

3.2.3 Simultaneous Localization and Mapping

Simultaneous localization and mapping (SLAM) helps in autonomous navigation for cases where either GPS fails or the vehicle has no information about its surrounding environment. SLAM consists of a feedback system where sensors obtain measurements of the AV's surroundings in real time, analyze them to map the local environment, and make decisions accordingly [15]. It is a type of sequential model or algorithm that seeks to assemble a set of states from a set of measurements [16]. With the quantities and the information on previous states provided, as well as on the environment, the vehicle's route is plotted.

A learning process among the conditions and measurements is required for an accurate representation for the navigation system. A recursive algorithm called the Kalman filter (that is, a sort of Bayes filter) is the most widely adopted methodology for SLAM to provide state estimation of the host vehicle. As a function of uncertainty, a prediction is made that is improved over time within the system, where the uncertainty represents a weight given to the current state estimate and previous measurements, known as the Kalman gain [15].

The methodology uses the history of the system's state, control inputs, and observations. The Kalman filter works in two steps: measuring and predicting. The prediction method estimates the current position based on previous positions and also the current control input. A final estimation of this state is made based on the current and previous observations and on uncertainty, for which an observation model is used [16].

3.2.4 Trajectory Planning and Collision Avoidance

Using time and velocity parameters, a trajectory can be defined as the state sequence visited by the vehicle. A moving object must identify and bypass obstacles in order to create an effective route, which is not yet a completed task. Real-time collision avoidance route planning of a vehicle's visits to subsequent possible states, supporting its kinematic and dynamic constraints over the complete navigation, can be termed trajectory planning.

Considering linear and nonlinear control systems for path planning, the widely used approaches include model predictive control (MPC) and behavior-based models that can be managed in a complex environment with behaviors that are easy to design and test. As a function of the position and speed of the moving vehicle, the maneuver of the wheeled object is characterized, which includes every complex task like maintaining a straight path, detecting and changing lanes, turning the vehicle, using emergency braking, and overtaking, by maintaining a collision-free path. The controller is defined over the speed, position, and path profile that are required to be maintained even in the presence of instability and an unconstrained environment, thereby generating a feasible path on which to drive the vehicle safely. Real-time decision-making to move over the path traced through the spaces where the vehicle can drive easily is the major purpose of maneuver planning.

The steering commands to generate a collision-free nominal path ensuring the vehicle's stability are the cynosure of the controller. Predictions of the upcoming constrained environmental conditions must be made, incorporating the dynamics over the current steering conditions to attain a safe path. Figure 3.3 is a simple illustration of such an objective, where the subject avoids the obstacle nodes intelligently and follows a safe path generated within the constrained environment.

FIGURE 3.3   Collision avoidance using the rapid exploring random tree method.

The rapid exploring random tree is a computationally less expensive path planner that generates the shortest optimal path between the start and the goal node. Following is the pseudo code that has been implemented to get the result as shown in Figure 3.3.

Pseudo Code
1. goalNode #region that identifies success
2. counter = 0 # iteration counter
3. no_of_iter = n # iteration limit
4. graph(vert, edge) # graph with edges and vertices as arguments
5. while counter < no_of_iter:
6. new_waypoint = randomPosition()
7. if isinObstacle(new_waypoint) == True:
8. continue
9. nearest_waypoint = nearest(graph(vert, edge), new_waypoint) # search nearest waypoint
10. link = chain(new_waypoint, nearest_waypoint)
11. graph.append(link)
12. if new_waypoint in goalNode:
13. return graph
14. return graph

The nodes (blue dots) are initialized in random fashion, and each node is connected to the closest available node. With each node created, the algorithm checks if it is an obstacle node (one of the large circles). The algorithm terminates successfully when the node lies around the goal region or reaches the iteration limit. If a path exists between the start and the goal node, the algorithm promises to generate it.

The workflow of path planning to maneuver through traffic could be pipelined in the following manner:

1. *Perception and prediction:* With integrated sensor readings, information about external environmental objects like position and velocity can be gathered. This helps the controller to predict and generate a safe path for the vehicle's movement.

2. *Behavioral forethought:* The system reaches a conclusion drawn from the insights and translates them into a scene. Based on this, the planner makes suggestions for the car to maneuver along the predicted route.

3. *Trajectory planning:* Using the scores of the potential parameters, such as accuracy, precision, and recall, and analyzing feasibility in terms of safety, comfort, and efficiency, a probable trajectory is created.

4. *Controlling:* The final decision is sent to the controller to regulate the actuators to move the vehicle over the defined path.

3.3 SENSOR FUSION FOR AUTONOMOUS NAVIGATION

Integration of two or more diverse sensors, such as camera, LIDAR, and RADAR, is called sensor fusion, which makes the entity a sensory device [17]. Sensor fusion allows AVs to perceive the external environment so as to provide a safe drive. Believing in their own advantages, a multitude of technologies or sensors is required to provide the redundancy of measured readings that is required to sense the environment for safe movement [18]. With the implementation of a sensor fusion framework, improved accuracy is achieved in applications like object detection and position estimation [19]. The fusion system with individual ranges is shown in Figure 3.4.

Automotive sensors can be classified as active sensors and passive sensors. Active sensors emit wave energy and perceive the objects that reflect that energy. RADAR is an active sensor that uses radio waves to detect obstacles present in the beam range when the waves are reflected back. Passive sensors do not radiate any wave; instead, they gather information based on the detection of vibration, light, heat, etc. One example of a passive sensor is a simple camera or thermal camera.

3.3.1 Camera Sensor

Nearly all AVs present today are equipped with different types of cameras, both single and multiple, for various applications like lane, roadside, and pedestrian detection. Many of them include wide-angle cameras for constructing a 360° view of the environment. Information captured through cameras is fed to various algorithms that can be trained to accomplish various tasks. In other words, the camera becomes the driver's vision.

Cameras make the system intelligent by enabling it to perform complex tasks like classifying road and nonroad areas, detecting walkers, understanding traffic signs and symbols,

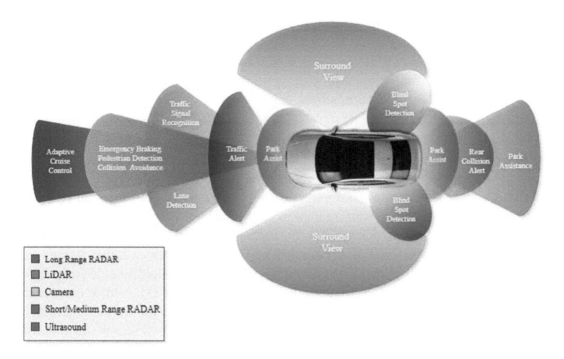

FIGURE 3.4   Sensor fusion system with individual ranges [see Ref. 37].

and identifying other details like footpaths and speed breakers. Also, for high-end applications, a 3-D camera is included in the system to capture higher-level information in order to perform depth imaging–based tasks. With the help of various artificial intelligence (AI) techniques like the convolutional neural network (CNN) and reinforcement learning, an AV can be trained to recognize its surroundings in order to make decisions accordingly [20]. Various methodologies have been proposed to get a complete real-time 360° view of a vehicle's surroundings. Hee Lee et al. [21], for example, have published about the fusion of four fish-eye cameras calibrated to obtain localization, online obstacle detection, and computation over dense maps. There are also infrared cameras that are meant to perform in dark surroundings, providing the obvious advantage of using infrared rays, which are helpful in a foggy environment.

3.3.2 Radio Detection and Ranging Sensor

RADAR is a vital sensing technology for ADAS because of its powerful recognition ability, extensive range, and robust ability to detect environmental variations [22]. RADAR is a radio-wave sensor that detects objects within a large radius, thereby measuring their position and speed. It is based on the Doppler effect, which measures the change in the frequency of the wave if the vehicle moves toward or away from the host object. However, it cannot determine the characteristics of the sensed object and is a low-resolution sensor.

There are short-range and long-range RADARs that are installed in the vehicles to provide an omnidirectional view, each pursuing different functionalities. For applications like blind-spot monitoring and parking assistance, short-range RADAR (with an approximate frequency of 24 GHz) is used, whereas for tasks like brake assistance, a long-range type

(77 GHz) is preferred [23]. In an unclear environment due to, for example, fog or rain, RADAR works best compared to other sensors and is used for localization with the implementation of algorithms like the extended Kalman filter (EKF) [24].

3.3.3 Inertial Measurement Unit Sensor

The inertial measurement unit (IMU) sensor is capable of characterizing the movement of the vehicle along the yaw, pitch, and roll axes. It calculates orientation, inclination, altitude, and acceleration along the X, Y, and Z axes. The IMU sensor is mounted in a fixed position within the structure of a SDC so that it is aware of its fastened placement. From this fixed position, the IMU will keep track of the movement and position of the car.

It provides "localization" facts (i.e., data about the orientation, inclination, altitude, and acceleration of the autonomous vehicle). The controller then combines this data with the map to make the vehicle aware of surrounding objects. Since the vehicle is dependent on its steering and heading direction, accelerating the vehicle in an undesired direction may direct the vehicle to the wrong lane. Thus, to inspect these, fusion of the IMU sensor is required, as it will provide dynamic controllability to the system through the sensor's strength of accurate calculation of attitude and position. The addition of an IMU sensor will allow the vehicle to deal with complex unstructured environments like mountainous steep regions or skidding regions where tires lose traction, increasing the probability of accidents.

Tesla, a visionary SDC company, believes in "No LIDAR Technology": that is, it refrains from using the costly LIDAR sensors. Rather, in such systems, clusters of inertial sensors and cameras are needed to maintain an accuracy level that could have been obtained more easily by using LIDAR. For example, an IMU with a thermal camera can be integrated to detect moving objects [25]. This would deal with continuous oscillations in accuracy and precision levels in an uncertain environment.

3.3.4 Light Detection and Ranging Sensor

A LIDAR sensor is a laser-based sensor that functions similar to RADAR. It is primarily used for generating dynamic 2-D as well as 3-D environments for the host system over a range up to several meters. In addition, pedestrians can be recognized by implementing 3-D LIDAR, which can be trained using complex AI algorithms like support vector machine (SVM) to learn their behavior and take action accordingly [26]. These advantages incline SDC manufacturers such as Waymo, Hyundai, and Uber to opt for LIDAR over any other technologies.

The instrument throws off rapid laser pulses that reflect back from the objects and are detected by the photodetector. It measures the distance of the objects using the time of flight of the laser in a round-trip, using Equation (3.4):

$$d = \frac{c \times (t.o.f)}{2} \qquad (3.4)$$

where d denotes the distance of the object from the sensor, $c = 3 \times 10^8$ m/s is the speed of light, and $t.o.f.$ represents the time of flight, which is the time taken by the pulse to reach the object; the division by 2 represents the first half of the complete round-trip. Along with this computation, the sensor's attitude and altitude are also noted, as they contribute to the integrity of the data collected to build the map. The LIDAR sensor is capable of carrying out rapid successive calculations and then transporting them to form a cluster of points replicating a 3-D view of the environment. This allows the vehicle to perceive everything in its surroundings and hence is crucial [27].

The LIDAR sensor is generally mounted on the rooftop of the vehicle to get clearer readings of the desired surroundings. It also comes with a spinning unit meant for power transfer to each pulse, in order to protect eyes from the lasers, though the safety rating depends on various other parameters like pulse duration, divergence angle, and exposure direction.

3.3.5 Global Positioning System Sensor

A group of artificial satellites orbiting in space sends instantaneous data about position and time from their high orbits. These satellites have been termed the global navigation satellite system (GNSS), which includes the GPS. It is a "constellation" of approximately thirty well-spaced satellites that circumnavigate the earth and make it possible for a ground receiver to pinpoint its geographic location. The location accuracy varies from 100 to 10 m for most of the equipment.

One may think that if the SDC has an IMU, then maybe it does not require a GPS sensor for localization. But surprisingly, having both is crucial. The IMU can measure only the relative position and movement. But the GPS tells about the absolute position and movement of the vehicle. In other words, the GPS determines where the vehicle specifically is, while the IMU states how far it has moved from one position to another position. For the use of dead reckoning, one needs to have some good starting position. Dead reckoning refers to calculating the host's relative position with respect to its previous state and then optimizing it based on the predicted or known speed over elapsed time. The IMU in a SDC will use the GPS to provide that starting position. The GPS sensor is prone to errors, however, so a collection of them needs to be employed for the localization task to improve accuracy from redundant observations. A series of other sensors is also installed such as the IMU, whose main function is to keep track of the rotational parameters and acceleration. Similarly, motion sensors, cameras, and a road-map database are added to minimize the errors [28].

The GPS sensor is also crucial in applications when there are no lanes present in the road or when the lanes at an intersection point are curved rather than being the straight lanes for which the algorithm might have been designed. Therefore, Lee et al. [29] proposed a method for the localization of AVs that can be useful where assessment is based on detection of lanes involving nonlinear models and stop lines.

3.3.6 Ultrasonic Sensor

The ultrasonic sensor works on a principle similar to those of RADAR and LIDAR, but it uses ultrasound in place of light. Moreover, it can be used to get knowledge about the position of static objects, which could be helpful while parking the car. The detection and tracking of entities in the neighborhood of the vehicle has drawn considerable attention during the development of ADASs. With the installation of a linear arrangement of these ultrasonic sensors, object tracking could be accomplished by implementing a variation of the Kalman filter [30]:

$$dist = \frac{echo\ width\ (\mu s)}{58} \tag{3.5}$$

where *dist* represents the distance that the acoustic wave traveled and *echo width* is the time between transmission of the signal and reception of the echo (reflected) signal. Ultrasonic sensors are low-range sensors that emit short high-frequency sound pulses. For distance calculation, they use the same formula as for LIDAR and RADAR, with speed of light replaced by speed of sound. The time signal used by these sensors is translated into distance by the microcontroller using the relation mentioned above. They are ideal for near-distance low-speed applications such as parking, reversing, halting at traffic signals, and maintaining adequate distance from surrounding objects and vehicles.

3.4 DESIGN CHARACTERISTICS FOR AUTONOMOUS VEHICLES

The functional architecture of an SDC with ADAS is the framework that determines the functionalities of the system with its connections and works to accomplish the task [31, 32]. The design architecture of an AV can be roughly characterized as hardware planning and software planning, both of which can be further divided into additional subsets, as shown in Figure 3.5.

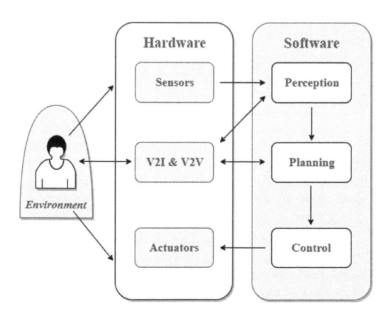

FIGURE 3.5   Architecture of autonomous vehicle.

3.4.1 Hardware Architecture

- *Sensors:* Sensors, as already discussed, are the components that enable the system to accumulate the required data about the surrounding environment. These include GPS sensors, IMU sensors, distance measurement unit (DMU) sensors, cameras, LIDAR sensors, and RADAR sensors that are fused in almost any self-driving technology, an approach called sensor fusion. The intelligent system combines these observations to improve accuracy by analyzing the redundancy in data or adds to them if needed.

- *Vehicle-to-vehicle, vehicle-to-infrastructure, and vehicle-to-network communication:* V2X technology allows the system to communicate bidirectionally with the components and also with the external environment, calculating the distance to passing cars and determining absolute and relative speed, which could help in crash avoidance. Additionally, it makes the system "attentive" to abrupt actions such as the sudden appearance of pedestrians or stray animals, the approach of an adjacent vehicle from a wrong direction, and the occurrence of potholes, road breaks, etc. Vehicle-to-network communication connects the vehicle to the cellular infrastructure and to the cloud so that the drivers can take the advantage of in-vehicle services like traffic updates and media streaming.

- *Actuators:* These are responsible for controlling the mechanical movement of the AVs, that is, they make the vehicle move. Based on their source of energy, they can be pneumatic, hydraulic, or thermal actuators. Electric motors can be rotatory actuators. Their application can be found in motoring, braking, and steering systems.

3.4.2 Software Architecture

Software architecture makes the system intelligent enough to make decisions. This is carried out with the following subdivisions of the architecture:

- *Perception:* It provides the AV with the ability to comprehend the sensory data obtained from mounted sensors, such as classifying the object in a captured frame as a vehicle, person, or animal, which can be further labeled as road and nonroad.

- *Scheduling:* It gives the AV the power of decision-making. The planning system works by combining the perception data and processes it to take suitable action such as, for example, identifying objects, predicting a crash, monitoring blind spots [33], and/or determining the vehicle's motion vector. The planning and execution of such decisions are performed through complex AI algorithms like reinforcement learning, support vector machines, etc.

- *Control:* The control system is responsible for activating the appropriate actuators to cause desired movement from the information obtained from the previous stages. Consider a situation where a speed breaker appears. The control system causes the vehicle to decelerate by the application of brakes. This knowledge is translated into action based on prior experience or preloaded instructions for such situations.

3.5 SAFETY ISSUES RELATED TO AUTONOMOUS VEHICLES

The advancement of self-driving technology is progressing at a fast pace. The current market has successfully introduced certain features to achieve autonomy at levels 3 and 4. Though continuous improvements are deployed to the infrastructure and machinery by the industry leaders; complete safety and security is still a prime concern in order to attain a complete driverless driving experience [34]. In order to gain passenger's faith, the product needs to assure their complete safety throughout the journey. For such confidence, the manufacturers need to cover all the safety bullet-points, which is itself a challenging task.

Before commercializing, on-road testing is indispensable, requiring the vehicle to be tested for an "uncertain" number of miles to meet suitable safety standards. This uncertainty is a major hindrance, as it requires countless dry runs to validate a certain failure rate.

Besides this, since the autonomy of the vehicle would require vehicle-to-network infrastructure, the probability of cyberattacks could arise. Hence, network security needs to be tackled for safety repercussions. Additionally, the vehicle requires continuous maintenance by the owner to leverage the complete efficiency of the revolutionary technology of the SDC.

To conceptualize safety in SDCs, companies need to benchmark themselves against safety standards from the International Organization for Standardization (ISO) and its national member organizations [35]. Table 3.2 provides an insight into safety guidelines.

TABLE 3.2   Safety Guidelines

	Safety Standard	Description
ISO 26262	Functional Safety	It focuses on failures due to malfunctions at the system hardware and software levels and on the responses designed to manage failures through analyzing development, production, and diagnostics.
ISO/PAS 21448	Safety of the Intended Functionality (SOTIF)	This extension of ISO 26262 covers ADAS functionality. It handles the faults generated by unexpected operating behavior even if there is no equipment fault present.
National Highway Traffic Safety Administration (NHTSA)		A few of the relevant safety elements addressed by the NHTSA are data recording, vehicle cybersecurity, operational design domain, system safety, and object and event detection and response.
Regional and Global New Car Assessment Programs (NCAP)		Regional NCAPs deal with safety practices in particular markets. European NCAP covers independent vehicle safety evaluation for that region. Some of the NCAP recommendations cover automatic emergency steering, autonomous emergency braking, V2X, driver monitoring, child presence detection, simulation, and pedestrian and cyclist safety.

3.6 CONCLUSION

The transportation industry is undergoing a revolution with the inauguration of self-driving vehicles. As we discussed, the integration of a number of sensors, the control of actuators, and the use of powerful processors are essential to achieving complete autonomy, together with passenger safety and comfort. By incorporating various sensors, the perception models are improved to the point that AVs are smart enough to make critical judgments online and hence have higher reliability. With advanced architecture, engineers enable AVs to more accurately identify their surroundings and threats. Table 3.3 presents an overall chapter brief.

TABLE 3.3   Overall Chapter Brief

Section	Section Name	Headings discussed	Conclusion
Section 3.1	Introduction	Level 0 to Level 5	SAE divides vehicles by degree of automation, ranging from "Driver Only" (level 0) to "Full Automation" (level 5). Currently, we have level 3 vehicles that provide limited conditional automation capabilities.
Section 3.2	Features of Autonomous Vehicles	Adaptive Cruise Control	Adaptive cruise control systems have the ability to adjust the vehicle's speed unlike conventional cruise control and also allow it to maintain adequate stopping distances.
		Lane Detection	Algorithm, such as the Canny edge and Harris corner detection algorithms, helps the car to detect lanes. Other methods are deep learning algorithms that re now being used by researchers.
		SLAM	Localization, the major challenge that roboticists face. enables the car to know where it is exactly. Hence, performing multiple localization algorithms is required, which is computationally complex. In addition, mapping of the surroundings is equally important. The car is equipped with range sensors and a camera setup to build a precise map.
		Obstacle Avoidance and Path Planning	Path planning with collision avoidance is one of the research areas that mainly focuses on making the car reach its destination. Path planners like RRT and the dynamic window approach are used in a major way to carry out this operation.
Section 3.3	Sensor Fusion for Autonomous Navigation	Range Sensors, Camera, Laser Sensors	Precise localization and mapping cannot be achieved without integration of multiple sensors. Analyzing and plotting redundant values from sensors with Kalman filtering and particle filters helps the car to achieve the task with increased efficiency and speed.
Section 3.4	Design Characteristics	V2X, Software and Hardware Architecture	Intelligent architecture must consider safety aspects, robust structure, fast internal and external communication, and overall heat-handling capacity.
Section 3.5	Safety Issues related to Autonomous Vehicle	Various Safety Standards at National, Regional, and International Levels	SDCs cannot be launched if they fail to meet various safety standards. The section mentions some of these safety assessments that are considered before designing and manufacturing.

REFERENCES

1. Anderson, J. M., et al. Autonomous Vehicle Technology: A Guide for Policymakers. Santa Monica, CA: RAND Corporation, 2014.
2. Ziębiński, Adam, Cupek, Rafał, Grzechca, Damian and Chruszczyk, Lukas. "Review of advanced driver assistance systems (ADAS)." AIP Conference Proceedings, 1906, 120002, 2017. doi: 10.1063/1.5012394.
3. Wang, Junmin and Rajamani, R. "Adaptive cruise control system design and its impact on highway traffic flow." Proceedings of the 2002 American Control Conference (IEEE Cat. No. CH37301), Anchorage, AK, vol. 5, pp. 3690–3695, 2002. doi: 10.1109/ACC.2002.1024501.
4. Thapa, Vikas, Sharma, Abhishek, Gairola, Beena, Mondal, Amit Kumar, Devalla, Vindhya and Patel, Ravi Kumar. "A review on visual odometry techniques for mobile robots: Types and challenges." Recent Advances in Electrical & Electronic Engineering, vol. 12, no. 1, 2019. doi: 10.2174/2352096512666191004142546.
5. Thomas, Cris, Bharadwaj, Rahul, Mondal, Amit K., Sharma, Abhishek, Omkar, S.N. and Devalla, Vindhya. "Design and development of voice control system for micro unmanned aerial vehicles." 2018 Aviation Technology, Integration, and Operations Conference, p. 4231, 2018.
6. Gern, Axel, Moebus, R. and Franke, U. "Vision-based lane recognition under adverse weather conditions using optical flow." Intelligent Vehicle Symposium, vol. 2, pp. 652–657, 2002.
7. Han, Jaehyun, Kim, Dongchul, Lee, Minchae and Sunwoo, Myoungho. "Enhanced road boundary and obstacle detection using a downward-looking LIDAR sensor." IEEE Transactions on Vehicular Technology, vol. 61, pp. 971–985, 2012. doi: 10.1109/TVT.2012.2182785.
8. Liu, Guoliang, Wörgötter, Florentin and Markelic, Irene. "Stochastic lane shape estimation using local image descriptors." IEEE Transactions on Intelligent Transportation Systems, vol. 14, pp. 13–21, 2013. doi: 10.1109/TITS.2012.2205146.
9. Hassan, Bassem, Gausemeier, Jürgen, Abdelgawad, Kareem, Berssenbrügge, Jan and Grafe, Michael. "A design framework for developing a reconfigurable driving simulator." International Journal on Advances in Systems and Measurements, vol. 8, no. 1 & 2, 2015.
10. Maag, C., Muhlbacher, D., Mark, C., and Kruger, H. "Studying effects of advanced driver assistance systems (ADAS) on individual and group level using multi-driver simulation." IEEE Intelligent Transportation Systems Magazine, vol. 4, no. 3, pp. 45–54, 2012. doi: 10.1109/MITS.2012.2203231.
11. Péter, G., Kiss, B. and Tihanyi, V. "Vision and odometry based autonomous vehicle lane changing." 2019 Eleventh International Conference on Ubiquitous and Future Networks (ICUFN), Zagreb, Croatia, pp. 102–107, 2019. doi: 10.1109/ICUFN.2019.8806159.
12. Yadav, A. K. and Szpytko, J. "Safety problems in vehicles with adaptive cruise control system." Journal of KONBiN, vol. 42, no. 1, pp. 389–398, 2017.
13. Prince, Simon J. D. Computer Vision: Models, Learning and Inference. Cambridge: Cambridge University Press, 2012.
14. Kanjee, R., Bachoo, A. K. and Carroll, J. "Vision-based adaptive cruise control using pattern matching." 2013 6th Robotics and Mechatronics Conference (RobMech), Durban, pp. 93–98, 2013. doi: 10.1109/RoboMech.2013.6685498.
15. Durrant-Whyte, H. and Bailey, T. "Simultaneous localization and mapping: Part I." IEEE Robotics and Automation Magazine, vol. 13, no. 2, pp. 99–108, 2006.
16. Bailey, T. and Durrant-Whyte, H. "Simultaneous localization and mapping (SLAM): Part II." IEEE Robotics & Automation Magazine, vol. 13, no. 3, pp. 108–117, 2006. doi: 10.1109/MRA.2006.1678144.
17. Kocić, J., Jovičić, N. and Drndarević, V. "Sensors and Sensor Fusion in Autonomous Vehicles." 2018 26th Telecommunications Forum (TELFOR), Belgrade, pp. 420–425, 2018. doi: 10.1109/TELFOR.2018.8612054.

18. Gustafsson, F. Statistical Sensor Fusion. Lund, Sweden: Lund University, 2010.
19. Burlet, J. and Fontana, M. Dalla. "Robust and efficient multi-object detection and tracking for vehicle perception systems using RADAR and camera sensor fusion." IET and ITS Conference on Road Transport Information and Control (RTIC 2012), London, pp. 1–6, 2012. doi: 10.1049/cp.2012.1553.
20. Stroupe, A. W., Martin, M. C. and Balch, T. "Distributed sensor fusion for object position estimation by multi-robot systems." Proceedings 2001 IEEE International Conference on Robotics and Automation (Cat. No.01CH37164), Seoul, South Korea, vol. 2, pp. 1092–1098, 2001. doi: 10.1109/ROBOT.2001.932739.
21. Hee Lee, G., Faundorfer, F. and Pollefeys, M. "Motion estimation for self-driving cars with a generalized camera." Proceedings of the IEEE Conference on Computer Vision and Pattern Recognition, pp. 2746–2753, 2013.
22. Zhou, Taohua, Mengmeng Yang, Kun Jiang, Henry Wong, and Diange Yang. "MMW RADAR-based technologies in autonomous driving: A review." Sensors, vol. 20, no. 24, p. 7283, 2020
23. Ginsburg, B. P., et al. "A multimode 76-to-81 GHz automotive RADAR transceiver with autonomous monitoring." 2018 IEEE International Solid-State Circuits Conference (ISSCC), San Francisco, CA, pp. 158–160, 2018. doi: 10.1109/ISSCC.2018.8310232.
24. Ward, E. and Folkesson, J. "Vehicle localization with low cost RADAR sensors." 2016 IEEE Intelligent Vehicles Symposium (IV), Gothenburg, pp. 864–870, 2016. doi: 10.1109/IVS.2016.7535489.
25. Lenac, K., Maurović, I. and Petrović, I. "Moving objects detection using a thermal camera and IMU on a vehicle." 2015 International Conference on Electrical Drives and Power Electronics (EDPE), Tatranska Lomnica, pp. 212–219, 2015. doi: 10.1109/EDPE.2015.7325296.
26. Wang, Heng, Wang, Bin, Liu, Bingbing, Meng, Xiaoli and Yang, Guanghong. "Pedestrian recognition and tracking using 3D LIDAR for autonomous vehicle." Robotics and Autonomous Systems, vol. 88, pp. 71–78, 2017.
27. Gao, H., Cheng, B., Wang, J., Li, K., Zhao, J. and Li, D. "Object classification using CNN-based fusion of vision and LIDAR in autonomous vehicle environment." IEEE Transactions on Industrial Informatics, vol. 14, no. 9, pp. 4224–4231, 2018. doi: 10.1109/TII.2018.2822828.
28. Jo, K., Chu, K. and Sunwoo, M. "GPS-bias correction for precise localization of autonomous vehicles." 2013 IEEE Intelligent Vehicles Symposium (IV), Gold Coast, QLD, pp. 636–641, 2013. doi: 10.1109/IVS.2013.6629538.
29. Lee, B.-H., Song, J.-H., Im, J.-H., Im, S.-H., Heo, M.-B. and Jee, G.-I. "GPS/DR error estimation for autonomous vehicle localization." Sensors, vol. 15, pp. 20779–20798, 2015.
30. Li, S.E., Li, G., Yu, J., Liu, C., Cheng, B., Wang, J. and Li, K. "Kalman filter-based tracking of moving objects using linear ultrasonic sensor array for road vehicles." Mechanical Systems and Signal Processing, vol. 98, pp. 173–189, 2018.
31. Munir, Farzeen, Azam, Shoaib, Hussain, Muhammad, Sheri, Ahmed and Jeon, Moongu. "Autonomous vehicle: The architecture aspect of self driving car." SSIP 2018: Proceedings of the 2018 International Conference on Sensors, Signal and Image Processing, pp. 1–5, 2018. doi: 10.1145/3290589.3290599.
32. Behere, S. and Torngren, M. "A functional architecture for autonomous driving." 2015 First International Workshop on Automotive Software Architecture (WASA), Montreal, QC, pp. 3–10. doi: 10.1145/2752489.2752491.
33. Bierstedt, Jane, Gooze, Aaron, Gray, Chris, Peterman, Josh, Raykin, Leon and Walters, Jerry. "Effects of next-generation vehicles on travel demand and highway capacity." FP Think Working Group, vol. 8, pp. 1–10, 2014.

34. Koopman, P. and Wagner, M. "Autonomous vehicle safety: An interdisciplinary challenge." IEEE Intelligent Transportation Systems Magazine, vol. 9, no. 1, pp. 90–96, 2017.

35. Koopman, Philip, Ferrell, Uma, Fratrik, Frank and Wagner, Michael. "A safety standard approach for fully autonomous vehicles." International Conference on Computer Safety, Reliability, and Security, Cham, Switzerland: Springer, pp. 326–332, 2019.

36. Udacity. An open source self-driving car, 2017.

37. Mafrica, Stefano. "Bio-inspired visual sensors for robotic and automotive applications." PhD diss., Aix-Marseille Université, 2016.

CHAPTER 4

Object Detection, Tracking and Trajectory Prediction for Autonomous Driving

Sridevi M and Sugirtha T

National Institute of Technology
Tiruchirappalli, India

Hazem Rashed

Valeo R&D
Cairo, Egypt

B Ravi Kiran

Navya
France

Senthil Yogamani

Valeo Vision Systems
Galway, Ireland

CONTENTS

DOI: 10.1201/9781003048381-5

4.1   INTRODUCTION

Object detection based on Convolutional Neural Network (CNN) has been successfully employed in autonomous driving systems. Vehicle class is considered the most important object, and it is necessary to detect and track all the vehicles around the ego car. Typically, at least four cameras around the car (front, rear, left, and right) are used for surround-view detection, and objects have to be tracked across the cameras (e.g., from rear to left to front). There are many challenges due to the highly dynamic environment such as occlusion, object pose changes, and multi-camera perspective changes. In a classical approach, a state-based tracking method such as a Kalman filter is employed as an independent module. Recently, CNN-based tracking approaches have been successful and have a strong potential to be integrated into a unified CNN detection and tracking multi-task model. Additionally, it is important to predict the trajectory of surrounding vehicles to plan maneuvers for safe automated driving. This chapter discusses unified vehicle detection, tracking, and trajectory prediction of objects around the ego vehicle and includes sections that explain individual tasks in detail. Also we discuss unified modeling approaches and provide future directions.

Autonomous vehicles capture the surrounding objects via cameras or sensors mounted on it [49, 51]. Three primary sensors used in autonomous vehicles are: the camera, LIDAR, and RADAR. There are different types of cameras such as monocular RGB, stereo, RGB camera with depth sensor (RGB-D), and fish-eye cameras. The autonomous driving system takes a sequence of frames from the video captured by sensors. The object detection phase classifies and labels all the objects in the frame. The tracking phase creates tracks by associating the detections obtained in the previous step. The trajectory prediction phase performs motion modeling and creates trajectories for the identified objects. Figure 4.1 illustrates the pipeline of the three main tasks to predict the trajectory of surrounding objects in autonomous driving, and Figure 4.2 shows the taxonomy of the various detection, tracking,

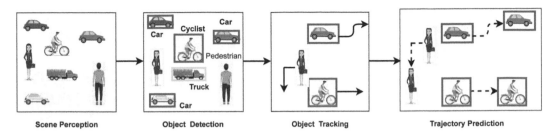

FIGURE 4.1   Generic pipeline for trajectory prediction in autonomous driving.

and trajectory prediction methods being used in autonomous driving systems that will be discussed in the subsections of this chapter. Autonomous driving has hard real-time constraints, and it is necessary to design efficient CNNs [8].

FIGURE 4.2   Taxonomy of multiple tasks in autonomous driving and unified models.

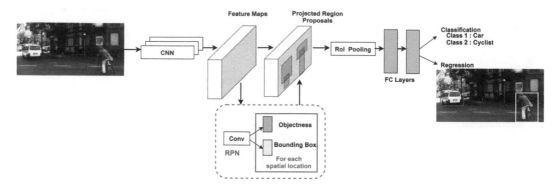

FIGURE 4.3   Architecture of Faster R-CNN: Two-stage detector [see Ref. 98].

4.2 2D OBJECT DETECTION

Object detection is the first and foremost problem in autonomous driving systems. It involves predicting the location of the target object along with its class in the given image. The alternative semantic segmentation is not covered in this chapter, and we refer the reader to refs [102, 103]. State-of-the-art methods for object detection based on deep learning can be broadly classified into two types: (1) two-stage detectors and (2) single-stage detectors. Figures 4.3 and 4.4 show the architecture of the most popular two-stage detector, Faster-RCNN [98], and single-stage detector, SSD [77].

- *Overview from the Perspective of Autonomous Driving:* Object detection is performed by autonomous vehicles in real-time to navigate through the surrounding environment. Object classification is crucial for the navigation system to make decisions. For instance, pedestrians need to be distinguished because they have a different motion model than that of vehicles. Tight but slow maneuvers are expected from pedestrians; however, wide and fast maneuvers can be performed by moving vehicles. Such information is critical for deciding which trajectory to plan. Other objects need to be localized and classified as well, such as traffic lights and traffic signs due to interaction

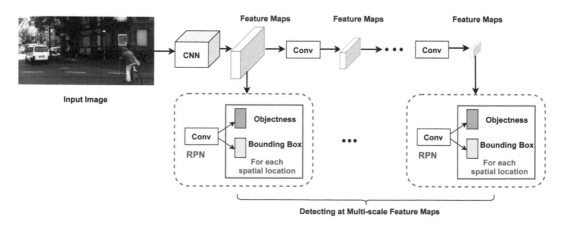

FIGURE 4.4   Architecture of SSD: One-stage detector [see Ref. 77].

TABLE 4.1   Classification of CNN-Based Object Detection Methods

Single-Stage Detectors	Two-Stage Detectors	Multistage Detectors	Deformable Part-Based Detectors	Keypoint-Based Detectors
SSD [77]	R-CNN [41]	Cascade R-CNN [10]	DPM-CNN [42]	CornerNet [65]
YOLO9000 [96]	Fast R-CNN [40]	CRAFT [130]	DeepIDNet [89]	ExtremeNet [136]
RetinaNet [76]	Faster R-CNN [98]	CC-Net [87]	DP-FCN [84]	CenterNet [28]
SqueezeDet [124]	R-FCN [25]	Multipath Net [133]	Deformable	
SPP-Net [48]		Multiregion CNN [39]	convnets [26]	
OverFeat [99]		HyperNet [58]		
DSSD [36]		IoU-Net [54]		
MDSSD [24]		Hybrid task cascade [16]		
DETR [11]				
EfficientDet [109]				

with those signs in different driving scenarios. Although object detection has gained huge attention in autonomous driving applications, state- of-the-art algorithms still have some limitations in realistic scenarios. Such scenarios include small objects that comprise risk of collision, but are hard to detect. Occluded and grouped objects are also hard to distinguish and might cause false negatives due to deformation of such objects compared to the objects used in training data. Table 4.1 gives the classification of CNN-based object detection methods based on the number of stages involved in the framework as well as deformable part–based and keypoint-based detection methods.

4.2.1 Two-Stage Detectors

In this approach, the object detection task is split into two stages: (i) extraction of Regions of Interest (RoIs) and (ii) classification and regression of the RoIs. Regions with CNN features (R-CNN) [41] was the first two-stage approach introduced. It generates RoIs using selective search and performs RoI classification using a deep convolution network-based classifier. It involves complex computations, which makes it slow. Fast R-CNN [40] and SPP-Net [48] improved R-CNN [41] by extracting RoIs from the feature maps. SPP-Net [48] deployed a spatial pyramid pooling (SPP) layer to handle images of arbitrary sizes and aspect ratios. It applies the SPP layer over the feature maps generated from convolution layers and outputs fixed-length vectors required for fully connected layers. It eliminates fixed-size input constraints and can be used in any CNN-based classification model. However, Fast R-CNN and SPP-Net are not end-to-end trainable, as they depend on a regional proposal approach. Faster R-CNN [98] solved this limitation by introducing a region proposal network (RPN), which made end-to-end training possible. RPNs generate RoIs by regressing a set of reference boxes called anchor boxes. The efficiency of Faster R-CNN [98] is further improved by R-FCN [25], which replaced fully connected (FC) layers with a fully convolutional network (FCN).

4.2.2 Single-Stage Detectors

Unlike two-stage detectors, single-stage detectors eliminate the RoI extraction stage and directly carry out classification and regression of the anchor boxes; that is, the RoI pooling step is excluded, and object detection is performed using a single network. OverFeat [99], a feature extractor for computer vision applications, proposed a unified framework to perform three tasks—classification, localization, and detection—using a multiscale, sliding window approach. You Only Look Once (YOLO) is a single-stage detector with three versions released at the time of writing this chapter. YOLOv1 [41] divides the input image into grids and predicts the bounding box (BB) directly by regression and classification. YOLO9000 (YOLOv2) [96] improves the performance by introducing batch normalization and replaces fully connected layers of YOLOv1 with anchor boxes for BB prediction. YOLOv3 [97], a faster and more accurate object detector than previous versions, uses Darknet-53 as its feature extraction backbone. YOLOv3 can detect small objects with multiscale predictions, which is a major drawback in earlier versions like YOLOv1 and YOLOv2. Figure 4.5 shows the architecture of YOLO3 [97], which extracts features at three scales to detect small, medium, and large objects. A single-shot multibox detector (SSD) [77] places dense anchor boxes over the input image and extracts feature maps from multiple scales. It then classifies and regresses the anchor boxes to predict the BB. The deconvolutional SSD (DSSD) [36] replaces the VGG network of the SSD [77] with Residual-101. It is then augmented with a deconvolution module to integrate feature maps from an early stage with the deconvolution layers. It outperforms SSD in detecting small objects. MDSSD [24] further extends DSSD [36] with a fusion block to handle feature maps at different scales. RetinaNet [76] introduced focal loss to address foreground and background class imbalance during training. It matches or surpasses the accuracy of state-of-the-art two-stage detectors while running at faster speeds. The architecture shares "anchors" from RPN and builds an FCN with a feature pyramid network (FPN) on top of the ResNet backbone. SqueezeDet [124] focused on small model size, speed, and accuracy,

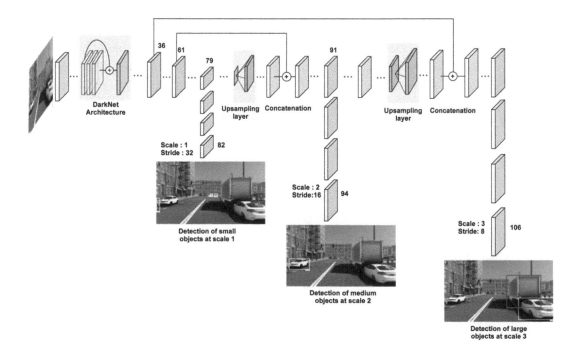

FIGURE 4.5   Architecture of YOLOv3: Single-stage detector [see Ref. 97].

making it suitable for detecting objects in autonomous driving. It follows YOLOv1 [41] in its detection pipeline and designed a ConvDet layer to generate region proposals with comparatively fewer parameters than YOLO. EfficientDet [109] is a one-stage detector with EfficientNet as its backbone. It proposed a weighted bidirectional FPN to fuse multiscale features and compound scaling, which jointly scales up all networks' depth, width, and resolution. Recently, the DEtection Transformer (DETR) [11] works on a direct set prediction paradigm. It adopts transformer-based encoder-decoder architecture and follows a bipartite matching loss function to give unique predictions. The performance is better than Faster-RCNN [98] on large objects.

4.2.3 Multistage Detectors

As the name implies, the detectors in this category deploy a sequence of CNNs at different levels for detection. Cascade R-CNN [10] extends R-CNN [41] with multiple stages. At each stage, the training data is sampled, and the intersection over union (IoU) threshold is increased. It escalates the hypotheses by adopting iterative BB regression. CRAFT [130] implemented two tasks—namely, proposal generator and classifier—to improve the quality of proposal generation and detection by deploying a cascaded structure with RPN and two Fast R-CNNs. CC-Net [87] is composed of many cascade stages, as shown in Figure 4.6. It has two levels of cascade: (i) early cascade and (ii) contextual cascade. Shallow layers reject easy RoIs, and therefore, hard samples are handled easily by latter stages. A multipath network [133] has also been built with Fast R-CNN [40] as its base and includes a few modifications like skip connections, foveal region, and loss function. Information streams across multiple paths in the network, which enables the classifier to function at different scales. Ref [39] proposed a multiregion CNN model that includes an iterative BB regression mechanism that alternates between box scoring and coordinate refinement. HyperNet [58] is a multistage architecture that jointly performs region proposal and object detection by creating hyper feature maps. IoU-Net [54] accomplishes progressive BB regression with a stand-alone IoU predictor that can then be integrated with any of the FPN-based [75] CNN architecture for object detection.

4.2.4 Deformable Part–Based Detectors

Handling deformation properties of dynamic objects helps to improve the detection performance. A deformation layer is proposed for pedestrian detection in [88]. Deep-Pyramid DPM [42] is a single CNN that maps an input image pyramid to a detection score pyramid by constructing a distance transform pooling layer. DeepIDNet [89] proposed a deformable

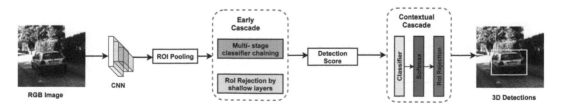

FIGURE 4.6   Architecture of CC-Net: Multistage detector [see Ref. 87].

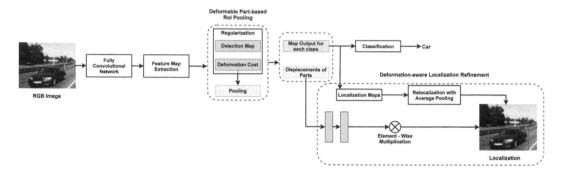

FIGURE 4.7   Architecture of DP-FCN: Deformable-part-based detector [see Ref. 84].

part–based CNN for object detection by designing a deformation-pooling layer to learn the geometric deformations of all instances of a part. DP-FCN [84] further improves it by introducing a deformable part–based RoI pooling layer and deformation-aware localization, as shown in Figure 4.7. The model is fully convolutional and end-to-end trainable. It focuses on discriminative elements. Deformable ConvNets [26] supports CNNs to learn dense spatial transformations, which can then be used in object detection tasks. It introduced two modules—(1) deformable convolution and (2) deformable RoI pooling—which help CNNs to efficiently model geometric transformations.

4.2.5 Keypoint-Based Detectors

Keypoints replace anchor boxes in single-stage detectors. Most one-stage detectors place dense anchor boxes over images to predict BBs. For example, RetinaNet [76] and DSSD [36] require nearly 100k and 40k anchor boxes, respectively. These detectors also introduce many hyperparameters. CornerNet [65] overcome these limitations by detecting objects as paired keypoints that represent the top left and bottom right corners of the BB of the object. It uses an hourglass network as its backbone and introduces corner pooling to localize corners. It groups the keypoints with associative embedding. CenterNet [28] extends CornerNet by representing each object as a triplet—a pair of corners and a center keypoint, as shown in Figure 4.8. It introduced center pooling and cascade corner pooling to make corners recognize visual patterns of objects. On the other hand, ExtremeNet [136] detects BBs by the extreme top, left, bottom, and right points and midpoint of all objects. They deploy geometric grouping based on DPM [35].

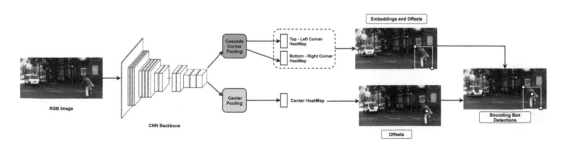

FIGURE 4.8   Architecture of CenterNet: Keypoint-based detector [see Ref. 28].

TABLE 4.2   Classification of 3D Object Detection Methods Based on Number of Stages

Single-Stage 3D Detectors	Two-Stage 3D Detectors	Map-Based Detectors
PIXOR [129]	Point R-CNN [100]	HDNET [128]
Stereo RCNN [73]	GS3D [71]	BirdNET [4]
	Pseudo LIDAR [122]	BirdNET+ [3]
	MV3D [19]	
	Accurate Mono3D [80]	
	3D BB by GC [32]	

4.3 3D OBJECT DETECTION

3D object detection provides adequate information for scene perception, motion prediction, and trajectory planning in autonomous driving applications. Today most autonomous vehicles are equipped with LIDAR and RADAR sensors that yield accurate depth information for the surrounding objects. Monocular cameras use semantic properties of the scene to predict depth or indirectly make use of depth estimation [60–62] to localize in 3D.

4.3.1 Classification Based on Number of Stages

Table 4.2 shows the classification of 3D object detectors based on number of stages and of map-based 3D object detectors.

- *Single-stage 3D detectors:* PIXOR [129], a proposal-free dense object detector, uses a fully connected network to produce pixel-wise 3D detections from bird's-eye-view (BEV) representations of the LIDAR point cloud. Figure 4.9 shows the architecture of PIXOR. Stereo-RCNN [73] extends Faster R-CNN [98] for stereo inputs that jointly perform detection and association of the left and right camera images.

- *Two-stage 3D detectors:* Unlike single-stage 3D object detection (3DOD) methods, Point R-CNN [100] performs 3DOD in two stages: (1) 3D proposal generation and (2) proposal refinement. It takes raw point cloud data as input and generates 3D proposals directly. Figure 4.10 shows the architecture of Point R-CNN. GS3D [71]

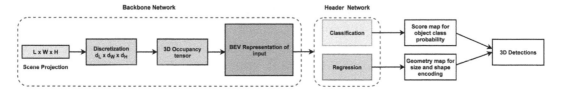

FIGURE 4.9   Architecture of PIXOR: Single-stage 3D object detector [see Ref. 129].

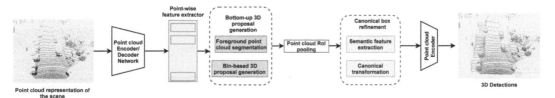

FIGURE 4.10   Architecture of Point R-CNN: Two-stage 3D object detector [see Ref. 100].

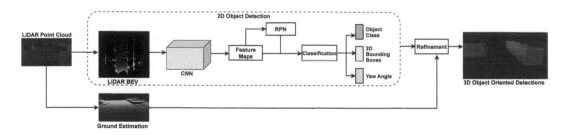

FIGURE 4.11   Architecture of BirdNET: Map-based 3D object detector [see Ref. 4].

takes monocular RGB images as input. The detection network has two stages: (i) feature extraction from the 2D box and projected guidance and (ii) 3D box refinement, as shown later in Figure 4.14. A CNN model and a refinement model are deployed in corresponding stages. Rather than concentrating on quality of input, pseudo LIDAR [122] considers representation to provide high-quality 3DOD. The network can take either stereo or monocular camera images as input. It generates a pseudo-LIDAR representation by predicting the depth map and projecting to a LIDAR coordinate system. In the second stage, this pseudo LIDAR representation can predict 3D BBs when combined with any LIDAR-based detection method. Another method that focuses on representation is the MV3D [19] network. The detector has two stages: 3D proposal and multiview fusion. It takes three inputs: (i) a BEV map, (ii) a front-view representation of the LIDAR point cloud, and (iii) an RGB image, as shown later in Figure 4.16. It fuses two representations to predict 3D BBs. Accurate Mono3D [80] presented a two-stage 3D detection framework that takes point-cloud representations of monocular image as input. Ref [32] proposed a two-stage method to get 3D perception using cascaded geometric constraints (GC) and filtering out incorrect 2D detections.

- *Map-based 3D OD methods:* A prebuilt map of a scene provides a strong prior for static infrastructure that can be subtracted out to detect dynamic objects [95] better. HD-NET [128] presented a single-stage detector that exploits semantic and geometric features from existing high-definition (HD) maps that an autonomous driving system can access. It also proposed an online map prediction module if it is not available in prior. The BirdNET [4] framework consists of three stages: (i) BEV generation, (ii) an inference subnetwork, and (iii) Post Processing. BirdNET+ [3] presented an end-to- end two-stage 3DOD framework. It integrated the post processing step in BirdNET [4] with the inference stage. Figures 4.11 and 4.12 show the architectural differences between BirdNET and BirdNET+. All these methods take BEV representations of the LIDAR point cloud as input to provide 3D detections.

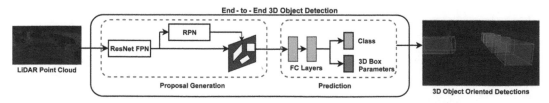

FIGURE 4.12   Architecture of BirdNET+: Map-based 3D object detector [see Ref. 3].

TABLE 4.3   Classification of 3D Object Detection Methods Based on Input

LIDAR-based	Monocular-based	Stereo-based	Multimodal-based	RGB-D based
Vote3D [117]	3D RCNN [63]	3D OP [17]	FractalNet [64]	Frustum PointNet [92]
Vote3D Deep [30]	Deep 3D box [85]	Stereo RCNN [73]	Deeply-Fused Nets [118]	Deep sliding shapes [107]
VeloFCN [70]	Mono 3D [18]		MV3D (LIDAR and RGB) [19]	Learning-rich feat [46]]
3D FCN [67]	Accurate mono3D [80]		RandomForest [43]	Sliding shapes [106]
PointNet [93]	GS3D [71]			
VoxelNet [137]	DeepMANTA [14]			
Point R-CNN [100]				
3D IoU-Net [72]				

4.3.2 Classification Based on Input

Detectors take images captured by sensors (discussed in Section 1.1) fixed on autonomous vehicles. A few detection algorithms take input from multiple sensors to improve performance, which is referred to as multimodal input. Table 4.3 shows the classification of 3D Object detection methods based on the nature of the input data provided to the detection system.

- *LIDAR-based 3D OD methods:* Vote3D [117] forms a voxel 3D grid by clustering the point cloud input. A sliding window finds feature vectors, which are then fed to the SVM classifier. Vote3DDeep [30] detects objects in the point cloud using CNNs that are built with a feature-centric voting algorithm. It eliminates the discretization process in Vote3D. VeloFCN [70] projects a front view of the range scan data to a 2D point map. It then predicts BBs using a 2D FCN. Ref [67] extends the FCN to 3D and helps in detecting 3D BBs of vehicles in autonomous driving systems. Point R-CNN [100] and PointNet [93] take raw point cloud data as input. Frustum PointNet [92] applies PointNet to estimate 3D BBs by extracting frustum point clouds from 2D detections, as shown later in Figure 4.17. VoxelNet [137] partitions raw point clouds into 3D voxels and gets 4D tensor representations by transforming points inside each voxel. The RPN then produces 3D detections, as shown in Figure 4.13. 3D IoU-Net [72] generates 3D proposals from the LIDAR point cloud. It estimates 3D BBs by IoU-sensitive feature learning and IoU assignment mismatching.

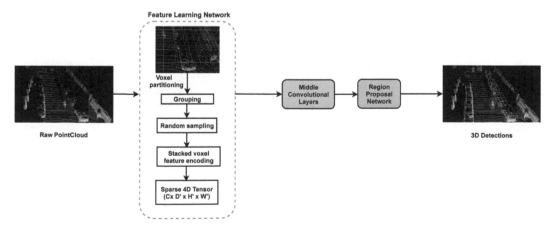

FIGURE 4.13   Architecture of VoxelNet: LIDAR-based 3D object detector [see Ref. 137].

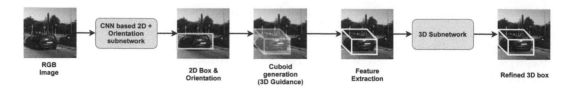

FIGURE 4.14 Architecture of GS3D: Monocular-based 3D object detector [see Ref. 71].

- *Monocular-based 3D OD methods:* Given a single monocular image, DeepMANTA [14] produces 2D detections and extracts feature vectors that jointly do many tasks like part localization, visibility, and 3D template prediction. Deep3DBox [85] crops the 2D box to determine size and orientation. It predicts location with a requirement that the 3D box should firmly fit into the 2D BB. 3D-RCNN [63] is a unified network based on inverse graphics that computes the 3D box in a single forward pass. Accurate Mono3D [80] encodes monocular images to the point cloud and uses PointNet [93] to estimate the 3D box. In contrast, GS3D [71] determines an accurate 3D box directly from the RGB image without point cloud or stereo data, as shown in Figure 4.14. It estimates the 3D box with the projection matrix and basic cuboid called guidance. Mono3D [18] takes single monocular images as input and generates candidate class-specific object proposals. It proposed an energy minimization approach to estimate 3D BBs.

- *Stereo-based 3D OD methods:* Stereo cameras provide accurate depth information when compared to monocular cameras, which makes them more suitable for autonomous driving applications. 3D OP [17] formulates an energy function using object size priors, the ground plane context, and depth information. 3D proposals are generated by minimizing the energy function. It then jointly regresses to the object pose and 3D BB coordinates. Stereo R-CNN [73] takes left-right photometric aligned images provided by a stereo camera as input. It takes dense object constraints of stereo images into account and estimates the 3D box using sparse keypoints and left-right 2D boxes. Figure 4.15 shows the architecture of Stereo R-CNN.

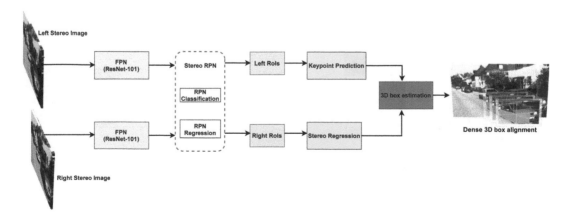

FIGURE 4.15 Architecture of Stereo R-CNN: Stereo-based 3D object detector [see Ref. 73].

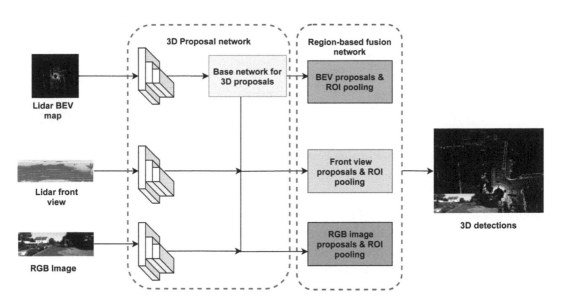

FIGURE 4.16   Architecture of Multiview 3D: Multimodal input-based 3D object detector [see Ref. 19].

- *Multimodal input-based 3D OD methods:* FractalNet [64] repeatedly iterates the base module to construct a network. Deeply-Fused Nets [118] constructs a deeply fused neural network that can learn multiscale representations by integrating shallow and deep subnetworks. MV3D [19], on the other hand, takes three inputs: (1) a BEV representation of the LIDAR point cloud, (2) a LIDAR front-view image, and (3) an RGB image. It applies the same base network to each column, as shown in Figure 4.16. Ref [43] generates multimodal representations by combining RGB and depth maps. It then extracts multicue features that are merged with different object models to get a multiview model for detecting objects.

- *RGB-D-based 3D OD methods:* Ref [106] generalizes R-CNN to RGB-D images and makes a CNN to learn rich features represented by height, angle, and disparity. Ref [107] proposed a generic 3D OD algorithm for RGB-D images that extracts a depth map from collected Computer Aided Design (CAD) models and features from the 3D point cloud and does classification using Exemplar-Support Vector Machine (SVM). Handcrafted features and many exemplar classifiers makes the detector slow. Ref [46] replaces handcrafted features with 3D ConvNets, which learns depth and color features efficiently. Authors of Ref [46] were the first to introduce 3D RPN and a joint object recognition network (ORN) to regress 3D BBs directly from 3D proposals. Frustum PointNet [92] applies 2D detectors on RGB images to get 2D object regions. It defines the 3D search space by lifting 2D BBs to the plane within depth sensor range called the frustum and forms a frustum point cloud with all points inside the frustum. The architecture generates a 3D box from the RGB image and depth data using three modules: (i) frustum proposal, (ii) 3D instance segmentation, and (iii) amodal 3D box estimation. Figure 4.17 shows the architecture of Frustum PointNet.

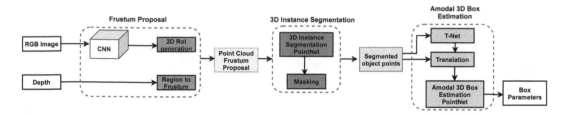

FIGURE 4.17   Architecture of Frustum PointNet: RGB-D-based 3D object detector [see Ref. 92].

4.4 OBJECT TRACKING

Bounding box detections of objects from the detection phase are given as input to the tracker. It generates tracks for the corresponding detections. Various tracking algorithms are tabulated in Table 4.4. A few of them do single-object tracking (SOT). However, multiple-object tracking (MOT) provides adequate support for autonomous driving applications. With MOT algorithms, it is possible to track different objects such as cars, pedestrians, cyclists, trucks, and traffic signs in the driving scenario.

- *Overview from the Perspective of Autonomous Driving:* Tracking for autonomous driving applications aims at accurate identification and localization of both dynamic and static objects in the scene. The tracking role is crucial, especially for dynamic obstacles. Static obstacles can be avoided once they are detected. On the other hand, dynamic obstacles have to be monitored across several sequential frames. The input from various frames helps the autonomous driving system understand the motion model of each object in the scene. This will help the system predict the location of the object in the upcoming time frames. The navigation system should plan its trajectories in a way that does not cause collision risk in the current state and in the future states as well. Tracking is also helpful where autonomous driving scenes are characterized with high occlusion levels. A vehicle can be monitored using the sensors for a specific time frame, and then the same vehicle can disappear behind a large truck. Tracking keeps the vehicle in memory and helps predict when the vehicle will be visible again. This information is crucial for the navigation system to avoid high collision risks.

Tracking can be performed on map space as well as on image space. Map-level tracking is useful in the cases where there are multiple sensor inputs that are fused together in one single map. Different sensors such as LIDAR, camera, and ultrasonic sensors [91]

TABLE 4.4   Classification of Generic Object Tracking Methods

Tracker Name	Year	SOT	MOT	Online	Off-line	Approach
GOTURN [50]	2016	✓			✓	Regression-based approach
SORT [6]	2016		✓	✓		Pragmatic approach based on Kalman Filter
DeepSORT [123]	2017		✓	✓		Hypothesis-tracking methodology
STAM-MOT [22]	2017		✓	✓		Spatial-temporal attention mechanism (STAM)
MDP-Framework [126]	2015		✓	✓		Markov decision process (MDP)
FCNT [119]	2015	✓			✓	Heat maps for target localization

perform object detection separately and generate output features that are then fed into a sensor fusion algorithm [29, 94]. The algorithm takes into consideration the limitations of each sensor and generates a single map describing the surrounding scene for a predefined time frame relative to the location of the ego vehicle. The generated features can be tracked using multiple approaches such as Kalman filters and particle filters depending on the nature and motion models of the features. The scope of this chapter is to focus on image-based tracking techniques, as demonstrated in upcoming sections.

4.4.1 General Tracking Methods

Most neural networks for tracking were trained online. Online training leads to slow tracking. GOTURN [50] trained a neural network off-line with selected videos and images to learn appearance and motion relationships. The network can track generic objects during testing. Online fine-tuning is not required. It is the first tracker that runs at 100 fps. The network takes a cropped search region from the present frame and a target object from the last frame and predicts the location of the target inside the search region. Figure 4.18 shows the architecture of the GOTURN tracker. SORT [6] applied the Kalman filter and Hungarian algorithm for frame-to-frame data association. It adopted an overlap of BBs as its association metric. A typical shortcoming of SORT is that it results in ineffective tracking during occlusions. Deep-SORT [123] overcomes this limitation by alternating the association metric with appearance and motion information and thus is able to track objects even in a prolonged occlusion scenario. It learnt the deep association metric by off-line pretraining with MARS [134], which is a large-scale reidentification dataset. STAM-MOT [22] performs MOT with a CNN-based single-object tracker. It handles the tracking drift and intercommunication among targets using a spatial attention map. Ref [126] models the lifetime of an object as decision-making in the Markov decision process (MDP). It executes MOT by assembling multiple MDPs. FCNT [119] performs SOT by jointly considering the properties of convolutional layers at different levels to alleviate drifts in tracking.

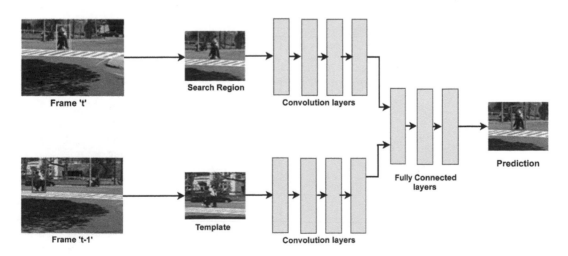

FIGURE 4.18   Architecture of GOTURN: Generic object tracker [see Ref. 50].

4.4.2 Siamese Network-Based Tracking

Siamese-based trackers are mainly useful in autonomous driving where multiple cameras are deployed to capture the surrounding environment. They help to identify whether the objects that appear in different views are the same. A Siamese network compares the features encoded in two branches. Table 4.5 lists various Siamese-based trackers.

GOTURN [50] applied a Siamese network to extract features. SiamFC [5] adopted a fully convolutional Siamese network for tracking. It performs tracking at 80 fps. As a result of its success, several updated models were proposed. CFNet [115] improves tracking accuracy by adding a correlation layer to SiamFC [5]. DSiam [45] learns the Siamese network in dynamic mode. SA-Siam [47] introduces a two-fold Siamese network with two branches—semantic and appearance—that are trained separately to learn the features and are combined during test time. Motivated by RPN for object detection, SiamRPN [69] is the first region proposal-based tracker that integrates a Siamese network and an RPN that

TABLE 4.5   Siamese Network–Based Object Trackers

Tracker Name	Year	SOT	MOT	Online	Off-line	Approach	Stages
Siamese Track RCNN [101]	2020		✓	✓		Re-identification and tracking	2
Siam FC [5]	2016	✓		✓		Discriminative Stochastic Gradient Descent (SGD) approach	1
Siam RPN [69]	2018	✓		✓		One-shot detection	1
DaSiamRPN [138]	2018	✓		✓		Local-to-global search region	Multiple
Siam Cascaded RPN [31]	2019	✓			✓	Siam and cascaded RPN	Multiple
Siam RPN++ [68]	2019	✓			✓	Spatially aware sampling strategy	1
Siamese CNN [66]	2016	✓			✓	Tracking by detection	2
Siam R-CNN [116]	2020	✓	✓		✓	Tracking by re-identification	2
Siam CAR [44]	2020	✓			✓	Both proposal- and anchor-free	2
DSiam [45]	2017	✓		✓		Fast transformation learning	1
SA-Siam [47]	2018	✓		✓		Appearance and semantic features	1
CF-Net [115]	2017	✓		✓		Correlation filter based–learning	1
GOTURN [50]	2016	✓			✓	Regression-based tracker	1
SINT [110]	2016	✓		✓		Learns matching functions	1
SiamKPN [74]	2020	✓			✓	Cascade KPN head and heat map	3
SiamMask [121]	2019	✓		✓		Siam FC and binary segmentation	1

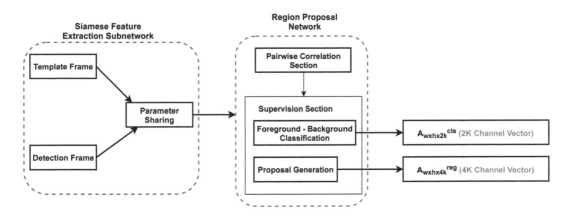

FIGURE 4.19   Architecture of SiamRPN: Siamese network-based object tracker [see Ref. 69].

formulates online tracking as one-shot learning; it is depicted in Figure 4.19. SiamRPN performs tracking at higher fps. Yet it suffers when handling the distractors that appear similar to the target. SiamRPN [69] is made aware of distractors by DaSiamRPN [138]. It extends SiamRPN [69] by increasing hard negative samples, which makes the tracker more robust and suitable for long-term tracking. The above-mentioned approaches that modified SiamFC [5] adopt AlexNet [59] as their backbone network. In contrast, Siam RPN++ [68] uses ResNet. Siamese Cascaded RPN [31] deployed a sequence of RPNs to perform classification and regression in a sequential manner. It leverages multilevel features by a novel feature transfer block for each RPN. Siam R-CNN [116] presented a tracking framework by combining Faster R-CNN [98] and a Siamese network. SINT [110] formulated tracking as a learning paradigm by matching candidate and target patches. Recently, SiamKPN [74], the first anchor-free Siamese-based tracker that follows the cascading of a keypoint prediction network (KPN) heads for prediction modeling.

4.5 TRAJECTORY PREDICTION TECHNIQUES

In autonomous driving applications, trajectory prediction is an important phase that forecasts the position of surrounding vehicles after a few seconds. Table 4.6 shows four categories of trajectory prediction methods that can be applied for autonomous driving.

- *Overview from the Perspective of Autonomous Driving:* The main objective of trajectory prediction in autonomous driving is to predict the future states of the objects surrounding the ego vehicle for a specific time frame. The predicted time frame should be large enough to minimize the risk of collision with any of the surrounding objects. Conventional navigation systems depend on minimization of cost functions, which represent collision risk. Having the future trajectory of each object in the

TABLE 4.6   Classification of Trajectory Prediction Methods

Attention-Based	Social Pooling-Based	Graph-Based	Trajectory Set-Based
Multihead attention [57]	Social LSTM [1]	SPAGNN [12]	CoverNet [90]
Generic attention-based [81]	Convolutional social pooling [27]	ChauffeurNet [2]	Trajectory sets and domain knowledge [7]
	RRNN [82]	VectorNet [37]	

surrounding scene as prior information significantly reduces the space of available trajectories for planning. This in turn helps provide smooth trajectories with no sudden maneuvers due to unanticipated motion by the surrounding objects.

4.5.1 Attention-Based Methods

[57] deployed multihead attention-based nonlocal social pooling that models only the vehicle interactions that are significant to the target vehicle. Ref [81] extends [57] by applying an attention mechanism to explicitly derive intercommunication of the surrounding vehicles to produce multiple possible trajectories.

4.5.2 Motion Forecasting by Social Pooling

Social Long Short-term Memory (LSTM) [1] was proposed to predict trajectories of pedestrians in a crowd based on their previous positions. It encodes each trajectory with an LSTM block. A social-pooling layer connects all LSTMs and shares hidden states of surrounding agents between LSTMs. It uses a fully connected layer for a social tensor. Ref [27] proposed convolutional social pooling that applies convolutional and max pooling layers to the social tensor. Ref [82] presented a relational recurrent neural network-based encoder-decoder framework for predicting vehicle trajectories.

4.5.3 Graph-Based Methods

SPAGNN [12] explicitly models social interactions among agents to enable detection and behavior prediction by leveraging a graph neural network (GNN). ChauffeurNet [2], a recurrent-based neural network, predicts trajectories using midlevel 2D representations of all objects in the environment. VectorNet [37] transforms agent trajectories to vector representation and deploys a hierarchical GNN that operates on HD maps to predict vehicle behavior.

4.5.4 Trajectory Set-Based Behavior Prediction

CoverNet [90] is a multimodal approach that performs classification over a set of trajectories. It predicts the future behavior of the target using current and past states of all agents, including yaw rate, speed, and acceleration. It overcomes the issue of "mode collapse" in the regression model. Figure 4.20 shows the architecture of CoverNet. Ref [7] extends CoverNet [90] by incorporating domain knowledge and penalizes off-road predictions with auxiliary loss.

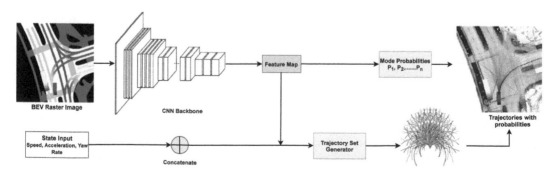

FIGURE 4.20 Architecture of CoverNet: Trajectory set–based behavior prediction [see Ref. 90].

4.6 UNIFIED MODELING

Though many existing methods accomplish detection, tracking, and trajectory prediction independently, a few recent researchers proposed a unified framework to execute them in joint fashion. Some of them do detection and tracking jointly, while others do all three tasks simultaneously. Various unified framework models are tabulated in Table 4.7.

4.6.1 Multitask Model

The multitask model helps to solve various perception tasks in autonomous driving, which significantly improves the performance with reduced computational complexity. It solves multiple tasks by considering similarities between independent tasks.

- *Joint Detection and Tracking (JDT) models:* [56] presented a JDT framework that adopts SSD to output appearance features and RNN to associate the detections to tracks. Track-RNN [33] combines CNN and RNN for JDT by formulating the tracking as an MDP. It considers a motion prior model to improve the accuracy of BB predictions. RetinaTrack [78] uses one-stage RetinaNet as its base detector and adds instance-level embeddings to perform data association. Ref [34] proposed a correlation-based tracker that extends an R-FCN [25] detector to achieve a multitasking model. It applies RoI pooling to generate per-frame detections and RoI tracking to generate across-frame-tracklets. Ref [52] presented a JDT framework to predict trajectories of vehicles in 3D space. It efficiently handles reidentification of occluded

TABLE 4.7   Unified Models for Multitask Learning

Model	Tasks Supported			Input to the System	Architecture	2D	3D	Year
	Detect	Track	Trajectory Prediction					
							✓	2019
Joint mono det and track [52]	✓	✓		Sequence of monocular images	Faster RCNN+LSTM	✓		2018
Joint det and online MOT [56]	✓	✓		detections from SSD	SSD+RNN	✓		2018
Detect to track [34]	✓	✓		Two or more frames	R-FCN	✓		2020
RetinaTrack [78]	✓	✓		associate detections directly	Retinanet+FPN		✓	2018
FaF Net [79]	✓	✓	✓	4D tensor and temporal data	Models temporal data and decodes tracklet		✓	2018
IntentNet [13]	✓		✓	raw sensor data	Two-stream network+ HD maps		✓	2020
MotionNet [125]	✓	✓	✓	sequence of LIDAR sweeps	spatio-temporal (STPN)		✓	2020
CenterTrack [135]	✓	✓		pair of images and heat map	CenterNet+ conditional tracking	✓	✓	2020

vehicles. CenterTrack [135] proposed a point-based framework that learns association jointly with detection. It adopts CenterNet [28] to localize object centers and represents each object by the center point of its BB.

- *Joint Detection, Tracking and Trajectory Prediction (JDT+TP) models:* FaFNet [79] takes BEV representation of multiple frames and carries out 3D convolutions across space and time to generate 3D BBs. It lessens computational complexity by sharing computations among all the three tasks. As a result of this work, IntentNet [13] proposed a fully convolutional neural network to reason about the intention of traffic participants. MotionNet [125] is a BB-free approach that uses BEV maps to jointly perform perception and future motion prediction with a spatial-temporal pyramid network.

- *Sample output:* Figure 4.21 shows the output of detection, tracking, and trajectory prediction on a sample video. Parts a and b in Figure 4.21 are the input frames from a video sequence. The inputs were processed by a YOLOv3 and DeepSORT framework. Figure 4.21c shows the output of detection and tracking with estimated (pink) and ground truth (white) BBs. Figure 4.21d has the trajectory line drawn for the detected track.

4.6.2 Datasets

Designing a dataset for an autonomous driving application to cover diverse scenarios is a challenging task [113]. In case of adverse weather, an enhancement step may be needed to

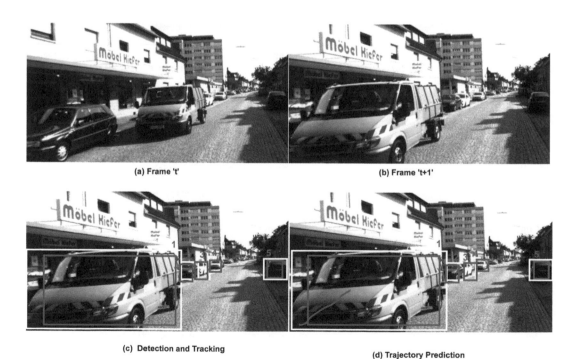

(a) Frame 't' (b) Frame 't+1'

(c) Detection and Tracking (d) Trajectory Prediction

FIGURE 4.21 Sample output for trajectory prediction using YOLOv3 and DeepSORT. (a) Current frame 't' (b) Next frame 't+1' (c) Output of detection and tracking (d) Trajectory prediction for the detected track.

improve the quality of the images [114]. Several data sets were released for scene understanding in autonomous driving applications. They provide camera information, video sequences, and significant annotations for various tasks. For example, BDD100K [132] supports ten tasks, and WoodScape [131] provides annotations for nine tasks—notably, depth estimation, semantic segmentation, and 3DOD—to evaluate autonomous driving algorithms. Table 4.8 provides a summary of a few autonomous driving datasets.

4.6.3 Towards a Unified Model

The multitask models discussed above do either two tasks or three tasks in a unified manner. In the future, unified algorithms can be built using CNNs by sharing an encoder among all three tasks (detection, tracking, and trajectory prediction) of autonomous driving. There is a lot of recent research in multitask networks, especially for resource-limited applications such as the autonomous driving application. A multitask network is able to perform multiple tasks jointly by sharing specific parts of the network. A common approach is to share the network encoder among all the tasks. This is due to the fact that the network encoder performs feature task-agnostic extraction for the input modality. Multiple network heads are attached to the network encoder, allowing task-specific features to be learned during training. This architecture saves computation due to minimizing the number of parameters needed for feature extraction of multiple tasks to only one encoder, as demonstrated in ref [15]. Moreover, parallel tasks may benefit each other, due

TABLE 4.8 Summary of Autonomous Driving Datasets

Dataset	Year	Images	Classes	Tasks Supported				Camera Information				Trawffic[a]		
				Detect	Track	Lane	SS	RGB	LIDAR	GPS	Video	U	R	H
CityScape [23]	2016	25k	30	✓			✓	✓	✓	✓		✓		
KITTI [38]	2012	diff sizes	8	✓	✓	✓	✓	✓	✓	✓	✓	✓	✓	✓
ApolloScape [120]	2018	>140k	8–35			✓	✓				✓	✓	✓	✓
nuScenes [9]	2020	40k	23		✓			✓	✓	✓	✓	✓		
Waymo Open Dataset [108]	2020	1M	4	✓	✓			✓	✓			✓		
Lyft Level 5 [55]	2019	323k	9	✓	✓			✓	✓			✓		
Mapillary Vistas [86]	2017	25k	100			✓	✓	✓				✓	✓	
BDD100K [132]	2020	10 k	40	✓	✓	✓	✓	✓		✓	✓	✓	✓	✓
KAIST urban [53]	2018	19 video	—		✓				✓	✓	✓	✓		
KAIST Multispectral [21]	2015	10 video	3			✓	✓	✓	✓	✓	✓	✓		
WoodScape [131]	2019	40		✓	✓	✓	✓					✓		

[a] U, urban; R, rural; H, highway.

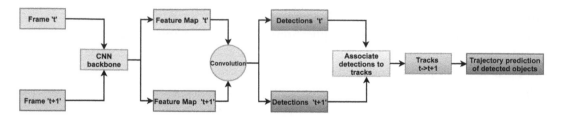

FIGURE 4.22   Generic architecture for a unified model of trajectory prediction using CNN.

to enforcing the shared encoder to learn multiple cues that are important for perception. For instance, it has been proven by ref [104] that joint training of motion segmentation and object detection increases the accuracy of motion segmentation over that of motion segmentation learned separately. This is due to the fact that object detection imposes some kind of attention to the objects rather than segmenting separate pixels. In ref [20], weight sharing has been studied for multiple input streams. The network accepts two RGB images for multitask learning. Instead of a separate encoder for each input, the network uses shared weights between the two encoders, allowing memory to be saved while maintaining the same performance. Multitask learning has been studied for motion segmentation, object detection, semantic segmentation, road classification, soiling, and instance segmentation in refs [15, 20, 83, 112, 127], where it has shown significant improvements. In ref [105], a unified multitask model for visual perception is discussed in detail. Finally, a recent multitask dataset [131] for surround-view fish-eye images for autonomous driving has been released to motivate research in that area. Motivated by these, we propose to design a unified model for trajectory prediction, as illustrated in Figure 4.22. In addition, adversarial techniques can be used to generate a broad variety of possible trajectories [111].

4.7 CONCLUSION

In this chapter, we demonstrated the importance of three crucial tasks—namely, object detection, tracking, and trajectory prediction. Various use-cases have been illustrated highlighting the benefit of the three algorithms for autonomous driving applications. A detailed review for recent state-of-the-art algorithms for each of the three tasks has been presented, showing the benefit of each one. A comparison among the datasets used for such tasks has also been presented. We hope this study helps to develop more robust algorithms for autonomous driving in the future.

REFERENCES

1. Alexandre Alahi, Kratarth Goel, Vignesh Ramanathan, Alexandre Robicquet, Li Fei-Fei, and Silvio Savarese. Social LSTM: Human trajectory prediction in crowded spaces. In *The IEEE Conference on Computer Vision and Pattern Recognition (CVPR)*, June 2016.
2. Mayank Bansal, Alex Krizhevsky, and Abhijit S. Ogale. ChauffeurNet: Learning to drive by imitating the best and synthesizing the worst. *CoRR*, abs/1812.03079, 2018.
3. Alejandro Barrera, Carlos Guindel, Jorge Beltrán, and Fernando García. BirdNET+: End-to-end 3D object detection in LIDAR bird's eye view. *ArXiv*, abs/2003.04188, 2020.

4. J. Beltrán, C. Guindel, F. M. Moreno, D. Cruzado, F. García, and A. De La Escalera. BirdNET: A 3D object detection framework from LIDAR information. In *2018 21st International Conference on Intelligent Transportation Systems (ITSC)*, pages 3517–3523, 2018.

5. Luca Bertinetto, Jack Valmadre, João F. Henriques, Andrea Vedaldi, and Philip H. S. Torr. Fully-convolutional Siamese networks for object tracking. *CoRR*, abs/1606.09549, 2016.

6. A. Bewley, Z. Ge, L. Ott, F. Ramos, and B. Upcroft. Simple online and realtime tracking. In *2016 IEEE International Conference on Image Processing (ICIP)*, pages 3464–3468, 2016.

7. Freddy A. Boulton, Elena Corina Grigore, and Eric M. Wolff. Motion prediction using trajectory sets and self-driving domain knowledge. *ArXiv*, abs/2006.04767, 2020.

8. Alexandre Briot, Prashanth Viswanath, and Senthil Yogamani. Analysis of efficient CNN design techniques for semantic segmentation. In *Proceedings of the IEEE Conference on Computer Vision and Pattern Recognition Workshops*, pages 663–672, 2018.

9. Holger Caesar, Varun Bankiti, Alex H. Lang, Sourabh Vora, Venice Erin Liong, Qiang Xu, Anush Krishnan, Yu Pan, Giancarlo Baldan, and Oscar Beijbom. nuScenes: A multimodal dataset for autonomous driving. In *Proceedings of the IEEE/CVF Conference on Computer Vision and Pattern Recognition (CVPR)*, June 2020.

10. Zhaowei Cai and Nuno Vasconcelos. Cascade R-CNN: Delving into high quality object detection. In *The IEEE Conference on Computer Vision and Pattern Recognition (CVPR)*, June 2018.

11. Nicolas Carion, F. Massa, Gabriel Synnaeve, Nicolas Usunier, Alexander M. Kirillov, and Sergey Zagoruyko. End-to-end object detection with transformers. *ArXiv*, abs/2005.12872, 2020.

12. Sergio Casas, Cole Gulino, Renjie Liao, and Raquel Urtasun. Spatially-aware graph neural networks for relational behavior forecasting from sensor data. *ArXiv*, abs/1910.08233, 2019.

13. Sergio Casas, Wenjie Luo, and Raquel Urtasun. IntentNet: Learning to predict intention from raw sensor data. In *CoRL*, 2018.

14. Florian Chabot, Mohamed Chaouch, Jaonary Rabarisoa, Celine Teuliere, and Thierry Chateau. Deep MANTA: A coarse-to-fine many-task network for joint 2D and 3D vehicle analysis from monocular image. In *The IEEE Conference on Computer Vision and Pattern Recognition (CVPR)*, July 2017.

15. Ranveer Chandra and Paramvir Bahl. MultiNet: Connecting to multiple IEEE 802.11 networks using a single wireless card. In *IEEE INFOCOM 2004*, volume 2, pages 882–893, IEEE, 2004.

16. Kai Chen, Jiangmiao Pang, Jiaqi Wang, Yu Xiong, Xiaoxiao Li, Shuyang Sun, Wansen Feng, Ziwei Liu, Jianping Shi, Wanli Ouyang, Chen Change Loy, and Dahua Lin. Hybrid task cascade for instance segmentation. In *The IEEE Conference on Computer Vision and Pattern Recognition (CVPR)*, June 2019.

17. X. Chen, K. Kundu, Y. Zhu, H. Ma, S. Fidler, and R. Urtasun. 3D object proposals using stereo imagery for accurate object class detection. *IEEE Transactions on Pattern Analysis and Machine Intelligence*, 40(5):1259–1272, 2018.

18. Xiaozhi Chen, Kaustav Kundu, Ziyu Zhang, Huimin Ma, Sanja Fidler, and Raquel Urtasun. Monocular 3D object detection for autonomous driving. In *Proceedings of the IEEE Conference on Computer Vision and Pattern Recognition (CVPR)*, June 2016.

19. Xiaozhi Chen, Huimin Ma, Ji Wan, Bo Li, and Tian Xia. Multi-view 3D object detection network for autonomous driving. In *The IEEE Conference on Computer Vision and Pattern Recognition (CVPR)*, July 2017.

20. Sumanth Chennupati, Ganesh Sistu, Senthil Yogamani, and Samir A. Rawashdeh. Multinet++: Multi-stream feature aggregation and geometric loss strategy for multi-task learning. In *Proceedings of the IEEE Conference on Computer Vision and Pattern Recognition Workshops*, pages 11–21, 2019.

21. Y. Choi, N. Kim, S. Hwang, K. Park, J. S. Yoon, K. An, and I. S. Kweon. Kaist multi-spectral day/night data set for autonomous and assisted driving. *IEEE Transactions on Intelligent Transportation Systems*, 19(3):934–948, 2018.

22. Qi Chu, Wanli Ouyang, Hongsheng Li, Xiaogang Wang, Bin Liu, and Nenghai Yu. Online multi-object tracking using CNN-based single object tracker with spatial-temporal attention mechanism. In *The IEEE International Conference on Computer Vision (ICCV)*, Oct. 2017.

23. Marius Cordts, Mohamed Omran, Sebastian Ramos, Timo Rehfeld, Markus Enzweiler, Rodrigo Benenson, Uwe Franke, Stefan Roth, and Bernt Schiele. The Cityscapes dataset for semantic urban scene understanding. In *Proceedings of the IEEE Conference on Computer Vision and Pattern Recognition (CVPR)*, June 2016.

24. Lisha Cui. MDSSD: Multi-scale deconvolutional single shot detector for small objects. *Science China Information Sciences*, 63, 2020.

25. Jifeng Dai, Yi Li, Kaiming He, and Jian Sun. R-FCN: Object detection via region-based fully convolutional networks. In D. D. Lee, M. Sugiyama, U. V. Luxburg, I. Guyon, and R. Garnett, editors, *Advances in Neural Information Processing Systems 29*, pages 379–387, Curran Associates, 2016.

26. Jifeng Dai, Haozhi Qi, Yuwen Xiong, Yi Li, Guodong Zhang, Han Hu, and Yichen Wei. Deformable convolutional networks. In *The IEEE International Conference on Computer Vision (ICCV)*, Oct. 2017.

27. Nachiket Deo and Mohan M. Trivedi. Convolutional social pooling for vehicle trajectory prediction. In *The IEEE Conference on Computer Vision and Pattern Recognition (CVPR) Workshops*, June 2018.

28. Kaiwen Duan, Song Bai, Lingxi Xie, Honggang Qi, Qingming Huang, and Qi Tian. CenterNet: Keypoint triplets for object detection. In *The IEEE International Conference on Computer Vision (ICCV)*, Oct. 2019.

29. Khaled El Madawi, Hazem Rashed, Ahmad El Sallab, Omar Nasr, Hanan Kamel, and Senthil Yogamani. RGB and LIDAR fusion based 3d semantic segmentation for autonomous driving. In *2019 IEEE Intelligent Transportation Systems Conference (ITSC)*, pages 7–12, IEEE, 2019.

30. M. Engelcke, D. Rao, D. Z. Wang, C. H. Tong, and I. Posner. Vote3Deep: Fast object detection in 3D point clouds using efficient convolutional neural networks. In *2017 IEEE International Conference on Robotics and Automation (ICRA)*, pages 1355–1361, 2017.

31. Heng Fan and Haibin Ling. Siamese cascaded region proposal networks for real-time visual tracking. In *The IEEE Conference on Computer Vision and Pattern Recognition (CVPR)*, June 2019.

32. Jiaojiao Fang, Lingtao Zhou, and Guizhong Liu. 3D bounding box estimation for autonomous vehicles by cascaded geometric constraints and depurated 2D detections using 3d results. *ArXiv*, abs/1909.01867, 2019.

33. Kuan Fang. Track-RNN: Joint detection and tracking using recurrent neural networks. 2016.

34. Christoph Feichtenhofer, Axel Pinz, and Andrew Zisserman. Detect to track and track to detect. In *The IEEE International Conference on Computer Vision (ICCV)*, Oct. 2017.

35. P. F. Felzenszwalb, R. B. Girshick, D. McAllester, and D. Ramanan. Object detection with discriminatively trained part-based models. *IEEE Transactions on Pattern Analysis and Machine Intelligence*, 32(9):1627–1645, 2010.

36. Cheng-Yang Fu, Wei Liu, Ananth Ranga, Ambrish Tyagi, and Alexander C. Berg. DSSD: Deconvolutional single shot detector. *ArXiv*, abs/1701.06659, 2017.

37. Jiyang Gao, Chen Sun, Hang Zhao, Yi Shen, Dragomir Anguelov, Congcong Li, and Cordelia Schmid. VectorNet: Encoding HD maps and agent dynamics from vectorized representation. In *The IEEE/CVF Conference on Computer Vision and Pattern Recognition (CVPR)*, June 2020.

38. A. Geiger, P. Lenz, C. Stiller, and R. Urtasun. Vision meets robotics: The KITTI dataset. *International Journal of Robotics Research*, 32(11):1231–1237, Sept.2013.

39. Spyros Gidaris and Nikos Komodakis. Object detection via a multi-region and semantic segmentation-aware CNN model. In *The IEEE International Conference on Computer Vision (ICCV)*, Dec. 2015.

40. Ross Girshick. Fast R-CNN. In *The IEEE International Conference on Computer Vision (ICCV)*, Dec. 2015.

41. Ross Girshick, Jeff Donahue, Trevor Darrell, and Jitendra Malik. Rich feature hierarchies for accurate object detection and semantic segmentation. In *The IEEE Conference on Computer Vision and Pattern Recognition (CVPR)*, June 2014.

42. Ross Girshick, Forrest Iandola, Trevor Darrell, and Jitendra Malik. Deformable part models are convolutional neural networks. In *The IEEE Conference on Computer Vision and Pattern Recognition (CVPR)*, June 2015.

43. A. González, D. Vázquez, A. M. López, and J. Amores. On-board object detection: Multicue, multimodal, and multiview random forest of local experts. *IEEE Transactions on Cybernetics*, 47(11):3980–3990, 2017.

44. Dongyan Guo, Jun Wang, Ying Cui, Zhenhua Wang, and Shengyong Chen. SiamCAR: Siamese fully convolutional classification and regression for visual tracking. In *Proceedings of the IEEE/CVF Conference on Computer Vision and Pattern Recognition (CVPR)*, June 2020.

45. Qing Guo, Wei Feng, Ce Zhou, Rui Huang, Liang Wan, and Song Wang. Learning dynamic Siamese network for visual object tracking. In *The IEEE International Conference on Computer Vision (ICCV)*, Oct. 2017.

46. Saurabh Gupta, Ross Girshick, Pablo Arbeláez, and Jitendra Malik. Learning rich features from RGB-D images for object detection and segmentation. In David Fleet, Tomas Pajdla, Bernt Schiele, and Tinne Tuytelaars, editors, *Computer Vision—ECCV 2014*, pages 345–360, Cham, Springer International Publishing, 2014.

47. Anfeng He, Chong Luo, Xinmei Tian, and Wenjun Zeng. A twofold Siamese network for real-time object tracking. In *The IEEE Conference on Computer Vision and Pattern Recognition (CVPR)*, June 2018.

48. K. He, X. Zhang, S. Ren, and J. Sun. Spatial pyramid pooling in deep convolutional networks for visual recognition. *IEEE Transactions on Pattern Analysis and Machine Intelligence*, 37(9):1904–1916, 2015.

49. Markus Heimberger, Jonathan Horgan, Ciarán Hughes, John McDonald, and Senthil Yogamani. Computer vision in automated parking systems: Design, implementation and challenges. *Image and Vision Computing*, 68:88–101, 2017.

50. David Held, Sebastian Thrun, and Silvio Savarese. Learning to track at 100 FPS with deep regression networks. *CoRR*, abs/1604.01802, 2016.

51. Jonathan Horgan, Ciarán Hughes, John McDonald, and Senthil Yogamani. Vision-based driver assistance systems: Survey, taxonomy and advances. In *2015 IEEE 18th International Conference on Intelligent Transportation Systems*, pages 2032–2039, IEEE, 2015.

52. Hou-Ning Hu, Qi-Zhi Cai, Dequan Wang, Ji Lin, Min Sun, Philipp Krahenbuhl, Trevor Darrell, and Fisher Yu. Joint monocular 3D vehicle detection and tracking. In *Proceedings of the IEEE/CVF International Conference on Computer Vision (ICCV)*, Oct. 2019.

53. J. Jeong, Y. Cho, Y. Shin, H. Roh, and A. Kim. Complex urban LIDAR data set. In *2018 IEEE International Conference on Robotics and Automation (ICRA)*, pages 6344–6351, 2018.

54. Borui Jiang, Ruixuan Luo, Jiayuan Mao, Tete Xiao, and Yuning Jiang. Acquisition of localization confidence for accurate object detection. In *The European Conference on Computer Vision (ECCV)*, Sept. 2018.

55. R. Kesten, M. Usman, J. Houston, T. Pandya, K. Nadhamuni, A. Ferreira, M. Yuan, B. Low, A. Jain, P. Ondruska et al. Lyft level 5 av dataset 2019. *urlhttps://level5.lyft.com/dataset*, 2019.

56. Hilke Kieritz, Wolfgang Hubner, and Michael Arens. Joint detection and online multi-object tracking. In *Proceedings of the IEEE Conference on Computer Vision and Pattern Recognition (CVPR) Workshops*, June 2018.

57. Hayoung Kim, Dongchan Kim, Gihoon Kim, Jeongmin Cho, and Kunsoo Huh. Multi-head attention based probabilistic vehicle trajectory prediction. *ArXiv*, abs/2004.03842, 2020.

58. Tao Kong, Anbang Yao, Yurong Chen, and Fuchun Sun. HyperNet: Towards accurate region proposal generation and joint object detection. In *The IEEE Conference on Computer Vision and Pattern Recognition (CVPR)*, June 2016.

59. Alex Krizhevsky, Ilya Sutskever, and Geoffrey E. Hinton. ImageNet classification with deep convolutional neural networks. In *Proceedings of the 25th International Conference on Neural Information Processing Systems (NIPS'12)*, volume 1, page 1097–1105, Curran Associates, 2012.

60. Varun Ravi Kumar, Sandesh Athni Hiremath, Markus Bach, Stefan Milz, Christian Witt, Clément Pinard, Senthil Yogamani, and Patrick Mäder. FisheyeDistanceNet: Self-supervised scale-aware distance estimation using monocular fish-eye camera for autonomous driving. In *2020 IEEE International Conference on Robotics and Automation (ICRA)*, pages 574–581, IEEE, 2020.

61. Varun Ravi Kumar, Stefan Milz, Christian Witt, Martin Simon, Karl Amende, Johannes Petzold, Senthil Yogamani, and Timo Pech. Monocular fisheye camera depth estimation using sparse LIDAR supervision. In *2018 21st International Conference on Intelligent Transportation Systems (ITSC)*, pages 2853–2858, IEEE, 2018.

62. Varun Ravi Kumar, Senthil Yogamani, Markus Bach, Christian Witt, Stefan Milz, and Patrick Mader. UnRectDepthNet: Self-supervised monocular depth estimation using a generic framework for handling common camera distortion models. *arXiv preprint, arXiv:2007.06676*, 2020.

63. Abhijit Kundu, Yin Li, and James M. Rehg. 3D-RCNN: Instance-level 3D object reconstruction via render-and-compare. In *The IEEE Conference on Computer Vision and Pattern Recognition (CVPR)*, June 2018.

64. Gustav Larsson, Michael Maire, and Gregory Shakhnarovich. FractalNet: Ultra-deep neural networks without residuals. *CoRR*, abs/1605.07648, 2016.

65. Hei Law and Jia Deng. CornerNet: Detecting objects as paired keypoints. In *The European Conference on Computer Vision (ECCV)*, Sept. 2018.

66. Laura Leal-Taixe, Cristian Canton-Ferrer, and Konrad Schindler. Learning by tracking: Siamese CNN for robust target association. In *Proceedings of the IEEE Conference on Computer Vision and Pattern Recognition (CVPR) Workshops*, June 2016.

67. B. Li. 3D fully convolutional network for vehicle detection in point cloud. In *2017 IEEE/RSJ International Conference on Intelligent Robots and Systems (IROS)*, pages 1513–1518, 2017.

68. B. Li, Wei Wu, Q. Wang, Fangyi Zhang, Junliang Xing, and J. Yan. SiamRPN++: Evolution of Siamese visual tracking with very deep networks. *2019 IEEE/CVF Conference on Computer Vision and Pattern Recognition (CVPR)*, pages 4277–4286, 2019.

69. Bo Li, Junjie Yan, Wei Wu, Zheng Zhu, and Xiaolin Hu. High performance visual tracking with Siamese region proposal network. In *The IEEE Conference on Computer Vision and Pattern Recognition (CVPR)*, June 2018.

70. Bo Li, Tianlei Zhang, and Tian Xia. Vehicle detection from 3D LIDAR using fully convolutional network. *CoRR*, abs/1608.07916, 2016.

71. Buyu Li, Wanli Ouyang, Lu Sheng, X. Zeng, and X. Wang. GS3D: An efficient 3D object detection framework for autonomous driving. *2019 IEEE/CVF Conference on Computer Vision and Pattern Recognition (CVPR)*, pages 1019–1028, 2019.

72. Jiale Li, Shujie Luo, Ziqi Zhu, Hang Dai, Andrey S. Krylov, Yong Ding, and Ling Shao. 3D IoU-Net: IoU guided 3D object detector for point clouds. *ArXiv*, abs/2004.04962, 2020.

73. Peiliang Li, Xiaozhi Chen, and Shaojie Shen. Stereo R-CNN based 3D object detection for autonomous driving. *2019 IEEE/CVF Conference on Computer Vision and Pattern Recognition (CVPR)*, pages 7636–7644, 2019.

74. Qiang Li, Zekui Qin, Wen bo Zhang, and Wen Zheng. Siamese keypoint prediction network for visual object tracking. *ArXiv*, abs/2006.04078, 2020.

75. Tsung-Yi Lin, Piotr Dollar, Ross Girshick, Kaiming He, Bharath Hariharan, and Serge Belongie. Feature pyramid networks for object detection. In *The IEEE Conference on Computer Vision and Pattern Recognition (CVPR)*, July 2017.

76. Tsung-Yi Lin, Priya Goyal, Ross B. Girshick, Kaiming He, and Piotr Dollár. Focal loss for dense object detection. *CoRR*, abs/1708.02002, 2017.

77. Wei Liu, Dragomir Anguelov, Dumitru Erhan, Christian Szegedy, Scott Reed, Cheng-Yang Fu, and Alexander C. Berg. SSD: Single shot multibox detector. In Bastian Leibe, Jiri Matas, Nicu Sebe, and Max Welling, editors, *Computer Vision—ECCV 2016*, pages 21–37, Cham, Springer International Publishing, 2016.

78. Zhichao Lu, Vivek Rathod, Ronny Votel, and Jonathan Huang. RetinaTrack: Online single stage joint detection and tracking. In *The IEEE/CVF Conference on Computer Vision and Pattern Recognition (CVPR)*, June 2020.

79. Wenjie Luo, Bin Yang, and Raquel Urtasun. Fast and furious: Real time end-to-end 3D detection, tracking and motion forecasting with a single convolutional net. In *The IEEE Conference on Computer Vision and Pattern Recognition (CVPR)*, June 2018.

80. Xinzhu Ma, Zhihui Wang, Haojie Li, Pengbo Zhang, Wanli Ouyang, and Xin Fan. Accurate monocular 3D object detection via color-embedded 3D reconstruction for autonomous driving. In *The IEEE International Conference on Computer Vision (ICCV)*, Oct. 2019.

81. K. Messaoud, I. Yahiaoui, A. Verroust, and F. Nashashibi. Attention based vehicle trajectory prediction. In *IEEE Transactions on Intelligent Vehicles*, pages 1–12, 2020.

82. K. Messaoud, I. Yahiaoui, A. Verroust-Blondet, and F. Nashashibi. Relational recurrent neural networks for vehicle trajectory prediction. In *2019 IEEE Intelligent Transportation Systems Conference (ITSC)*, pages 1813–1818, 2019.

83. Eslam Mohamed, Mahmoud Ewaisha, Mennatullah Siam, Hazem Rashed, Senthil Yogamani, and Ahmad El-Sallab. InstanceMotSeg: Real-time instance motion segmentation for autonomous driving. *arXiv preprint, arXiv:2008.07008*, 2020.

84. Taylor Mordan, Nicolas Thome, Matthieu Cord, and Gilles Hénaff. Deformable part-based fully convolutional network for object detection. *ArXiv, abs/1707.06175*, 2017.

85. Arsalan Mousavian, Dragomir Anguelov, John Flynn, and Jana Kosecka. 3D bounding box estimation using deep learning and geometry. In *The IEEE Conference on Computer Vision and Pattern Recognition (CVPR)*, July 2017.

86. Gerhard Neuhold, Tobias Ollmann, Samuel Rota Bulo, and Peter Kontschieder. The Mapillary Vistas dataset for semantic understanding of street scenes. In *Proceedings of the IEEE International Conference on Computer Vision (ICCV)*, Oct. 2017.

87. Wanli Ouyang, Kun Wang, Xin Zhu, and Xiaogang Wang. Chained cascade network for object detection. In *The IEEE International Conference on Computer Vision (ICCV)*, Oct. 2017.

88. Wanli Ouyang and Xiaogang Wang. Joint deep learning for pedestrian detection. In *Proceedings of the IEEE International Conference on Computer Vision (ICCV)*, Dec. 2013.

89. Wanli Ouyang, Xiaogang Wang, Xingyu Zeng, Shi Qiu, Ping Luo, Yonglong Tian, Hongsheng Li, Shuo Yang, Zhe Wang, Chen-Change Loy, and Xiaoou Tang. DeepID-Net: Deformable deep convolutional neural networks for object detection. In *The IEEE Conference on Computer Vision and Pattern Recognition (CVPR)*, June 2015.

90. Tung Phan-Minh, Elena Corina Grigore, Freddy A. Boulton, Oscar Beijbom, and Eric M. Wolff. CoverNet: Multimodal behavior prediction using trajectory sets. In *The IEEE/CVF Conference on Computer Vision and Pattern Recognition (CVPR)*, June 2020.

91. Maximilian Pöpperli, Raghavendra Gulagundi, Senthil Yogamani, and Stefan Milz. Capsule neural network based height classification using low-cost automotive ultrasonic sensors. In *2019 IEEE Intelligent Vehicles Symposium (IV)*, pages 661–666, IEEE, 2019.

92. Charles R. Qi, Wei Liu, Chenxia Wu, Hao Su, and Leonidas J. Guibas. Frustum pointnets for 3D object detection from RGB-D data. In *The IEEE Conference on Computer Vision and Pattern Recognition (CVPR)*, June 2018.

93. Charles R. Qi, Hao Su, Kaichun Mo, and Leonidas J. Guibas. PointNet: Deep learning on point sets for 3D classification and segmentation. In *The IEEE Conference on Computer Vision and Pattern Recognition (CVPR)*, July 2017.

94. Hazem Rashed, Mohamed Ramzy, Victor Vaquero, Ahmad El Sallab, Ganesh Sistu, and Senthil Yogamani. FuseMODNet: Real-time camera and LIDAR based moving object detection for robust low-light autonomous driving. In *Proceedings of the IEEE International Conference on Computer Vision Workshops*, pages 2393–2402, 2019.

95. B. Ravi Kiran, Luis Roldao, Benat Irastorza, Renzo Verastegui, Sebastian Suss, Senthil Yogamani, Victor Talpaert, Alexandre Lepoutre, and Guillaume Trehard. Real-time dynamic object detection for autonomous driving using prior 3D-maps. In *Proceedings of the European Conference on Computer Vision (ECCV)*, pages 567–582, 2018.

96. Joseph Redmon and Ali Farhadi. YOLO9000: Better, faster, stronger. In *The IEEE Conference on Computer Vision and Pattern Recognition (CVPR)*, July 2017.

97. Joseph Redmon and Ali Farhadi. YOLOv3: An incremental improvement. *CoRR*, abs/1804.02767, 2018.

98. Shaoqing Ren, Kaiming He, Ross Girshick, and Jian Sun. Faster R-CNN: Towards real-time object detection with region proposal networks. In C. Cortes, N. D. Lawrence, D. D. Lee, M. Sugiyama, and R. Garnett, editors, *Advances in Neural Information Processing Systems 28*, pages 91–99, Red Hook, NY, Curran Associates, 2015.

99. Pierre Sermanet, David Eigen, Xiang Zhang, Michael Mathieu, Rob Fergus, and Yann LeCun. OverFeat: Integrated recognition, localization and detection using convolutional networks. *arXiv*, abs/1312.6229, 2013.

100. Shaoshuai Shi, Xiaogang Wang, and Hongsheng Li. PointRCNN: 3D object proposal generation and detection from point cloud. In *The IEEE Conference on Computer Vision and Pattern Recognition (CVPR)*, June 2019.

101. Bing Shuai, Andrew G. Berneshawi, Davide Modolo, and Joseph Tighe. Multiobject tracking with Siamese Track-RCNN. *arXiv*, abs/2004.07786, 2020.

102. Mennatullah Siam, Sara Elkerdawy, Martin Jagersand, and Senthil Yogamani. Deep semantic segmentation for automated driving: Taxonomy, roadmap and challenges. In *2017 IEEE 20th International Conference on Intelligent Transportation Systems (ITSC)*, pages 1–8, IEEE, 2017.

103. Mennatullah Siam, Mostafa Gamal, Moemen Abdel-Razek, Senthil Yogamani, and Martin Jagersand. RTSeg: Real-time semantic segmentation comparative study. In *2018 25th IEEE International Conference on Image Processing (ICIP)*, pages 1603–1607, IEEE, 2018.

104. Mennatullah Siam, Heba Mahgoub, Mohamed Zahran, Senthil Yogamani, Martin Jagersand, and Ahmad El-Sallab. MODNet: Motion and appearance based moving object detection network for autonomous driving. In *2018 21st International Conference on Intelligent Transportation Systems (ITSC)*, pages 2859–2864, IEEE, 2018.

105. Ganesh Sistu, Isabelle Leang, Sumanth Chennupati, Senthil Yogamani, Ciarán Hughes, Stefan Milz, and Samir Rawashdeh. NeurALL: Towards a unified visual perception model for automated driving. In *2019 IEEE Intelligent Transportation Systems Conference (ITSC)*, pages 796–803, IEEE, 2019.

106. Shuran Song and Jianxiong Xiao. Sliding shapes for 3d object detection in depth images. In David Fleet, Tomas Pajdla, Bernt Schiele, and Tinne Tuytelaars, editors, *Computer Vision— ECCV 2014*, pages 634–651, Cham, Springer International Publishing, 2014.

107. Shuran Song and Jianxiong Xiao. Deep sliding shapes for amodal 3D object detection in RGB-D images. In *The IEEE Conference on Computer Vision and Pattern Recognition (CVPR)*, June 2016.

108. Pei Sun, Henrik Kretzschmar, Xerxes Dotiwalla, Aurelien Chouard, Vijaysai Patnaik, Paul Tsui, James Guo, Yin Zhou, Yuning Chai, Benjamin Caine, Vijay Vasudevan, Wei Han, Jiquan Ngiam, Hang Zhao, Aleksei Timofeev, Scott Ettinger, Maxim Krivokon, Amy Gao, Aditya Joshi, Yu Zhang, Jonathon Shlens, Zhifeng Chen, and Dragomir Anguelov. Scalability in perception for autonomous driving: Waymo Open Dataset. In *Proceedings of the IEEE/CVF Conference on Computer Vision and Pattern Recognition (CVPR)*, June 2020.

109. Mingxing Tan, Ruoming Pang, and Quoc V. Le. EfficientDet: Scalable and efficient object detection. In *The IEEE/CVF Conference on Computer Vision and Pattern Recognition (CVPR)*, June 2020.

110. Ran Tao, Efstratios Gavves, and Arnold W. M. Smeulders. Siamese instance search for tracking. In *The IEEE Conference on Computer Vision and Pattern Recognition (CVPR)*, June 2016.

111. Michal Uřičář, Pavel Křížek, David Hurych, Ibrahim Sobh, Senthil Yogamani, and Patrick Denny. Yes, we GAN: Applying adversarial techniques for autonomous driving. *Electronic Imaging*, 2019(15):48–1, 2019.

112. Michal Uřičář, Pavel Křížek, Ganesh Sistu, and Senthil Yogamani. SoilingNet: Soiling detection on automotive surround-view cameras. In *2019 IEEE Intelligent Transportation Systems Conference (ITSC)*, pages 67–72, IEEE, *2019.*

113. Michal Uřičář, David Hurych, P. Křížek, and Senthil Yogamani. Challenges in designing datasets and validation for autonomous driving. In *Proceedings of the 14th International Joint Conference on Computer Vision, Imaging and Computer Graphics Theory and Applications (VISAPP)*, volume 5, pages 653–659, INSTICC, SciTePress, 2019.

114. Michal Uřičář, Jan Ulicny, Ganesh Sistu, Hazem Rashed, Pavel Krizek, David Hurych, Antonin Vobecky, and Senthil Yogamani. Desoiling dataset: Restoring soiled areas on automotive fisheye cameras. In *Proceedings of the IEEE International Conference on Computer Vision Workshops*, pages 4273–4279, 2019.

115. Jack Valmadre, Luca Bertinetto, Joao Henriques, Andrea Vedaldi, and Philip H. S. Torr. End-to-end representation learning for correlation filter based tracking. In *The IEEE Conference on Computer Vision and Pattern Recognition (CVPR)*, July 2017.

116. Paul Voigtlaender, Jonathon Luiten, Philip H. S. Torr, and Bastian Leibe. Siam R-CNN: Visual tracking by re-detection. In *The IEEE/CVF Conference on Computer Vision and Pattern Recognition (CVPR)*, June 2020.

117. Dominic Zeng Wang and Ingmar Posner. Voting for voting in online point cloud object detection. In *Robotics: Science and Systems*, 2015.

118. Jingdong Wang, Zhen Wei, Ting Zhang, and Wenjun Zeng. Deeply-fused nets. *ArXiv*, abs/1605.07716, 2016.

119. Lijun Wang, Wanli Ouyang, Xiaogang Wang, and Huchuan Lu. Visual tracking with fully convolutional networks. In *The IEEE International Conference on Computer Vision (ICCV)*, Dec. 2015.

120. P. Wang, X. Huang, X. Cheng, D. Zhou, Q. Geng, and R. Yang. The ApolloScape open dataset for autonomous driving and its application. *IEEE Transactions on Pattern Analysis and Machine Intelligence*, pages 2702–2719, 2019.

121. Q. Wang, L. Zhang, Luca Bertinetto, W. Hu, and P. Torr. Fast online object tracking and segmentation: A unifying approach. *2019 IEEE/CVF Conference on Computer Vision and Pattern Recognition (CVPR)*, pages 1328–1338, 2019.

122. Yan Wang, Wei-Lun Chao, Divyansh Garg, Bharath Hariharan, Mark Campbell, and Kilian Q. Weinberger. Pseudo-LIDAR from visual depth estimation: Bridging the gap in 3D object detection for autonomous driving. In *The IEEE Conference on Computer Vision and Pattern Recognition (CVPR)*, June 2019.

123. N. Wojke, A. Bewley, and D. Paulus. Simple online and realtime tracking with a deep association metric. In *2017 IEEE International Conference on Image Processing (ICIP)*, pages 3645–3649, 2017.

124. Bichen Wu, Forrest Iandola, Peter H. Jin, and Kurt Keutzer. SqueezeDet: Unified, small, low power fully convolutional neural networks for real-time object detection for autonomous driving. In *The IEEE Conference on Computer Vision and Pattern Recognition (CVPR) Workshops*, July 2017.

125. Pengxiang Wu, Siheng Chen, and Dimitris N. Metaxas. MotionNet: Joint perception and motion prediction for autonomous driving based on bird's eye view maps. In *The IEEE/CVF Conference on Computer Vision and Pattern Recognition (CVPR)*, June 2020.

126. Yu Xiang, Alexandre Alahi, and Silvio Savarese. Learning to track: Online multi-object tracking by decision making. In *The IEEE International Conference on Computer Vision (ICCV)*, December 2015.

127. Marie Yahiaoui, Hazem Rashed, Letizia Mariotti, Ganesh Sistu, Ian Clancy, Lucie Yahiaoui, Varun Ravi Kumar, and Senthil Yogamani. FisheyeMODNet: Moving object detection on surround-view cameras for autonomous driving. *arXiv preprint, arXiv:1908.11789*, 2019.

128. Bin Yang, Ming Liang, and Raquel Urtasun. HDNET: Exploiting HD maps for 3D object detection. In Aude Billard, Anca Dragan, Jan Peters, and Jun Morimoto, editors, *Proceedings of the 2nd Conference on Robot Learning*, volume 87 of *Proceedings of Machine Learning Research*, pages 146–155, PMLR, Oct. 2018.

129. Bin Yang, Wenjie Luo, and Raquel Urtasun. PIXOR: Real-time 3D object detection from point clouds. In *The IEEE Conference on Computer Vision and Pattern Recognition (CVPR)*, June 2018.

130. Bin Yang, Junjie Yan, Zhen Lei, and Stan Z. Li. Craft objects from images. In *The IEEE Conference on Computer Vision and Pattern Recognition (CVPR)*, June 2016.

131. Senthil Yogamani, Ciaran Hughes, Jonathan Horgan, Ganesh Sistu, Padraig Varley, Derek O'Dea, Michal Uricar, Stefan Milz, Martin Simon, Karl Amende, Christian Witt, Hazem Rashed, Sumanth Chennupati, Sanjaya Nayak, Saquib Mansoor, Xavier Perrotton, and Patrick Perez. WoodScape: A multi-task, multi-camera fisheye dataset for autonomous driving. In *Proceedings of the IEEE/CVF International Conference on Computer Vision (ICCV)*, Oct. 2019.

132. Fisher Yu, Haofeng Chen, Xin Wang, Wenqi Xian, Yingying Chen, Fangchen Liu, Vashisht Madhavan, and Trevor Darrell. BDD100K: A diverse driving dataset for heterogeneous multitask learning. In *Proceedings of the IEEE/CVF Conference on Computer Vision and Pattern Recognition (CVPR)*, June 2020.

133. Sergey Zagoruyko, Adam Lerer, Tsung-Yi Lin, Pedro H. O. Pinheiro, Sam Gross, Soumith Chintala, and Piotr Dollár. A multipath network for object detection. *CoRR, abs/1604.02135*, 2016.

134. Liang Zheng, Zhi Bie, Yifan Sun, Jingdong Wang, Chi Su, Shengjin Wang, and Qi Tian. MARS: A video benchmark for large-scale person re-identification. In *The European Conference on Computer Vision (ECCV)*, 2016.

135. Xingyi Zhou, Vladlen Koltun, and Philipp Krähenbühl. Tracking objects as points. *ArXiv, abs/2004.01177*, 2020.

136. Xingyi Zhou, Jiacheng Zhuo, and Philipp Krahenbuhl. Bottom-up object detection by grouping extreme and center points. In *The IEEE Conference on Computer Vision and Pattern Recognition (CVPR)*, June 2019.

137. Yin Zhou and Oncel Tuzel. VoxelNet: End-to-end learning for point cloud based 3D object detection. In *The IEEE Conference on Computer Vision and Pattern Recognition (CVPR)*, June 2018.

138. Zheng Zhu, Qiang Wang, Bo Li, Wei Wu, Junjie Yan, and Weiming Hu. Distractor-aware Siamese networks for visual object tracking. In *The European Conference on Computer Vision (ECCV)*, Sept. 2018.

CHAPTER 5

ADAS Vision System with Video Super Resolution

Need and Scope

Mrunmayee V. Daithankar and Sachin D. Ruikar

Walchand College of Engineering

Sangli, India

CONTENTS

5.1 INTRODUCTION

The concern about road security and the protection of lives is increasing gradually due to intensified mobility, unfocused driving, and control over the vehicle. As per a World Health Organization (WHO) report on the global status of road injuries and safety, the key fact is that roughly 1.35 million persons lose their lives every year due to road accidents [1]. These deaths cause significant financial harm to victims' families and to entire countries. The reasons behind this scene include uncontrolled speed of the vehicle, unsafe road construction, disregard of traffic rules, unsafe driving caused by the driver's drowsiness, and

DOI: 10.1201/9781003048381-6

vehicles with fewer safety features. The government aims to decrease this number by 2030 by supporting technical advances in the unsafe vehicles. This interest led to the development of advanced driver-assistance systems (ADASs), which are intended to offer requisite information, caution, and instinctive intrusion to lessen the severity of an accident. Each system is a collection of numerous intelligent units integrated in the vehicle itself [2]. The developments in the vision system and even machine learning–based automotive systems are mainly focused on services and not on quality of input—i.e. video resolution. The focus of this study is mainly on the vision system and video super resolution. It provides a systematic look at the basics, recent developments, challenges, and scope of the vision system, with video resolution as the key parameter. The motive behind exploring this area is that new researchers in the area of image or video processing will benefit from the information provided and be motivated to contribute in the same growing area.

5.1.1 ADAS at a Glance

ADASs involve numerous sensors, handling components and actuators that help drivers to avoid accidents and to drive cautiously. The actuators are responsible for applying the necessary mechanical actions in the system after getting processed information from various sensors like LIDAR and infrared (IR) and visible cameras. The ADAS is shown in Figure 5.1, which introduces four important components: sensors, processors, the decision-making component, and the actuator. The role and sample components of the system are included in figure with the services offered, including lane deviation warning (LDW), traffic sign recognition (TSR), and driver's behavior status [3]. One can say that awareness about danger is the outcome of the automotive vision system. The input to the vision system is video streams collected from front, rear, and side cameras fitted on the vehicle. The challenges associated with the system are increased data rates, the availability

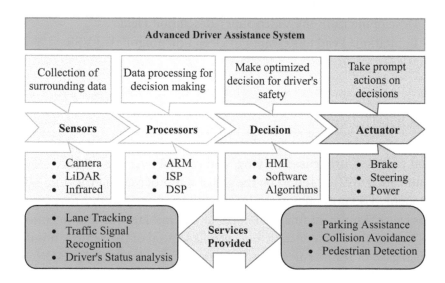

FIGURE 5.1 Advanced driver assistance system at a glance.

TABLE 5.1 Pedestrian or Vehicle Detection Summary

Ref. No.	Publication Year	Method/Model Preferred	Image Size	Accuracy
5	2019	CNN	720 Pixel	76%
6	2018	CNN	362 × 480	78.6%
7	2018	SVM	320 × 97	70%
8	2017	CNN	1242 × 375	68.1%
9	2016	CNN	1242 × 375	76.7%

of memory, the need for high-speed data processing and communication, and low-quality video streams [4]. The possibility exists that lower-resolution videos may be responsible for the ineffective decisions made by the system's services.

5.1.2 Services by ADAS

The ADAS provides many services, some of which are introduced in following paragraphs. Each service is summarized in tables where methods, accuracy, and image size are explored. The need of quality images in such services is introduced briefly in section 5.3.1.

The presence of extensive and uneven obstacles at varying distances on roads, like vehicles and pedestrians, increases difficulties in driving. Thus, on-road object detection to streamline the recognition of the targets and lane tracing is an imperative technology for vehicle security and driver suitability [5, 6]. However, it is challenging to identify the road situation exactly because restricted feature maps are used to identify objects. Object detection methods are developed from the basics up to the deep learning-based approaches [7–9]. Some recent deep learning–based literature is summarized in Table 5.1.

The number of unfocused driving accidents has surpassed those caused by drunk driving, speeding, and not wearing a seat belt. Drivers are considered to be inattentive when they are not concentrating on driving. Driving distractions are of three types. Manual distractions occur when the driver's hands are off the wheel due to drinking, eating, etc. Visual distraction occurs when the driver stares away from the road. In the last type, cognitive distraction, the driver's mind is not entirely attentive to the driving job [10–13]. The literature related to driver behavior analysis is summarized in Table 5.2.

Traffic symbol recognition has been a common problem for smart vehicles [14]. Particularly for TSR which offers worthwhile information like directions and warnings for self-governing driving and driver support systems. This field has drawn on navigation

TABLE 5.2 Driver Status Detection Summary

Ref. No.	Publication Year	Method/Model Preferred	Image Size	Accuracy
10	2018	CNN	224 × 224	89%
11	2018	CNN	64 × 64	92%
12	2017	CNN	640 × 480	91.2%
13	2015	SVM	576 × 720	8.44% FPR

TABLE 5.3 Traffic Signal Detection Summary

Ref. No.	Publication Year	Method/Model Preferred	Image Size	Accuracy
14	2018	CNN	1280 × 720	82.8%
15	2018	—	256 × 455	92.22%
16	2018	SVM	1360 × 800	90.85%
17	2018	Squeeze Net	542 × 412	81% mAP
18	2017	MB-LBP	640 × 480	78.34%

logics for rational vehicles, where traffic signs can be treated as diverse landmarks for plotting and localization [15–18]. Work related to TSR is summarized in Table 5.3.

Road detection is habitually employed in combination with lane detection to regulate the drivable regions. Even if some existing study based on bulky deep learning models attained great accuracy using the road detection data set, it would frequently have to deal with various challenges that show the scope of research needed in the field [19–23]. Some of the information is summarized in Table 5.4.

The technology is on the verge of development from manual analysis of images to automatic analysis by deep learning-based approaches.

5.2 VISION SYSTEM OF ADAS

The vision system within the ADAS acts as the heart of the vehicle. Automotive industrialists generally place the camera system on their high-end models as a minimum requirement, with various purposes like backup protection and front collision warning. Unsurprisingly, additional innovative applications entail higher-end processing units, and the manufacturer has higher production costs. Nevertheless, as security legislation calls for enhancements, camera systems will gradually appear in lower-end vehicles and soon will be routine in several vehicle variants [24]. Texas Instruments sees a growing trend to obtain multiple sensor inputs and fuse them to build more accurate conclusions and recognize critical circumstances. The high-tech progressions in the sensor mechanisms, explicitly in vision-centered ADAS, have vast significance in the automotive market.

The vision system has various components, each with a specific task. According to its application and expectations, each component is of different quality and has different features. The general components of the system are shown in Figure 5.2.

The important components of the system are the automotive cameras and image signal processor (ISP). The camera monitoring system collects data from the surroundings and

TABLE 5.4 Lane Detection and Tracking Summary

Ref. No.	Publication Year	Method/Model Preferred	Image Size	Accuracy
19	2019	Depthwise conv.	—	60%
20	2019	Hardware mapping	1080 Pixel	91.60% mAP
21	2018	CNN	1392 × 512	53% RMSE
22	2016	Deep NN	240 × 360	89.32% mAP
23	2016	Knowledge transfer	240 × 180	77%

Abbreviation: NN, neural network.

| Camera Module | | Video Streams | | Image Signal Processor | | Decision Algorithms | | Input to Actions by Actuator |

FIGURE 5.2   General components of the vision system.

gives it to the ISP in the form of video streams to be analyzed for further decisions. Feature extraction, enhancement, and filtering are among the processes required of the ISP. The system entails handling numerous successive frames and uses a group of dense and refined processes to scrutinize the image and reach a conclusion for the ADAS to work [24–27].

The important component is the ADAS decision algorithm, where the processed data—i.e. feature maps of the image signal—are analyzed with the standard feature maps for the purpose of decision-making. The decisions are further fed to actuators for actions to maintain driver safety.

5.2.1 Camera Modules

The cameras, which are also known as an eye of the ADAS, are fitted over and inside the vehicle to capture internal and external views. The types of cameras vary depending on the services provided by the system. Each camera has a specific purpose based on its features [24]. The information about types of cameras used in the ADAS and their applications is summarized in Table 5.5.

As this study focuses on the processing of images, the next section concerns the image signal processor.

5.2.2 Image Signal Processor

The appearance of collected images or video frames is altered by digital image processing in accord with each application's requirement. Processing the image signal enhances the original images, conversion from low-quality images, and prepares master images for display or printing. This can be achieved with pixel-level modification such as the tuning of brightness and contrast, gamma improvement, histogram adjustment, and color rectification.

The process is supported by many other statistics and algorithms that assist in setting the appropriate spotlight and focus. The algorithms set up different sensors and artifacts linked with each lens to improve the picture quality of the image/video, as various cameras have sensors with unlike features. In the ADAS, front camera systems are principally used for the finding and tracing of pedestrians, ground level detection, LDW, and TSR [2]. This creates a novel set of prerequisites for the imaging sensor and image signal processer (ISP) to process raw data. In the situation of cell phones, ISPs use a sequence of algorithms to handle the steps from the raw images to those that offer a pleasurable viewing feel to the individual eye and brain. The ISP pipelines of front cameras and cell phones differ in their features and requirements. These differences mean cameras can improperly process video streams, which leads to inefficient decisions and servicing [24–27].

With automated driving features, vision-based ADAS systems make drivers feel safe and informed [1, 2]. However, the failure of the system can cause the loss of someone's life,

TABLE 5.5   Summary of Camera Types with Features and Applications

Type	Features	Application
Exterior	• Provides information about the external environment where the vehicle is navigating	Cross traffic alert, traffic sign recognition
Interior	• Captures the occupants in the vehicle	Driver status monitoring
Side View	• Field of view is greater than 160° • Front, rear, left, and right views collect more information about the scene	Lane marking detection, object detection
Single View	• Field of view is less than 60° • Traditional camera handles the front view	Object detection
Mono	• Traditional single camera is used but provides in-depth estimation of scene • Less expensive but less efficient than stereo camera	Adaptive cruise control
Stereo	• Two or more lenses with a distinct image sensor for each lens • More expensive than mono due to extra cameras and processing hardware • More accurate in-depth scene estimation and increased robustness	Automotive emergency breaking, adaptive cruise control
Active	• Active cameras with active night vision to illuminate the scene in low lighting conditions	Advanced functioning of ADAS in low light
Passive	• Uses light from the environment and operates within the visible electromagnetic spectrum • Degrades the quality of the image in low lighting	General ADAS functioning in environmental lighting
Low Speed	• Operates at 25 to 30 frames per second • For low lightning conditions	For displaying view to user
High Speed	• Operates at 60 frames or more per second	Automotive emergency breaking, adaptive cruise control
Stand-Alone	• Provides relevant data to user without fusion of the data with another sensor system	Display camera with traditional system
Fusion	• Data fusion between the system's different sensors	Advanced ADAS for accuracy

which is not acceptable. So accuracy should be the major parameter of analysis. The vision of Texas Instruments is to provide improved digital and image signal processors that can run various high-performance algorithms at one time and with low complexity in order to improve the ADAS's real-time analysis. According to the surveyed literature, the system still needs developments related to camera data fusion, low power consumption, and government commands for car safety, as the effectiveness of provided services has not reached the level required [24].

5.2.3 Challenges in Vision System

• Because numerous sensors are available from different sellers, along with a well-developed group of algorithms with enormous parameters, there are substantial challenges in effectively blending image data to attain the best visual feature.

• Unlike with cell phones, the typical digital camera's ISP feature lacks the general processing algorithms to properly process video streams.

- The choice of algorithm depends on the frame rate, speed of the vehicle, requirement of interframe motion, computational load of the algorithm, and update rate required from the function itself.

- Embedding all processing blocks through the combination of hardware and software techniques is necessary to progress as a factual time system.

- An invasion of high-quality cell phone and tablet displays in the customer space has placed the bar of buyers' hopes very high in terms of analogous color loyalty, signal to noise ratio, and resolution in functions like rearview and surrounding scene cameras.

5.3 VIDEO SUPER-RESOLUTION CONCEPT

Super resolution (SR) is the way to obtain an extreme-resolution image or a chain of such images from a collection of low-resolution images. The SR theory is ill-posed and having converse routine. The degradation of an image leads to ground-level quality exposures, and the contrary process for restoration is presented by the video resolution improvement model in Figure 5.3. Super resolution gives an image or video of elevated quality with more particulars about the scene, which is essential for exact analysis [28].

The mathematical basis for the super-resolution model is given by Equation 5.1:

$$Y_k = \mathrm{DHF}_k X + V_k \tag{5.1}$$

where Y_k is the kth low-quality revelation of the scene, H is the blur aspect due to the camera features, D is decimation, F_k is warping, X is the high-resolution image, and V_k is the noise factor. This mathematical equation is solved reversely to get X by reducing the effects of D, H, F, and V. The different techniques for resolution enhancement under development are discussed in section 5.3.2.

5.3.1 Need of SR in ADAS Vision System

Resolution enhancement relies on either hardware or software developments. The hardware properties like display components, sensor type, and optics of imaging tools are sensible for the resolution of the image. The modification of the hardware has reached to the

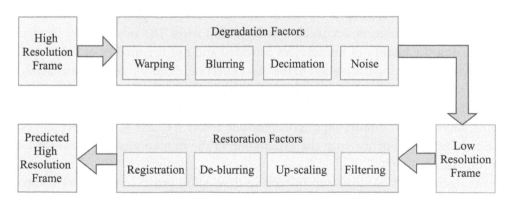

FIGURE 5.3 The super-resolution model.

optimum solution, so no scope of improvement in hardware. Hardware changes lead to complexity and product cost. To avoid limitations of this type on resolution enhancement, one can take advantage of offline resolution upgrading procedures. In this type of SR, digital signal processing is used to restore and reform the image [28].

The ISP is the heart of the vision system for the services supported, affecting the quality of input video streams through systematic processing. The input coming from different imaging sensors/cameras needs to be optimized for further processing to enhance visual effect on different displays and to provide appropriate information for the decision-making algorithms of the ADAS. The manufacturer wants to avoid increased production costs in top-level models, and provision of maximum facilities in lower end models limits the hardware excellence and storing devices capacity in the vehicles [24–27]. The manufacturing limitations affect the video quality as well as the overall analysis of video streams. On the other hand, customers need good visuals on high-definition displays. The overall efficiency in the ADAS depends on efficient services provided by the vision system with accurate analysis of visuals received. The details in the visuals like objects, edges, and color are the features that are going to be processed for further analysis and decision-making, so the resolution of these is the important factor for exact information [1, 2, 27]. The feature maps extracted from low-quality streams do not having sufficient information to be compared with standard feature maps, leading to inefficient decisions by software algorithms.

The digital automotive camera market has been overrun by low-budget analog cameras whose low quality does not come near that of even economical cell phones. The advanced resolution digital camera sector, restricted to high-end automobiles, is normally sustained by both intelligent sensors (i.e. those with built-in ISPs) and individual ISPs constructed by the sensor maker. These chips are bound to the sensor and yet are incapable to match the expressively developed image quality beliefs. Further, they lack in the fusion and in handling horsepower wanted for a single chip [24–27].

The camera monitoring system preferred by the ADAS gives a maximum resolution of 2.6 MP, which is not sufficient to analyze details and make accurate decisions. The quality of input streams is even decreasing due to compression, transfer, etc. According to the literature, most of the developments in ADAS services are getting attention, but the enhancement of the quality of input had not been the focus of research. This enables elaboration of the ADAS concept from a new point of view [24]. The data provided in Tables 5.1–5.4 shows the image resolution, accuracy, and algorithm used. The work always has focused on improving the quality of the services provided and not the quality of the input data. This area needs additional attention to the exact effect of resolution on image analysis, efficiency of services, computational capacity of algorithms, etc. The necessity for accompanying visual display creates new disputes earlier not present in conventional ADAS analytics systems. Good visual quality highlights pleasant ambiance, less noise, sharp edges, etc. These requirements openly map the exploration of the human visual system with super resolution [27].

Texas Instruments has taken an interest in developing processors that are compatible for the fusion of unlike featured input data from different cameras, have low complexity as well as low power consumption, and include algorithms with the computational load-handling capacity [26]. This need leads to embedding the video quality process and therefore the rise of the super-resolution concept in the ADAS area. The developments in this field are covered in next section.

5.3.2 Developments in the Video Super-Resolution Field

The enhancement of frame resolution can be carried out using either single-frame or multiframe technology. In multiframe resolution enhancement, subpixel moves among consecutive frames are used to reconstruct a single frame without blur. The algorithms of super resolution are explored according to their domain; spatial or frequency. The frequency domain–based methods use feature-level processing. The transformation of the image domain for feature extraction can be done with the help of discrete Fourier transform (DFT), discrete cosine transform (DCT), and discrete wavelet transform (DWT), depending on the need of the application and the system's computational capacity [28]. The spatial domain algorithms deal with pixel-level processing, which requires greater memory and more computations. But because of the requirement of automation and the speedy process, the focus of this study is the emerging trend of deep learning-based techniques. The deep learning approach relies on processing either spatial or feature level information or embedding both types of information. The input data provided for processing is restricted by parameters like processing speed, accuracy requirement, applications, and computational load of the algorithm. For video super resolution (VSR), several frames offer more scene data than a single frame, and there is intraframe spatial as well as interframe temporal reliance. Thus, the present work rests on optical flow, ascertaining and recurrent methods, etc. The blend of optical flow methods and CNN is studied by Liao et al. [29] for high-resolution (HR) pixel generation. VSRnet [30] uses the motion compensation algorithm of Druleas [31] and CNNs for consecutive frame processing in predicting HR frames. VSRnet confirms that pretraining of CNN over images can limit the time needed to handle a bulky video record. This requires fewer video records for training to achieve promising results. The detailed motion estimation between the low-resolution (LR) frames is the essential step in almost all VSR algorithms. These algorithms are believed to protect the optical flow over time. This source is used to form an equation that relates spatial and temporal gradients for optical flow. These equations are resolved to predict a restricted fidelity of optical flow [31–34]. The most recent SR work is based on CNN, which estimates the optical flow of video frames. These methods regularly study the motion and alliance of multiple frames for super resolution. However, this two-step approach has the flaw that the first phase controls the overall performance.

Many authors have tried to directly train the networks for the motion compensation. For example, spatial temporal convolutional network (STCN) [35] combines a deep CNN and a bidirectional long short-term memory (LSTM) [36] to separate spatial and temporal data. Frame recurrent video super resolution (FRVSR) [37] uses formerly assumed HR approximations to rebuild the succeeding HR frames by two deep CNNs in a recurrent way. The bidirectional recurrent convolutional network (BRCN) [38] works with a bidirectional outline and a custom recurrent neural network (RNN) and conditional CNN to exhibit the spatial-temporal dependencies. The bidirectional networks are always more complex than fully connected feed forward networks, but accuracy increases at the cost of complexity, which reduces the feasibility of the network in many applications.

The dense varieties of the structure and pixel associations,, handover the SR effects from one frame to contiguous frames, and fast-tracks the hi-tech SR algorithms with minor performance failure by Zhang and Sze [39]. Jo et al. [40] produced active up-sampling filters and the HR residual image grounded on the confined spatiotemporal regions of individual pixels, and sidestep explicit motion recompense. This VSR literature summarizes the techniques and their compatibility, but deep study will motivate further developments in this area, allowing the ADAS to provide more proficient automotive services. The limitations of previous work always lead to in-depth investigation of the corresponding field. Some of the flaws are summarized in next section.

5.3.3 Limitations Lead to Research in Deep Learning–Based VSR

- The absolute utilization of space-time information connecting the LR sequence is ignored in CNN- based techniques. A straight association and a single memory unit inside the network are responsible for this drawback of CNN. For complete use of space-time correlations among neighboring LR exposures and to expose additional practical particulars, one needs competent algorithms.

- The most recent SR work is based on CNN that estimates the optical flow of video frames. These methods often consider motion and alignment of multiple frames for super resolution. However, this two-step tactic has the weakness that the first step restricts the overall performance.

- Use of LSTM increases hardware complexity and restricts the practical utility of applications such as the ADAS where speed and accuracy both are important parameters.

- Deeper networks with a number of parameters increase the complexity of the system.

- Single image super resolution (SISR) algorithms restrict the use of spatiotemporal information, which results in flickering output and no pleasing visuals.

- The restrictive input fields of networks can't handle arbitrary input sequences, and this restricts the practical utility of algorithms.

- A competent algorithm is needed that handles any size of video with less complexity, as embedding steps like frame resizing, registration, and resolution enhancement for better performance lead to reduced speed and increased memory requirements.

- The exact use of and the need for quality images and image-processing techniques in the ADAS should be the subject of in-depth research.

5.4 SUMMARY

The ADAS is hugely popular due to safety measures that lead to more practical use of the system. An optimum solution that bridges the gap between customers' requests and manufacturers' limitations is needed. Finding such solutions is the researchers' interest;

hence, here is a contribution from the author side about the basics of the ADAS and the need for better image resolution for better performance. The research community is still trying to create the best driver assistance services, and it needs to focus on developing efficient preprocessing steps and ensuring key information is not lost during processing. Providing more details about the scene is the major aim of super resolution, which focuses on embedding this concept with the new emerging trend of the ADAS. This embedding exposes the massive scope of research needed in the field, as detailed input data results in better analysis of the information and increases the overall performance of the system, but not many have explored this area. Here are the small efforts taken by the authors to explore the groundbreaking combination of two main concepts like VSR and ADAS.

REFERENCES

1. World Health Organization, "Road traffic injuries," 7 February 2020. Link: who.int/newsroom/factsheets/detail/road-traffic-injuries
2. World Health Organization, Global Status Report on Road Safety 2018, ISBN 978-92-4-156568-4.
3. S. Raviteja and R. Shanmugha Sundaram, "Advanced driver assistance system," in Proceedings of the Second International Conference on Intelligent Computing and Control Systems (ICICCS 2018), 2018, ISBN:978-1-5386-2842-3.
4. Rahul Kala, On-road Intelligent Vehicles, Butterworth-Heinemann, 27 April 2016, eBook ISBN: 9780128037560. http://dx.doi.org/10.1016/B978-0-12-803729-4.00004-0.
5. J. Xu, P. Wang, H. Yang, and A. M. López, "Training a binary weight object detector by knowledge transfer for autonomous driving," 2018 [Online]. Available: http://arxiv.org/abs/1804.06332.
6. Y. Koo, C. You, and S. Kim, "OpenCL-darknet: An OpenCL implementation for object detection," in Proc. IEEE Int. Conf. Big Data Smart Comput. (BigComp), Jan. 2018, pp. 631–634.
7. D. Nazir, M. Fizza, A. Waseem, and S. Khan, "Vehicle detection on embedded single board computers," in Proc. 7th Int. Conf. Comput. Commun. Eng. (ICCCE), Sep. 2018, pp. 480–485.
8. H. E. Kim, Y. Lee, H. Kim, and X. Cui, "Domain-specific data augmentation for on-road object detection based on a deep neural network," in Proc. IEEE Intell. Vehicles Symp. (IV), Jun. 2017, pp. 103–108.
9. B. Wu, A. Wan, F. Iandola, P. H. Jin, and K. Keutzer, "Squeeze Det: Unified, small, low power fully convolutional neural networks for real-time object detection for autonomous driving," in Proc. IEEE Conf. Comput. Vis. Pattern Recognit. Workshops (CVPRW), Jul. 2017, pp. 446–454.
10. M. García-García, A. Caplier, and M. Rombaut, "Sleep deprivation detection for real-time driver monitoring using deep learning," in Proc. Int. Conf. Image Anal. Recognit., in Lecture Notes in Computer Science, vol. 10882, 2018, pp. 435–442.
11. D. Tran, H. Manh Do, W. Sheng, H. Bai, and G. Chowdhary, "Realtime detection of distracted driving based on deep learning," IET Intell. Transp. Syst., vol. 12, no. 10, Dec. 2018, pp. 1210–1219.
12. B. Reddy, Y.-H. Kim, S. Yun, C. Seo, and J. Jang, "Real-time driver drowsiness detection for embedded system using model compression of deep neural networks," in Proc. IEEE Conf. Comput. Vis. Pattern Recognit. Workshops (CVPRW), Jul. 2017, pp. 438–445.
13. K. Selvakumar, J. Jerome, K. Rajamani, and N. Shankar, "Real-time vision based driver drowsiness detection using partial least squares analysis," J. Signal Process. Syst., vol. 85, no. 2, Dec. 2015, pp. 263–274.
14. H. S. Lee and K. Kim, "Simultaneous traffic sign detection and boundary estimation using convolutional neural network," IEEE Trans. Intell. Transp. Syst., vol. 19, no. 5, May 2018, pp. 1652–1663.

15. D. Yudin and D. Slavioglo, "Usage of fully convolutional network with clustering for traffic light detection," in Proc. 7th Medit. Conf. Embedded Comput. (MECO), vol. 169, nos. 3–4, Jun. 2018, pp. 1–6.

16. H.-M. Weng and C.-T. Chiu, "Resource efficient hardware implementation for real-time traffic sign recognition," in Proc. IEEE Int. Conf. Acoust. Speech Signal Process. (ICASSP), Apr. 2018, pp. 1120–1124.

17. K. Yi, K. Z. Jian, S. Chen, Y. Yang, and N. Zheng, "Knowledge-based recurrent attentive neural network for small object detection," 2018, arXiv:1803.05263 [Online]. Available: https://arxiv.org/abs/1803.05263.

18. H. Novais and A. R. Fernandes, "Community based repository for georeferenced traffic signs," in Proc. Encontro Português Computação Gráfica Interação (EPCGI), Oct. 2017, pp. 1–8.

19. Y. Gu, Q. Wang, and S. Kamijo, "Intelligent driving data recorder in smartphone using deep neural network-based speedometer and scene understanding," IEEE Sensors J., vol. 19, no. 1, Jan. 2019, pp. 287–296.

20. Y. Zhou, Y. Lyu, and X. Huang, "RoadNet: An 80-mW hardware accelerator for road detection," IEEE Embedded Syst. Lett., vol. 11, no. 1, Mar. 2019, pp. 21–24.

21. M. Oeljeklaus, F. Hoffmann, and T. Bertram, "A fast multi-task CNN for spatial understanding of traffic scenes," in Proc. 21st Int. Conf. Intell. Transp. Syst. (ITSC), Nov. 2018, pp. 2825–2830.

22. A. Gurghian, T. Koduri, S. V. Bailur, K. J. Carey, and V. N. Murali, "DeepLanes: End-to-end lane position estimation using deep neural networks," in Proc. IEEE Conf. Comput. Vis. Pattern Recognit. Workshops (CVPRW), Jun. 2016, pp. 38–45.

23. G. Ros, S. Stent, P. F. Alcantarilla, and T. Watanabe, "Training constrained deconvolutional networks for road scene semantic segmentation," 2016, arXiv:1604.01545 [Online]. Available: https://arxiv.org/abs/1604.01545.

24. Jonathan Horgan, Ciaran Hughes, John McDonald, and Senthil Yogamani, "Vision-based driver assistance systems: Survey, taxonomy and advances," in IEEE 18th Int. Conf. Intell. Trans. Syst., 2015.

25. "Advanced driver assistance systems (ADAS) guide 2015," SLYY044A, Texas Instruments, 2015. Available: http://www.ti.com/lit/sl/slyy044a/slyy044a.pdf.

26. Mihir Mody, Shashank Dabral, Mayank Magla, Hetul Sanghvi, Niraj Nandan, Kedar Chitnis, Brijesh Jadhav, Raja Shekhar Allu, and Gang Hua, "High quality image processing system for ADAS," Automotive Processor Business, Texas Instruments, IEEE, 2019, doi: 10.1109/CONECCT47791.2019.9012938.

27. Mihir Mody, Niraj Nandan, Shashank Dabral, Hetul Sanghvi, Rajat Sagar, Zoran Nikolic, Kedar Chitnis, Rajasekhar Allu, and Gang Hua, "Image signal processing for front camera based automated driver assistance system." in 2015 IEEE 5th Int. Conf. Consum. Electron. – Berlin (ICCE-Berlin), 2015, pp. 158–159, doi: 10.1109/ICCE-Berlin.2015.7391221.

28. Mrunmayee V. Daithankar and Sachin D. Ruikar, "Video super resolution: A review," ICDSMLA 2019, Springer Nature Singapore Private Ltd. 2020 Lecture Notes in Electrical Engineering 601, 2019.

29. R. Liao, X. Tao, R. Li, Z. Ma, and J. Jia, "Video super-resolution via deep draft-ensemble learning," in Int. Conf. Comput. Vision, 2015.

30. A. Kappeler, S. Yoo, Q. Dai, and A. K. Katsaggelos, "Video superresolution with convolutional neural networks," in IEEE Trans. Comput. Imaging, vol. 2, 2016.

31. M. Drulea and S. Nedevschi, "Total variation regularization of local global optical flow," in Proc. IEEE Conf. Intell. Transp. Syst. (ITSC), 2011, pp. 318–323.

32. D. Liu, Z. Wang, Y. Fan, X. Liu, Z. Wang, S. Chang, X. Wang, and T. S. Huang, "Learning temporal dynamics for video super resolution: A deep learning approach," IEEE Trans. Image Process., vol. 27, 2018.

33. S. Baker, D. Scharstein, J. P. Lewis, S. Roth, M. J. Black, and R. Szeliski, "A database and evaluation methodology for optical flow," Int. J. Comput. Vis. 92 (1), 2011, pp. 1–31.

34. D. Sun, S. Roth, and M. J. Black, "Secrets of optical flow estimation and their principles." in Proc. IEEE Comput. Soc. Conf. Comput. Vis. Pattern Recog., 2010, pp. 2432–2439.

35. J. Guo and H. Chao, "Building an end-to-end spatial-temporal convolutional network for video super-resolution," in Proc. AAAI Conf. Art. Intelligence, 2017.

36. A. Graves, S. Fernández, and J. Schmidhuber, "Bidirectional LSTM networks for improved phoneme classification and recognition," in ICANN, 2005.

37. M. S. Sajjadi, R. Vemulapalli, and M. Brown, "Frame-recurrent video super-resolution," in CVPR, 2018.

38. Y. Huang, W. Wang, and L. Wang, "Bidirectional recurrent convolutional networks for multi-frame super-resolution," in NIPS, 2015.

39. Z. Zhang and V. Sze, "Fast: A framework to accelerate super resolution processing on compressed videos," in CVPRW, 2017.

40. Y. Jo, S. W. Oh, J. Kang, and S. J. Kim, "Deep video super resolution network using dynamic up sampling filters without explicit motion compensation," in CVPR, 2018.

CHAPTER 6

Lane Detection, Prediction, and Path Planning

Any Gupta and Ayesha Choudhary

Jawaharlal Nehru University
New Delhi, India

CONTENTS

6.1 INTRODUCTION

Lane detection and tracking, along with lane prediction, makes an intelligent vehicle complete and robust. Lane detection is described as identifying the lane markings printed on a road, whereas lane tracking is the tracking of the lanes within and across the frames. A lane departure warning system (LDWS) requires accurate information regarding the labeled lane markings printed on the road and is very essential for an advanced driver-assistance system (ADAS). It helps the driver make decisions regarding vehicle movement. The purpose of creating a robust and accurate system for lane detection is to alert the driver in lane-changing scenarios and contribute to reducing the accidents that occur due to driver's error. If this kind of framework is integrated into intelligent vehicles, then it will surely increase the safety of the people driving on the road.

DOI: 10.1201/9781003048381-7

There is no tool or system available that gives information regarding the further tracks on the road that a vehicle is going to pass. This is the reason a lane detection and tracking framework should detect lanes accurately in real time and provide the correct lane information to the driver without any delay. However, one has to face many more challenges while building this kind of framework, as there is not any specific pattern of lane printing. The lanes can be marked in a continuous manner or in a dotted manner in either white or yellow. Sometimes the lanes can be occluded by surrounding vehicles or by snow, fog, etc., creating an obstacle to finding the lanes. Varying illumination caused by sunlight and shadows can also make it difficult to detect the lane markings on the road. Furthermore, there can be the case where the lane markings are not present. Therefore, it is necessary to do lane prediction to be able to make the LDWS and ADAS more robust and to enable these systems to continue working smoothly.

Lane prediction can be described as accurately predicting the lanes where the lanes are not present on the road. We suggest using an incremental clustering algorithm based on an unsupervised learning technique for lane detection and tracking that takes the frames from the camera as input and produces the accurate result for any type of lanes, including those that curve. It is totally based on real-time scenarios and does not require an a priori lane model. We use the vehicle tracks and the last detected lane markings to accurately predict the lane markings so that the driver can be given a lane departure warning, even when the lanes are not actually visible or present. We detect the vehicle using the YOLOv3 object detection technique [1] and track them using parameters such as color of the vehicle, area, orientation, vehicle centroid, and vehicle position in the lane.

Another important component of autonomous driving vehicles is the ability to estimate the pose (position and orientation) of the ego vehicle in real time. As the driver is driving, he needs to decide whether he wants to remain in same lane or whether he needs to change lanes. Therefore, he needs to plan the path in real time. At a point in time, when the driver needs to make the decision whether or not to change lanes, our system is there to assist him based on the current traffic situation and detected/predicted lane and will help him plan the future path accordingly.

Lane detection and prediction using vehicle detection and tracking may provide static information on the real-time surrounding view, which can be helpful for path planning. These things will be the add-on features in intelligent vehicles and help to make them more robust and accurate. Therefore, lane detection and prediction, along with vehicle detection and tracking, are fundamental parts of the ADAS. Also, they play an essential role in assisting map generation, localization, and route planning in intelligent vehicles.

6.2 LITERATURE SURVEY

This section describes the techniques associated with lane detection and tracking, vehicle detection and tracking, lane prediction, and path planning. Hasabnis et al. [2] proposed a lane detection technique in which they used the Canny edge detection algorithm to detect lane edges on the road and hysteres thresholding to segment the lane pixels from the image. Then they applied Hough transform to detect lane markings. Wang et al. [3] proposed a search-based optimization algorithm for ego-lane detection by extracting the road shape from OpenStreetMap, which represents a lane model. Moreover, Lu et al. [4] proposed a multilane detection algorithm in which they performed lane detection using a feature geometric uncertainty algorithm and prevented false detection using a random sample consensus (RANSAC) algorithm.

Ma et al. [5] demonstrated a framework by taking bird's-eye view of the lanes using inverse perspective mapping. After that, they applied edge detection followed by image segmentation to extract the pixels of lanes. Finally, they fitted the lane by polynomial by calculating the deviation angle of the lanes from the road center. Jiang et al. [6] preprocessed the image to extract the pixels of lanes, and then they applied an improved Hough transform and R-LSDR method together for lane detection and a Kalman filter to track them. Wu et al. [7] used vehicle trajectories to detect the lanes on the road. They applied 3-D density statistic filtering for foreground extraction.

Vehicle detection and tracking is helpful for lane prediction for an ADAS. Yao et al. [8] extracted the lane segments from a continuous driving scenario and performed the lane change analysis using information on vehicle parameters and lane segments. Satzoda and Trivedi [9] trained their model on complete vehicle images, which makes their system sensitive to partially visible vehicles in the frame in night vision The authors of [9] and [10] both considered color and geometrical information to detect the vehicle and train the AdaBoost detector on Haar-like features of gray-level images for the same. Satzoda and Trivedi [11] took several types of information into consideration, such as type of lane markings, speed and angle of vehicle motion, and lane and vehicle position, for lane prediction in further frames. Furthermore, Bar and Trivedi [12] also trained the AdaBoost detector on pixel-level details of clusters of vehicles, which are created by using color and some geometrical information on the vehicles.

Chen and Meng [13] performed vehicle detection by combining and applying features from three techniques: the accelerated segment test (FAST); hue, saturation, and value (HSV) color space for object (vehicle) extraction; and the histogram of gradients (HoG) method. The detected vehicles are tracked by the forward and backward tracking (FBT) method. It is really challenging to detect objects at night using a camera. The framework of Kosaka and Ohashi [14] used the Laplacian of Gaussian operator to detect vehicles at night and then used support vector machines (SVMs) to classify those vehicles. Tian et al. [15] applied the Kalman filter to track the vehicle, which is detected by taking its color and texture into consideration. Kampker et al. [16] proposed a framework for multiobject (including vehicles) detection and tracking by clustering the objects in the frame. They captured the environment using 3-D LIDAR to overcome the problems of occlusion and over segmentation.

Some lane prediction is performed using deep neural networks. John et al. [17] applied neural networks to extract color and depth features of the road surface. This information also helped in lane prediction in the presence of occlusion. Gurghian and Murali [18] also applied neural networks for lane prediction by taking into consideration parameters such as the distance of the vehicle from the lane and the lane angle. They trained the neural network by annotating some artificial lanes with synthetic background. McCall and Trivedi [19] predicted lanes using lane texture information and vehicle position. They applied steerable filters for lane detection and tracking. Li et al. [20] applied inverse perspective mapping (IPM) to get a bird's-eye view of the image, which helped them to get the position and orientation of the lanes. Further, they used a combination of neural network—i.e., a multitask deep convolutional network and a recurrent neural network—for lane estimation. We propose a simple geometric algorithm for lane prediction by performing the lane and vehicle detection using Spatio temporal clustering and compare our framework with [20].

Further, we describe the techniques for path planning that have been introduced by various researchers. Khairdoost et al. [21] applied long short-term memory (LSTM) for path planning, which included left/right lane changes, left/right turns, and continuous straight driving. They used the data on driver's gaze and surrounding vehicles for this purpose. Gilitschenski et al. [22] did trajectory prediction with deep-context maps that are trained with the predictor in parallel. Their map is capable of finding a location beyond the visual context cues. Messaoud et al. [23] gave a solution to path planning when a vehicle is surrounded by multiple other vehicles on the road. They proposed a multihead attention method based on features of the surrounding vehicle and map-based context, which helped the driver to make future driving decisions on the road.

Nakamura et al. [24] proposed a framework for planning vehicle trajectory to avoid collisions. For this purpose, they took the history of the speed, position, and trajectory of each surrounding vehicle and predicted if there would be any possibility of collision. They sent this information to the ego vehicle, and a modified trajectory was calculated. Deo et al. [25] also considered the information of surrounding vehicles, such as speed and position, for path planning. Menner et al. [26] proposed a framework in which they used maximum likelihood estimation and a posterior distribution for further path planning. Messaoud et al. [27] used the combination of multihead attention and LSTM for path planning. They used the surrounding vehicle trajectories and their records of driving behavior and decided the path accordingly.

For path prediction, lateral control plays an important role in that it allows the vehicle to keep the lane or overtake. Authors of [28–31] consider longitudinal and lateral motions of the vehicle in helping the driver to make decisions. Xu et al. [28] proposed a hybrid of the Gaussian mixture model and the continuous hidden Markov model to analyze the lane-changing behavior of the vehicle by dividing the trajectories into small lane units. Authors of [30] performed real-time simulation for tuning the information regarding longitudinal and lateral vehicle motion in various driving conditions for accurate path planning. Moreover, Sefati et al. [31] predicted vehicle motion with the help of two techniques—Monte Carlo value iteration (MCVI) and successive approximations of the optimal policies (SARSOP)—and proposed a decision-making framework based on a Bayesian network.

6.3 PROPOSED WORK

We now explain our combined novel framework for lane detection, tracking, and lane prediction. We propose a spatiotemporal incremental clustering (STIC) algorithm [32] for lane detection and tracking, whereas we do lane prediction [33] using the information on vehicle tracking and detected lane markings. Afterward, we use the vehicle detection and tracking information, along with last detected lanes, to explain our ideas regarding path planning. We arrange this section in three subsections: 6.3.1, Lane Detection and Tracking; 6.3.2, Lane Prediction (including 6.3.2.1, Vehicle Detection; 6.3.2.2, Vehicle Tracking; and 6.3.2.3, Lane Prediction Using Vehicle Detection and Tracking); and 6.3.3, Lane Detection and Prediction-Based Path Planning.

6.3.1 Lane Detection and Tracking

Lane detection identifies the lanes in a frame, whereas lane tracking tracks the same lane throughout the video. Lane detection and tracking is helpful in lane-changing scenarios, in which it notifies the driver if the ego vehicle is coming too close to the lane edge. Here we elaborate our unsupervised learning–based algorithm [32], which works for different types of lanes, such as double-marked, dash-marked, and solid printed lanes.

We chose our region of interest by considering that the lanes are always present in the lower part of the frame. Therefore, we cropped the images such that the lower part is processed through the video, decreasing the time complexity of our algorithm by reducing the number of pixels in the frame. We then converted this RGB-cropped image to gray scale to make the thresholding process smooth. Due to this conversion, all the different colors of the lanes get uniform resolution. The gray-scale process is followed by a noise reduction step in which we apply a Gaussian smoothing kernel of size 3×3 to remove the noise present in the image. It performs well, as it does not let the important features disappear and it removes unnecessary sharp features from the image.

Furthermore, we performed the segmentation on the image resulting from the previous step. We applied adaptive thresholding, which resulted in a binary image containing only black-and-white regions, as shown in Figure 6.1. The white portion contained the lanes, road markings, and bright-colored vehicles as well as some noise. We considered the lanes relevant and filtered out the irrelevant parts in further processing.

The white region of the segmented image contained high-intensity pixel objects other than lane markings, such as guardrails and areas of sunlight, that are irrelevant for our task. We needed to filter these objects out, as these could increase the time complexity of our algorithm. We performed contour detection on the segmented image and calculated

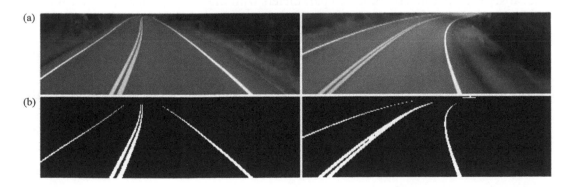

FIGURE 6.1   (a) Original images, (b) segmented output of the original images. (Adapted from [32].) [See Ref. 34.]

the orientation of the contours using principal component analysis (PCA). We have referred to the contours as connected components in some places. The lanes may vary in size, as there may be continuous and discontinuous lanes, which results in contours of various sizes. The small contours may exist due to the bright-colored objects that may be far away from the camera, whereas the large contours may exist due to sunlight or artificial light on the road. We considered these contours as irrelevant objects and filtered them out. Further, we clustered the lanes and proposed a STIC algorithm coupled with curve-fitting on the fly.

In the STIC algorithm [32], we performed clustering in such a way that the contours were clustered in first frame, and we clustered the contours of the upcoming frames on the basis of these cluster previously created in the first frame (Algorithm 1).

Algorithm 1 Psuedocode of our algorithm
```
1: procedure MY PROCEDURE
2 for i = 1 do                          ▷ i is frame number
3: Make clusters of connected components using orientation and
distance measured as SSE.
4: top:
5: for i = 2 to last frame do
6: for j = 2 to last cluster do ▷ compare each connected component
of iᵗʰ frame to jᵗʰ cluster using orientation and distance
7: if (comparison error < threshold)
8: cluster[j] ← (connected component of iᵗʰ frame).
9: goto top.                           ▷ no more further comparison
10: endif
11: else create new cluster
12: endfor
13: endfor
```

We considered a few parameters for performing clustering, such as orientation and distance, which is calculated as the sum of the squared errors (SSE). This distance was measured between the new contour and the existing contours in a cluster. If any contour did not satisfy the threshold of these two parameters with the existing cluster, then it was put in new cluster as its first element. Now we describe the STIC algorithm.

At time $m = 1$, we let $C^1 = \{C_1^1, C_2^1, \ldots, C_n^1\}$, where $n \geq 1$, having orientation as $O^1 = \{O_1^1, O_2^1, \ldots, O_n^1\}$, represent contours in the initial frame. Then we clustered them in the following way.

The first contour C_1^1 represented first cluster L_1 with the cluster orientation β_1. The remaining contours in $C^1 = \{C_2^1, \ldots, C_n^1\}$ were clustered as follows.

For C_2^1, O_2^1 was compared with β_1, and distance was calculated in terms of the SSE by fitting a curve on C_1^1 *and* C_2^1 using Equation 6.1.

$$Sum\,of\,squared\,error = \sum_{l=1}^{m}(k_{l(observed)} - k_{l(predicted)})^2 \qquad (6.1)$$

The observed value in Equation 6.1 represented the contour's pixels, whereas the predicted points were calculated using curve $f(j)$, found using Equation 6.2.

$$f(j) = b_0 + b_1 j + b_2 j^2 + \cdots + b_i j^i \qquad (6.2)$$

If the above computation satisfied the threshold limit of β_1 and SSE, then C_2^1 was part of L_1; otherwise, it was put in new cluster L_2 as its first element. Similarly, we clustered the rest of the contours on C^1 and made clusters as $L^m = \{L_1, L_2, \ldots, L_s\}$, where $s \geq 1$ having orientation $\beta^m = \{\beta_1, \beta_2, \ldots, \beta_s\}$. The cluster orientation represents the average orientation of all the contours in it.

The clusters created at the mth frame helped to do further clustering and work as a prebuilt set of clusters for the $(m+1)^{th}$ frame. We used the least square fitting method for curve fitting and computed SSE. We decided whether a cluster depicts a lane or not by seeing the length of the fitted curve and orientation of the respective cluster. The clusters that represented lanes were labeled lane clusters. We show an example of our algorithm in Figure 6.2.

We kept K as the limit of the contours in a clusters to make the framework efficient and adaptable. Also, we deleted the contours that existed in the cluster for more than F number of frames. By doing so, we made our algorithm efficient in terms of space complexity. The

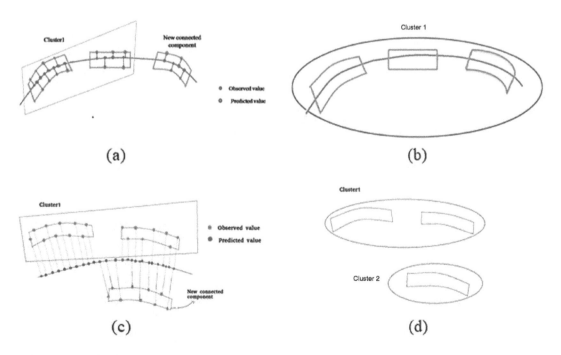

FIGURE 6.2 This diagram explains our STIC algorithm [see Ref. 32]. (a) Cluster 1 and a new contour that needs to be clustered. SSE is calculated between the two. (b) If SSE is within the threshold, then the new contour is part of the existing cluster. (c) If SSE does not satisfy the threshold limit, (d) this new contour is part of a new cluster.

values of K and F were experimentally decided. If a cluster did not take any new contours for T time steps due to the frequent changes in lane orientation, then we deleted such clusters and optimized the algorithm in terms of time and space. We showed the lanes by fitting a curve on the lane clusters using the least square fitting technique. Our algorithm did not take a priori information about lanes and gave good results for straight, curved, continuous, and discontinuous lanes.

6.3.2 Lane Prediction

Lane prediction means to predict the lanes where the lanes are not printed or visible on the road. Lane prediction is an essential part of LDWSs. Sometimes there is an absence of lane markings on the road, or they are not clearly visible because the paint has worn off or there is occlusion due to heavy vehicle traffic on the road. In such cases, it is possible that the lane does not get detected on the road, and therefore, we propose to predict the lane [33] to enable the LDWS and the ADAS to continue working smoothly. We assumed that the lane was detected to a certain extent and further that because of occlusion or wear and tear, the lane was not clearly visible. Therefore, we used the information on the detected lane in the past and the presence of the vehicle in front to be able to predict the lane. For this purpose, we first did vehicle detection and tracking, which is described in following subsection.

6.3.2.1 Vehicle Detection

We detected the vehicle in parallel to the lane detection process by applying the YOLOv3 object detection method [1]. It is a fast and accurate technique to detect the objects in the frame, and also it is known as a one-stage object detector because it processes the full frame at once by applying the convolutional neural network to it instead of putting it in multiple locations. It divides the image into regions and applies logistic regression for predicting the bounding box and confidence for each region. YOLOv3 uses Darknet-53 custom deep learning 53-layer architecture, which is trained on ImageNet [35] database. In total, YOLOv3 contains a 106-convolutional-layer architecture that considers the inter-section over union (IOU) value as 0.5 and results in a mean average precision (MAP) on this value.

We trained the YOLOv3 model on one class—i.e., vehicle—using a transfer learning approach and a pretrained darknet53.conv.74 weight file for this purpose. We set the value of some parameters for training, such as the batch as 24, the subdivisions as 8, and the filters as 18. We annotated the images on vehicle class and trained the model for 500 epochs on a learning rate of 0.001. The trained model gave precision as 0.98, recall as 0.99, and f1-score as 0.98 on the threshold value of 0.85.

As the frame was captured, YOLOv3 detected all the vehicles with bounding boxes on them, as shown in Figure 6.3a. We extracted the vehicles using bounding box coordinates and got the relevant information that was needed for tracking the vehicles. Furthermore, the detected vehicles in the frame were tracked by our incremental clustering approach, which is explained in next step.

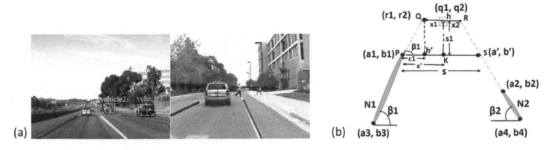

FIGURE 6.3   (a) Vehicle detection and tracking on LISA data set. (b) Geometrical structure of lanes and detected vehicle used for lane prediction. (Adapted from [33].) [See Ref. 36.]

6.3.2.2 Vehicle Tracking

We computed some parameters from the extracted vehicle in the vehicle detection step and tracked the vehicle using these parameters. We considered area, color, angle, centroid, and position of the vehicle as parameters to track the vehicle. We computed the distance between the centroid of the vehicle and the detected lane markings (section 6.3.1) present on the sides of the vehicle to determine the vehicle position as represented. The importance of the vehicle position lies in the fact that the vehicle should be tracked as the same vehicle even if it changes lanes.

The vehicle H_i^j represented the ith vehicle in j^{th} frame and had parameters like $\{T_i^j, E_i^j, S_i^j, C_i^j\}$, where orientation was represented as T_i^j, centroid as E_i^j, position as S_i^j, and color as C_i^j. The set $H^j = \{H_1^j, H_2^j, \ldots, H_n^j\}$ represented the vehicle detected in the jth frame—i.e., f_j—and was treated as the initial set of clusters. We took this initial set of clusters with the above-mentioned vehicle parameters into consideration as we performed the incremental clustering for vehicle tracking in the following manner.

$H^{j+1} = \{H_1^{j+1}, H_2^{j+1}, \ldots, H_n^{j+1}\}$ was the set of detected vehicles in frame f_{j+1}, and $\{T_i^{j+1}, E_i^{j+1}, S_i^{j+1}, C_i^{j+1}\}$ contained the parameters of a vehicle H_i^{j+1}. Now the color and position of vehicles H_i^j and H_i^{j+1} were matched, and if they matched, then the orientation and distance between these vehicles were computed. If this computation came under their threshold, then H_i^{j+1} became part of the cluster H_i^j. Otherwise, we performed the same procedure with other sets of clusters in frame f_j. We computed the distance between the vehicles using Euclidean distance, as shown in Equation 6.3.

$$d(E_i^j, E_i^{j+1}) = \sqrt{(b_1 - a_1)^2 + (b_2 - a_2)^2} \tag{6.3}$$

where $E_i^j = (a_1, b_1)$, $E_i^{j+1} = (a_2, b_2)$.

If H_i^{j+1} did not satisfy the threshold for any of the clusters present in frame f_j, it was put in new cluster H_{n+1}^{j+1} as its initial element.

We followed the same process for clustering the other vehicles in f_{j+1}, and in similar way, we clustered the vehicles for vehicle tracking within and across frames on the fly. The track of the vehicle was given by the centroid of the vehicle recently inserted in the cluster.

We computed the difference between the coordinates of detected lane markings and the centroid of the vehicle to continuously check if the vehicle was in the same lane or not. Also, our clustering technique made sure whether it was the same vehicle that had changed lanes or whether it was some other vehicle. In this way, our clustering-based vehicle tracking framework contributed in lane-changing scenarios.

6.3.2.3 Lane Prediction Using Vehicle Detection and Tracking

We performed lane prediction using the vehicle detection and tracking information along with the lanes detected in the past. The procedure for our lane prediction method is as follows.

In Figure 6.3b, we represented the detected lanes as N_1 and N_2, having their major axis coordinates as (a_1,b_1), (a_2,b_2) and (a_3,b_3), (a_4,b_4), respectively. The lanes have orientations β_1 and β_2. The tracked vehicle H, having the centroid as (q_1,q_2), was present in between the lanes N_1 and N_2. We wanted to find out the coordinates of points Q and R, which would be the starting points for further predicting lanes N_1 and N_2. For this purpose, we first computed the distances x_1 and x_2, which included computing the value of distance s and the coordinates of point $S(a', b')$.

We then performed some geometric computation for the above-mentioned parameters. As in Figure 6.3b, geometrically $b'=b_1$ and $a' = \dfrac{b_4 - b'}{\tan\beta_2}$; therefore, the distance $s = a' - a_1$. K represented the perpendicular point from H to the line between P and S; therefore, it had coordinates (q_1,b_1) or (q_1,b'), which further helped to compute the perpendicular distance $s_1 = b_1 - q_2$. In the region $PQHK$, distance c_1 was calculated as $\dfrac{s_1}{\tan\beta_1}$ and x' as $q_1 - a_1$. Finally, the distance x_1 gave the value as $x' - c_1 = x' - \dfrac{s_1}{\tan\beta_1}$. Similarly, the value of x_2 was computed.

Furthermore, the point $Q(r_1,r_2)$ was calculated as $r_1 = q_1 - x_1$ and $r_2 = q_2$, which acted as the starting point of the predicted lane with orientation β_1. This point was extended to the base of this frame, and the y-coordinate of the end point of the predicted lane was considered as the base point of the frame. The lane prediction result is shown in Figure 6.4.

(a) **(b)**

FIGURE 6.4 This dataset does not have lane markings in some places. We detected and predicted the lanes in (a), and on the basis of these predicted lanes, we predicted the lanes in (b), where there are no lane markings. (Adapted from [33].) [See Ref. 41.]

There can be more than one prediction for the lane due to the presence of more than one vehicle on both sides of a lane. We compared the predicted lanes with actual detected lanes for computing accuracy of the framework, and we show the results in the experimental section (section 6.4).

6.3.3 Lane Detection and Prediction-Based Path Planning

As the driver is driving, he needs to decide whether he wants to remain in same lane or to change lanes. Therefore, he needs to plan the path in real time. At a point in time, when the driver needs to decide whether to change lanes, our system is there to assist him. Based on the current traffic situation and detected/predicted lanes, it determines whether or not the driver can change lanes and plans the future path accordingly.

Our lane detection and prediction framework may provide static information on the real-time surrounding view, which can be helpful for path planning. We propose some points that explain various situations while performing lane changes.

a. *Left or right lane change:* While driving, if the driver wants to change lanes in the left or right direction, then the path-planning framework has to sense the surrounding situation and instruct the driver accordingly. This framework should first check whether or not the vehicle is in between the lanes by seeing the detected or predicted lanes on the road because it is necessary to drive the vehicle in correct lane to avoid accidents. Afterward, the framework should check the surrounding vehicle condition. As in Figure 6.5, the ego vehicle has no other vehicle to its immediate left, and there is enough distance (a safe distance is around 3 seconds distance, which allows time to react to any mishap) between the front and ego vehicles. Therefore, the path-planning framework should instruct the driver to move to the lane to the left, as shown in Figure 6.5. At the end of the lane change, the framework should again check the vehicle position and alert the driver about the same.

b. *Right lane change:* Similarly in Figure 6.6, the ego vehicle is trying to change to the lane to the right. Since there is a vehicle coming in on the right side, the

FIGURE 6.5 Left lane change scenario.

FIGURE 6.6   Right lane change scenario.

path-planning framework should get information about the incoming vehicle and sense the distance between the vehicles. Until the driver has a safe distance in which to change lanes with no vehicle to his immediate right, he should stay in the current lane. In Figure 6.6, the red vehicle is fairly far away from the ego vehicle. Therefore, it changes lanes in last frame.

c. *Left or right turn:* Left and right turns of the vehicle may involve lane change properties. The path-planning framework should start informing the driver 800 meters (a distance that mostly depends on traffic) before the upcoming turn needs to be made. It should sense the traffic on the road and accordingly should instruct the driver when to start moving the vehicle to the left or right in order to make the necessary turn. In Figure 6.7a, there is no vehicle to the left of the ego vehicle, and the front vehicle is a safe distance beyond the ego vehicle. Therefore, in this case the driver should change to the lane to the left and make a left turn. Similarly, the conditions are appropriate to move to the lane to the right and make a right turn in Figure 6.7b.

The above scenarios show clearly that information on the lane and surrounding vehicles can be helpful to the driver making decisions on the road, such as whether or not to make a lane change.

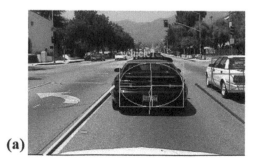
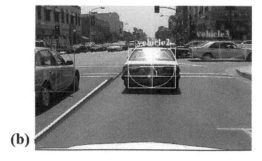

FIGURE 6.7   (a) Left turn scenario. (b) Right turn scenario.

6.4 EXPERIMENTAL RESULTS

We ran our experiments on an Intel Core i7-7500U CPU at 3GHz with 16GB RAM and NVIDIA GeForce GTX 1060 GPU. We performed lane detection and tracking on four internet downloaded videos—data set [34], data set [37], data set [38], and data set [39]—whereas the lane prediction was performed on two publicly available datasets—the Caltech data set [40] and LISA data set [36]—and one internet video data set [41]. The data sets and the performance of our framework are described below.

First, we describe the experiments done for lane detection one by one. We took real-time internet videos for this purpose. The first row of Figure 6.8 represents the lane detection results on data set [34], which consists of 250 frames of resolution 320 × 240 having

FIGURE 6.8 (a), (b), (c) and (d) represents lane detection on different datasets. Each color portrays a lane cluster. (Adapted from [32].) [see Ref. 34, 37, 38, 39.]

TABLE 6.1 Performance of Our STIC Algorithm

Data Sets	Total Frames	Correct Detection	Wrong Detection	False Detection	Processing Time (s)	Frames/ Second	Time/Frame (ms)
Data set [34]	250	244 (97.6%)	6 (2.4%)	0 (0%)	8	32	31.25
Data set [37]	403	394 (97.76%)	7 (1.73%)	2 (0.51%)	12	34	29.5
Data set [38]	550	541 (98.31%)	5 (0.90%)	4 (0.73%)	21	27	37.03
Data set [39]	995	977 (98.19%)	11 (1.10%)	7 (0.71%)	40	25	40

continuous lanes. The video of this data set contains a lot of sunlight and shadows in many places, which made the segmentation part challenging to perform. Our STIC algorithm was able to process this data set in 8 seconds, as shown in Table 6.1. Furthermore, data set [37] consists of 403 frames of size 320 × 240 having mostly low-contrast images and varying brightness in some frames. This also made the segmentation part hard to perform. The average speed of our framework for processing this data set was around 31 frames per second.

Data set [38] consists of dotted middle lanes and solid side lanes with 550 frames having resolution 320 × 240. For processing the middle lane of this data set, we used the history of past C contours. This data set resulted in very small and very large contours due to the presence of side guardrails, which made it challenging to extract the relevant objects from the frame.

When there were many noisy contours present in the frame, the resulting lanes sometimes deviated from the true lanes by a small margin.

Data set [39] is captured in an even illumination condition and has continuous lanes with 995 frames in total. The speed performance of our algorithm processes is shown in Table 6.1.

Table 6.1 represents overall performance of the lane detection task on the above-mentioned data sets. In this table, correct detection represents the detected lanes that map accurately over true lanes. If the detected lanes are not positioned over the marked lanes, then it results in a wrong detection. The false detection represents the scenario when an object other than a lane is detected as a lane.

Now we explain the experiments with our lane prediction framework on the Caltech data set [40], LISA data set [36] and data set [41]. The Caltech data set [40] is captured in various locations in Southern California with sunlight and shadows and has 526 images of vehicles with the resolution of 320 × 240 pixels. We annotated 350 images of the total frames for training the YOLOv3 model [1] and kept the rest of the images for testing purpose. YOLOv3 detects each vehicle in the form of bounding box coordinates. We extracted the vehicles using the coordinates for further tracking. We got 98.6% vehicle detection accuracy and processed the whole data set within 15 seconds, including the vehicle tracking and lane prediction. This data set changes the location very frequently, and therefore, a vehicle is not present in more than two frames. This resulted in a lot of new clusters of vehicles. We kept the information of few frames for vehicle tracking.

Figure 6.9 clearly shows the accurate results of lane prediction. which are very much similar to those for lane detection. We computed true positives, false positives, and false

FIGURE 6.9 Lane detection, prediction, vehicle detection and tracking, and lane prediction on the Caltech data set (a and b) and LISA data set (c and d). (a) The lane detection is shown by maroon and blue, whereas the lane prediction is shown by yellow and orange. (b) The lane detection is shown by maroon, yellow, and dark blue, whereas the lane prediction is shown by orange and sky blue. (c) The lane detection is shown by maroon and light yellow, whereas the multiple lane prediction is shown by yellow, green, orange, pink, and red. (b) The lane detection is shown by maroon and blue, whereas the multiple lane prediction is shown by orange, yellow, green, and violet. (Adapted from [33].) [see Ref. 36, 40.]

negatives to measure the performance of our coupled framework on lane prediction, as shown in Table 6.2. We compared our framework with Li et al. [20] by computing receiver operating characteristics (ROC) curves on the Caltech data set [40] and show the results in Figure 6.10. Li et al. [20] predicted the lanes using two neural networks and achieved area under the curve (AUC) as 0.96, whereas our framework resulted in an output of 0.98 AUC.

The LISA-Q Front FOV video data set [36] is a combination of three videos, labeled as dense, sunny, and urban and having 1,600, 300 and 300 frames, respectively. We trained

TABLE 6.2 The Performance of Our Framework on Vehicle Detection and Lane Prediction

Methods	Vehicle Detection Performance						Lane Prediction Performance		
	Caltech [40]		LISA [36]		Data Set [41]		Caltech [40]	LISA [36]	Data Set [41]
	Train	Test	Train	Test	Train	Test			
TP	99.6%	98.6%	98.5%	99.2%	98.7%	98.2%	98.9%	98.5%	98.8%
FN	0.12%	1.2%	1.3%	0.7%	0.5%	1.3%	-	-	-
FP	2.2%	1.9%	2.8%	1.6%	2.4%	2.1%	4.9%	5.5%	1.9%

Abbreviations: FN, False negative; FP, False positive; TP, True positive.

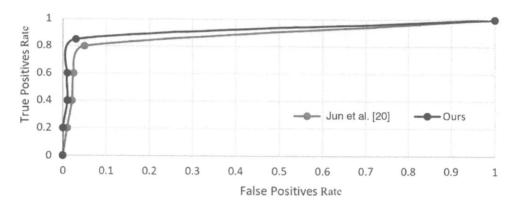

FIGURE 6.10   ROC curves for Li et al. and our framework. (Adapted from [33].) [see Ref. 20.]

the YOLOv3 model by annotating 1,600 images and kept the remaining images for testing purposes. The YOLOv3 model gave 99.2% vehicle detection accuracy. Our framework processed this data set for vehicle tracking and lane prediction within 20 seconds. The videos of this data set were captured in a consecutive manner, resulting in fewer clusters for vehicle tracking throughout the video. The lane prediction output of this data set is shown in Figure 6.9.

Furthermore, we processed data set [41], which is an internet video having a total of 2,000 frames, by selecting 1,200 frames to train the YOLOv3 model and keeping the rest for testing purposes. This data set has very light-colored lane markings, and still our framework predicted the lane accurately, as can be seen in Figure 6.4 (second row). YOLOv3 gave 98.3% vehicle detection accuracy on this data set.

6.5 CONCLUSION

In this chapter, we proposed an integrated framework for lane detection, prediction and path planning. We performed lane detection using the proposed STIC algorithm. In real time, there can be scenarios where lanes are not properly drawn on the road or may be very light in color. Then we need to predict the lanes in these scenarios. For this purpose, we performed vehicle detection using the YOLOv3 [1] object detection technique and tracked the vehicles by clustering them using some parameters. Furthermore, we used the vehicle tracking and lane detection information to predict the lanes. We achieved 98.9% accuracy in lane prediction. The experimental results clearly show the performance of our framework. At the end, we used the lane detection and prediction information to make some points regarding decision-making in path planning.

REFERENCES

1. https://pjreddie.com/darknet/yolo/.
2. Hasabnis, C., Dhaygude, S., and Ruikar, S. Real-Time Lane Detection for Autonomous Vehicle Using Video Processing. In S. Fong, N. Dey, and A. Joshi (eds.), ICT Analysis and Applications: Lecture Notes in Networks and Systems, vol. 93, Springer, 2020.
3. Wang, X., Qian, Y., Wang, C., and Yang, M. Map-Enhanced Ego-Lane Detection in the Missing Feature Scenarios. arXiv preprint, arXiv:2004.01101, 2020.

4. Lu, H., Ding, G., Tan, X., and Qin X. A Real-Time Multi-lane Detection Approach Using Features Geometric Uncertainty and Stereo Vision. In Proceedings of IEEE International Conference on Control and Robotics Engineering (ICCRE), pp. 202–206, 2020.
5. Ma, N., Pang, G., Shi, X., and Zhai, Y. An All-Weather Lane Detection System Based on Simulation Interaction Platform. IEEE Access, vol. 8, 2018.
6. Jiang, L., Li, J., and Ai, W. Lane Line Detection Optimization Algorithm Based on Improved Hough Transform and R-least Squares with Dual Removal. In Proceedings of IEEE Advanced Information Technology, Electronic and Automation Control Conference (IAEAC), vol. 1, pp. 186–190, 2019.
7. Wu, J., Xu, H., and Zhao, J. Automatic Lane Identification Using the Roadside LiDAR Sensors. IEEE Intelligent Transportation Systems Magazine, vol. 12, no. 1, 2020.
8. Yao, W., Zeng, Q., and Aioun, F. On-Road Vehicle Trajectory Collection and Scene-Based Lane Change Analysis: Part II. IEEE Transactions on Intelligent Transportation Systems, vol. 18, no. 1, pp. 206–220, 2017.
9. Satzoda, R. K., and Trivedi, M. M. Looking at Vehicles in the Night: Detection & Dynamics of Rear Lights. IEEE Transactions on Intelligent Transportation Systems, pp. 1–11, 2016.
10. Satzoda, R. K., and Trivedi, M. M. Multipart Vehicle Detection Using Symmetry-Derived Analysis and Active Learning. IEEE Transactions on Intelligent Transportation Systems, vol. 17, no. 4, pp. 926–937, 2016.
11. Satzoda, R. K., and Trivedi, M. M. Drive Analysis Using Vehicle Dynamics and Vision-Based Lane Semantics. IEEE Transactions on Intelligent Transportation Systems, vol. 16, no. 1, pp. 9–18, 2015.
12. Bar, E., and Trivedi, M. M. Learning to Detect Vehicles by Clustering Appearance Patterns. IEEE Transactions on Intelligent Transportation Systems, vol. 16, no. 5, pp. 2511–2521, 2015.
13. Chen, X., and Meng, Q. Robust Vehicle Tracking and Detection from UAVs. In Proceedings of International Conference of Soft Computing and Pattern Recognition (SoCPaR), pp. 241–246, 2015.
14. Kosaka, N., and Ohashi, G. Vision-Based Nighttime Vehicle Detection Using CenSurE and SVM. IEEE Transactions on Intelligent Transportation Systems, vol. 16, no. 5, pp. 2599–2608, 2015.
15. Tian, B., Li, Y., Li, B., and Wen, D. Rear-View Vehicle Detection and Tracking by Combining Multiple Parts for Complex Urban Surveillance. IEEE Transactions on Intelligent Transportation Systems, vol. 15, no. 2, pp. 597–606, 2014.
16. Kampker, A., Sefati, M., Rachman, A. S., Kreisköther, K., and Campoy, P. Towards Multi-object Detection and Tracking in Urban Scenario under Uncertainties, In VEHITS, pp. 156–167, 2018.
17. John, V., Liu, Z., and Kidono, K. Real-Time Road Surface and Semantic Lane Estimation Using Deep Features. Signal, Image and Video Processing, vol. 2, no. 6, pp. 1133–1140, 2018.
18. Gurghian, A., and Murali, V. N. DeepLanes: End-To-End Lane Position Estimation Using Deep Neural Networks, In Proceedings of IEEE Conference on Computer Vision and Pattern Recognition, pp. 38–45, 2016.
19. McCall, J. C., and Trivedi, M. M. Video-Based Lane Estimation and Tracking for Driver Assistance: Survey, System, and Evaluation. IEEE Transactions on Intelligent Transportation Systems, vol. 7, no. 1, 2006.
20. Li, J., Mei, X., and Tao, D. Deep Neural Network for Structural Prediction and Lane Detection in Traffic Scene. IEEE Transactions on Neural Networks and Learning Systems, vol. 28, no. 3, 2017.
21. Khairdoost, N., Shirpour, M., Bauer, M. A., and Beauchemin, S. S. Real-Time Maneuver Prediction Using LSTM. IEEE Transactions on Intelligent Vehicles, 2020.
22. Gilitschenski, I., Rosman, G., Gupta, A., Karaman, S., and Rus, D. Deep Context Maps: Agent Trajectory Prediction Using Location-Specific Latent Maps. IEEE Robotics and Automation Letters, 2020.

23. Messaoud, K., Deo, N., Trivedi, M. M., and Nashashibi, F. Multi-head Attention with Joint Agent-Map Representation for Trajectory Prediction in Autonomous Driving. arXiv preprint, arXiv:2005.02545, 2020.
24. Nakamura, A., Liu, Y. C., and Kim, B. Short-Term Multi-vehicle Trajectory Planning for Collision Avoidance. IEEE Transactions on Vehicular Technology, 2020.
25. Deo, N., Rangesh, A., and Trivedi, M. M. How Would Surround Vehicles Move? A Unified Framework for Maneuver Classification and Motion Prediction. IEEE Transactions on Intelligent Vehicles, vol. 3, no. 2, pp. 129–140, 2018.
26. Menner, M., Berntorp, K., Zeilinger, M. N., and Di Cairano, S. Inverse Learning for Data-Driven Calibration of Model-Based Statistical Path Planning. IEEE Transactions on Intelligent Vehicles, 2020.
27. Messaoud, K., Yahiaoui, I., Verroust, A., and Nashashibi, F. Attention Based Vehicle Trajectory Prediction. IEEE Transactions on Intelligent Vehicles, 2020.
28. Xu, T., Wen, C., Zhao, L., Liu, M., and Zhang, X. The Hybrid Model for Lane-Changing Detection at Freeway Off-Ramps Using Naturalistic Driving Trajectories. IEEE Access, vol. 7, pp. 103716–103726, 2019.
29. Baldi, S., Rosa, M. R., Frasca, P., and Kosmatopoulos, E. B. Platooning Merging Maneuvers in the Presence of Parametric Uncertainty. IFAC-PapersOnLine, vol. 51, no. 23, pp. 148–153, 2018.
30. Rachman, A. S., Idriz, A. F., Li, S., and Baldi, S. Real-Time Performance and Safety Validation of an Integrated Vehicle Dynamic Control Strategy. IFAC-PapersOnLine, vol. 50, no. 1, pp. 13854–13859, 2017.
31. Sefati, M., Chandiramani, J., Kreisköther, K., Kampker, A., and Baldi, S. Towards Tactical Behavior Planning under Uncertainties for Automated Vehicles in Urban Scenarios. In Proceedings of IEEE International Conference on Intelligent Transportation Systems (ITSC), pp. 1–7, 2017.
32. Gupta, A., and Choudhary, A. Real-Time Lane Detection Using Spatio-temporal Incremental Clustering, In Proceedings of IEEE International Conference on Intelligent Transportation Systems (ITSC), pp. 1–6, 2017.
33. Gupta A., and Choudhary, A. A Framework for Lane Prediction Based on Vehicle Detection and Tracking. In Proceedings of National Conference on Computer Vision, Pattern Recognition, Image Processing and Graphics (NCVPRIPG), 2019.
34. https://youtu.be/SqLdiPZgxw4.
35. http://www.image-net.org/.
36. Sivaraman, S., and Trivedi, M. M. A General Active Learning Framework for On road Vehicle Recognition and Tracking. IEEE Transactions on Intelligent Transportation Systems, vol. 11, no. 2, 2010.
37. https://youtu.be/V8X-WFExRf8.
38. https://www.youtube.com/watch?v=T6c0o7iR2u4.
39. https://youtu.be/IUMnutNRSlk.
40. Caltech computational vision Caltech 2001. [Online]. Available: http://www.vision.caltech.edu/html-files/archive.html.
41. https://www.youtube.com/watch?v=NS7ymLOPT-I.

CHAPTER 7

PRN-SORB-SLAM

A Parallelized Region Proposal Network-Based Swift ORB SLAM System for Stereo Vision-Based Local Path Planning

Kishorjit Nongmeikapam

Indian Institute of Information Technology
Heingang, India

Wahengbam Kanan Kumar

North Eastern Regional Institute of Science and Technology
Nirjuli, India

Aheibam Dinamani Singh

National Institute of Technology
Imphal, India

CONTENTS

DOI: 10.1201/9781003048381-8

In this chapter, a fast and efficient stereo vision–based simultaneous localization and mapping system that can be operated in real time is presented. The major takeaway is the significant reduction in the computational cost and the error in the resulting trajectory, which is realized via a new scheme of feature extraction cum matching technique between any two successive frames. The oriented BRIEF (ORB) descriptors does not vary with scale and rotation and result in highly reduced computational costs in comparison to popular feature extraction techniques. A parallelized region proposal network–based ORB feature extraction technique is proposed in which a significantly smaller number of bounding boxes are produced on the currently rectified stereo image and the next stereo frame for selective extraction of features and then matching. The use of a stereo image pair can provide better results than a monocular system for determining a trajectory while resulting in much less error. The region proposal network–based ORB visual odometry technique proposed here is quite quick in parsing through a stereo image pair data set consisting of 1,700 images in comparison to other popular feature extraction techniques. This setup promises a considerable reduction in cost against those systems that rely on LIDAR-based path planning.

7.1 INTRODUCTION

Simultaneous localization and mapping (SLAM) is capable of enabling mobile robots to make wise path-planning and navigation decisions. Over the past decade, a lot of concepts, ranging from SLAMs based on light detection and ranging (LIDAR) to monocular vision–based SLAMs, have been proposed by researchers worldwide. They have shown several state-of-the-art results that have enabled robots to navigate in their environment amidst various kinds of obstacles. However, several issues need addressing before deploying such algorithms for commercial usage. One key issue that researchers have identified is that the use of LIDAR technology is quite costly in comparison to those technologies that employ cameras. LIDAR-based SLAM algorithms have shown above-average state-of-the-art performance. While some of them have been employed in real-time applications, others have shown the inability to be integrated into the system due to high cost and complexity. Recently, the advent of monocular vision–based SLAM algorithms for path planning has shown great potential, since they result in much less cost in comparison to their LIDAR counterparts.

However, despite the immense cut in cost, several issues need to be addressed before vision-based SLAMs can be used for real-time path planning. For instance, classifying between static and dynamic objects can aid in understanding more about the surrounding. Localization is an operation performed by autonomous vehicles using a combination of different modules such as inertial sensing provided by accelerometers and gyroscopes and wheel odometry provided by joint encoders. Two issues here are that inertial sensors face drifting and wheels responsible for providing odometry tends to sink and slip. Some crucial factors to be remembered while developing a SLAM algorithm are as follows. Provision must be made for observing corresponding map points from among the subset of keyframes. An increase in the level of complexity is seen with the number of keyframes; however, it must not be at the cost of extracting redundant scene features or map points.

It is also essential that the corresponding features be spread well with significant parallax and that an abundant number of loop closure matches be present to provide a strong network configuration. For better nonlinear optimization, a good estimation of the initial number of keyframe poses and locations is essential. Finally, a local map and the ability to perform swift global optimization for closing loops in real time are also essential.

SLAM through the eyes of visual odometry (VO) is of two types: monocular VO (single camera) and stereo VO (two synchronized cameras). VO relies on a good level of feature extraction from the images in order to track them in sequential frames. This technique of tracking an ego vehicle using such a sequence of images is known as ego-motion estimation. An example that can be cited is the determination of the position of an ego car concerning the street signs or lanes in the road. It is quite important to determine the ego motion to facilitate autonomous navigation of robots or vehicles. It involves the use of either monocular or stereo VO with the sequence of images under consideration. Briefly speaking, features are extracted from two successive image frames to construct an optical flow. In case a stereo camera is used, the images derived from the left and right cameras are merged to form a single camera. The same process is carried out for the next frame-pair, after which the previously rectified and the currently rectified image frames are used together to develop an optical flow. The use of stereo vision has many advantages over monocular vision, including providing more information about depth and reducing error. The process of constructing optical flow require that features be detected in the first frame or image and then matched to features in the second image. Using the information about feature matching, optical flow is created. The optical flow field will highlight how feature descriptors tend to diverge from the focus of expansion. The focus of expansion, which is created gradually using many such successive image frames, indicates the direction along which the ego camera is moving and thereby provides an estimate of the overall path traversed.

Despite the evolution of monocular VO, certain crucial difficulties arise when using a single camera, and thus, stereo VO vastly outperforms it. Some challenges encountered by monocular VO are as follows. First, scale estimation through either object recognition or ground-plane estimation is challenging work filled with many uncertainties, since objects must be tracked over a longer period. Second, objects that are in dynamic motion pose a different kind of challenge in that many outliers can be introduced; these are inherently difficult to identify immediately and therefore tracks may need to be carefully maintained, which is time-consuming. Third, poor estimation of pose and measurements, which are quite noisy, necessitates the robustification of the triangulation and estimation procedure. Lastly, the construction of good-quality tracks relies on the ability of the monocular camera to perform the initial feature points estimation.

Recovering a global metric scale, on the other hand, by using a stereo VO system is quite easy, since it has a constant known baseline. In rare cases, however, the use of only local data may provide some anomalous vulnerability for deducing distances. It is relatively easier to identify moving objects, but they also face the same problem. Noisy frames, which may occur occasionally, usually present fewer problems, since the distance of objects can be triangulated once again after a couple of frames by estimating depths using the stereo camera. Another strong trait of the stereo vision system is that redundancy arising from field overlapping aids in stabilizing tracks. Therefore, several challenges faced by monocular systems in each frame are greatly reduced in the stereo VO system.

However, despite the challenges resolved by stereo VO, there are venues where monocular VO finds application. An advantage of stereo VO is that exact estimation of a trajectory is possible, while in the case of monocular VO accurate estimation is possible only up to a few scale factors. For instance, it can be said that an ego camera has moved by a meter in x, two units in y, and so on. Distance estimation using a stereo vision system gets converted to the monocular case when objects are faraway in comparison to the distance between the camera pair. For example, using a stereo camera system for a very small robot is quite useless; here using a single camera–based system is most likely the better option. A trend among enthusiasts nowadays is the use of monocular VO for developing smaller and smaller drones.

The contribution proposed in this chapter is discussed here. An ability to process a stereo image pair swiftly is made possible despite undergoing processes such as correlation, rectification, prefiltering, feature extraction and matching, and 3- point triangulation. The credit for this ability can be attributed chiefly to two factors: the use of a region proposal–type structure for selective extraction of features of an image and the use of oriented BRIEF (ORB) features, which is shown to be intrinsically fast in comparison to other feature extraction techniques. As a result, this chapter uses the term PRN-SORB, which is an abbreviation for parallelized region proposal network– based Swift ORB. Another important feature that works in close conjunction with the PRN-SORB is the use of a clique-based inliers detection technique for matching, which has yielded a good level of trajectory matching against the ground truth. This section is responsible for providing a complete trajectory. Therefore, it can be said that such type of VO or SLAM technique can be further upgraded for implementation in a real-time scenario. This kind of setup promises a considerable reduction in cost compared to those systems that rely on LIDAR-based path planning. This chapter is organized as follows. Following this introduction to VO, SLAM, and the strengths and weaknesses associated with both monocular and stereo vision setups, Section 7.2 presents a literature review. Section 7.3 described the proposed procedure, while Section 7.4 highlights the detailed implementation strategy employed and the results obtained. In conclusion, Section 7.5 highlights the contributions.

7.2 LITERATURE REVIEW

Several VO-based SLAM algorithms, which are based on either monocular vision or stereo vision, have been proposed by researchers. However, their techniques had serious limitations, as mentioned in the previous section. Nister et al. demonstrated and implemented a feature-based image motion tracking algorithm for estimating the trajectory of ground vehicles [1]. A stereo odometry technique was proposed by Matthies [2] that works by extracting and tracking features between sequential images. The technique after upgrading was outfitted into the JPL Mars Exploration Rover to serve as its VO system [3]. It is also being used in the Mars Science Lab [4]. Hirschmuller et al. proposed a stereo vision–based algorithm that relied on matching extracted features for detecting inliers [5]. The current work uses an inlier detection system for a faster and easier point-to-point inlier test scheme. Authors of [6] performed a survey of some techniques for recognizing places. Their study concluded that methods based on image appearance—i.e., those based on matching features between images—can be scaled up for larger environments than techniques based on image-to-map or map-to-map methods. The bag of visual words [7] can be cited as an example of the appearance-based technique. The probabilistic approach FAB-MAP [8], which is an adaptation of the bag of visual words, is well known for its higher efficiency. The technique DBoW2 [9] is another adaptation of the bag of visual words technique and uses features extracted using the BRIEF descriptors [10] and FAST feature descriptor [11]. These feature extractors have been proven to be faster by one order of magnitude in comparison to those bag of visual words approaches that use popular techniques such as SURF [12] and SIFT [13]. Even though VO techniques employing such handcrafted features have shown robustness and efficiency, they have two major deficiencies: i.e., their invariance toward scale and rotation. This inability limits estimation of in-plane trajectories and loop closure detection from similar viewpoints. A good variant of the BRIEF feature descriptor is the one that solves both issues of the ORB descriptor, which is also the chief component of the present work. These ORB binary features have shown to speed up matching in SLAM algorithms. To compute depth in an image, a technique such as the monocular SLAM must create a map, which is usually performed by tracking a known structure [14]. Using inverse depth parameterization [15], feature points that have the highest matching score must be extracted. Two instances of initializing features are as follows: (1) recovering the relative pose of the ego camera using the technique provided by Faugeras and Lustman [16] from a homography by assuming local scene planarity [17, 18] and (2) computing a matrix [19, 20] that models general and planar scenes using the five-point algorithm provided by the authors of [21]. However, neither of these techniques performs well under low parallax but instead encounters the twofold ambiguity solution issue when the extracted key points are close to the center of the camera [22].

Authors in [14, 15, 23, 24] used filtering-based techniques for performing VO or monocular SLAM in which map feature locations extracted using key points and the pose of the ego camera were jointly estimated. A drawback with such methods was the production of very little new information despite the greater power consumption they inherit intrinsically for processing adjacent frames. Instead of yielding meaningful information efficiently, they accumulated linearization errors. Better alternatives have been proposed by researchers in [17, 25] by estimating maps using only some selected number of frames. The operation was costly in terms of time but gave good optimization results. For the same computational cost, techniques that are based on keyframes are found to be more accurate [26]. In another state-of-the-art monocular SLAM technique proposed by Strasdat et al. [27], a GPU-implemented optical flow served as a front-end module. It was then followed by FAST feature descriptors extraction cum matching, along with a motion-only bundle adjustment. They implemented a sliding window–type bundle adjustment as the back end, in which pose graph optimization bearing similarity constraints was used for solving loop closures. The technique innately corrected the phenomenon of scale drift faced by monocular SLAM algorithms. Song et al. [28] proposed a technique that used

ORB feature descriptors with a back end that is based on a temporal sliding window–type bundle adjustment. To prevent the problem of monocular scale drift, the distance between the ground and the ego camera is already known beforehand. In comparison to all the above, the work by authors in [27] provided the most computationally effective solution by retaining only the keyframes that are nonredundant.

7.3 PROPOSED FRAMEWORK

A stereo vision–based VO SLAM system is proposed in this chapter. The novelty of the technique lies in the huge reduction in time to parse all the adjacent stereo image pairs and the close resemblance to the actual ground-truth trajectory while using the ORB features. The reduction in time is due to the extraction of features from only the pre-defined regions of both the current and the previous scene/frame, which shows parallel nature. Also, the use of ORB [29] feature descriptors for feature matching and subsequently detection of inlier points provides a greater number of good matches in comparison to the use of popular feature descriptors such as KAZE [30], BRIEF [10], and SURF [12].

The development of the proposed PRN-SORB-SLAM—i.e., parallelized region proposal network–based swift ORB SLAM—which utilizes a stereo-vision setup to project a trajectory for local path planning is elaborated in detail in this section. The implementation procedure, consisting of the values of certain parameters along with their results, is highlighted in Section 7.4.

7.3.1 Input

Unlike a monocular camera vision setup, which utilizes a single-image stream, the current technique requires the presence of two images. It has a left stream and a right stream originating from two stereo cameras mounted side by side, providing a wider view in comparison to its monocular counterpart. Let I_l^t and I_r^t denote the images captured by the left camera and right camera at time t. Similarly, I_l^{t+1} and I_r^{t+1} are the images obtained from the same camera setup at time $t + 1$.

7.3.2 Obtaining Depth Information from Stereo Images

The depth perception and formation of a fused image from a given stereo image pair work on the triangulation principle. The left and right cameras, which have projective optics, are placed side by side in order to overlap their fields of view at the desired object distance. An illustration of such a setup appears in Figure 7.1 to aid understanding. The two cameras capture the same scene but from different viewpoints, which results in a spatial mismatch at the right side or left side of the image tensor.

Every pixel in both images is connected to the corresponding camera's center of projection by two rays emanating through the 3D space. Two tasks must be completed in order to compute the 3D position or depth of the scene. Initially, it is determined if every pixel in the left image is present in the right image; in case every pixel is not identified in both images, then there is a disparity between the two image pairs (Figure 7.2). Then the place where each pixel in the left image resides in the right image is identified. Second,

FIGURE 7.1 A scene consisting of paper cones that is captured by a stereo imaging camera. The center of projection of each image can be seen. Rays from the tip of two cones being projected to both the left and the right camera images are also shown.

to compute the place of intersection of ray points associated with the pixels of the right and left cameras, the exact geometry of the cameras must be known. Therefore, before the stereo image undistortion, rectification, and other sequential processes unfold, the calibration process for computing geometry must be performed; this is done only once.

- *Calibration:* A calibration object, usually a planar plate having a chessboard-like black-and-white color pattern, is required to perform the stereo calibration process. The next step is to capture synchronous left and right image pairs by utilizing different patterns like orientation, position, and distances. The 3D poses of all the patterns that are observed in this process, along with the precise construction or model of the stereo setup, are then computed using the position of the black-and-white pattern's dots in pairs and their known locations on the calibration plate. The model of the stereo setup has information about the intrinsic parameters of each camera such as focal length, distortion, rotation, and shift between the left and right camera. The data obtained from the calibration process can be used for triangulating the pixels that are common to both the images and then gradually for recovering the 3D coordinates with respect to the camera.

FIGURE 7.2 A sample stereo image pair showing disparity. While the vertical lines remain the same, the feature matches along the horizontal lines.

- *Rectification:* In this process, the original images obtained from the left and right cameras are warped so that epipolar lines are properly aligned to the rows of the image. Though the process leading to the formation of the final or fused rectified image is quite long, it involves only two broad tasks: undistortion and rectification. The rectified left and right images can be thought of more as images that can be produced by a perfectly aligned perspective camera. Image distortion due to lens imperfectness is compensated for through the process of undistortion, using parameters obtained from the calibration process. On the other hand, rectification reduces the issues faced during the disparity map or stereo matching computation. After the process of undistortion and rectification, the epipolar lines are now aligned parallel to the rows of the image. Computation of an image disparity map is then undertaken by searching for matching blocks.

Triangulating image points requires that pixels common to both the left and the right images be identified. The simplest technique is to take a small patch from the left image and parse across the right image in a sliding window fashion to obtain the best match possible. However, parsing through patch by patch for every adjacent image would consume a tremendous amount of time. For instance, in Figure 7.1 the tip of the cone that is seen in the left image is also easily visible in the upper half or the right image. Intuitively, it is not necessary to look for the same tip in the bottom half of the right image. The geometrical arrangement of the two projective cameras is such that there is a constraint to search in a one-dimensional line parallel to the image rows in the right image, which is also called the epipolar line. The epipolar lines, even though straight, usually have different orientations across an image, which occurs when the camera sensors are neither identically oriented nor perfectly coplanar. To further increase the speed of such a correspondence search, the geometry of the camera obtained after calibration can be used and then interfaced with the perspective image transformation, keeping in mind that epipolar lines must be aligned with the image scanlines. This procedure is called rectification. Therefore, by looking at this scanline, the white cone's tip can be readily located on the right image.

- *Disparity Map Construction via Block Matching:* The pixels of the left image can be matched to their similar counterpart on the same scanline. However, matching on a pixel-by-pixel basis is not discriminative enough, so matching is usually performed by using masks or windows (e.g., 3×3 pixels) around each pixel and comparing them to all possible windows in the right image on the same row. Instead of searching over the entire row, the search is limited to a few pixels present on the left side of the x-coordinate of the left image pixel. This mode of searching is faster and constrains the depth range where image points can be triangulated. In case a unique and sufficiently good match is found, the association of the common pixels is stored in the form of an offset between the x-locations. The map constructed in this way is called the disparity map, and the technique is termed stereo matching, since only local spatial information present around a central pixel is utilized. A region is said to be sufficiently common between the left and right images when it is extremely different in comparison to another region of the same image pair. In this sense, the technique of local stereo matching suffers from the problem of accumulating repetitive or poor texture. A better technique that can also be considered is global stereo matching, which can exploit

FIGURE 7.3   A disparity map computed on frames from the KITTI VO data set.

neighboring spatial information. This technique, instead of simply matching patches between the stereo image pairs, determines the matches with the neighboring pixels to the left and right in one step. The global method considers that adjacent pixels have flat or similar depths and that the surfaces are smooth throughout. They therefore make use of a lesser amount of surface texture and hence deliver more precise results—specifically at boundaries. Despite this merit, an issue with the global stereo matching technique is its comparatively greater power consumption and complexity in implementation compared to that of the local stereo matching technique.

A brief process for determining disparity is described here. A pixel residing at a spatial position (x,y) can be perfectly matched to another pixel located in its stereo image counterpart at a position $(x + d,y)$. The location (x,y) on the disparity map now contains the information value d. The value of y remains the same, as the stereo images has now been rectified. Thus, the disparity for each pixel can be defined as $d = x_l - x_r$, where x_l and x_r are the x-coordinates of the left and right images, respectively. The sliding window protocol is used for computing disparities. An $n \times n$ window or mask is laid on top of every pixel on which their values are stored. The same $n \times n$ window is laid on top of the right image at precisely the same location and then moved horizontally until the sum of absolute differences (SAD) is minimized. The semiglobal block matching algorithm proposed by [31] is used in the current work. Figure 7.3 shows a disparity map constructed from the an image pair of the KITTI VO dataset.

7.3.3 Region Proposal

Computing feature descriptors from all over the vast expanse of an image in order to match two successive frames consumes time and results in a redundant number of features. To cut the time consumption, a region proposal–type architecture is proposed herein. The percentage of similarity between pixels in any two adjacent images is well over 80%, since generally more than 30 frames are captured per second by the camera. Suppose two adjacent images are considered, and for each image, the edge box [32] algorithm produces a finite number of proposals. The algorithm inevitably yields an enormous number of region proposals; however, since the level of similarity between any two adjacent images is quite high, it would be redundant to use many proposals for matching. Therefore, the number of regions proposed by the edge box algorithm is reduced to a very small number—i.e., less than or equal to 20 for the current work. Two conditions are set for selecting the 20 proposed boxes. (1) Initially, about 100 of the strongest boxes are proposed by setting the appropriate parameters of the edge box algorithm. The parameters used for the edge box algorithm are explained in Section 7.4. (2) From among the 100 boxes, the top 20 boxes are selected by setting a minimum threshold size equal to one-sixth of the image size under consideration. The next step is to match the 20 proposals from each of the two images to create 10 of the most similar pairs.

The edge box algorithm can make bounding box predictions using the structured forest technique [33], which generates an edge map from the input image. The generated maps are fed into the edge box algorithm to predict bounding boxes by considering the number of contours present inside a region of the generated edge map. In addition to the edge box algorithm, the authors proposed an objectness prediction score that uses the number of edges contained inside a box and subtracts the overlapping contours that are located at the boundary of box. Using 1,000 proposals, they achieved an object recall over 96% by setting a threshold value equal to 0.5.

7.3.4 Feature Detection

Among the main design themes of the proposed system is the use a single-feature extraction technique (i.e., ORB feature descriptors) for mapping and tracking, which are responsible for recognition of place by performing frame rate relocalization and loop detection. This process is quite efficient in that sense that the requirement for performing depth interpolation from recognition features is completely done away with. To implement the process in a real-time scenario, a critical requirement is the ability to perform feature extraction in under 33 ms per image and the ORB feature descriptor meets this requirement. This is quite contrary to popular feature descriptors such as SIFT (300 ms) [34], SURF (300 ms), and A-KAZE (100 ms). Other feature extractors such as BRIEF and LDB [35] are not invariant to rotation and hence should be avoided. Therefore, the only viable option for the current technique is to use ORB features, which are 256-bit descriptors with oriented multiscale FAST corners. This makes them quite fast for computing and matching procedures while at the same time they have significantly good invariance to viewpoints. This functionality has imparted a wide baseline for matching, thereby boosting accuracy.

An interesting thing noticed while moving the feature detector over the expanse of the image under consideration is that there is a high probability that rich or high-scoring features will be accumulated only in certain regions, whereas other regions may have fewer or absolutely no representations at all. Such a response is not appropriate for our algorithm because of our assumption that an image is truly static, which simply means that features must be recovered from all over the image. Therefore, the process of "bucketing" is employed, in which an image is divided into roughly 100×100 pixel grids, and a maximum of 20 features from these patches or grid are extracted, thereby maintaining uniformity during feature distribution.

7.3.5 Feature Description and Matching

The feature descriptors are fed into the KLT tracking algorithm so that it can look for matching corners in the next $t + 1$ frame. In other words, the corners present in the frame I^t are tracked in the next frame I^{t+1}. Let F^t and F^{t+1} denote the two sets of features detected in I^t and I^{t+1}, respectively. In the current work, feature detection is done in one frame and is matched or tracked in the next adjacent frame. Then the process of feature extraction in the next frame starts and again tracked in the next, and so on.

7.3.6 Triangulation of 3D Point Cloud

The 3D coordinates of all the points that make up the extracted features F^t and F^{t+1} are computed. These two sets of features are used with the left image, using their corresponding disparity value and the projection matrices of the left and right cameras P_1 and P_2. The initial step is to form the reprojection matrix Q by using information from projection matrices P_1 and P_2.

$$Q = \begin{bmatrix} 1 & 0 & 0 & -c_x \\ 0 & 1 & 0 & -c_y \\ 0 & 0 & 0 & -f \\ 0 & 0 & -1/T_x & 0 \end{bmatrix} \tag{7.1}$$

where

c_x = x-coordinate of the optical center of the left camera (in pixels)
c_y = y-coordinate of the optical center of the left camera (in pixels)
F = focal length of the first camera
T_x = x-coordinate of the right camera with respect to the first camera (in meters)

We use the following relation to obtain the 3D coordinates of every feature in F_i^t and F_i^{t+1}:

$$\begin{bmatrix} X \\ Y \\ Z \\ 1 \end{bmatrix} = Q \times \begin{bmatrix} x \\ y \\ d \\ 1 \end{bmatrix} \tag{7.2}$$

Let the set of point clouds obtained be referred to as W^t and W^{t+1}.

No matter the type of matching technique employed, the end product is always the relationship between pixels present in the right and left images, which is stored by the disparity map. The disparity map stores the difference or offset of pixels between the left and right images, which can be used with the computed or calibrated geometry of the camera to produce the actual 3D coordinates of each of the pixels. This type of conversion is termed reprojection. The point resulting from the intersection of the pair of rays emanating from the left and right pixels is called a point cloud, which is usually stored in the form of a three-channel image pixel to accommodate neighboring point clouds also.

7.3.7 The Inlier Detection Step

Contrary to other VO techniques where outliers are detected, the current work uses an inlier detection procedure. The scene is assumed to a rigid one, and thus, the time

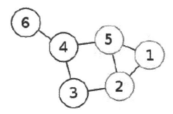

FIGURE 7.4   What a clique looks like.

instances t and $t + 1$ is also unchanged. This means that the distance between a pair of features located in the point cloud W^t is same as that between its corresponding points located in the point cloud W^{t+1}. A 3D triangulation error can also result when this distance is not similar; this occurs then one of the two features is mobile. A maximum set of consistency matrix M can be formed such that $M_{ij} = 1$ if the distance between points i and j in same in both point clouds; otherwise, $M_{ij} = 0$.

Now the largest subset from the original point clouds is selected in such a way that all the points conform with one another; i.e., each element in the resulting consistency matrix is reduced to 1. This is like the maximum clique problem, which has an adjacency matrix M. A clique is defined as a subset of a graph whose nodes are interconnected. The simplest way to understand a clique would be to view it as a graph whose nodes are persons in a social network and to be able to find a person, one has to know who his friends are. An example of a clique is given in Figure 7.4

A greedy heuristic is applied to render a clique that is very close to the optimal solution. It goes through the following procedure:

1. The node having the maximum degree is selected, and a clique is initialized to hold it.

2. The subset of nodes that are connected to all other nodes in the existing clique is determined.

3. From the subset so created, the node that is interconnected to the greatest number of nodes in the clique is selected. Finally, steps 2 and 3 are repeated until no new nodes can be added to the clique.

7.3.8 Computation of Rotational Matrix and Translation Vector

The Levenberg-Marquardt nonlinear least squares minimization process is used to minimize the reprojection error, which is used to determine the translation vector (t) and rotational matrix (R).

$$\varepsilon = \sum_{F^t, F^{t+1}} \left(j_t - PTw_{t+1} \right)^2 + \left(j_{t+1} - PT^{-1}w_t \right)^2 \tag{7.3}$$

where

ε = reprojection error
F_i^t, F_i^{t+1} = features in the left image at times t and $t + 1$
j_t, j_{t+1} = 2D homogenous coordinates of the features F_i^t, F_i^{t+1}

w_t, w_{t+1} = 3D homogeneous coordinates of the features F_i^t, F_i^{t+1}
$P = 3 \times 4$ projection matrix of left camera
$T = 4 \times 4$ homogenous transformation matrix

The deduced values of R and t are considered valid when these two conditions are satisfied: first, the minimum number of features present in the clique is 8; and second, ε is less than a predefined threshold. Adding these constraints reduces noise in the data.

7.4 EXPERIMENTAL EVALUATION

Our system has been validated extensively by means of a visual assessment data set from KITTI, which comprises 1,700 stereo images. The size of each image is 1241×376. Our system runs on a Core i-7700HQ CPU with 16GB RAM and NVIDIA GTX 1050Ti GPU. Figures 7.5 and 7.6 illustrate the process taking place, starting with the image input from each stereo camera and continuing up to the feature-matching stage between two successive frames. Figures 7.5a and 7.6a are the sample adjacent images captured by the right camera, while Figures 7.5b and 7.6b are those of left camera.

The next move is to gradually rectify the stereo image. The downloaded data set contains the stereo calibration parameter required to correct both images. To assess and rebuild the 3D point cloud, the cameras on the left and the right have to be corrected. Row-aligned and horizontally epipolar lines have corrected images. This promotes the measurement of inequality by reducing the quest field for matches to one dimension. Corrected images also can be combined in an anaglyph, using red/cyan stereo glasses to see the 3D effect. The color-composite monitor displays the distinct pixels in both images in Figure 7.5c and 7.6c. The left image shows the color contrast between red and cyan in the left image. There is an apparent offset between the images in orientation and location. It is intended that the images be translated so that they appear in the same rows in all images. The rectification process must create a set of points that correspond between the two images. In order to create these correspondences, we gather interest points in both images and choose potential matches between them. The SURF feature descriptor is used for this role, describing the blob-like functions for the left and right photos. In Figures 7.5d and 7.6d, the position and scale of the 30 SURFs are illustrated in the right image. In Figures 7.5e and 7.6e are the 30 SURFs in the left image. It should be remembered that not every identified feature can be compared, either because the two pictures were not detected or because a camera movement did not identify those pictures. The left and right photos are compared functionally to render a plausible point fit. SAD is used to classify the indexes of corresponding functions. The putative matches display the points at the top of the composite image, mixing the stereo images, in Figures 7.5f and 7.6f. Notice that most matches are correct, but there are also some outliers.

Epipolar limits must be reached by the points appropriately paired. This means that the required line of epipolarity must be an object. The Random Sample Consensus (RANSAC) algorithm is used to estimate the key matrix and inliers that satisfy the epipolar restriction by defining 10,000 parameters, a 0.1 distance threshold, and 99.99% confidence. In corrected stereo images, a pair of matching dots can be put on the same pixel axis. The next move is to calculate the projective shifts from right and left. The undistorted and rectified versions

FIGURE 7.5 The stereo image rectification procedure for image pair 1. (a) Image obtained by right camera, (b) image obtained by left camera, (c) composite image (left image is red; right image is cyan), (d) 30 strongest SURF features in the right image.

FIGURE 7.5 *(Continued)* (e) 30 strongest SURF features in the left image, (f) putatively matched points, (g) inlier points, (h) disparity map.

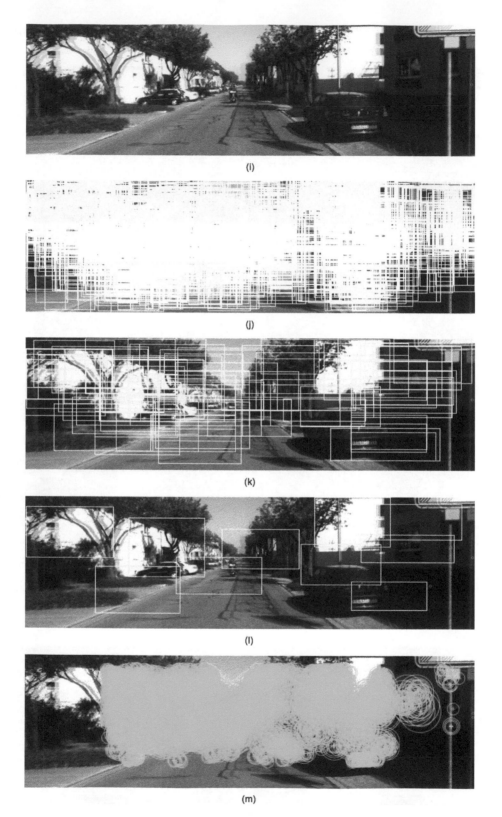

FIGURE 7.5 (i) rectified stereo image (left image is red; right image is cyan), (j) initial proposals using edge box algorithm, (k) selection of top 80 bounding boxes, (l) retention of top scoring bounding boxes, and (m) selection of strongest ORB features.

FIGURE 7.6 The stereo image rectification procedure for image pair 2. (a) Image obtained by right camera, (b) image obtained by left camera, (c) composite image (left image is red; right image is cyan), (d) 30 strongest SURF features in the right image.

(e)

(f)

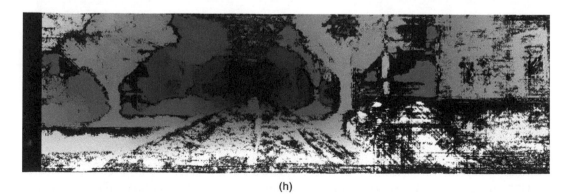

(g)

(h)

FIGURE 7.6   (e) 30 strongest SURF features in the left image, (f) putatively matched points, (g) inlier points, (h) disparity map.

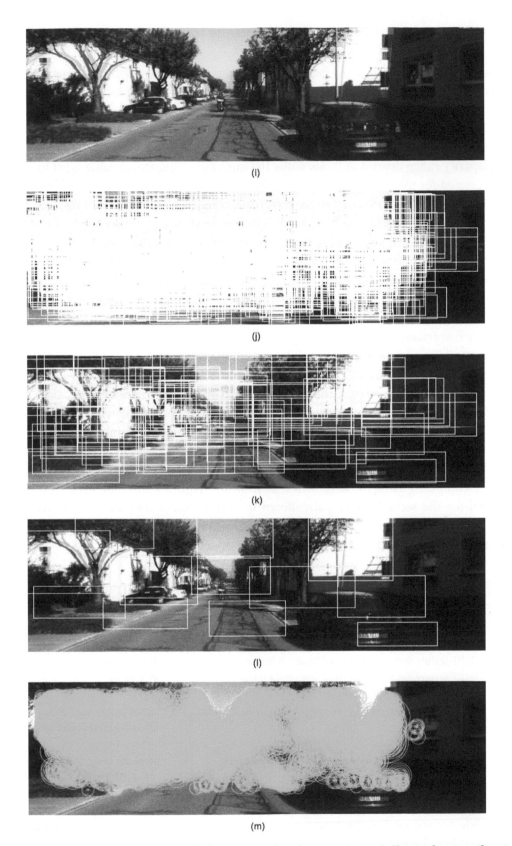

FIGURE 7.6 (i) rectified stereo image (left image is red; right image is cyan), (j) initial proposals using edge box algorithm, (k) selection of top 80 bounding boxes, (l) retention of top scoring bounding boxes, and (m) selection of strongest ORB features.

of the left and right images are measured using the calculated projective transformations. Corrected stereo images are then used to create the 3D scene reconstruction disparity diagram. The distance to the respective pixel on the right image for each pixel in the left image is called the difference and is commensurate with the distance from the camera to the corresponding point of the planet. The difference map is determined by seminal matching, with the disparity range defined as 0–48, while the minimum uniqueness value is set to 20. The maps created for the two image pairs are Figures 7.5h and 7.6h. The disparity chart is now used to create the final corrected stereo picture pair version, as shown in Figures 7.5i and 7.6i.

To speed up the task of matching features between two adjacent scenes or frames located in the trajectory, ORB feature descriptors are computed over some selected regions instead of deriving features from all over the image. This process is explained in detail here. Initially, the edge box algorithm is used on the rectified images shown in Figures 7.5i and 7.6i to compute bounding box proposals. The parameters alpha, beta, and minimum score of the edge box algorithm are set to 0.65, 0.75, and 0.1, respectively, after which 2,000 bounding boxes each are obtained. The bounding boxes are overlaid on the rectified images, as shown in Figures 7.5j and 7.6j. The proposed bounding boxes are arranged in descending order of their score, after which a selection criterion is used. The top 80 bounding boxes whose size is greater than one-sixth of the number of rows and columns are retained. Figures 7.5k and 7.6k show the top 80 bounding boxes for the two scenes under consideration. Then, by maintaining an overlap threshold value equal to 0.1, the best-performing bounding boxes are further selected. This process results in the retention of around 10 boxes for the first image pair under consideration, shown in Figure 7.5l. A total of 6,711 ORB feature descriptors are computed using these 10 boxes, as shown in Figure 7.5m. Similarly, 12 boxes are retained for the second image pair, shown in Figure 7.6l. A total of 8,236 ORB feature descriptors are computed using these 12 boxes, as shown in Figure 7.6m. Table 7.1 shows a summary of the techniques and parameters mentioned above.

TABLE 7.1 Summarized Computational Analysis of Techniques, Parameters, and Results for Deriving ORB Features from the Stereo Image Pair in Figure 7.5

Step	Description	Parameters
1	Stereo image rectification	
2	SURF feature descriptors derived from left image	30 features
3	SURF feature descriptors derived from right image	30 features
4	Matching features descriptors	
5	Fundamental matrix and inlier computation using RANSAC algorithm	10,000 parameters, distance threshold 0.1, confidence 99.99%
6	Matching inlier points	
7	Disparity map construction using self-global matching	Disparity range 0–48, minimum uniqueness 20
8	Rectified stereo image	
9	Region proposal using edge box algorithm on the rectified image	Produced 2,000 bounding boxes
10	Selection of top 80 bounding boxes.	80 bounding boxes selected
11	Selection of best regions using threshold overlap value of 10%.	10 bounding boxes retained
12	Computation of ORB feature descriptors from these 10 boxes.	Total 6,711 features

FIGURE 7.7 Matched features between image pair 1 and image pair 2.

The ORB feature descriptors extracted from rectified image 1 and rectified image 2 are now matched, resulting in a total of 755 matches. Figure 7.7 shows the putatively matched ORB features. Similarly, for every adjacent frame, the above activities are performed, followed by feature tracking, triangulation of the 3D point cloud, and inlier detection. This process of ego camera tracking is followed for every frame, and the results are updated to create the complete trajectory, as shown in Figure 7.8. The trajectory achieved using the

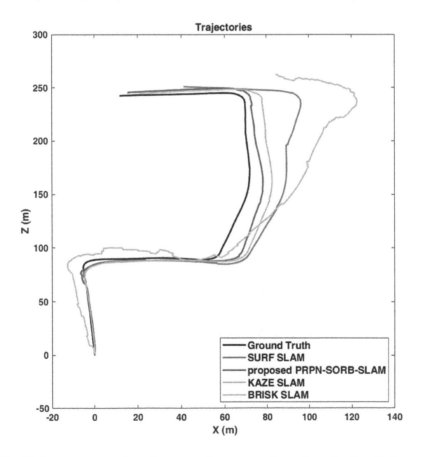

FIGURE 7.8 Trajectory comparison between the proposed result and other feature extraction techniques.

TABLE 7.2   Comparative Performance of Various Types of Feature Descriptors (Best Values Indicated in Bold)

Parameter	SURF	BRISK	KAZE	Proposed ORB
Time consumption (s)	155.3	259.541	639.24	**85.43**
Error in trajectory	24.9195	34.2625	15.6352	**11.4055**

proposed SLAM technique (dark blue) is plotted for comparison with the ground truth, which is shown in black. In addition to the ORB features, other popular feature descriptors such as SURF, KAZE, and BRIEF were also implemented to check their trajectories against the ground-truth trajectory. The use of ORB features as the core extractor of the proposed VO technique results in the trajectory that most resembles that of the ground truth. From Table 7.2, the error due to the use of ORB features is just 11.4055, which shows better performance than all the three techniques. The use of ORB features also shows the lowest overall time consumption, requiring just 85.43 seconds to parse all of the 1,700 image pairs.

7.5 CONCLUSION

Some features of the current approach worth emphasizing are as follows. First, the algorithm runs very quickly, as it has stereo-vision processing abilities such as correlation, rectification, and prefiltering. Also, the use of the region proposal network for selective extraction of ORB features further speeds up operation in comparison to those algorithms where extraction is carried out from the complete image area. Table 7.2 shows that the use of ORB features yields the lowest time consumption, just 85.43 seconds for 1,700 frames. Second, to select a good number of high-quality matches, inliers are detected instead of rejecting outliers. The clique-based technique also works well for frames having around 90% outliers, which would have added complexities to the RANSAC-style techniques. Third, the technique is subjected to strong validation checks that safeguard it against immediate or unanticipated failures. The clique inlier threshold, reprojection error, size of feature descriptor, and minimum number of features are the key parameters that drive the algorithm. It is also good that these parameters do not exhibit a high level of sensitivity, and one can determine values that can result in comparatively more unreported failures. The run time of the algorithm, which starts at the initial frame and continues up to the 1,700th frame, is mainly driven by the proposed feature-extraction scheme and the type of extractor used. The trajectory is tracked and updated continuously, using two adjacent frames, until the overall trajectory of the ego camera is computed through successive integration of the homogenous transformation matrix. At a higher frame rate, this limitation can decrease accuracy. A solution, however, is to make use of bundle adjustment. However, it uses a sliding window that results in a high latency, as the estimated pose is updated only when the window leaves the frame.

Therefore, through the current work, a new stereo SLAM algorithm that uses a parallel region proposal type of feature-extraction technique is illustrated and evaluated using the KITTI odometry evaluation data set. The low latency and error demonstrated using PRN-SORB features show that this technique can effectively process outdoor scenes. ORB features can also provide a sufficient number of good matches for recognizing places until there is a severe change in viewpoint. Also, they are quite fast in extracting, matching, and tracking between adjacent scenes, and there is no requirement for using parallel computing or accelerating using a GPU.

ACKNOWLEDGMENT

This work is supported by a grant from the Ministry of Electronics and Information Technology (MeitY), Government of India, vide reference no. 4(6)/2018-ITEA.

REFERENCES

1. Nister, David, Oleg Naroditsky, and James Bergen. 2006. "Visual Odometry for Ground Vehicle Applications." Journal of Field Robotics. https://doi.org/10.1002/rob.20103.
2. Matthies, L. 1989. Dynamic Stereo Vision. PhD thesis, Dept. of Computer Science, Carnegie Mellon University. CMU-CS-89-195.
3. Maimone, Mark, Yang Cheng, and Larry Matthies. 2007. "Two Years of Visual Odometry on the Mars Exploration Rovers." Journal of Field Robotics. https://doi.org/10.1002/rob.20184.
4. Johnson, Andrew E., Steven B. Goldberg, Yang Cheng, and Larry H. Matthies. 2008. "Robust and Efficient Stereo Feature Tracking for Visual Odometry." In Proceedings—IEEE International Conference on Robotics and Automation. https://doi.org/10.1109/ROBOT.2008.4543184.
5. Hirschmuller, Heiko, Peter R. Innocent, and Jon M. Garibaldi. 2002. "Fast, Unconstrained Camera Motion Estimation from Stereo without Tracking and Robust Statistics." In Proceedings of the 7th International Conference on Control, Automation, Robotics and Vision, ICARCV 2002. https://doi.org/10.1109/icarcv.2002.1238577.
6. Williams, Brian, Mark Cummins, Joste Neira, Paul Newman, Ian Reid, and Juan Tardos. 2009. "A Comparison of Loop Closing Techniques in Monocular SLAM." Robotics and Autonomous Systems. https://doi.org/10.1016/j.robot.2009.06.010.
7. Nister, David, and Henrik Stewtenius. 2006. "Scalable Recognition with a Vocabulary Tree." In Proceedings of the IEEE Computer Society Conference on Computer Vision and Pattern Recognition. https://doi.org/10.1109/CVPR.2006.264.
8. Cummins, Mark, and Paul Newman. 2011. "Appearance-Only SLAM at Large Scale with FAB-MAP 2.0." International Journal of Robotics Research. https://doi.org/10.1177/0278364910385483.
9. Gtalvez-Ltopez, Dorian, and Juan D. Tardos. 2012. "Bags of Binary Words for Fast Place Recognition in Image Sequences." IEEE Transactions on Robotics. https://doi.org/10.1109/TRO.2012.2197158.
10. Calonder, Michael, Vincent Lepetit, Christoph Strecha, and Pascal Fua. 2010. "BRIEF: Binary Robust Independent Elementary Features." In Lecture Notes in Computer Science (Including Subseries Lecture Notes in Artificial Intelligence and Lecture Notes in Bioinformatics). https://doi.org/10.1007/978-3-642-15561-1_56.
11. Rosten, Edward, and Tom Drummond. 2006. "Machine Learning for High-Speed Corner Detection." In Lecture Notes in Computer Science (Including Subseries Lecture Notes in Artificial Intelligence and Lecture Notes in Bioinformatics). https://doi.org/10.1007/11744023_34.
12. Bay, Herbert, Andreas Ess, Tinne Tuytelaars, and Luc Van Gool. 2008. "Speeded-Up Robust Features (SURF)." Computer Vision and Image Understanding. https://doi.org/10.1016/j.cviu.2007.09.014.
13. Lowe, David G. 2004. "Distinctive Image Features from Scale-Invariant Keypoints." International Journal of Computer Vision. https://doi.org/10.1023/B:VISI.0000029664.99615.94.

14. Davison, Andrew J., Ian D. Reid, Nicholas D. Molton, and Olivier Stasse. 2007. "MonoSLAM: Real-Time Single Camera SLAM." IEEE Transactions on Pattern Analysis and Machine Intelligence. https://doi.org/10.1109/TPAMI.2007.1049.

15. Civera, Javier, Andrew J. Davison, and J. M. Martínez Montiel. 2008. "Inverse Depth Parametrization for Monocular SLAM." IEEE Transactions on Robotics. https://doi.org/10.1109/TRO.2008.2003276.

16. Faugeras, O. D., and F. Lustman. 1988. "Motion and Structure from Motion in a Piecewise Planar Environment." International Journal of Pattern Recognition and Artificial Intelligence. https://doi.org/10.1142/s0218001488000285.

17. Klein, Georg, and David Murray. 2007. "Parallel Tracking and Mapping for Small AR Workspaces." In 2007 6th IEEE and ACM International Symposium on Mixed and Augmented Reality, ISMAR. https://doi.org/10.1109/ISMAR.2007.4538852.

18. Forster, Christian, Matia Pizzoli, and Davide Scaramuzza. 2014. "SVO: Fast Semi-Direct Monocular Visual Odometry." In Proceedings—IEEE International Conference on Robotics and Automation. https://doi.org/10.1109/ICRA.2014.6906584.

19. Tan, Wei, Haomin Liu, Zilong Dong, Guofeng Zhang, and Hujun Bao. 2013. "Robust Monocular SLAM in Dynamic Environments." In 2013 IEEE International Symposium on Mixed and Augmented Reality, ISMAR 2013. https://doi.org/10.1109/ISMAR.2013.6671781.

20. Lim, Hyon, Jongwoo Lim, and H. Jin Kim. 2014. "Real-Time 6-DOF Monocular Visual SLAM in a Large-Scale Environment." In Proceedings—IEEE International Conference on Robotics and Automation. https://doi.org/10.1109/ICRA.2014.6907055.

21. Nister, David. 2004. "An Efficient Solution to the Five-Point Relative Pose Problem." IEEE Transactions on Pattern Analysis and Machine Intelligence. https://doi.org/10.1109/TPAMI.2004.17.

22. Longuet-Higgins, Hugh Christopher. 1986. "The Reconstruction of a Plane Surface from Two Perspective Projections." Proceedings of the Royal Society of London. Series B. Biological Sciences 227, no. 1249, 399–410.

23. Chiuso, Alessandro, Paolo Favaro, Hailin Jin, and Stefano Soatto. 2002. "Structure from Motion Causally Integrated over Time." IEEE Transactions on Pattern Analysis and Machine Intelligence. https://doi.org/10.1109/34.993559.

24. Eade, Ethan, and Tom Drummond. 2006. "Scalable Monocular SLAM." In Proceedings of the IEEE Computer Society Conference on Computer Vision and Pattern Recognition. https://doi.org/10.1109/CVPR.2006.263.

25. Mouragnon, E., M. Lhuillier, M. Dhome, F. Dekeyser, and P. Sayd. 2006. "Real Time Localization and 3D Reconstruction." In Proceedings of the IEEE Computer Society Conference on Computer Vision and Pattern Recognition. https://doi.org/10.1109/CVPR.2006.236.

26. Strasdat, Hauke, J. M. M. Montiel, and Andrew J. Davison. 2012. "Visual SLAM: Why Filter?" Image and Vision Computing. https://doi.org/10.1016/j.imavis.2012.02.009.

27. Strasdat, Hauke, J. M. M. Montiel, and Andrew J. Davison. 2011. "Scale Drift-Aware Large Scale Monocular SLAM." In Robotics: Science and Systems. Robotics: Science and Systems VI, 2, no. 3, 7.

28. Song, Shiyu, Manmohan Chandraker, and Clark C. Guest. 2013. "Parallel, Real-Time Monocular Visual Odometry." In Proceedings—IEEE International Conference on Robotics and Automation. https://doi.org/10.1109/ICRA.2013.6631246.

29. Rublee, Ethan, Vincent Rabaud, Kurt Konolige, and Gary Bradski. 2011. "ORB: An Efficient Alternative to SIFT or SURF." In Proceedings of the IEEE International Conference on Computer Vision. https://doi.org/10.1109/ICCV.2011.6126544.

30. Alcantarilla, Pablo F., Jesus Nuevo, and Adrien Bartoli. 2013. "Fast Explicit Diffusion for Accelerated Features in Nonlinear Scale Spaces." In BMVC 2013—Electronic Proceedings of the British Machine Vision Conference 2013. https://doi.org/10.5244/C.27.13.

31. Birchfield, Stan, and Carlo Tomasi. 1999. "Depth Discontinuities by Pixel-to-Pixel Stereo." International Journal of Computer Vision. https://doi.org/10.1023/A:1008160311296.
32. Zitnick, C. Lawrence, and Piotr Dollar. 2014. "Edge Boxes: Locating Object Proposals from Edges." In Lecture Notes in Computer Science (Including Subseries Lecture Notes in Artificial Intelligence and Lecture Notes in Bioinformatics). https://doi.org/10.1007/978-3-319-10602-1_26.
33. Dollar, Piotr, and C. Lawrence Zitnick. 2013. "Structured Forests for Fast Edge Detection." In Proceedings of the IEEE International Conference on Computer Vision. https://doi.org/10.1109/ICCV.2013.231.
34. Lowe, David G. 2004. "Distinctive Image Features from Scale-Invariant Keypoints." International Journal of Computer Vision. https://doi.org/10.1023/B:VISI.0000029664.99615.94.
35. Yang, Xin, and Kwang Ting Cheng. 2012. "LDB: An Ultra-Fast Feature for Scalable Augmented Reality on Mobile Devices." In ISMAR 2012—11th IEEE International Symposium on Mixed and Augmented Reality 2012, Science and Technology Papers. https://doi.org/10.1109/ISMAR.2012.6402537.

Ontology-Based Indoor Domain Model Representation and Reasoning for Robot Path Planning Using ROS

Gayathri Rajendran, Uma Vijayasundaram, and Bettina O'Brien

Pondicherry University
Puducherry, India

CONTENTS

DOI: 10.1201/9781003048381-9

8.1 INTRODUCTION

Artificial intelligence (AI) has become one of the emerging technologies in the field of path planning. Path planning deals with the problem of sequential planning to provide an optimal path for a robot in complex and uncertain environments (Moon & Lee, 2019). Robotics can be used as a common method to overcome diverse obstacles in the real world like natural disasters, man-made disasters, earthquakes, tsunamis, volcanoes, and transportation problems.

For example, in pandemic situations (2019–2020), robots are utilized in many scenarios and act like humans. During this period, humanoid robots are providing requirements such as sanitizer, foods, and medicines to the patients in hospitals. UVD Robot is used to decontaminate surfaces by spraying disinfectant in an autonomous mode and thereby protects persons, objects, vehicles, etc. Robots help clean the house (i.e., objects, windows, and floors), spray disinfectant in residential areas, support quarantined patients, and help people overcome the pandemic situations. Also, we can add constraints (e.g., an 8-feet distance) in human-robot interaction during communication, serving, manipulation tasks, etc.

The most challenging tasks are planning the paths and predicting the obstacles in uncertain environments. To be able to manage all the possible obstacles and to be dynamic, the robot needs to know the environmental scenarios in which it has to navigate. So representing knowledge of an entire domain is essential for performing efficient robot navigation (Gayathri & Uma, 2018). But representing and providing knowledge of a whole domain knowledge is a challenge in robotic navigation. This chapter explains an approach to this aspect that enables efficient path planning. Knowledge representation and reasoning has played a vital role in AI systems. Ontology, a knowledge base, provides complete domain knowledge that can be represented efficiently using ontology languages such OWL-DL

(Gayathri & Uma, 2019a), OWL-Lite, and OWL-Full. Section 8.2 explains in detail this knowledge representation and reasoning.

Traditional navigation mapping approaches include metric, topological, and semantic maps (Kuric, Bulej, Saga & Pokorny, 2017). To efficiently plan the optimal path, a robot requires semantic information on the domain in which semantic labels are interconnected. Hence, a mobile robot includes semantic information that leads to semantic navigation (Crespo, Barber & Mozos, 2017). The idea of semantic navigation is to decompose the environment into different regions, thus helping a robot to navigate toward the goal while passing through the obstacles on the map.

Generally, the ontology-based model is used for representing the domain knowledge, and the sampling-based algorithm is used for effective path planning (Yang, Qi, Song, Xiao, Han & Xia, 2016). To improve the contextual awareness of mobile robots during semantic navigation, in this chapter we propose a three-layer perceptive autonomous navigation framework based on ontology (representation and reasoning), an action planner (i.e., a planning domain and definition language, or PDDL, planner), and motion-planning algorithms (i.e., sampling-based algorithms). The system architecture used in our approach is shown in Figure 8.1.

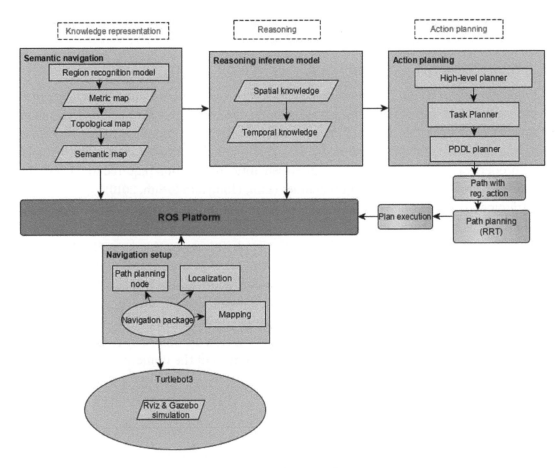

FIGURE 8.1   Perceptive autonomous navigation framework.

This chapter provides a comprehensive explanation of the following. Domain modeling is covered in Section 8.2. This section explains how a robot can recognize places such as rooms with different objects in regions using ontology. The reasoning inference model is used to improve the contextual awareness of mobile robots based on spatiotemporal properties. Spatiotemporal data is the key information in the field of robotics, as it improves the intelligence of mobile robots during navigation. The inherent time and space properties of spatiotemporal data are identified using the contextual information in domain knowledge. The contextual information helps to enhance planning efficiency and to increase the massive intelligence of robots through spatiotemporal reasoning. This is explained in Section 8.3. The possible actions generated using the temporal domain knowledge, when augmented with the PDDL planner, help the robot to move toward the target node and to find the optimal path with minimum computational time by using sampling-based algorithms. This is explained in Section 8.4. The fourth section also explains the rapidly exploring random tree (RRT) algorithm. Moreover, the indoor environment can be designed and simulated in the Robot Operating System (ROS) using Gazebo and Rviz simulators. The special features of simulators and packages and the details about the graphical interface are given in Section 8.5. This chapter also provides details about the experiment conducted and the results obtained. Thus, this chapter provides a comprehensive account of ontology-based semantic knowledge representation and reasoning, the PDDL planner, the RRT algorithm, and simulators.

8.2 ONTOLOGY-BASED DOMAIN KNOWLEDGE REPRESENTATION

Ontology is used to create hierarchical concepts with geometrical features. Ontology provides explicit and implicit semantic knowledge and involves applying reasoning techniques that enable the derivation of new information from existing relations. Ontology allows the sharing and reuse of domain knowledge and enables the definition of classes, individuals, and properties (relations) with the enhanced semantic information required to retrieve the contextual concepts in a meaningful manner (Lim, Hong Suh & Suh, 2010).

Ontology is increasingly used for representing domain knowledge in various applications such as path planning, diagnosis, search and rescue, and object manipulation. The ontology-based domain model infers the implicit information by performing reasoning on the relations that are specified in the form of logical facts (Sun, Zhang & Chen, 2019). Generally, the ontology-based domain model is used for various purposes such as classification, information retrieval, pattern design, and decision-making. Ontological concepts, individuals, and their properties are formally defined using the ontological languages—namely, Resource Description Framework (RDF) and Web Ontology Language (OWL). The spatial representation of the domain model is showed in Figure 8.2.

8.2.1 Domain Modeling

The elements of the domain model are entity, class, individual, and data, object, and annotation properties. The different levels of domain knowledge abstraction are shown in Figure 8.3.

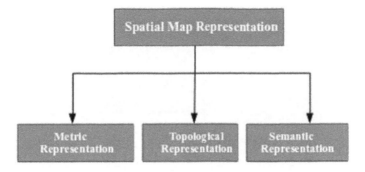

FIGURE 8.2   Spatial organization of domain knowledge.

- *Entity:* Represents an object in OWL ontology
- *Class:* Represents the hierarchical classes in ontology
- *Individual:* Represents an individual or instances in ontology
- *Object property:* Represents a role between domain and range classes
- *Data property:* Represents a data type with the corresponding value in ontology
- *Annotation property:* Describes the asserted knowledge in ontology

8.2.1.1 Geometric Model Representation (Metric Map)

The low-level layer of the domain model is called the metric map. In the metric map, the lines are used to represent the boundaries (walls) of the configuration space. A sample indoor domain model built using the Gazebo simulator is shown in Figure 8.4. Simultaneous localization and mapping (SLAM) is used to build a metric map with geometric features to reliably localize a robot on the map (Guimarães, de Oliveira, Fabro, Becker & Brenner,

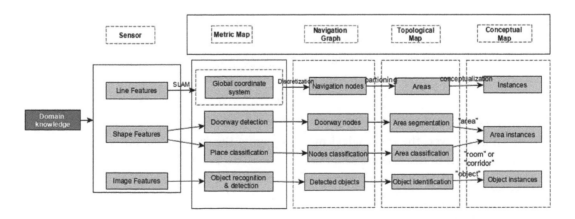

FIGURE 8.3   Different levels of domain modeling.

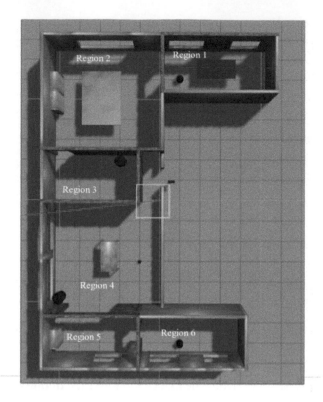

FIGURE 8.4   Indoor domain model designed using Gazebo.

2016). The metric map created using the SLAM algorithm is shown in Figure 8.5. In the metric map, a robot retrieves the geometric features through sensors. The geometric features such as walls, points, and lines are considered obstacles during navigation.

8.2.1.2 Road Map (Navigation Graph)

The second-level layer, the navigation graph, is used to connect the discrete nodes in the workspace. The workspace is divided into two spaces—namely, obstacle-free space and obstacle space. The obstacle space denotes the area in the space occupied by objects or entities. Object-free space denotes the collision-free space where a robot navigates to reach the goal. The navigation graph is based on the road-map model.

8.2.1.3 Topological Model Representation (Topological Map)

The third-level layer, the topological map, segments the indoor workspace into distinct regions. It is used to discretize a set of nodes into areas, and the nodes are interconnected to form a graph. In the topological map, all the nodes are discretized and connected from start point to goal point through the doorway node. The topological area, along with the identified objects, is passed to the conceptual map, which relates the class instances with their respective categories.

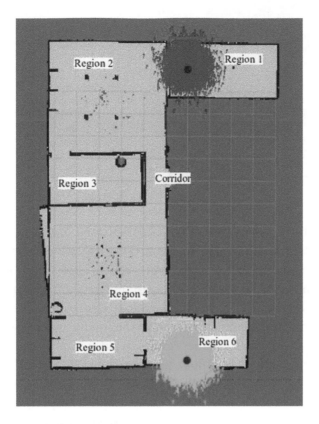

FIGURE 8.5   Metric map created using Rviz.

8.2.1.4 Semantic Model Representation (Semantic Map)

Ontology plays a vital role in semantic knowledge representation and reasoning (Lim, Hong Suh & Suh, 2010). Generally, vague representations of domain knowledge may result in incomplete information, uncertainty, imprecise prediction, and ambiguous knowledge. Semantic knowledge provides more meaningful contextual information about the domain. Ontology represents the contextual domain information such as spatial locations, line features, objects' positions, laser and image attributes, path, and the robot's activity/ behaviors. For intelligent indoor robotic navigations, the semantic perception and reasoning process must include the semantic map (i.e., meaningful information mapping), the reasoning process (i.e., region retrieval), and the path-finding process. The semantic map plots an indoor domain and functionally relates its domain characteristics, such as features, object locations, rooms, and the specified tasks, with a desired goal. The OpenStreetMap (OSM) is the most promising tool for mapping both indoor and outdoor domains (Naik, Blumenthal, Huebel, Bruyninckx & Prassler, 2019).

The semantic approach provides comprehensive domain knowledge in order to execute a situation-aware navigation (i.e., a feature-based navigation). There are many approaches used for indoor and outdoor domain descriptions using ontologies. Tenorth et al. (Tenorth, Kunze, Jain & Beetz, 2010) proposed the KNOWROB architecture for performing a complex task (i.e., an egg-cracking problem) in an indoor environment.

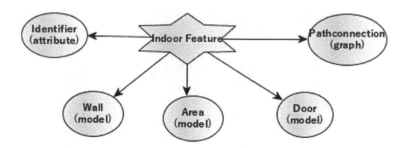

FIGURE 8.6 The hierarchy of domain knowledge.

8.2.1.5 Conceptual Map

The highest-level abstraction, called the conceptual map, defines the abstract domain knowledge. The abstract relations are encoded in OWL-DL, which describes the taxonomic concepts (i.e., regions and room types) and instances (i.e., individual objects) of an indoor environment in a manner that resembles human understanding of spatial categorization in a real-world workspace. The conceptual ontology defines hierarchical concepts using *Is-a* hierarchy relations and identifies the object types on the basis of locations represented using *Has-a* relationship (Crespo, Barber & Mozos, 2017).

The terminological knowledge (TBox) and assertional knowledge (ABox) are used to identify the conceptual concepts and their instances of hierarchical ontology. TBox represents the concepts, and ABox specifies the instances. The conceptual map derives a higher-level knowledge by combining with the metric and topological maps (Kuric, Bulej, Saga & Pokorny, 2017).

There are many ontology-based knowledge frameworks that have been proposed for representing domain knowledge in indoor environments. Robotic context is classified into two levels of abstraction—namely, low-level and high-level context. Low-level context is a primitive context that can directly represent domain knowledge and doesn't require any other type of contextual information. For example, geometric primitives of domain properties such as physical locations and objects are considered low-level context.

In Figure 8.6, the root of the ontology concepts are designed using Protege. The concepts are collections of classes and their individuals. An individual is an object, and roles are binary relations between classes. The high-level context is derived from the conceptual map shown in Figure 8.6. Ontological reasoning can be achieved through reasoners based on logical rules.

8.3 REASONER

A reasoner (i.e., a plan or program) derives logical consequences from asserted facts or axioms (Dentler, Cornet, Ten Teije & De Keizer, 2011). Typically, reasoners support both classification and debugging queries. The most promising reasoners are Pellet, RacerPro, Fact++, Hermit, and SWRL-IQ. Reasoners can perform inference over spatial and temporal relations.

In this section, we explain a set of spatiotemporal properties—i.e., RCC-8 and Allen's interval relations. According to RCC-8 calculus, the intersection of two concepts that are spatially connected can be represented via spatial properties such as *overlaps*, *within*, *contains*, and *disjoint*. In the domain model, the features are functionally related with the individuals. Each instance of a class such as a rectangle, polygon, round, square, or line is identified via a geometric property—namely, *hasgeometry*.

8.3.1 Characteristics

Reasoners are used to solve logical problems, and they validate all the possible inference procedures. The main features of reasoners are soundness and completeness (Dentler, Cornet, Ten Teije & De Keizer, 2011). Generally, the inference rules can be expressed using OWL-DL, RDF, and SWRL (Zhai, Ortega, Martínez & Castillejo, 2018). Ontology offers various functional axioms such as transitivity, symmetry, antisymmetry, reflexivity, and irreflexivity.

8.3.2 Rule-Based Engine

The rule-based engine can be expressed with a set of logical rules used to derive a new pattern. The different kinds of rules are expressed in conjunctive ($\land$) and disjunctive ($\lor$) normal forms. Reasoning is performed using forward and backward chaining (Zhai, Ortega, Martínez & Castillejo, 2018). The forward chaining algorithm uses the known facts and derives a valid conclusion. Backward chaining is the reverse of forward chaining and finds a known fact that supports the goal.

- Advantages of Reasoning

  - Reduces the redundant information

  - Helps in discovering the context in knowledge content

  - Infers new knowledge

  - Enhances the reusability of the domain model

- Disadvantage of Reasoning

  - Can result in wrong information due to inconsistency and redundancy in the knowledge base

8.3.3 Inference Model

8.3.3.1 Knowledge Representation

Knowledge representation includes three main subsystems—namely, the perception subsystem, the communication subsystem, and the conceptual mapping. The perception subsystem extracts domain information (i.e., perception features) from sensor data. The communication subsystem is used for natural language dialogue, and the conceptual semantic map links knowledge representation and sensor-based maps.

8.3.3.1.1 Spatial Properties   SpatialObjectProperty denotes the spatial relations (RCC-8) (Cohn, Bennett, Gooday & Gotts, 1997) such as overlaps and intersects that are used to relate the individuals of one class with other subclasses. The RCC-8 relations are listed in

TABLE 8.1   Spatial Relations Representation

RCC-8	Spatial Relations of (A, B)	Topological Relations Property	Directional Relations Property	Distance Relations Property
DC = disconnected	A DC B ≡ disjoint	InContGeneric	AboveOf	Very-close
EC = externally	A EC B ≡ touches	InCenterOf	belowOf	close,
connected	A TPP B ≡ within	OnPhysical	behind	far,
TPP = tangential proper part	A nTTP B ≡ within	OutsideOf	inFrontOf	very-far
nTTP = nontangential proper part	A PO B ≡ overlaps	InsideOf	toTheLeftOf	
PO = partially overlapping	A EQ B ≡ equals		toTheRightOf	
EQ = equal	A TPPi B ≡ contains		toStraightOf	
TPPi = tangential proper part inverse	A nTTpi B ≡ contains			
nTTPi = nontangential proper part inverse				

Table 8.1. High-level context is represented using object properties that are specified using the logical axioms in a hierarchical domain ontology. The high-level context of an object property can be designed using the Protege tool and is presented in Figure 8.7.

Some properties related to object properties are as follows:

- SubObjectProperty is a subproperty of the object property.

- EquivalentObjectProperties specifies the two equivalent object properties.

- InverseObjectProperties specifies that an object property is an inverse of another object property. (For example, the "before" relation is an inverse of the "after" relation.)

FIGURE 8.7   Spatial object property for the domain model.

- ObjectPropertyDomain specifies the domain class of an object property.

- ObjectPropertyRange specifies the range class of an object property.

- ObjectPropertyMember specifies the individual values of an object property.

- ObjectPropertyAttribute indicates object property attributes, which are transitive, functional, symmetric, and equivalent properties.

8.3.3.1.2 Temporal Properties   In this section, we discuss the rich set of temporal operators in Allen's interval algebra. Temporal relations representation can be either point (or instant) based or interval based (Allen, 1983). The point-based representation consists of a set of temporal operators such as *equals* (=), *before* (<), and *after* (>) relations. The interval-based operators are based on Allen's interval theory, which includes properties such as *before*, *meets*, *overlaps*, and *contains*, which are the inverse roles of *after*, *ismetby*, *overlappedby*, and *during*, respectively.

A temporal relation is a time interval that can be conceptualized as discrete or continuous, linear or cyclical, absolute or relative, or qualitative or quantitative relations. The ontology-based domain model is combined with temporal reasoning relations to describe a set of composition relations using chain operators. Allen's relations between temporal intervals are expressed in Table 8.2. The composition chain property can be achieved by specifying the chain operator (*o*).

For instance, if the relation *R1* holds between *A* and *B* entities and the relation *R2* holds between *B* and *C* entities, the entities *A* and *C* are related by the *R3* relation.

$$R1(A,B) o R2(B,C) \rightarrow R3(A,C) \tag{8.1}$$

A qualitative temporal relation between time intervals is generally unpredictable (i.e., the exact duration of event (*A* and *B*) or (*A* or *B*) is unknown). Allen's relations are based on the qualitative method. To reduce the ambiguity of Allen's relations such as "after" and "before," Uma and Aghila (2014) proposed the use of REseT ordering relations to increase the expressiveness and access the order of intervals.

Reasoning over temporal relations is an NP-hard problem. Time is represented in ontologies using temporal description logic (TDL), temporal RDF, and 4-D fluent. The 4-D

TABLE 8.2   Allen's Interval-Based and Point-Based Representation

Point-Based Relations	Interval-Based Relations (Relationship—Inverse relationship)	Expression $[a] = [s1, e1], [b] = [s2, e2]$
Equals (=)	Before (a,b)—After (b,a)	$(e1 < s2) \wedge (e2 > s1)$
Before (<)	Meets (a,b)—MetBy (b,a)	$(e1 = s2) \wedge (e2 = s1)$
After (>)	Overlaps (a,b)—OverlappedBy(b,a)	$s1 < s2 \wedge e1 < e2 \wedge e1 < s2$
	Contains (a,b)—During (b,a)	$s1 < s2 < e2 < e1$
	Starts (a,b)—StartedBy(b,a)	$s1 = s2 \wedge e1 < e2$
	Finishes (a,b)—FinishedBy (b,a)	$s1 > s2 \wedge e1 = e2$
	Equals (a,b)	$s1 = s2 \wedge e1 = e2$

TABLE 8.3   Action-Related Properties

Pre-actors	Post-actors
ObjectActedOn	Post-conditions
objectAddedTo	ActionOnObject
detectedObject	MovementTranslation
objectRemoved	PickingUpAnObject
Inputs	TurningAnObject
- Move	FlippingSomething
- Pickup	
- Moveholding	
- Place	
- Transformedobject	
Doneby	Robot
	TargetPosture
fromLocation	ToLocation
fromState	ToState
OutputsRemaining	Outputs
	OutputsCreated

fluent approach enables modeling of domain dynamics and represents the time aspects as the fourth dimension. TDL infers a new relation from the composition of existing temporal relations by using chain operators (*o*) as well as by validating the path consistency.

8.3.3.1.3 Action Representation   Action can define the abstract schema that can be generated from instructions given by humans. Temporal actions such as the initial time of an action and the duration of an action, as well as the goal of an action, are extremely important for robots that take action in the environment. The hierarchy of action-related properties is shown in Table 8.3.

8.3.3.2 Semantic Web Reasoners

The most popular ontology reasoners—namely, Pellet, Hermit, and RacerPro—are based on the tableaux-based algorithm (Möller & Haarslev, 2009). These reasoners handle both quantitative and qualitative relations and are commonly used by DL reasoners. They infer a new relation from the asserted knowledge of a domain in which the classes and their individuals are related with the help of properties and are implemented using SWRL rules. The special characteristics of reasoners are shown in Table 8.4. The Pellet and RacerPro reasoners support classification and rule-based approaches and also verify the inconsistencies that exist in the ontologies.

Pellet, an open-source software, depends on the tableaux algorithm. It supports expressive description logics—i.e., OWL-DL. Pellet is the first reasoner that supports the OWL-DL language, and it also supports the extended version of OWL 2. Fact++ (Fast classification of Terminologies) implements the tableaux-based terminological knowledge, and it offers partial support for assertional knowledge. RacerPro (Rename Aboxes and Concept Expression Reasoner) implements the terminological and assertional knowledge, and it supports optimization techniques. RacerPro is a commercial software that also supports

TABLE 8.4   Semantic Web Reasoner Characteristics

Semantic Web Reasoners	Methodology	Parameters	Consistency	Response Time	Rule Support
Fact++	Tableau algorithm	Soundness and completeness	Yes	Slower than Hermit	No
Hermit	Hypertableau	Efficiency, correctness and consistency, soundness and completeness	Yes	Faster than Fact++ but slower than Pellet	Yes
Pellet	Tableau	Efficiency, incremental classification, correctness and consistency, soundness and completeness	No	Faster than Hermit but slower than RacerPro	Yes
RacerPro	Tableaux	Efficiency, correctness, consistency, soundness, and completeness	No	High	Yes
SWRL-IQ	SWRL rules	Efficiency, correctness, consistency, soundness, incremental classification	No	High	Yes

the OWL-DL reasoner. Hermit is a Java-based technique and is based on the tableau reasoning algorithm.

8.3.3.3 Ontology Languages

Ontological languages support two kinds of properties—namely, object and data properties. Object properties specify the relationships among the individuals. Data properties relate the individuals with predefined data-type values or literals, which include strings, integers, and Boolean literals. The ontology languages such as RDF, RDF Schema (RDFS), OWL, SPARQL, Description Logic, and SWRL rules are used in various semantic web applications (Lim, Hong Suh & Suh, 2010). The OWL expression supports various sublanguages—namely, OWL DL, OWL Full, and OWL Lite. OWL Lite is based on first-order predicate logic. OWL DL is the larger fragment of the first-order logic (FOL). OWL Full is a combination of both approaches with RDF features.

Description Logic (DL) is based on FOL, which can define facts in an expressible manner. The basic components of DL include the concepts or classes, the individuals or objects, and their properties or roles. The expressive DL query constructs a set of relations and verifies the inference rules, path consistency, and instances. The expressive DL language supports the Boolean-type constructors existential ($\exists$) and universal ($\forall$) restriction and the Boolean operators disjunction ($\lor$), conjunction ($\land$), and negation ($\neg$).

The inference rules can be specified using an ontological query language such as SWRL. SWRL is the preferred expressive rule language for representing complex relations. SWRL rules recursively connect a set of logical rules to express the complex relationships. They are designed for specifying logical rules and support the semantic ontologies and rule interchange format (RIF). SWRL rules can be expressed by using Horn clauses. A Horn clause is a disjunction of literals with at most one positive literal. "All humans are mortal" can be written as the Horn clause $\forall x(human\ (X) \rightarrow mortal\ (X))$.

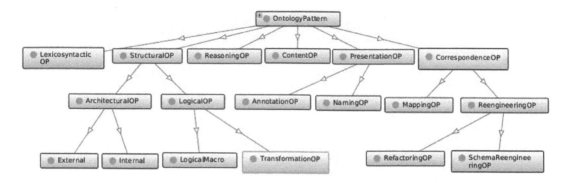

FIGURE 8.8   The hierarchy of ontology design patterns.

SWRL rules are implemented in OWL and are capable of deriving spatiotemporal relations and detecting incompatible assertions (Zhai, Ortega, Martínez & Castillejo, 2018). When an ontology language such as OWL is combined with SWRL rules, it provides sound and complete reasoning, which ensures path consistency over qualitative reasoning relations.

A SPARQL query is based on the RDF language, which extracts the triplets using the "SELECT" keyword and the set of conditions using the "where" keyword. The syntax of SPARQL is similar to that of the SQL language.

```
For example: SELECTSCRIPT query
SELECT object FROM kitchen
WHERE {
      above (table, object)
      }
```

8.3.3.4 Ontology Design Pattern

This section presents design patterns by discussing the classes, properties, and axioms. Ontology-based semantic knowledge provides additional information by using design patterns to improve the path-planning process. The ontology design pattern (ODP) approach provides a well-documented axiomatic pattern that can be shared and tested. It consequently maintains interoperability even when we use multiple ontologies together.

ODPs characterize the different axioms of asserted knowledge, which is defined by recurring patterns or a combination of axioms used to draw satisfiable inferences (Vinu, Sherimon, Krishnan & Takroni, 2014). The different types of ODPs are shown in Figure 8.8, and some are compared in Table 8.5.

TABLE 8.5   Comparison between Ontology Design Patterns

ContentOP	LogicalOP
Conceptual design pattern	Logical design pattern
Content-dependent	Content-independent
Specialization	Generalization

ODP classes and properties are determined by the semantic class and n-ary semantic relation (i.e., property). A set of specialization operations in the ODPs consists of import, specialization, and composition. The n-ary relation supports sequential ordering of events.

8.4 PLANNING

Planning is assembling an order of actions that will achieve the desired goal. It is a formal specification of a planning problem, and it represents entities such as classes, functions, properties, relations, and actions of the domain. A planning problem contains a set of variables V, a set of actions A, the start state I_s, and the goal state I_g. The planner contains the complete global plan, and it keeps executing the plan until the sequence of actions is satisfied. It is used to generate plans and execute the actions based on the declared domain specification.

For example, during the COVID-19 period, planning was done for self-navigating vehicles such as drones that were used extensively in outdoor environments for various purposes such as monitoring places, capturing locations, and finding vehicle data.

8.4.1 Constraints-Based Planning

Planning with differential constraints such as action-sequence constraints (Moon & Lee, 2019), semantic constraints, and trajectory constraints leads to minimum search times when solving planning problems. Such types of constraints-based planning remove the inconsistency and redundancy a problem. Generally, planning can be categorized as either task planning or motion planning.

8.4.2 Task Planner

Action sequences are planned by the task planner (Tenorth, Kunze, Jain & Beetz, 2010). Several planners such as PDDL, LAMA, FF, and ASP-based planner are used in task planning. In this chapter, we focus mainly on the PDDL planner, which performs better on tasks with longer solutions.

8.4.2.1 PDDL

PDDL is a classical representation is derived from the STRIPS planner. It supports the domain axioms and hierarchical relations and is a standard language for representing the deterministic planning domains and problems. PDDL has two files—namely, the domain and the problem files. The domain file includes the actions and predicate conditions necessary to accomplish the task. The problem file is used for declaring the start and goal state in the environment.

8.4.2.1.1 PDDL Components   The component of an action language is designed to construct a set of propositions in an action description language. The following propositions are as follows:

- *Objects:* These are things or entities in the domain world.
- *Start state:* This is the initial state for solving a planning problem.
- *Goal state:* The goal state can be executed after performing the actions.
- *Actions:* Actions can be specified in terms of predicates and effects.

For example:

Objects: r – robot,

Reg1, Reg2 – Region

Action Description: The robot can navigate from Reg1 to Reg2.

Precondition: Region (Reg1), Region (Reg2), and at-robot (Reg1) are true.

Effect: at-robot (Reg2) becomes true. at-robot (Reg1) becomes false.

Everything else doesn't change.

In PDDL:

```
(:action move :parameters (?Reg1? Reg2)
:precondition (and (Region? Reg1) (Region? Reg2)
        (at-robot? Reg1))
:effect (and (at-robot? Reg2)
        (not (at-robot? Reg1)))
```

The domain knowledge source can be regularized in PDDL that can be defined by using the predicates.

The planning properties of the domain elements are as follows:

hasGeometric(Reg, obj): Represents the geometric features by considering the objects or material properties such as windows, points, colors, and lines placed in the location

isConnected(Reg1, Reg2): Represents the path between two regions

isGoingTo(Reg, n): Represents the symbolic action command (i.e., "goto") to navigate a robot to the goal state

visited(R, n): Denotes a place the robot (R) has visited

hasPath(Reg1, Reg2): Traverse to the location (Reg2) from the current location (Reg1)

For example, a mobile robot can navigate in an indoor domain that consists of a set of regions (i.e., rooms) that are adjacent to each other. The regions are connected to each other via a doorway.

Alternatively, the regions can be directly connected to each other in such a way that access is always possible from any location in one region to any other location (Jiang, Zhang, Khandelwal & Stone, 2019).

Reg1 is reachable from Reg2 if Reg1 is directly connected to Reg2 or if Reg1 and Reg2 share the same doorway (i.e., Dway) and it is open. Moreover, the accessible property is both commutative (i.e., Reg1 is reachable from Reg2 if Reg2 is reachable

TABLE 8.6   Domain and Problem Models

Domain Model	Problem Model
It contains the actions—i.e., moves between any two regions—and must satisfy the associative and transitive properties. acc(Reg1,Reg2,n) :- connected(Reg1,Reg2). acc(Reg1,Reg2,n) :- open(Dway,n), hasdoor(Reg1,Dway), hasdoor(Reg2,Dway). acc(Reg1,Reg2,n) :- acc(Reg2,Reg1,n). acc(Reg1,Reg2,n) :- acc(Reg1,Reg3,n), acc (Reg3,Reg2,n).	It contains the instance to be solved. (: derived (acc? Reg1 - region? Reg2 - region) (or (connected? Reg1? Reg2) (exists (?Dway - doorway) (hasdoor? Reg1? Dway) (hasdoor? Reg2? Dway)) (acc? Reg2? Reg1) (exists (?Reg3 - region) (and (acc? Reg1? Reg3) (acc? Reg3? Reg2)))))

from Reg1) and associative (i.e., if both Reg1 and Reg2 are reachable from Reg3, then they are reachable from each other). The recursive function of the associative property can be expressed in PDDL and is defined in the domain and problem models shown in Table 8.6.

The domain knowledge can be formalized in PDDL defined using the following predicates:

hasdoor(Reg,Dway): The hasdoor predicate specifies that the region (Reg) has a doorway (Dway) through which to navigate to an adjacent location. The hasdoor expression of the PDDL statement is defined as

(hasdoor? Reg - region? Dway - doorway).

isConnectedTo (Reg1,Reg2): The ConnectedTo predicate specifies that region 1 (Reg1) is directly connected to region 2 (Reg2) by a door. The PDDL statement is expressed as

(connected? Reg1 - region? Reg2 - region).

at(R,n): at is used to indicate that the robot is at region Reg at timestep n in the high-level plan. This predicate is inertial (i.e., the robot remains in region Reg if there is no evidence showing that it is not in region Reg anymore), and the predicate property is defined in PDDL as

(at? Reg - region, n) :- (at? Reg - region, n-1), (not-at? Reg - region, n).

visited(Rm,n): Once the robot visits a room (Rm), this predicate holds true until the planning process completes. The visited term describes the goal conditions. The persistence property is defined in PDDL as (visited? Rm - room, n-1).

isGoingTo(Reg2,n): This action specifies that the robot (or agent) should travel to region Reg2 at timestep n. The precondition states that the robot must be in a region Reg1 from which region Reg2 is reachable. Once the robot reaches region Reg2, the goal condition visited is set to true for that region. The preconditions and effects of the PDDL statement is expressed as follows:

```
(:action goto
    :parameters (?A - agent? Reg1  - region? Reg2 - region)
    :precondition (exists (?Reg1 - region)
                          (and (at? A? Reg1)
                               (acc? Reg1? Reg2)))
    :effect (and (at? A? Reg2)
                 (forall (?Reg1 - region)
                         (when (at? Reg1)
                               (not (at? A? Reg1))))
                 (visited? Reg2)
                 (forall (?Dway - doorway)
                         (not (canopen? Dway)))))
```

8.4.3 Motion Planner

Control-based plans and action-sequence-based plans are typically used in the motion plan. The motion plan deals with the trajectory constraints during navigation. The semantic constraints can control a robot and guides it to trace a path that ensures safe navigation. This outcome is sent to the control system of the robot to perform collision prediction or avoidance, acceleration limitation, motion in the right direction, and efficient decision-making.

8.4.3.1 Classical Path-Planning Algorithms

There are five classes of path-planning algorithms: sampling-based, node-based, mathematical model–based, bio-inspired, and multifusion-based algorithms (Yang, Qi, Song, Xiao, Han & Xia, 2016). Sampling-based algorithms are applied in many scenarios such as disaster environments, search and rescue tasks, and path planning in indoor and outdoor environments. In our previous work (Gayathri & Uma, 2019b), we implemented sampling-based algorithms and found that RRT provided the minimum search time and distance compared with other sampling-based approaches. Generally, the RRT algorithm repeats the sample process until it finds the goal locations.

8.4.3.1.1 Rapidly Exploring Random Tree Algorithm   RRT is part of the sampling-based algorithm in which the nodes are denoted as samples, and it randomly selects the samples toward the goal point in the configuration space (X). RRT generates samples from an initial point (X_i) that continues the tree construction process until either it finds the target (X) or the search time ends. The RRT algorithm is integrated with the PDDL planner in order to solve the sequential order within the search process. A robot executes the ordered events based on the specified preconditions and actions. It navigates when its defined sequence of domain conditions is satisfied. The RRT motion planner verifies that the plan is valid for navigation. If the plan is valid, RRT generates a constrained sequence of paths. Otherwise, the robot's recovery behavior of switching back to target tracing occurs. The sampling-based RRT algorithm with action-sequence constraints is implemented in ROS for efficient robot navigation.

8.5 ONTOLOGY-BASED ROBOTIC NAVIGATION USING ROBOT OPERATING SYSTEM (ROS)

The ontology-based domain knowledge source with perceivable sensor data will provide sufficient information about the domain for efficient robot navigation using ROS. This section explains ROS in detail.

8.5.1 ROS

ROS provides a framework for hardware and software (Guimarães, Rodrigo, André, João, Thiago & Vinícius, 2016). It is a generic software framework for programming robots in various applications for industry, education, the military, agriculture, and indoor and outdoor navigation. It is an open-source software, and it also provides a different set of software libraries and tools that can be used to build robotic systems. In ROS, the accurate robot model is created from the URDF and SRDF files. The Unified Robot Description Format (URDF) is used to describe the physical properties of a robot and is based on the XML format. The Semantic Robot Description Format (SRDF) represents the semantic information (i.e., the set of joints) of the robot model, which is data useful for motion planning. ROS supports many simulators such as V-Rep, Webots, Gazebo, and OpenRave. ROS has several tools to inspect and debug messages. The most powerful visualization tool is ROS Visualization (Rviz), which allows one to view the Gazebo simulator for ROS.

8.5.1.1 Perception and Sensors

Perception involves sensing the environment and assessing its situation through sensors—namely, laser range scanners and cameras. These sensors perceive the domain information, which is evaluated using different techniques. The laser-scanned data is processed and creates the low-level layer of spatial representation. The processed laser-based data is used for detecting and avoiding the obstacles in the path. Finally, the camera-acquired images are examined by a computer vision component in the process of object recognition or detection.

During navigation, a robot tries to perceive objects with the help of sensors. Here the laser scanner is used for place classification, and the camera is used for object recognition. Generally, objects play an important role in the semantic map. The recognized objects aid in deducing the subregions in an indoor environment. For example, generally the living room is larger than all other rooms and contains a stable object such as a sofa or TV set.

The semantic SLAM approach extracts the geometrical (i.e., polygonal or rectangular) features from the laser scanner in order to classify the region with respect to objects. In indoor domains, the corridors and rooms are classified as regions based on the laser observation data so that a robot is reliably localized. For the classification of a region in which objects are present, the objects are denoted using invariant (static) features at the coordinate position (x, y). This approach is called a supervised approach, as the robot is trained in an indoor environment. The concepts (rooms, corridors, and hallways) and relations (properties) are represented using ontology.

8.5.1.2 ROS 3-D Simulation

Rviz is a 3-D visualizer that is used to visualize a robot. It allows visualization of the laser data, map data, transform data, and data from different sensors for robotic models. Gazebo is an actual real-world physics simulator that is used for building 2-D and 3-D domain models with different features.

8.5.1.3 The Parameter of ROS

8.5.1.3.1   Move_Base   The move_base package contains the local and global planners. The global planner traces the path from the current position to the goal point with the lowest cost when compared with the global costmap. Hence, the local planner detects more obstacles than the global costmap, and it creates the optimal trajectory with the least cost.

8.5.1.3.2 Global and Local Costmaps   Global and local costmaps represent the environment and the localized robot's position, respectively. The local costmap represents the obstacles predicted on a map (2-D plane). It ensures there is a security inflation radius (an area surrounding each obstacle) so that the robot will not collide with any objects during robotic navigation.

8.5.1.4 Mapping and Localization

8.5.1.4.1   SLAM (Simultaneous Localization and Mapping Algorithm)   The SLAM algorithm is used to create metric maps of its environment and is used in robot navigation to reach high-level autonomy, reliable navigation, and safe localization (Crespo, Barber & Mozos, 2017). It uses gmapping and hector_mapping to create these maps. Maps are classified into three paradigms—namely, the metric, topological, and hybrid mapping paradigms, which were discussed in detail in Section 8.2. The SLAM algorithm extracts the geometric primitives from the laser scanner and applies a particle filter or Kalman filter to integrate feature measurements. The geometric features correspond to walls, and contour features represent the height and width of the objects. Walls are static features of the environment and are used to keep the robot localized. All the domain features are stored in the global metric map with an absolute frame. The SLAM algorithm maps the geometric features such as lines, shapes, edges, and points that denote the objects, individuals, or obstacles present in the indoor domain. The laser-based scanner provides a 360° view of the space. The actual robot location is determined using adaptive Monte Carlo localization.

8.5.1.4.2 Adaptive Monto Carlo Localization (AMCL)   Adaptive Monte Carlo localization (AMCL) is a localization system that depends on the Monte Carlo localization approach. It uses a particle filter to determine robot positions and represents these locations on a static map.

8.5.1.5 ROS Integration Framework

8.5.1.5.1   Open Motion Planning Library (OMPL)   The ROS-OMPL interface has more advanced features. The open motion planning library (OMPL) supports two types of motion planners (Sucan & Moll, 2012). The first planner supports the motion controls

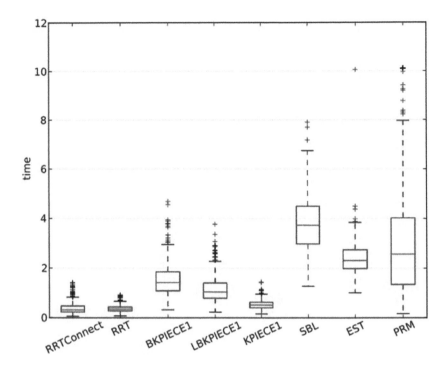

FIGURE 8.9   The benchmark of geometric planners.

(i.e., PathControl) while planning, and the other planner does not control motion. Specifically, the RRT algorithm is used to plan motions both with and without controls. Various geometric planning algorithms are executed in OMPL, as shown in the Figure 8.9. The snapshot of the RRT configuration using OMPL is shown in Figure 8.10. RRT has shorter execution times when compared with other algorithms.

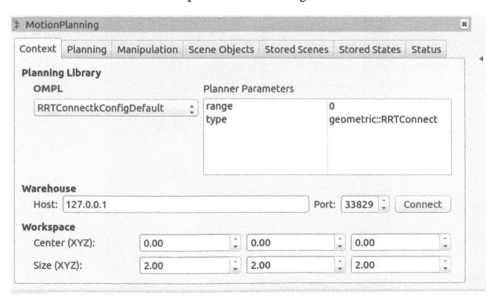

FIGURE 8.10   The RRT configuration using OMPL.

8.6 EXPERIMENTAL RESULTS AND ANALYSIS

The experiment was conducted in ROS for robotic navigation. ROS and the parameter for the ROS navigation stack have been explained in detail in Section 8.5. In ROS, the environment is built using a Gazebo simulator where a robot navigates using the RRT algorithm with action-sequence constraints declared using PDDL. The constrained shortest path between Regions 1 and 2 is shown in Figure 8.11. The path connection between Regions 2 and 3 is shown in Figure 8.12. Finally, the optimal path between Regions 4 and 5 is shown in Figure 8.13.

8.6.1 Graphical Analyses

The path-planning algorithm was analyzed with respect to path length and execution time by considering the number of rooms visited by a robot at timestamp n in the high-level plan, as shown in Figures 8.14 and 8.15. The execution time and the distance to the destination are shown in Table 8.7.

The distance covered by the robot from the initial to the target region is shown in Figure 8.14. The time taken to visit the number of regions is shown in Figure 8.15.

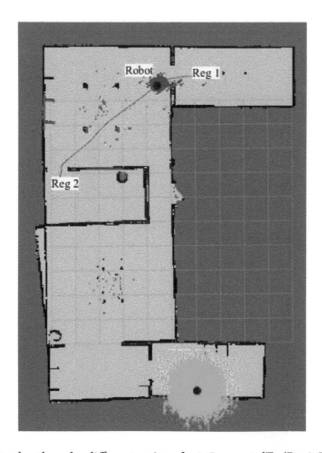

FIGURE 8.11   Optimal path under different regions for isConnectedTo (Reg1, Reg2).

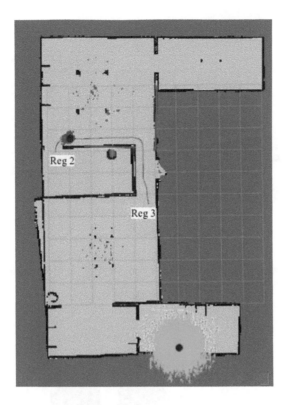

FIGURE 8.12   Optimal path under different regions for isConnectedTo (Reg2, Reg3).

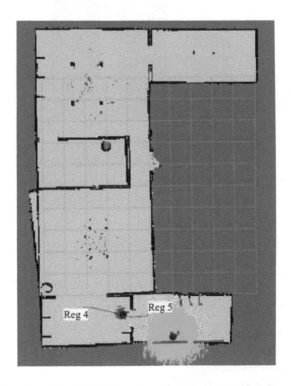

FIGURE 8.13   Optimal path under different regions for isConnectedTo (Reg4, Reg5),

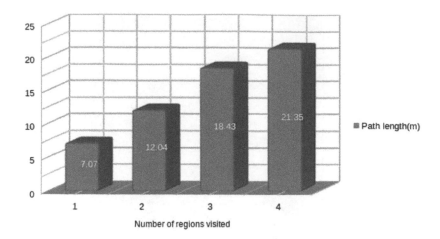

FIGURE 8.14   Distance analyses of path finding considering different regions.

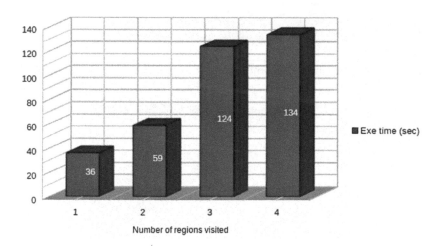

FIGURE 8.15   Execution time analyses of path finding with constraints.

TABLE 8.7   Path Connection between Regions Based on PDDL with RRT

PDDL Action	Execution Time (sec)	Length (m)
isConnectedTo (Reg1, Reg2)	36	7.07
isConnectedTo (Reg2, Reg3)	23	4.97
isConnectedTo (Reg3, Reg4)	65	6.39
isConnectedTo (Reg4, Reg5)	10	2.92

8.7 CONCLUSION

This chapter has discussed the details related to ontology-based knowledge representation and reasoning techniques with action constraints that are relevant to robotic navigation. Planning representation and the uses of the PDDL language have been explained in detail. Different types of knowledge representation and reasoning techniques relevant to the robotics have been discussed. Representation of various robotic simulators along with their special features has been provided. The performance of RRT path-planning algorithms was analyzed by considering domain constraints given by PDDL. The features of the planning domains and the problem file that improve the planning efficiency for robotic navigation were considered. The results demonstrate that a robot can navigate in a collision-free path and satisfy the action constraints with help of a PDDL planner, which can be improved and reinforced by applying sampling-based path-planning algorithms.

REFERENCES

Allen, James. 1983. "Maintaining Knowledge about Temporal Intervals." *Communications of the ACM* 26 (11): 832–43.

Cohn, Anthony G., Brandon Bennett, John Gooday, and Nicholas Mark Gotts. 1997. "Qualitative Spatial Representation and Reasoning with the Region Connection Calculus." *GeoInformatica* 1 (3): 275–316. https://doi.org/10.1023/A.

Crespo, Jonathan, R. Barber, and O. M. Mozos. 2017. "Relational Model for Robotic Semantic Navigation in Indoor Environments." *Journal of Intelligent & Robotic Systems* 86 (3): 617–39.

Dentler, Kathrin, Ronald Cornet, Annette Ten Teije, and Nicolette De Keizer. 2011. "Comparison of Reasoners for Large Ontologies in the OWL 2 EL Profile." *Semantic Web* 2 (2): 71–87.

Gayathri, R., and V. Uma. 2018. "Ontology Based Knowledge Representation Technique, Domain Modeling Languages and Planners for Robotic Path Planning: A Survey." *ICT Express* 4 (2): 69–74. https://doi.org/10.1016/j.icte.2018.04.008.

Gayathri, R., and V. Uma. 2019a. "A Review of Description Logic-Based Techniques for Robot Task Planning." In *Integrated Intelligent Computing, Communication and Security*, 101–7. Springer Singapore. https://doi.org/10.1007/978-981-10-8797-4.

Gayathri, R., and V. Uma. 2019b. "Performance Analysis of Robotic Path Planning Algorithms in a Deterministic Environment." *International Journal of Imaging and Robotics* 19 (4): 83–108.

Guimarães, Rodrigo Longhi, André Schneider de Oliveira, João Alberto Fabro, Thiago Becker, and Vinícius Amilgar Brenner. 2016. "ROS Navigation: Concepts and Tutorial." In *Robot Operating System (ROS)*, Springer, Cham, 121–60.

Jiang, Yu-qian, Shi-qi Zhang, Piyush Khandelwal, and Peter Stone. 2019. "Task Planning in Robotics: An Empirical Comparison of PDDL- and ASP-Based Systems." *Frontiers of Information Technology & Electronic Engineering* 20 (3): 363–73.

Kuric, Ivan, Vladimir Bulej, Milan Saga, and Peter Pokorny. 2017. "Development of Simulation Software for Mobile Robot Path Planning within Multilayer Map System Based on Metric and Topological Maps." *International Journal of Advanced Robotic Systems* 14 (6): 1–14. https://doi.org/10.1177/1729881417743029.

Lim, Gi Hyun, Il Hong Suh, and Hyowon Suh. 2010. "Ontology-Based Unified Robot Knowledge for Service Robots in Indoor Environments." *IEEE Transactions on Systems, Man, and Cybernetics, Part A: Systems and Humans* 41 (3): 492–509. https://doi.org/10.1109/TSMCA.2010.2076404.

Möller, Ralf, and Volker Haarslev. 2009. "Tableau-Based Reasoning." In *Handbook on Ontologies* Springer, Berlin, 509–28. https://doi.org/10.1007/978-3-540-92673-3_23.

Moon, Jiyoun, and Beom Hee Lee. 2019. "PDDL Planning with Natural Language-Based Scene Understanding for UAV-UGV Cooperation." *Applied Sciences (Switzerland)* 9 (18): 3789. https://doi.org/10.3390/app9183789.

Naik, Lakshadeep, Sebastian Blumenthal, Nico Huebel, Herman Bruyninckx, and Erwin Prassler. 2019. "Semantic Mapping Extension for OpenStreetMap Applied to Indoor Robot Navigation." In *Proceedings—IEEE International Conference on Robotics and Automation*, 3839–45. https://doi.org/10.1109/ICRA.2019.8793641.

Sucan, Ioan Alexandru, and Mark Moll. 2012. "The Open Motion Planning Library." *IEEE Robotics & Automation Magazine* 19 (4): 72–82. https://doi.org/10.1109/MRA.2012.2205651.

Sun, Xiaolei, Yu Zhang, and Jing Chen. 2019. "RTPO: A Domain Knowledge Base for Robot." *Electronics* 8 (10): 1105.

Tenorth, Moritz, Lars Kunze, Dominik Jain, and Michael Beetz. 2010. "KNOWROB-MAP— Knowledge-Linked Semantic Object Maps." In *10th IEEE-RAS International Conference on Humanoid Robots*, 430–35.

Uma, V., and G. Aghila. 2014. "Event Order Generation Using Reference Event Based Qualitative Temporal (REseT) Relations in Time Event Ontology." *Open Computer Science* 4 (1): 12–29. https://doi.org/10.2478/s13537-014-0202-9.

Vinu, P. V., P. C. Sherimon, Reshmy Krishnan, and Youssef Saad Takroni. 2014. "Pattern Representation Model for N-Ary Relations in Ontology." *Journal of Theoretical and Applied Information Technology* 60 (2): 231–36.

Yang, Liang, Juntong Qi, Dalei Song, Jizhong Xiao, Jianda Han, and Yong Xia. 2016. "Survey of Robot 3D Path Planning Algorithms." *Journal of Control Science and Engineering*. https://doi.org/10.1155/2016/7426913.

Zhai, Zhaoyu, José Fernán Martínez Ortega, Néstor Lucas Martínez, and Pedro Castillejo. 2018. "A Rule-Based Reasoner for Underwater Robots Using OWL and SWRL." *Sensors* 18 (10): 3481. https://doi.org/10.3390/s18103481.

CHAPTER 9

Automated Guided Autonomous Car Using Deep Learning and Computer Vision

Anubha Parashar and Vidyadhar Aski

Manipal University Jaipur
Jaipur, India

Apoorva Parashar

Maharshi Dayanand University
Rohtak, India

CONTENTS

DOI: 10.1201/9781003048381-10

9.1 INTRODUCTION

A smart car generally has two controlling units that dictate its actions, the controllers of low magnitude and high magnitude. The controller of high magnitude takes input from its components—i.e., the driver (in this case the camera), the surroundings such as the traffic, and the sensors in place. Then, after deducing the correct actions to be taken, it sends signals to the low-level controller, which controls the brakes, steering, engine, and throttle [1]. To do this successfully, controllers needs to understand driver psychology—e.g., how and when a specific maneuver is necessary, which changes with the terrain and the area in which the car is driving—since driver temperament and driving style cannot be universally generalized. To understand and correctly predict such outcomes is risky. Studies show that if the driver is given even an extra half a second before a collision, 60% of accidents can be avoided, and this percentage increases to 90% if one second of warning time can be provided [2]. Such results stress the importance of timely and correct decisions, but the conventional architecture of a smart car system faces problems in this area. Also, when cars rely on so many sensors, it is difficult for them to adapt to new surroundings and to reconfigure the system to achieve a different goal based on learning that occurs on the move, especially when noisy sensor data is received [3]. The foundation of the end-to-end approach was laid almost 14 years ago when a project sponsored by the Defense Advanced Research Projects Agency (DARPA) created DAVE) [4], an autonomous car that ran along an alley filled with junk [5]. The project demonstrated that this approach was viable and adequate for the functioning of a smart car. The end-to-end approach thus provided alternatives that were uncomplicated and also easier to test [6]. With the advancement in technology, the approach achieved similar functionality more skillfully and with limited resources. At the center of this end-to-end learning is the convolutional neural network (CNN), which performs the driver's actions based on the training. The data was not hard to collect, and the system itself could be reproduced efficiently at a low cost, which made it possible to do rigorous experimentation. The data from the system could also be shared with another system of the same kind to improve performance.

One of the breakthroughs in navigating autonomous vehicles happened because of using CNN [4, 6–16]. In order to navigate the vehicle while providing complete passenger safety, the CNN model has been deployed and trained as well as tested. This model maps the complete driving model in real time by collecting information about driving behavior and taking images from the angle of the steering wheel and camera [6, 10, 17–29]. Vehicle performance is heavily dependent on the data set; i.e., if the vehicle encounters a new hazardous situation (one on which the model has not been trained), the system will not provide a good analysis, and an accident might happen. There are a lot of reasons that the system might malfunction and crash, such as software failure or camera sensor impairment.

The rest of this chapter proceeds as follows. In the literature review, we explore the ultramodern models used for self-driving vehicles. We also touch on the limitations of models based on conventional deep neural networks (DNNs). Then we gave introduce the approach preferred in this study and describe the CNN architecture used for autonomous driving. In order to validate our method, we provide the testing and training results along with the real-time simulation of the vehicle drive.

9.2 LITERATURE REVIEW

This journey to make a smart autonomous vehicle began with the invention of modern cruise control in 1948 [30]. Many dedicated steps have been taken since then to make self-driving cars a reality. The autonomous land vehicle in a neural network (ALVINN diversified the field by combining end-to-end learning [31] with a neural network to enable it to solve any issue [10]. DARPA then gave perspective to what can be achieved with the technical know-how of the time [4, 32]. In the recent past, when CNN was trained to map camera pixels so they could be interpreted directly as guiding orders [6], it demonstrated the reliability of this approach in contrast to the more modular alternatives [33].

One of the most used techniques for self-driving vehicles consists of the deep neural network (DNN) [34]. A lot of car companies like Ford, Tesla, BMW, and Volvo swear by DNN. Many other firms such as Uber, Lyft, and Google are also deploying DNNs in their autonomous vehicles [35]. The working of such systems is based on the accurate transfer of information from RADAR, cameras, and LIDAR as input to the DNN, such as a recurrent neural network (RNN) or CNN [36]. The information is processed by the system in order to control the angle of the steering wheel and the velocity of the vehicle being driven. For instance, the models used by Udacity make use of both RNN- and CNN-based technique, whereas the models created by NVEDIA make use of only a CNN model for processing the input data used to take command of the steering wheel [37]. Our study has made use of a model based on a CNN just like that of DAVE-2 (made by NVEDIA).

A DNN-based system can sometimes misread the given data and cause treacherous consequences [38]. A lot of studies have been done on DNN-based models and they have determined that these systems are vulnerable to erroneous data and can malfunction easily [39]. For instance, we can disrupt a DNN-based system by adding a small inaccuracy in the image, causing the system to categorize it in a different group [40]. It has also been found that objects can be morphed physically by attackers in order to cause glitches in DNN-based self-driving systems [41]. These low-cost techniques used by attackers can cause inaccuracy in measuring distances, resolution, and angles. Likewise, barricades or debris present on the road can lead the system to produce incorrect outputs (Figure 9.1) [42–47].

9.3 PROPOSED METHODOLOGY

We proposed to use a toy car and mounted a Raspberry Pi on top of it. An 8 MP camera was inserted in the raspberry pi and attached in a way that gave it a clear view of the road ahead. An ultrasonic sensor was attached on the hood of the car to detect any obstructions on the road.

The car could be driven by a remote control (the one that came with the toy car) or could be driven autonomously (by applying DNNs). An Arduino Uno microcontroller board was used in this experiment to collect the data from the remote (the data here was input for the Arduino).

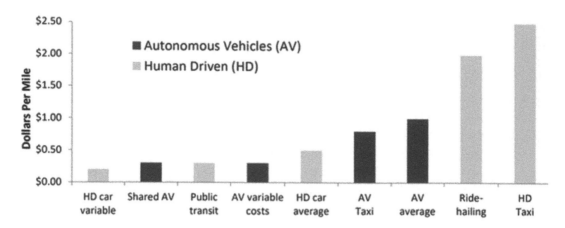

FIGURE 9.1   Comparison of driving costs.

A Wi-Fi module was also latched onto the Arduino in order to connect it to the built-in Wi-Fi of the Raspberry Pi. This way the Raspberry Pi would have access to the data coming from the remote control (data from the Arduino through Wi-Fi) and from the ultrasonic sensor (which would detect any road debris) as well as input data on the road (from the camera mounted on the Raspberry Pi).

The road was made with a sheet of black paper, and details were painted on it. Some barricades and debris were used to create obstructions. The model was trained on various road paths—straight, curved left, curved right, and circular. Testing was done in phases, and after completion, the model was given a final test path with a broad curvature.

9.3.1 Data Collection

Initially, Udacity's Self-Driving Car Simulator was used to generate the training data needed to test the equipment and the plan of action [48]. It gives the user the liberty to drive a car on preset tracks, and the data corresponding to how you drive is collected frame by frame.

The data also contains steering angle and acceleration on each frame. This data helped actualize the direction of this study and formulate the kind of data the project needed so that it could be mapped onto directions. Thus, the data had to be generated independently and was specific to the need of the project [49]. There were two major reasons for this. First, the remote-control car was not taking directions in the form of steering angle but rather only left and right. Second, the camera angle played an important role in how the car understood the road ahead, which greatly affected its decision-making capabilities.

Data was collected from the next set of tests by transmitting direction commands to car's remote and thus to the car via a laptop computer. The camera view was visible on the screen of a remote device using the VNC viewer to stream the camera's input [7]. The car was steered on self-laid tracks of different orientations that were similar to but not the same as those on which the car had been tested. The tracks mimicked unmarked roads and the environment where the car would be tested, and at times the car had to stop or turn to avoid having a collision or going off-road [50].

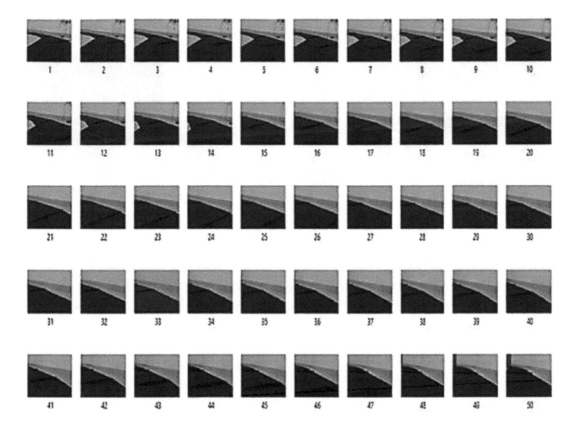

FIGURE 9.2   Sample section of the collected data set.

The frames were captured by the Pi camera staged on a remote-control vehicle, which also documented directions at every moment that were time-synchronized and embedded in the final data set. This was repeated on diverse tracks until a useful amount of data was collected. Thus, the data set had frames containing the tracks as viewed by the Pi camera along with the directions, as shown in Figure 9.2 [51].

9.3.2 Feature Extraction

In each image, unnecessary data was cropped out; i.e., the height of the images was reduced in order to increase the contributing information in the frame, and the images were resized so that less memory was occupied.

The images were then converted into the YUV color system, as it allows a systematic decrease in the quantity of information necessary to constitute images of equivalent quality [52]. To increase the sample data, images containing turns were flipped with the corresponding directions (Figure 9.3).

The brightness of undecided frames was increased to random degrees to account for the changes in lighting conditions, and the same procedure was followed to reduce the brightness of random images in order to make the model more robust.

Furthermore, Gaussian blur was applied to each frame to smooth the image and to reduce noise in the captured frame. Also, it was observed that a disproportionately large

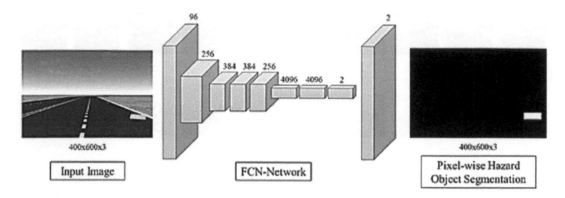

FIGURE 9.3 Feature extraction model using object detection and segmentation.

amount of the recorded data corresponded to the car driving in a straight direction as compared to that recorded while the car was making a right or left turn. Thus, the data had to be normalized to make the scales even and avoid the possibility of a biased model [53].

9.3.3 CNN Architecture

The CNN was trained on our collected data following the VGG16 model. It had 16 layers and used the softmax function as the classification layer, as shown in Figures 9.4 and 9.5. Transfer learning was implemented by freezing the top layer in order to give the desired output.

9.4 DISCUSSION AND RESULTS ANALYSIS

9.4.1 Experimental Setup

For this experiment, we used a toy car and mounted a Raspberry Pi on top of it. An 8 MP camera was inserted in the Raspberry Pi and attached in a way that it gave a clear view of the road ahead. An ultrasonic sensor was attached on the hood of the car to detect any obstructions on the road. The car could be driven by a remote control (the one that came with the toy car) or could be driven autonomously (by applying DNNs). An Arduino Uno microcontroller board was used in this experiment to collect the data from the remote (the data here was input for the Arduino). A Wi-Fi module was also latched onto the Arduino in order to connect it to the built-in Wi-Fi of the Raspberry Pi. This way the Raspberry Pi had access to the data coming from the remote control (data from the Arduino through Wi-Fi)

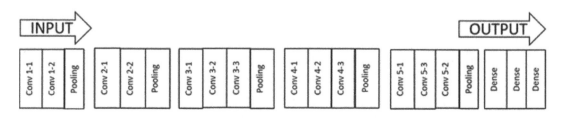

FIGURE 9.4 Deep learning layers used in the project.

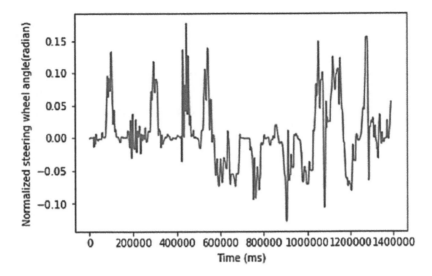

FIGURE 9.5   Results from the training data set captured the curvature of the steering wheel after normalization.

and from the ultrasonic sensor (for detecting any road lumber) as well as input data on the road (from the camera mounted on Raspberry Pi). The road was made with a sheet of black paper, and details were painted on it. Some barricades and debris were used to create obstructions. The model was trained on various road paths—straight, curved left, curved right, and circular. Testing was done in phases, and after completion, the model was given a final test path with a broad curvature, shown in Figure 9.6

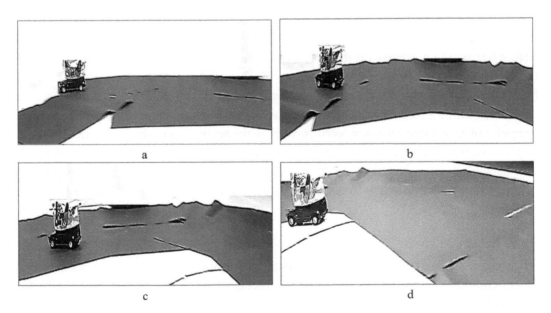

FIGURE 9.6   (a) The car is unable to detect the road on the right-hand side so it makes a left turn. (b) The car is on a circular curvature. (c) The car makes a sharp left turn. (d) The car is shown in a mismatched scenario.

9.4.1.1 Input Component (Camera)

A Pi camera attached to the Model B+ board of the Raspberry Pi, which draws its power from an external power bank, was used to collect input data. The camera was fitted on top of the car in such a way that it provided vision to the car and was over-looking the road and the immediate surroundings. The client program that runs on Raspberry Pi was used to send frames to the neural network, which was also stored in the Pi.

9.4.1.2 Processing Unit (Raspberry Pi)

A computer's processing unit manages numerous chores: inputting the data, training the neural network, projecting the data via commands, and sending the resultant commands to the remote control for the final movement, as shown in Figure 9.1.

9.4.1.3 Unit of Autonomous Vehicle Control

The controller of the car used contained a switch for turning it on and off. The Raspberry Pi was used to simulate button-press actions by soldering the jumper cables to the remote and then connecting them to four general-purpose input/output (GPIO) pins that were selected to collect the pin chips of the remote, communicating actions like turn left, move ahead, turn right, and move back. When the GPIO pins emitted a low signal, it meant that the pins had been given a supply from the ground, whereas a high signal denoted that chip resistance had no effect on the ground [54]. The model returned the resultant commands to the Pi using the serial interface, and the Pi then output the signal as high or low after reading the input command, mimicking the act of driving the autonomous vehicle by pressing buttons.

9.4.2 Simulation

Before testing the hardware on the actual field, the working of the model and the systems in place had to be tested. To achieve this, a video was fed to the training model frame by frame that corresponded to the directions generated by the CNN.

After obtaining these results, it was apparent that the basic functionality had reached the point of acceptable accuracy, as confirmed by the accuracy graphs shown in Figures 9.7 and 9.8. However, due to the hardware restrictions—i.e., having only left, right, forward, and backward controls—no concrete conclusions could be drawn from this effort, and field testing was the only way to be able to understand the working and the shortcomings in detail.

9.4.3 Results Analysis

After rigorous test runs on tracks different from those on which the car was trained, it was concluded that the car was able to function competently in a controlled environment. The neural network was also working correctly and gave better results than those obtained by previous studies, as shown in Table 9.1. The only complications faced pertained to the type of car used, which it was later determined could be comfortably resolved.

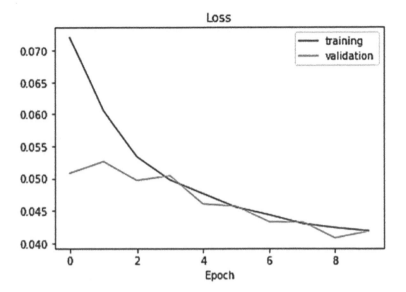

FIGURE 9.7   The result given by the CNN for every frame.

After testing and training the data, a data set of images was obtained from the first trial of our self-driving vehicle. The data set consisted of videos and images with similar structure to the tracks we used in driving vehicle. The test data was used to evaluate the accuracy of the model. A new curvature of the road (on a sheet of black paper) was introduced for each test case. After several tests, we noticed that the accuracy increased and that with every tryout, the car started to make more precise turns. The car drove effortlessly and dodged the obstructions in the lane with apt precision.

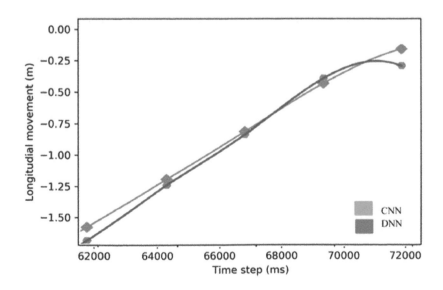

FIGURE 9.8   Accuracy comparison between CNN and DNN.

TABLE 9.1   A Comparison of the Accuracy of the Current Study with That of Others

	Title of Paper	Accuracy
Muller et al. (2006) [55]	Off-Road Obstacle Avoidance through End-to-End Learning	75%
Mori et al. (2019) [56]	Visual Explanation by Attention Branch Network for End-to-End Learning-Based Self-Driving	79%
Xu et al. (2017) [57]	End-to-End Learning of Driving Models from Large- Scale Video Datasets	84.6%
Bojarski et al. (2016) [6]	End to End Learning for Self-Driving Cars	88%
Ours	Automated Guided Autonomous Car Using Deep Learning and Computer Vision	98%

9.5 CONCLUSION

The learning approach used here in building a self-driving vehicle from beginning to end is an effective alternative to the traditional one. The car learned driving mannerisms and could detect the road without the need for explicit labels, and it gave viable results in a limited time frame, making the approach also very cost-effective [58]. The project thus developed should be viewed as independent of the vehicle, like a compressed natural gas kit, as the vision was to develop a setup that could be incorporated into any vehicle, given that its acceleration and direction could be controlled. More work needs to be done on how to make the hardware implement the product of the neural network more precisely.

Some researchers think that the future of vehicles is electric energy-saving vehicles. Today we rely heavily on fossil fuels to run our vehicles, but because these fuels are nonrenewable, they should be used judiciously. By consuming fossil fuels, we are not only exhausting our resources but also adding to air pollution. With electric vehicles, we may think we will have a one less problem to worry about, but believing that vehicles that run on electricity will not cause any harm is incorrect. An automobile running on electric current produces particulate discharge from use of the breaks and wear and tear on the tires, and this emission is also hazardous.

Analysts indicate that it will be about 25 years before autonomous vehicles make up half the automobile market and probably 40 years before there is an autonomous cars. In the coming years, we might see drivers getting rid of vehicles that are not smart and self-driving. It is obvious that at first, autonomous vehicles will be very costly, and only the affluent will have the luxury of using them. There are numerous upsides of self-driving vehicles, but first and foremost, with less reliance on drivers, there will be fewer to no chances of accidents occurring, as the algorithm will have peak precision. Also, this will bring a sense of relief for nondrivers. Nevertheless, unless autonomous vehicles become a common thing, they will not be affordable to moderate-income people/organizations. For these vehicles to be feasible, they need to be flooding the auto market.

REFERENCES

1. Pan, Y., C. A. Cheng, K. Saigol, K. Lee, X. Yan, E. Theodorou, and B. Boots. 2017. Agile Autonomous Driving Using End-to-End Deep Imitation Learning. arXiv preprint, arXiv:1709.07174.
2. Desai, S., and S. Desai. 2017. Smart vehicle automation. *International Journal of Computer Science and Mobile Computing, 6*(9), pp. 46–50.
3. Hussain, R., and S. Zeadally. 2018. Autonomous cars: Research results, issues, and future challenges. *IEEE Communications Surveys & Tutorials, 21*(2), pp. 1275–1313.
4. Lecun, Y., E. Cosatto, J. Ben, U. Muller, and B. Flepp. 2004. DAVE: Autonomous Off-Road Vehicle Control Using End-to-End Learning. Final Technical Report, Net-Scale Technologies http://www.cs.nyu.edu/yann/research/dave/dave-final-report.pdf.
5. Jackel, L. D., E. Krotkov, M. Perschbacher, J. Pippine, and C. Sullivan. 2006. The DARPA LAGR program: Goals, challenges, methodology, and phase I results. *Journal of Field Robotics, 23*(11–12), pp. 945–973.
6. Bojarski, M., D. Del Testa, D. Dworakowski, B. Firner, B. Flepp, P. Goyal, L. D. Jackel, M. Monfort, U. Muller, J. Zhang, and X. Zhang. 2016. End to End Learning for Self-Driving Cars. arXiv preprint, arXiv:1604.07316.
7. Gurghian, A., T. Koduri, S. V. Bailur, K. J. Carey, and V. N. Murali. 2016. DeepLanes: End-to-end lane position estimation using deep neural networks. 2016 IEEE Conference on Computer Vision and Pattern Recognition Workshops (CVPRW), Las Vegas, NV, pp. 38–45.
8. Huang J., et al. 2017. Speed/accuracy trade-offs for modern convolutional object detectors. 2017 IEEE Conference on Computer Vision and Pattern Recognition (CVPR), Honolulu, HI, pp. 3296–3297.
9. Billones, R. K. C., A. A. Bandala, E. Sybingco, L. A. G. Lim, A. D. Fillone, and E. P. Dadios. 2017. Vehicle detection and tracking using corner feature points and artificial neural networks for a vision-based contactless apprehension system. 2017 Computing Conference, London, pp. 688–691.
10. Pomerleau, D. A. 1988. ALVINN: An autonomous land vehicle in a neural network. Advances in Neural Information Processing Systems 1 (NIPS 1988), pp. 305–313.
11. Rowley, H. A., S. Baluja, and T. Kanade. 1998. Neural network-based face detection. *IEEE Transactions on Pattern Analysis and Machine Intelligence, 20*(1), pp. 23–38.
12. Sharifara, A., M. S. Mohd Rahim, and Y. Anisi. 2014. A general review of human face detection including a study of neural networks and Haar feature-based cascade classifier in face detection. 2014 International Symposium on Biometrics and Security Technologies (ISBAST), pp. 73–78.
13. Baykal, S. I., D. Bulut, and O. K. Sahingoz. 2018. Comparing deep learning performance on BigData by using CPUs and GPUs. 2018 Electric Electronics, Computer Science, Biomedical Engineerings' Meeting (EBBT), Istanbul.
14. Mo, Y. J., J. Kim, J. K. Kim, A. Mohaisen, and W. Lee. 2017. Performance of deep learning computation with TensorFlow software library in GPU-capable multi-core computing platforms. 2017 Ninth International Conference on Ubiquitous and Future Networks (ICUFN), pp. 240–242.
15. Gong, T., T. Fan, J. Guo, and Z. Cai. 2017. GPU-based parallel optimization of immune convolutional neural network and embedded system. *Engineering Applications of Artificial Intelligence, 62*, pp. 384–395.
16. Ertugrul, E., U. Kocaman, and O. K. Sahingoz. 2018. Autonomous aerial navigation and mapping for security of smart buildings. 2018 6th International Istanbul Smart Grids and Cities Congress and Fair (ICSG), Istanbul, pp. 168–172.
17. Turker, T., O. K. Sahingoz, and G. Yilmaz. 2015. 2D path planning for UAVs in RADAR threatening environment using simulated annealing algorithm. 2015 International Conference on Unmanned Aircraft Systems (ICUAS), pp. 56–61.

18. Bresson, G., Z. Alsayed, L. Yu, and S. Glaser. 2017. Simultaneous localization and mapping: A survey of current trends in autonomous driving. *IEEE Transactions on Intelligent Vehicles*, *2*(3), pp. 194–220.

19. Choudhury, S., S. P. Chattopadhyay, and T. K. Hazra. 2017. Vehicle detection and counting using Haar feature-based classifier. 2017 8th Annual Industrial Automation and Electromechanical Engineering Conference (IEMECON), Bangkok, pp. 106–109.

20. Tefft, B. C. 2016. The prevalence of motor vehicle crashes involving road debris, United States, 2011–2014. *AAA Foundation for Traffic Safety*, (24), pp. 1–10.

21. Bertozzi, M., A. Broggi, and A. Fascioli. 2000. Vision-based intelligent vehicles: State of the art and perspectives. *Robotics and Autonomous Systems*, *32*(1), pp. 1–16. https://doi.org/10.1016/S0921-8890(99)00125-6.

22. Dagan, E., O. Mano, G. P. Stein, and A. Shashua. 2004. Forward collision warning with a single camera. *IEEE Intelligent Vehicles Symposium, 2004*, pp. 37–42. https://doi.org/10.1109/IVS.2004.1336352.

23. Tatarek, T., J. Kronenberger, and U. Handmann. 2018. Functionality, advantages and limits of the Tesla Autopilot. https://www.semanticscholar.org/paper/Functionality-%2C-Advantages-and-Limits-of-the-Tesla-Tatarek-Kronenberger/3f6d7ec8f532aeabb8a0cb0c8820126648398093

24. Krizhevsky, A., I. Sutskever, and G. E. Hinton. 2012. ImageNet classification with deep convolutional neural networks. Advances in Neural Information Processing Systems 25 (NIPS 2012), pp. 1–9. https://doi.org/http://dx.doi.org/10.1016/j.protcy.2014.09.007.

25. Yang, Z., Y. Zhang, J. Yu, J. Cai, and J. Luo. 2018. End-to-end multi-modal multi-task vehicle control for self-driving cars with visual perception. arXiv:1801.06734.

26. Bhavsar, P., P. Das, M. Paugh, K. Dey, and M. Chowdhury. 2017. Risk analysis of autonomous vehicles in mixed traffic streams. *Transportation Research Record: Journal of the Transportation Research Board*, *2625*(1), pp. 51–61. https://doi.org/10.3141/2625-06.

27. Yao, J., S. Fidler, and R. Urtasun. 2012. Describing the scene as a whole: Joint object detection, scene classification and semantic segmentation. Proceedings of the 2012 IEEE Computer Society Conference on Computer Vision and Pattern Recognition, pp. 702–709. https://doi.org/10.1109/CVPR.2012.6247739.

28. Zhang, M., Y. Zhang, L. Zhang, C. Liu, and S. Khurshid. 2018. DeepRoad: GAN-based metamorphic testing and input validation framework for autonomous driving systems. Proceedings of the 33rd ACM/IEEE International Conference on Automated Software Engineering, pp. 132–142. https://doi.org/10.1145/3238147.3238187.

29. Sak, H., A. Senior, and F. Beaufays. 2014, Long short-term memory recurrent neural network architectures for large scale acoustic modeling. 15th Annual Conference of the International Speech Communication, pp. 338–342. arXiv:1402.1128.

30. Udacity, Inc. n.d. Self driving car. https://github.com/udacity/self-driving-car.

31. Takahashi, N., Shibata, N., and Nonaka, K. 2020. Optimal configuration control of planar leg/wheel mobile robots for flexible obstacle avoidance. *Control Engineering Practice*, *101*, p. 104503.

32. Carlini, N., and D. Wagner. 2017. Towards evaluating the robustness of neural networks. Proceedings—IEEE Symposium on Security and Privacy, pp. 39–57. https://doi.org/10.1109/SP.2017.49.

33. Papernot, N., P. McDaniel, X. Wu, S. Jha, and A. Swami. 2016. Distillation as a defense to adversarial perturbations against deep neural networks. Proceedings—2016 IEEE Symposium on Security and Privacy (SP 2016), pp. 582–597. https://doi.org/10.1109/SP.2016.41.

34. Athalye, A., N. Carlini, and D. Wagner. 2018. Obfuscated gradients give a false sense of security: Circumventing defenses to adversarial examples. arXiv:1802.00420v4.

35. Papernot, N., P. McDaniel, S. Jha, M. Fredrikson, Z. B. Celik, and A. Swami. 2016. The limitations of deep learning in adversarial settings. Proceedings—2016 IEEE European Symposium on Security and Privacy (EURO S and P 2016), pp. 372–387. https://doi.org/10.1109/EuroSP.2016.36.

36. Eykholt, K., I. Evtimov, E. Fernandes, B. Li, A. Rahmati, C. Xiao, A. Prakash, T. Kohno, and D. Song. 2018. Robust physical-world attacks on deep learning models. 2018 IEEE/CVF Conference on Computer Vision and Pattern Recognition, pp. 1625–1634 https://doi.org/10.1109/CVPR.2018.00175.

37. Geiger, A., P. Lenz, C. Stiller, and R. Urtasun. 2013. Vision meets robotics: The KITTI dataset. *International Journal of Robotics Research*, 32(11), pp. 1231–1237. https://doi.org/10.1177/0278364913491297.

38. Cordts, M., M. Omran, S. Ramos, T. Rehfeld, M. Enzweiler, R. Benenson, U. Franke, S. Roth, and B. Schiele. 2016. The Cityscapes dataset for semantic urban scene understanding. 2016 IEEE Conference on Computer Vision and Pattern Recognition (CVPR), pp. 3213–3223. https://doi.org/10.1109/CVPR.2016.350.

39. Guo, Y., Y. Liu, T. Georgiou, and M. S. Lew. 2018. A review of semantic segmentation using deep neural networks. *International Journal of Multimedia Information Retrieval*, 7(2), pp. 87–93. https://doi.org/10.1007/s13735-017-0141-z.

40. Caesar, H., J. Uijlings, and V. Ferrari. 2016. Region-based semantic segmentation with end-to-end training. Lecture Notes in Computer Science (Including Subseries Lecture Notes in Artificial Intelligence and Lecture Notes in Bioinformatics), vol. 9905, pp. 381–397. https://doi.org/10.1007/978-3-319-46448-0_23.

41. Girshick, R., J. Donahue, T. Darrell, and J. Malik. 2014. Rich feature hierarchies for accurate object detection and semantic segmentation. Proceedings of the 2014 IEEE Computer Society Conference on Computer Vision and Pattern Recognition, pp. 580–587. https://doi.org/10.1109/CVPR.2014.81.

42. Long, J., E. Shelhamer, and T. Darrell. 2015. Fully convolutional networks for semantic segmentation. Proceedings of the 2015 IEEE Computer Society Conference on Computer Vision and Pattern Recognition, pp. 3431–3440. https://doi.org/10.1109/CVPR.2015.7298965.

43. Eigen, D., and R. Fergus. 2015. Predicting depth, surface normals and semantic labels with a common multi-scale convolutional architecture. 2015 IEEE International Conference on Computer Vision (ICCV), pp. 2650–2658. https://doi.org/10.1109/ICCV.2015.304.

44. Liu, Y., Y. Guo, and M. S. Lew. 2017. On the exploration of convolutional fusion networks for visual recognition. Lecture Notes in Computer Science (Including Subseries Lecture Notes in Artificial Intelligence and Lecture Notes in Bioinformatics), vol. 10132, no. 1, pp. 277–289. https://doi.org/10.1007/978-3-319-51811-4_23.

45. Dai, J., K. He, and J. Sun. 2015. BoxSup: Exploiting bounding boxes to supervise convolutional networks for semantic segmentation. Proceedings of the 2015 IEEE International Conference on Computer Vision, pp. 1635–1643. https://doi.org/10.1109/ICCV.2015.191.

46. Papandreou, G., L.-C. Chen, K. P. Murphy, and A. L. Yuille. 2015. Weakly- and semi-supervised learning of a deep convolutional network for semantic image segmentation. 2015 IEEE International Conference on Computer Vision (ICCV), pp. 1742–1750. https://doi.org/10.1109/ICCV.2015.203.

47. Khoreva, A., R. Benenson, J. Hosang, M. Hein, and B. Schiele. 2017. Simple does it: Weakly supervised instance and semantic segmentation. Proceedings—30th IEEE Conference on Computer Vision and Pattern Recognition (CVPR 2017), pp. 1665–1674. https://doi.org/10.1109/CVPR.2017.181.

48. Udacity, Inc. n.d. Self-Driving Car Simulator. https://github.com/udacity/self-driving-car-sim. Accessed on 5 Feb. 2019.

49. Eraqi, H. M., M. N. Moustafa, and J. Honer. 2017. End-to-end deep learning for steering autonomous vehicles considering temporal dependencies. 31st Conference on Neural Information Processing Systems (NIPS), pp. 1–8. arXiv:1710.03804.

50. Teichmann, M., M. Weber, M. Zoellner, R. Cipolla, and R. Urtasun. 2018. MultiNet: Real-time joint semantic reasoning for autonomous driving. 2018 IEEE Intelligent Vehicles Symposium (IV), pp. 1013–1020. https://doi.org/10.1109/IVS.2018.8500504.

51. Siam, M., S. Elkerdawy, M. Jagersand, and S. Yogamani. 2018. Deep semantic segmentation for automated driving: Taxonomy, roadmap and challenges. Proceedings of the 2018 IEEE Conference on Intelligent Transportation Systems (ITSC), pp. 1–8. https://doi.org/10.1109/ITSC.2017.8317714.

52. Podpora, M., G. P. Korbas, and A. Kawala-Janik. 2014. YUV vs RGB: Choosing a color space for human-machine interaction. *FedCSIS Position Papers, 18*, pp. 29–34.

53. Zhang, Jiakai. 2019. *End-to-end learning for autonomous driving*. Dissertation, New York University.

54. Wang, Zheng. 2018. Self driving RC car. https://zhengludwig.wordpress.com/projects/self-driving-rc-car/.

55. Muller, U., Ben, J., Cosatto, E., Flepp, B., and Cun, Y. L. 2006. Off-road obstacle avoidance through end-to-end learning. In Advances in neural information processing systems, pp. 739–746.

56. Mori, Keisuke, et al. 2019. Visual explanation by attention branch network for end-to-end learning-based self-driving. 2019 IEEE intelligent vehicles symposium (IV). IEEE.

57. Xu, H., Gao, Y., Yu, F., and Darrell, T. 2017. End-to-end learning of driving models from large-scale video datasets. In Proceedings of the IEEE conference on computer vision and pattern recognition (pp. 2174–2182).

58. Rajasekhar, M. V., and A. K. Jaswal. 2015. Autonomous vehicles: The future of automobiles. 2015 IEEE International Transportation Electrification Conference (ITEC), pp. 1–6.

CHAPTER 10

Deep Learning for Obstacle Avoidance in Autonomous Driving

Mallika Garg

Indian Institute of Technology Roorkee
Roorkee, India

Jagpal Singh Ubhi

Sant Longowal Institute of Engineering and Technology
Longowal, India

Ashwani Kumar Aggarwal

Sant Longowal Institute of Engineering and Technology
Longowal, India

CONTENTS

DOI: 10.1201/9781003048381-11

Autonomous driving is one of the hot areas of research and business in the modern era. In the past few decades, huge advancements have been made in this area. When driving, a human is required to keep an eye on the road and detect the obstacles coming in his path. So in autonomous vehicle driving, it is extremely significant to detect, recognize, track, and localize static and dynamic obstacles such as other vehicles, animals, trees, signboards, pedestrians, and buildings in order to avoid these obstacles. This can be done using various deep learning techniques, in which the images of the scene are provided as input to the system, and information such as the position, size, and category of the obstacle is taken as output used by the system to guide further action of the autonomous vehicle.

Some of the leading-edge algorithms and techniques for dealing with obstacles will be discussed in this chapter. Computer vision has played a significant role in many tasks needed for autonomous vehicle driving; nevertheless, several issues and challenges need to be addressed for autonomous driving to be safe and feasible in diverse environments. Vision-based obstacle detection, avoidance, and depth prediction present a significant visual relationship. The objects with different depths to the camera have different attributes (pose, size, and definition). Nowadays, researchers in this field are evaluating the performances of their algorithms on various datasets for autonomous driving such as the KITTI dataset, Caltech pedestrian dataset, nuScenes, and Waymo open multimodal sensor dataset. This chapter will discuss various real-time challenges in the context of obstacle detection for autonomous driving such as small objects, occlusion, shadows, object size variations, and loss of depth information while projecting a three-dimensional scene on a two-dimensional plane. Along with high accuracy, obstacle detection should occur at high speed to ensure safe navigation during self-assisted driving. After object detection, an object avoidance strategy is deployed to avoid the detected obstacle. More recent methods like region-based convolutional neural networks (R-CNNs) use region proposal methods to locate an object in an image and then classify that object in a particular class. Various region proposal networks such as Fast R-CNN, Faster R-CNN, You Only Look Once (YOLO), and single-shot detector will be discussed. In this chapter, we also define various deep learning solutions provided for the above-mentioned challenges in this field. The advances in computing resources have boosted the research in this field. The resulting systems are less costly and more reliable, accurate, and flexible. Finally, this chapter considers its main focus, on deep learning for obstacle detection, elaborating different models that have been adapted to improve the performance of the system.

10.1 INTRODUCTION

Autonomous vehicles can play a key role in urban transportation frameworks, as they offer the potential for extra security, expanded profitability and productivity, more prominent availability, better street proficiency, and a positive effect on nature. Research in autonomous systems has resulted in sensational advances in just a few years because of the increases in accessible computing power and decrease in expenses related to detecting and sensing innovations. All this has brought the field closer to the mechanical availability of completely self-sufficient vehicles.

The self-driving car has to detect different kinds of vehicles, road signs, road signals, and pedestrians on the road, among other things. For this, various detection algorithms are deployed to perceive the various obstacles in a fast and accurate manner. This minimizes the risk of accidents, as now the self-assisted vehicle can detect the obstacles in its path. The advances in computing technology and modern devices have been the main improvement that generated enthusiasm for this field. Finally, the subject of this chapter is deep learning for obstacle detection, which concerns the selection of models and algorithms that can have their parameters tuned to improve the recommended performance criterion. The motivation behind this chapter is to study the algorithms used to detect, classify, and track the obstacles for self-driving vehicles. Different devices like cameras, sensors, laser scanners, and the global positioning system/inertial navigation system (GPS/INS) are utilized to assemble information from the scene. Detection can be done on various types of objects coming in the nearby vicinity of the autonomous vehicle. For each type of obstacle, different algorithms and datasets, such as the following, are used:

1. *Road detection:* The main issue for the autonomous or self-driving vehicle is road detection [12], which means the surface of the road on which the vehicle drives has to be detected.

2. *Road markings detection:* Symbolic road markings (SRMs) are the images painted on the lanes to assist the driver in safely securely driving the vehicle. These road markings are painted in bright hues or colors—for the most part, in white or yellow. These may incorporate arrow marks, zebra crossings, traffic signs, railway crossings, speed limits, merge signs, and Ped and Xing signs [1].

3. *Obstacle detection:* Obstacle detection includes the detection of pedestrians, animals, other vehicles, and objects in the nearby vicinity of the vehicle.

10.1.1 Road Detection

Road detection is a significant undertaking for self-sufficient automobile applications. Street detection implies finding a street area without previous information on street geometry and incorporates a couple of essential steps. In particular, road localization computes the position and size of the autonomous driving system (ADS) relative to the street parameters, while lane tracking upgrades the street boundaries from previous street boundaries and dimensions. Video-based lane detection continuously draws attention to this subject, since it has numerous benefits in contrast to dynamic sensors. Moreover, two kinds of detection methodologies have been developed: one for well-organized lanes marked with path markings and one for unstructured lanes.

There are various algorithms for lane detection and tracking. In many models of independent vehicles all over the world, road detection and driving are two independent categories. Though traditional frameworks did not depend on the fundamental of lane recognition, instructions were given based on the road images. For instance, an intelligent automobile developed by Carnegie Mellon University and named autonomous land vehicle in a neural net (ALVINN), had a network with one hidden layer [23]. In this model, the input layer of the network had dimensions of 30 × 32, and the output was a linear representation of the direction of the automobile's movement, with the goal that the self-driving automobile would be able to navigate safely on a track. In training, the vehicle could self-sufficiently follow a path. This framework allowed the autonomous vehicle to drive on different street types under various conditions. The results for road detection were compared and indicated that the adaptive random Hough transform (ARHT) [18] was more effective than the genetic algorithm [19].

A large portion of the work on representative street identification and acknowledgment follows the two stages of object recognition: i.e., object detection and object classification. In [1], Ahmad et al. examine the utilization of convolutional neural networks (CNNs) to characterize painted representative street markings. Traditional work on road marking recognition is for the most part dependent either on layout coordination or on feature extraction in sequence with classifier training, which isn't generally viable. But with the neural networks and their achievement in ADS frameworks, it is normal to examine the appropriateness of the network for road marking recognition. In contrast to other research, the main focus is exclusively on road marking recognition, which is broadly investigated and is dependent on features of the inverse perspective mapping (IPM) pictures. Figure 10.1 shows examples of the traffic signs and symbols used.

10.1.2 Vehicle and Object Detection and Tracking

Vehicle and object detection is a salient and prominent research area for ADS. Detection systems are being used in driver-assistance systems and self-driving automobiles. However, achieving robust detection in the real world is really a challenging task. Some vision-based sensors have the potential to estimate the distance between the self-assisted vehicle and

FIGURE 10.1   Various traffic signs and symbols.

an object. But these vision sensors are dependent on weather conditions and lighting or illumination of the scene. Single-vision sensors are not able to estimate the exact distance and position of the object, since depth information is not gathered by these sensors. To deal with the various limitations of different sensors, a multimodal sensor strategy is often used for detection and tracking.

Basic practices in framework design have been established throughout the years. A large portion of the ADS separate the huge undertaking of self-driving into subcategories and utilize various sensors and techniques on different modules. Nowadays, end-to-end driving schemes have been developed in contrast to modular schemes. Deep neural networks are being used in a large number of applications. In the ADS object detection module, the speed of detection and recognition plays an important role. Along with this, the speed and direction of the obstacle are estimated [6].

The remainder of this chapter consists of three sections, two of which have subsections. Section 10.2 discusses the detection and classification of obstacles in the path of the autonomous vehicle, issues and challenges related to obstacle detection, and datasets used in obstacle detection. Section 10.3 considers the algorithms for obstacle avoidance using deep learning, different deep learning architectures that involve CNN and its variants, and the detailed YOLO algorithm for obstacle avoidance. Section 10.4 provides concluding remarks.

10.2 OBSTACLE DETECTION

As already mentioned in section 10.1, obstacles seen by the autonomous vehicle can be of any type. They may be traffic signs, road markings, pedestrians, trees, other vehicles, etc. All of them can be detected by object detection frameworks. There are various feature extraction techniques and training algorithms available for object detection. These detection algorithms can be based on machine learning and deep learning–based approaches. In autonomous vehicle driving, it is extremely important to detect, recognize, track, and localize static and dynamic obstacles.

Before going into object detection in an ADS, it is necessary to have some knowledge of computer vision. Following are a few terms used in computer vision:

1. *Object classification:* In this technique, each object in an image is classified as a particular category or class and assigned a probability that the object will fall into that category in the image. It essentially answers the question "What objects are in the image or frames of the video?" and indicates the probability that each resembles the objects in the class to which is it assigned.

2. *Object localization:* This method can predict where the object is in the image, along with the probability it belongs to a particular class. This answers to question "What objects are in the image, and where are they located?" A bounding box describes the exact location of each object.

3. *Object detection:* In a real-life scenario, we may have to find multiple objects and their positions in an image. Object detection combines object classification and

localization for multiple-object images. In this, the locations of multiple objects are specified by multiple bounding boxes, with each having a class label.

4. *Instance segmentation:* Instance segmentation extracts the actual instance of the object from the image. In detection, the bounding box that is drawn may include some portions of the background along with the object, but in instance segmentation, the instance of the object is separated from the image.

There are many applications where object detection and recognition is required: e.g., face detection, human detection, traffic monitoring, ADS, optical character recognition, and traffic sign recognition. The whole procedure of road tracking and navigating relies on three key issues: localization, mapping, and object tracking. Localization is the process of locating the position of the ADS in its surroundings. Mapping involves being able to get an idea of the surroundings. Tracking static and moving objects includes being able to identify and track these objects during navigation.

There are numerous applications where object identification and acknowledgment is needed: e.g., face identification, human discovery, traffic observing, ADS, optical character acknowledgment, and traffic sign acknowledgment. The cycle of way following and self-sufficient vehicle direction relies on three things: restriction, planning, and following moving objects. Restriction is a way of distinguishing the situation of the self-ruling vehicle in its environment. Planning incorporates the option to comprehend the environment. Following moving objects includes the option to distinguish and track the moving objects. In this section, our principal focus is article recognition in ADS.

10.2.1 Obstacle Detection in Autonomous Vehicles

This chapter presents a huge range of research work on detecting and avoiding obstacles in the path of autonomous vehicles using deep learning frameworks. In deep learning, the objective is to update the weights of a deep neural network during training and to recognize the obstacle from a 2-D image or a 3-D point cloud acquired from cameras and light detection and ranging (LiDAR) devices, respectively. There are numerous deep learning frameworks available for obstacle detection. Depending on the type of data, they can be classified as supervised or unsupervised learning. Supervised learning utilizes labeled data, while unsupervised learning does not require labeled data. During training, the network weights are updated for each instance until the error during training convergences and reaches an optimal value.

Zou et al. [30] propose a robust framework for lane detection in the multiple frames of a driving scene. The algorithm uses a combination of a CNN with a state-of-the-art recurrent neural network (RNN). The CNN extracts the features from each frame of multiple continuous frames. The features are then given as input to a double-layer long short-term memory (LSTM) block to predict the lane. In this method, the multiple consecutive images play a significant role in the detection. A similar method that uses the combination of CNN and RNN is discussed in [17]. In this, the road images are first divided into a number of continuous slices before feeding them to the CNN.

Despite using a combination of CNN and RNN, independent networks can be used for object detection and avoidance. Muller et al. [21] describe a vision-based obstacle avoidance system for off-road obstacles in extremely diverse situations. This model uses a CNN that takes input from two color stereo cameras. The CNN learns the local and shift-invariant features with minimal training of the network. The robot is a 50cm off-road truck. An RNN-based model is presented in [25]. It incorporates RNNs for lane keeping and obstacle avoidance.

10.2.2 Issues and Challenges in Obstacle Detection

Navigation of vehicles with no human assistance in indeterministic environments is really a challenging task. There are various issues and challenges that occur in object detection in ADS [29]:

1. The natural factors—for instance, climate conditions such as shadows, rain, and fog and human conduct—are profoundly random and hard to determine.

2. The ADS sometimes fails due to an incorrect estimation of the speed of a vehicle coming from the opposite direction.

3. Sometimes the object detection module is not able to recognize the object due to shadows, haze, etc.

4. Accidents have increased due to takeovers, which is still a problem that needs to be solved.

5. In the case of an unavoidable mishap, it is very difficult for the ADS to decide in what manner the framework should carry on for the correct navigation.

Along with these issues, an ideal opportunity to arrive at the destination, fuel consumption, comfort, and driving rules expand the complexity. Whether all these things can be considered in a single-object detection algorithm is really an unanswered question.

10.2.3 Datasets used in Obstacle Detection

Datasets are important for scientists and designers, as a large number of the methods and apparatuses must be tried and tested before the autonomous vehicle is developed. Ordinarily, sources of information are given as input to a multitude of calculations and algorithms with different aims and target outputs. The typical flow of developing an algorithm involves training, testing, and then approving the algorithm independently on different datasets. As an illustration, the raw images from a source can be given as input to the detection network to detect and track the nearby vehicles and objects. After this, this information can be utilized for arranging the resources of the vehicle to follow the trajectory. Despite the fact that these two processes are associated with the same vehicle, the obstacle detection network can be trained and tested independently to develop the full algorithm. There is a huge number of datasets that are well suited to the purpose of training a neural network for object detection and recognition.

A few of the regularly utilized datasets for object detection ad recognition are ImageNet [10] and COCO [20]. While these conventional image datasets can be used for training the model, they lack the adequate context needed to test the effectiveness of ADS. So nowadays researchers in this field have developed datasets for autonomous driving, such as the KITTI dataset, Caltech pedestrian dataset, nuScenes, and Waymo open multimodal sensor dataset. nuScenes is the latest urban driving dataset with image and LiDAR sensors [4]. It consists of 1,000 scenes having 25 classes and attributes with 3-D bounding boxes. Overall, it contains about 1.4 million images, 400,000 LiDAR sweeps, 1.3 million RADAR sweeps, and 1.1 million bounding boxes in 40 keyframes.

The PASCAL VOC dataset [11] was one of the first datasets to highlight a lot of information with applicable classes for the ADS. Pascal VOC 2012 is a publicly available dataset for object detection and image segmentation tasks. There is lot of variations in size, shape, position, orientation, illumination, and occlusion in the VOC datasets. It has images with 20 image classes, and all images were taken from the Flickr's website. The total number of annotated images is 11,540, with 5,717 training images and 5,823 validation images. The total number of annotated objects is 27,450, so it contains an average of 1,372 objects per class.

The KITTI Vision Benchmark [13] in 2012 added a huge number of labeled driving scenes, which were missing in the earlier datasets. This dataset was acquired by driving a vehicle in the rural areas and on the highways around the midsized city of Karlsruhe, Germany. It contains 7,481 training images with 3-D bounding boxes. There is a maximum of 15 cars and 30 pedestrians in an image.

UC Berkeley DeepDrive [28] is an ongoing dataset with annotated images. It consists of 100,000 videos of more than 1,000 hours of driving, along with trajectory information. This dataset contains annotated images for instance segmentation, image tagging, domain adaptation, lane detection, drivable area segmentation, object detection, semantic segmentation, multiobject detection tracking, multiobject segmentation tracking, and imitation learning.

For sematic understanding of street scenes, Mapillary Vistas [22] is used. It is an enormous image dataset having 25,000 high-resolution images with 152 object categories. Another dataset having LiDAR, images, and driving information is the LiVi-Set [5]. CommonRoad [2] and SHRP2 [3] are other benchmarks. Some other driving datasets for training ADS are the 100-car study [16] and NUDrive [26].

10.3 OBSTACLE AVOIDANCE USING DEEP LEARNING

Real-time obstacle or hindrance evasion is a central concern in guiding autonomous vehicles; however, it remains a challenge. So the decision-making device plays a vital role in ADS by dealing with the complex dynamics of the environment and the unknown navigation situations. As a human-computer interaction (HCI) system, an ADS is required to work in an environment surrounded by humans or other vehicles. Therefore, obstacle avoidance has gained much attention where the ADS performs object avoidance on real-time stationary or moving obstacles to reach the destination. A lot of research has been

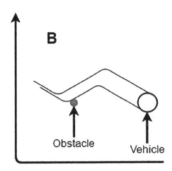

FIGURE 10.2   Single-obstacle avoidance scheme. (A) shows the motion trajectories of the autonomous vehicle in the case of no obstacle avoidance algorithm. (B) Shows the motion trajectories in the case of an obstacle avoidance algorithm [see Ref. [27].

done, providing the promising results shown in Figures 10.2 and 10.3. However, there are some issues in all obstacle avoidance algorithms that need to be resolved:

1. The algorithms are not robust with regard to changes and uncertainty in the nearby surroundings and environment.

2. The control mechanism of the ADS is too complex for a real-time application because of sensor fusion which are complicated to be deployed in a real-time device.

3. The algorithms already designed [7] for obstacle avoidance consider some hypothetical situations that are still not real-time applicable.

Xu et al. [27] propose an algorithm that considers deep RNN to control the ADS navigation. Critical point sets are used to represent the distances between the robot and obstacles. After that, the obstacle avoidance scheme is customized by the inequality constraints. Multiple constraints are considered in order to formulate the control problem as quadratic programming. To solve these quadratic-programming issues online, a deep RNN is established. This model is able to avoid real-time obstacles while following a predefined direction.

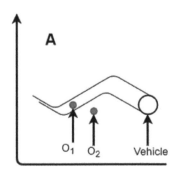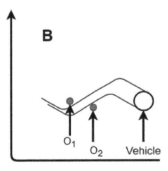

FIGURE 10.3   Multiple-obstacle avoidance scheme. (A) shows the motion trajectories of the autonomous vehicle in the case of no obstacle avoidance algorithm. (B) shows the motion trajectories in the case of an obstacle avoidance algorithm [see Ref. [27].

10.3.1 Deep Learning Architectures and Their Variants

In this section, we consider various deep neural networks that can be used for obstacle avoidance. More recent methods like regions with CNN features (R-CNN) [15] use region proposals for simple and scalable object detection. Increased speed is enabled by Fast R-CNN [14]. It is built on R-CNN and effectively classifies object proposals using deep learning at a speed nine times faster than that of R-CNN on a VGG16 network. These methods depend on region proposal algorithms. In the next step, a region proposal network (RPN) is used along with the object detection algorithm in Faster R-CNN [24].

In R-CNN, given an input image, a bottom-up region proposal is used to localize and segment the objects present in the image. The CNN generates 2,000 regions using the selective search algorithm. Each pixel of the proposed region is wrapped in a bounding box of a specific size. A feature representation of 2000×4098 is then fed to the CNN for feature extraction, and the features extracted are then passed to the support vector machine (SVM) for prediction of the object present in the proposed region.

Along with objects in the region proposals, offset values are predicted by R-CNN. However, there are certain problems with R-CNN:

1. Though the model produces good results, it is quite slow, and computational costs are high.

2. Since the proposal region is wrapped, the exact size of the object cannot be estimated.

3. It takes around 47 seconds to test each image, so it is less reliable for real-time applications.

4. The selective search algorithm is fixed, so it can generate false or poor region proposals.

The computational costs of R-CNN are very high, as the 2,000 region proposals are fed to the CNN, so to tackle this issue of R-CNN, the whole image is fed to the CNN, and the feature map is produced in Fast R-CNN. Then the feature map is used to locate the region proposals, which are then given to a fully connected layer. This is how region of interest (RoI) is obtained and then used to predict the class of the proposed region.

Both these networks are based on region proposals, and the process takes as much time as the detection algorithm. Also, the selective search algorithm is also fixed, not learned, which affects the results. So a further enhancement in speed has been proposed by introducing an RPN. The RPN does not add any cost to the region proposals, as they utilize the layers of the detection network used for the region proposal and do not require their own layers. After this, the classification procedure is same as that of Fast R-CNN.

10.3.2 YOLO Architecture

Faster R-CNN is much faster than other networks, so much so that now it can be used in most of the real-world applications—e.g., self-driving cars and robots—where the performance of the system depends on the object detection algorithm. Further proposed as an improvement is the use of a single-shot detectors, which are even faster and less costly. While they are less accurate, they requires less power for detection, which makes them reliable for real-time applications. In these algorithms, no selection of region proposals is done in the image; rather, the classes and bounding boxes for the whole image are predicted at once. This makes detection even faster than with classification algorithms. This algorithm is called YOLO. The YOLO-based object detector is so fast that it can be used for any real-time object detection application, like in autonomous vehicles.

YOLO splits the image into several cells, typically using an S*S grid. Each grid cell predicts the bounding boxes along with the confidence scores for each box, which is the intersection over union (IoU) between the predicted bounding box and the real ground truth box, where IoU is given in Equation 10.1:

$$IoU = \frac{Size\,of\,intersection}{Size\,of\,union\,area} \tag{10.1}$$

The label for each grid cell is an eight-dimensional output vector: four dimensions are for the bounding box center's x and y coordinates and the width and height of the bounding box, one is for the confidence score, and three are for the class probability (if it is a three-class problem). This vector is given as output for each bounding box, so the size of output vector is eight times the number of bounding boxes. The bounding boxes in the cell may or may not contain an object. Bounding boxes with lesser probability are then eliminated using a non-max suppression method.

There are two networks of YOLO. The base network works on 45 frames per second and is better than real-time. The fast version of YOLO works at a higher rate of 155 frames per second, although with less accuracy as compared to the base model. Further enhancement is proposed in YOLO in different versions: YOLO 9000, YOLOv3, YOLOv4, and YOLOv5. While not all these versions are discussed in this chapter, they can be used for obstacle detection in autonomous vehicles.

10.3.3 YOLO for Autonomous Vehicle Applications

As already discussed, YOLO can be used for multiclass problems. These classes can be cars, buses, pedestrians, motorcycles, trucks, traffic lights, background, and many more things if they are used for autonomous vehicle applications. Let us assume that we are building a car detection system for a self-driving car. For the sake of understanding, suppose we are dealing with only three classes: pedestrian, bicycle, and cars. In this case, the class label is a three-dimensional vector, in which one dimension is 1 and the rest are 0. This is illustrated in Figure 10.4. Here we are using one hot encoding for class labels, which means c = 3 is represented as 0, 0, 1 for the car class.

Choi et al. [8] uses the state-of-the-art YOLOv3 with a Gaussian parameter for accurate and fast object detection for ADS. The Gaussian parameter is modeled with the bounding box (bbox) of YOLOv3, which helps to increase the detection accuracy of the framework. In addition, the framework predicts the localization variability that symbolizes the reliability of bounding box. The mean average precision (mAP) is increased on the KITTI and

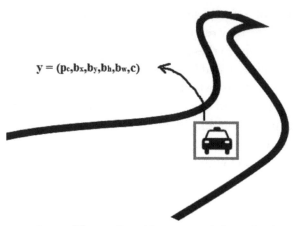

$y = (p_c, b_x, b_y, b_h, b_w, c)$

$p_c = 1$: confidence of an object present in bounding box
$c = 3$: class of object (here 3 for car)

FIGURE 10.4   YOLO detection for an autonomous vehicle.

Berkeley Deep Drive (BDD) datasets when compared to the precision of the conventional YOLOv3. Similarly, Ciberlin et al. [9] used the Viola–Jones algorithm and YOLOv3 algorithm for object detection from the front-view camera. Four groups were divided from nine detectors, which achieved precision and recall values of 0.88 and 0.86 for vehicle detection, 0.9 and 0.92 for pedestrian detection, 0.80 and 0.84 for traffic light detection, and 0.9 and 0.89 for traffic sign detection.

10.4 CONCLUSION

In this chapter on deep learning frameworks for ADS, we have indicated some of the recent trends in the existing systems. We can conclude from this chapter that several deep neural network models have already been proposed for object detection and avoidance. Despite the shortcomings that these systems pose, they can be considered tremendous achievements in this area. The localization, mapping, and detection algorithms still lack accuracy and efficiency. Anything that is not an ideal road condition poses a challenge for autonomous vehicles. Still if ideal conditions are not reached, proposing an algorithm that is significant in overcoming the drawbacks of state-of-the-art methods or proposing an alternative to state-of-the-art methods is worthwhile.

In the future, various enhancements to the existing algorithms for lane detection can be made. The various levels of autonomous vehicles have been achieved to date except level 5, which is a fully autonomous vehicle, and this area needs more research. Many improvements and advances are required for a self-driving vehicle to fully achieve level 5. The development of a completely self-governing driving framework will require a few other segments besides the absolutely independent obstacle detection and avoidance system described here. The system reviewed in this chapter is only one segment of a future framework that will incorporate map building, visual odometry, way finding, and different systems for navigating trajectories.

REFERENCES

1. Touqeer Ahmad, David Ilstrup, Ebrahim Emami, and George Bebis. Symbolic road marking recognition using convolutional neural networks. In *2017 IEEE Intelligent Vehicles Symposium (IV)*, pages 1428–1433. IEEE, 2017.

2. Matthias Althoff, Markus Koschi, and Stefanie Manzinger. CommonRoad: Composable benchmarks for motion planning on roads. In *2017 IEEE Intelligent Vehicles Symposium (IV)*, pages 719–726. IEEE, 2017.

3. Alan Blatt, John Pierowicz, Marie Flanigan, Pei-Sung Lin, Achilleas Kourtellis, Chanyoung Lee, Paul Jovanis, James Jenness, Martha Wilaby, John Campbell, et al. Naturalistic driving study: Field data collection. Technical report, National Academies of Sciences, Engineering, and Medicine, 2015.

4. Holger Caesar, Varun Bankiti, Alex H. Lang, Sourabh Vora, Venice Erin Liong, Qiang Xu, Anush Krishnan, Yu Pan, Giancarlo Baldan, and Oscar Beijbom. nuScenes: A multimodal dataset for autonomous driving. In *Proceedings of the IEEE/CVF Conference on Computer Vision and Pattern Recognition*, pages 11621–11631. IEEE, 2020.

5. Yiping Chen, Jingkang Wang, Jonathan Li, Cewu Lu, Zhipeng Luo, Han Xue, and Cheng Wang. LiDAR-video driving dataset: Learning driving policies effectively. In *Proceedings of the IEEE Conference on Computer Vision and Pattern Recognition*, pages 5870–5878. IEEE, 2018.

6. Hong Cheng. *Autonomous Intelligent Vehicles: Theory, Algorithms, and Implementation.* Springer Science & Business Media, 2011.

7. Yin Cheng and Weidong Zhang. Concise deep reinforcement learning obstacle avoidance for underactuated unmanned marine vessels. *Neurocomputing*, 272:63–73, 2018.

8. Jiwoong Choi, Dayoung Chun, Hyun Kim, and Hyuk-Jae Lee. Gaussian YOLOv3: An accurate and fast object detector using localization uncertainty for autonomous driving. In *Proceedings of the IEEE International Conference on Computer Vision*, pages 502–511. IEEE, 2019.

9. Juraj Ciberlin, Ratko Grbić, Nikola Teslić, and Miloš Pilipović. Object detection and object tracking in front of the vehicle using front view camera. In *2019 Zooming Innovation in Consumer Technologies Conference (ZINC)*, pages 27–32. IEEE, 2019.

10. Jia Deng, Wei Dong, Richard Socher, Li-Jia Li, Kai Li, and Li Fei-Fei. ImageNet: A large-scale hierarchical image database. In *2009 IEEE Conference on Computer Vision and Pattern Recognition*, pages 248–255. IEEE, 2009.

11. Mark Everingham, Andrew Zisserman, Christopher K. I. Williams, Luc Van Gool, Moray Allan, Christopher M. Bishop, Olivier Chapelle, Navneet Dalal, Thomas Deselaers, Gyuri Dorkó, et al. The 2005 PASCAL Visual Object Classes Challenge. In *Machine Learning Challenges Workshop*, pages 117–176. Springer, 2005.

12. Carlos Fernandez, David Fernandez-Llorca, and Miguel A Sotelo. A hybrid vision-map method for urban road detection. *Journal of Advanced Transportation*, 2017, Hindawi Publishers, 2017. DOI: https://doi.org/10.1155/2017/70.

13. Andreas Geiger, Philip Lenz, and Raquel Urtasun. Are we ready for autonomous driving? The KITTI vision benchmark suite. In *2012 IEEE Conference on Computer Vision and Pattern Recognition*, pages 3354–3361. IEEE, 2012.

14. Ross Girshick. Fast R-CNN. In *Proceedings of the IEEE International Conference on Computer Vision*, pages 1440–1448. IEEE, 2015.

15. Ross Girshick, Jeff Donahue, Trevor Darrell, and Jitendra Malik. Rich feature hierarchies for accurate object detection and semantic segmentation. In *Proceedings of the IEEE Conference on Computer Vision and Pattern Recognition*, pages 580–587. IEEE, 2014.

16. Sheila G Klauer, Feng Guo, Jeremy Sudweeks, and Thomas A Dingus. An analysis of driver inattention using a case-crossover approach on 100-car data. Technical report, 2010.

17. Jun Li, Xue Mei, Danil Prokhorov, and Dacheng Tao. Deep neural network for structural prediction and lane detection in traffic scene. *IEEE Transactions on Neural Networks and Learning Systems*, 28(3):690–703, 2016.

18. Qing Li, Nanning Zheng, and Hong Cheng. Lane boundary detection using an adaptive randomized Hough transform. In *Fifth World Congress on Intelligent Control and Automation (IEEE Cat. No. 04EX788)*, volume 5, pages 4084–4088. IEEE, 2004.

19. Qing Li, Nanning Zheng, and Hong Cheng. Springrobot: A prototype autonomous vehicle and its algorithms for lane detection. *IEEE Transactions on Intelligent Transportation Systems*, 5(4):300–308, 2004.

20. Tsung-Yi Lin, Michael Maire, Serge Belongie, James Hays, Pietro Perona, Deva Ramanan, Piotr Dollár, and C Lawrence Zitnick. Microsoft COCO: Common objects in context. In *European Conference on Computer Vision*, pages 740–755. Springer, 2014.

21. Urs Muller, Jan Ben, Eric Cosatto, Beat Flepp, and Yann Cun. Off-road obstacle avoidance through end-to-end learning. In *Advances in Neural Information Processing Systems*, volume 18, pages 739–746, 2005.

22. Gerhard Neuhold, Tobias Ollmann, Samuel Rota Bulo, and Peter Kontschieder. The Mapillary Vistas dataset for semantic understanding of street scenes. In *Proceedings of the IEEE International Conference on Computer Vision*, pages 4990–4999. IEEE, 2017.

23. Dean A Pomerleau. Progress in neural network-based vision for autonomous robot driving. In *Proceedings of the 1992 Intelligent Vehicles Symposium*, pages 391–396. IEEE, 1992.

24. Shaoqing Ren, Kaiming He, Ross Girshick, and Jian Sun. Faster R-CNN: Towards real-time object detection with region proposal networks. In *Advances in Neural Information Processing Systems*, volume 28, pages 91–99, 2015.

25. Ahmad El Sallab, Mohammed Abdou, Etienne Perot, and Senthil Yogamani. Deep reinforcement learning framework for autonomous driving. *Electronic Imaging*, 2017(19):70–76, 2017.

26. Kazuya Takeda, John H. L. Hansen, Pjnar Boyraz, Lucas Malta, Chiyomi Miyajima, and Hüseyin Abut. International large-scale vehicle corpora for research on driver behavior on the road. *IEEE Transactions on Intelligent Transportation Systems*, 12(4):1609–1623, 2011.

27. Zhihao Xu, Xuefeng Zhou, and Shuai Li. Deep recurrent neural networks based obstacle avoidance control for redundant manipulators. *Frontiers in Neurorobotics*, 13:47, 2019.

28. Fisher Yu, Wenqi Xian, Yingying Chen, Fangchen Liu, Mike Liao, Vashisht Madhavan, and Trevor Darrell. BDD100k: A diverse driving video database with scalable annotation tooling. *arXiv preprint, arXiv:1805.04687*, 2(5):6, 2018.

29. Ekim Yurtsever, Jacob Lambert, Alexander Carballo, and Kazuya Takeda. A survey of autonomous driving: Common practices and emerging technologies. *IEEE Access*, 8:58443–58469, 2020.

30. Qin Zou, Hanwen Jiang, Qiyu Dai, Yuanhao Yue, Long Chen, and Qian Wang. Robust lane detection from continuous driving scenes using deep neural networks. *IEEE Transactions on Vehicular Technology*, 69(1):41–54, 2019.

CHAPTER 11

An Array of Processed Channel for Multiple Object Detection and Distance Estimation in a Video Using a Homographic Mono Camera System

Wahengbam Kanan Kumar

North Eastern Regional Institute of Science and Technology
Itanagar, India

Aheibam Dinamani Singh

National Institute of Technology
Imphal, India

Kishorjit Nongmeikapam

Indian Institute of Information Technology
Imphal, India

CONTENTS

DOI: 10.1201/9781003048381-12

11.1 INTRODUCTION

Image processing for enhancing contours of natural and synthetic objects occurring in images for proper detection by computer vision algorithms is still a challenge. Every image has edges that demarcate boundaries between various regions. It makes them eligible to be recognized as curved objects with their own very distinct contours [1]. Methods for enhancing and analyzing the shapes for these objects are crucial for detecting objects. Objects are detected using popular techniques such as line profile, linear filtering, and template matched filtering. Contour tracing algorithms use a set of pixels that are refined by using a sequence of nonmaximal suppression and thresholding operation [2–6]. A wide variety of feature extraction techniques have been recently employed for differentiating between various types of objects present in urban road scenes. Some techniques that may be cited are scale invariant feature transform (SIFT) [7], Haar features [8], Gabor features [9], log-Gabor [10], and the histogram of oriented gradients (HOG) [11]. Features belonging to a class are used for classifying test images by testing against a network trained using many such features in a suitable machine-learning method. The support vector machine (SVM) [12], extreme learning machine [13], k-nearest neighbor (kNN) [14], random forest [15], and deep learning architectures [16] are well-known training methods. Sensitivity to variation in luminance is one of the main drawbacks of the Haar features as it yields excess features. Gabor filters have numerous advantages. They have a massive number of features that are formed by a combination of different values of θ and λ. Using the gradient region information contained in images, it is also possible to develop a lane detection algorithm. A color image processing technique that enhances pixel intensity at the lanes was developed; however, the technique failed in cases of multiple illuminations such as reflection in water during heavy rainfall at nighttime [17]. In another technique, pixels with weak illuminance were compensated by using a saturated image [18]. New color space was proposed using differences in red-green-blue (RGB) color channels for studying the distribution of lane markers and roads. This helped with better extraction of lane marking using a Gaussian-distributed model [19]. For compensating gradient depression, histogram equalization is used in [20]. A technique for detecting lanes was proposed in [21] by maintaining a larger border gradient between road boundaries and lanes. A limitation with this method is its sensitivity to variations in daylight due to the fixed value of empirically deduced RGB weights. A technique for correcting γ in a standard gray scale image is proposed in which the coefficients were generated by self-clustering and fuzzy C-means (FCM) algorithms. A limitation of this technique is seen when pixels belonging to lanes and roads fall into the same cluster [22].

In recent years, visual saliency has evoked interest among many researchers, especially due to its effective applications such as scene classification [23], image annotation [24], and tracking of objects visually [25, 26]. It is true that the introduction of several state-of-the-art deep learning techniques has successfully increased visual saliency tremendously. However, it is not able to preserve boundaries of salient objects against a cluttered background. The above issues are handled quite effectively using deep learning-based techniques. The lower layers of a convolutional neural network (CNN) have a fine spatial resolution, but the information about structures related to the objects are cluttered; whereas the deeper layers have a less spatial resolution but higher semantic information about an object. These methods are based on fusing channel-wise semantic information for integrating high-level information with low-level information [27–30]. However, these techniques do not provide enough attention to boundary areas, so the use of low-level features is not able to provide distinct boundaries. A method for detecting a pedestrian with a reduced false-positive rate was proposed in refs. [31, 32]. Despite having a high detection rate and frame rate of 80% and 15 frames per second (fps), respectively, on the National Institute for Research in Computer Science and Automation (INRIA) pedestrian data set, a demerit is its high computational cost. Recently, it has been realized that the pooling layers of CNN are not dependent on the scale and rotation of the system; rather, they depend on the training data set. In a recurrent-convolutional neural network (R-CNN), feature vectors are extracted from different regions and fed into a CNN. For each class, deep learned features are extracted and used as feature vectors for an SVM classifier. They performed well for object localization problems but had a very low frame rate of around 5 fps. The problems associated with the single-stage and multiple-task losses were solved in the fast R-CNN model by using region of interest (ROI) and stochastic gradient descent algorithm to speed up execution. The faster R-CNN, on the other hand, uses a region proposal network (RPN) with convolutional layers for computing proposals using the deep net. Compared with the above three, a much faster object detection, which could predict the category of an object and its location at a single glance, was introduced. It was called You Look Only Once (YOLO). It considers the problem of object detection as a regression problem using the ground truth bounding boxes. Each of the boxes is associated with a class probability. It also uses GoogLeNet as the base network capable of performing in real time with a good level of accuracy. Some limitations associated with it are (1) its insensitivity to curvatures, edges, and orientation of objects; (2) spatial constraints on the bounding box for localizing smaller objects; and (3) inability to cope with newer objects having different aspect ratios [33–35].

The use of anchor boxes in some deep learning-based object detection methodology is shown to increase speed and efficiency for multiple object detection. The anchor boxes are populated densely at the neuron of each output feature map and have an associated confidence value of classification. Critical parameters such as anchor width and height are mostly determined empirically. In faster R-CNN [33], three scales have been used, i.e., (12, 82), (25, 62), and (51, 22), with three aspect ratios (1:1, 1:2, and 2:1); whereas in the single shot detector (SSD) technique, the aspect ratios are 1:3 and 3:1 for different feature maps [36]. The initial version of YOLO did not have any anchor boxes [34]. The second version used hard k-means clustering on the ground truth boxes to deduce the size of anchors. Anchors for object detectors have to be adapted according to the domains in which they are aimed at employing, for example, in case of text detection, which uses aspect ratios equal to 5:1 and 1:5 [37]. In case of face detection, the suitable anchor ratio is 1:1 as faces are square in almost all the cases [38, 39]. Training begins after empirically determining the appropriate width and height of anchors. Wrongful deduction of anchors can lead to a reduction in frame rate and, at worst, it could lead to a decrease in object detection.

In this chapter, a novel, and an optimized approach for detecting objects using a combination of low level, high frequency, and a fuzzy-Gabor-based gradient feature with contour reinforcement (FGGFCR) technique is investigated. The low-level representation corresponds to the simple RGB image, the high-frequency representation consists of most of the contours in the image, and the FGGFCR consists of a good number of prominent features and edges that can represent an image. These images are grouped to form the "array of processed channels (AOPC)," which is a graphical workflow demonstrated in Figure 11.1. The full potential of this representation is exploited by training these features into a deep learning architecture. Before starting the training phase, the number and dimensions of anchors are optimized using a two-stage clustering-based optimization procedure, which leads to an increase in performance and speed of detection.. Finally, a technique for detecting distance using a mono camera setup that shows promising performance in the real-time video is proposed.

This chapter is organized as follows: Section 11.1 gives an overview and critique of some related works, Section 11.2 describes the proposed methodology, Section 11.3 shows the experimentation and discussion. This chapter concludes with Section 11.4.

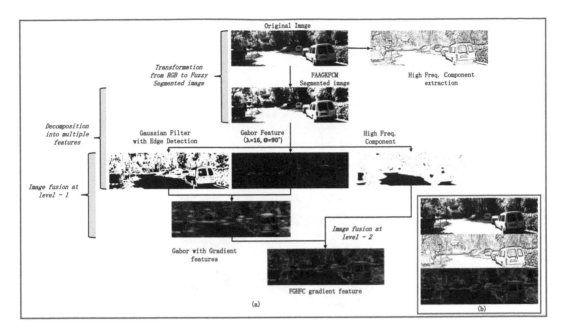

FIGURE 11.1   (a) Graphical workflow of the AOPC algorithm and (b) sample AOPC of a single image for training the deep learning network.

11.2 METHODOLOGY

The sequential workflow described in this chapter starts from the AOPC as described in Section 11.2.1. It consists of three different representations of the standard RGB images. Each of the three forms acts as a channel for training an optimized, deep learning framework as proposed in Section 11.2.2.2. Finally, using the bounding boxes of the detected objects and intrinsic and extrinsic parameters of the camera in the homographic projection, the distance of objects is determined. The proposed workflow is shown in Figure 11.2.

11.2.1 Array of Processed Channels

The AOPC consists of three separate representations (or channels) of the standard RGB picture: (1) the standard RGB, (2) the high-frequency feature, and (3) the FGGFCR channel. The use of AOPC allows the training of a deep learning model with three types of images instead of using the RGB version alone. It is true that deep learning based on RGB provides a strong classification result; however, the existence of multiple-colored patterns in the RGB image can lead to a misunderstanding of minor edges with the actual contours of the area. This can inhibit a deep learning network from minutely learning features of an object. The high frequency contains many of the edges derived from the RGB images, and the FGGFCR contains the most significant edges that can represent object patterns. A joint parametric and non-parametric deep learning is used here. For a parametric approach, deep learning explores spatial features through the use of standard RGB images. On the other hand, the same network also uses handcrafted FGGFCR features with deep learning spatial exploitation to learn more features. The main objective of the AOPC is to encourage a deep learning network to learn a variety of features that may represent an entity. It

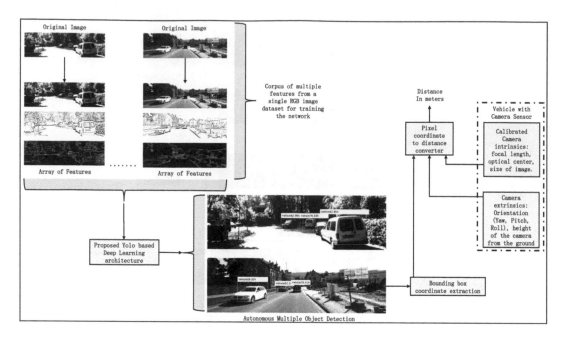

FIGURE 11.2   Summarized view of the proposed object detection with distance estimation using a mono camera system.

also helps the object detection model to leverage the strength of both parametric and non-parametric features. AOPC is a better alternative than using only a standard RGB image data set for training a deep learning framework. This is because it is superior and consists of more features arising due to the use of three channels. Use of an additional channel guarantees better and richer representation, and the simple feature guarantees faster computation. A sample illustration of the AOPC for a single RGB image is shown in Figure 11.1b. The effect of varying numbers of clusters on the FGGFCR features is highlighted in Figure 11.3. Sections 11.2.1.1 and 11.2.1.2 describe the second and third channels mentioned earlier.

11.2.1.1 High-Frequency Component

High frequency is the second channel in the AOPC. Let I and R be the input RGB and reference images, respectively, O is the output image, which is the linear transform of R centered at the kth pixel in the window, and w_k is given as

$$O_i = a_k r_i + b_k, \forall i \in w_k \tag{11.1}$$

where $a_k = \dfrac{\frac{1}{|w|}\Sigma_{i \in w_k} R_i I_i - \mu_k I'_k}{\sigma_k^2 + \varepsilon}$, $b_k = I'_k - a_k \mu_k$. (a_k, b_k) are constant linear coefficients in the square window w_k of radius r. The following objective function is minimized iteratively so that Equation (11.1) can yield a solution

$$E(a_k, b_k) = \sum_{i \in w_k} \left((a_k R_i + b_k - I_i)^2 + \varepsilon a_k^2 \right), \tag{11.2}$$

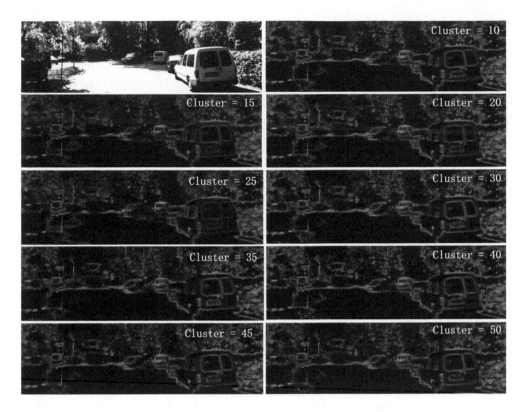

FIGURE 11.3 Effect of varying numbers of clusters on the FGGFCR features. Qualitative results are recorded in Table 11.1.

where ε prevents a_k from getting a larger value. σ_k^2 and μ_k are the variance and mean of reference (R) in the window, and $w_k.I_k' = \frac{1}{|w|}\sum_{i\in w_k} I_i$ is the average if I is input in the window w_k.

For all the patches of w_k within the image, (a_k, b_k) is computed and the filter output is now given by

$$O_i = \frac{1}{|w|} \sum_{k:i\in w_k} \left(a_i R_i + b_k\right) \tag{11.3}$$

$$= a_i' R_i + b_i', \tag{11.4}$$

where $a_i' = \frac{1}{|w|}\sum_{k\in w_i} a_k$ and $b_i' = \frac{1}{|w|}\sum_{k\in w_i} b_k$.

a_k, b_k, and O_i from Equations (11.1) and (11.4) represent image filtering with O being the low-frequency component I (input image). If I' is the gray scale transformation of O, then the desired high-frequency (HF) component can be realized by applying gamma correction

$$I_{hf} = 1 + (eps/100)\frac{1}{\left(I' + \dfrac{eps}{100}\right)}, \tag{11.5}$$

where $eps = 2.2204e{-}16$.

11.2.1.2 Fuzzy-Gabor-Based Gradient Feature with Contour Reinforcement

FGGFCR is the third channel in the proposed AOPC. A sequential illustration of the workflow of this channel is shown in Figure 11.4. The different stages are described sequentially in the following subsections. Initially, the input RGB image is transformed into the LAB color space to yield three tristimulus channels, i.e., L (Luminance), A (Chrominance), and B (Chrominance).

11.2.1.2.1 The FAAGKFCM Algorithm   The fast and automatically adjustable Gaussian radial basis function kernel-based fuzzy C-means (FAAGKFCM) algorithm was proposed in our earlier work for image segmentation in ref. [41]. The major benefits of this method are increased contrast, resilience to noise, and improved edge connectively, among others. These features are a must for creating the robust FGGFCR technique.

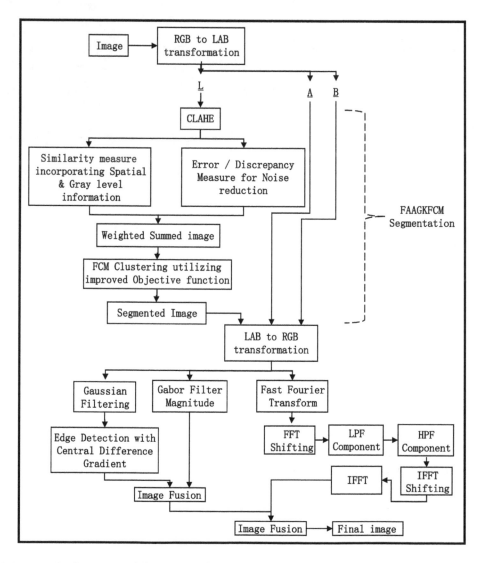

FIGURE 11.4   Architecture of the proposed FGGFCR algorithm.

Therefore, in this chapter it is extended to the urban road scene. The algorithm follows the basic steps of the FCM algorithm; however, instead of the original image, a new weighted image is used.

The **weighted summed image** is the final filtered image formed by the FAAGKFCM algorithm and is expressed as

$$\xi_i = \frac{\left[\sum_{k \in N_{iD}} w_k\right]\left[\sum_{j \in N_{is}} S_{ij} x_k\right] + \left[\sum_{j \in N_{is}} S_{ij}\right] w_i}{\left[\sum_{j \in N_{is}} S_{ij}\right]\left[\sum_{k \in N_{iD}} w_k\right]}$$

(11.6)

where ξ_i represents the gray scale pixel intensity of the ith pixel in L. Similarly, ξ_j represents the intensities of the neighboring pixels ξ_i. N_{is} and N_{iD} are pixels that belong to the local window for S_{ij} and w_i, respectively. S_{ij} and w_i are two weighing factors that are responsible for maintaining the correlation between pixels for suppressing noisy pixels and anti-blurring.

- *Local Similarity (S_{ij})* Local similarity determines spatial and gray-level similarity between ith and jth pixels. Let us assume that x_i and x_j are the gray scale intensities of the central and jth pixels in a window. S_{ij} can be defined as the product of S_{s_ij} and S_{g_ij}, i.e.

$$S_{ij} = S_{s\_ij} \cdot S_{g\_ij},$$

(11.7)

S_{s_ij} is the spatial relationship that exists between pixels belonging to the local window. It is directly proportional to the distance between the central pixel and each pixel of the window. It can be expressed as $S_{s\_ij} = \exp\left(\frac{-\max(|p_j - p_j|,|q_j - q_j|)}{\lambda_s}\right)$, where (p_i, q_i) is the pixel coordinate of the ith pixel and λ_s is a factor showing the wide of S_{s_ij}. In our entire experimental work the value of S_{s_ij} is set to 3.

S_{g_ij} is the pixel gray-level relationship that exists between pixels belonging to the window. It is defined as $S_{g\_ij} = \exp\left(\frac{-\|x_i - x_j\|^2}{\lambda_g \cdot \sigma_{g\_i}^2}\right)$, where $\sigma_{g\_i} = \sqrt{\frac{\sum_{j \in N_i} \|x_j - x_i\|^2}{N_R}}$, λ_g is a scaling factor. It takes values in the range of 0.5–6 with a step size of 0.5. σ_{g_i} indicates the degree of homogeneity within the local window, and N_i is the number of pixels falling in the window and N_R is the cardinality.

- *Discrepancy Estimation Measure (w_j)* In the discrepancy estimation measure discrepancy denotes saturated and unwanted artifacts present in an image. The heterogeneity between any central pixels and that of the surrounding pixels is defined as

$$D_i = \frac{\sum_{k \in N_i} (x_k - x_i')^2}{N_R * (x_i')^2},$$

(11.8)

where x_k is the pixel intensity of any pixel around N_{iD} inside the window, the cardinality of N_{iD} is N_R, and x_i' is the average gray scale intensity. The weighting factor w_i can be expressed as

$$w_i = \exp\left(\sum_{k \in N_{i}, i \neq k} D_k\right)$$

- *Objective Function* The clustering objective function shown below is minimized iteratively until the membership values (u_{ij}) and centers v_j converge into an appropriate solution. The objective function J is given by

$$J = 2\left[\sum_{i=1}^{N}\sum_{j=1}^{c} u_{ij}^m \left(1 - K(x_i, v_j)\right) + \sum_{i=1}^{N}\sum_{j=1}^{c} \xi_i u_{ij}^m \left(1 - K(x_i', v_j)\right)\right], \qquad (11.9)$$

where $u_{ij} = \dfrac{\left((1-K(x_i,v_j)) + \xi_i(1-K(x_i',v_j))\right)^{\frac{-1}{(m-1)}}}{\sum_{k=1}^{c}\left((1-K(x_i,v_k)) + \xi_i(1-K(x_i',v_k))\right)^{\frac{-1}{(m-1)}}}$ and $v_j = \dfrac{\sum_{i=1}^{N} u_{ij}^m\left(K(x_i,v_j)x_i + \xi_i K(x_i',v_j)x_i'\right)}{\sum_{i=1}^{N} u_{ij}^m\left(K(x_i,v_j) + \xi_i K(x_i',v_j)\right)}$.

An illustration of the FAAGKFCM segmented image is shown in Figure 11.1a. Let this new image be denoted by "*I*".

11.2.1.2.2 Gaussian Filtering and Edge Detection A two-dimensional (2D) Gaussian smoothing filter with a standard deviation of 1.1 is used on *I*, and then a central difference gradient operation is applied. This new image is denoted by I_{grad}. The result of the operation is shown in Figure 11.1a.

11.2.1.2.3 Gabor Filter Array Gabor features are suitable for representing textures and discrimination because their orientation and frequency are contextually similar. They find applications in a wide range of pattern analysis-based applications [42–44]. The merit of Gabor features are rotation, intensity of illumination, translation, scale, and ability to withstand a change in illumination and noise associated with images. The expression for the 2D Gabor filter is given below,

$$G(x, y) = \frac{f^2}{\pi \gamma \eta} \exp\left(-\frac{x'^2 + \gamma^2 y'^2}{2\sigma^2}\right) \exp(j2\pi fx' + \phi) \qquad (11.10)$$

where $x' = x\cos\theta + y\sin\theta$ and $y' = x\sin\theta + y\cos\theta$. f represents the frequency of the sine factor, θ is the orientation, ϕ is the phase offset, σ is the standard deviation, and γ is an aspect ratio that denotes ellipticity of the function. In the current work, 21 filters are employed resulting from various combinations of $\lambda = 2, 4, 6, 8, 10, 12, 16$ and $\theta = 0°, 45°,$ 90°. After empirical deduction as recorded in Section 11.3.1.3, $\lambda = 16$ and $\theta = 90°$ are selected as the best suitable values for the current data set. This new image is denoted by I_{gabor}.

11.2.1.2.4 *First-Level Image Fusion*   Using the simple technique of overlaying images on top of each other, an image fusion operation is performed between I_{grad} and I_{gabor}. The result of this first-level fusion is illustrated in Figure 11.1a. This new image is now denoted by I_{1f}.

11.2.1.2.5 *High-Pass Filter Component from Fast Fourier Transform*   Fast Fourier transform (FFT) is applied to I'. A Gaussian low-pass filter component is determined from the shifted version of the FFT signal using the relation following relation:

$$L = \exp\left(\frac{-\left((X - C_x)^2 + (Y - C_y)^2\right)}{(2R)^2}\right) \tag{11.11}$$

where X and Y are rows and columns of input image, respectively. $C_x = 0.5 \times Y$ and $C_y = 0.5 \times X$ and R is the filter size, which is set as 10 in this case. Now, the high-pass filter mask, which is $H = 1 - L$ is multiplied by the shifted FFT signal. The next operations are inverse FFT shifting and inverse FFT, which yields the high-frequency signal component as shown in Figure 11.1a. The new image is denoted by I_{hp}.

11.2.1.2.6 *Second-Level Image Fusion*   The same image fusion operation mentioned previously is applied on I_{gabor} and I_{hp}. This results in the formation of the proposed FGGFCR image feature. Graphical illustrations are shown in Figures 11.1a and 11.10. As realized from the earlier procedure, multiple features are combined into a single image to form the final reinforced gradient image.

11.2.2 Multiple Object Detection

Three of the most important parameters for efficient detection of objects in an image are (1) identification of features that represent different regions in an image, (2) selection of suitable anchor sizes, and (3) architecture for training and detection. In the current work, the AOPC algorithm is used to create a corpus of the image data set by using the data set proposed in ref. [45]. Details about the original data set are described in Section 11.3.1.1. A technique for selection of an optimal number of anchors along with a suitable anchor for the current data set is described in Section 11.2.2.1. Finally, training is done using the corpus, anchors, and the deep learning framework described in Section 11.2.2.2.

11.2.2.1 Selection and Optimization of Anchors

The use of multiple feature types and optimized anchors in a deep learning network can result in fast and accurate detection of multiple objects in an image. The use of anchor boxes for object detection is gaining immense popularity. Anchor boxes give a faster mode of detection compared with other frameworks that use the sliding window and region-based approaches. Therefore, in this section, a method for estimating the optimal number of anchor boxes along with their sizes is being described.

11.2.2.1.1 Anchor Box   Anchor boxes are basically bounding boxes that have a fixed height to width aspect ratio. They are used for detecting objects of specific classes. During the detection phase, the chosen anchor boxes are tiled all over the image. For every box some attributes, such as probability or confidence scores, intersection of union (IoU), and offset values, are detected. Based on these attributes, the non-maximal suppression technique is used for selecting a unique set of predicted bounding boxes. It enables easier detection of objects that fall into a wide range of scales because predictions of anchor boxes are computed at once, which alleviates the need to use sliding window-type scanning [46]. Detection frameworks that use anchors are most suited for real-time application because they sum up the process of detecting, feature extraction and encoding, and classifying into one system.

11.2.2.1.2 Proposed Procedure   About 5745 ground-truth boxes are labeled manually for supervising networks to learn two different classes (i.e., person and vehicle). The probability that many of these boxes have nearly similar aspect ratios hints at the possibility of group-ing such similar boxes into clusters. In the current work, a two-stage clustering process is employed, i.e., FCM and k-medoids clustering stages. Although FCM is quite popular, the use of k-medoids is quite uncommon. The basic idea employed in k-medoids clustering is to determine k representatives for all the k number clusters from distribution of n number of aspect ratios. The next step is to associate each of the (n-k) objects to a suitable cluster by taking the k representatives as a reference and taking the mean value of objects in every cluster. The algorithm minimizes the absolute error which can be written as

$$E = \sum_{i=1}^{k} \sum_{p \in C} |p - O_i|, \tag{11.12}$$

where p is one of the n objects and O_i is the representative object or center of the cluster C_i.

Figure 11.5b shows the workflow for empirically estimating the best number and values of the anchors. Initially, all the 5745 bounding boxes are stacked column-wise in an array, after which only the width and height values from all the rows are retained. The resulting array, which consists of only width and height, is fed into four different FCM algorithms with different cluster sizes, i.e., 100, 150, 200, and 250. When 100 clusters are used, all of the 5745 bounding boxes are represented by 100 best candidates. Similarly, 150, 200, and 250 are the resulting representatives for the 5745 boxes after the clustering operation. To refine the clusters further, a second-stage clustering procedure using the k-medoids clus-tering algorithm uses the results obtained due to the FCM clustering operation. In other words, k-medoids clustering is performed separately for 100, 150, 200, and 250 candidates as shown in Figure 11.5b. Each of the four k-medoid clustering operations is run by 20 times, i.e., k = 1:20, and for each run, the mean IoUs are calculated. In other words, the value of k that has the maximum value of IoU is selected as the best number of clusters into which all of the 5745 boxes can be grouped. This best number of clusters corresponds to the optimal number of anchors that can best represent the current data set.

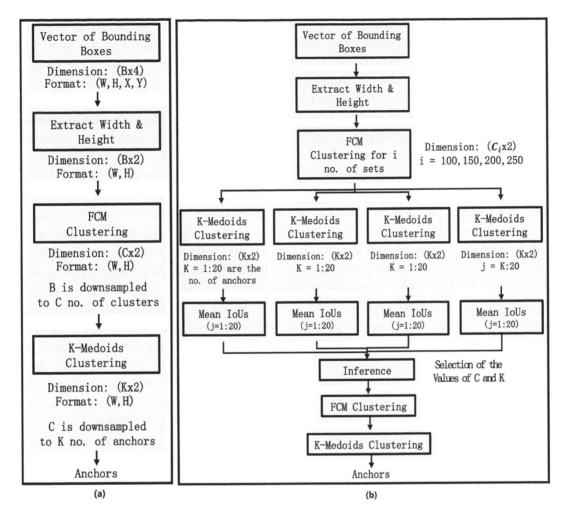

FIGURE 11.5 Basic workflow for (a) selection of anchor using determined values of C and k and (b) determination of optimal values of C and K for anchor selection.

After selecting the best value of C (i.e., FCM cluster) and K (i.e., k-medoids cluster), the next step is to arrange bounding boxes in vector form column-wise to extract width and height from the array, to perform FCM clustering using the optimal number of C, and to perform k-medoids clustering on the $C \times 2$ data using the optimal value of k. The result of the clustering operation is the anchors [50]. Choosing the optimal number of anchors is of extreme importance in empirical analysis. The mean IoU is a suitable and good quality index that has been used for this purpose.

11.2.2.2 Proposed Multiple Object Detection Framework

Deep learning-based object classification and detection models have been shown to be quite promising for multiple object detection, because they are trained using low-level or mid-level or high-level features in an end-to-end fashion. It is evident from recent work that richer features start to appear as the depth of layers increase. It is also realized that it is not easy to achieve more accuracy by just adding a greater number of layers. The case of the vanishing gradient was a severe case, which hindered convergence. It was, however, addressed by adding normalized and intermediate normalization layers. Another issue is that use of many layers does not always increase accuracy, rather, it tends to become constant. This is not due to overfitting; instead of adding more layers it induces error. Therefore, a remedy to this is to use good features for training. Current work shows that using a better feature-oriented training set as an alternative to the standard RGB with a deep learning framework results in a higher level of accuracy. Figure 11.6 shows the proposed deep learning framework. The input to the network is a corpus created using the proposed AOPC algorithm. The size of each image in the network is 320×96. The standard color augmentation technique is used to resize these images, and this is done to match the size of the input layer, which is $224 \times 224 \times 3$. Prior to activation and at the end of each convolution layer, batch normalization has been adopted. The network has three different convolutional layer groupings that are repeated a finite number of times: (1) convolutional layers $[1 \times 1 \times 64]$, $[3 \times 3 \times 64]$, $[1 \times 1 \times 256]$; (2) convolutional layers $[1 \times 1 \times 128]$, $[3 \times 3 \times 128]$, $[1 \times 1 \times 512]$; and (3) convolutional layers $[1 \times 1 \times 256]$, $[3 \times 3 \times 256]$, $[1 \times 1 \times 1024]$. In all the three sets, there is a 3×3 filter that has the same size output feature map, and the filter elements are doubled for preserving the complexity per layer. The downsampling operation is done by using a convolutional layer and max-pooling layer with stride equal to 2. The 149th layer is the "YOLO v2 transform layer." It has the capability to constrain the prediction of locations, thus making the network stable. This layer extracts pre-trained features or activations from the 148th layer. The convolutional layer constrains the predictions of location so that they fall within the limits of bounds of the ground truth, thus making the network stable. The final or 150th layer is the output layer; it further refines the locations of bounding boxes using a single-stage type multiple object detection network. They are faster than well-known two-stage detectors such as R-CNN and faster R-CNN. The proposed network uses anchor boxes that have the following benefits: (1) IoU, (2) anchor offsets, and (3) class probability. Therefore, the proposed object detection network has two subnetworks: (1) a feature extraction network using the deep convolutional network architecture from layers 1 to 148 and (2) a YOLO v2-based final detection network.

11.2.3 Distance Estimation Using Monocular Camera Vision

This section proposes a technique for estimating distance using a monocular camera vision system.

11.2.3.1 Some Definitions

11.2.3.1.1 Vehicle Coordinate System   Suppose that (X_v, Y_v, Z_v) defines a vehicle coordinate system: X_v axis directs along the front facing direction of the vehicle, Y_v-axis directs toward the left, and Z_v directs to the upward direction of the vehicle. The origin is on the surface of the road just below the focal point or center of the camera.

11.2.3.1.2 Pitch Angle   It is the angle between X_v Y_v (i.e., the horizontal) plane and the camera's optical axis of the vehicle in degrees.

No.	Layer	Feature
1	Input	224x224x3
2	Conv.	7x7x64
3	B. N.	
4	ReLU	
5	M. P.	3x3, S=2
6	Conv.	1x1x64
7	B. N.	
8	ReLU	
9	Conv.	3x3x64
10	B. N.	
11	ReLU	
12	Conv.	1x1x256
13	Conv.	1x1x256
14	B. N.	
15	B. N.	
16	Add	Element Wise
17	ReLU	
18	Conv.	1x1x64
19	B. N.	
20	ReLU	
21	Conv.	3x3x64
22	B. N.	
23	ReLU	
24	Conv.	1x1x256
25	B. N.	
26	Add	Element Wise
27	ReLU	
28	Conv.	1x1x64
29	B. N.	
30	ReLU	
31	Conv.	3x3x64
32	B. N.	
33	ReLU	
34	Conv.	1x1x256
35	B. N.	
36	Add	Element Wise
37	ReLU	
38	Conv.	1x1x128
39	B. N.	
40	ReLU	
41	Conv.	3x3x128
42	B. N.	
43	ReLU	
44	Conv.	1x1x512
45	Conv.	1x1x512
46	B. N.	
47	B. N.	
48	Add	Element Wise
49	ReLU	
50	Conv.	1x1x128
51	B. N.	
52	ReLU	
53	Conv.	3x3x128
54	B. N.	
55	ReLU	
56	Conv.	1x1512
57	B. N.	
58	Add	Element Wise
59	ReLU	
60	Conv.	1x1x128
61	B. N.	
62	ReLU	
63	Conv.	3x3x128
64	B. N.	
65	ReLU	
66	Conv.	1x1x512
67	B. N.	
68	Add	Element Wise
69	ReLU	
70	Conv.	1x1x128
71	B. N.	
72	ReLU	
73	Conv.	3x3x128
74	B. N.	
75	ReLU	
76	Conv.	1x1x512
77	B. N.	
78	Add	Element Wise
79	ReLU	
80	Conv.	1x1x256
81	B. N.	
82	ReLU	
83	Conv.	3x3x256
84	B. N.	
85	ReLU	
86	Conv.	1x1x1024
87	Conv.	1x1x1024
88	B. N.	
89	B. N.	
90	Add	Element Wise
91	ReLU	
92	Conv.	1x1x256
93	B. N.	
94	ReLU	
95	Conv.	3x3x256
96	B. N.	
97	ReLU	
98	Conv.	1x1x1024
99	B. N.	
100	Add	Element Wise
101	ReLU	
102	Conv.	1x1x256
103	B. N.	
104	ReLU	
105	Conv.	3x3x256
106	B. N.	
107	ReLU	
108	Conv.	1x1x1024
109	B. N.	
110	Add	Element Wise
111	ReLU	
112	Conv.	1x1x256
113	B. N.	
114	ReLU	
115	Conv.	3x3x256
116	B. N.	
117	ReLU	
118	Conv.	1x1x1024
119	B. N.	
120	Add	Element Wise
121	ReLU	
122	Conv.	1x1x256
123	B. N.	
124	ReLU	
125	Conv.	3x3x256
126	B. N.	
127	ReLU	
128	Conv.	1x1x1024
129	B. N.	
130	Add	Element Wise
131	ReLU	
132	Conv.	1x1x256
133	B. N.	
134	ReLU	
135	Conv.	3x3x256
136	B. N.	
137	ReLU	
138	Conv.	1x1x1024
139	B. N.	
140	Add	Element Wise
141	ReLU	
142	Conv.	3x3x1024
143	B. N.	
144	ReLU	
145	Conv.	3x3x1024
146	B. N.	
147	ReLU	
148	Conv.	1x1x1024
149	YOLO	Transform Layer
150	YOLO	OUTPUT

FIGURE 11.6   Proposed deep learning architecture.

11.2.3.1.3 Yaw Angle   It is the angle between the camera's optical axis and the X_v-axis of the vehicle in degrees.

11.2.3.1.4 Roll Angle   It is the angle measured around the camera's optical axis in degrees.

11.2.3.1.5 Height   It is the perpendicular distance between the surface of the road and camera's focal point in meters.

11.2.3.2 Camera's Intrinsic and Extrinsic Parameters Calibration

The parameter optical center and focal length make up the intrinsic parameter of a camera. Height, pitch, yaw, and roll are the extrinsic parameters of a camera. The technique proposed in ref. [39] is used to estimate their accurate values. The intrinsic parameters are fairly simple to deduce compared with the extrinsic parameters. Suppose $[c_x, c_y]$ is a two-element vector given in pixels. It denotes the camera's principal point. The focal length (F) of the camera can also be specified as $[f_x, f_y]$, which is a two-element vector in pixels. F is in millimeters and $[s_x, s_y]$ are the number of pixels

$$f_x = F \times s_x \tag{11.13}$$

$$f_y = F \times s_y \tag{11.14}$$

The steps for deducing the extrinsic parameters are summarized as follows.

11.2.3.2.1 Place Checkerboard   Initially, a checkerboard pattern is captured and printed on a plain paper. The checkerboard used for determining intrinsic parameters are the same. Suppose (Xp, Yp) is the coordinate of the checkerboard. The way of placing (or orientating) it in front of the camera is shown in Figure 11.7. The Xp- and Yp-axes are aligned with Xv- and Yv-axes. The Xv-axis directs outward from the vehicle, whereas the Yv-axis directs toward the left direction. Placement of the *checkerboard can be* done two ways, horizontal and vertical.

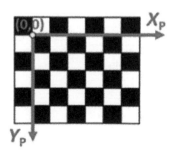

FIGURE 11.7   Orientation of checkerboard for calibration.

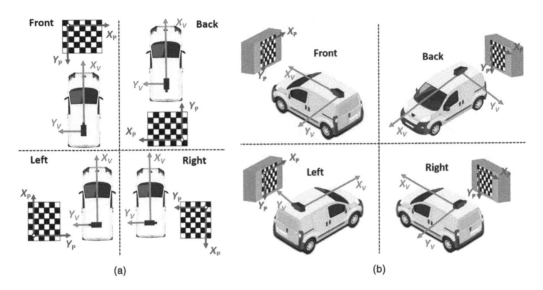

FIGURE 11.8 Extrinsic camera parameters calibration using (a) horizontal orientation and (b) vertical orientation of the checkerboard.

11.2.3.2.2 Estimating Extrinsic Parameters   After placing the checkerboard in the positions as shown in Figure 11.8, images are captured by using the monocular camera. Key points detected from these images along with the intrinsic parameters and the $[x, y]$ coordinates of the checkerboard are used in ref. [39] to determine the extrinsic parameters. The parameters height, pitch, yaw, and roll are now calibrated.

11.2.3.3 Distance Estimation

The extrinsic parameters deduced earlier are used with homographic projection to deduce distance of every object in the image frame. Using the homogenous representation, a point (x, y) can be expressed in the 3D form as $x = (x_1, x_2, x_3)$, where $x = x_1/x_3$ and $y = x_2/x_3$. This point lies on the plane P^2. Therefore, homography is simply a mapping of points that are a part of the plane P^2. Authors in ref. [43] opined that a projectivity occurs from $P^2 \rightarrow P^2$ if any point belonging to P^2 (i.e., x vector) is mapped to a 3×3 non-singular matrix with a value H_x. H is also called as the homography matrix.

11.2.3.4 Proposed Transformation between Camera Plane and Road Plane

The transformation between a road plane (n) and an image plane (π) is described in this section. The relation between the vehicle coordinate system and the road plane is shown in Figure 11.9 graphically, where (X_v, Y_v, X_v) is the coordinate of the vehicle, and the X_v-axis is directed toward the driving direction in the road X_R, the Y_v-axis is directed downward orthogonal with the plane of the road Y_R, and the Z_v-axis is perpendicular with the driving direction down the road Z_R. The vehicle coordinate is modeled as the X_R-axis is aligned with the X_v-axis and the Y_R-axis is aligned with the Y_v-axis. Therefore, a 3D point vector $X_W = (X, Y, Z)$ can be expressed as $X_W = (X_R, Y_R, h_v)$, where, h_v is the height of the camera mounted on the ego car measured from the ground. The central projection between X_W

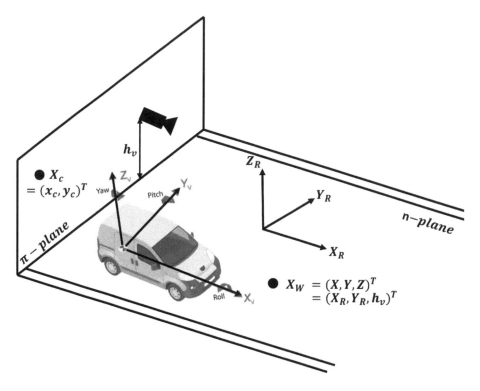

FIGURE 11.9 The vehicle coordinate system.

and another point $X_c = (x_c, y_c)$ lying in the camera plane can be defined using the simple pinhole model $x_{im} = Kx_c$, where x_{im} is the image transformed into the pixel coordinate system, K is the calibration matrix containing the intrinsic parameters [43], and x_c is given by the following equation:

$$x_c = PX_w, \qquad (11.15)$$

where $X_w = R^T xc - R^T t = |R^T| - |R^T t| x_c$ and $R = \begin{bmatrix} 1 & 0 & 0 \\ 0 & \cos\theta & \sin\theta \\ 0 & -\sin\theta & \cos\theta \end{bmatrix}$, $t = \begin{bmatrix} 0 \\ h_c \\ 0 \end{bmatrix}$. P is the projec-

tion matrix of the camera that provides the relationship between x_c and X_w. It consists of a translation matrix $t_{3\times1}(h_c)$, $P = [R(\phi,\theta,\psi)|t(h_c)]$, where ϕ,θ,ψ define roll, pitch, and yaw angles and a rotation matrix, $R_{3\times3(\phi,\theta,\psi)}$. In the current case, yaw and roll are zero, hence, x_c is simplified as

$$x_c = [R_{3x3} | t_{3x3}] \begin{bmatrix} X_w \\ 1 \end{bmatrix}_{4\times1} = RX_w + t. \qquad (11.16)$$

Solving Equation (11.15) now yields the coordinate of any point (X_R, Y_R) on the plane of the road.

$$\begin{bmatrix} 0 \\ h_c \\ 0 \end{bmatrix}_{2\times1} = \begin{bmatrix} x_c p_{33} - p_{13} & x_c p_{31} - p_{11} \\ -y_c p_{33} + p_{33} & -y_c p_{31} + p_{21} \end{bmatrix}_{2\times2}^{-1} \times \begin{bmatrix} x_c(p_{32}h_c + p_{34}) + p_{12}h_c + p_{14} \\ y_c(p_{33}h_c + p_{34}) - p_{22}h_c - p_{24} \end{bmatrix}_{2\times1}$$

After obtaining the values of (X_R, Y_R) using a simple measurement technique, distance X_R from the center of the camera is computed.

11.2.3.5 Determination of Pitch Angle

The pitch angle is approximated by using the vanishing point as follows [41]:

$$vp_h^*(\phi, \theta, \psi) = \begin{bmatrix} \dfrac{\cos\phi\sin\psi - \sin\phi\sin\theta\cos\psi}{\cos\theta\cos\psi}, & \dfrac{-\sin\phi\sin\psi - \cos\phi\sin\theta\cos\psi}{\cos\theta\cos\psi} \end{bmatrix}^T \quad (11.17)$$

If roll and yaw angles are zero, then

$$vp_h^*(\phi = 0, \theta, \psi = 0) = \begin{bmatrix} \dfrac{0}{\cos\theta}, & -\dfrac{\sin\theta}{\cos\theta} \end{bmatrix}. \quad (11.18)$$

11.3 EXPERIMENTAL EVALUATION AND DISCUSSION

This section discusses the implementation and experimental results of the proposed methodology.

11.3.1 Array of Processed Channels

The results of the implementation of the proposed AOPC technique is discussed in the following section.

11.3.1.1 Data Set

The data set proposed in ref. [45] is used in the current work. The authors' data sets consist of data for optical flow; stereo; and visual odometry by driving around highways, city, and rural areas. The images gathered by the left camera of their stereo camera, which consists of 14,999 images, are used for the current work. Of these images, 7481 and 7518 are used for testing and training, respectively. To demonstrate the performance of the proposed object detection method and for comparing with other research, ground truth boxes are manually annotated as belonging to either a vehicle or a person. Of the 7072 boxes, 5745 and 1327 are for vehicle and person, respectively. The original dimension of the images in the data set is 370×1224.

11.3.1.2 Implementation Results for High-Frequency Component Technique

Images are downsized to 96 × 320. The size of the window is 10 × 10. The newly created 7518 high-frequency images are added to the original 7518 RGB images. The total training image now doubles to 15036. This results in doubling the number of bounding boxes.

11.3.1.3 Implementation Using the Proposed FGGFCR Technique

The original dimension of the images in the data set is 370 × 1224 and is downsized to 96 × 320 for faster training. The size of the window is 10 × 10. Another set of FGGFCR gradient component images for all 7518 RGB training images is created. Now the total data set for training up to this point becomes 7518(RGB) + 7518(HFC) + 7518(FGGFCR), which is equal to 22,554 images. The number of bounding boxes is tripled, i.e., 21,216.

The quantitative evaluation measures used for evaluation are the (1) blind/referenceless image spatial quality evaluator (BRISQUE), (2) naturalness image quality evaluator (NIQE), (3) perception-based image quality evaluator (PIQE), and (4) structural similarity index (SSIM). BRISQUE is a no-reference image quality score, and a smaller score indicates better perceptual quality [51]. NIQE is a no-reference image quality score, and a smaller score indicates better perceptual quality [52]. Authors in ref. [53] proposed the PIQE index, which is also a no-reference image quality score, but it is inversely correlated to the perceptual quality of an image. A low-score value indicates high perceptual quality, and a high-score value indicates low perceptual quality. SSIM is used for measuring image similarity between two images, and a higher value indicates better image quality. Objective image quality assessment refers to automatically predicting the quality of distorted images as would be perceived by an average human.

11.3.1.3.1 Impact of Varying Number of Clusters   The effect of varying the number of clusters on the FGGFCR technique is highlighted in this section. The cluster is varied from 10 to 50 as shown in Table 11.1. The implementation result in image 1 is shown in Figure 11.3. Information carried by images due to varying cluster is different. It is not easy to choose the optimal cluster by a simple visual comparison, therefore, BRISQUE, NIQE, and PIQE indices are used for empirically deducing the best cluster. For image 1, the BRISQUE, NIQE, and PIQE indexes are best at clusters 10, 15, and 15, respectively. Image 1 shows good performance when the number of clusters equal to 15 is used. Similarly, images 2–5 show good performance at clusters 15, 45, 35, and 10, respectively. Most of the data set shows better performance at the lower cluster. Therefore, for creating the FGGFCR image corpus, cluster 15 is selected.

11.3.1.3.2 Impact of Various Combination of λ and θ of the Gabor Filter Array   Selection of appropriate values of λ and θ is critical for extracting the best feature using the appropriate Gabor filter. The best performing pair is selected from among 21 different pairs that are realized by using seven scales of λ (i.e., 2, 4, 6, 8, 10, 12, and 16) and three orientations of θ (i.e., 0°, 45°, and 90°). For each of the five images considered in Table 11.1, 21 different

TABLE 11.1   Impact of a Varying Number of Clusters on the RGB Images.

Image	Cluster	BRISQUE	NIQE	PIQE
1	10	**27.9585**	5.1982	55.7707
	15	28.0263	**4.0352**	**46.2728**
	20	36.7685	4.6301	55.4130
	25	34.0972	4.4785	51.9609
	30	37.6220	4.6459	56.3185
	35	37.3999	5.135	55.572
	40	39.7150	4.8677	58.4196
	45	37.3846	4.4273	52.7822
	50	30.5596	4.5241	51.6006
2	10	33.1495	4.0717	53.8239
	15	**32.0344**	4.4131	**51.7515**
	20	33.7187	4.1395	54.5410
	25	39.4347	4.3162	56.7533
	30	33.3494	4.7636	55.3198
	35	32.2657	3.9289	52.8525
	40	33.4047	4.0407	54.8589
	45	33.7610	**3.8377**	56.5761
	50	33.0969	3.9157	51.6098
3	10	32.0477	4.5733	39.6700
	15	38.1049	4.062	31.8393
	20	29.4752	3.9936	31.7415
	25	30.7128	4.0905	34.0792
	30	30.9330	4.3506	34.5617
	35	29.3512	4.2614	39.3662
	40	31.6925	3.9302	31.2460
	45	33.4929	**3.7672**	**31.1439**
	50	**21.8036**	4.5908	36.2686l
4	10	31.3471	4.8583	55.7465
	15	**30.5213**	4.4062	55.8944
	20	31.1243	4.7013	56.2108
	25	37.5542	4.9666	58.3626
	30	32.1285	4.4472	55.8308
	35	34.4164	**4.0771**	**54.1770**
	40	39.1388	5.3924	59.2731
	45	40.2923	4.9019	56.7073
	50	37.8836	5.2244	54.2313
5	10	27.6033	**3.9201**	**52.0512**
	15	35.5131	4.6000	53.6804
	20	32.4930	5.4043	58.1875
	25	27.4881	4.1642	53.1727
	30	29.6314	4.3624	54.4239
	35	32.3447	4.4231	53.8174
	40	32.9522	4.0076	54.6554
	45	33.0040	4.1823	54.3216
	50	**26.9554**	4.3292	55.7204

Note: Bold numerals indicates the best scores of BRISQUE, NIQE and PIQE indices from
among the nine (9) different clusters.

TABLE 11.2   SSIM Indices for Different Combinations of (Lambda, Theta) the Gabor Filter Array Used in the FGGFCR Gradient Feature Extraction Technique

	1	2	3	4	5	6	7
Image	**(2, 0)**	**(4, 0)**	**(6, 0)**	**(8, 0)**	**(10, 0)**	**(12, 0)**	**(16, 0)**
1	0.242	0.237	0.238	0.234	0.236	0.242	0.250
2	0.151	0.148	0.148	0.152	0.158	0.156	0.157
3	0.175	0.164	0.164	0.174	0.179	0.176	0.177
4	0.170	0.165	0.168	0.167	0.168	0.169	0.177
5	0.173	0.168	0.169	0.168	0.169	0.173	0.179

variants and SSIM indices for each image are deduced. They are recorded in Tables 11.2–11.4. The 21 combinations of (λ, θ) are $(2, 4°)$, $(4, 0°)$, $(6, 0°)$, $(8, 0°)$, $(10, 0°)$, $(12, 0°)$, $(16, 0°)$, $(2, 45°)$, $(4, 45°)$, $(6, 45°)$, $(8, 45°)$, $(10, 45°)$, $(12, 45°)$, $(16, 45°)$, $(2, 90°)$, $(4, 90°)$, $(6, 90°)$, $(8, 90°)$, $(10, 90°)$, $(12, 90°)$, and $(16, 90°)$.

For image 1, the highest value of SSIM (i.e., 0.2614) is found when $\lambda = 2$ and $\theta = 90°$. Similarly, for images 2–5, the optimal value of SSIM occurs at the pairs $(\lambda = 10, \theta = 90°)$, $(\lambda = 2, \theta = 45°)$, $(\lambda = 16, \theta = 90°)$, and $(\lambda = 16, \theta = 90°)$, respectively. Depending on the number of occurrences, $\lambda = 16$ and $\theta = 90°$ have been selected for use in the current data set. The nine variants of the RGB image in Figure 11.3 have been derived using $\lambda = 16$ and $\theta = 90°$. An optimal combination of cluster number, θ-λ pair can successfully extract a high-level feature that is capable of representing only the useful regions of an image. Implementation results on image 1 and 2 are shown by the fourth rows of Figure 11.10.

Additionally, in is Figure 11.10, the different levels of representation of each of the RGB images are shown. For instance, the first row is the original RGB image, the second row is the simple gradient on RGB image, the third row is the high-frequency component feature extraction discussed earlier, and the fourth row is the proposed FGGFCR gradient feature. It is important to note that the use of FGGFCR or RGB or high frequency alone is not recommended as they represent different classes. The deep learning network, which is proposed in the upcoming section, learns features not only from the RGB component but also high-level representations and reinforced gradient features of the FGGFCR of the objects within the bounding boxes. This enables learning of different types of representations of an object, which results in better object detection capability. Therefore, the AOPC for a single image, which is proposed here, is a vector obtained by stacking the RGB, high frequency,

TABLE 11.3   SSIM Indices for Different Combinations of (Lambda, Theta) the Gabor Filter Array Used in the FGGFCR Gradient Feature Extraction Technique (Contd. from Table 11.2).

	8	9	10	11	12	13	14
Image	**(2, 45)**	**(4, 45)**	**(6, 45)**	**(8, 45)**	**(10, 45)**	**(12, 45)**	**(16, 45)**
1	0.259	0.254	0.247	0.244	0.245	0.249	0.248
2	0.159	0.154	0.151	0.151	0.150	0.150	0.152
3	0.190	0.183	0.180	0.174	0.173	0.172	0.170
4	0.183	0.181	0.183	0.184	0.187	0.187	0.190
5	0.183	0.170	0.167	0.169	0.170	0.176	0.187

TABLE 11.4   SSIM Indices for Different Combinations of (Lambda, Theta) the Gabor Filter Array Used in the FGGFCR Gradient Feature Extraction Technique (Contd. from Table 11.3).

Image	15 (2, 90)	16 (4, 90)	17 (6, 90)	18 (8, 90)	19 (10, 90)	20 (12, 90)	21 (16, 90)
1	0.261	0.246	0.240	0.237	0.240	0.242	0.249
2	0.160	0.153	0.157	0.161	0.164	0.161	0.163
3	0.186	0.177	0.165	0.161	0.163	0.166	0.171
4	0.183	0.173	0.175	0.178	0.177	0.179	0.192
5	0.188	0.174	0.171	0.171	0.176	0.179	0.189

and the FGGFCR gradient feature, as shown in Figure 11.1b. The proposed AOPC is implemented on the image corpus mentioned previously to yield a total of 22,554 image features, which is three times when an RGB variant is used alone (i.e., 7518).

11.3.2 Multiple Object Detection with Distance Deduction

This section demonstrates the implementation results of the proposed object and distance detection procedures.

11.3.2.1 Optimal Anchor Determination

Determination of optimal size and number of anchor boxes is critical for faster and accurate detection for networks based on R-CNN and YOLO. The 7072 bounding boxes are

FIGURE 11.10   (a) RGB image; (b) simple RGB gradient feature extraction; (c) high-frequency component (HFC) (d) proposed FAAGKFCM with Gabor HFC gradient feature extraction on RGB image.

TABLE 11.5   Anchors for Different Values of Cluster (C)

Anchor No.	C = 100	C = 150	C = 200	C = 250
1	60,34	45,25	76,43	78,43
2	20,13	30,20	59,34	44,26
3	44,27	102,50	44,27	58,34
4	108,50	71,40	21,15	106,49
5	30,20	53,32	101,50	32,20
6	84,45	20,13	34,20	17,13
Mean IoU	**0.78**	**0.77**	**0.79**	**0.81**

Note: Selection is done by considering the highest mean IoU. The anchors given in the table are shown in the format (width, height).

all stacked in vector form after which the procedure for selection of best size and number of anchors is performed using four different clusters (i.e., C = 100, 150, 200, and 250) and anchors in the range of 1–20. An empirical deduction is now performed. (1) The maximum number of anchors for evaluation is set to 20 to widen the field of searching. An instance of this can be seen in Figure 11.11, where the C = 100 IoUs for different anchors are plotted. (2) All the individual IoUs are accumulated together to determine the mean IoU for that particular cluster. Table 11.5 shows the mean IoUs for different values of clusters (C).

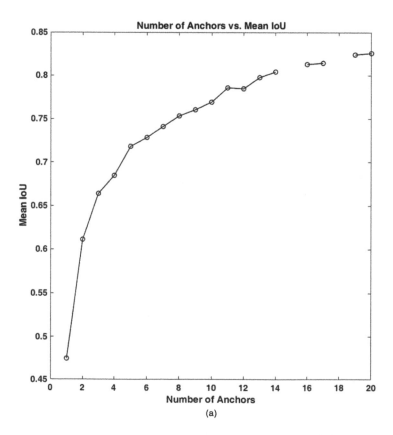

FIGURE 11.11   Mean IoU of different number of anchors for varying number of FCM clusters. (a) 100 clusters.

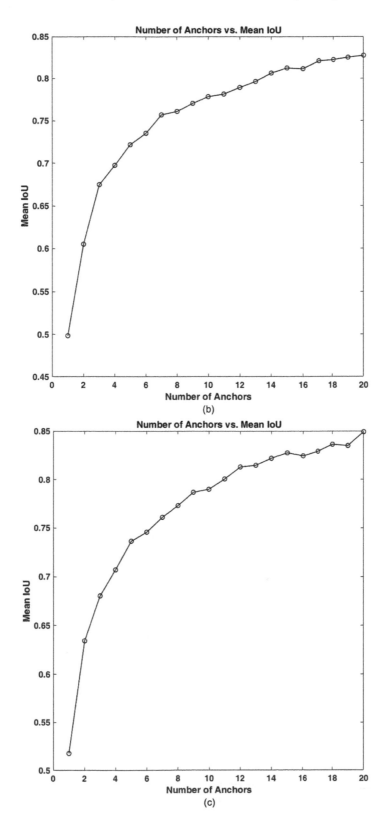

FIGURE 11.11   *(Continued)* (b) 150 clusters, (c) 200 clusters.

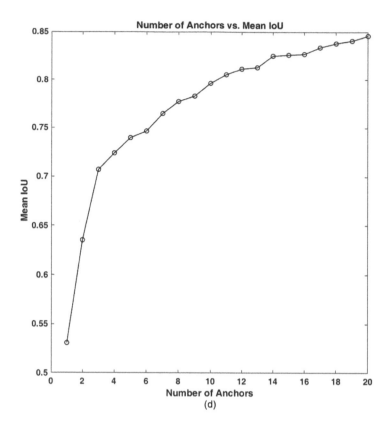

FIGURE 11.11   *(Continued)* (d) 250 clusters.

(3) For each cluster and the IoUs of each anchor, the best performing number of anchors is determined. The mean IoU should be greater than 0.5 to ensure that anchor boxes overlap well with the boxes in the training data. An increasing number of anchors improves the mean IoU but at the cost of increased computational time, and chances of overfitting.

For measuring the trade-off between the varying number of anchors and IoU, the k-medoids operation is swept within the range of 1–20. In Figure 11.11, if $C = 100$, anchor numbers from 3 to 5 provide a mean IoU over 0.7, whereas for the remaining anchors, the slope does not change abruptly. So, for C = 100, the best performing number of anchors is 5, and the mean IoU as recorded in Table 11.5 is 0.78. Similarly, $C = 150$, 200, and 250 also shows the best performing number of anchors as 5, 4, and 6, respectively. Therefore, $C = 250$ and $k = 6$ are selected as they have the highest mean IoU. The final value of anchors obtained by using this optimal value of C and k are (78, 43), (44, 26), (58, 34),(106, 49), (32, 20), and (17, 13).

11.3.2.2 Multiple Object Detection

Three separate training sets are used to demonstrate the effectiveness of the proposed method: (1) RGB data set, which consists of about 7518 images with 7072 manually annotated bounding boxes; (2) RGB combined with HFC has 22,554 images with 21,216 bounding boxes, and (3) proposed AOPC (RGB, HFC, FGGFCR), which consists of 22,554 images with 21,216 bounding boxes. The use of training set (3) increases the training data set by threefold. This also increases confidence scores associated with each bounding box at the final layer. Various combinations of channels with a different type of state-of-the-art detector are carried out to determine the best among them in terms of frame rate and accuracy. As mentioned in Section 11.2.2.1, the first 148th layer is trained for classifying the two categories (i.e., vehicle and person). The following training parameters are used: minibatch size is 32, the learning rate is constant at 1e-2, epochs are 20, and training images in each data set are shuffled for every epoch. For each of the three data sets, the network converges within 20 epochs. The six anchors that are deduced in the p section are used. Rich deep features are extracted from the 148th layer, which is a $1 \times 1 \times 1024$ convolutional layer. These features are used by the 149th and 150th YOLO layers to predict the class probability and bounding boxes at the final layer. The height and width of the bounding box are normalized with respect to the width and height of the image so that they may fall within the range of 0 and 1. The training was done with a single NVIDIA GeForce GTX 1050 Ti GPU with one Core i7-7700HQ CPU. Training converged in approximately 4 hours when only standard RGB was used. Training took place for approximately 8 hours for RGB with an HFC, whereas it took approximately 12 hours using the proposed AOPC features. The training parameters were the same for all the three combinations of the training data set mentioned earlier.

11.3.2.2.1 Testing   There are 7481 RGB test images used for determining the mean average precision (mAP). In the test set, 4024 and 1222 manual ground truth annotations are made to represent the vehicle and person category, respectively. An mAP of 57.64% was shown when testing against network trained using the RGB data set only. Although it was 59.48% and 68.37% using the RGB + HFC and proposed AOPC data set, respectively. These results are shown in Table 11.6.

TABLE 11.6   Comparison of Accuracy and Frame Rate of the Proposed Object Detection Technique with Some State-of-the-Art Techniques

| Method | Features | Training | | Accuracy | FPS |
		Data Set	B box	mAP (%)	
R-CNN [54]	RGB	7518	7072	31.21	3
	RGB, HFC	15036	14144	33.14	3
	Proposed AOPC	22554	21216	36.74	3
F R-CNN [33]	RGB	7518	7072	37.65	4
	RGB, HFC	15036	14144	37.85	4
	Proposed AOPC	22554	21216	39.32	4
YOLO [34]	RGB	7518	7072	52.65	16
Proposed	RGB	7518	7072	57.64	19
	RGB, HFC	15036	14144	59.48	19
	Proposed AOPC	22554	21216	68.37	19

Note: B box refers to bounding boxes.

FIGURE 11.12 Demonstration of object detection on two sample images (a) "Vehicle" category. (b) "Person" category.

In Figure 11.12(a), all the vehicles in the frame are detected. Vehicles located at a longer distance are also detected with a high confidence score of 79.41%. In the second picture, all the people walking on the road are detected quite easily. IoU will decrease if the center of the anchor and bounding box differ. Another issue is that some ground truth boxes may be missed if the width or stride between anchor boxes is large, despite having small anchor boxes. To solve this issue, the threshold of IoU is decreased from 50% to 40%.

The proposed technique is also implemented on a video stream in our PC having a single NVIDIA GeForce GTX 1050 Ti GPU with one Core i7-7700HQ CPU and 16GB RAM. The frame rate is found to be approximately 19 fps. Among the 297 frames contained in the video, 99 had objects. The results in four such frames out of 99 are shown in Figure 11.13, which shows that the object along with its distance from the ego vehicle is detected.

11.3.2.3 Distance Deduction
The following procedure is used for estimating distance between the ego vehicle and the detected vehicles. (1) Calibration of the camera is done to determine the intrinsic properties. In the current work, focal length is 800×800 pixels, and the optical center is 320×240. (2) The extrinsic parameters are determined. In the current work, pitch = 14°, yaw = 14°, roll = 0°, height = 2.18 m above the ground. (3) A frame is read from the video and passed to the trained detector. If there is/are object(s) belonging to the category, then it is trained to recognize the same. The detector then returns the bounding box coordinates along with the width and height of the object(s). (4) Using the coordinates (XY) of the

FIGURE 11.13   Demonstration of object detection along with their distance from the ego-vehicle. The distance between object and the ego-vehicle is computed as (a) 11.69m at a distance of −2.15m on the right side of the road's principal axis, (b) 13.23m at a distance of −2.16m on the right side of the road, (c) 13.23m at a distance of 5.03m to the left side of the road, and (d) 15.09m at a distance of 0.34m to the left side of the road.

detected object(s) (the extrinsic and intrinsic camera parameters with the homographic projection), the distance of these objects from the ego vehicle is deduced. XY are pixels in the image. The distance is in meters.

A benefit of this approach is the removal of dependency on complex stereovision for estimating distance. Calibration, triangulation, and, above all, cost are major factors associated with stereovision.

In Figure 11.13(a), two operations are seen primarily. (1) Vehicle detection is done with a confidence score of 61.18%. (2) Using the coordinates of the detected bounding box, the distance of the object is found to be 11.69 m in front of the ego vehicle, and 2.15 m to the right side of the X_v-axis. Similarly, in the right top image of Figure 11.13, the same object is a little bit farther than the previous frame. This object is now detected with a confidence score of 62.78% at about 13.23 m in front, and 2.16 m toward the right side of the X_v-axis. In the left picture on the bottom of Figure 11.13, the vehicle is detected at a distance of about 13.23 m and 5.03 m to the left side of the X_v-axis with a confidence score of about 53.25%. Finally, in the last image (right side, bottom), a vehicle is detected at about 15.09 m in front of the ego car with a confidence score of approximately 71.75%. The vehicle is located at 0.3 4 m to the right side of the X_v-axis.

11.4 CONCLUSION

Throughout this chapter, it has been demonstrated that the use of multiple features for representing objects along with the optimal number and size of anchors can solve the problems faced by some popular object detection algorithms. Limitations faced by these algorithms are insensitivity to the orientation of objects, spatial constraints placed by the bounding box, the inability to learn high-level features for object classification, and the inability to learn with a limited set of data. All of these result in a low frame rate and reduced convergence rate. The object detection with the proposed monocular camera-based distance detection procedure is quite effective for real-time implementation. The FGGFCR algorithm, which is based on image clustering-based segmentation followed by reinforcing contours of objects with Gabor and filtered HFCs, also managed to successfully replace the traditional edge detection algorithm. Another important feature realized through this chapter is that use of multiple levels of clustering operation for selection of the optimal value of anchors increased the frame rate compared with other research works. Through the current work, it is established that the use of image processing tools along with an optimized deep learning framework can increase performance appreciatively. Also, the practical feasibility of the proposed object detection technique with mono camera-based distance deduction is explored by implementing several images and a video stream.

ACKNOWLEDGMENT

This work is supported by a grant from the Ministry of Electronics and Information Technology (MeitY), The Government of India, vide reference no. 4(6)/2018-ITEA.

REFERENCES

1. Candes E., and D. Donoho, "Curvelets – A Surprisingly Effective Nonadaptive Representation of Objects with Edges," Technical Report, California Institute of Technology, Pasadena, 1999.
2. Laishram, Romesh, Wahengbam Kanan Kumar, Anshuman Gupta, and Khairnar Vinayak Prakash. 2014. "A Novel MRI Brain Edge Detection Using PSOFCM Segmentation and Canny Algorithm." In Proceedings – International Conference on Electronic Systems, Signal Processing, and Computing Technologies, ICESC 2014. https://doi.org/10.1109/ICESC.2014.78.
3. Nongmeikapam, Kishorjit, Wahengbam Kanan Kumar, Ranita Khumukcham, and Aheibam Dinamani Singh. 2018. "An Unsupervised Cluster-Wise Color Segmentation of Medical and Camera Images Using Genetically Improved Fuzzy-Markovian Decision Relational Model." Journal of Intelligent and Fuzzy Systems, 35, 1, 1147–1160. https://doi.org/10.3233/JIFS-17968.
4. Kumar, Wahengbam Kanan, Kishorjit Nongmeikapam, and Aheibam Dinamani Singh. 2020. "An Urban Parametric Scene Parsing Technique through an Improved Multispectral Image Fusion." SSRN Electronic Journal, 44–49. https://doi.org/10.2139/ssrn.3516699.
5. Kumar, Wahengbam Kanan, Kishorjit Nongmeikapam, and Aheibam Dinamani Singh. 2019. "Enhancing Scene Perception Using a Multispectral Fusion of Visible–near-Infrared Image Pair." IET Image Processing, 13, 13, 2467–2479. https://doi.org/10.1049/iet-ipr.2018.5812.
6. Kumar, Wahengbam Kanan, Kishorjit Nongmeikapam, and Aheibam Dinamani Singh. 2020. "Selecting a Suitable Image Enhancement Tool for Near-Infrared Urban Scenes." SSRN Electronic Journal, 40–43. https://doi.org/10.2139/ssrn.3516693.

7. Bugdol, Marcin D., Pawel Badura, Jan Juszczyk, Wojciech Wieclawek, and Maria J. Bienkowska. 2018. "System for Detecting Vehicle Features from Low Quality Data." Promet – Traffic – Traffico, 30, 1, 11–20. https://doi.org/10.7307/ptt.v30i1.2430.

8. Wen, Xuezhi, Ling Shao, Yu Xue, and Wei Fang. 2015. "A Rapid Learning Algorithm for Vehicle Classification." Information Sciences, 295, 395–406. https://doi.org/10.1016/j.ins.2014.10.040.

9. Sun, Zehang, George Bebis, and Ronald Miller. 2005. "On-Road Vehicle Detection Using Evolutionary Gabor Filter Optimization." IEEE Transactions on Intelligent Transportation Systems, 6, 2, 125–137. https://doi.org/10.1109/TITS.2005.848363.

10. Arrospide, Jon, and Luis Salgado. 2013. "Log-Gabor Filters for Image-Based Vehicle Verification." IEEE Transactions on Image Processing, 22, 6, 2286–2295. https://doi.org/10.1109/TIP.2013.2249080.

11. Arrtospide, Jon, Luis Salgado, and Massimo Camplani. 2013. "Image-Based on-Road Vehicle Detection Using Cost-Effective Histograms of Oriented Gradients." Journal of Visual Communication and Image Representation, 24, 7, 1182–1190. https://doi.org/10.1016/j.jvcir.2013.08.001.

12. Zhang, Rong Hui, Feng You, Fang Chen, and Wen Qiang He. 2018. "Vehicle Detection Method for Intelligent Vehicle at Night Time Based on Video and Laser Information." International Journal of Pattern Recognition and Artificial Intelligence, 32, 04, 1850009. https://doi.org/10.1142/S021800141850009X.

13. Zhu, Wentao, Jun Miao, Jiangbi Hu, and Laiyun Qing. 2014. "Vehicle Detection in Driving Simulation Using Extreme Learning Machine." Neurocomputing, 128, 160–165. https://doi.org/10.1016/j.neucom.2013.05.052.

14. Kim, Jisu, Jeonghyun Baek, and Euntai Kim. 2015. "A Novel On-Road Vehicle Detection Method Using _ HOG." IEEE Transactions on Intelligent Transportation Systems, 16, 6, 3414–3429. https://doi.org/10.1109/TITS.2015.2465296.

15. Liu, Kang, and Gellert Mattyus. 2015. "Fast Multiclass Vehicle Detection on Aerial Images." IEEE Geoscience and Remote Sensing Letters, 12, 9, 1938–1942. https://doi.org/10.1109/LGRS.2015.2439517.

16. Zhang, Huaizhong, Chunbo Luo, Qi Wang, Matthew Kitchin, Andrew Parmley, Jesus Monge-Alvarez, and Pablo Casaseca-de-la-Higuera. 2018. "A Novel Infrared Video Surveillance System Using Deep Learning Based Techniques." Multimedia Tools and Applications, 77, 20, 26657–26676. https://doi.org/10.1007/s11042-018-5883-y.

17. Yoo, Hunjae, Ukil Yang, and Kwanghoon Sohn. 2013. "Gradient-Enhancing Conversion for Illumination-Robust Lane Detection." IEEE Transactions on Intelligent Transportation Systems, 14, 3, 1083–1094. https://doi.org/10.1109/TITS.2013.2252427.

18. Sun, Tsung Ying, Shang Jeng Tsai, and Vincent Chan. 2006. "HSI Color Model Based Lane-Marking Detection." In IEEE Conference on Intelligent Transportation Systems, Proceedings, ITSC. https://doi.org/10.1109/itsc.2006.1707380.

19. Cheng, Hsu Yung, Bor Shenn Jeng, Pei Ting Tseng, and Kuo Chin Fan. 2006. "Lane Detection with Moving Vehicles in the Traffic Scenes." IEEE Transactions on Intelligent Transportation Systems, 7, 4, 571–582. https://doi.org/10.1109/TITS.2006.883940.

20. Borkar, Amol, Monson Hayes, and Mark T. Smith. 2009. "Lane Detection and Tracking Using a Layered Approach." In Lecture Notes in Computer Science (Including Subseries Lecture Notes in Artificial Intelligence and Lecture Notes in Bioinformatics). https://doi.org/10.1007/978-3-642-04697-1_44.

21. Kim, Zu Whan. 2008. "Robust Lane Detection and Tracking in Challenging Scenarios." IEEE Transactions on Intelligent Transportation Systems, 9, 1, 16–26. https://doi.org/10.1109/TITS.2007.908582.

22. Wang, Jyun Guo, Cheng Jian Lin, and Shyi Ming Chen. 2010. "Applying Fuzzy Method to Vision-Based Lane Detection and Departure Warning System." Expert Systems with Applications. https://doi.org/10.1016/j.eswa.2009.05.026.

23. Siagian, Christian, and Laurent Itti. 2007. "Rapid Biologically-Inspired Scene Classification Using Features Shared with Visual Attention." IEEE Transactions on Pattern Analysis and Machine Intelligence. https://doi.org/10.1109/TPAMI.2007.40.

24. Fang, Hao, Saurabh Gupta, Forrest Iandola, Rupesh K. Srivastava, Li Deng, Piotr Dolltar, Jianfeng Gao, et al. 2015. "From Captions to Visual Concepts and Back." In Proceedings of the IEEE Computer Society Conference on Computer Vision and Pattern Recognition. https://doi.org/10.1109/CVPR.2015.7298754.

25. Borji, Ali, Simone Frintrop, Dicky N. Sihite, and Laurent Itti. 2012. "Adaptive Object Tracking by Learning Background Context." In IEEE Computer Society Conference on Computer Vision and Pattern Recognition Workshops. https://doi.org/10.1109/CVPRW.2012.6239191.

26. Mahadevan, Vijay, and Nuno Vasconcelos. 2013. "Biologically Inspired Object Tracking Using Center-Surround Saliency Mechanisms." IEEE Transactions on Pattern Analysis and Machine Intelligence, 35, 3, 541–554. https://doi.org/10.1109/TPAMI.2012.98.

27. Wang, Tiantian, Ali Borji, Lihe Zhang, Pingping Zhang, and Huchuan Lu. 2017. "A Stagewise Refinement Model for Detecting Salient Objects in Images." In Proceedings of the IEEE International Conference on Computer Vision. https://doi.org/10.1109/ICCV.2017.433.

28. Liu, Nian, and Junwei Han. 2016. "DHSNet: Deep Hierarchical Saliency Network for Salient Object Detection." In Proceedings of the IEEE Computer Society Conference on Computer Vision and Pattern Recognition. https://doi.org/10.1109/CVPR.2016.80.

29. Zhang, Pingping, Dong Wang, Huchuan Lu, Hongyu Wang, and Xiang Ruan. 2017. "Amulet: Aggregating Multi-Level Convolutional Features for Salient Object Detection." In Proceedings of the IEEE International Conference on Computer Vision. https://doi.org/10.1109/ICCV.2017.31.

30. Hou, Qibin, Ming Cheng, Xiaowei Hu, Ali Borji, Zhuowen Tu, and Philip H.S. Torr. 2019. "Deeply Supervised Salient Object Detection with Short Connections." IEEE Transactions on Pattern Analysis and Machine Intelligence, 41, 4, 815–828. https://doi.org/10.1109/TPAMI.2018.2815688.

31. Viola, Paul, and Michael Jones. 2001. "Rapid Object Detection Using a Boosted Cascade of Simple Features." In Proceedings of the IEEE Computer Society Conference on Computer Vision and Pattern Recognition. https://doi.org/10.1109/cvpr.2001.990517.

32. Viola, Paul, Michael J. Jones, and Daniel Snow. 2005. "Detecting Pedestrians Using Patterns of Motion and Appearance." International Journal of Computer Vision, 63, 2, 153–161. https://doi.org/10.1007/s11263-005-6644-8.

33. Ren, Shaoqing, Kaiming He, Ross Girshick, and Jian Sun. 2017. "Faster R-CNN: Towards Real-Time Object Detection with Region Proposal Networks." IEEE Transactions on Pattern Analysis and Machine Intelligence, 39, 6, 1137–1149. https://doi.org/10.1109/TPAMI.2016.2577031.

34. Redmon, Joseph, and Ali Farhadi. 2017. "YOLO9000: Better, Faster, Stronger." In Proceedings – 30th IEEE Conference on Computer Vision and Pattern Recognition, CVPR 2017. https://doi.org/10.1109/CVPR.2017.690.

35. Redmon, Joseph, Santosh Divvala, Ross Girshick, and Ali Farhadi. 2016. "You Only Look Once: Unified, Real-Time Object Detection." In Proceedings of the IEEE Computer Society Conference on Computer Vision and Pattern Recognition. https://doi.org/10.1109/CVPR.2016.91.

36. Liu, Wei, Dragomir Anguelov, Dumitru Erhan, Christian Szegedy, Scott Reed, Cheng Yang Fu, and Alexander C.Berg. 2016. "SSD: Single Shot Multibox Detector." In Lecture Notes in Computer Science (Including Subseries Lecture Notes in Artificial Intelligence and Lecture Notes in Bioinformatics). https://doi.org/10.1007/978-3-319-46448-0_2.

37. Liao, Minghui, Baoguang Shi, and Xiang Bai. 2018. "TextBoxes++: A Single-Shot Oriented Scene Text Detector." IEEE Transactions on Image Processing, 27, 8, 3676–3690. https://doi.org/10.1109/TIP.2018.2825107.

38. Najibi, Mahyar, Pouya Samangouei, Rama Chellappa, and Larry S. Davis. 2017. "SSH: Single Stage Headless Face Detector." In Proceedings of the IEEE International Conference on Computer Vision. https://doi.org/10.1109/ICCV.2017.522.

39. Zhang, Shifeng, Xiangyu Zhu, Zhen Lei, Hailin Shi, Xiaobo Wang, and Stan Z. Li. 2017. "S3FD: Single Shot Scale-Invariant Face Detector." In Proceedings of the IEEE International Conference on Computer Vision. https://doi.org/10.1109/ICCV.2017.30.

40. Ford, A., and A., Roberts. 1998. Colour space conversions. Westminster University, London, pp. 1–31.

41. Nongmeikapam, Kishorjit, Wahengbam Kanan Kumar, and Aheibam Dinamani Singh. 2018. "Fast and Automatically Adjustable GRBF Kernel Based Fuzzy C Means for Cluster-Wise Coloured Feature Extraction and Segmentation of MR Images." IET Image Processing, 12, 4, 513–524. https://doi.org/10.1049/iet-ipr.2017.1102.

42. Liu, Chengjun, and Harry Wechsler. 2002. "Gabor Feature Based Classification Using the Enhanced Fisher Linear Discriminant Model for Face Recognition." IEEE Transactions on Image Processing, 11, 4, 467–476. https://doi.org/10.1109/TIP.2002.999679.

43. Meshgini, Saeed, Ali Aghagolzadeh, and Hadi Seyedarabi. 2013. "Face Recognition Using Gabor-Based Direct Linear Discriminant Analysis and Support Vector Machine." Computers and Electrical Engineering, 39, 3, 727–745. https://doi.org/10.1016/j.compeleceng.2012.12.011.

44. Shen, Lin, Li Bai, and Michael Fairhurst. 2007. "Gabor Wavelets and General Discriminant Analysis for Face Identification and Verification." Image and Vision Computing, 25, 5, 553–563. https://doi.org/10.1016/j.imavis.2006.05.002.

45. Geiger, Andreas, Philip Lenz, and Raquel Urtasun. 2012. "Are We Ready for Autonomous Driving? The KITTI Vision Benchmark Suite." In Proceedings of the IEEE Computer Society Conference on Computer Vision and Pattern Recognition. https://doi.org/10.1109/CVPR.2012.6248074.

46. Zhong, Yuanyi, Jianfeng Wang, Jian Peng, and Lei Zhang. 2009. "Anchor Box Optimization for Object Detection." arXiv preprint arXiv:1812.00469.

47. Park, Hae Sang, and Chi Hyuck Jun. 2009. "A Simple and Fast Algorithm for K-Medoids Clustering." Expert Systems with Applications, 36, 2, 3336–3341. https://doi.org/10.1016/j.eswa.2008.01.039.

48. Zhang, Zhengyou. 2000. "A Flexible New Technique for Camera Calibration." IEEE Transactions on Pattern Analysis and Machine Intelligence, 22, 11, 1330–1334. https://doi.org/10.1109/34.888718.

49. Andrew, Alex M. 2001. "Multiple View Geometry in Computer Vision." Kybernetes, Dec. 1.https://doi.org/10.1016/S0143-8166(01)00145-2.

50. Hwangbo, Myung. 2012. "Vision-Based Navigation for a Small Fixed-Wing Airplane in Urban Environment." ProQuest Dissertations and Theses.

51. Mittal, Anish, Rajiv Soundararajan, and Alan C. Bovik. 2013. "Making a 'Completely Blind' Image Quality Analyzer." IEEE Signal Processing Letters, 20, 3, 209–212. https://doi.org/10.1109/LSP.2012.2227726.

52. Mittal, Anish, Anush Krishna Moorthy, and Alan Conrad Bovik. 2012. "No-Reference Image Quality Assessment in the Spatial Domain." IEEE Transactions on Image Processing, 21, 12, 4695–4708. https://doi.org/10.1109/TIP.2012.2214050.

53. Venkatanath, N., D. Praneeth, B. H. Maruthi Chandrasekhar, Sumohana S. Channappayya, and Swarup S. Medasani. 2015. "Blind Image Quality Evaluation Using Perception Based Features." In 2015 21st National Conference on Communications, NCC 2015. https://doi.org/10.1109/NCC.2015.7084843.

54. Girshick, Ross, Jeff Donahue, Trevor Darrell, and Jitendra Malik. 2014. "Rich Feature Hierarchies for Accurate Object Detection and Semantic Segmentation." In Proceedings of the IEEE Computer Society Conference on Computer Vision and Pattern Recognition. doi:10.1109/CVPR.2014.81.

CHAPTER 12

Stackelberg

Hidden Markov Model Approach for Behavior Prediction of Surrounding Vehicles for Autonomous Driving

R Syama and C Mala

National Institute of Technology Tiruchirappalli, India

CONTENTS

12.1 INTRODUCTION

Autonomous driving refers to self-driving vehicles that sense the environment and move without human intervention. The need for safe, energy-efficient, sustainable, and comfortable transportation services is the top reason for the development of autonomous vehicles. A mixed scenario exists in which the autonomous vehicles share the roads with human-driven vehicles. For safe and effective operation on roads, autonomous vehicles must be able to correctly predict the intention or future movement of the surrounding vehicles.

DOI: 10.1201/9781003048381-13

In a traffic environment, the vehicle will respond to the stimulus of the surroundings irrespective of whether it is a vehicle driven by a human or an autonomous vehicle. Human-driven vehicles may have several driving styles, and the same situation can be handled in distinct ways by distinct drivers. The driving choice may change for different passengers. Autonomous vehicles need to make decisions dynamically in the mixed scenario. They should also be adaptive to meet the requirements of different traffic scenarios. Adequate research has not been carried out on the adaptive and dynamic decision making for autonomous driving. The driving styles of human drivers are generally decided by the behavior of the drivers and environmental factors [1, 2].

Autonomous vehicles must behave like human drivers to provide safety in a mixed driving environment. The autonomous vehicle obtains the driving information from the surrounding vehicles and it applies a model to accurately predict the future behavior of the surrounding vehicles [4]. A game-theoretic approach can be applied to such a scenario, which can effectively investigate the actions of the vehicles. Limited research has been performed to predict the behavior of the vehicles by considering the influence of nearby vehicles. Considering this, this chapter proposes a method for predicting the behavior of surrounding vehicles based on the Stackelberg game and hidden Markov model (HMM). This method considers the recognition and prediction of driver behavior. The driver intention prediction is done by considering the interactions among the traffic vehicles. It solves the behavior prediction and recognition problem, which can be modeled using Gaussian mixture model (GMM)-HMM and making use of historical trajectory of the vehicle and the revenue function for different vehicle scenarios. Simulations are conducted to demonstrate the feasibility of the study.

12.2 RELATED WORKS

A great deal of research has been done in behavior prediction of vehicles in the autonomous driving systems because it is a critical step in the path planning for autonomous driving in advanced-driver assistance systems (ADAS). A wide variety of methods have been proposed to predict the behavior of vehicles in recent years. A number of machine learning-based algorithms are proposed to study the behavior of vehicles. The support vector machine (SVM)-based approach is proposed for the prediction of driving objectives [1, 3]. In ref. [4], the k-nearest neighbor-based lane change scenario is proposed to produce trajectory.

Several probabilistic-based approaches are used in behavior planning and prediction. A dynamic programming-based approach is implemented in ref. [4]. The problem is well studied and formulated to optimize the value, but it does not consider the participants on the road. Refs. [5, 6] propose the decision-making approaches based on the historical trajectory information of the vehicle. Deep learning approaches were also applied to the traffic scenarios to study the behavior of different participants. A generative adversarial network (GAN)-based approach is used in ref. [7]. The lane change problem is intensively studied in refs. [8, 9], which solve the problem by recurrent neural network (RNN) and long short term memory (LSTM), respectively. To model the lane change scenario better and to make the decision making more efficient, ref. [10] proposed a reinforcement learning-based approach that considers both autonomous and human drivers on the road. A game theory-based approach is suggested in ref. [11]. Adaptable generative prediction framework (AGen) is proposed in ref. [12] for better prediction efficiency. The computer vision approach is proposed in ref. [13]. Fuzzy logic-based approaches are proposed to implement human-like behavior for autonomous vehicles [14]. The parameters to achieve human driving behavior in autonomous vehicles were studied and modeled in ref. [15].

HMM-based approaches are also used in several studies because it can model human driving behavior. In ref. [16], driver intention prediction based on HMM is proposed. The system is implemented and tested on real data. The driver behavior at intersections is estimated in refs. [17, 18], which uses HMM and the hybrid state system (HSS). They studied the behavior of drivers at merging, because at the merging of lanes the vehicles need mutual interaction.

From the previously mentioned literature, it is inferred that limited works have been carried out in accurately predicting the behavior of the surrounding vehicles. None of the models specifically model the driver intention [19]. The response of the vehicles in a road, whether it is a vehicle driven by human or an autonomous vehicle, always depends on the surrounding environment and participants. A game theory approach is well suited to analyze the behavior because it always considers the behavior of other players in the system [2]. So this chapter proposes a method based on the game-theoretic approach and HMM, which better predicts the behavior of human vehicles in a mixed road scenario. To model human intentions better, GMM-HMM has been used for modeling and predicting the behavior considering the historical trajectory information. The game used in this chapter is the Stackelberg game, which is a non-cooperative game that can model the traffic scenario well. This chapter's contributions can be summarized as follows: (1) to improve the prediction accuracy by using a method that is based on the game-theoretic approach and HMM; (2) revenue functions are designed for modeling the intents of the driver and are combined with HMM to predict future behavior; and (3) the Next Generation SIMulation (NGSIM) data set is used for extracting useful parameters for training HMM and for revenue function, and simulations are done for validation.

12.3 PROPOSED WORK

12.3.1 Stackelberg Game

Game theory can be described as the mathematical modeling that expresses the cooperation between intelligent and logical agents. These methods can be used in a variety of decision- making processes because of their ability to produce optimal solutions while interacting with multiple agents. This branch of mathematics was initially used in economics, but now it is applied in almost all fields of science. With the advancements in technology, it is widely used in all areas of computer science. Game theory is suitable for modeling human behavior, which makes it the logical selection among a number of alternatives.

In autonomous driving, the interaction between the vehicles can be considered as a game with multiple players in which each of the players has a specific strategy. The driving behaviors of different vehicles can be treated as a non-cooperative game in which each vehicle is independent and selects its strategy to maximize revenue regardless of other vehicles' strategies.

While on a road, drivers normally respond to what they see in front or in rearview mirrors. Traffic rules also affect the driver behavior such as speed limit, congestion, etc. [20]. Normally the driver in the front decides first before the drivers in the lane behind. This backward propagation of the information can be represented by the Stackelberg game, and thus generates a hierarchical decision process. It can be utilized to solve the traffic problems and design an individual driver behavior model because it is pertinent to the information from the roads. It is a strategic game in which one player fixes the strategy and others respond to this strategy sequentially. The player who fixes a certain strategy is known as the "leader," and others who respond to the leader's strategy are called "followers." The leader is the player who is active at the first level and chooses the strategy that gives the best response. In the subsequent levels, the followers react to the leader's strategy. They also try to generate the best response. The leader updates the strategy to obtain the best cost, i.e., minimize the cost. The solution to this game is known as "Stackelberg equilibrium." By solving the equilibrium the most likely behavior can be obtained.

The Stackelberg game can be considered as the hierarchical decision order among players. Assume two players A and B in which A is the leader who commits its strategy before B commits and B is the follower. B maximizes the revenue based on the strategy that the leader selects. The vehicles can make the decision independently and select their strategy in such a way that it will maximize their revenue. The revenue values considered in this chapter are free headway and collision index. The vehicles do not know how much they are going to achieve while choosing a strategy, but they choose a strategy expecting they will produce the maximum revenue out of the strategy. Thus, the expected utility can be expressed as the sum of the product of the revenues of all combinations of behaviors and their occurrence probability. The vehicle calculates the utility value given by each behavior and picks the behavior with the maximum value.

Figure 12.1 shows the behavior prediction framework using the Stackelberg game and HMM.

12.3.1.1 Background Design

The Stackelberg game can be formally defined as $G = (P,S,R)$, where $P = (p_1, \ldots p_i \ldots p_n)$ represents the finite set of players, $S = (s_1, \ldots s_i \ldots s_n) \in S, s_i$ represents the strategy of the player p_i, and $R = (r_1, r_2 \ldots r_n)$ is the revenue function of the players.

Figure 12.2 shows a three-lane road where three vehicles, A, B, and C, are moving where car A has information priority to car B and car C has information priority to A. In this figure, vehicle A is the autonomous vehicle that is surrounded by the human-driven vehicles. The Stackelberg model can be applied to this scenario in which each driver has a strategic move considering the leader's strategy. There exist as many games as the number of drivers, which is shown in Figure 12.3.

These vehicles also have a maximum of three actions based on their lane of movement in the road. Each vehicle will have different behaviors based on the position of the vehicle

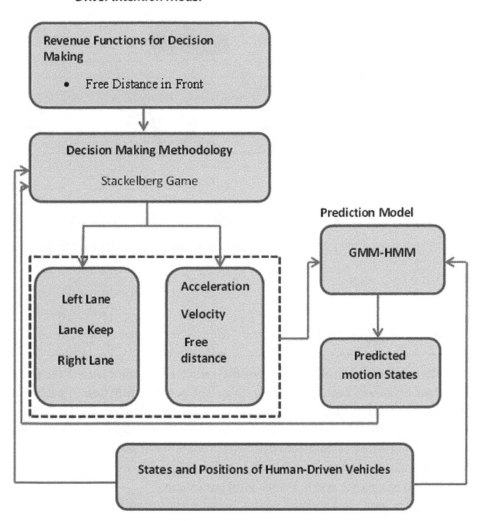

FIGURE 12.1   Behavior prediction framework.

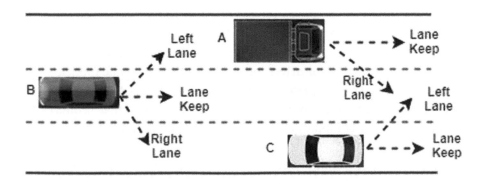

FIGURE 12.2   Vehicle ordering and interaction.

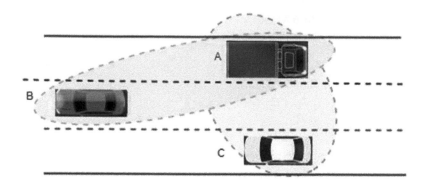

FIGURE 12.3   Multiple games.

on the road and the environment. The different behaviors (B_i) of the vehicles in Figure 12.3 can be:

- $\mathbf{B_A}$= {Lane keep, Right}

- $\mathbf{B_B}$ = {Lane keep, Right, Left}

- $\mathbf{B_C}$ = {Lane keep, Left}

Therefore, the total number of behaviors of the vehicles in such a lane is the product of the number of behaviors each vehicle can have. The revenue function of each vehicle is obtained as the combination of the behaviors of vehicles in the road.

The behavior of the vehicles is not known in advance, and each of the vehicles has a probability for choosing a certain behavior. This probability of selecting a certain behavior by each vehicle can be represented by $p(B_A)$, $p(B_B)$, $p(B_C)$. The drivers can be rational or irrational. The driving style also is a behavioral parameter.

The Stackelberg game is a dynamic game because the reward values change continuously depending on the driving situation. The vehicles do not share their reward values because they have different strategies and each tries to generate the optimal value. The vehicles ahead may also consider the autonomous vehicle as a game player in a different game and respond to its actions.

12.3.2 Revenue Function Design

Some performance parameters are considered in this chapter to model the decision-making process. The cost function for driver intention prediction can be modeled by revenue function, which depends on the performance parameters. It is based on the expected utility theory, which states that a player always chooses a strategy that produces the highest revenue. Each vehicle computes the revenue for the different permitted strategies and chooses the best one.

Positive and negative revenue are taken into account in this game-theoretic approach. The positive revenue includes the free distance that each vehicle has in front [3], attaining the vehicle speed [2, 19], etc. The negative revenue consists of the risk of having an accident, loss of comfort, etc. [21]. The revenue of a driver always depends on its own behavior and the behavior of other vehicles in and around the vehicle; thus, the revenue function can best describe the interaction among vehicles.

In the proposed scenario, the revenue function that describes the driver intention is defined as:

$$R'(T) = w_1 d + w_2 c \qquad (12.1)$$

where T is the scenario and d and c are the free distance and collision index. Here the free distance gives the positive revenue to the driver, whereas the collision index gives negative revenue.

12.3.2.1 Free Distance in Front

Generally all the drivers want more free distance in front [21]; thus, the free distance can be treated as a positive revenue that the measures the driver intention to get more space. This can be defined as:

$$d = \begin{cases} min(d_r, d_v) & \text{if there is a vehicle ahead} \\ d_v & \text{otherwise} \end{cases} \qquad (12.2)$$

where d_v denotes the visibility distance and d_r denotes the distance between the vehicles under consideration.

12.3.2.2 Collision Index

Once the driver decides which lane it wants to move into, it has to check the sides so that it can identify whether any vehicles are approaching to avoid the collision. If the vehicle is fast enough to overtake the subject vehicle, then it cannot change the lane even though it has enough free distance in front. This can be considered as a negative utility. From the studies it observed that the collision index can be defined as:

$$c = \begin{cases} 0 & \text{Satisfy safety condition} \\ -\dfrac{1}{d_{min}} & \text{does not satisfy safety condition,} \end{cases} \qquad (12.3)$$

where the d_{min} is the nearest distance between the vehicle and the surrounding vehicle.

The revenue function parameters w_1 and w_2 are obtained from the training results of NGSIM data, which is shown in the Table 12.1.

TABLE 12.1   Revenue Function Parameter

w_1	w_2
0.061	6.25

12.3.3 GMM-HMM Construction and Training

Driver behavior recognition is based on GMM-HMM. It is a probability distribution model that uses a discrete random variable for expressing the state of the system. In the Markov model, the system state at any moment depends on the previous instant. The probability distribution of all random variables in the HMM model can be represented as [2]:

$$P(O|Q) = \prod_{i=1}^{T} (o_i | q_i)$$

(12.4)

where $Q = q_0, q_1, q_2 \ldots, q_r$ is the hidden state sequence and $O = o_1, o_2, \ldots o_r$ is the observation sequence.

This can be determined by giving state transition probability, observation probability, and initial state distribution. The initial state distribution is the probabilities of s_i at the initial moment and can be represented as [2]:

$$p_i = P(q_1 = s_i)$$

(12.5)

The state transition probability is the probability to go from state i to state j [2]:

$$a_{i,j} = P(q_{n+1} = s_j | q_n = s_i).$$

(12.6)

They are represented by matrix A. The observation probability describes the probability of a certain observation x, if the model is in state s_i.

HMMs can predict the future intention of the surrounding vehicle. The mobility features are extracted from the data set and are given to the training/testing data. The training data set is divided into subsets based on the given intentions and are trained. In this approach, HMM is trained for each of the intentions of the driver, which are considered as Lane Keep, Left, and Right.

The information that is received from autonomous vehicles and other nearby vehicles can be used for training. The locations of the vehicles are taken and the location coordinates of each vehicle for a certain period of time is recorded. Preprocessing on the same data can be done to select some of the features such as velocity, acceleration, the free distance between vehicles and number of lanes, etc. These features can be used to obtain the prediction result.

In this chapter, N number of mobility features for each vehicle is taken. The features can be represented as a matrix [2]:

$$V = \left[\boldsymbol{V_1}^T, \ldots \boldsymbol{V_n}^T \ldots \boldsymbol{V_N}^T \right]$$

(12.7)

where $n = 1, 2, \ldots, N$. This defines the features of one vehicle where each V_i represents the feature at an interval of time $t = 1 \ldots T$. The mobility feature matrix of a vehicle can be represented as:

$$F = \left[\boldsymbol{V^1}, \ldots \boldsymbol{V^i} \ldots \boldsymbol{V^L} \right]$$

(12.8)

The mobility feature matrix F includes the features of both the autonomous vehicle and the nearby vehicle.

Continuous HMM can be used to model the continuous distribution, and it is represented by GMM; thus, it is written as GMM-HMM. The GMM parameters are computed applying maximum likelihood estimation. The Gaussian distribution fits the probability density function of mobility features. Each column in the mobility feature matrix F denotes the features of type i of all vehicles and can be represented as f. This probability density function $P(f)$ can be derived as [7]:

$$\sum_{m=1}^{M}\sum_{p=1}^{Q}w_{n,p,m}p(f\,|\,N) \qquad (12.9)$$

where $w_{n,p,m}$ represents the weight of the pth state, which is modeled by the mth Gaussian component of the mobility feature n. For training, Gaussian distribution that fits the probability density function for each mobility feature is used.

The historical information can be used to predict the behavior of targeted vehicle. Features of the surrounding vehicles in the same interval are used together to predict the targeted vehicle's intention. The past evidence of autonomous vehicle features and surrounding vehicle features are used as the observation of HMM [22]. This is given as the input to the prediction algorithm. The prediction accuracy can be improved by giving the historical traces of both the selected vehicle and nearby vehicles. The probability of each scenario can be generated by the Forward algorithm. The most likely behavior HMM is selected as the driving intention and it is represented as

$$i = arg_{\max}\left(P\big(O\,|\,\lambda_i\big)\right) \qquad (12.10)$$

where i is the driving intention and in this approach it can have three values, i.e., $i \in \{1,2,3\}$ that represent Line Keep, Left, and Right, respectively. The intention represented by i gives the intention of the targeted vehicle.

The proposed method has used an NGSIM data set, which is an initiative of the U.S. Federal Highway Administration for model training. It stores different information about the vehicle and its mobility information [23]. Preprocessing is done to eliminate the noise present in the data and to obtain the vehicle coordinates and the acceleration and velocity information. The lane change information is extracted from the data set.

12.4 SIMULATION AND PERFORMANCE ANALYSIS

The proposed methods are tested by simulating two scenarios that are built and tested in MATLAB® and Simulink. For simulation, a road with three lanes is considered.

12.4.1 Scenario

In the selected scenario, a lane change in a road merge is used where the autonomous vehicle predicts the behavior of the human-driven vehicle in the adjacent lane and decides to change its lane. The scenario is shown in Figure 12.4. In the designed scenario, A is the

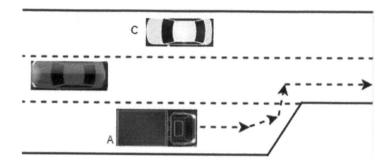

FIGURE 12.4   Testing scenario.

autonomous vehicle and B is the human-driven vehicle. Initially, A has a speed of 28 km/h and B has the same speed, which is going straight. Then there is a road merge in the path, so A has to make a lane change in between. It considers the free distance between the cars and it will check whether there is as chance that B may overtake it. If it is safe to perform the lane change, then A will do so by gradually increasing its speed. The driving styles also affect the decision making. If the driver is irrational, then the lane change by the targeted vehicle will be sudden and there will be an immediate increase of the acceleration of the vehicle. If the driver is rational, then the change in acceleration will be linear and the vehicle will guarantee safety. In Stackelberg equilibrium, the behavior of a targeted vehicle will depend on the behavior of human the vehicle. Here, the decision making is just like human decision making.

The information we have considered for simulation is given in Table 12.2. From the Figure 12.5, it is clear that the human-driven vehicle keeps the straight lane and the autonomous vehicle gradually increases the speed to change the lane and then keeps the constant speed.

Figure 12.6a and b shows how the different driving styles affect the speeds of the vehicles. For irrational driving, there is a sudden and high change in the speed, whereas for rational driving, the speed change is gradual and remains constant after lane change.

Figure 12.7 compares the probabilities of Lane Change and Lane Keep behaviors of the proposed approach and the HMM approach. The Lane Keep probability of maintaining the lane decreases as the time increases and lane change to left probability increases as the vehicle reaches the lane intersection; thereafter it maintains constant. The prediction results show that the prediction time for the proposed method is less compared with the prediction time of HMM. The actual prediction occurs a few seconds before the vehicle starts changing the lane. The lane change probability of the proposed approach starts to increase long before recognition probability of HMM.

TABLE 12.2   Information for Simulation

The autonomous vehicle changes the lane since the speed of the human vehicle is constant	
Initial speed of vehicles $V_{Autonomous} = V_{human} = 28$ km/h	Total simulation time 12 s
Initial coordinate positions of vehicle	Trajectory prediction time 5 s
$(X_A, Y_A) = (18.32, 1.8)$ $(X_B, Y_B) = (0, 4.4)$	

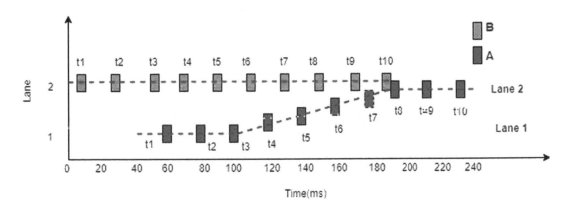

FIGURE 12.5   Trajectories of the vehicles.

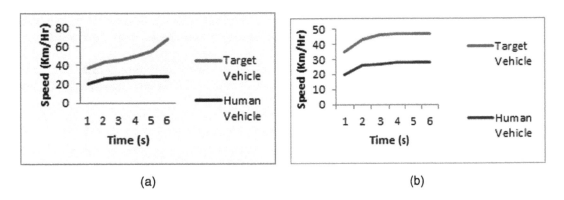

FIGURE 12.6   (a) Irrational driving style and (b) rational driving style.

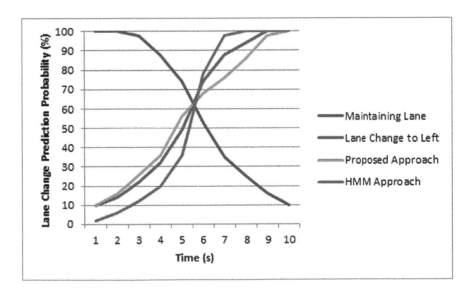

FIGURE 12.7   Lane change probability for proposed method and HMM.

12.5 CONCLUSION

This chapter proposes a game-theoretic approach using the Stackelberg game and HMM for prediction of the surrounding vehicle behavior in a mixed scenario. The vehicle behavior in different scenarios is studied and a non-cooperative game-theoretic approach is proposed to model the scenarios. The GMM-HMM is used to train the parameters for recognition of the behavior of vehicles using the NGSIM data set. Simulation results show that the proposed game-theoretic approach predicts the vehicle behavior better compared with HMM.

REFERENCES

1. A. Turnwald, and D. Wollherr, "Human-like motion planning based on game theoretic decision making," International Journal of Social Robotics, 2019, vol. 11, pp. 151–170.
2. S. Zhang, Y. Zhi, R. He, and J. Li, "Research on traffic vehicle behavior prediction method based on game theory and HMM," IEEE Access, 2020, vol. 8, pp. 30210–30222.
3. N. Li, D. W. Oyler, M. Zhang, Y. Yildiz, I. Kolmanovsky, and A. R. Girard, "Game theoretic modeling of driver and vehicle interactions for verification and validation of autonomous vehicle control systems," IEEE Transactions on Control Systems Technology, 2018, vol. 26, no. 5, pp. 1782–1797.
4. Y. Jeong, and K. Yi, "Target vehicle motion prediction-based motion planning framework for autonomous driving in uncontrolled intersections," IEEE Transactions on Intelligent Transportation Systems, 2019, vol. 22, no. 1, pp. 168–177.
5. W. Si, T. Wei and C. Liu, "AGen: adaptable generative prediction networks for autonomous driving," IEEE Intelligent Vehicles Symposium (IV), Paris, 2019.
6. E. Cheung et al., 2018. "Classifying driver behaviors for autonomous vehicle navigation," 2018 IEEE/IRSJ International Conference on Intelligent Robots and Systems, Madrid, Spain, 2019.
7. J. Hong, B. Sapp, and J. Philbin, "Rules of the road: predicting driving behavior with a convolutional model of semantic interactions," IEEE/CVF Conference on Computer Vision and Pattern Recognition (CVPR), Long Beach, CA, 2019.
8. S. Mozaffari, O. Al-Jarrah, M. Dianati, P. Jennings, and A. Mouzakitis, "Deep learning-based vehicle behaviour prediction for autonomous driving applications: a review," IEEE Transactions on Intelligent Transportation Systems, 2020, pp. 1–15.
9. X. Li, X. Ying, and M. C. Chuah, "GRIP: graph-based interaction-aware trajectory prediction," IEEE Intelligent Transportation Systems Conference (ITSC), Auckland, New Zealand, 2019, pp. 3960–3966.
10. X. Geng, H. Liang, B. Yu, P. Zhao, L. He, and R. Huang, "A scenario-adaptive driving behavior prediction approach to urban autonomous driving," Applied Sciences., 2017, vol. 7, pp. 426. https://www.mdpi.com/2076-3417/7/4/426.
11. Q. Deng, and D. Söffker, "Modeling and prediction of human behaviors based on driving data using multi-layer HMMs," IEEE Intelligent Transportation Systems Conference (ITSC), Auckland, New Zealand, 2019, pp. 2014–2019.
12. Z. Wu, C. Li, J. Chen, and H. Gao. "Learning driving behavior for autonomous vehicles using deep learning based methods," IEEE 4th International Conference on Advanced Robotics and Mechatronics (ICARM), Toyonaka, Japan, 2019, pp. 905–910.
13. D. Tran, W. Sheng, L. Liu, and M. Liu, "Hidden Markov model based driver intention prediction system," IEEE International Conference on Cyber Technology in Automation, Control, and Intelligent Systems (CYBER), Shenyang, China, 2015, pp. 115–120.
14. Y. Liang, M. Reyes, and J. Lee, "Real-time detection of driver cognitive distraction using support vector machines," IEEE Transactions on Intelligent Transportation Systems, 2007, vol. 8, no. 2, pp. 340–350.

15. Y. Liao, S. Li, G. Li, W. Wang, B. Cheng, and F. Chen, "Detection of driver cognitive distraction: an SVM based real time algorithm and its comparison study in typical driving scenarios," in the Proceedings of 2016 IEEE Intelligent Vehicles Symposium (IV), 2016, pp. 394–399.
16. T. Toledo, H. N. Koutsopoulos, and M. Ben-Akiva, "Integrated driving behavior modeling," Transportation Research Part C: Emerging Technologies, 2007, vol. 15, no. 2, pp. 96–112.
17. E. Schmerling, K. Leung, W. Vollprecht, and M. Pavone, "Multimodal probabilistic model-based planning for human-robot interaction," International Conference on Robotics and Automation (ICRA), Brisbane, Australia, 2018.
18. R. Schubert, "Evaluating the utility of driving: Toward automated decision making under uncertainty," IEEE Transactions on Intelligent Transportation Systems, 2012, vol. 13, no. 1, pp. 354–364.
19. J. Ho, and S. Ermon, "Generative adversarial imitation learning," In Proceedings of the 30th International Conference on Neural Information Processing Systems, (NIPS'16), Curran Associates Inc., Red Hook, New York, 2016, pp. 4572–4580.
20. M. Wang, S. P. Hoogendoorn, W. Daamen, B. van Arem, and R. Happee, "Game theoretic approach for predictive lane-changing and car-following control," Transportation Research Part C: Emerging Technologies, 2015, vol. 58, pp.73–92.
21. P. Kumar, M. Perrollaz, S. Lefevre, and C. Laugier, "Learning-based approach for online lane change intention prediction," 2013 IEEE Intelligent Vehicles Symposium (IV 2013), Gold Coast City, Queensland, Australia, 2013, pp. 797–802.
22. T. Gindele, S. Brechtel, and R. Dillmann, "A probabilistic model for estimating driver behaviors and vehicle trajectories in traffic environments," 13th International IEEE Conference on Intelligent Transportation Systems, Funchal, Portugal, 2010.
23. X. Xu, L. Zuo, X. Li, L. Qian, J. Ren, and Z. Sun, "A reinforcement learning approach to autonomous decision making of intelligent vehicles on highways," IEEE Transactions on Systems, Man, and Cybernetics: Systems, 2020, vol. 50, no. 10, pp. 3884–3897. doi:10.1109/TSMC.2018.2870983.

CHAPTER 13

Recent Verification and Validation Methodologies for Advanced Driver-Assistance Systems

Franz Wotawa, Florian Klück, and Martin Zimmermann

Graz University of Technology
Graz, Austria

Mihai Nica, Hermann Felbinger, and Jianbo Tao

AVL LIST GmbH
Graz, Austria

Yihao Li

Ludong University
Yantai, China

CONTENTS

DOI: 10.1201/9781003048381-14

13.1 RECENT VERIFICATION AND VALIDATION METHODOLOGIES FOR ADVANCED DRIVER-ASSISTANCE SYSTEMS

Ensuring quality of dependable systems is generally considered a non-trivial task, especially in the context of safety-critical systems like cars or airplanes where any fault that is not revealed during development may harm people. In automated and autonomous driving the situation becomes even more complicated requiring new quality assurance methodologies. Wotawa (2016) discussed this issue arguing that in case of autonomous systems there is no external supervision if a system has to fallback in case of failure. Hence, there it is necessary to verify not only the expected behavior of the system but also the system's behavior in case of unintended interactions with its environment. As a consequence, it is important to verify all potential critical interactions. This seems to be an almost impossible task in general due to the search space.

Kalra and Paddock (2016) argued that an autonomous vehicle should be tested for a particular number of miles (i.e., 275 million) for verification purposes; the number of miles is estimated by the fatality rate of human driving in the United States and assuming an autonomous vehicle has a much lower rate of mileage. An implicit assumption behind Kalra and Paddock (2016) is that when an autonomous vehicle drives a fixed number of miles, it has to experience many critical situations, which unfortunately is not necessarily the case. For example, when always driving in the same area we most likely never see all the issues that may arise in practice, like slightly different stop signs or different driving behavior of other vehicles, which may depend on the country. In addition, testing a car for 275 million miles may also be rather unrealistic considering there is only a small fleet of autonomous vehicles.

As a consequence, we have to come up with specific methods that allow testing the behavior of autonomous vehicles in a realistic setup requiring the least amount of effort but still be able to detect critical traffic situations that may reveal a failure. Such approaches should also come together with certain guarantees allowing us to determine when to stop testing (at least to a certain extent). In this chapter, we discuss two recent approaches for testing automated and autonomous vehicles that have been recently published. Both approaches rely on providing critical scenarios of interactions between the driving system and its environment. One approach utilizes ontologies for this purpose, describing the environment comprising concepts, like roads, crossings, pedestrians, or other cars, that can be divided into a static and a dynamic part. This approach allows for generating test cases, i.e., driving scenarios, from the ontologies directly, which can be simulated afterward for detecting crashes or near-crash situations without harming people. The other approach relies on searching for critical interactions. Both approaches can be fully automated in terms of test generation and test execution.

We organize this chapter as follows. First, we discuss the preliminaries of software testing, and the particular case of advanced driver-assistance systems (ADASs). Afterward, we introduce the two approaches, i.e., ontology-based testing and search-based testing, as well as other testing approaches. Finally, the last section summarizes this chapter.

13.1.1 Preliminaries

Before introducing the different approaches to ADAS testing, we must first discuss the preliminaries. We start by giving an overview of testing used for verifying and validating software and systems. Afterward, we briefly outline challenges of ADAS testing, in particular using an autonomous emergency braking (AEB) system as our running example.

13.1.1.1 Software and System Testing

Testing software and systems has been an active research area of great practical relevance for several decades. Depending on the requirements, we may have a different view on how and when to test. The sole purpose of testing is to find an input stimulus for a given software or system that leads to a wrong behavior of the software or system. It is well known that testing itself is only able to reveal bugs but never prove a software or system to be correct. Nevertheless, testing is a required activity of quality assurance that can still be carried out even for complicated or complex systems. For a more detailed discussion about testing and some of the methods used, we refer the interested reader to (Myers 2004).

On an abstract level, testing comprises two activities, i.e., the generation of test cases and their execution. A test case is composed of an input stimulus and the expected output behavior. Test execution takes a test case and operates the software or system using the input stimuli. It compares the actual behavior of the software or system with its expected one, and in case of divergence a fault is revealed. In this case, we say a test case is a failing one, and a passing one otherwise. Note that accordingly to Myers (2004) a test case not only comprises the input and outputs, but also all means necessary for carrying out the test case. This includes bringing a system into a particular state from which a test is executed, or explaining in detail how execution has to be done. It is important to ensure that a test case, if executed correctly, always has to guarantee to lead to the same behavior of the software or system. Otherwise, a test may be considered a failing test case revealing a non-deterministic behavior.

As already stated, testing requires diligently searching for test cases that reveal a faulty behavior. In more detail, we are usually interested in inputs according to the specification of the software or system in which the concrete implementation fails to behave as expected, i.e., again as given in the specification. However, in practice we are also interested in the behavior of a system when we use an input that is outside its specification. In such cases, we expect the software or system to come up with a certain error message, but not to cause a crash or any other behavior. Test cases following the specification are called positive test cases, whereas the others are called negative test cases. When testing systems appropriately, we have to consider both positive and negative test cases.

There have been many approaches published for generating test cases like model-based testing (Utting and Legeard 2010), combinatorial testing (Kuhn et al. 2013), or fuzz testing (Takanen et al. 2008). Whereas the first two approaches are mainly used to generate positive test cases, fuzz testing mainly focuses on generating test cases that are outside the given specification. The question is whether we can use these methods directly for ADAS testing or in a modified form. To answer this question, we further discuss the challenges of ADAS testing in more detail.

13.1.1.2 Challenges of ADAS Testing

ADASs like an AEB come with a gained autonomy and may also integrate methodologies and tools originating from artificial intelligence (AI), like vision sensors. Originally, automotive standards like ISO 26262 (2011) introducing automotive safety integrity levels (ASILs) do not allow AI technology to be integrated in case of safety-critical functions. However, standards are evolving and AI technology has become more and more important with increasing autonomy of vehicles. Ideally, and to be prepared for future applications, we have to come up with testing approaches for ADASs that are able to be used for fully autonomous vehicle testing.

Testing ADASs and other systems with a higher degree of autonomy potentially relying on AI technology requires testing its parts, including the AI first. This step may comprise using testing techniques applied to machine learning implementations. However, at the system level we have to come up with a testing technique that is agnostic with respect to the underlying technology used. Therefore, we are not discussing the topic of AI testing in particular but how to ensure testing the ADAS in general. We discuss the challenges considering the following two obvious requirements for ADASs.

13.1.1.2.1 ADASs Should Work Correctly Everywhere on Earth (or at Least in Many Countries)   A consequence of this requirement is to consider different types of roads, road markings, traffic signs, and other aspects like traffic on highways or rural areas. In addition, we have to consider other environmental issues like weather conditions or signs that have been modified or partially occluded. In all such cases an autonomous vehicle still has to work appropriately. This holds also for ADASs. An AEB must work during day and night. It must be independent from clothes pedestrians wear. Lighting conditions shall never have an impact on the final behavior of the AEB. Hence, the challenge here is to consider diverse situations and potential interactions between parameters or concepts used in the environmental description.

13.1.1.2.2 ADAS Have to Be Safe   Under no circumstances is an ADAS allowed to harm people. This can partially be achieved by allowing drivers to overrule the systems; this cannot be achieved in case of full autonomy. Nevertheless, in both cases we have to test all kinds of scenarios to be sure that there is no scenario in which the ADAS may behave unsafely. In general, such a challenge is not feasible in practice. First, there is a potentially infinite number of scenarios we may have to consider. Second, we do not know in advance what scenarios we are missing. We may only take care of some but not all cases, which may lead to unintended crashes or situations. The latter challenge is well known and usually is resolved using a database of crashes together with their causes order to avoid trouble occurring more than once. However, this approach requires that we deal with fatalities until reaching a level of confidence in our crash database, which seems to not be the best choice.

In the following we outline the AEB function we are going to use as running example and discuss how validation is currently carried out. The AEB function is a vehicle safety function. It uses the equipped sensors of the vehicle to detect the objects and avoid the potential collision situation. The system will take actions instead of the human driver to prevent from emergency situations. As a famous organization vehicle safety performance evaluation, Euro NCAP[1] provides a safety performance assessment by means of rating. Regarding the AEB system, Euro NCAP provided test protocols for AEB C2C[2] systems and AEB VRU[3] systems (Euro New Car Assessment Programme (NCAP) 2017a, b). The AEB C2C protocol depicts the most frequent accident scenarios of car-to-car rear end collision. It consists of different scenarios such as CCRs,[2] CCRm,[2] and CCRb.[2] CCRs describes a scenario during which a vehicle drives forward toward another stationary vehicle. In the CCRm scenario, the leading vehicle is moving, whereas CCRb means the leading vehicle is braking. On the other hand, the AEB VRU case consists of the scenarios CPFA,[4] CPNA,[4] CPNC,[4] and CPLA.[4] In the protocols the scenario testing values are also defined, such as ego vehicle speed (the vehicle running the system under test [SUT] function) or the speed of the front vehicle. All these variable parameter values are documented in the protocols.

Even in the case that the NCAP scenarios cover typical applications of the AEB and more complicated ones, there are two aspects that are critical from the perspective of testing. First, we may ask ourselves about the completeness of the used scenarios, and, second, there are potential variations in the scenarios that reveal a faulty behavior. For example, it may make a difference exactly where a car is moving in a lane or when a pedestrian is crossing. Hence, even when only focusing on NCAP scenarios we need methods that can vary parameters in a smart way for detecting really critical situations in which an AEB or another ADAS is not working as expected.

In summary, the challenge of ADAS testing is to come up with critical scenarios that may reveal crashes or other unacceptable faults. We may consider environmental models that capture all potential concepts occurring in today's traffic. From this knowledge ADAS testing becomes either a search for criticality making use of evaluation or optimization functions capturing how close the ADAS causes a crash, or a combinatorial search that considers combinations of various concepts assuming that faults are usually revealed when making use of a specific combination. In the next section, we discuss testing approaches based on these principles. We start with ontology-based testing utilizing combinatorial testing, explain search-based approaches, and finally summarize other testing approaches for ADASs.

13.1.2 Recent Approaches of ADAS Testing

13.1.2.1 Ontology-Based Testing

Generally speaking, ontology-based testing combines ontology construction with a combinatorial testing mechanism. According to Feilmayr and Wöß (2016), an ontology is "a formal, explicit specification of a shared conceptualization that is characterized by high semantic expressiveness required for increased complexity." In the autonomous driving domain, ontologies have been used differently and variously. Xiong et al. (2016) provided an ontology to be used for scenario orchestration modeling and reasoning. In Bagschik et al. (2017) the author discussed the usage and utilization of ontologies for various applications for automated driving vehicles. Geyer et al. (2014) proposed an ontology concept including scenery, scene, situation, and scenario description for cooperative vehicle guidance systems. Li et al. (2011) presented an ontology to generate test cases for GUIs. Nguyen et al. (2008) introduced a test generation framework based on ontology for multi-agent systems. Other researchers (i.e., Nasser 2007; Blomqvist et al. 2012; de Souza et al. 2013; 2014; and Vasanthapriyan et al. 2017) used ontologies for different software testing activities. Meanwhile, combinatorial testing is able to offer the capabilities of detecting all faults triggered by interactions of parameters for different ordinary systems (Kuhn et al. 2009, 2013). Satish et al. (2017) presented a rule-based approach to obtain a CT input model including parameters and their values from use case specification and diagrams, sequence diagrams (Satish et al. 2017), and UML activity diagrams (Satish et al. 2013). Moser et al. (2010) expressed that the ontology-based approach is more effective compared with the traditional static approach based on the evaluation of two different application domains. Li et al. (2020) presented the details regarding automatic conversion from an ontology to its corresponding CT input model.

13.1.2.1.1 The Ontology-Based Testing Process   To carry out a comprehensive ontology-based testing process for autonomous driving and ADASs, it is important to follow a defined and standardized procedure starting from the construction of ontology for driving scenario modeling to the generation of the test scenario, and finally test execution. An overview of the underlying testing process is presented in Figure 13.1 (based on Klück et al. 2018).

In brief, there are three phases:

Phase 1: Ontology construction. In phase 1, a domain ontology has to be built to capture the environment of the SUT to a certain degree of necessary detail. A simplified definition of ontologies comprises concepts, and composition and inheritance relations. For composition there is a smallest and largest arity between the concepts, i.e., *minarity* and *maxarity*, respectively. This environment-based ontology will then be used for concrete test generation and execution. The ontology forms the basis for the

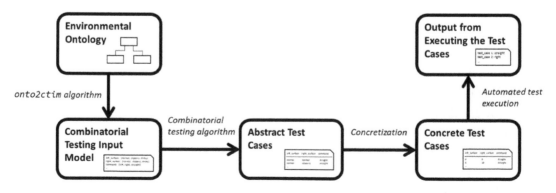

FIGURE 13.1   Ontology-based testing process overview.

subsequent automated test case generation of the entire process. Using ontologies, the collected information, i.e., the domain-related influence factors, are structured hierarchically as concepts and subsets. Figure 13.2 shows the graphic representation of concept, attributes, inheritance, and composition using UML2 syntax. As shown in this figure, concepts correspond to the graph vertices and relations (inheritance and composition) to the edges of the graph. The relations comprise two concepts and a type, which can be interpreted as directed edges. Concepts can have attributes and attributes have their own type such as string or integer. To build the CT input model in a more efficient way, only enumeration types are used, which means that elements of the enumeration for an attribute need to be specified. The ontology is then converted into an input model for CT test case generation.

Phase 2: Test scenario generation. The concepts described in the ontology form the basic instances of the input model, which consists of parameters, attributes, and domain elements. When the construction is completed, a CT input model for test generation will be formed from its ontology. For every concept in an ontology, a CT input model (i.e., M^{CT}) comprises its variables (i.e., V^{CT}) with their respective domains (i.e., DOM^{CT}) and constraints (i.e., $CONS^{CT}$; $M^{CT} = (V^{CT}, DOM^{CT}, CONS^{CT})$). Two algorithms CT_ONT1 (Wotawa and Li 2018) and CT_ONT2 (Felbinger et al. 2019) were introduced for ontology conversion. Because CT_ONT2 is derived from CT_ONT1 with better scalability (Li et al. 2020), CT_ONT2 (i.e., renamed as *onto2ctim*) will be used for the rest of this chapter. Generally speaking, in the *onto2ctim* algorithm, the domains, variables, and constraints of a composer (or lower level) concept cumulatively form as that of its directly related composer (or high level) concept. The

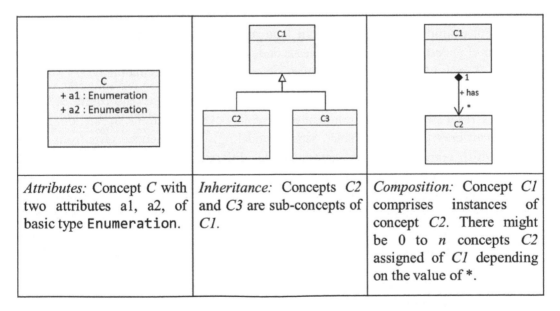

| *Attributes:* Concept *C* with two attributes a1, a2, of basic type **Enumeration**. | *Inheritance:* Concepts *C2* and *C3* are sub-concepts of *C1*. | *Composition:* Concept *C1* comprises instances of concept *C2*. There might be 0 to *n* concepts *C2* assigned of *C1* depending on the value of *. |

FIGURE 13.2   Basic terms and definitions to form an ontology. (From Li et al. 2020.)

complete *onto2ctim* algorithm is shown below (the source code of the algorithm can be obtained online[5]).

Function *onto2ctim (c, O, k)* (from Li et al. 2020)

INPUT: *Concept c, the corresponding ontology O, and a combinatorial strength of k.*
OUTPUT: *A CT input model for n.*

Line01:   Set V^{CT} and $CONS^{CT}$ as empty.
Line02:   **for** all attributes $a \in \omega(c)$ **do**
Line03:   Include c_a into V^{CT}.
Line04:   Set $DOM^{CT}(c_a)$ as $dom(c_a)$
Line05:   **end for**
Line06:   **if** c is not a leaf concept **then**
Line07:   **for** all relations (c, c') in R with type i **do** // inheritance relationship
Line08:   Include c' into V^{CT}
Line09:   Include ε into $dom(c)$
Line10:   Include $dom(c)$ into $DOM^{CT}(c)$
Line11:   Call function **onto2ctim(c', O, k)**
Line12:   **end for**
Line13:   **for** all relations (c, c') in R with type c **do** // other relationship
Line14:   Include variables c'_1 into c'_m to V^{CT}.
Line15:   **for** $i=1$ to m **do**
Line16:   Include ε into $dom(c'_i)$
Line17:   Include $dom(c'_i)$ into $DOM^{CT}(c)$
Line18:   Include $CONS^{CT}(c'_i)$ into $CONS^{CT}(c)$
Line19:   Call function **onto2ctim(c'_i, O, k)**
Line20:   **end for**
Line21:   **end for**
Line22:   **end if**
Line23:   **return** $(V^{CT}, DOM^{CT}, CONS^{CT})$

When using a CT algorithm to generate different combinations for test generation, some of them are not valid from the domain semantic, and must be excluded from the resulting test set. For example, if there is only one lane generated under a specific case, the configuration of pedestrians walking on the second or third lane is not a valid combination. Current CT tools like ACTS only allow users to specify constraints manually.

Phase 3: Test execution framework. The virtual test environment consists of the SUT and the virtual simulated environment (e.g., vehicle dynamic, traffic simulation, three-dimensional [3D] environment, sensor modeling). The generated tests from phase 2, which represent driving scenarios under different situations, are converted into the corresponding input files for the virtual test environment. Using the virtual test environment and the input files, the ADAS functions are tested and assessed under different test scenarios. Based on feedback from the execution, information regarding test case quality can be obtained, e.g., the number of scenarios leading to crashes. This information can later be used as an indicator for future improvement of the SUT.

13.1.2.1.2 Case Study   In this section, a detailed case study is conducted based on a prototype AEB. In the following we present the three different steps necessary to make use of ontology-based testing for verifying the AEB.

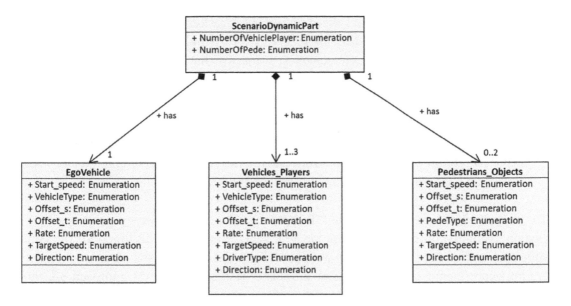

FIGURE 13.3 Formed AEB ontology using Euro NCAP scenarios and a UML. (From Tao et al. 2019.)

- *Ontology construction*: The ontology for the AEB system is tailored to cover all the scenarios defined in Euro NCAP protocols C2C and VRU. Figure 13.3 shows the construction of the ontology for AEB. There are four concepts and three compositional relations in the constructed ontology describing all the participants in the scenario. At the top of the figure, concepts *NumberOfVehiclePlayer* and *NumberOfPede* are, respectively, defined. These parameters specify the number of participants to be used in the generated test scenario. Specifically, *NumberOfVehiclePlayer* varies from 1 to 3 and *NumberOfPede* varies from 0 to 2. Zero pedestrians are considered because in C2C scenarios there are no pedestrians involved. The three composer or high level concepts in the ontology define the following objects: pedestrians, vehicle players, and ego vehicle. For each concept all the dynamic moving information (e.g., the position as well as type of the objects) will be defined correspondingly. The value range and representative values of the parameter are mainly taken from the Euro NCAP protocol.

- *Test generation and execution/simulation*: Next, the test suite is created using "Load Matrix for Software," a combinatorial testing tool from AVL that is based on the IPOG algorithm from AVL. Using the obtained CT input model, 993 test cases are generated in total with a combinatorial strength of 2. We used AVL VSM for vehicle dynamic simulation in the virtual test environment, and VTD from VIRES is used as the virtual driving environment platform. The SUT (AEB function) is compiled into functional mockup interface (FMI) format for the co-simulation. AVL Model. CONNECT is used as the co-simulation platform, which connects all of the software and components together with the AEB function. Later these generated test cases are converted into XML files based on the specification of ASAM OpenScenario, an open file format used to describe scenarios for virtual driving simulations. These converted XML files are executable test scenarios that contain all the information from the original test cases. As a result, a total number of 993 scenarios were created for simulation execution on the virtual driving environment platform with a combinatorial strength of 2.

- *Test execution and results:* As an outcome of the simulation, 35 crash cases were identified out of the 993 test cases. Crash cases are times inside the simulation a physical collision took place. The remaining cases are non-crash cases.

To evaluate the performance of the CT approach, 10 additional experiments were carried out using the random test generation approach for the same AEB function. The same simulation setup and configurations were used. For a clear comparison, each random generation experiment consists of the same number of test cases as the CT approach, i.e., 993 test cases. For random test generation, the test cases are generated randomly based on a uniform distribution. To have a comparable test case set, two steps were implemented in generating the random test cases. First, the parameters were taken from the same input model from the CT approach. The value for each parameter is selected randomly from its domain, which was defined in the CT input model. Initial random test cases without any combination constraints were then generated.

Second, during CT generation the same constraints were applied to remove some combinations. These constraints are also applied to the generated initial test cases, and the invalid test cases, including the constrained parameter combinations, are removed. In the end the same number of random test cases with the same constraints are fed to the simulation execution. Figure 13.4 shows the overview of the comparison results regarding the obtained number of crash cases from execution. As clearly observed, overall CT detected

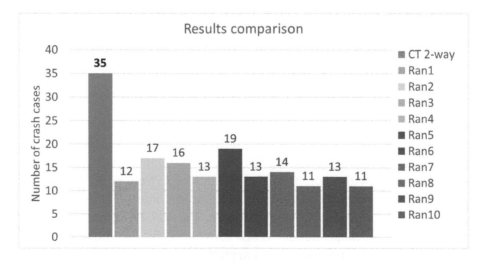

FIGURE 13.4   Crash case results comparison: CT approach versus random test generation.

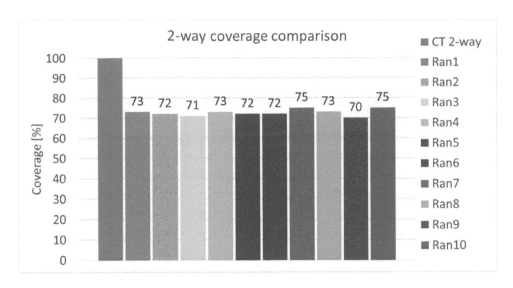

FIGURE 13.5   Results comparison of two-way coverage.

more crash cases than the random testing approach. From the CT approach 35 crash cases were obtained, whereas random approaches detected crash cases from 11 to 19 with an average number of around 14.

Furthermore, the two-way coverage of the generated test suites was compared as well. Figure 13.5 illustrates the two-way coverage comparison results. Due to the generation concept, the CT two-way test suite covered all the two-way parameter tuples, but the generated random test suites did not cover all the two-way parameter tuples. On average 28% of two-way tuples are missing in the generated random suites. In addition, the obtained crash cases were analyzed in detail. A total of 176 detected crash cases, which were included in the CT and the random test suites were investigated. From the analysis six failure scenarios were identified, as shown in Table 13.1. FS1 to FS4 are the collisions that happen between the ego vehicle and the front vehicle. The differences between them are the impact points and the number of side parking vehicles. FS5 and FS6 are the failure scenarios in which the collisions happen with the pedestrians crossing from the left or right side.

From the results of the AEB experiments we see that ontology-based testing can be effectively used to detect faults in ADASs. Compared with random testing ontology-based testing returns already more faults for a combinatorial strength of 2.

TABLE 13.1   Detected Failure Scenarios

Failure Scenario (FS)	Description
FS1	Collision with front vehicle - right rear side (two parking vehicles)
FS2	Collision with front vehicle - right rear side (one parking vehicle)
FS3	Collision with front vehicle - middle rear side (one parking vehicle)
FS4	Collision with front vehicle - left rear side (one parking vehicle)
FS5	Collision with pedestrian - crossing from left
FS6	Collision with pedestrian - crossing from right

13.1.2.2 Search-Based Testing

For the development of complex software, researchers and practitioners often face challenges related to inconsistent requirements, competing constraints, or a problem formulation that excludes deriving solutions analytically. In that case, computing the perfect solution is sometimes either impossible or practically infeasible. However, in search-based software engineering (SBSE) near-optimal or "good enough" solutions, that fall within the range of acceptable deviations, can be achieved by applying metaheuristic search techniques such as genetic algorithms (GAs), simulated annealing (SA), and tabu search (TS). In fact, a broad body of software engineering problems can be reformulated as a computational search problem (Clarke et al. 2003). To reformulate a software engineering problem as a computational search problem we first need to create a representation of problem parameters (candidate solutions) that is accessible to symbolic manipulation (e.g., floating-point numbers or binary code) and second a suitable metric, also called fitness function or cost function, to measure the quality of a potential solution (Harman 2001, 2004). The fitness function specifies what is considered to be a good solution and iteratively guides the search toward better and eventually near-optimal solutions. Depending on the representation of problem parameters, different SBSE methods can be applied such as GAs, TS, SA and ant colony optimization (ACO).

- *GAs*: GAs (Goldberg 1989) follow the process of natural selection, using evolutionary inspired operators such as mutation, crossover, and selection. In general, GAs work as follows: a population of chromosomes (i.e., candidate solutions) is processed and a score (fitness) is assigned to each chromosome in the population, according to the cost function. The fitness of a chromosome depends on how well it solves the problem at hand. Based on their individual fitness score, suitable chromosomes are selected for reproduction. If two chromosomes are selected for crossover, they exchange parameter sequences with each other to produce offspring for the next population. If a chromosome is selected for mutation, a parameter value within the chromosome is randomly exchanged, based on some predefined mutation probability. Figure 13.6 shows a graphic representation of crossing and mutation. Following this process, the GA optimizes populations of chromosomes until a near-optimal solution is found (Mitchell 1999).

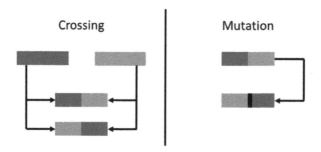

FIGURE 13.6   Basic principle of crossing and mutation. On the left two chromosomes get crossed by exchanging parameter sequences between them. On the right a chromosome is mutated by changing a parameter.

- *TS:* TS (Glover 1986) is a general heuristic procedure for efficiently guiding the search for near-optimal solutions in a complex search space. When TS iteratively explores a set of candidate solutions, it is repeatedly making moves from one solution *s* to another solution *s'*, located in the near-neighborhood of *s*. Moves are carried out with the aim to efficiently reach a near-optimal solution, based on the cost function. One core element of TS is the use of adaptive memory to forbid certain moves in the neighborhood space. In contrast to GA, TS follows a single trajectory in the search space by only considering one candidate solution per iteration (Glover et al. 1993).

- *SA:* Like GA, SA (Kirkpatrick et al. 1983) is inspired by a natural process. The working principal of SA is inspired by the physical annealing of materials. First, the solid material is brought to a very high temperature until its structure melts. Second, the material is cooled down according to a particular temperature decreasing scheme to reach a solid state with minimum energy (i.e., solid state with an optimal crystal structure). During the search for the global optimum of a given function, SA also accepts bad solutions on an interim basis. Transferred to the physical annealing of materials, a low level of energy represents a good solution. Therefore, the initial solution is modified until a new better solution is found that results in a lower level of energy. For higher temperatures, worse solutions are more likely to be accepted, maintaining the possibility to again leave a local optimum on the search for the global optimum. However, the temperature parameter decreases over time, therefore, the chance to leave local optima decreases over time as well (Delahaye et al. 2018; Klück et al. 2019a).

- *ACO:* The searching behavior of ACO algorithms (ACOAs) (Dorigo et al. 1996) is inspired by the natural process of how ant colonies organize their search for food in the surrounding environment. Every now and then, ants tend to leave established paths during the search for food and deposit portions of pheromones. Other ants are encouraged to follow a path with higher concentrations of pheromones. Because shorter paths can be traversed quicker and therefore receive more pheromone per unit time, the path's pheromone concentration steadily increases over time, which results in a positive feedback loop that reinforces shorter paths.

  In ACOAs, the evolutionary operators are not directly applied to solutions as is done in GA. Instead, the solution space is modified based on decision variable values that have resulted in good solutions in previous iterations. In this way, completely new solutions are generated in each iteration, rather than modifying (good) solutions from previous iterations (Maier et al. 2019).

A study by Arora and Saha (2016) on applications of major SBSE techniques in last decade showed that metaheuristic techniques have been successfully applied in different phases of the software development process for a wide range of software development activities such as project management, software cost, and effort estimation as well as automated test case generation. Notably, the majority of studied applications are linked to the wider range of software testing. In addition, Zeller (2017) argued that for testing at a system level, search-based techniques are best suited as they avoid the combinatorial explosion of conditions and parameters compared with random or constraint-based testing techniques.

In the following we outline several reasons why search-based testing methods, with a focus on evolutionary algorithms (EAs), are a good choice for finding near-optimal solutions to software testing problems in a very efficient manner. First, EAs are population based, meaning that a population comprising numerous diverse candidate solutions is used to explore the search space on the outlook for the *globally optimal solution*. Due to that, EAs are able to explore *large and rugged search spaces* very efficiently, where, for instance, exhaustive methods would fail. Furthermore, EAs can be applied both on *discrete and continuous variables*, which is beneficial for a larger range of real-world applications. Because the candidate solutions in a population exchange information with each other (e.g., crossover in GAs) *promising regions of the search space* are identified, enabling the search to concentrate on these regions in subsequent iterations. Another great advantage is that the workflow of EAs is very intuitive, and they can easily be *linked with existing simulation models* only requiring a two-way coupling between the optimization algorithm and the simulation model. Furthermore, the searching behavior of EAs can be customized to the problem at hand by modeling the cost function to simultaneously consider multiple criteria for a good solution (Maier et al. 2019).

However, there are also challenges and certain limitations when using EAs for search-based testing. Large search spaces require a huge population of candidate solutions and a great number of iterations to eventually evolve optimal solutions, which is *computationally demanding*. Another challenge is that specifying the fitness function as well as constraints to the EA *requires a certain amount of domain knowledge* to generate valid solutions. Furthermore, EAs need to be tuned carefully to find a suitable *balance between the exploration and exploitation properties*. Finally, there is *no guarantee in finding the (near-) optimal solution* in finite time because the EA may constantly select locally optimal candidate solutions to produce offspring and therefore get trapped in these regions.

13.1.2.2.1 Related Work   Search-based testing was already used in the mid-1990s to generate test data that fulfills specific requirements, e.g., a certain level of coverage (Roper et al. 1995; Sthamer 1995). Briand et al. (2005) presented one of the first specialized domains for using the GA. The authors used it to stress test a real-time system and had great success. In 2010, Harman and McMinn (2010) performed a theoretical study on search-based optimization techniques for software test data generation and compared a GA, a global search, and the hill-climbing algorithm, which is a local search. Also, in 2010 Ali et al. (2010) performed a systematic review on the application of search-based testing techniques and proposed a framework for data collection to compare different approaches. In the following years, search-based testing was more specialized for specific application domains. Harman et al. (2010) used the technique to test automotive functions, e.g., a door lock control, and Matinnejad et al. (2016) showed that time-continuous Simulink models could also efficiently be tested with GAs.

ADAS testing methods were first proposed to only be based on existing data, e.g., data from a crash database, and translating this data to simulation (Stellet et al. 2015). Masuda

(2017) analyzed state-of-the-art research on ADAS testing regarding the test methods listed in ISO/IEC/IEEE 29119-4. This list already included generative testing methods like random testing and combinatorial testing, but search-based testing methods were still absent. One of the first papers that proposed search-based testing for ADAS was by Ben Abdessalem et al. (2016). In recent years, a few other papers using search-based testing for ADAS have been published (Bühler and Wegener 2003; Mullins et al. 2017; Gambi et al. 2019). However, a comparison between different search-based approaches and different testing techniques is missing in the literature.

13.1.2.2.2 General Approach   ADAS testing is challenging for multiple reasons. First, the system's potential input space is very large, even infinitely large if we want to perform a full system test. Second, more and more ADASs are enhanced or replaced by machine learning techniques. Although machine learning techniques perform well, we still lack an understanding of what these techniques are really doing. Without understanding how they work, it is hard to predict corner cases or potential failures of the enhanced ADAS.

For the first mentioned problem, state-of-the-art automated test case generation methods (e.g., full factorial) fail because, although they guarantee full coverage, they generate too many tests. Executing all of these tests is not feasible in a reasonable time. For example, a full factorial test with an input space of only seven parameters and seven values for each of these parameters produces 823,543 test cases. If each test case took 1 minute to execute, it would take nearly 2 years to execute all test cases. The second mentioned problem makes it almost impossible for humans to write test cases that cover all corner cases. As we can see from recent publications (Su et al. 2019), small, seemingly arbitrary, changes in the input space can lead to a complete system failure.

We, therefore, propose to use search-based methods for automated test case generation to test an ADAS. In the literature, we see that, generally, search-based testing methods perform well for system testing, such as ADASs. They provide good coverage of the input space with reduced testing effort, such that it is feasible to execute all test cases.

In our work, a test case consists of two parts: the input stimulus describing the specific driving scenario, which the ADAS should handle, and the result of a cost function that measures how critical a test case was. This result can be fed into an oracle function to find out if this is the expected behavior. Each input stimulus constitutes multiple parameters, e.g., speed of a pedestrian. Together with a static description of the driving scenario, e.g., a straight road, the test case can be simulated in a 3D simulation environment. During simulation, we measure different metrics, e.g., the distance between two vehicles. These measurements are used as the cost function. For example, a well-known measurement to estimate a driving situation's criticality is time to collision (TTC) (Vogel 2003). In Figure 13.7, we present a high-level overview of the search-based testing workflow.

The general idea of testing ADASs with search-based testing methods is to translate the testing problem into an optimization problem. First, an initial set of test cases is generated. These test cases are evaluated based on the chosen cost function. The evaluation's feedback is then used to generate a new set of test cases by either modifying existing test cases or creating new ones. Test cases generated that way usually are more critical than the

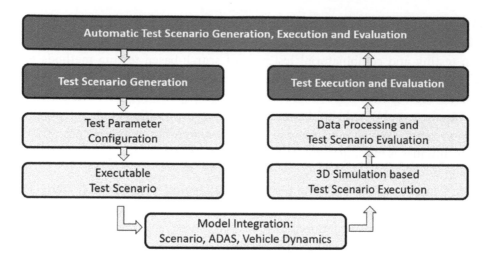

FIGURE 13.7 Overview of the search-based testing workflow describing the underlying tool chain for automatic test scenario generation, 3D-based simulation, and test result evaluation. (From Klück et al. 2019b.)

initial set of test cases. By repeating this process multiple times, each new iteration will produce more critical test cases than the previous iteration. This can be repeated either until a fixed number of test cases are generated or the behavior of the system differs from the expected behavior, i.e., a threshold for the cost function is reached (e.g., a TTC smaller than 1 second).

13.1.2.2.3 Findings in Our Work   In Klück et al. (2019b), we introduced the general concept of search-based testing for ADASs and provided first empirical results to show that search-based methods are viable for ADAS testing. Our experimental setup was modeled based on the previously mentioned Euro NCAP test protocol, which is the standard for testing AEB systems. More specifically, this setup focused on the CCR test protocol. The driving scenario consists of a straight road with two vehicles; one is equipped with the AEB function and the other is a leading test vehicle. Parameters for this scenario include, for example, the initial speed of both vehicles, starting distance between the vehicle, speed change rate of the vehicles, and many more. In total, the driving scenario was parameterized by eight different parameters from the continuous domain.

The GA depicted below was used as the search-based testing method. An exemplary implementation in Python using the open source library DEAP is available on GitHub.[6] The parameters of the scenario were directly encoded as parameters in a chromosome. The start population was generated at random. For selection we used a tournament selection of five, which selects five individuals at random and keeps the best of those five. This is repeated until enough individuals are selected. We used the uniform cross-function for crossing two chromosomes, which switches the same parameter from two chromosomes at random. The mutation was done by randomly generating a new value for parameters in a chromosome. As there is no general rule on finding a good crossing and mutation probability, we searched for good values by trial and error. Because of its applicability, we used the TTC as the fitness function for the evaluation of the chromosomes.

Algorithm *GeneticAlgorithm (G, generate, select, evaluate, cross, mutate)* (Klück et al. 2019a)

Require: *G: Number of generations that should be run,, generate(): method for generating the seed population, select(P): method that selects a new population from an old population (P), evaluate(P): method for evaluating the population (P), cross(P): method for crossing the population (P), and mutate(P): method for mutating a population (P).*

```
1:      Let P be generate()
2:      Call evaluate(P)
3:      for g=0 to G do
4:          Let P be select(P)
5:          Let P be cross(P)
6:          Let P be mutate(P)
7:          Call evaluate(P)
8:      end for
```

Our experiments consist of two different test situations. First, we simulated a situation where there is only a small test budget (in terms of time) available. For this situation, we generated an initial population of 21 test cases and let the genetic algorithm run for five generations; in total, this produced 106 test cases. The second situation simulates an available higher test budget. We generated an initial population of 106 test cases and let the GA run for 10 generations, in total for 1060 test cases. To benchmark our results, we generated the same amount of test cases purely at random.

Our experiments showed that the GA produced more critical test cases in the TTC range between 0s and 1s than the random generation (see Figures 13.8 and 13.9). This result was expected because a GA behaves close to a random generation of test cases in the first few generations. However, in the later generations, a GA focuses on the critical parameter space and generates far more critical test cases than a random generation could.

The lowest TTC for the smaller test budget was produced by the random approach. In contrast, for the higher test budget, the lowest TTC was generated by the GA. However, in both cases, the difference was small, and the GA generated far more test cases that were

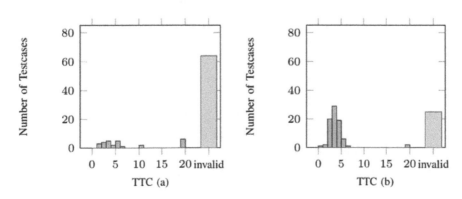

FIGURE 13.8   Histogram of the resulting TTC distribution for a small test budget. (a) Random testing and (b) GA tests. (From Klück et al. 2019a.)

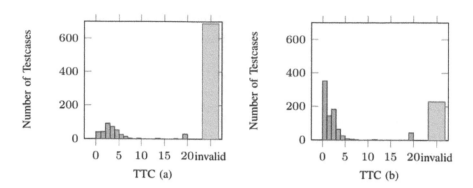

FIGURE 13.9 Histogram of the resulting TTC distribution for a large test budget. (a) Random testing and (b) GA tests. (From Klück et al. 2019a.)

close to the minimum TTC value. This result also reinforces our previous observation that a GA performs better the more generations it runs.

The random generation outperforms the GA in terms of how many test cases must be generated until a critical test case is found. On average, 32 randomly generated test cases were enough for generating a critical test case. For the high test budget, this is fewer test cases than our initial population.

To conclude, in Klück et al. (2019a) we showed that in general search-based methods can be used for ADAS testing. However, our driving scenario seems to be too simple to show a GA's benefit, as the random generation also quickly generated critical test cases.

In Klück et al. (2019a), extending our previous work, we created a more complex driving scenario and compared a GA, not only with a random generation, but also with two versions of SA. With a more complex scenario, we could show that a GA has superior performance, in terms of test executions needed to find a critical test case, compared with random testing and both SA algorithms.

To increase our driving scenario's complexity, we extended the previous scenario by the Euro NCAP vulnerable road users test protocol. This protocol also includes two pedestrians crossing the road and two cars parked alongside the road. A pedestrian can cross the road either before, between, or behind these cars. With this addition, the scenario has 16 parameters in total, making this scenario twice as complex as our previous scenario.

The first version of the SA is the standard SA algorithm, the second version of SA used an improved algorithm proposed by Locatelli (2000). In this algorithm, not only the temperature is decreased, but also the parameter space, from which new solutions can be drawn, is reduced over time.

In this chapter, we were not interested in the algorithms' general performance, but how fast, or in other words, with how many test executions they can find a critical test case. In a real-world situation, this is a crucial factor when deciding which approach should be used. Therefore, we run every algorithm until a critical scenario, this time, a TTC smaller than 0.3 seconds, was found, or a maximum of 500 test cases was generated. We stopped the GA even mid-generation if one of the stopping-criteria was reached.

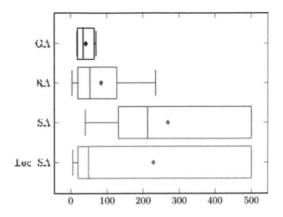

FIGURE 13.10 Comparison of the GA, random generation (RA), SA, and Locatelli's improved SA (Loc. SA). The *x*-axis shows how many tests were executed until a critical test case was found. (From Klück et al. 2019a.)

From the results depicted in Figure 13.10 we can see that the GA outperforms the other approaches; its low variance makes it a good choice. The random generation was in one instance faster than the GA; however, with an average of over 80 test cases until a critical test case was found, it is far worse than the GA with a maximum of 70 test cases needed. The result of the SA algorithms lets us believe that this algorithm is not suitable for generating test cases for ADAS. However, the result of Locatelli's improved algorithm is interesting: either the algorithm finds a suitable solution fast, i.e., fewer than 50 test cases, or not at all. This is indicated by the low median and high average results of the algorithm. We believe this is because it is tough for the algorithm to recover from an unsuitable starting seed; however, if there is a suitable starting seed, it quickly converges to a good solution. Further improvement to this algorithm could also lead to good results.

This chapter could confirm our previous claim that search-based methods and, especially, a GA, is suitable for ADAS testing. We showed that for a complex scenario, a GA significantly outperforms a random generation. Furthermore, we showed that the standard SA algorithm is not suitable for ADAS testing. However, improved versions of the SA algorithm could be viable for this purpose.

To compare search-based testing with other state-of-the-art testing methods, we compared a GA with combinatorial testing. In Felbinger et al. (2019) we qualitatively compared the two testing methods to help select the right method for a particular task. Both methods used the AEB function and driving scenario described in previous paragraphs.

To use a GA, a suitable representation of the parameters must be found. Furthermore, a good crossing function, mutation function, and cost function must be designed. All these tasks are not trivial, and some trial and error is inevitable. In contrast, for combinatorial testing, only an input model is required. Therefore, the setup of combinatorial testing is usually easier than for a GA.

Using the AEB function and driving scenario, both methods could reveal test cases that caused the ADAS to misbehave. Combinatorial testing produces test cases with different reasons for a crash, e.g., a test case in which the collision happens with a pedestrian and another test case in which the collision happens with a car. However, all 993 generated test cases must be executed to find all of them.

In contrast, the GA only produces test cases with the same or a similar reason for a crash. However, it already generates critical test cases within 106 test case executions.

A benefit of combinatorial testing is that the full input space is covered with respect to the input model and the combinatorial strength. This means using combinatorial testing, and we either know that the ADAS is faulty or the ADAS is safe with respect to the input model and the combinatorial strength. In contrast, for search-based methods, we cannot give such guarantees.

13.1.2.3 Other Approaches

Ben Abdessalem et al. (2016) used a multi-objective search together with neural networks to test a visual pedestrian detection system. Their proposed algorithm uses neural network-based predictions to alleviate expensive simulations in which particular solutions from the search space can be pruned. Vishnukumar et al. (2017) presented a methodology to bring together test and validation of independent systems as well as the complete system during the entire development process. Available real test data were used to derive and sort the test scenarios with the help of pretrained machine learning/deep neural network systems. The trained AI core is expected to lower human workload and errors; furthermore, it makes the process of generating, sorting, and standardizing new test data, test cases, and test scenarios more efficient. Gangopadhyay et al. (2019) used Bayesian optimization for test case identification for a Society of Automotive Engineers (SAE) Level 4 low-speed automated driving (LSAD) system. Given a test scenario, the proposed method observes the output of the SUT and learns safety parameter values. Later those values are used to generate test cases that violate the safe boundaries of the system. Rocklage et al. (2017) combined combinatorial interaction testing and trajectory planning to create a feasibility checker, which can generate test cases. Bach et al. (2016) aimed at describing driving scenarios as abstract positions and temporal descriptions that can be used for early validation. They use a movie-base omniscient view, which is composed of sequential acts. Each act contains states and interactions of elements in the act as well as the scenery. Transitions between acts are triggered by certain events. For consistency checks a rule set has to be provided. Furthermore, from this rule set, test cases can be generated semi-automatically.

13.2 CONCLUSION AND FUTURE RESEARCH

In this chapter, we discussed the case of ADAS testing in general, where we focused on the two most recent testing methodologies, i.e., ontology based and search based. Both approaches are used for generating critical test cases. Ontology-based testing utilizes the findings of combinatorial testing assuming that systems usually fail in case of certain combinations of parameters or concepts. Search-based testing relies on an evaluation function for guiding the search toward the direction of a solution. In case of ADASs the evaluation function should be able to map a scenario to be close or further away from a crash. Both approaches can be fully automated and coupled with a simulation engine to execute the generated tests in an automated fashion. Along with discussing the approaches, we also summarized findings showing that the approaches can be effectively used for testing ADASs considering the implementation of an AEB function.

Future research has to come up with guarantees and estimations of residual risks when using these testing methods. In case of ontology-based testing we may come up with the combinatorial strength and ontology coverage as a means for estimating when we do stop testing. In case of search-based testing, the number of generated tests and the closeness to crashes may indicate the quality of obtained tests. However, in both cases further experimental studies using different ADASs are required.

ACKNOWLEDGMENTS

The financial support by the Austrian Federal Ministry for Digital and Economic Affairs, the National Foundation for Research, Technology and Development and the Christian Doppler Research Association is gratefully acknowledged.

NOTES

1. The European New Car Assessment Programme.
2. C2C, car-to-car; CCRs, Car-to-car rear stationary; CCRm, car-to-car rear moving; CCRb: car-to-car rear braking (https://cdn.euroncap.com/media/1569/aeb-test-protocol-v-10.pdf, p. 13).
3. Vulnerable-Road-User (https://cdn.euroncap.com/media/21509/euro-ncap-aeb-vru-test-protocol-v101.pdf, p. 16ff).
4. CPFA, car-to-pedestrian farside adult; CPNA: car-to-pedestrian nearside adult; CPNC: car-to-pedestrian nearside child; CPLA: car-to-pedestrian longitudinal adult.
5. https://github.com/QAMCAS/onto2ctim
6. https://github.com/QAMCAS/ADAS-Testing-Genetic-Algorithm-Example

REFERENCES

S. Ali, L. L. C. Briand, H. Hemmati and R. K. Panesar-Walawege. "A Systematic review of the application and empirical investigation of search-based test case generation." IEEE Transactions on Software Engineering, 36(6): 742–762, 2010.

I. Arora and A. Saha. "A review of applications of search based software engineering techniques in last decade." 5th International Conference on Reliability, Infocom Technologies and Optimization, 2016.

J. Bach, S. Otten and E. Sax. "Model based scenario specification for development and test of automated driving functions." 2016, IEEE Intelligent Vehicles Symposium (IV), Gothenburg, 2016, pp. 1149–1155. doi: 10.1109/IVS.2016.7535534.

G. Bagschik, T. Menzel and M. Maurer. "Ontology based scene creation for the development of automated vehicles." 2018 IEEEE Intelligent Vehicles Symposium (IV), Changshu, China, 2018.

R. Ben Abdessalem, S. Nejati, L. C. Briand and T. Stifter. "Testing advanced driver assistance systems using multi-objective search and neural networks." 2016, 31st IEEE/ACM International Conference on Automated Software Engineering (ASE), Singapore, 2016, pp. 63–74.

E. Blomqvist, A. S. Sepour and V. Presutti. "Ontology testing methodology and tool." 18th International Conference on Knowledge Engineering and Knowledge Management, 2012, pp. 216–226.

L. C. Briand, Y. Labiche and M. Shousha. "Stress testing real-time systems with genetic algorithms." 7th Annual Conference on Genetic and Evolutionary Computation (GECCO '05), 2005, pp. 1021–1028.

O. Bühler and J. Wegener. "Evolutionary functional testing of an automated parking system." Proceedings of the International Conference on Computer, Communication and Control Technologies and the 9th International Conference on Information Systems Analysis and Synthesis, Florida, 2003.

J. Clarke et al. "Reformulating software engineering as a search problem." IEE Proceedings Software, 15(3): 161–175, 2003.

D. Delahaye, S. Chaimatanan and M. Mongeau. 2018. "Simulated Annealing: From Basics to Applications." In J. Y. Potvin and M. Gendreau (eds). Handbook of Metaheuristics. International Series in Operations Research & Management Science, Springer, Berlin.

E. F. de Souza. "Knowledge management applied to software testing: an ontology based framework." Ph.D. dissertation, National Institute for Space Research, 2014.

E. F. de Souza, R. A. Falbo and N. L. Vijaykumar. "Using ontology patterns for building a reference software testing ontology." 17th IEEE International Enterprise Distributed Object Computing Conference Workshops, 2013, pp. 21–30.

M. Dorigo, V. Maniezzo and A. Colorni. "Ant system: optimization by a colony of cooperating agents." IEEE Transactions on Systems, Man, and Cybernetics, Part B (Cybernetics), 26(1):29–41, 1996.

European New Car Assessment Programme (Euro NCAP). 2017a. Test Protocol – AEB Systems, Version 2.0. Brussels, Belgium.

European New Car Assessment Programme (Euro NCAP). 2017b. Test Protocol – AEB VRU Test Version 2.0.2. Brussels, Belgium.

C. Feilmayr and W. Wöß. "An analysis of ontologies and their success factors for application to business." Data & Knowledge Engineering, 1–23, 2016.

H. Felbinger et al. "Comparing two systematic approaches for testing automated driving functions." 2019, IEEE International Conference on Connected Vehicles and Expo (ICCVE), Graz, Austria, 2019, pp. 1–6.

A. Gambi, M. Mueller and G. Fraser. "Automatically testing self-driving cars with search-based procedural content generation." 28th ACM SIGSOFT International Symposium on Software Testing and Analysis (ISSTA 2019), 2019, pp. 318–328.

B. Gangopadhyay, S. Khastgir, S. Dey, P. Dasgupta, G. Montana and P. Jennings. "Identification of test cases for automated driving systems using Bayesian optimization." 2019, IEEE Intelligent Transportation Systems Conference (ITSC), Auckland, New Zealand, 2019, pp. 1961–1967. doi: 10.1109/ITSC.2019.8917103.

S. Geyer, M. Baltzer, B. Franz, S. Hakuli, M. Kauer, M. Kienle, S. Meier, T. Weissgerber, K. Bengler, R. Bruder, F. Flemisch and H. Winner. "Concept and development of a unified ontology for generating test and use-case catalogues for assisted and automated vehicle guidance." IET Intelligent Transport Systems, 8(3): 183–189, 2014.

F. Glover. "Tabu Search – Part 1." ORSA Journal on Computing, 1: 190–206, 1986. https://doi.org/10.1287/ijoc.1.3.190

F. Glover, E. Taillard and E. Taillard. "A user's guide to Tabu search." Annals of Operations Research, 41:1–28, 1993.

D. E. Goldberg. 1989. Genetic Algorithms in Search. Optimization and Machine Learning. Addison-Wesley Longman, Boston.

M. Harman. "Search-based software engineering." Information and Software Technology, 833–839, 2001.

M. Harman, et al. "Metrics are fitness functions too." Proceedings of the 10th International Symposium on Software Metrics, Chicago, IL, 2004, pp. 58–69.

M. Harman, S. G. Kim, K. Lakhotia, P. McMinn and S. Yoo. "Optimizing for the number of tests generated in search based test data generation with an application to the Oracle Cost Problem." 2010, Third International Conference on Software Testing, Verification, and Validation Workshops, Paris, 2010, pp. 182–191.

M. Harman and P. McMinn. "A theoretical and empirical study of search-based testing: local, global, and hybrid search." IEEE Transactions on Software Engineering, 36(2):226–247, 2010.

ISO 26262. Road vehicles functional safety. International Organization for Standardization, Geneva, 2011.

N. Kalra and S. M. Paddock. "Driving to safety: How many miles of driving would it take to demonstrate autonomous vehicle reliability?" Transportation Research Part A: Policy and Practice, 94:182–193, 2016.

S. Kirkpatrick, C. D. Gelatt Jr. and M. P. Vecchi. "Optimization by simulated annealing." Science, 220(4598):671–680, 1983.

F. Klück, Y. Li, M. Nica, J. Tao and F. Wotawa. "Using ontologies for test suites generation for automated and autonomous driving functions." Proceedings of the 29th IEEE International Symposium on Software Reliability Engineering (ISSRE2018), 2018.

F. Klück, M. Zimmermann, F. Wotawa and M. Nica. "Genetic algorithm-based test parameter optimization for ADAS system testing." 19th IEEE International Conference on Software Quality, Reliability and Security, QRS 2019. 418–425, 2019a.

F. Klück, M. Zimmermann, F. Wotawa and M. Nica. 2019b. "Performance Comparison of Two Search-Based Testing Strategies for ADAS System Validation." In: C. Gaston, N. Kosmatov and P. Le Gall (eds), Testing Software and Systems. ICTSS 2019. Lecture Notes in Computer Science, vol. 11812. Springer, Cham.

D. Kuhn, R. Kacker and Y. Lei. Introduction to Combinatorial Testing. Chapman & Hall/CRC Innovations in Software Engineering and Software Development Series, Taylor & Francis, Boca Raton, FL, 2013.

D. Kuhn, R. Kacker, Y. Lei and J. Hunter. "Combinatorial software testing." Computer, 94–96, 2009.

H. Li, H. Guo, F. Chen, H. Yang and Y. Yang. "Using ontology to generate test cases for GUI testing." International Journal of Computer Applications in Technology, 42(2/3): 213–224, 2011.

Y. Li, J. Tao and F. Wotawa. "Ontology-based test generation for automated and autonomous driving functions." Information and Software Technology, 117, 2020.

M. Locatelli. "Simulated annealing algorithms for continuous global optimization: convergence conditions." Optimization Theory and Applications, 121–133, 2000.

H. R. Maier, S. Razavi, Z. Kapelan, L. S. Matott, J. Kasprzyk and B.A. Tolson. "Introductory overview: optimization using evolutionary algorithms and other metaheuristics." Environmental Modelling & Software, 114:195–213, 2019.

S. Masuda. "Software testing design techniques used in automated vehicle simulations." 2017, IEEE International Conference on Software Testing, Verification and Validation Workshops (ICSTW), Tokyo, 2017, pp. 300–303.

R. Matinnejad, S. Nejati, L. C. Briand and T. Bruckmann. "Automated test suite generation for time-continuous Simulink models." 2016, IEEE/ACM 38th International Conference on Software Engineering (ICSE), 2016, pp. 595–606.

M. Mitchell. 1999. An Introduction to Genetic Algorithms. A Bradford Book. The MIT Press, Cambridge, MA.

T. Moser, G. Dürr and S. Biffl. "Ontology-based test case generation for simulating complex production automation systems." 22nd International Conference on Software Engineering & Knowledge Engineering, 2010, pp. 478–483.

G. E. Mullins, P. G. Stankiewicz and S. K. Gupta. "Automated generation of diverse and challenging scenarios for test and evaluation of autonomous vehicles." 2017 IEEE International Conference on Robotics and Automation (ICRA). Singapore, 2017, pp. 1443–1450.

G. J. Myers. 2004. The Art of Software Testing (2nd ed.). Wiley, Hoboken NJ.

V. H. Nasser. "Ontology-based unit test generation." Master's thesis, Amirkabir University of Technology, Tehran, Iran, 2007.

C. D. Nguyen, A. Perini and P. Tonella. "Ontology-based test generation for multiagent systems." 7th International Conference on Autonomous Agents and Multiagent Systems, May 2008, pp. 1315–1318.

E. Rocklage, H. Kraft, A. Karatas and J. Seewig. "Automated scenario generation for regression testing of autonomous vehicles." 2017, IEEE 20th International Conference on Intelligent Transportation Systems (ITSC), Yokohama, 2017, pp. 476–483. doi: 10.1109/ITSC.2017.8317919.

M. Roper, I. Maclean, A. Brooks, J. Miller and M. Wood. "Genetic algorithms and the automatic generation of test data." Seminars in Arthritis and Rheumatism, 1995.

P. Satish, M. Basavaraja, M. S. Narayan and K. Rangarajan. "Building combinatorial test input model from use case artefacts." 10th IEEE International Conference on Software Testing, Verification and Validation Workshops, 2017, pp. 220–228.

P. Satish, A. Paul and K. Rangarajan. "Extracting the combinatorial test parameters and values from UML sequence diagrams." 7th IEEE International Conference on Software Testing, Verification, and Validation Workshops, 2014, pp. 88–97.

P. Satish, K. Sheeba and K. Rangarajan. "Deriving combinatorial test design model from UML activity diagram." 6th IEEE International Conference on Software Testing, Verification and Validation Workshops, 2013, pp. 331–337.

J. E. Stellet, M. R. Zofka, J. Schumacher, T. Schamm, F. Niewels and J. M. Zöllner. "Testing of advanced driver assistance towards automated driving: A survey and taxonomy on existing approaches and open questions." 2015 IEEE 18th International Conference on Intelligent Transportation Systems, 2015, pp. 1455–1462.

H.-H. Sthamer. 1995. "The automatic generation of software test data using genetic algorithms." PhD thesis, University of Glamorgan, Wales.

J. Su, D. V. Vargas and K. Sakurai. "One pixel attack for fooling." IEEE Transactions on Evolutionary Computation, 23(5):828–841, 2019.

A. Takanen, J. DeMott and C. Miller. 2008. Fuzzing for Software Security Testing and Quality Assurance. Artech House, Inc., Norwood, MA.

J. Tao, Y. Li, F. Wotawa, H. Felbinger and M. Nica. "On the industrial application of combinatorial testing for autonomous driving functions." 2019, IEEE International Conference on Software Testing, Verification and Validation Workshops (ICSTW), 2019.

M. Utting and B. Legeard. 2010. Practical Model-Based Testing: A Tools Approach. Morgan Kaufmann, Burlington, MA.

S. Vasanthapriyan, J. Tian, D. Zhao, S. Xiong and J. Xiang. "An ontology-based knowledge sharing portal for software testing." 17th IEEE International Conference on Software Quality, Reliability and Security (Companion Volume), 2017, pp. 472–479.

H. J. Vishnukumar, B. Butting, C. Müller and E. Sax. "Machine learning and deep neural network—artificial intelligence core for lab and real-world test and validation for ADAS and autonomous vehicles: AI for efficient and quality test and validation." 2017 Intelligent Systems Conference (IntelliSys), London, 2017, pp. 714–721. doi: 10.1109/IntelliSys.2017.8324372.

K. Vogel. "A comparison of headway and time to collision as safety indicators." Accident Analysis & Prevention, 427–433, 2003.

F. Wotawa. Testing Autonomous and Highly Configurable Systems: Challenges and Feasible Solutions, Chapter 22. In: D. Watzenig and M. Horn (eds), Automated Driving, Springer International Publishing, Cham, Switzerland, 2016. doi:10.1007/978-3-319-31895-0 22.

F. Wotawa and Y. Li. "From ontologies to input models for combinatorial testing." Proceedings of the 30th IFIP International Conference on Testing Software and Systems (ICTSS), Cadiz, Spain, Oct. 1–3, 2018.

Z. Xiong, V. V. Dixit and S. T. Waller. "The development of an ontology for driving context modelling and reasoning." 2016 IEEE 19th International Conference on Intelligent Transportation Systems (ITSC), Nov 2016, pp. 13–18.

A. Zeller. "Search-based testing and system testing: a marriage in heaven." IEEE/ACM 10th International Workshop on Search-Based Software Testing (SBST), 2017, pp. 49–50.

II

ADAS and AV Legal Issues and Liabilities

CHAPTER 14

Human Factors of Automated Driving Systems

Stefan Brandenburg

Technische Universität Berlin
Berlin, Germany

CONTENTS

14.1 INTRODUCTION

Automated driving is a vision with a long history. In 1965, General Electric advertised the GM Firebird II, the first vehicle that could maintain its speed and lateral control without driver input. The vehicle achieved speed control via a speedometer and lateral vehicle control by sensing magnets that were placed beneath the road surface. However, the GM Firebird II remained a vision, partly because it demanded specific infrastructure like induction loops in the road (Kröger, 2015).

Starting from the mid-1980s, the increase of computing power enabled a large step toward vehicle automation. Vehicles improved their ability to sense their environment and connected to other transports and the infrastructure. The successive introduction of partial automation disentangled vehicles from fixed infrastructure components like induction loops. Additionally, legislation formed the legal presumptions for automated driving in past years. On an international level, politicians added an amendment to paragraph 8 of the Vienna Convention on road traffic. Drivers can hand over the controls of their vehicle to automated driving systems, "…when such systems can be overridden or switched off by the driver" (United Nations Economic Commission for Europe, 2014, p. 9). Subsequently,

DOI: 10.1201/9781003048381-16

national governments adopted that regulation, paving the way to the widespread implementation of automated driving.

Today, vehicles can take over parts of the driving task. However, skillful drivers will continue to guarantee traffic safety for the following reasons: technical issues in detecting other traffic participants (Campbell et al., 2010), proper handling of unexpected events (Koopman & Wagner, 2017), and incomplete communication of automated vehicles with each other and the infrastructure (Zhang et al., 2018). Additional challenges arise when drivers hand over vehicle control to automated driving systems and vice versa. Those transitions are associated with significant losses in traffic safety (Eriksson & Stanton, 2017a).

The level of automation strongly affects the magnitude of automation challenges. The Society of Automotive Engineers defines six levels of vehicle automation: no driving automation, driver assistance, partial driving automation, conditional driving automation, high driving automation, and full driving automation (SAE International, 2018). The classification mainly defines the roles and responsibilities of drivers and their vehicles. It is also a basis for communication, automation construction, and legislation. Level 3 (L3) vehicle automation is especially important for transportation safety. Drivers permanently and fully command their vehicles at lower levels. Here, the automation produces parts of the longitudinal and lateral vehicle guidance. Drivers are not allowed to engage in non–driving-related tasks (NDRTs) like reading or writing messages on their smartphones. In contrast, the vehicle handles the driving task completely for a certain period at higher levels. Drivers do not have to focus on the driving task at all times. They may engage in NDRTs. In case of an emergency, the vehicle can establish a minimum risk state by reducing speed and stopping at the roadside (Gasser et al., 2012; SAE International, 2018). L3 automation is different in terms of the allocation of vehicle control of drivers and vehicles. The automation manages parts of the driving task and drivers may engage in NDRTs. However, they must be ready at all times to take over the control of their vehicle whenever it reaches its system limits. Drivers, therefore, have to monitor their vehicles' driving performance and their interaction with other artifacts like smartphones or books in parallel.

Human factors research has revealed that drivers mainly engage in visually demanding NDRTs in these situations, like watching a DVD or reading (Jamson et al., 2013; Petermann-Stock et al., 2013). Research on peoples' performance in secondary task settings has revealed that their achievements decrease in each of the tasks compared with their sole execution. The most substantial achievement reductions appear when operators use the same resources for the information uptake from different sources or the reaction to various stimuli at the same time (Wickens, 2008). In automated driving, NDRTs that use visual resources, like reading a newspaper, compete against the surveillance of the vehicle. Operating a smartphone or using in-vehicle entertainment systems affects drivers' readiness to engage in steering if necessary. The design of human–machine interfaces (HMIs) can help to reduce these challenges regarding the drivers' resources. Human factors research on HMI design is supposed to be one of the most important efforts for the success of automated vehicles (Casner et al., 2016; Noy et al., 2018).

14.2 HUMAN FACTORS RESEARCH IN AUTOMATED DRIVING

In the last decade, human factors research in automated driving has revealed many results. Dividing the ongoing task of driving into an episode of automated driving with several stages helps to sort these findings and to derive blind spots (Brandenburg et al., 2017). Figure 14.1 visualizes an episode of automated driving, including its four stages.

An episode of automated driving begins with manual driving (Figure 14.1, stage 1). Drivers operate their vehicles and activate driver assistance systems, if available. The handover to the vehicle automation (Figure 14.1, stage 2) marks the end of stage one. Drivers experience automated driving after handing over vehicle control to the automation (Figure 14.1, stage 3). Now they can engage in NDRTs but are obliged to monitor the performance of their vehicle. Drivers also have to take over vehicle control if the automation presents a takeover request (TOR) (Gasser et al., 2012; SAE International, 2018). The shift of control from the vehicle to the motorist (Figure 14.1, stage 4) terminates the stage of automated driving. The drivers' takeover can be the start of a new episode of automated driving.

The four stages of an episode of automated driving, therefore, group in the two driving modes, manual and automated driving, and the two transitions of control between these driving modes, handover and takeover. Human factors research has accumulated findings for each of the four stages; however, substantial blind spots still exist, motivating future studies.

14.2.1 Manual Drive and Handover to the Automated Vehicle

The first stage of an episode of automated driving does not differ from manual driving, except that drivers can hand over the control of their vehicle to the automation, if possible. Online surveys revealed that many of the respondents could imagine using automated driving functions. For example, Payre et al. (2014) found that 68% of the interviewees would like to use vehicle automation. More specifically, drivers wanted to hand over control at monotonous highways or in very stressful situations, like in traffic jams. Another survey by Fraedrich et al. (2016) revealed similar results. Here, respondents also aimed to use vehicle automation on highways and in urban areas. Moreover, they stated that they could imagine using longitudinal vehicle automation rather than lateral. Kuehn et al. (2017) asked the participants of a driving simulator study about their intended use of automated vehicles. Drivers wanted to use vehicle automation at highways and good weather and road conditions. Buckley et al. (2018) also combined a driving simulator and a survey study. Their results revealed that the participants' perceived behavioral control and trust in automation determined their intention to use automated driving functions.

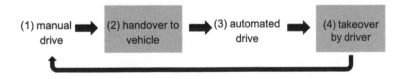

FIGURE 14.1 An episode of automated driving including its four stages.

Trust in automation is closely related to automation usage (Hergeth et al., 2015, 2016, 2017; Körber et al., 2018; Körber & Bengler, 2014). In their review on safety blind spots of automated driving, Noy et al. (2018) argued that the concept of driver trust needs special attention in human factors research. Drivers have to trust and accept automated vehicles before they can use them appropriately. In general, studies investigated the role of driver trust in automation usage analytically (Noy et al., 2018) and driving simulator studies (Hergeth et al., 2015, 2016, 2017; Körber et al., 2018; Körber & Bengler, 2014); on-the-road investigations are still rare.

Summing up, drivers' willingness to hand over vehicle control to the automation was studied using surveys (Dikmen & Burns, 2016; Fraedrich et al., 2016; Payre et al., 2014) and interviews (Buckley et al., 2018; Kuehn et al., 2017). These studies are essential as they deliver an estimate of the acceptance of automated vehicles. However, they require participants to imagine their interaction with a technology that most of them did not yet experience. The authors of survey studies, therefore, highlight that most drivers' assessments of vehicle automation will change with practical automation experience (Buckley et al., 2018; Payre et al., 2014).

Studies only begin to examine drivers' willingness to hand over vehicle control in real traffic. For example, an ethnographic study by Lee et al. (2016) assessed the trust of front-seat passengers in a prototype of an automated vehicle driving in real traffic. Results revealed that passengers did not fully trust the vehicle after 6 days. The authors concluded that the HMI design must eliminate sources of mistrust to allow drivers to trust (Lee et al., 2016).

A recent study by Schott et al. (2018) assessed drivers' handover behavior in real traffic. The authors invited participants to drive a Tesla Model S at various highway and rural road sections. They also assessed some aspects of the drivers' personalities, like affinity to technology (Franke et al., 2019) and five personality traits (Rammstedt & John, 2007). The authors found that drivers were willing to hand over complete vehicle control to the automation on highways, aligning with findings of previous surveys (Fraedrich et al., 2016; Kuehn et al., 2017; Payre et al., 2014). Also, drivers were more willing to hand over longitudinal control only on rural roads. Moreover, a higher affinity to technology score was related to increased use of vehicle automation. In contrast, a higher score on neuroticism led to less use of vehicle automation (Schott et al., 2018).

Evaluating drivers' handover behavior in real traffic is, therefore, one of the blind spots in human factors research at the first stage of an episode of automated driving. Another blind spot relates to the samples that human factors studies used. On-the-road studies mostly used early adopters with high knowledge about vehicle automation and interest in new technologies (Schott et al., 2018; Dikmen & Burns, 2016). Whether their results apply to other samples of drivers as well should be subjected to investigation. Finally, future studies should examine the factors that promote or hinder automation usage in real traffic. HMI design (Lee et al., 2016) and road and driver characteristics (Schott et al.,2018) are important. Simulator studies showed that traffic density (Gold et al., 2016; Körber et al., 2016) and the visibility of the driving situation (Brandenburg & Roche, 2020) affect drivers' interactions with automated vehicles. Upcoming studies should evaluate whether these factors also impact drivers' willingness to use vehicle automation.

14.2.2 Driving Automatically

L3 (and higher) automated vehicles offer open spaces to drivers; they can engage in NDRTs (Merat et al., 2012; SAE International, 2018). A survey by Zeeb et al. (2016) revealed that drivers associate automated driving with talking to passengers, relaxing, watching videos, and reading text messages. In a driving simulator study, drivers intensified their engagement in NDRTs with increasing levels of automation (Carsten et al., 2012). Jamson et al. (2013) showed that drivers listened to the radio and watched DVDs significantly more often during automated compared with manual driving. The drivers' engagement in NDRTs during automated driving affects their driver state. Their heart rate and subjective feelings of strain decrease with increasing vehicle automation (Carsten et al., 2012). Also, the drivers' gazes wander from the middle of the road to the NDRT and to the roadside (Carsten et al., 2012; Jamson et al., 2013; Louw et al., 2015; Merat et al., 2012).

Moreover, driver states also change without engaging in NDRTs. In a driving simulator study, drivers' lateral and longitudinal performances decreased after a 20-minute episode of automated driving (Brandenburg & Skottke, 2014). Possibly drivers have to motivate themselves intrinsically to concentrate and monitor the actions of their vehicles during automated driving (Saxby et al., 2013). Neubauer et al. (2012) examined whether designed driver-vehicle interactions help to reduce adverse automation effects. Results showed that the alternating activation and deactivation of the automation increased driver fatigue compared with manual driving. Another simulator study supports the claim that driver fatigue increases during vehicle automation (Vogelpohl & Vollrath, 2017). Additionally, automated driving also affects drivers' situation awareness (Neubauer et al., 2012; Noy et al., 2018; Saxby et al., 2013). Endsley (1995) defined situation awareness as the "... perception of the elements in the environment within a volume of time and space, the comprehension of their meaning, and the projection of their status in the near future" (p. 36). Drivers, therefore, might have problems in representing their current driving situation and forecasting its development. These problems, in turn, affect drivers' takeover behavior after TORs (Merat et al., 2014).

Inappropriate driver reactions after TORs are the most important effects of changes in the driver state. Visual NDRTs that are performed during automated driving, increase drivers' reaction times to TORs compared with manual driving (Kuehn et al., 2017). The presence of NDRTs during automated driving leads to higher numbers of crashes (Radlmayr et al., 2014) and smaller time-to-collisions regarding an obstacle (Körber et al., 2016) compared with their absence. Similar results are assumed for drives without NDRTs (Vogelpohl et al., 2016).

In summary, automated driving affects the drivers' state independently of the presence and absence of NDRTs. However, driving simulator studies generated most of the empirical evidence, posing the question of whether these results also apply for real driving scenarios. Drivers seem to concentrate more on driving and less on NDRTs in real driving scenarios than they do in the driving simulator (Naujoks et al., 2016). Thus, future studies should evaluate whether automated driving affects the drivers' state in real-world settings in the same way it does in the driving simulator.

14.2.3 Takeover of Vehicle Control

Human factors research dedicated most of its attention to the fourth section of an episode of automated driving, the takeover of vehicle control by the drivers. This section can be further divided into four cases following the two criteria: initiation of takeovers (vehicle or driver) and criticality of the driving situation (low or high). The first criterion depicts the two ways of possible transitions of control. On the one hand, the vehicle must present a TOR to the driver when it reaches its system limits (SAE International, 2018). On the other hand, drivers are allowed to resume the controls of their vehicles whenever they want (Gasser et al., 2012; United Nations Economic Commission for Europe, 2014). The second criterion considers the criticality of the driving situation. It strongly affects driver reactions to TORs; for example, drivers steer and brake more strongly in critical compared with uncritical driving situations (Epple et al., 2018; Roche & Brandenburg, 2018). Table 14.1 depicts the four cases of takeover situations in the fourth section of an automated driving episode.

In the first case, automated vehicles present TORs in uncritical driving situations. This occurs with the automation reaching its system limits because of dirty or missing lane markings or worsening of the weather. Planned transitions of control will also happen when drivers reach the end of the stretch of the road where L3 automated driving is possible, like a highway exit. Empirical studies rarely address these types of planned transitions. For example, Brandenburg and Epple (2019) examined the design of TORs for planned transitions. They found that drivers prefer speech-based, auditory TORs utilizing two separate steps.

The second case in Table 14.1 describes driver-initiated transitions of control in uncritical driving situations. This could happen for several reasons; for example, drivers could take over vehicle control when becoming tired. They might feel that driving their own could make them alert. Moreover, studies revealed that about one-third of drivers would like to partially hand over vehicle control to the automation (Fraedrich et al., 2016; Payre et al., 2014). Reasons for keeping vehicle control include reservations about automated driving functions, feelings of loss of control (Noy et al., 2018), and uncertainty about the functioning of the automation. However, investigations assessing empirical data for driver-initiated takeovers in uncritical driving situations are still missing.

The third case in Table 14.1 represents vehicle-initiated takeovers in critical driving situations. The vast majority of human factors research addresses this scope (Brandenburg et al., 2017). On the one hand, the research centers on the behavior and subjective experience of drivers during takeovers and subsequent manual driving. On the other hand, it concentrates on factors that affect the drivers' behaviors and experiences in these situations. These factors include, but are not limited to, NDRTs during automated driving, characteristics of the takeover situation, and the design of TORs.

TABLE 14.1 Four Cases of Takeover Situations in the Fourth Section of an Episode of Automated Driving

		Criticality of the Driving Situation	
		Low (Uncritical)	High (Critical)
Initiation of takeovers	**Vehicle**	Case 1	Case 3
	Driver	Case 2	Case 4

In the literature, takeover time is one of the main criteria of driver behavior after TORs. It is a central measure for drivers' takeover performances. Reviews on takeover times report several periods that drivers need to take back control of their vehicles. Eriksson and Stanton (2017b) list takeover times ranging from 1.14 to 15 seconds with a mean takeover time of 2.96 seconds (standard deviation [SD] = 1.96). Another review of Vogelpohl et al. (2016) reported takeover times of 1.66 to 30 seconds. These reviews reveal that takeover times differ vastly, depending on the definition of their measurement. Drivers must perceive and understand a takeover first. In parallel, they can start preparing a reaction. After finishing the processing of the request, drivers can execute their reactions (Zeeb et al., 2015). Takeover times vary depending on the definitions of the responses that drivers have to perform, including glancing at the device presenting the TOR, touching the pedals or the steering wheel, or some kind of driving action. Therefore, some authors additionally report the time point at which most drivers (i.e., 95%) performed a takeover; it was 10 seconds across several studies (Brandenburg & Chuang, 2019; Petermann-Stock et al., 2013).

Moreover, NDRTs increase takeover times (Feldhütter et al., 2017; Vogelpohl & Vollrath, 2016). They also lead to lower speeds (Merat et al., 2012; Vogelpohl & Vollrath, 2016), inaccurate lane keeping (Zeeb et al., 2016), and fewer glances on the road (Carsten et al., 2012; Jamson et al., 2013; Louw et al., 2015; Merat et al., 2012). These findings suggest that studies on driver responses to TORs in critical driving situations should always consider the effects of NDRT.

Other studies revealed that traffic density affects driver performance after TORs. The presence of other vehicles leads to increased takeover times, shorter time-to-collisions, and more accidents than the absence (Gold et al., 2016; Körber et al., 2016). Other drivers impact the takeover performance of drivers and should, therefore, be considered in future research.

Finally, many studies examined the effects of the design of the HMI of TORs on driver behavior. The HMI design affects automation acceptance (Casner et al., 2016; Merat et al., 2014) and influences drivers' understanding regarding the capabilities and constraints of the technology (Noy et al., 2018). For example, studies investigated the modalities for presenting TORs (i.e., visual, auditory, haptic). In an online survey, Bazilinskyy et al. (2018) found that respondents prefer speech-based, acoustic requests in uncritical takeover situations. In critical situations, they favored multimodal designs. A driving simulator study by Roche et al. (2018) showed that speech-based, acoustic TORs led to more glances at the road than visual-auditory requests. However, the investigation also revealed that the modality of the NDRT affects driver behavior after taking over vehicle control. Visual tasks distracted drivers more than auditory. Other studies examined the number of steps of TORs (Brandenburg & Roche, 2020; Epple et al., 2018; Walch et al., 2015). Here, one-step requests, demanding drivers to take back vehicle control at once, are compared with two-step systems presenting a preliminary warning before an alert. The results of these experiments revealed that drivers prefer two-step over one-step procedures (Brandenburg & Chuang, 2019; Walch et al., 2015). Moreover, drivers' takeover performances are higher with two-step procedures compared with one-step ones. They react a little slower but brake and steer less strong (Brandenburg & Roche, in 2020; Epple et al., 2018).

The fourth and last case in Table 14.1 denotes driver-initiated takeovers in critical driving situations. They can occur when drivers' automation trust is not sufficient. A preliminary study by Roche et al. (2020) showed that driver interventions in highly dynamic maneuvers of automated vehicles lead to dangerous driving situations. Drivers steer and brake stronger than necessary, causing instability of the vehicle and increasing the likelihood of accidents. Driver-initiated takeovers in critical situations should, therefore, be subjected to future human factors research.

In summary, driver takeovers of vehicle control were studied extensively in the past; however, human factors research centered on a few types of transitions only. Sorting the existing literature into a scheme of four cases demonstrated that most studies examined vehicle-initiated takeovers in critical driving situations. Considering this type of emergency transition of control certainly is very important. However, reliable vehicle automation will mostly lead to planned transitions in uncritical and less critical situations. Human factors research has not yet examined this case extensively (Table 14.1, case 1). Another large blind spot in research addresses driver-initiated takeovers in uncritical (Table 14.1, case 2) and critical (Table 14.1, case 4) driving situations. Again, from a legal point of view, drivers can interrupt vehicle automation at any time. The research revealed that automated driving impacts drivers' ability to manage lateral and longitudinal vehicle control. Future research should examine these transitions because they are potential threats to traffic safety.

14.3 FUTURE CHALLENGES TO HUMAN FACTORS IN AUTOMATED DRIVING

Human factors research in automated driving generated a large body of evidence. However, many challenges need to be addressed in the future. Short-term issues include the transfer of knowledge from surveys and the simulator to field studies (Brandenburg & Roche, in 2020; van Nes et al., 2010). Driver behavior in real traffic might be different from the behaviors reported in surveys or shown in the simulator. Simulators are well suited for preliminary studies as they allow researchers to manipulate the desired environments at relatively little risk and cost (van Nes et al., 2010). They deliver prefatory results. Future studies should replicate and validate them in on-the-road tests. For example, the results of Naujoks et al. (2016) suggested that distracted drivers behave safer in real driving situations compared with the simulator. Also, Eriksson et al. (2017) reported that drivers executed takeovers faster in an on-road driving scenario than in the simulator.

Another short-term challenge is the communication of automated vehicles with vulnerable road users like pedestrians and cyclists. Drivers and pedestrians regularly communicate via speed choice, eye gazes, and hand gestures to avoid confrontations. However, this communication does not necessarily work with the (inattentive) drivers of automated vehicles. Their vehicles do not recognize the signals of vulnerable road users. A new strand of human factors research, therefore, examines interfaces that communicate the awareness and intent of automated vehicles to people (Ackermann et al., 2019; Habibovic et al., 2018; Mahadevan et al., 2018). Future work should focus on these design issues fostering automation acceptance and preventing accidents.

A third short-term issue addresses the interactions of regular drivers with the automated vehicles of others, or the so-called mixed traffic. To date, studies model the traffic flow of vehicles with and without automated driving capabilities. Some of them even incorporate driver characteristics like their skills and personality (Sharma et al., 2018). Still, these models can be improved by considering the accumulating knowledge regarding driver interactions with automated vehicles.

Concerning the mid-term challenges of human factors research in automated driving, behavioral adaptation effects become important. The first results of driving simulator research revealed that drivers change their behavior with the repeated experience of takeover situations (Roche et al., 2018). Drivers even seem to be able to transfer their takeover behavior across situations (Brandenburg & Roche, 2020). However, these are preliminary results from a few simulator studies. Future empirical work should examine drivers' behavioral adaptation in on-the-road-studies.

The HMI design of automated vehicles remains a mid-term challenge, although many studies examined its effects on driver behavior. The literature provides many cues on proper design solutions. For example, empirical evidence promoted speech-based, acoustic HMIs for vehicle-initiated uncritical takeover situations (Brandenburg & Epple, 2019) and for the stage of automated driving (Lee et al., 2016). These HMIs were also superior for takeovers in critical driving situations (Epple et al., 2018) and behavioral adaptation processes (Roche et al., 2018). Also, evidence has accumulated favoring a two-step takeover process over a one-step one (Brandenburg & Epple, 2019; Brandenburg & Roche, 2020; Walch et al., 2015). However, to date, no study investigated the merits of an HMI that is consistent across all four stages of an episode of automated driving (see Figure 14.1). The issue of HMI design should be subjected to future research because it strongly influences driver trust and automation utilization (Lee et al., 2016; Noy et al., 2018).

Finally, there are long-term challenges to human factors research in automated driving. They include but are not limited to issues that might arise from prolonged automation usage and new technological developments like the implementation of artificial intelligence in automated vehicles. Long-term automation usage might lead to the misaligned calibration of driver trust. Over time, drivers could rely on vehicle automation too much, or they might not trust it at all (Noy et al., 2018). Also, long-term usage might elicit effects similar to the ones described as ironies of automation (Bainbridge, 1983). For example, this could mean that drivers lose their driving skills because they rely on their vehicles' abilities. It could also mean that drivers lose their understanding of the capabilities and constraints of their vehicles with increasing automation usage.

Finally, new developments like the successive implementation of artificial intelligence challenge the results of human factors studies. To date, empirical studies used automated systems that do not change over time or adapt to specific driving situations. However, artificially intelligent algorithms improve the vehicles' perception of the environment and the planning of actions. They contribute to the advance of camera and decision processes with increasing experience (Meiring & Myburgh, 2015). It seems to be a matter of time until these changes on an algorithmic level impact the vehicle's behavior in a way that is important for the driver to realize and understand. Then, HMI would become adaptive. Whether drivers can interact with adaptive HMI in all kinds of situations is not clear yet.

14.4 SUMMARY AND CONCLUSIONS

Automated driving is a vision with a long history and, possibly, with a prosperous future. The empirical evidence that was presented in this chapter summarized the main points of the current state-of-the-art knowledge regarding human factors research in this domain. It also listed blind spots in this research field. For this purpose, it divided an episode of automated driving into four stages: (1) manual driving, (2) handover to the vehicle, (3) automated driving, and (4) takeover by driver. Sorting the empirical evidence into these stages demonstrated that relatively few studies examined the first two stages, several investigations assessed driver behavior in the third stage, and by far most of the evidence was accumulated in the fourth stage. However, the close examination of that fourth stage revealed that many studies focused on the drivers' behavior after vehicle initiated takeovers in critical driving situations. Few investigations evaluated driver behavior in uncritical takeover situations and driver-initiated takeovers, despite these cases occurring more often than takeovers in critical situations.

Moreover, the section on short, medium, and long-term challenges for human factors research in automated driving listed additional topics, like replications of survey and simulator research in field studies, HMI design issues, drivers' long-term adaptation to automated driving, and the possible impact of artificial intelligence on the interactions of drivers with their automated vehicles.

The main conclusions of this chapter are, therefore, that human factors research should focus on (1) the first two stages of an episode of automated driving, (2) more cases of control transitions from the automation to the drivers, (3) the design of proper internal and external HMI, and (4) future challenges like artificial intelligence. Future human factors research should gather empirical results in the respective fields to delete some of the blind spots that this chapter highlighted. This work is necessary for the development of automated driving so that it can achieve some of the benefits that are associated with it.

REFERENCES

Ackermann, C., Beggiato, M., Schubert, S., & Krems, J. F. (2019). An experimental study to investigate design and assessment criteria: What is important for communication between pedestrians and automated vehicles? *Applied Ergonomics, 75*, 272–282. https://doi.org/10.1016/j.apergo.2018.11.002

Bainbridge, L. (1983). Ironies of automation. *Automatica, 19*(6), 775–779. https://doi.org/10.1016/0005-1098(83)90046-8

Bazilinskyy, P., Petermeijer, S. M., Petrovych, V., Dodou, D., & de Winter, J. C. F. (2018). Take-over requests in highly automated driving: A crowdsourcing survey on auditory, vibrotactile, and visual displays. *Transportation Research Part F: Traffic Psychology and Behaviour, 56*, 82–98. https://doi.org/10.1016/j.trf.2018.04.001

Brandenburg, S., & Chuang, L. (2019). Take-over requests during highly automated driving: How should they be presented and under what conditions? *Transportation Research Part F: Traffic Psychology and Behaviour, 66*, 214–225. https://doi.org/10.1016/j.trf.2019.08.023

Brandenburg, S., & Epple, S. (2019). Drivers' individual design preferences of takeover requests in highly automated driving. *I-Com, 18*(2), 167–178. https://doi.org/10.1515/icom-2018-0028

Brandenburg, S., & Roche, F. (2020). Behavioral changes to repeated takeovers in automated driving: the drivers' ability to transfer knowledge and the effects of takeover request process. *Transportation Research Part F: Psychology and Behaviour, 73*, 15–28. https://doi.org/10.1016/j.trf.2020.06.002

Brandenburg, S., Roche, F., & Thüring, M. (2017). Kognitionspsychologische Erkenntnisse zum hochautomatisierten Fahren – eine Übersicht. *VDI-Berichte, 2312*, 277–292.

Brandenburg, S., & Skottke, E.-M. (2014). Switching from manual to automated driving and reverse: Are drivers behaving more risky after highly automated driving? *17th International IEEE Conference on Intelligent Transportation Systems (ITSC)*, Qingdao, China, 2978–2983. https://doi.org/10.1109/ITSC.2014.6958168

Buckley, L., Kaye, S.-A., & Pradhan, A. K. (2018). Psychosocial factors associated with intended use of automated vehicles: A simulated driving study. *Accident Analysis & Prevention, 115*, 202–208. https://doi.org/10.1016/j.aap.2018.03.021

Campbell, M., Egerstedt, M., How, J. P., & Murray, R. M. (2010). Autonomous driving in urban environments: Approaches, lessons and challenges. *Philosophical Transactions of the Royal Society A: Mathematical, Physical and Engineering Sciences, 368*(1928), 4649–4672. https://doi.org/10.1098/rsta.2010.0110

Carsten, O., Lai, F. C. H., Barnard, Y., Jamson, A. H., & Merat, N. (2012). Control task substitution in semiautomated driving: Does it matter what aspects are automated? *Human Factors, 54*(5), 747–761. https://doi.org/10.1177/0018720812460246

Casner, S. M., Hutchins, E. L., & Norman, D. (2016). The challenges of partially automated driving. *Communications of the ACM, 59*(5), 70–77. https://doi.org/10.1145/2830565

Dikmen, M., & Burns, C. M. (2016). Autonomous driving in the real world: experiences with Tesla autopilot and summon. *Proceedings of the 8th International Conference on Automotive User Interfaces and Interactive Vehicular Applications*, 225–228. https://doi.org/10.1145/3003715.3005465

Endsley, M. R. (1995). Toward a theory of situation awareness in dynamic systems. *Human Factors, 37*(1), 32–64.

Epple, S., Roche, F., & Brandenburg, S. (2018). The sooner the better: Drivers' reactions to two-step take-over requests in highly automated driving. *Proceedings of the Human Factors and Ergonomics Society Annual Meeting, 62*, 1883–1887. https://doi.org/10.1177/1541931218621428

Eriksson, A., Banks, V. A., & Stanton, N. A. (2017). Transition to manual: Comparing simulator with on-road control transitions. *Accident Analysis & Prevention, 102*, 227–234. https://doi.org/10.1016/j.aap.2017.03.011

Eriksson, A., & Stanton, N. A. (2017a). Driving performance after self-regulated control transitions in highly automated vehicles. *Human Factors, 59*(8), 1233–1248. https://doi.org/10.1177/0018720817728774

Eriksson, A., & Stanton, N. A. (2017b). Takeover time in highly automated vehicles: Noncritical transitions to and from manual control. *Human Factors, 59*(4), 689–705. https://doi.org/10.1177/0018720816685832

Feldhütter, A., Gold, C., Schneider, S., & Bengler, K. (2017). How the Duration of Automated Driving Influences Take-Over Performance and Gaze Behavior. In C. M. Schlick, S. Duckwitz, F. Flemisch, M. Frenz, S. Kuz, A. Mertens, & S. Mütze-Niewöhner (Eds.), *Advances in Ergonomic Design of Systems, Products and Processes* (pp. 309–318). Springer, Berlin Heidelberg. https://doi.org/10.1007/978-3-662-53305-5_22

Fraedrich, E., Cyganski, R., Wolf, I., & Lenz, B. (2016). *User Perspectives on Autonomous Driving: A Use-Case-Driven Study in Germany* (Arbeitsbericht No. 187). HU Berlin, Berlin.

Franke, T., Attig, C., & Wessel, D. (2019). A personal resource for technology interaction: Development and validation of the Affinity for Technology Interaction (ATI) scale. *International Journal of Human–Computer Interaction, 35*(6), 456–467. https://doi.org/10.1080/10447318.2018.1456150

Gasser, T. M., Arzt, C., Ayoubi, M., Bartels, A., Bürkle, L., Eier, J., Flemisch, F., Häcker, D., Hesse, T., Huber, W., Lotz, C., Maurer, M., Ruth-Schumacher, S., Schwarz, J., & Vogt, W. (2012). *Rechtsfolgen zunehmender Fahrzeugautomatisierung: Gemeinsamer Schlussbericht der Projektgruppe* (Bundesanstalt für Straßenwesen, Ed.). Wirtschaftsverlag NW, Bremerhaven.

Gold, C., Körber, M., Lechner, D., & Bengler, K. (2016). Taking over control from highly automated vehicles in complex traffic situations: The role of traffic density. *Human Factors, 58*(4), 642–652. https://doi.org/10.1177/0018720816634226

Habibovic, A., Lundgren, V. M., Andersson, J., Klingegård, M., Lagström, T., Sirkka, A., Fagerlönn, J., Edgren, C., Fredriksson, R., Krupenia, S., Saluäär, D., & Larsson, P. (2018). Communicating intent of automated vehicles to pedestrians. *Frontiers in Psychology, 9*, 1336. https://doi.org/10.3389/fpsyg.2018.01336

Hergeth, S., Lorenz, L., & Krems, J. F. (2017). Prior familiarization with takeover requests affects drivers' takeover performance and automation trust. *Human Factors, 59*(3), 457–470. https://doi.org/10.1177/0018720816678714

Hergeth, S., Lorenz, L., Krems, J. F., & Toenert, L. (2015). Effects of take-over requests and cultural background on automation trust in highly automated driving. *Proceedings of 8th International Driving Symposium on Human Factors in Driver Assessment, Training, and Vehicle Design*, 331–337. http://drivingassessment.uiowa.edu/sites/default/files/DA2015/papers/051.pdf

Hergeth, S., Lorenz, L., Vilimek, R., & Krems, J. F. (2016). Keep your scanners peeled: Gaze behavior as a measure of automation trust during highly automated driving. *Human Factors, 58*(3), 509–519. https://doi.org/10.1177/0018720815625744

Jamson, A. H., Merat, N., Carsten, O. M. J., & Lai, F. C. H. (2013). Behavioural changes in drivers experiencing highly-automated vehicle control in varying traffic conditions. *Transportation Research Part C: Emerging Technologies, 30*, 116–125. https://doi.org/10.1016/j.trc.2013.02.008

Koopman, P., & Wagner, M. (2017). Autonomous vehicle safety: An interdisciplinary challenge. *IEEE Intelligent Transportation Systems Magazine, 9*(1), 90–96. https://doi.org/10.1109/MITS.2016.2583491

Körber, M., Baseler, E., & Bengler, K. (2018). Introduction matters: Manipulating trust in automation and reliance in automated driving. *Applied Ergonomics, 66*, 18–31. https://doi.org/10.1016/j.apergo.2017.07.006

Körber, M., & Bengler, K. (2014). Potential individual differences regarding automation effects in automated driving. *Proceedings of the XV International Conference on Human Computer Interaction - Interacción '14*, 1–7. https://doi.org/10.1145/2662253.2662275

Körber, M., Gold, C., Lechner, D., & Bengler, K. (2016). The influence of age on the take-over of vehicle control in highly automated driving. *Transportation Research Part F: Traffic Psychology and Behaviour, 39*, 19–32. https://doi.org/10.1016/j.trf.2016.03.002

Kröger, F. (2015). Das automatisierte Fahren im gesellschaftsgeschichtlichen und kulturwissenschaftlichen Kontext. In M. Maurer, J. C. Gerdes, B. Lenz, & H. Winner (Eds.), *Autonomes Fahren* (pp. 41–67). Springer Berlin Heidelberg. https://doi.org/10.1007/978-3-662-45854-9_3

Kuehn, M., Vogelpohl, T., & Vollrath, M. (2017). Takeover times in highly automated driving (level 3), *International Technical Conference on the Enhanced Safety of Vehicles*, Detroit, MI, 1–11.

Lee, J., Kim, N., Imm, C., Kim, B., Yi, K., & Kim, J. (2016). A question of trust: an ethnographic study of automated cars on real roads. *Proceedings of the 8th International Conference on Automotive User Interfaces and Interactive Vehicular Applications – Automotive'UI 16*, 201–208. https://doi.org/10.1145/3003715.3005405

Louw, T., Kountouriotis, G., Carsten, O., & Merat, N. (2015). Driver inattention during vehicle automation: how does driver engagement affect resumption of control? *Proceedings of the 4th International Conference on Driver Distraction (DDI2015) and Inattention*, 9–11.

Mahadevan, K., Somanath, S., & Sharlin, E. (2018). Communicating awareness and intent in autonomous vehicle-pedestrian interaction. *Proceedings of the 2018 CHI Conference on Human Factors in Computing Systems - CHI' 18*, 1–12. https://doi.org/10.1145/3173574.3174003

Meiring, G., & Myburgh, H. (2015). A review of intelligent driving style analysis systems and related artificial intelligence algorithms. *Sensors, 15*(12), 30653–30682. https://doi.org/10.3390/s151229822

Merat, N., Jamson, A. H., Lai, F. C. H., & Carsten, O. (2012). Highly automated driving, secondary task performance, and driver state. *Human Factors, 54*(5), 762–771. https://doi.org/10.1177/0018720812442087

Merat, N., Jamson, A. H., Lai, F. C. H., Daly, M., & Carsten, O. M. J. (2014). Transition to manual: Driver behaviour when resuming control from a highly automated vehicle. *Transportation Research Part F: Traffic Psychology and Behaviour, 27*, 274–282. https://doi.org/10.1016/j.trf.2014.09.005

Naujoks, F., Purucker, C., & Neukum, A. (2016). Secondary task engagement and vehicle automation – Comparing the effects of different automation levels in an on-road experiment. *Transportation Research Part F: Traffic Psychology and Behaviour, 38*, 67–82. https://doi.org/10.1016/j.trf.2016.01.011

Neubauer, C., Matthews, G., Langheim, L., & Saxby, D. (2012). Fatigue and voluntary utilization of automation in simulated driving. *Human Factors: The Journal of the Human Factors and Ergonomics Society, 54*(5), 734–746. https://doi.org/10.1177/0018720811423261

Noy, I. Y., Shinar, D., & Horrey, W. J. (2018). Automated driving: Safety blind spots. *Safety Science, 102*, 68–78. https://doi.org/10.1016/j.ssci.2017.07.018

Payre, W., Cestac, J., & Delhomme, P. (2014). Intention to use a fully automated car: Attitudes and a priori acceptability. *Transportation Research Part F: Traffic Psychology and Behaviour, 27*, 252–263. https://doi.org/10.1016/j.trf.2014.04.009

Petermann-Stock, I., Hackenberg, L., Muhr, T., & Mergl, C. (2013). Wie lange braucht der Fahrer? Eine Analyse zu Übernahmezeiten aus verschiedenen Nebentätigkeiten während einer hochautomatisierten Staufahrt [How long does the driver take? An analysis of take-over times from different secondary tasks during a highly automated drive in a traffic jam]. *6th Conference on Driver Assistance Systems. The way to automatic driving.*

Radlmayr, J., Gold, C., Lorenz, L., Farid, M., & Bengler, K. (2014). How traffic situations and non-driving related tasks affect the take-over quality in highly automated driving. *Proceedings of the Human Factors and Ergonomics Society Annual Meeting, 58*(1), 2063–2067. https://doi.org/10.1177/1541931214581434

Rammstedt, B., & John, O. P. (2007). Measuring personality in one minute or less: A 10-item short version of the Big Five Inventory in English and German. *Journal of Research in Personality, 41*(1), 203–212. https://doi.org/10.1016/j.jrp.2006.02.001

Roche, F., & Brandenburg, S. (2018). Should the urgency of an auditory-tactile takeover request match the situational criticality? *2018 21st International Conference on Intelligent Transportation Systems (ITSC)*, 1035–1040. https://doi.org/10.1109/ITSC.2018.8569650

Roche, F., Somieski, A., & Brandenburg, S. (2018). Behavioral changes to repeated takeovers in highly automated driving: Effects of the takeover request-design and the non-driving related task-modality. *Human Factors, 61*(5), 839–849. https://doi.org/10.1177/0018720818814963

Roche, F., Thüring, M., & Trapp, A. K. (2020). What happens when drivers of a highly-automated vehicle take over control in critical brake situations? *Accident Analysis & Prevention, 144*, 105588.

SAE International. (2018). *Taxonomy and Definitions for Terms Related to Driving Automation Systems for On-Road Motor Vehicles (J3016).* https://www.sae.org/standards/content/j3016_201806/

Saxby, D. J., Matthews, G., Warm, J. S., Hitchcock, E. M., & Neubauer, C. (2013). Active and passive fatigue in simulated driving: Discriminating styles of workload regulation and their safety impacts. *Journal of Experimental Psychology: Applied, 19*(4), 287–300. https://doi.org/10.1037/a0034386

Schott, R.M., Brandenburg, S., Thüring, M., Schröder, F., & Telle, F. (2018). Who is driving whom? Highly automated driving transitions from manual to automation in reality and the impact of situation, personality and the driving experience. In R. Wiczorek, D. Manzey, L. Onnasch, K. Brookhuis, A. Toffetti, & D. DeWaard. *Annual Meeting of the Human Factors Ergonomics Society (HFES) Europe Chapter – Book of Abstracts.* 29.

Sharma, A., Ali, Y., Saifuzzaman, M., Zheng, Z., & Haque, Md. M. (2018). Human Factors in Modelling Mixed Traffic of Traditional, Connected, and Automated Vehicles. In D. N. Cassenti (Ed.), *Advances in Human Factors in Simulation and Modeling* (Vol. 591, pp. 262–273). Springer International Publishing, Cham, Switzerland. https://doi.org/10.1007/978-3-319-60591-3_24

United Nations Economic Commission for Europe. (2014). *Report of the sixty-eighth session of the Working Party on Road Traffic Safety.* https://www.unece.org/fileadmin/DAM/trans/doc/2014/wp1/ECE-TRANS-WP1-145e.pdf

van Nes, N., Brandenburg, S., & Twisk, D. (2010). Improving homogeneity by dynamic speed limit systems. *Accident Analysis & Prevention, 42*(3), 944–952. https://doi.org/10.1016/j.aap.2009.05.002

Vogelpohl, T., & Vollrath, M. (2016). *Übernahmezeiten beim hochautomatisierten Fahren* (No. 57; Unfallforschung Kompakt, p. 20). Unfallforschung der Versicherer.

Vogelpohl, T., & Vollrath, M. (2017). *Tiredness and level 3—Automated driving* (No. 70; Unfallforschung kompakt, p. 20). Gesamtverband der Versicherungswirtschaft e.V.

Vogelpohl, T., Vollrath, M., Kühn, M., Hummel, T., & Gehlert, T. (2016). *Übergabe von hochautomatisiertem Fahren zu manueller Steuerung Teil 1. Review der Literatur und Studie zu Übernahmezeiten.* Unfallforschung der Versicherer GDV.

Walch, M., Lange, K., Baumann, M., & Weber, M. (2015). Autonomous driving: Investigating the feasibility of car-driver handover assistance. *Proceedings of the 7th International Conference on Automotive User Interfaces and Interactive Vehicular Applications,* 11–18. https://doi.org/10.1145/2799250.2799268

Wickens, C. (2008). Multiple resources and mental workload. *Human Factors, 50*(3), 449–455. https://doi.org/10.1518/001872008X288394

Zeeb, K., Buchner, A., & Schrauf, M. (2015). What determines the take-over time? An integrated model approach of driver take-over after automated driving. *Accident Analysis & Prevention, 78,* 212–221. https://doi.org/10.1016/j.aap.2015.02.023

Zeeb, K., Buchner, A., & Schrauf, M. (2016). Is take-over time all that matters? The impact of visual-cognitive load on driver take-over quality after conditionally automated driving. *Accident Analysis & Prevention, 92,* 230–239. https://doi.org/10.1016/j.aap.2016.04.002

Zhang, S., Chen, J., Lyu, F., Cheng, N., Shi, W., & Shen, X. (2018). Vehicular communication networks in the automated driving era. *IEEE Communications Magazine, 56*(9), 26–32. https://doi.org/10.1109/MCOM.2018.1701171

CHAPTER 15

Human Factors of Vehicle Automation

Sunil Kr. Sharma

Indian Railway
Kolkata, India

Sunil Kr. Singh

Panjab University
Chandigarh, India

Subhash C. Panja

Jadavpur University
Kolkata, India

CONTENTS

DOI: 10.1201/9781003048381-17

15.1 INTRODUCTION

Autonomous vehicles (AVs) have immense potential to improve transportation safety and enhance its quality by using resources more productively. It can radically change the transportation arrangement in the near future. This change does not embody only a technological break but embraces cultural changes and thus includes a significant role for human factors. At present, automation is impacting all three major modes of transportation, viz. air, railways, and roadways. In fact, automation is already being successfully used in air traffic, which marks the shifting of responsibility of functions to the technical system and changing human roles to more of a supervisory control exercise. Parallel developments are now emerging in rail and road transportation sectors. However, the role of the human factors, which is a fundamental issue in successful automation, has yet to be clearly defined and established in these fields. AVs fundamentally alter the cognitive demands that are put on vehicle drivers. In addition, passengers and other road users' experiences also change while interacting with AVs. It is, therefore, essential that automation challenges pertaining to human factors should be understood and addressed so that AVs can be successfully utilized to improve the transportation sector.

Studies conducted in relation to the aviation and unmanned vehicle and rail automation can help in informing the design and development of AVs as these areas also involve interesting human factor challenges (Trimble et al., 2014). However, these studies cannot be directly transferred to the field of AVs because of inherent characteristic differences among them. Autonomous driving is now a reality in railroad transport with the automation of train control and protection systems (Bucsky, 2018). The Kobe Port Island Line was run for the first time in 1981 without any on board staff while carrying passenger train. This was defined as an unattended train operation (UTO; Powell et al., 2016). Presently, about one-fourth of existing metros have at least one UTO (Union Internationale des Transports Publics [UITP], 2018). In driverless train operation (DTO), starting and stopping operations are automated, but human intervention is required to operate the doors and drive the train in case of emergencies. Train automation is referred to the process that transfers the responsibility for managing train operations from the human operator to the automated control system. Different forms of automation in railway and road transportation are organized into a hierarchy of grades or levels. Based on grade of automation for railways (UITP, -2018; NSAI Standards, 2009) and level of automation for vehicles (National Highway Traffic Safety Administration [NHTSA], 2013), hierarchy details are presented in Table 15.1 for conceptualizing the automation continuum.

A similar kind of approach seems to be adopted to define automation continuum for both parts of ground automation, viz. rail and road transportation. It connotes that the role of human drivers and capabilities change as the form or grade of automation advances. It also signifies that all AVs are not capable and intelligent enough to drive themselves and require manual assistance or intervention in different forms. For example, level 1 automation incorporates features like adaptive cruise control (ACC) and lane keeping assist, which help drivers in controlling lateral and longitudinal motion, and averting unsafe lane change maneuvers. These are essentially function-specific automation features that

TABLE 15.1   Automation Continuum

Railroad Vehicles	Grade/Level of Automation	Road Vehicles
Driver without automatic train protection	0	All functions are completely controlled by drivers
Driver with automatic train protection	1	One function is automated
Automatic train operation and protection with driver to attend emergencies	2	More than one vehicle function is automated; however, driver is constantly attentive
Driverless train operation	3	Driving function sufficiently automated and takes full control of safety critical functions
Unattended train operation	4	Vehicle driven by itself without a driver

assist drivers in reference to these functions. Similarly, in level 3, vehicles such as Google's Driverless Car, a driver is required to take back vehicle control when its technical competence reaches the defined limit. Hence, human involvement and AV performance should be reviewed and studied in a cooperative perspective for improving its social acceptability and future utilization. Further, it hints at feasibility of developing an integrated AV and rapid rail transport with existing public transit networks in the future. A proper understanding of human factors and contextual perspective can help in this regard.

Regarding contextual perspective, one may appreciate its impact on human-automation interaction from the field of aviation in which automation is designed with two different philosophies by Airbus and Boeing (Orlady & Barnes, 1997). Simply stated, automation can adopt two strikingly different contextual perspectives in managing human-automation interaction, assisting rather than replacing the human operator. The operators are allowed to utilize the safe flight envelope to the fullest. In Boeing's case, the pilot remains the final decision maker or final authority to change the control limits, whereas in Airbus, automation takes back the control when the flight envelope reaches the defined limits. Unlike other modes, road transport is self-organizing where unambiguous rules cannot be framed for many situations, which makes it difficult for drivers to timely respond to emergencies. Further, AVs may also be run on different business models like private and commercial taxies, buses, or freights, or integrated "origin to destination" transport systems, etc. In fact, some companies like Uber and Lyft have been trying to develop a model similar to shared AVs in their operations where human drivers would be responsible for routing, relocation, operation times, and many other decisions (Faisal et al., 2019). This is similar to rail automation except that signalers or operational managers rather than drivers may decide a change in route or stoppage, etc. Such varied human-automation contexts will involve diverse roles and necessitate developing different capabilities to manage the technology and exercise controls. It is therefore required to develop the coping ability to manage the technology by communicating through appropriate technical fluency and effective training programs.

In the existing body of literature, inferences have been drawn from the study of use cases that serve as proxies for "typical usage scenario" for autonomous driving. These scenarios are conceptualized on the basis of assumption of mixed operations of transportation with different levels of automation. Wachenfeld et al. (2016) attempted to categorize them into four broad scenarios: (1) autonomous valet parking, (2) interstate pilot with a human driver for extended availability, (3) full automation with a human driver for extended availability, and (4) vehicle on demand. In this regard, a significant number of projects have been undertaken by various governments and private organizations. Apart from simulating research and development of AVs, these studies have shown that AVs with higher automation capabilities are not very far from reality. However, their reliability is yet to be established and some of the challenges need to be resolved. For instance, drivers who rely heavily on highly automated systems may fail to utilize their manual driving skills in the long run (Parasuraman et al., 2000). Although automation aims to ease the driver's work, this may not always be advantageous for driving nor may this necessarily result in improved road safety (Cunningham & Regan, 2015). Because of low workload, boredom may also be a factor for drivers in periods of automation. Consequently, drivers may tend to focus on the activities other than monitoring and supervising. Actually, during automated motion, the driver may encounter passive fatigue, which supposedly arises from low cognitive load and the lack of direct control over the tasks being supervised (Desmond & Hancock, 2001). This inattentiveness and reduced vigilance may lead to difficulties for drivers when they need to intervene and take the control during failures. This occurs due to a sudden and unexpected increase in cognitive load, which the driver may find difficult to deal with, which possibly may result in accidents (Young & Stanton, 1997). Another issue pertains to the capability of AV to interpret road users' intensions. No explicit communication channel exists between AV and road users. Interactions in vehicular traffic and its societal acceptance are not only affected by the AV's design aspects but also on how they are understood or misunderstood. Moreover, drivers may misuse AVs and regulatory measures and design solutions need to be devised for dealing with these situations.

Recent research (Merat et al., 2012; Färber, 2016; Spulber, 2016; Wada, 2016; Cunningham & Regan, 2017; Flemisch et al., 2017; Hoffman & Hancock, 2017; Bucsky, 2018; Bourrelly et al., 2019; Faisal et al., 2019; Hancock et al., 2019; Kurpiers et al., 2020) has been published that has highlighted the importance of the role of human factors in the field of vehicle automation. The literature review reveals that they have identified several important human factors that affect human-automation interaction. Spulber (2016) identified trust and reliance, situational awareness, and behavior adaptation as the most important factors in relation to an AV's deployment. They have further highlighted that aviation automation can offer valuable insights that can be used in ground automation. Hancock et al. (2019) emphasized that design processes should focus on achieving the trust in AVs. Automation will not always yield positive results; for example, higher automation may lead to reduced diver's attention, lower awareness, and excessive trust in automation (Merat et al., 2009a,b; 2012). Rouchitsas and Alm (2019) have reviewed the empirical work conducted on the use of external human-machine interface for communicating with pedestrians and they recommended using external surface to improve the interaction between AVs and multiple road users. El-Rewini et al. (2014) have elaborated on the cybersecurity challenges and intra-vehicular security threats. The review findings also highlight that it is not easy to predict how AVs will behave in unfamiliar situations and clearly define how the evolving AVs technology will affect the technological transformation of a transportation system. Moreover, there still remains an ambiguity about the role of human factors in automation.

In this background, this work attempts to contribute to the existing body of knowledge by presenting a comprehensive summary of human factor issues that have potential bearing on promoting safe and effective use, reducing the security concerns, improving the acceptability, and extending the availability of AVs. The review indicates that most of the earlier studies have viewed the human-automation context from a competitive perspective. However, authors advocate for adopting a human-centered approach toward automation and highlight the need for addressing the associated human factors and upgrading the design aspects to improve readiness of the driver to take over the vehicle command when automation fails and develop better communication among AVs, operators, and road users. This chapter also suggests introducing the concept of resilience in human-automation interaction in the context of mixed-autonomy transportation environment. Human operators need to be kept in the loop as backup architecture for building resilience in the AV. Automation design should consider the fact that algorithmic oversight cannot completely replace human monitoring at the current stage of AV development. Cunningham & Regan (2015) pointed out that the fundamental issue pertains to designing automation to make the driver aware of automation capabilities. In this regard, taking a cue from the railroad and aviation automation, it is suggested that training can play a significant role in counteracting the adverse effect of negative behaviors, such as skill degradation, low situation awareness (SA), automation misuse, etc.

Coming back to the human-centered perspective of implementing automation, main challenges relate to making a driver understand the AV's capability and limitations, organizing the AVs' communication with other system users, and maintaining alertness despite passive fatigue and low cognitive load. The subsequent section documents the key human factor challenges. It then discusses the future research agenda and makes some suggestions about the objective of addressing these human factor issues. This chapter is expected to help researchers and practitioners in this regard.

15.2 HUMAN FACTORS: ROLE AND CHALLENGES

With the technological advancements, highly capable systems like maneuver-based automation, cameras, and sensors dynamically generate a map of the surroundings and search for a suitable path for the AVs. These cars utilize various sensors, complex algorithms, machine learning systems, and powerful processors to make decisions regarding motion planning, i.e., planning of path, route, trajectory, or maneuver and choosing the best sequence of actions. These algorithms essentially try to search for a path; avert obstructions; and provide the best global route to ensure safety, comfort, and efficiency (Varaiya, 1993). Automation thereby relieves human drivers from much of the decision making and other activities, and human intervention is needed in case of automation failures. However, it is required to develop an understanding about the challenge of managing human performance for achieving automation benefits. Learning from rail automation, it is noted that human performance for safety-critical events can be managed either through technology or through human resource management. The first choice embraces measures like automating controls and operations to take care of human errors and safety-critical functions. However, automated systems may fail to understand and read human intentions. Therefore, many but not all errors or mistakes or inconsistencies can be accounted for and prevented. For example, confusion and lack of understanding about the characteristics and capabilities of automation mode may sometimes lead to serious errors within automation. In this regard, human-centered automation provides the path for better cooperation and coordination between humans and automated system (Flemisch et al., 2014). Stated simply, it highlights that the technological advancements can serve as an extension of human senses and cognition to improve mobility. The human resource approach implies identifying the challenges and implementing the procedures that address those human-automation aspects that cause errors and failures. Such an approach can help in achieving higher safety and better performance. The following sections discuss the relevant factors and challenges in the human element of AVs to facilitate improved understanding.

15.2.1 Necessity of Manual Intervention

Driver errors, infrastructure, and vehicle design are said to be the main contributing factors in road accidents. Bucsky (2018) documented that the European Truck Accident Causation study found that human factors are the main causal factor in 85.2% of cases. Automation can assist in reducing the crash frequencies with the help of advanced sensors and intelligent systems like forward collision, adaptive highlights, and lane departure warning systems.

Several technological evolutions are used to assist drivers in regard to lane keeping, lane changing, intelligent speed adaptation, lane departure warning, and emergency braking improve the longitudinal and lateral comfort and security for a safe and comfortable journey. These critical decisions are made through planning algorithms, integrated within the AV's navigation, situation understanding, and decision-making modules. However, AVs cannot drive reliably and safely in all traffic conditions (Cunningham & Regan, 2017). Human operators will therefore be required to stay in the loop for successfully handling the situation when the AV's capabilities fail. In fact, the driver can be assigned various roles, such as actively participating and passive yet attentive observance as per the requirement. However, this aspect has not yet been settled in the automated vehicle literature.

Further, human controllers need not be inside the vehicles; rather, they may be remotely working away from the actual vehicles as is done in emerging drone technology (Riley & Endsley, 2005). For example, signal controls also remotely set the route for driverless trains in case of railroad transport. However, regardless of the location of the controller, human operators have to maintain required levels of SA suited to the ambient environmental demands at all times because when such a human intervention will be required as a backup architecture is still not predictable (Hancock et al., 2019). In this context, it is again stated that the possibility that the AV software algorithm may not work resiliently when the operational envelope varies or environmental conditions worsen cannot be ignored. Sensors and programmable actuators cannot match human operators in terms of resilience to contextual changes. As a result, these vehicles would lack the tactical human decision making that might lead to suboptimal performance; for instance, poor road markings or signage and extreme weather like heavy rainfall or a snowstorm may significantly harm the functioning of the vision algorithm in today's autonomous cars. Deterioration or suboptimal condition of the various components of the infrastructure may result in various undesirable outcomes like disruptions, delays, etc. Hence, there is a need for integrating resilience perspective in future studies. Resilience is a desirable system property of the transportation sector. The concept of resilience is presently applied in various physical, social, and ecological disciplines. The resilience concept has assumed further significance in view of extreme weather events, which are now causing more serious disruptions. Moreover, various weather-induced disruptions like extreme rainfall, extreme temperature, heavy snow, cyclones, storms, etc., cannot be accurately predicted. Consequently, the transportation sector is required to take into consideration these disruptions to build up resilience for fulfilling their objective of safely taking passengers to their destinations.

In case of the sociotechnical system, resilience is defined as the capacity to continue to evolve and fulfill its operational mission despite the difficult conditions, serious constraints, or events, and sometimes severe damages or losses (Ruault et al., 2012). It can also be considered as the system's ability to reduce its failure probabilities, failure consequences, and speeding up recovery time (Bruneau et al., 2003). Thus, resilience connotes the persistence of a system whereby it realizes its operational objectives by flipping from the existing equilibrium state to another steady state while facing a disruption. It also reflects the ability of a system to successfully face the disruption and speedily recover by quickly adapting to the sudden disturbance (Sharma et al., 2021). In case of AVs, this may involve rerouting of the vehicle or switching over to manual mode operation or operating at a lower grade of automation to reduce the negative consequences of various disruptive events like automation failure, unauthorized attempts to access control system architecture by an unknown entity, weather disturbances, road blockage, or some other traffic disruptions. Resilience building exercises usually involve developing the understanding system, identifying the probable failures and disruptive events, and designing appropriate strategies to deal with them. Various techniques like anticipatory failure determination and theory of inventive problem solving, which provide a system approach, may be tried in this regard to analyze unexpected events that may disrupt a complex system.

Further, human operators, if kept in the loop, can definitely contribute to AV-based transportation system resilience. When the AV's software algorithmic oversight fails or mechanistic capabilities of the contemporary hardware's sensors reach their respective designed thresholds, on board human operators would be contributing through their innovative problem-solving capabilities. Possibly, differing forms of "smart infrastructures" can be developed and used to share these control and navigation responsibilities. The understanding of contextual reliability of different versions of AV automation and semi-automation developed by different companies is yet to be crystallized. In these circumstances, one is left with the alternative of conducting restricted sample-based testing for deriving general inferences from partial evaluation coverage and thereby building resilience by having one or more humans in the loop (Hoffman & Hancock, 2017). However, future research studies are required to find how AVs will adapt and recover from disruptive events or failures and thereby suggest appropriate resilience-building measures. This need will assume urgency when integrated "end to end" or "origin to destination oriented" transport system will emerge and AVs will serve alongside other modes of transportation like trains, escalators, elevators, ships, etc., to cater to the transport needs of the society.

15.2.2 Vulnerability of Drivers

The basic objective of automation aims at delegating the vehicle driving responsibility to automated systems for providing safe and efficient transport solutions. As discussed earlier, AVs' potential to provide a safe and reliable journey is sourced in the fact that a large number of serious accidents happen due to human errors in all safety-critical systems. However, possibilities of human errors cannot be entirely eliminated even in automated systems. In fact, automation may lead to a different set of human factor challenges that can have serious consequences. Using AVs for greater safety benefits requires developing an understanding of the driver's role and required capabilities to successfully manage the technology and exercise controls. Drivers' vulnerabilities to errors may arise due to a variety of factors like erroneous classification of situation, mode identification errors, automation surprise, and a lack of understanding and skills that are necessary for predicting the development of situations. For example, if the drivers are slow in detecting the problems associated with automation and struggle to recognize the problem, they may fail to attend an unexpected automation transition breakdown. In such a condition, the driver's performance would depend on the level of SA and capability, as well as factors like boredom and fatigue, which are induced when the driver remains out of the loop during the period of automation. These factors are described in the following subsections.

15.2.2.1 Boredom

Vehicle automation has significantly lowered the driver workload and is said to have contributed to increasing the safety in supervisory control settings. However, increased automation may lower the diver's attention toward monitoring and supervising the autonomous driving as he or she might engage in other activities, like a task that is more enjoyable such as listening to music(Merat et al., 2012). Actually, the low cognitive and physical workload may cause boredom in periods of automated driving. Boredom is closely associated with the driver's reduced vigilance. Vigilance is defined as readiness to detect and react to all minor changes happening at arbitrary time periods in the AVs (Mackworth, 1957). Alternatively, boredom is referred to a transient affective state in which one feels that one has nothing to do, or too little to do, or to do something uninteresting, which one would rather not do at that time, or simply does not feel like doing anything in particular yet wishes to be entertained (Fisher, 1987). Thus, it can also be thought as an unkind temporary state reflecting lack of interest in an existing task. In such conditions, the driver may become more vulnerable to low awareness of the automation state and resultant mode confusion. Hence, boredom and fatigue can cause attention and reaction time impairments leaving the driver to be inadequately prepared for handling sudden automation failures and takeover requests. Therefore, more focused research is required for developing a deeper and wider understanding of the various risks associated with long periods of inactivity and boredom.

15.2.2.2 Situational Awareness, Automation Surprise, and Mode Confusion

SA is dynamically built from the information and knowledge about the present state of the AV and the events occurring in the nearby surroundings. It encompasses the relevant parameters of AV and states of the surrounding environment. The concept was originally introduced in the aviation industry to define an important precondition for driving safely. SA is defined as the perception of the elements of the environment within a volume of time and space, the comprehension of their meaning, and the projection of their status in the near future (Endsley, 1988, 1995). A human operator is required to perceive and identify the relevant aspects of the surroundings and understand the situation, which not only serves as the basis for his decision making but also affects the performance of related operations. Therefore, SA is indispensable for developing a full understanding of the situation, which helps in anticipating its further development. When the situation alters dynamically, mental representation of the situation repeatedly interacts with the perceived environment, operator's previous experience, and operator's active exploration. It indicates that a cognitive representation of the present situation and its future development is created by using knowledge stored in the long-term memory (Schömig & Metz, 2013). Hence, it can also be considered as an externally directed consciousness that is helping the driver to adapt readily to the dynamically changing situation. Further, SA can be hypothesized to have various levels of awareness: perceiving relevant information, integrating perceived information, and developing the understanding and predicting the future state. Regarding safe AV driving, the SA is concerned with gathering meaningful knowledge of an unpredictable dynamic situation, which a driver uses to timely respond to and guide the AV. While operating an AV, the driver must be attentive about the various states of the automation processes, functions, surrounding conditions like road conditions, foggy or raining conditions, distance coordination with other vehicles, etc. This vital information assists the driver in driving the vehicle in the safest and best way. For instance, if something unusual has happened in and around an AV, the driver is required to be very attentive to uncover that something is not going well and is expected to immediately switch over the controls from automation to manual mode, so that required action can be taken to avoid any mishap like an accident, collision, etc. A greater SA means more attentiveness of the driver toward AVs, which lowers the risk of unsafe driving, whereas a lower SA leads to higher risk. To illustrate, while driving an AV if the driver engages himself in some other task like listening to music, talking on the mobile phone, looking outside, or some other interesting activities and assumes that the vehicle is fully controlled by the automated system and would be operating safely, he is more likely to miss automation failures and face automation surprise. Basically, automation surprise is a state in which automation does not act as per user's expectations. Carsten and Martens (2019) categorized automation surprises into two categories: "absence of expected actions" and "presence of unexpected actions." In the first category, the system fails to perform a specific action without any apparent safety risk; for example, when the AV is not picking up speed after passing the speed restriction area.

The second category involves situations in which the AV system does not perform according to the operator's expectation and heightens the driver's arousal and stress, for example, increasing the speed when it is required to control the speed for changing the lane or taking a turn. There might be serious consequences if the operator does not have full awareness of the AV's operational envelope in such cases. However, it is impractical to believe that the human driver will continually supervise the automation system; instead, it may be preferred to put some alarm notification system in the AV (Kurpiers et al., 2020). The alarm notifications are usually suggested to be installed with an automated system that notifies/alerts the driver if some problem occurs in the automation process, so that vehicle control may be taken back within a stipulated time.

Inadequate SA and lack of required skills of the driver may give rise to a condition of mode confusion. Mode confusion is a serious safety issue that refers to automation wonder, where the system is not acting as per the defined automation rules. Mode confusion is reported to occur in various domains such as nuclear power plants, aviation, and automotive. In this condition, the driver may not able to understand how the vehicle is actually running. The confusion reflects the driver's assumptions about how the AV should be operating are not true. For example, if a driver is reversing a vehicle without actually looking back with an incorrect assumption that the reverse sensors would alert the driver about any possible risk (Cunningham & Regan, 2015). Mode confusion can also be characterized as a type of automation surprise. In fact, it may embrace the situations in which the operators incorrectly assumed that the vehicle was in an automated mode, although in reality it was not. Insufficient cues to notify the driver about changes in automation mode and the existing state of automation may also lead to mode confusion (Bredereke & Lankenau, 2002). Therefore, it would be beneficial to develop what is referred to as technological fluency by Hancock et al. (2019), which is considered as a combination of common semantic grounds for discourse, an understanding of the automation capabilities, and the critical inquiry skills needed to make sense of the AV's technology. These initiatives can help build the SA to ensure the safety of the driver as well as the AV if any failure condition is not taken care of by the automated system.

15.2.2.3 Automation Overreliance and Skill Degradation

Automation overreliance refers to the state of excessive trust being placed on the automated system. Overreliance occurs when the driver's trust in the automation goes beyond the automation's actual capabilities. Consequently, the driver does not verify the AV's performance or verifies it inadequately. The overreliance usually arises from the belief and false expectation that an automated system will pre-warn about failures and can prevent consequent disasters. This may lead to reduced SA and/or result in degraded skill of the driver. With the overreliance, drivers tend to feel that automation is working safely and the probability of any error is negligible. As a result, the driver may engage himself in other activities (Rudin-Brown & Parker, 2004) rather than monitoring the AV performance during the vehicle movement. In the process, the driver becomes vulnerable to distractions and engages in unsafe behavioral practices. Therefore, overreliance is considered as one of the negative behavioral effects that can be disadvantageous to safe operations. In this regard, it is stated that SA facilitates proper monitoring of the system and helps in developing the ability to timely control AV performance whenever required. Stated simply, whether the driver possesses sufficient knowledge about the present state of the automated system and its functions along with his or her own responsibility, i.e., awareness of how the automation is functioning and knowledge of what he is expected to do in case of failures. Although overreliance is considered undesirable, low trust, on the other hand, may lead to technology being ignored or low usage and negating the related benefits with its use (Parasuraman & Riley, 1997). Hence, it is necessary to build an optimum level of trust in the technology.

The importance of trust is amplified by the fact that these vehicular robots will grow into more complex systems for ensuring their safe function in more difficult future contexts like dense urban routes (Hancock et al., 2019). It will be an important critical human factor challenge to maintain an optimum level of trust in the AV's performance.

Associated with overreliance, skill degradation is another important human factor challenge. Because of long automation periods of driving, drivers may not use or get the chance to use or practice their manual driving skills. The neglect of manual driving skills may deteriorate the psychomotor dexterity and cognitive skills that are necessary to manually execute an activity successfully and safely (Parasuraman et al., 2000). In fact, long automated driving periods may induce the deterioration of reaction time in the drivers and generate passive fatigue (Bourrelly et al., 2019). The diminished skills may further increase operators' reliance on AVs' automated system.

In such circumstances, the possibility of driving skill degradation may become very high, which may in turn adversely affect the SA. Stated simply, overreliance on automation usually results in shrinking the attention resources that are necessary for maintaining required SA and for safe manual driving. When the operator takes back control of the AV, the cognitive load increases suddenly and attention resources might be insufficient for ensuring a safe transition and subsequent driving. In the aviation industry, automation is said to have resulted in a variety of problems like poor decision making, reduced manual-flying skills, and possible erosion of confidence, when automation abruptly starts malfunctioning or disengages during an emergency (Spulber, 2016). Hence, pilots are regularly required to disconnect the automation to facilitate refreshing their knowledge and thwarting skill degradation (Barley, 1990). Moreover, it is highly suggested that drivers must upgrade their skills, both manual driving skills and technological skill, to maintain their SA. So that in the conditions of automation failure the driver possesses the skills to react immediately to smoothly take back the control to avoid the accidents and drive the vehicle with full safety. Apart from long-term effects, automation may also lead to transient degradation of skills. In this regard, it is recommended that training programs need to be carefully designed to play a vital role in reducing the automation impact on skill degradation.

15.2.2.4 Motion Sickness

Motion sickness is one of the important human factors associated with automated driving. However, only a few studies have been done on motion sickness in automated driving. Actually, AV offers greater freedom and flexibility to drivers in the cabin where no manual driving controls are required. As a result, in an automated vehicle, the driver is a passenger (Wada, 2016). The passengers of a vehicle have the propensity of getting motion sickness during vehicle movement. Motion sickness is a condition in which passengers develop the symptoms of light-headedness, vomiting, faintness, and sensation of other physical discomforts. It stems mainly from the conflicting visual and vestibular inputs (Benson, 1999). It has significant consequences like deterioration of the ability to anticipate the movement direction (Golding & Gresty, 2005), dizziness, spatial disorientation, difficulty in controlling the movements, etc.

Motion sickness is therefore an important human factor in highly automated vehicles and can pose a serious challenge. The chance of motion sickness could be high in those AVs that are supposed to be operated at level 3 or higher levels of automated driving. In these AVs, the driver does not necessarily pay attention to the control system or is engaged in monitoring the traffic situation (Wada, 2016). In such cases, the driver becomes a passenger and engages in a rest or using a mobile phone or engages in other non-driving activities like other passengers for a long time. As a result of the lack of controllability and conflicts between sensory inputs, an AV driver becomes susceptible to motion sickness (Iskander et al., 2019). These facts highlight a need for providing a comfortable experience for the passengers to ensure advancement of the AV to its full extent and improving its acceptability.

15.2.2.5 Personalization of Automation

As AVs are still evolving, different manufacturers are developing automated systems in diverse ways by using the latest technologies. Display and automation-function settings need to be made customizable or configurable according to the operator's preference to ensure that drivers can interact with the technology efficiently (Saffarian et al., 2012), which can encourage automation acceptability. Put simply, this issue pertains to determining the extent of standardization or diversification of automated operations and interfaces. The general approach in advanced driver assistance systems is to design the system for the average driver (Hasenjäger and Wersing, 2017). However, this approach is generic in nature and tends to neglect individual differences among drivers. Drivers may differ considerably both in terms of interpersonal differences and intrapersonal differences. Therefore, the concept of cooperative automation may be used to provide selective assistance functions based on direct requests such as speech commands (Biester, 2008). At the same time these automated systems should be consistent in their behavior so as not to cause automation surprise for drivers and road users. The diversity and personalization of automated systems would generate interoperability issues (Burns, 2014). Hence, further research is required regarding the issue of personalization of automation embracing key issues like designing the interface between drivers and personalized AVs for promoting safe driving styles, improving the AV's usability, and acceptability by adapting to individual preferences.

15.2.3 Automation Acceptability

Acceptance of AVs is a vital issue as it will determine the extent of their diffusion into society. Several studies have been conducted for evaluating the role of various aspects associated with automation in affecting their acceptance. Beller et al. (2013) studied the effect of communicating automation uncertainty in the context of driver-automation interaction. They found that the automation system can benefit from presenting relevant information. The system that provides information to operators is viewed as more acceptable and trustworthy than the system that takes over vehicle controls without giving alert or notice (Verberne et al., 2012). If AVs are not perceived as useful and reliable, drivers may not use them and negate all associated benefits (Regan et al., 2014). Weinstock et al. (2012) studied the role of aesthetics by manipulating aesthetic parameters in an imperfect automation system. Their findings concluded that aesthetics do not have much of a role in building trust and improving the acceptability of automation.

Perceived ease of use (Xu et al., 2018) and perceived usefulness (Panagiotopoulos & Dimitrakopoulos, 2018) are also found to have influence AVs' acceptability or acceptance intention in case of autonomous driving. Acceptability can be enhanced in the future by giving more freedom to users and addressing their safety concerns. The AV's capability to handle unanticipated events, legal liability for drivers and owners, and security issues like software vulnerability for hacking are some other issues that are receiving considerable research attention (Cunningham & Regan, 2017). Society and transport infrastructure differ across countries and across regions within a country. Such variations will lead to a varied level of acceptability of any new technology including AV proliferation. Therefore, AVs' compatibility needs to be further studied in different regions (Peng et al., 2020). Acceptability is also said to be influenced by gender and age differences. Compared with elderly people, young people have a more positive attitude toward AVs (Liu et al., 2019). In fact, peoples' attitudes are also one of the most powerful predicting factors of their intention to use AVs. Webb et al. (2019) observed that commuters and young couples have more interest in shared AVs, whereas couples with children are less interested to do so.

Safety is another key factor in the decision to use a particular type of vehicle (Vrkljan & Anaby, 2011). Safety concerns, if not addressed, can be a potential deterrent. Many drivers still remain concerned and do not opt to use the new technology because of apprehension about technology's limitations and sensor degradation. Verberne et al. (2012) have highlighted that trustworthiness serves as a mediator while determining the effect of shared driving goals and automation level on acceptability. Commuters' travel habits and transport needs may also influence acceptance in case of shared AVs. The previous discussion reveals that there are a number of psychological factors including a range of issues like safety concerns, infrastructure availability, costs, and technology that may influence the acceptance of AV technology. In regard to social acceptance, one has to appreciate the role of informal communication in the circumstances for which either formal rules are not available or rules programmed in the software architecture cannot serve the requirements. For instance, drivers of vehicles can handle congestion situations by cooperating with others through non-verbal signals or by talking to each other.

Examples also include cases in which human operators can compensate for each other's errors and save the collision or potential accident. In addition, non-verbal communications like gestures, symbols, glances, facial expressions, etc., also play a vital role in communicating one's intension. These non-verbal cues and their meanings may vary vastly across cultures and countries. As a result, a broad array of glances, actions, or a sequence of actions is used for informal communication among road users, which are manifested in driving behavior (Fäber, 2016). This makes it mandatory for AVs to learn region-specific culture and symbols and have the provision of periodically updating them to improve their usability, as no standard rules can be framed for these non-verbal cues.

From the studies conducted regarding communication efficacy of the external human-machine interface, it is found that communication interface benefits the pedestrians in their interaction with AVs. However, both optimal communication interface specifications and standard procedures for evaluating their usefulness are still lacking (Rouchitsas & Alm, 2019). Rather than providing explicit advice, relevant, unambiguous and intelligible information on a scalable interface is to be provided to support communication with road users (Habibovic et al., 2018; Holländer, 2019). Advanced communication interfaces may be developed for efficiently interacting with the road user that will help in maximizing the safety and efficiency of road users and improve their trust and acceptance of AV technology (Coeugnet et al., 2018; Rouchitsas and Alm, 2019). Future research work should keep these requirements in their ambit.

15.2.4 Automation Misuse and Vulnerabilities

Prolonged use of automation systems can lead to misuse of automation by operators that can lead to monitoring failures and decision biases. Parasuraman and Riley (1997) classified uses of automation into four distinct types: use, misuse, abuse, and disuse. Users and stakeholders might misuse (e.g., overreliance or too much trust), disuse (e.g., low trust or distrust), or abuse it. Abusing automation includes instances of introducing automation without considering its consequences. Users do not follow critical assumptions and bank on the automation inappropriately (Spulber, 2016) in case of the automation's misuse. Thus, misusing involves placing too much trust on automation and, while misusing, operators may engage in other tasks. Consequently, overreliance in automation capabilities might lead to misuse through inappropriate application of automation and compromise safety. For instance, the operator uses the automation mode to a roadway area which lies outside the AV's operational envelope (Trimble et al., 2014). This highlights the need of training and education of drivers and users for developing the automation capabilities and limitations.

In this regard, driver state assessment (DSA) technology can also be used to monitor driver's alertness on a real-time basis and improve the safety performance by inducing desired behavior. Driver performance can be monitored by using either direct or indirect methods. Mueller et al. (2021) recommended for using a combination of indirect and direct methods for attaining highest accuracy and reliability of detecting driver disengagement. Indirect methods using parameters like lane departure frequency, steering wheel input, ignition cycle duration since the start, and driver's response time to respond to attention reminders can be used according to some predetermined criteria, whereas eye gaze and eyelid closure, head orientation, etc., are monitored through direct methods. DSA can monitor operators' alertness and attention level to reorient their attention in case they become distracted or inattentive (Rauch et al., 2009).

With more sophisticated and reliable automation, it will be increasingly difficult for drivers to maintain the necessary vigilance (Carsten & Martens, 2019). In view of the safety risks associated with driving automation, it is essential to monitor the operator-vehicle interface and provide detailed information about automation limitation as AVs can come across difficult road conditions that may surpass their operational boundaries. However, future research work is required to evaluate the effectiveness of technological interventions for realizing AVs' potential safety benefits. Preventing AVs' misuse is therefore a major human-factor challenge for users, industry, and public authorities.

Increasing digitalization of technical systems would lead to emergence of vulnerability to intentional disruptions and external cyberattacks. These systemic risks from the digital world are well known and can have serious consequences. The AV control systems architecture may be hacked by extremists and psychopaths or may be infiltrated during cyber warfare by exploiting vulnerabilities present in various entry points of AV technologies such as databases, remote communication technologies, and control software. In fact, two researchers, Charlie Miller and Chris Valasek, remotely gained control of a Chrysler Jeep Cherokee that was running at high speed and made it stop. When automation and communication technologies will be commonly used in vehicles, interest in discovering vulnerabilities might probably increase due to financial motivation (Parkinson et al., 2017). Cyberattacks on the sensing and communication layers of automation control can adversely affect the functionality and impair the security leading to various risks (El-Rewini et al., 2020). For example, these risks may include unauthorized manipulation, installation of malware, and remotely controlling various safety-related functions like brakes, steering, engine ignition, and power transmission, which might result in unpredictable attack scenarios and other serious safety risks. In such situations, the divers will find it difficult to comprehend the AV's behavior and understand the unusual situation. However, protective measures are technically feasible and need researchers' in-depth attention in future studies.

15.3 CONCLUSION AND FUTURE RESEARCH AGENDA

This chapter highlights the fact that careful consideration of human factors would be helpful in maximizing the social benefits of vehicle automation. An inadequate consideration of these factors may not yield desired results. As algorithmic oversight may fail to notice unusual events lying outside the AV's software architecture, the role of human operator would be difficult to eliminate, at least at the current stage. The role and responsibilities of the human and the AV are witnessing an important and crucial evolution (Spulber, 2016). However, this work finds that a consensus is yet to be formed regarding the nature of human-automation interaction. Therefore, future research efforts are required to first define the role of human operators according to the level of automation in AVs, i.e., capabilities of automation. It calls for defining the role of human operator such as actively supervising, intermittently sharing driving responsibility, or an observant passenger. As AVs may be capable of higher-order decision making at higher levels of automation, it is necessary to inform the driver about its capability at each level. Human factor challenges related to vehicle automation level 2 and 3 were studied under an NHTSA-funded project by using prototypes on a test track (Blanco et al., 2015). The main challenges that were uncovered were how to communicate takeover requests to drivers and how to reorient their attention from distractions. However, these studies, although focusing on important aspects, do not address the overall design objectives of fighting the distraction. These are important design aspects that may impact smooth transition of the AV's control and inadequate consideration may create difficulties. For instance, alert timing is an important factor and the alert needs to be properly timed to provide adequate time to drivers to successfully respond and reengage themselves. If an alert timing is too early, it may be perceived as a false alarm and is very likely to be ignored by the driver. In this regard, Fitch (2015) in his commercial report containing reviews of current concepts and designs and views of various system developers and researchers brought out the significance of human-automated machine interactions in safe operation of AVs and highlighted it as a unique feature for differentiating various brands.

Hence, AV researchers need to adopt a careful human-interaction design approach for encouraging an operator and a user-centered perspective. Future studies may take up the issue of communicating this intention as well. Dense urban traffic scenarios would involve significant "automation-road users' interaction" and therefore road users are also required to have an interpretation of the situation, which is consistent with AVs and AV operators. If road users interpret differently or develop an awareness that is not consistent with automation working, AV and road user interactions are most likely to breakdown. In fact, misinterpretation is said to have a significant role in pedestrian incidents and accidents (Habibovic & Davidsson, 2012).

Some of the main concerns revealed from the review of the existing literature are driving skill degradation, poor decision-making skills, and confidence erosion when automation suddenly fails. The important psychological factors that affect operator performance are boredom and fatigue and overreliance on automated system. Preventing misuse of AVs is also another vital challenge that is yet to be addressed. In the context of AV accidents, responsibility attribution between automation and human operator will be another significant challenge. This is another complex human-automation interaction aspect that also embraces several legal and technical issues. More research attention is needed in ascertaining how to use design aspects, education and training, and licensing procedures as a remedial measure for preventing adverse effects of these factors.

Design factors should also consider suitably modifying the driving environment making it capable of supporting operators in terms of providing adequate communication and reorient the attention from distraction to keep the operator in the loop. In addition, it should provide a common semantic ground for dialogue, facilitating technological know-how and making sense of automation systems (Hancock et al., 2019). This is essentially required for building an understanding about AVs among manufacturers, operators, users, legislators, regulatory bodies, and the public, which is necessary for developing not only expertise but also building optimum trust. It is suggested that various stakeholders, like manufacturers, design experts, researchers, and public authorities, should view AV automation as a cooperative effort between humans and technology. In this cooperative interaction context, human operators may be assigned an important and active role to optimize the human-technology interaction and extend the availability of automated driving. In fact, most of the earlier findings emphasized the need for keeping the driver in the loop, except in case of fully automated vehicles (Merat et al., 2009a,b; Nees, 2015; Spulber, 2016). Based on the earlier research findings, the following suggestions are made for improving human-automation interaction and AV performance:

- Establish the nature of shared responsibility among human-automation interaction in various levels of automation.

- Organize information around the operator's responsibility structure.

- Provide assistance through timely alerts or notification for improving the understanding of driving situation.

- Supporting development of awareness of the whole environment to enable the operator to correctly project the situation development.

- Combine visual, auditory, and tactile information for activating operators' cognitive schemas for improving operators' response time and reorient their attention.

- Make AVs capable of learning and updating non-verbal cues.

- Use a training program to improve understanding of automation capabilities and limitations.

- Design training and develop design adaptations to prevent skill degradation, boredom, and low SA.

- Improve software security to prevent data misuse and reduce the possibility of system hacking.

Regarding successful performance and desired level of acceptance, training can definitely play a very vital role. The training should contain specific modules for differing levels of automation and counteract the long-term impacts of automation on skill degradation. The training will have a key role in making AVs a safe and acceptable alternative and addressing human factor challenges from an end-user's perspective. The issue of trust is going to be further magnified in future context as AVs are going to be more and more complex.

As seen in the other fields, aircraft crews receive rigorous training for each specific aircraft type, although various types may be clustered for the purpose of a "type rating" because of their underlying similarity within a manufacturer (EASA, 2017). Similarly, locomotive drivers also undergo intensive training to acquire the skill for running different types of locomotives, such as electric or diesel-electric locomotives, and to develop an understanding of various operational aspects in railways. Their skill and knowledge are refreshed through periodic specific refresher training and counseling. In case of automated train operations, Karvonen et al. (2011) found that drivers observe, interpret, anticipate, and respond to events in the surrounding environment and serve as an important link. Their role cannot be ignored while migrating to a fully automated metro system as it can adversely affect the service quality and operation safety. Similarly, the gradual deployment of automation will necessitate a progressive or periodic and continuous training, rather than one-off and initial training (Spulber, 2016). This will have implications for the licensing requirement of AV operators. Although it seems strange, it cannot be assumed that the drivers operating new AVs will always be engaged, informed, and ready to respond to take the appropriate decisions. As a result, when automation systems needs an operator's intervention, he or she may either fail to act or may actually make the matter worse by inadequate responses. In this context, the role of training has become more important and significant. Actually, training can be effectively used to make a driver aware of the essential capabilities and limitations of automated systems and realize that they may not be perfectly reliable in all circumstances (Rudin-Brown & Parker, 2004; Endsley, 2017). Problems associated with boredom, fatigue, low SA, and difficulty in maintaining skill levels should also be made a part of the training program and drivers need to be informed about these problems and adverse behavioral adaptation effects.

As the automated devices are not still completely safe and reliable, the driver is required to take control and resume vehicle driving in case of automation failure. Following this stand, humans and automated vehicles are required to monitor each other and mutually communicate their intents as co-pilots (Spulber, 2016). In fact, some researchers suggest that the more AV technology advances, the better feedback system needs to be provided to make them observable to the operators. It would have a favorable effect on the SA, trust, and reliance (Verberne et al., 2012; Beller et al.,2013; Spulber, 2016). Haptic feedback is found to be the most effective method to keep the driver informed (Spiessl, 2011). The automation-human interaction design aspect should give due consideration to the loss of SA as factors like information overload, attentional tunneling, misplaced salience, complexity creep, requisite memory trap (e.g., overload of working memory), errant mental models, and other stressors like sudden workload, fatigue, anxiety, etc., affect driving performance (Endsley et al., 2003). However, it is also to be decided how much unfolding conflicts should be communicated to drivers that may crop up concurrently or occur at very short intervals as it may confuse the operator and affect his or her reaction time very adversely (Fitch et al., 2014). Personalization of automation is an essential key area of research in automation where a person may be allowed to customize automation settings to increase or decrease automation levels. In fact, many automobile companies are developing automated systems that offer greater diversity and customization in automation settings as per driver preference. In this way, drivers may set or adjust their own preferred automation level for driving the vehicle; this will increase people's acceptance toward automation. Schoettle and Sivak (2014) conducted a public opinion survey, which provided valuable but worrisome insights. Their findings indicate safety consequences such as vehicles getting confused by the sudden occurrence of unexpected events, software vulnerability, and legal liability for drivers and owners are the factors that have received substantial attention and might adversely affect public trust and acceptance of AV technology.

With the fast-paced technological changes, the gap between stakeholders' expectations about AVs and what is put in service is continually increasing which, in turn, is further aggravating the criticality of the problem (Hancock et al., 2019). Accordingly, human-automation interaction is still evolving, therefore, the role of human operators is yet not well defined. The ambiguity needs to be addressed urgently to minimize the risks posed by lack of clarity and to effectively devise training programs and create design interventions for increasing trust and acceptability. A large number of issues like safety concerns, infrastructure availability, costs, software vulnerability, and a host of psychological factors are found to be vital in determining the acceptability and successful utilization of AVs. The important psychological factors requiring consideration are boredom and inattention, low SA, mode confusion, skill degradations, and overreliance on the technology. Learning from other fields, it is inferred that training needs to be carefully designed to make operators understand AV capabilities and limitations and loss of skills to build the trust and prevent overreliance. It might become necessary to refresh the knowledge, although it might have cost consequences. Along with the changes in the training, driver licensing will also undergo changes following the deployment of automation. Future researchers should devote their effort for improving our understanding of AV safety and security issues, potential automation misuses and surprises, and devising countermeasures to reduce driver distraction and overreliance. This chapter has identified a number of human factor challenges and made suggestions for future research studies. All stakeholders, such as manufacturers, researchers, policy makers, financers, and regulatory bodies, have to come together to address the wide spectrum of problems by taking human factor challenges and the user's point of view into consideration. The technological fluency and research involving these factors can facilitate the joint effort toward the development of human-automation interaction design, training and education, and addressing other concerns. Research efforts with a holistic perspective with due consideration of human factor challenges can immensely help in ensuring a safe and successful adoption and penetration of AVs into society.

REFERENCES

Barley, S. 1990. The Final Call: Air Disasters… When Will They Ever Learn? Sinclair-Stevenson, London.

Beller, J., Heesen, M. & Vollrath, M. 2013. "Improving the driver–automation interaction: An approach using automation uncertainty." *Human Factors*, Vol. 55, No. 6, pp. 1130–1141.

Biester, L. 2008. "Cooperative automation in automobiles," PhD dissertation, Humboldt-Universitat zu Berlin.

Blanco, M., Atwood, J., Vasquez, H. M., Trimble, T. E., Fitchett, V. L., Radlbeck, J, Fitch, G. M., Russell, S. M., Green, C. A., Cullinane, B. & Morgan, J. F. 2015. Human factors evaluation of level 2 and level 3 automated driving concepts. Report No DOT HS 812 182. National Highway Traffic Safety Administration, Washington, DC.

Bourrelly, A., Jacobé de Naurois, C., Zran, A., Rampillon, F., Vercher, J., et al. 2019. "Long automated driving phase affects take-over performance." *Intelligent Transport Systems*, Vol. 13, No. 8, pp. 1249–1255.

Bredereke, J. & Lankenau, A. 2002. A Rigorous View of Mode Confusion. Computer Safety, Reliability and Security: SAFECOMP 2002, Volume 2434 of Lecture Notes in Computer Science, Springer-Verlag, London, pp. 19–31.

Bruneau, M., Chang, S. E., Eguchi, R. T., Lee, G. C., O'Rourke, T. D., Reinhorn, A. M., Shinozuka, M., Tierney K., Wallace, W. A. & von Winterfeldt, D. 2003. "A framework to quantitatively assess and enhance the seismic resilience of communities." *Earthquake Spectra*, Vol. 19, No. 4, pp. 733–752.

Bucsky, P. 2018. "Autonomous vehicles and freight traffic: Towards better efficiency of road, rail or urban logistics?" *Urban Development Issues*, Vol. 58, pp. 41–51. doi:10.2478/udi-2018-0022.

Burns, P. 2014. "Safety and human factors challenges for emerging vehicle technologies." Presented at the 2014 International Conference on Urban Traffic Safety, Alberta, Canada.

Carsten, O. & Martens, M. H. 2019. "How can humans understand their automated cars? HMI principles, problems and solutions." *Cognition, Technology & Work*, Vol. 21, pp. 3–20. https://doi.org/10.1007/s10111-018-0484-0.

Coeugnet, S., Cahour, B. & Kraïem, S. 2018. "A psycho-ergonomic approach of the street-crossing decision-making: Toward pedestrians' interactions with automated vehicles," in Proceedings of the 20th Congress of the International Ergonomics Association, Springer, Cham, pp. 132–141. doi:10.1007/978-3-319-96074-6_14.

Cunningham M. & Regan M. A. 2015. "Autonomous vehicles: human factors issues and future research," in Proceedings of Australasian Road Safety Conference, Gold Coast, Australia.

Cunningham, M. L. & Regan, M. A. 2017. "Driver distraction and inattention in the realm of automated driving." *IET Intelligent Transport Systems*, Vol. 12, No. 6, pp. 407–413.

Desmond, P. A. & Hancock, P. A. 2001. Active and Passive Fatigue States. In: P. A. Hancock & P. A. Desmond (Eds.), Stress, Workload, and Fatigue. Lawrence Erlbaum, Mahwah, NJ, pp. 455–465.

EASA. 2017. "Type rating & license endorsement list—all aircraft, excluding helicopters." European Aviation Safety Agency, Cologne, Germany.

El-Rewini, Z., Plathottam, S. J., Sadatsharan, K., Ranganathan, P. & Selvaraj, D. F. 2020. "Cybersecurity challenges in vehicular communications." *Vehicular Communication*, Vol. 20. https://doi.org/10.1016/j.vehcom.2019.100214.

Endsley, M. R. 1988. "Situation awareness global assessment technique (SAGAT)". in Proceedings of the National Aerospace and Electronics Conference (NAECON). IEEE, New York, pp. 789–795.

Endsley, M. R. 1995. "Towards a theory of Situational Awareness in Dynamic Systems." *Human Factors*" Vol. 37, No 1, pp. 32–64

Endsley, M. R. 2017. "Autonomous driving systems: a preliminary naturalistic study of the Tesla model." *Journal of Cognitive Engineering and Decision Making*, 11, pp. 1–14.

Endsley, M. R., Bolstad, C. A., Jones, D. G., Riley, J. M. 2003. "Situation awareness oriented design: from user's cognitive requirements to creating effective supporting technologies". in Proceedings of the 47th Annual Meeting of the Human Factors and Ergonomics Society, HFES, Santa Monica, CA.

Faisal, A. I. M., Yigitcanlar, T., Kamruzzaman, M. & Currie, G. 2019. "Understanding autonomous vehicles: A systematic literature review on capability, impact, planning and policy." *Journal of Transport and Land Use*, Vol. 12. https://doi.org/10.5198/jtlu.2019.1405.

Färber, B. 2016. Communication and Communication Problems between Autonomous Vehicles and Human Drivers. In: M. Maurer, J. Gerdes, B. Lenz & H. Winner (Eds.), Autonomous Driving. Springer, Berlin, Heidelberg, pp. 125–144.

Fisher, C. D. 1987. Boredom: Construct, causes, and consequences. *Technical Report ONR-9*, Texas A & M University, College Station, TX.

Fitch, G. 2015. The HMI for the Automated Vehicle: Enabling Safe Interaction with Automated Vehicles. TU Automotive, London.

Fitch, G., Bowman, D. & Llaneras, R. 2014. "Distracted driver performance to multiple alerts in a multiple-conflict scenario." *Human Factors*, Vol. 56, No. 8, pp. 1497–1505.

Flemisch, F., Altendorf, E. Canpolat, Y., Weßel, G., Baltzer, M., Lopez, D., Herzberger, N. D., Irmgard, V., Gudrun, M., Schwalm, M. & Schutte, P. 2017. Uncanny and Unsafe Valley of Assistance and Automation: First Sketch and Application to Vehicle Automation.

In: C. M. Schlick, S. Duckwitz, F. Flemisch, M. Frenz, S. Kuz, A. Mertens & S. Mütze-Niewöhner (Eds.), Advances in Ergonomic Design of Systems, Products and Processes, Springer, Berlin, Heidelberg, pp. 319–334.

Flemisch, F. O., Bengler, K., Bubb, H., Winner, H. & Bruder, R. 2014. "Towards cooperative guidance and control of highly automated vehicles: H-Mode and Conduct-by-Wire." *Ergonomics*, Vol. 57, No. 1, pp. 343–360.

Golding, J. F. & Gresty, M. A. 2005. "Motion sickness." *Current Opinion in Neurology*, Vol. 18, pp. 29–34.

Habibovic, A. & Davidsson, J. 2012. "Causation mechanisms in car-to-vulnerable road user crashes: Implications for active safety systems." *Accident; Analysis and Prevention*, Vol. 49, pp. 493–500.

Habibovic, A., Andersson, J., Lundgren, V. M., Klingegård, M., Englund, C. & Larsson, S. 2018. "External vehicle interfaces for communication with other road users?," in Proceeding of the Automated Vehicles Symposium 2018, Springer, Cham, pp. 91–102. doi:10.1007/978-3-319-94896-6_9.

Hancock, P. A., Nourbakhsh, I. & Stewart, J. 2019. "In the future of transportation in an era of automated and autonomous vehicles." *PNAS*, Vol. 116, No. 16, pp. 7684–7691.

Hasenjäger, M. & Wersing, H. 2017. "Personalization in advanced driver assistance systems and autonomous vehicles: A review," in 2017 IEEE 20th International Conference on Intelligent Transportation Systems (ITSC), Yokohama, Japan. doi:10.1109/ITSC.2017.8317803.

Hoffman, R. R. & Hancock, P. A. 2017. "Measuring resilience." *Human Factors*, Vol. 59, pp. 564–581.

Holländer, K. 2019. "A pedestrian perspective on autonomous vehicles," in Proceedings of the 24th International Conference on Intelligent User Interfaces: Companion, ACM, New York, pp. 149–150.

Iskander, J., Attia, M., Saleh, K., Nahavandi, D., Abobakr, A., Mohamed, S., Asadi, H., Khosravi, A., Peng Lim, C. & Hossny, M. 2019. "From car sickness to autonomous car sickness: A review." *Psychology and Behaviour*, Vol. 62, pp. 716–726.

Karvonen, H., Aaltonen, I., Wahlström, M. & Salo, L. 2011. "Hidden roles of the train driver: A challenge for metro automation." *Interacting with Computers*, Vol. 23, No. 4, pp. 289–298.

Kurpiers, C., Biebl, B., Hernandez, J. M. & Raisch, F. 2020. "Mode awareness and automated driving—what is it and how can it be measured?" *Information*, Vol. 11, No. 5, p. 277.

Liu, P., Zhang, Y. & He, Z. 2019. "The effect of population age on the acceptable safety of self-driving vehicles." *Reliability Engineering & System Safety*, Vol. 185, pp. 341–347.

Mackworth, N. H. 1957. "Some factors affecting vigilance." *Advancement of Science*, Vol. 53, pp. 389–393.

Merat, N. & Jamson, A. H. 2009a. "How do drivers behave in a highly automated car?," in Proceedings of the Fifth International Driving Symposium on Human Factors in Driver Assessment, Training, and Vehicle Design. Big Sky, MT, pp. 514–521.

Merat, N. & Jamson, A. H. 2009b. "Is Drivers' situation awareness influenced by a fully automated driving scenario?, in "Human Factors, Security and Safety"." Human Factors and Ergonomics Society Europe Chapter Conference, Shaker Publishing, Soesterberg, the Netherlands. ISBN 978-90-423-0373-7.

Merat, N., Jamson, A. H., Lai, F. & Carsten, O. 2012. "Highly automated driving, secondary task performance and driver state." *Human Factors*, Vol. 54, pp. 762–771.

Mueller, A. S., Reagan, I. J. & Cicchino, J. B. 2021. "Addressing driver disengagement and system misuse: Human factors recommendations for Level 2 driving automation design." *Journal of Cognitive Engineering and Decision Making*, Vol. 15, No. 1, pp: 3–27.

National Highway Traffic Safety Administration (NHTSA). 2013. Preliminary Statement of Policy Concerning Automated Vehicles. NHTSA, Washington, DC.

Nees, M. 2015. "Sorry to Disappoint, but Driverless Cars Will Still Need Drivers." *Newsweek*, May, 10.

NSAI Standards. 2009. IEC 62267:2009. Railway applications – Automated urban guided transport (AUGT) – Safety requirements. https://infostore.saiglobal.com/preview/98696766638. pdf?sku=874084_SAIG_NSAI_NSAI_2078162.

Orlady, H. W. & Barnes, R. B. 1997. A methodology for evaluating the operational suitability of air transport flight deck system enhancements. SAE Technical Paper No. 975642. Society of Automotive Engineers, Warrendale, PA.

Panagiotopoulos, I. & Dimitrakopoulos, G. 2018. "An empirical investigation on consumers' intentions towards autonomous driving." *Transportation Research Part C: Emerging Technologies*, Vol. 95, pp. 773–784.

Parasuraman, R. & Riley, V. 1997. "Humans and automation: use, misuse, disuse, abuse." *Human Factors*, Vol. 39, No. 2, pp. 230–253.

Parasuraman, R., Sheridan, T. B. & Wickens, C. D. 2000. "A model of types and levels of human interaction with automation." *IEEE Transactions on Systems, Man, and Cybernetics – Part A: Systems and Humans*, Vol. 30, No. 3, pp. 286–297.

Parkinson, S., Ward, P., Wilson, K. & Miller, J. 2017. "Cyber threats facing autonomous and connected vehicles: future challenges." *IEEE Transactions on Intelligent Transportation Systems*, Vol. 18, No. 11, pp. 2898–2915. doi: 10.1109/TITS.2017.2665968

Peng, J., Gang, X., Yuexia, C., Yuji, S. & Fengping, Z. 2020. "The determinants behind the acceptance of autonomous vehicles: a systematic review." *Sustainability*, Vol. 12, p. 1719. doi:10.3390/su12051719.

Powell, J., Fraszczyk, A., Cheong, C. & Yeung, H. 2016. "Potential benefits and obstacles of implementing driverless train operation on the Tyne and Wear metro: a simulation exercise." *Urban Rail Transit*. Vol. 2, No. 3–4, pp. 114–127. doi:10.1007/s40864-016-0046.

Rauch, N., Kaussner, A., Krüger, H. P., Boverie, S. & Flemisch, F. 2009. "The importance of driver state assessment within highly automated vehicles," in Conference Proceedings of the 16th World Congress on ITS, Stockholm, Sweden.

Regan, M., Horberry, T. & Stevens, A. 2014. Driver Acceptance of New Technology: Theory, *Measurement and Optimisation*. CRC Press, Boca Raton, FL.

Riley, J. M. & Endsley, M. R. 2005. "Situation awareness in HRI with collaborating remotely piloted vehicles." Proceedings of the Human Factors and Ergonomics Society Annual Meeting, Vol. 49, pp. 407–411.

Rouchitsas, A. & Alm, H. 2019. "External human–machine interfaces for autonomous vehicle-to-pedestrian communication: a review of empirical work." *Frontiers in Psychology*, Vol. 10. doi:10.3389/fpsyg.2019.02757.

Ruault, J., Frédéric, V. & Dominique, L. 2012. "Sociotechnical systems resilience." *INCOSE International Symposium*, Vol. 22, No. 1, pp. 339–354. doi: 10.1002/j.2334-5837.2012.tb01341.x.

Rudin-Brown, C. & Parker, H. 2004. "Behavioural adaptation to adaptive cruise control (ACC): implications for preventive strategies." *Transportation Research Part F: Traffic Psychology and Behaviour*, Vol. 7, No. 2, pp. 59–76.

Saffarian, M., de Winter, J. & Happee, R. 2012. "Automated driving: human-factors issues and design solutions." *Proceedings of the Human Factors and Ergonomics Society Annual Meeting*, Vol. 56, No. 1, pp. 2296–2300.

Schoettle, B. & Sivak, M. 2014. A survey of public opinion about autonomous and self driving vehicles in the US, the UK, and Australia. Report No. UMTRI-2014-21. University of Michigan, Transportation Research Institute, Ann Arbor, MI.

Schömig, N. & Metz, B. 2013. "Three levels of situation awareness in driving with secondary tasks." *Safety Science*, Vol. 56, No. 2013, pp. 44–51.

Sharma, S. K., Poddar, S., Dwivedy, G. K., Panja, S. C. & Patra, S. N. 2021. Risk Reduction and Resilience Buildup in Railroad Transport. In: I. Pal, R. Shaw, R. Djalante & S. Shrestha (Eds.), Disaster Resilience and Sustainability. Springer, Amsterdam, Netherlands, pp: 509–562.

Spiessl, W. 2011. "Assessment and Support of Error Recognition in Automated Driving," thesis presented at the Ludwig-Maximilians-Universität München.

Spulber, A. 2016. Impact of automated vehicle technologies on driver skills. MDOT REQ. Report No. 1259, Connected and Automated Vehicle Industry Coordination Task C.2. Michigan Department of Transportation, Lansing MI.

Trimble, T. E., Bishop, R., Morgan, J. F. & Blanco, M., 2014. Human factors evaluation of level 2 and level 3 automated driving concepts: Past research, state of automation technology, and emerging system concepts. Report No. DOT HS 812 043. National Highway Traffic Safety Administration, Washington, DC.

Union Internationale des Transports Publics (UITP). 2018. Statistics brief. World report on metro automation. https://cms.uitp.org/wp/wp-content/uploads/2020/06/Statistics-Brief-Metro-automation_final_web03.pdf.

Varaiya, P. 1993. "Smart cars on smart roads: problems of control." *IEEE Transactions on Automatic Control*, Vol. 38, No. 2, pp. 195–207.

Verberne, F. M. F., Ham, J. & Midden, C. J. H. 2012. "Trust in smart systems: Sharing driving goals and giving information to increase trustworthiness and acceptability of smart systems in cars." *The Journal of the Human Factors and Ergonomics Society*, Vol. 54, No. 5, pp. 799–810.

Vrkljan, B. H. & Anaby, D. 2011. "What vehicle features are considered important when buying an automobile? An examination of driver preferences by age and gender." *Journal of Safety Research*, Vol. 42, pp. 61–65.

Wachenfeld, W., Winner, H., Chris Gerdes, J., Lenz, B., Maurer, M., Beiker, S., Fraedrich, E. & Winkle, T. 2016. Use Cases for Autonomous Driving. In: M. Maurer, J. Gerdes, B. Lenz & H. Winner (Eds.), Autonomous Driving. Springer, Berlin, Heidelberg, pp. 9–40.

Wada, T. 2016. Motion Sickness in Automated Vehicles. In: J. Edelmann, M. Plochl & P. E. Pfeffer (Eds.), Advanced Vehicle Control AVEC'16. CRC Press, London.

Webb, J., Wilson, C. & Kularatne, T. 2019. "Will people accept shared autonomous electric vehicles? A survey before and after receipt of the costs and benefits." *Economic Analysis and Policy*, Vol. 61, pp. 118–135.

Weinstock, A., Oron-Gilad, T. & Parmet, Y. 2012. "The effect of system aesthetics on trust, cooperation, satisfaction and annoyance in an imperfect automated system." *Work*, Vol. 41. pp. 258–265. doi: 10.3233/WOR-2012-0166-258.

Xu, Z., Zhang, K., Min, H., Wang, Z., Zhao, X. & Liu, P. 2018. "What drives people to accept automated vehicles? Findings from a field experiment." *Transportation Research Part C: Emerging Technologies*, Vol. 95, pp. 320–334.

Young, M. S. & Stanton, N. A. 1997. "Automotive automation: investigating the impact on drivers' mental workload." *International Journal of Cognitive Ergonomics*, Vol. 1, No. 4, pp. 325–336.

CHAPTER 16

Legal Issues Surrounding Cyber Security and Privacy on Automated Vehicle

Rakesh Kumar Chopra and Abhijeet Srivastava
University of Petroleum and Energy Studies
Dehradun, India

CONTENTS

DOI: 10.1201/9781003048381-18

In 1997, Sam Petroda, Chairman of International Telecom Union, said "I would like to talk on television and see on telephone." This became reality the world over when the telecom network in India was demonized and liberalized. Taking a step further in the technological revolution, there was also a move toward the automated vehicle. However, the idea of an automated vehicle was first envisaged by Norman Bel Geddes in 1939, when he said that there will be a time when cars would drive themselves. Many scholars believed that this was just a myth as no one expected that it would become a reality. Although it looks alluring, we must ask ourselves whether the world is ready for a driverless future. India is no different from the rest of the world in that it is also moving toward an advanced technological advancement and facing similar challenges

Therefore, it needs to be ensured that the system of automated vehicles suits the need of the society as every technology should have some control and protection by state for its effective implementation. Moreover, from a cyber security prospective, it cannot be disputed that such driverless cars operating through an interconnected central system are free from hacking, and there is a high probability that instead it will encourage hackers. The Federal Bureau of Investigation (FBI) in its recent reports has also predicted that hackers may use the automated technology either for overriding traffic speed limits or may use self-driving cars to turn these cars into driverless explosive cars; i.e., it may even become a challenge for national security. It is also likely that such unauthorized persons/entities may invade the privacy of the occupant by illegally obtaining a user's travel route history and personal details or instigate an attack on the user's system. Moreover, in such cases, it is the duty of the state to ensure that the data obtained by the telecom, insurance, or other entities are duly protected.

If we examine the Indian scenario there is no specific legislation nor rules and regulations to regulate these issues. Therefore, to proceed further on this topic, it is necessary to remember the quote of Mr. Obama: "If innovators want to gain public confidence on this technology so it's time for the legislators to strengthen cyber security laws for the protection of the personal information of the autonomous vehicle." For this statement to succeed, it must call on the car manufacturers to create a security consortium to share the information regarding potential cyber security threats.

In this chapter, an attempt is made to provide food for thought to the policy framers for developing an adequate framework to avoid the abuse of personal data of the users of automated vehicles. Because the author(s) come from a techno-legal prospective, they shall discuss subjects in a simplified manner so readers can understand the concepts and take them up further. Here author(s) shall embrace the idea for strengthening cyber security laws for this technology and then analyze the existing framework under Indian laws. The subject will be incomplete without having a glimpse of global legal scenarios on this subject (mainly in the United States) and its analysis in an Indian context. The shortcomings and challenges based on analysis shall be depicted as well as their how they should be implemented. Finally, there shall be suggestions about the way forward for future research.

16.1 INTRODUCTION

The world has witnessed an expeditious revolution in the automobile industry in the last few years. With the rapid advancement in autonomous technology integrated with artificial intelligence, this sector has successfully introduced advanced driver-assistance systems (ADASs) and autonomous vehicle (AV) technology, which was once considered a myth. AVs, which are widely known as self-driving car(s), are able to operate, navigate, and function without the constant need of human intervention.[1] There is no doubt that this technology is on the brink of its revolution, and it has come a long way since the creation of assembly line by Henry Ford in 1913.[2] Manufacturers like Toyota, Tesla, and Uber have successfully been able to introduce this driverless project to the complex city streets.[3]

The benefits of this technology are widely recognized, but there are several concerns regarding its hazardous risks and unintended consequences. One such concern are cyber security threats and privacy invasions. Many research reports suggest that the highly interconnected navigation system of an AV vehicle will encourage hackers to gain control over the entire network of the system.[4] The July 2015 hacking incident of a Jeep Cherokee has brought attention to vehicular cyber security threats.[5] It is noteworthy that this hacking was done on a semi-autonomous vehicle, thus we can easily anticipate that as more vehicles get connected the risk will only become amplified.

To date, several countries have started formulating policies for regulating AVs. Still, addressing key areas such as collection, use, and security of consumer data remains a challenge. This chapter will lay a foundation to analyze how this fast-paced technology will create new challenges for the legislators in setting new standards and regulations for the safe development and usage of AVs.

16.2 EMBRACING THE NEED TO STRENGTHEN CYBER SECURITY AND PRIVACY LAWS

Today, it is becoming increasingly difficult to open any news website without reading about cyber threats, privacy invasions, and third-party data access alerts. It is an undeniable fact that the scope and expense of addressing cyber security and privacy issues are increasing everyday with notable privacy invasions of almost every sector including both government and private. The automobile industry is no exception; however, before proceeding further, it is important to understand the difference between cyber security and privacy invasion. For example, a cyber security breach is said to be committed when a vehicle's operating system is hacked, and the hacker assumes total control over vehicle. The hacker may cause serious injury to an individual sitting inside the car. On the other hand, in the case of a privacy invasion, a driver's individual data could be transmitted to the unauthorized third party or privacy is breached, possibly resulting in the third party potentially tracking (drivers) consumers' whereabouts. The hacker could anticipate the driver's movement, which could impact the driver's reputation and loss of liberty.

A research report of white-hat hackers suggests that the connected cars will increase the chances of vulnerabilities that presently exist.[6] In one such experiment, the National Highway Traffic Safety Administration (NHTSA) bought an unaltered vehicle directly from the dealer in year 2014 and endeavored to hack its navigation system. The result of this experiments were published in 2015 revealing that at a mild speed of around 5–10 mph hackers could slightly take control over the entire system including steering, breaks, speed, locks, signals, radio, and Global Positioning System (GPS).[7] Consequently, after analyzing these results, the NHTSA determined that this technology will create an unreasonable risk to the security system of the vehicle because it provides access to a critical vehicle control system, which will lead to potential risks. The likelihood of exploitation of this technology could be foreseen due to the advent of the Internet and cellular access embedded into diagnostic ports, as hackers perceive it as a softer target compared with the vehicle itself. It is pertinent to note that any device that communicates from anywhere in the domain would give hackers another avenue to instill malware into the vehicle's network.[8]

We can witness the outcomes of this report in the case of *Cahen v. Toyota Motor Corp.*,[9] which came to light in 2015. A class action suit was filed against Ford and Toyota, contending that the network system of the AV was susceptible to being hacked by third parties, which puts customers' privacy rights at risk. It is noteworthy that these claims were completely based on the risk of cyber security threats and data breaches rather than physical safety risks. The plaintiff, Controller Area Network Bus (CAN Bus), claimed that this technology would expose all users to a privacy risk and cyber threats by allowing hackers to gain control over the internal electronic control unit (ECU) connections of the vehicle.[10] The court said that these situations are hypothetical and at present there is no such causality on the record. The plaintiff argued that[9] it is not prudent to wait for a hacker to prove that this defect could be dangerous. Honda was directed to bring back its cars to repair its deadly airbags, so Toyota and Ford should also be required to recall their cars to correct such a dangerous system.[9]

Although, this case was dismissed by the court, it still served as a good reminder for the upcoming litigation threats related to this technology for which legislators and policy makers must be ready to face in the near future. Manufacturers and technological companies must be ready to face such cyber security issues rising in the near future.

Many scholars may say that, seeing these repercussions, it is better to impose a ban on this technology.[11] However, the authors of this chapter completely disagree, because adoption of this technology will not only positively impact the road transport system but will also slash the accident and fatality rates by saving millions of lives around the world as per the statistics of the NHTSA.[12] AVs would also be a boon to physically challenged people as well as the elderly, infants, and pregnant women, which need special care and attention

Therefore, rather than slamming the breaks on innovations, legislators must create an adequate rules and regulatory mechanism to govern this technology and create public confidence by ensuring this technology is safe by taking into consideration the above-mentioned issues.

16.3 DECODING LITIGATION CHALLENGES IN THE WAY OF DRIVERLESS CARS

16.3.1 Understanding the Role of Product Liability Theory

In the previous section, we discussed how hackers may invade AVs by breaching cyber security norms. In such a situation, it becomes the duty of regulatory bodies or adjudicating authorities to take cognizance for such breaches against the manufacturers as observed in the case of *Cahen v. Toyota Motor Corp.*[9] Therefore, in the absence of any explicit framework pertaining to cyber security norms for AVs, the authors believe that courts may rely on various theories of civil liabilities based on tort laws like product liability theory while taking action against hackers causing cyber threats and privacy breaches.

The principles of product liability theory can be imposed on manufacturers and other persons who are involved in distribution of the product.[13] However, it is noteworthy that the court can only apply this theory on the products that have caused some physical injury.[14] This theory serves two broad principles: to compensate the injured party who has used the unsafe product and to encourage the companies by giving incentives for inculcating precaution in their products.[15] The rationale behind this principle is that because the manufacturer is in the best position to prevent any defect in the product, thus if any injury is caused by any product, then the manufacturer cannot escape from his liability in any situation. Therefore, while invoking product liability theory in cases of cyber threats and privacy invasions, courts have to determine whether the AV can be considered as a product and courts have to categorize the defects arising thereto in this technology.

16.3.2 Autonomous Vehicle: Is it a "Product" or a "Service" Under Torts?

In the last decades, when artificial technology was considered as science fiction, product liability theories used to draw a thin line between the injuries caused due to tangible and intangible products.[16] Due to this, computer software was not considered a product; rather, it was considered a service.[17] However, with the rapid development of technology, now software has been increasingly used in physical machines. According to the *Restatement Third of Torts,* a product is defined as tangible personal property commercially for use or consumption [emphasis added].[18] Moreover, it is pertinent to note that few items, like electricity, which is analogous to the distribution and use of any other physical product, are also taken in the ambit of product for the application of this principle. This rationale can also be supported by looking into the definition of product under the Uniform Commercial Code of the United States. This code defines that any computer software that is mass-marketed will be considered as a product; however, if it is manufactured for any specific purpose then it will be treated as a service.[19] Because computer software for AVs is manufactured for the public at large and keeping in mind that they are inseparable from the AV at the time of purchasing the vehicle, customers do not have the option to purchase the AV without the software. Thus, the customer has to completely rely on the manufacturers software to prevent unwanted cyberattacks and data breaches. Therefore, in light of this, the court(s) should consider an AV as a product rather than a service for the applicability of product liability theory under the law of tort.

16.3.3 How to Determine the Defects in Software-Driven Cars?

Based on the previous discussion, it can be concluded that the AV may be considered as a "product" under the law of tort; therefore, it is essential to analyze the defect that caused substantial injury to the affected person. Generally, to establish the manufacturer's liability in different circumstances, the defects are classified into the following three broad categories.

16.3.3.1 Warning Defects

Warning defects arise when the seller of the product breaches his or her duty to warn for any material risk associated with the product.[20] The seller shall be held liable for failure to warn or instruct, provided, if *firstly*, the reasonably anticipatable usage of the product creates an arbitrary risk of harm; *secondly*, either the probability of the danger or its severity should it occur is not apparent to the user; and *lastly*, the product carries insufficient warnings of the harm or instructions regarding the usage of the product.[21]

The rationale behind inclusion of this defect is based on the objective of efficiency in the tort law as it is usually presumes that the manufacturer is in a better position to identify the risk associated with the product.[21] Incorporating warning signals not only avoids an accident from occurring, but it also plays a prominent role in cost reduction to take appropriate measures. This can be better understood by referring to the case of *McLennan v. American Eurocopter Corp.*[22] In this case, a helicopter crashed due to the inadequacy of the fuel in it. The plaintiff sued the manufacturer of the helicopter alleging that the machine failed to give a warning sign of insufficient fuel to warn the pilot; as a result, he was unaware of the exhaustion of fuel, which led this crash.[22]

Similarly, one can also relate this case to the hacking incident of the Jeep Cherokee that took place in 2015. The jeep was running at a mild speed of 15–20 mph when suddenly intruders hacked the vehicle and took over entire control of the vehicle and accelerated it to a speed of 70 mph.[21] If manufacturers of this vehicle had incorporated a warning signal in its software, in case any unidentified third-party attempted a cyber intrusion, then the vehicle may have given an automatic warning sign to the customer (driver). This may have apprised the driver to take reasonable steps to prevent the cyber threat and data invasion.

16.3.3.2 Is It a Design Defect or a Manufacturing Defect?

Scrutinizing design and manufacturing defects in software-driven cars is a difficult task due to its intangible form.[23] For the purpose of investigation, we can simplify the complex nature of the software into four phases: (1) design, (2) coding, (3) testing, and (4) replication and distribution.[24] Any inconsistency in the former phases 1 and 2 will lead to a design defect and phases 3 and 4will lead to a manufacturing defect.[24]

16.3.3.2.1 Design Defect   To analyze the design defects in software, *Restatement (Third) of Torts* recommends the courts apply the Risk-Utility Test.[25] This principle says that a product is said to be defective when the foreseeable risk of harm of the product could have been avoided or reduced by adopting some reasonable alternative design.[25] Non-compliance of this principle renders the product not reasonably safe to use. Courts may evaluate the benefits of risk and utility of the product on the basis of major factors mentioned by New York's Court of Appeal[26]:

> (a) the usefulness of the product to the society at large and to the individual consumer; (b) the probability that it may cause harm injury; (c) accessibility of a safer design; (d) the capability for manufacturing and designing the product to make it safer but should also remain functional and priced judiciously; (f) the capacity of the plaintiff to evade harm by cautious usage; (g) the degree of awareness of the possible harm which can be attributed to the plaintiff; and (h) the ability of the manufacturer to range any cost related to improving the safety pertaining to design.[26]

In light of the above principles, the courts may assess whether the manufacturer has taken due care in making an adequate design and coding of the software that may lead to a cyber threat to the vehicle, as it is well established that any defect in the code and design of the software will lead to a defect in the entire product line.[24] We can relate this to the case of *Lone Star Bank v. Heartland Payment System*,[27] wherein the court concluded that hackers were able to invade the network because of the vulnerable coding done by the manufacturers.[27] Therefore, we need to examine the different aspects that can fall under the category of manufacturing defect.

16.3.3.2.2 Manufacturing Defect   When the concerned product does not satisfy the specifications issued by the manufacturer, it is said to be a manufacturing defect.[28] This defect occurs after finalizing the software of the technology of the AV, i.e., during testing, replication, and distribution.[29] The concept of a manufacturing defect is inspired by the Flaw Theory.[30] According to this, such defect involves products that are flawed, i.e., those products that do meet the specifications of the manufacturer and are identical to their mass-produced siblings.[31] This theory is based on the foundational principle of consumer expectancy, which states that a mass-produced product should not vary from its siblings in a manner which makes it dangerous than the other [emphasis added].[32]

At the time of testing, the manufacturer assesses the deficiency in the product. If he discovers any inadequacy in the software of the product then it is his duty to resend it to the coding phase to strengthen the loopholes.[33] Similarly, during the fourth phase (i.e., replication and distribution) the manufacturer induces the software in all its product lines. Any mistake while replicating the software in all the products will make that individual product hazardous.[24] Thus, in such situations the defect will be termed as a manufacturing defect.

16.3.3.3 Other Unidentifiable Defects

As mentioned earlier, these few defects are identifiable, but because of the complex structure of this technology, one also needs to understand and examine the unidentifiable defects, wherein it is not possible to pinpoint the defect causing injury to the plaintiff. In such situations, malfunction doctrine could suffice.[34] This theory is similar to the principle of *res ipsa loquitur* used in negligence. Here, the plaintiff needs to establish through this doctrine that firstly, the product in question has malfunctioned; secondly, the malfunction occurred during proper usage of the product; and thirdly, the product had not been misused or altered in a manner due which such malfunction occurred [emphasis added].[34]

The first condition could be proved by just establishing the fact that the accident occurred. However, the issue gets critical in proving the other two conditions. Manufacturers may defend that the AV was in fit condition at the time it left their control and may shift the onus to the unknown third party who has breached the cyber security of the vehicle. This raises another question of whether hackers created a sophisticated system to hack the vehicle or the defect in the vehicle, which helped them to gain control over it.

Although in such exceptional circumstances the burden of proof on the plaintiff is to just establish the circumstantial evidence against the manufacturer, one can observe this situation in Toyota's case in which the AV was unidentifiably accelerated and both plaintiff and manufacturer were unable to pinpoint any defect in the vehicle.[35] Applying this principle, the court in this case held Toyota liable for its failure to detect such unidentified acceleration.[36]

16.4 UNDERSTANDING THE SCOPE OF VARIOUS LEGISLATIONS OF DIFFERENT JURISDICTIONS TO MITIGATE CYBER SECURITY ISSUES

16.4.1 United States

The United States is one of the most developed nations in terms of introducing driverless technology or AVs.[37] In June 2011 Nevada became the first state to grant a license for the operation of AVs in the state.[38] The law of Nevada defines an autonomous vehicle as a vehicle that operates without human intervention by usage of the GPS, sensors, and artificial intelligence.[39] Followed by this, 19 other states in the United States, have also taken an initiative to enact laws pertaining to regulate AVs.[40] This section will lay out an analysis with respect to the legal framework adopted by the United States [emphasis added].

16.4.1.1 *Special Regulations that Directly Address Cyber Security and Data Breach Issues*

While introducing legislation on AVs, care has been taken wherein the manufacturer needs to provide a warranty clause where the vehicle is of merchantable quality and fit for the purpose for which it is intended. In the case of AVs, the law imposes an additional duty on the manufacturer that the vehicle is fit and free from cyber security standards and data breach issues, which can ordinarily be expected in this technological world, as the life and safety of the customer is paramount as the customer is ready and willing to pay for the product he or she requires.

16.4.1.1.1 The Security and Privacy in Your Car Act, 2019   The Security and Privacy in Your Car Act 2019 (SPY) was formulated with an objective to safeguard the consumers from privacy and cyber security threats from their motor vehicles, and for other purposes [emphasis added].[41] This act categorizes the cyber issues into three broad categories[42]: (1) cyber security standards, (2) cyber dashboard, and (3) privacy standards.

16.4.1.1.1.1. Cyber Security Standards This section begins by stating that all motor vehicles manufactured for sale in the United States shall act in accordance with the cyber security standards as set forth.[77] It further mandates that every AV should comply with the standards to protect the AV from getting hacked, prevent data breaches, and to detect and respond to hacking.[42] Non-compliance of these standards would incur a penalty to the manufacturer.[42]

16.4.1.1.1.2 Cyber Dashboard The cyber dashboard casts a mandatory duty on the manufacturer to make data protection policies clear and precise for consumers. The cyber dashboard policy states that it is the duty of every manufacturer to make consumers aware through a standardized, easy-to-understand graphic of the extent to which the motor vehicle protects the cyber security and privacy of the vehicle's owners, lessees, drivers, and passengers.[77] It has been observed in the past that due to complex privacy policies of the products, many consumers were not able to understand the policy.[43] Tesla's privacy policy is a glaring example of this. Tesla had given the privacy policies to their customers, and still the customers were unaware of the consequences of using an AV.[44] Experts opine that the only reason behind this unawareness was Tesla's lengthy legal documents, which were unlikely to be understood by the average consumer.[45] This encouraged legislators to ensure that the manufacturer should simplify the complicated language of these policies to make it easy to understand and implement.[45]

16.4.1.1.1.3 Privacy Standards It is essential to provide adequate standards for protecting customer privacy by providing a framework to fix the liability of the manufacturer. These standards are based on three pillars: (1) transparency, which is defined under the act as the vehicle providing clear notice to the owner of such vehicle with respect to the usage of driving data[42]; (2) consumer control, which is defined as the ability of the consumer to withdraw the usage of driving data without compromising the accessibility to the navigation tools[42]; and (3) this SPY Act also enumerates that a manufacturer who also includes an original equipment manufacturer should not use any data collected for any advertising purpose without the explicit authorization by the owner or lessee.[42]

16.4.1.1.2 The American Vision for Safer Transportation through Advancement of Revolutionary Technologies On October 6, 2017, the Senate Commerce Committee drafter legislation titled the AV Start Act recognizing the cyber threats and privacy invasions in AV technology. In this bill the Senate curbed out certain exceptions by grating power to state and local governments to enact laws and regulations for AVs unless already issued by the NHTSA. It is pertinent to note that, although the Senate bill includes cyber security provisions, it does not mention the data privacy concerns. However, under Section 10(c)(5) of the Act, it proposed to establish a working group who would be responsible for making recommendations. This working group consists of at least one member who represents a manufacturer of AVs. This is indeed a welcome step[46]; however, the latest position about the recommendations of the working group is not available.

16.4.1.2 Ancillary Framework Addressing Cyber Security and Data Breach Issues
In addition to the previously mentioned framework, cyber issues of AVs can also be regulated by the U.S. Federal Trade Commission (FTC). Section 5(a) of the Act grants powers to the FTC to prohibit all unfair methods of competition or deceptive acts or practices in or affecting commerce [emphasis added].[47] However, for the application of this provision, it is necessary to determine whether the FTC has power to control data security claims; if yes, then whether cyber security threats and data breaches fall under the ambit of "unfair" and "deceptive" practice.

16.4.1.2.1 Does the FTC Has Power to Regulate Data Security Claims?   This issue was first raised in the case of *FTC v. Wyndham Worldwide Corp.*,[48] wherein the FTC filed suit against Wyndham Worldwide Corporation for data breaches, alleging that they failed to safeguard the personal information of their customers. In 2012, hackers accessed unencrypted information of 619,000 accounts, which resulted in a loss of $10.6 million.[48] Rather than going for a settlement, Wyndham contested that the FTC had no power to take action on data security matters and relied on the case of Food and Drug Administration (FDA) v. Brown & Williamson Tobacco Corp [emphasis added][49], wherein the U.S. Supreme Court held that the FDA could not use its general powers pertaining to drugs to mandate disclaimers on tobacco packaging in the absence of any explicit legal authority over tobacco products [emphasis added].[49] The rationale behind this decision was that in past the FDA had disclaimed their authority on tobacco and Congress had already enacted a special legislation for tobacco wherein it had not given any authority to the FDA.[50] In the Wyndham case, likewise Congress did not gave special authority to the FTC to regulate data security cases. Therefore, Wyndham claimed that the FTC should not have jurisdiction to regulate the data security cases. However, the Supreme Court rejected these arguments and stated that the situation in the case of *Food and Drug Administration v. Brown & Williamson Tobacco Corp.* is not analogous to the present case. This is because, in the former case, Congress intended to remove the FDA from regulating tobacco, whereas in the Wyndham case they have not have given any express intention to deprive the FTC from regulating data security cases.[51] Additionally, unlike the FDA who denied their authority to regulate tobacco cases in the past, there was no submission given by the FTC.[48] Therefore, stating this rationale the U.S. Supreme Court held that the FTC has authority to regulate unfair data breach cases.

16.4.1.2.2 Do Cyber Security and Data Invasion Fall Under the Purview of "Unfair Data Practices" Under Section 5(a) of the FTC Act?   After determining the powers of the FTC to regulate data practices, it is important to assess whether cyber security threats fall under the purview of the FTC Act. Section 5(a) states that an act is unfair unless[51] (i) it results or is likely to result potential injury to consumers; (ii) such injury could not be reasonably avoidable by the consumers, and (iii) the injury is not outweighed by countervailing benefits to consumers or to competition [emphasis added]. The FTC has applied these principles as essential to prosecute a few companies in last decade. In the case of *TRENDnet, Inc.*,[52] the FTC alleged that they had violated Section 5(a) of the FTC Act, when a hacker was able to access Internet Protocol (IP) cameras sold by the respondents. Secondly, failure of TRENDnet to adequately test their software amounts to unfair practice because it may cause or is likely to cause harm to customers.[53] On this, the court held that since the respondent has miserably failed to arrange for reasonable security for preventing unauthorized access to the live feeds from its IP cameras, which respondent offered for the purpose of monitoring their homes and businesses, the acts and practices of the respondent constitutes unfair or deceptive acts or practices, which is in violation of Section 5(a) of the FTC Act, 15 U.S.C. § 45(a).[54] Therefore, AV technology developers must take into consideration that the high cost of better security will not by itself justify a secure failure.[55]

16.4.1.2.3 What Kind of Data Security Practices Are Considered as "Deceptive" Under Section 5(a) of the FTC Act? The FTC may initiate action against the company for deceptive practices, if a company is found giving false statements in their privacy policies that may mislead the customers.[56] A three-fold test is used for determining whether any act or practice is deceptive. First, the representation, omission, or practice must mislead or be likely to mislead the consumer. Second, the consumer's interpretation of the representation, omission, or practice must be reasonable under the circumstances. Third, the misleading representation, omission, or practice must be material [emphasis added].[57] This is equally relevant for the AV technology providers, as they might get tempted to oversell themselves by having a statement in their privacy policies that may be far away from the reality.

We can see this in the case of *Henry Schein Practice Solutions, Inc.*,[58] wherein the respondent provided their software for the dentist to perform a common task such as entering the patient data, insurance policies, diagnostic information, etc.[59] The respondent alleged in its privacy policy that its software, named "*Dentrix G5*," has sufficient capacity to protect the data of their customers.[60] However, in 2010 the FTC discovered that the respondent had never tested their software to protect the public from cyber security threats and data breaches in reality and it was examined that their software *Dentrix G5* was less secure and more vulnerable.[61] Due to this, it was not adequate and safe to protect the data of customers. Therefore, representation made by the corporation was misleading and thus deceptive under Section 5(a) of the FTC Act.[62]

16.4.2 Analysis of Indian Laws

Novus Drive was the first kind of AV in the country,[63] and it was mainly set up to carry visitors from one dome center in New Delhi in 2016. Although it was a welcome step for India, many scholars like Robert Bosch warned that seeing the condition of roads and traffic in India, autonomous technology would take more time compared with other countries.[64] Moreover, cyber security threat is another challenge for AVs in India. Presently, India is in a very nascent stage for developing the framework for the cyber security threats of AVs. However, the issues and challenges faced in the United States as discussed in previous sections are worth it for the Indian legislature to consider while formulating specific legislation on this subject. In this section, we will analyze certain legislations and bills on this subject.

16.4.2.1 Information Technology Act, 2000

In India, cyber security and data protection are primarily governed by the Information Technology Act, 2000. Presently, Section 66 of the Act classifies hacking as a situation when a third party with the mala fide intention causes harm or damage to any person by either altering or destroying his information.[65] Currently, cyber threats and privacy-related issues of connected vehicles are not covered under this section; however, the authors believe that in the absence of any specific legislation for AVs, remedy for such acts could only be given under this section.[65] With the advent of this technology, it is important for legislators to enlarge the scope of this provision accordingly.

16.4.2.2 Personal Data Protection Bill, 2019

As discussed in the previous sections, the issue pertaining to cyber security and privacy intrusion lies within the heart of the personal data of the consumer operating the AVs. Therefore, it is very relevant and important for the Indian legislators to classify what constitutes as "personal data." The Personal Data Protection Bill, 2019 defined personal data as data related to a natural person who is recognizable either directly or indirectly from the characteristic, irrespective of online or off-line, or any combination of such trait with any other information, and shall include any inference drawn from such data for the purpose of profiling.[66] The Bill intends to give certain rights to individuals for protecting their essential data from privacy invasion. These include the right to (1) acquire authorization from the data fiduciary on whether their personal data is processed or not; (2) strive for rectification of erroneous, inadequate, or old personal data; (3) have personal data transmitted to any other data fiduciary in certain circumstances; and (4) limit ongoing disclosure of their personal data by a fiduciary, in an event where the individual believes that such information is no longer necessary or where his consent is withdrawn.[65] It is pertinent to note that the Bill only authorizes the data fiduciary to process the individual's data after seeking his or her consent. However, this condition is not applicable if required by the State for providing benefits to the individual, for example, in case of litigation and for cases pertaining to medical emergency. To have strict implementation of the above provisions, the Bill has included that if any data are processed or transferred in violation of the provisions of the Bill, then such offense is punishable with a fine of Rs. 15 Crore or 4% of the annual turnover of the fiduciary, whichever is higher; this is a deterrent provisions for those misusers.

16.5 CHALLENGES DURING IMPLEMENTATION

16.5.1 Cost of Litigation

Keeping in mind the complex nature of the AV technology, finding an expert to testify with respect to any issue is challenging, i.e., it is difficult and expensive. As observed in the earlier sections, for proving product liability, two evidentiary issues are sine qua non, i.e., expert testimony issues and remedial measures.[67] For example, to prove any defect in the AV technology, the plaintiff will have to have any witness who is an expert and understands the complexities of the technology testify.[68] This may also require multiple experts at the same time to testify to the court and explain the functioning of the technology with respect to the matter beforehand. The plaintiff may also need a computer expert who understands the algorithm, an expert good with mathematics to rewrite the equation, an economist for weighing the costs of damage, and of course a specialist in AV technology.[69] The cost of these experts to testify in court may become burdensome for the plaintiff and could become a possible hurdle to bring the suit before the court.[70]

16.5.2 Third-Party Data Access

Another major challenge for the legislators is to formulate an adequate framework for third parties like Google, Verizon, etc., for protecting consumer data. As AVs will be constantly connected with the Internet for their functioning, such third parties will have access to the personal data of the consumers.[71] These third parties provides Internet broadband on which AVs will rely, thus giving a chance to more intruders to commit cyber threats and privacy invasion.[71] Therefore, this is another challenge for the legislators as they also have to formulate strict norms for protecting personal data of the consumers that is going to the Internet service providers.

16.5.3 Balancing the Liability of Manufacturer and Software Developer

Another important challenge is assessing the liability of the AV in case of any fault. As traditionally vehicles are under the control of a driver, they are accountable in case of any accident. However, in the case of AVs, the authors anticipate that courts may find it difficult to establish "liability" in case of cyberattacks and privacy invasions, as there are two parties involved (i.e., manufacturer and software developer).[72]

As observed in the previous section, the challenge lies in assessing what caused the defect to impose any liability to the abovementioned parties. In this context, an accident of a Toyota Camry in 2005 can be taken as an apt example wherein the accident was caused due to sudden acceleration and the courts faced difficulties in balancing liability between the manufacturer and software developer.[73]

16.6 WAY FORWARD AND RECOMMENDATIONS

There is a common saying that the technology is moving fast and the law is running behind. This is true like in nature where the plants and animals grow, but for their better nourishment and growth the necessary schemes are developed and implemented. To a large extent this also holds for technology for man to reach from Earth to space or have an automatic car be driven to any destination.

As we have discussed in the preceding sections, the technology possess a challenge for the law maker to implement; therefore, to say that the implementation of technology as per given legislation will fully satiate the needs of society cannot be answered affirmatively. There is no doubt that the introduction of AVs will not only decrease the accidents but will also provide an environment-friendly mode of transportation. However, to make the AV effective, it is necessary to connect with each other, through various platforms and surrounding infrastructure, and with a host of platforms through software code(s).

16.6.1 Liability of Manufacturer

Let us discuss the manufacturer point of view to avoid liability for a cyber breach as malicious hacking or user negligence. It is a matter of fact that the entire threat cannot be entirely eliminated despite taking every possible step. Therefore, it is essential that the vehicle manufacturer, original equipment manufacturer (OEM), and software manufacturers should consider the following steps to prevent a cyber breach liability[74]:

1. Identify the information that can lead to a breach and accordingly prepare an action plan as a response to such breach and prepare a breach response by both the software manufacturer and OEM by complying with the requirements imposed under the specific breach notification statutes, as it casts stringent consumer notification requirements. Therefore, compliance of the same is condition a priori including compliance with applicable statutory and regulatory requirements.

2. The AV industry is relatively unregulated and it focuses on broad guidelines for testing and development; therefore, while preparing the plan pertaining to cyber security, domestic and international statutes, regulations, and legal principles should also be taken into consideration, as a cyber breach can be from any jurisdiction. For example, the "privacy-by-design" approach endorsed by the FTC should be considered beforehand and an in-built security be created in AVs at the development stage. For this approach manufacturers and software developer/designers should assess the security risk assessment and test the security measures contemplated before launching their products.

3. The intended usage, integration, and requirements must be clear to software manufacturers, OEMs, and vehicle manufacturers. This will help fix the rights and obligations of the parties involved so that in case of cyber breach, the inter-see obligations can be fixed and accordingly the AV product can be given to customer with specific stipulations.

4. AVs will have a great deal of data to make them consumer friendly in the form of software codes and signals; therefore, it is essential to specify the role of all participants in the event of a breach. This includes the responsibility of the manufacturing chain or customer, and in case it falls to the supply chain, which has the obligation to notify consumers (i.e., vehicle manufacturer, OEMs, software manufacturer or the local bodies) who is responsible for the infrastructure. There is also a need to consider the interstate as well as overseas consumers regarding the applicability of laws in the event of a breach.

5. Engagement of counsel from the beginning will help avoid or minimize liability during litigation; therefore, an action plan can be foolproof and ready to the extent possible in the event of a breach.

6. A comprehensive policy involving all stakeholders should be enforced and the employees should be trained to take prompt action. It is appropriate to have a cyber liability insurance policy to cover damage to tangible property to minimize the risk.

With these steps and a calculated risk the vehicle can be placed in the market. However, these steps will be helpful in identifying responsibility (either the manufacturer chain or customer) by taking into consideration the development of technology along with appropriate legislation and judicial precedents on the subject.

16.6.2 Analysis on Liability Due to Breach

To place entire responsibility on the manufacturer of the AV is also not fair; however, for the AV it is essential that the software company, who is preparing the algorithm, should have the primary responsibility. Google and Samsung are two companies entering the AV market. The best approach is that the manufacturer either has a tie with the software company or owns a team to develop the product based on the software, or the manufacturer should manufacture the AV in discussion with a software company to cover the eventualities of cyber issues like hacking, terrorist attacks, or malware or decoding or any unwarranted control by third party.[74] After having this robust preparation, the AV is launched in the market. For cyber issues, the manufacturer and software company have to take preemptive steps about the contingencies or probabilities of cyberattacks and make the best foolproof system to remove any known threat and to a large extent the unknown threats as well. For this purpose, the insurance companies need to be convinced about the action plan and their readiness to provide such policies to the manufacturer and/or software company. Because fully automated AVs are driverless and may be used by a blind man, the quantum of risk by the customer is a challenge. However, except the liability cover by the manufacturer and its backend company, the rest of the liability may lie with the customer; unless otherwise decided by the court in a specific situation.

16.6.3 Regulatory Hurdles

In the area of cyber security, regulatory mechanisms are a mix blend of law, social norms, and software code applied to strong security standards established by technical experts. These mechanisms also cast a duty on manufacturers to formulate security measures and checks as per its established plan to be implemented during the design phase and finally development of the product, i.e., AVs. Because the technology moves at a faster pace and cyber attackers can create a debugging mechanism to control the AVs, the regulation must be dynamic, which takes into account the techno-legal developments and challenges to regulate the interest of stakeholders; in other words, these regulator mechanisms can be called responsive regulation or "smart regulations."[75]

Regulators use the conventional means as warning signals but also follow the regular review to see that the norms can effectively be monitored and followed, but this does not provide a foolproof system to control and combat cyber offenses completely.[76] Therefore, it is necessary to maintain a fine balance between flexibility and legal certainty, so that stakeholders have confidence in the methodology and approaches followed by regulators and or adjudicating authorities. The challenge before regulators is to intervene at appropriate moment the innovation is being executed, but the regulator should be satisfied with the security features before implementation, as can be seen in automatic cars.

One of the challenges that regulators face is whether manufacturers should follow the norms of public policy and social norms or norms for the development of technologies.

Therefore, it is necessary to manage risk regulation versus innovation stimulation, including privacy and autonomy of technology. Moreover, it is the duty of the regulator to be aware about the invisible challenges so that preemptive steps can be taken.

The European Union (EU) has formulated a regulatory framework that takes into account the human capabilities as well as the relevant technologies required for the regulatory framework. Once the capabilities are known and challenges are definite, the regulatory action will have to be concocted accordingly. It is necessary to judiciously differentiate aims of the intervention(s) and accept instruments focused on the main objective.

As far as the liability rule is concerned, it casts the duty of manufacturers to take into consideration the consequences of the harmful effect on others and therefore emphasizes safety and risk reduction *ex ante*, which includes cyberattacks or product failure for which the manufacturer has to compensate the third party. However, safety and compensation need to be looked at differently; safety is more linked to technical flaws or attacks impacting safety, whereas compensation for damage has to be seen from the point of view of all involved in the supply chain (i.e., the software developer, OEM, and AV manufacturer) and accordingly the stage-wise liability can be fixed, provided the customer has complied with the instruction manual. This is not a case of self-regulation. It is the onus of the regulator to take accountability to give correct direction regarding the technological developments. The regulator needs to be more interactive and dynamic and should involve more stakeholders as well as quasi-regulators such as industry associations, professional bodies, etc. No doubt more issues and concerns will be raised, but it provides a broad and varied perspective on the challenges met including the possible solutions, which may add to the acceptance of regulatory interferences by the appropriate stakeholders. In regulating technology-dominated fields, regulators should be technology neutral, which is the best way to deal with the modification that in itself requires self-reflection and may also need other supplementary measures. By consider all of these issues, it is expected that the regulator findings will be acceptable to stakeholders.

16.6.4 Future Scope of ADAS and AV Technology

No system or technology can be transplanted in any society unless it address local needs, awareness, utility, and the advantages and disadvantages of the same. As one of the famous jurisprudential thinkers, Savigny mentioned that law cannot be transplanted in society or enforced, unless the community is educated and feels the need for the same. This principle holds for AVs, both in terms of cost and comfort and the target segment of consumers. In India there is no codified legislation for AVs except the IT Act, 2000, which does not seems sufficient after taking into consideration the experience of developed nations mainly through case studies and legislation in the United States. Once Indian legislators are satisfied both from a technical and legal prospective, only then should this technology be implemented in India. Therefore, there is great scope for future research. Generally, it is said that technology changes the life of any society, but if technology comes first and law later, it creates an opportunity for hacking and misuse instead of benefits to the society.

16.7 CONCLUSION

It is difficult to answer whether AV technology is completely perfect or not, but it is indeed a stepping stone toward solving problems like parking, accidents, etc. However, as analyzed in this chapter, cyber security and privacy invasions could become the weakest link. We have observed in previous section that due to various issues about cyber security and privacy concerns, the journey for AV technology is certainly not an easy path. This reality check could be seen in the cases of the Jeep Cherokee, Toyota, and Tesla as discussed in earlier. Therefore, cyber security and data protection measures must be given priority in the emerging market of AV technology.

The authors here recommend that to make AVs successful the fundamental part of the design process should be the focus. There must be a strong incentive for strengthening the cyber security system design. The industry must also be ready for the worst-case scenario and should be prepared for large-scale coordinated attacks on AVs, which could be a setback for public confidence in the technology. Therefore, to make this development successful, legislators will have to play crucial role in framing necessary laws and regulations to protect consumers' personal data and protect them from cyberattacks. A harmonized framework will provide a level playing field for organizations and is positive for both consumers and the industry. Legislators, while developing a framework for cyber security and privacy issues, should address challenges for AVs as discussed in the preceding sections.

Thus, protection against cyber security and data privacy threats can only be achieved through a multi-stakeholder approach in which each participant who is connected in the functioning of the AVs should bear a degree of responsibility. It is not prudent to lay the full responsibility on either of the participants, such as the manufacturer who has to release AVs in the market, the software developer who is responsible for keeping the AV's application up to date, and legislators who must frame strong security requirements on the manufacturers and software developer. This responsibility has to be shared among each of the participants; therefore, using the above recommendations, we can reap the benefits of ADAS and AV technology and shape the future of AVs as a means of transportation in the society.

REFERENCES

* Ranade, A. "Call Me On My Computer." India Times, 2008. https://mumbaimirror.indiatimes.com/opinion/columnists/ajit-ranade/Call-me-on-my-computer/articleshow/15844881.cms.

1. Cunneen, M., Mullins, M., and Murphy, F. "Autonomous Vehicles and Embedded Artificial Intelligence: The Challenges of Framing Machine Driving Decisions." Applied Artificial Intelligence 33, no. 8 (2019): 706–731. https://doi.org/10.1080/08839514.2019.1600301.
2. "Henry Ford's Assembly Line: How It's Still Rolling Along 100 Years Later." Cbsnews.Com, 2013. https://www.cbsnews.com/news/henry-fords-assembly-line-how-its-still-rolling-along-100-years-later.
3. Harris, M. "How Google's Autonomous Car Passed the First U.S. State Self-Driving Test." IEEE Spectrum: Technology, Engineering, And Science News, 2014. https://spectrum.ieee.org/how-googles-autonomous-car-passed-the-first-us-state-selfdriving-test.
4. "CNN.Com – Toyota Unveils Car That Parks Itself – Sep. 1, 2003." Cnn.Com, 2003. http://www.cnn.com/2003/TECH/ptech/09/01/toyota.prius.reut/index.html.
5. Greenberg, A. "Hackers Remotely Kill a Jeep on the Highway—with Me In It." WIRED, 2015. https://www.wired.com/2015/07/hackers-remotely-kill-jeep-highway/.

6. Versprille, A. "Researchers Hack into Driverless Car System, Take Control of Vehicle." 2015. Nationaldefensemagazine.org. https://www.nationaldefensemagazine.org/articles/2015/5/1/2015may-researchers-hack-into-driverless-car-system-take-control-of-vehicle.

7. Valasek, C., and Miller, C. "Remote Exploitation of an Unaltered Passenger Vehicle." 2015. http://illmatics.com/Remote%20Car%20Hacking.pdf.

8. Mearian, L. "Securing Your Car From Cyberattacks Is Becoming a Big Business." Computerworld, 2020. https://www.computerworld.com/article/3081467/securing-your-car-from-cyberattacks-is-becoming-a-big-business.html.

9. *Cahen v. Toyota Motor Corp*; 147 F. Supp. 3d 955.

10. European Union Agency for Cybersecurity. "Cyber Security and Resilience of Smart Cars." Enisa.Europa.Eu, 2016. https://www.enisa.europa.eu/publications/cyber-security-and-resilience-of-smart-cars.

11. Brisc, N. "Why We Should Ban Autonomous Cars Now." The Irish Times 2019. https://www.irishtimes.com/business/innovation/why-we-should-ban-autonomous-cars-now-1.3987188.

12. Schoitsch, E., Schmittner, C., Ma, Z., and Gruber, T. 2016. The Need for Safety and Cyber-Security Co-Engineering and Standardization for Highly Automated Automotive Vehicles. Springer, pp. 251–261. https://www.researchgate.net/publication/300777848_The_Need_for_Safety_and_Cyber-Security_Co-engineering_and_Standardization_for_Highly_Automated_Automotive_Vehicles.

13. Butler, A. "Products Liability and the Internet of (Insecure) Things: Should Manufacturers be Liable for Damage Caused by Hacked Devices?" University of Michigan Journal of Law Reform 50, no. 4 (2017): 916. https://repository.law.umich.edu/mjlr/vol50/iss4/3.

14. In re Sony Gaming NetworksCustomer Data Sec. Breach Litig., 996 Supp. 2d 942, 966.

15. Sales, N.A. "Regulating Cyber Securities." Northwestern University Law Review 107, no. 4 (2013): 1533. https://scholarlycommons.law.northwestern.edu/nulr/vol107/iss4/1.

16. *James v. Meow Media, Inc.*, 300 F.3d 683, 701 (6th Cir. 2002); *Winter v. G.P. Putnam's Sons,* 938 F.2d 1033 (9th Cir. 1991).

17. *Watters v. TSR, Inc.,* 904 F.2d 378, (6th Cir. 1990).

18. Sales, N.A. "Regulating Cyber Securities." Northwestern University Law Review 107, no. 4 (2013): 1536. https://scholarlycommons.law.northwestern.edu/nulr/vol107/iss4/1.

19. *Advent Sys. Ltd. v. Unisys Corp.*, 925 F.2d 670; *Micro-Managers, Inc. v. Gregory,* 434 N.W.2d 97, 100.

20. *Liriano v. Hobart Corp.,* 700 N.E.2d 303, (N.Y. 1998).

21. Crane, D.A., Logue, K.D., and Pilz, B.C. "A Survey of Legal Issues Arising from the Deployment of Autonomous and Connected Vehicles." Michigan Telecommunications And Technology Law Review 23, no. 2 (2016): 282. https://repository.law.umich.edu/cgi/viewcontent.cgi?article=1226&context=mttlr.

22. *McLennan v. American Eurocopter Corp.*, 245 F. 3d 403 (5th Cir. 2001).

23. Mele, D. "The Quasi-Autonomous Car as an Assistive Device for Blind Drivers: Overcoming Liability and Regulatory Barriers." Syracuse Journal of Science & Technology Law 28, no. 2 (2013): 55. https://jost.syr.edu/wp-content/uploads/Mele-Final.pdf.

24. Scott, M. "Tort Liability for Vendors of Insecure Software: Has the Time Finally Come?" Maryland Law Review 67, no. 2 (2008): 459. https://digitalcommons.law.umaryland.edu/cgi/viewcontent.cgi?referer=https://www.google.com/&httpsredir=1&article=3320&context=mlr.

25. *Branham v. Ford Motor Co.*, 701 S.E.2d 5, 16–17 (S.C. 2010).

26. *Voss v. Black & Decker Mfg. Co.*, 450 N.E.2d 204, 208–09 (N.Y. 1983).

27. *Lone Star Bank v. Heartland Payment Sys.*, 729 F.3d 421 (5th Cir. 2013).

28. Kim, S. "Crashed Software: Assessing Product Liability for Software Defects in Automated Vehicles." Duke Law & Technology Law Review 16, no. 1 (2018): 305. https://scholarship.law.duke.edu/dltr/vol16/iss1/9.

29. Kreutzer, J. "Somebody Has to Pay: Products Liability for Spyware." American Business Law Journal 45, no. 1 (2008) 61–105. https://doi.org/10.1111/j.1744-1714.2008.00051.x.

30. Ryan, J.D. "The Emerging Intersection of Products Liability, Cybersecurity, and Autonomous Vehicles." Tennessee Law Review 85, no. 03 (2018): 822. https://www.beasleyallen.com/wp-content/uploads/ryan-duplechin-product-liability-intersection-products-liability-cybersecurity.pdf.

31. *Carroll v Fearon* [1999] ECC 73.

32. *Casey v. Toyota Motor Eng'g & Mfg. N. Am., Inc.*, 770 F. 3d 322, 329 (5th Cir. 2014).

33. *McCarthy v. Olin Corp.*, 119 F.3d 148, 154–55 (2d Cir. 1997).

34. Ryan, J.D. "The Emerging Intersection of Products Liability, Cybersecurity, and Autonomous Vehicles." Tennessee Law Review 85, no. 03 (2018): 823. https://www.beasleyallen.com/wp-content/uploads/ryan-duplechin-product-liability-intersection-products-liability-cybersecurity.pdf.

35. In re Toyota Motor Corp. Unintended Acceleration Mktg., Sales Practices, & Prod. Liab. Litig., 978 F. Supp. 2d 1053, 1100 (C.D. Cal. 2013).

36. Ross, B., Rhee, J., Hill, A.M., Katersky, A., and Chuchmach, M. "Toyota to Pay $1.2B for Hiding Deadly 'Unintended Acceleration'." ABC News, 2014. https://abcnews.go.com/Blotter/toyota-pay-12b-hiding-deadly-unintended-acceleration/story?id=22972214.

37. Schreurs, M.A., and Steuwer, S.D. "Autonomes Fahren." Ebook. Springer, 2015. https://link.springer.com/content/pdf/10.1007%2F978-3-662-45854-9_8.pdf.

38. Dillow, C. "Nevada Is the First State to Pass Driverless Car Legislation, Paving the Way For Autonomous Autos." Popular Science, 2011. https://www.popsci.com/cars/article/2011-06/nevada-passes-driverless-car-legislation-paving-way-autonomous-autos/.

39. Anderson, J.A., Nidhi, K., Stanley, K.D., Sorensen, P., Samaras, C., and Oluwatola Oluwatobi, A. Autonomous Vehicle Technology: A Guide For Policymakers, Rand Corporation. Santa Monica: Rand Corporation, 2016. https://www.rand.org/pubs/research_reports/RR443-2.html.

40. "Autonomous Vehicles Self-Driving Vehicles Enacted Legislation." Ncsl.Org, 2020. https://www.ncsl.org/research/transportation/autonomous-vehicles-self-driving-vehicles-enacted-legislation.aspx#:~:text=In%202018%2C%2015%20states%20enacted%2018%20AV%20related%20bills.&text=In%202016%2C%2020%20states%20introduced,legislation%20related%20to%20autonomous%20vehicles.

41. United State Congress House, The Security and Privacy in Your Car Act of 2019, S. 2182, 115th Cong. https://www.markey.senate.gov/imo/media/doc/SPY%20Car%20legislation.pdf.

42. Bollinger, B.J. "The Security and Privacy in Your Car Act: Will It Actually Protect You?" North Carolina Journal of Law and Technology 18, no. 5 (2017): 230. https://scholarship.law.unc.edu/cgi/viewcontent.cgi?article=1337&context=ncjolt.

43. "Privacy & Legal." Accessed 23 June 2020. https://www.tesla.com/about/legal.

44. National Cyber Security Alliance. "Results of Consumer Data Privacy Survey Reveal Critical Need for All Digital Citizens to Participate in Data Privacy Day." Prnewswire.Com, 2015. https://www.prnewswire.com/news-releases/results-of-consumer-data-privacy-survey-reveal-critical-need-for-all-digital-citizens-to-participate-in-data-privacy-day-300026888.html.

45. Bruening, P.J. and Culnan M.J. "Through a Glass Darkly: From Privacy Notices to Effective Transparency." North Carolina Journal of Law and Technology 17, no. 4 (2016): 568. https://scholarship.law.unc.edu/ncjolt/vol17/iss4/1.

46. Charfoos, A.D. and Derksen M.F. "How Well Does Your Car Know You? Privacy and Data Security Issues in Autonomous and Connected Vehicles," 2020. https://www.dykema.com/media/site_files/160_4834-8745-4796.4%20-%20MCity%20Privacy%20and%20Cybersecurity%20White%20Paper.pdf.

47. Federal Trade Commission Act, 1914. §05(a).

48. *FTC v. Wyndham Worldwide Corp*; 799 F.3d 236 (3d Cir. 2015).

49. *Food and Drug Administration v. Brown & Williamson Tobacco Corp.*, 529 U.S. 120 (2000).

50. Stevens, G. "The Federal Trade Commission's Regulation of Data Security Under Its Unfair or Deceptive Acts or Practices (UDAP) Authority." Congressional Research Service, 2014, 08. https://fas.org/sgp/crs/misc/R43723.pdf.

51. *"FTC v. Wyndham Worldwide Corp."* Harvardlawreview.Org, 2016. https://harvardlawreview. org/2016/02/ftc-v-wyndham-worldwide-corp/.
52. Complaint, Trendnet, Inc., No. C-4426, FTC No. 122 3090. https://www.ftc.gov/system/files/ documents/cases/140207trendnetcmpt.pdf.
53. Complaint, HTC America, Inc., No. C-4406, FTC No. 122 3049 (July 2, 2013). http://www.ftc. gov/sites/default/files/documents/cases/2013/07/130702htcdo.pdf.
54. Complaint, Trendnet, Inc., No. C-4426, FTC No. 122 3090 Para 19. https://www.ftc.gov/sys-tem/files/documents/cases/140207trendnetcmpt.pdf.
55. FTC Policy Statement on Unfairness, appended to Int'l Harvester Co., 104 F.T.C. 949, 1070 (1984). https://www.ftc.gov/public-statements/1980/12/ftc-policy-statement-unfairness.
56. Complaint, Henry Schein Practice Solutions, Inc., No. C-_, FTC No. 142 3161. https://www. ftc.gov/system/files/documents/cases/160105scheincmpt.pdf.
57. "Unfair and Deceptive Practices — Federal Trade Commission Act," 2018. https://www.fdic. gov/regulations/compliance/manual/7/vii-1.1.pdf.
58. Complaint, Henry Schein Practice Solutions, Inc., No. C-_, FTC No. 142 3161. https://www. ftc.gov/system/files/documents/cases/160105scheincmpt.pdf.
59. Complaint, Henry Schein Practice Solutions, Inc., No. C-_, FTC No. 142 3161, Para 04. https:// www.ftc.gov/system/files/documents/cases/160105scheincmpt.pdf.
60. Complaint, Henry Schein Practice Solutions, Inc., No. C-_, FTC No. 142 3161, Para 05. https:// www.ftc.gov/system/files/documents/cases/160105scheincmpt.pdf.
61. Complaint, Henry Schein Practice Solutions, Inc., No. C-_, FTC No. 142 3161, Para 07. https:// www.ftc.gov/system/files/documents/cases/160105scheincmpt.pdf.
62. Complaint, Henry Schein Practice Solutions, Inc., No. C-_, FTC No. 142 3161, Para 022. https://www.ftc.gov/system/files/documents/cases/160105scheincmpt.pdf.
63. "See India's First Autonomous Vehicle In Action – Novus Drive." Hitechroboticsystemz. Com, 2016. https://www.hitechroboticsystemz.com/novus-drive-autonomous-vehicle.html.
64. Vishal, K. "Autonomous Vehicle Policy: Here's Why India Needs to Step on the Gas. Yourstory.Com, 2018. https://yourstory.com/2018/01/autonomous-vehicle-policy-heres-india-needs-step-gas/.
65. Aporva. "A Background to Section 66A of the IT Act, 2000." Prsindia, 2015. https://prsindia. org/theprsblog/a-background-to-section-66a-of-the-it-act-2000.
66. Personal Data Protection Bill, 2019; § 3(28). http://164.100.47.4/BillsTexts/LSBillTexts/ Asintroduced/373_2019_LS_Eng.pdf.
67. Owen, D.G. "A Decade of Daubert." Denver University Law Review 80 (2003): 347–348. https://scholarcommons.sc.edu/cgi/viewcontent.cgi?article=1975&context=law_facpub.
68. *Watson v. Ford Motor Co.*, 699 S.E.2d 169, 174 (S.C. 2010).
69. Gurney, J.K. "Sue My Car Not Me: Products Liability and Accidents Involving Autonomous Vehicles." Journal of Law, Technology and Policy 2013, no. 2 (2013): 265. https://papers.ssrn. com/sol3/papers.cfm?abstract_id=2352108.
70. Sanders, J. "Adversarial Legalism and Civil Litigation: Prospects for Change." Law & Social Inquiry 28, no. 3 (2003): 723. https://www.jstor.org/stable/pdf/1215757.pdf.
71. Anderson, J.M., Nidhi, K., Stanley, K.D., Sorensen, P., Samaras, C., and Oluwatola Oluwatobi, A. Autonomous Vehicle Technology: A Guide For Policymakers, Rand Corporation. Santa Monica: Rand Corporation, 2016. https://www.rand.org/pubs/research_reports/ RR443-2.html.
72. Yeomans, G. "Autonomous Vehicles Handing Over Control: Opportunities and Risks for Insurance." Lloyds, 2014. https://www.lloyds.com/~/media/lloyds/reports/-emerging-risk-reports/autonomous-vehicles-final.pdf.
73. *Bookout v. Toyota Motor Corp.,* No. CJ-2008–7969, 2013 WL 5596096.
74. "Fisher Phillips: 8 Tips to Prevent Autonomous Vehicle Cyber Breach Liability." Fisherphillips. Com, 2018. https://www.fisherphillips.com/resources-articles-8-tips-to-prevent-autonomous-vehicle-cyber.

75. Leenes, R., Palmerini, E., Koops, B.J., Bertolini, A., Salvini, P., and Lucivero, F. "Regulatory Challenges of Robotics: Some Guidelines for Addressing Legal and Ethical Issues." Law, Innovation and Technology 9, no. 1 (2017): 1–44. https://doi.org/10.1080/17579961.2017.1304921.
76. Stigler, G. "The Theory of Economic Regulation." Bell Journal of Economics 2, no. 1 (1971). https://econpapers.repec.org/article/rjebellje/v_3a2_3ay_3a1971_3ai_3aspring_3ap_3a3-21.htm.
77. United State Congress House, The Security and Privacy in Your Car Act of 2019, S. 2182, 115th Cong. §05. https://www.govinfo.gov/content/pkg/BILLS-115hr3388eh/html/BILLS-115hr3388eh.htm.

CHAPTER 17

Human Factors in Autonomous Driving Systems

A User Perspective

Neeta Maitre

Cummins College of Engineering for Women
Pune, India

Neeraj Hanumante

Indian Institute of Technology Bombay
Mumbai, India

CONTENTS

17.1 INTRODUCTION

Automated driving systems (ADS) have been developed since the 1920s. The technology has seen its evolution through transmission of guiding signals, image processing algorithms like the Classification and Regression Trees (CART) Vision algorithm, Blocks World planning method, bifocal camera systems, and the Expectation-based Multifocal Saccadic (EMS) vision autonomy system. With the overall development of technological know-how specifically related to computer technology, this development process accelerated. However, in addition to the technological dimension, the ADS also has an equally crucial human dimension. This dimension encompasses both the elements of the automated road transport system: an ADS user and the non-ADS users of the road. In this chapter, the human factors in the ADS

DOI: 10.1201/9781003048381-19

from a user's perspective are discussed. The broad question investigated here is how do users take on the ADS. Specifically, how the psychology, economic, environmental, and social factors of the user environment affect the use of ADS are examined.

What benefits could ADS incur under ideal situations? These should include increased comfort and safety, reduced travel-related stress, efficient utilization of the resources such as vehicles and fuel, reduced requirement of the ownership, and a more inclusive driving experience for incapacitated users [1]. However, currently because of limited penetration of ADS, lack of infrastructure, and the nascent stage of technological development, these benefits cannot be realized to their fullest potential. In this regard, literature brought out the critical research areas for ADS and long-term recommendations for successful deployment of the ADS [2]. However, very few of research areas explicitly analyze the human factors that are related to ADS from the user perspective. The understanding of the user perspective is critical for the ADS development process. Here, this particular aspect is addressed and investigated, from a user perspective, as well as various dimensions of the ADS related to human factors.

In the next section, how the users perceive the different levels of automation is discussed. Then, the design principles of ADS are looked into from a user perspective in the third section. These sections probe different aspects of ADS from a user perspective with a holistic outlook. The penultimate section focuses on the psychosocial factors related to the user and the ADS. This chapter culminates with the authors' contribution.

17.2 LEVELS OF AUTOMATION

The modes of transportation have changed significantly over the ages in their speed and scale. However, transportation as a process has always been driven and directed by humans. Recently, with the advent of sophisticated technologies, efforts have been made to automate the driving process. Such efforts bring in a sea change in the role of humans, which was focused on driving the vehicle. Now with the assistance of the systems providing automation, their role is being shifted to being a passenger. This transformation process often becomes disharmonized due to inherent differences between the humans and the machines. Humans have an advantage in several aspects with respect to machines such as the ability to think, adapting to the situation, and perception. On the other hand, with proper maintenance, the machines can perform the same task tirelessly and consistently. Also, the machines do not get distracted. Hence, ADS should exploit these strengths and strive toward strengthening their weaknesses. How much the ADS can achieve this can be characterized in terms of the levels of automation.

SAE International, formerly known as the Society of Automotive Engineers, describes ADS in six levels, from 0 to 5, where level 0 represents no automation and level 5 represents the full driving automation. These are shown in Figure 17.1. This figure also shows the user perception of different ADS aspects in light of levels of automation. With an increase in the level of automation, the safety features are improved; as a result, the users' perceive them as safer. Simultaneously, elements providing comfort are also included in the ADS in an accelerated fashion. These developments require more investment for infrastructure buildup. Hence, the cost for a private user continues to increase with the level of ADS until the penetration of such technology becomes all pervasive. However, on the other hand, the

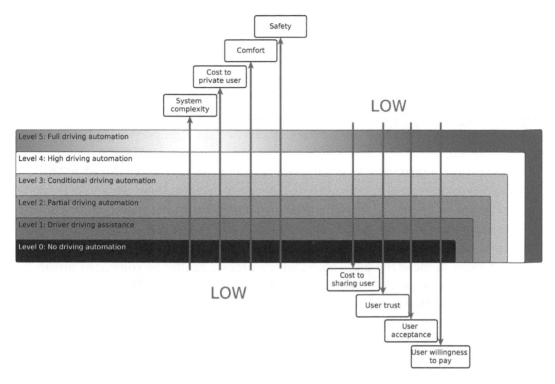

FIGURE 17.1   Levels of automation from a user perspective. Levels of automation with the keyword description is shown on the left. The arrows represent the increase, in the direction of arrow, in the particular aspect being represented.

cost of sharing the user is expected to reduce as the level of automation increases because of the optimized rerouting and reduced travel time.

From the users' perspective, the system complexity increases significantly with the level of automation. As a result, the users' understanding of how the vehicle or its components function remains at a comparatively rudimentary level. This factor, coupled with resistance to adopting newer technologies, creates a lack of trust in users toward ADS. This trust deficit also encompasses data privacy and security concerns. Subsequently, users' acceptance of ADS and their willingness to pay for ADS are adversely affected.

17.3 ADS ESSENTIALS

The systems of levels 3–5 bank on shared autonomy. Design principles are essential for developing such systems. In this section, first these design principles are briefly described and then each of them is discussed from the point of view of the user.

17.3.1 Design Principles

According to the first design principle, the team of human and machine should be considered cohesively. The situation awareness can be very well anticipated by human; hence, it can contribute to better handling of perception control problems. Perception is the point that allows a driver to control the actions and their consequences. It recommends prioritization of the development of human–machine interaction over the perception control. The evolution of ADS takes place through the learning process, which depends on the data obtained from various sensory systems. The second principle addresses this evolution process and suggests exploiting the modern machine learning techniques to develop each of the systems such as mapping, localization, scene perception, teleoperation, external human-machine interface, and so on. The overall goal of this evolution process is to move from a supervised learning system to a more independent semi-supervised and unsupervised system.

The next three principles focus on how the systems should be developed so that they can complement the humans in the process of driving. These are critical from a safety point of view. The system should be able to gauge the state and capabilities of humans. Moreover, ADS should be able to perceive the environment as a human and supplement this perception with additional information to facilitate the human to make the best choice. Such a process cannot be completed unless the human is aware of the capabilities and limitations of the ADS. The fifth principle builds on the four other principles and warrants the system to adapt itself to the human using the sensory and behavioral information and evolve to provide a deeply personal experience to the human.

The sixth principle branches off from the shared perception concept and insists on sharing how the system sees the world and its limitations so that a synergistic relationship can be built between the two. The last principle recommends the ADS development process to optimize both the safety and the enjoyment at the system level.

17.3.2 Benefits and Concerns

Figure 17.2 summarizes various design principles and sheds light on each of them from the users' perspective. Let us look at the benefits from a user perspective. First and foremost, because of the data-driven development and connected systems the, ADS facilitate

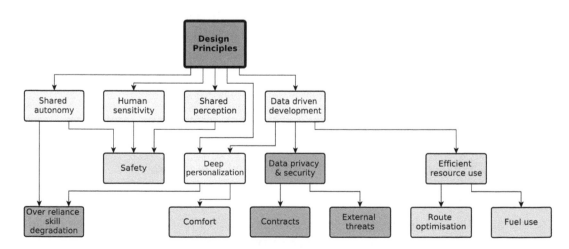

FIGURE 17.2   Design principles of ADS: benefits and the concerns associated with the design principles are depicted.

efficient use of available resources such as optimal routes leading to shorter transit times, and less congestion means lower fuel wastage. Hence, for a user, ADS can serve two purposes. First, its reduced transit times means users have more time available at their disposal. This a tangible economic benefit. However, this benefit also has social value. Availability of spare time can encourage users to enrich the lives of people around them and their own lives. Second, the optimal use of shared-access infrastructure (roads, highways, flyovers, bridges) can prolong their life; hence, it needs maintenance. As a result, under ideal conditions, the economic burden on the user, associated with building and maintenance of the infrastructure, in the form of taxes is expected to be reduced. Moreover, on a national level, such savings can be invested in other fields such as health, education, economic support programs for less affluent people, and so on. Thus, creating social value. The psychosocial aspects are discussed in detail in Section 17.4. However, these benefits to the user are not limited to economic and social dimensions, as lower congestion and shorter transit times lead to efficient use of fuel. Hence, emissions are expected to reduce. This environmental benefit has a global effect, but less pollution is expected to have positive effects on the health of the users.

Another critical aspect of the ADS is shared autonomy, where the human and machine work together. The system attempts to understand how the user perceives the surrounding. It also shares its perception of the surrounding with users, thus, providing them with a more holistic picture. As a result, users' safety is expected to increase. Such benefit depends on the synergy between the user and the system, that is, how well the user can understand the capabilities and limitations of the system and vice versa. This understanding of the user by the system leads to its deep personalization, hence, increasing the comfort level of the user during the travel. The comfort may come from the confidence in the system to carry out allocated tasks or from the optimized rerouting based on personal choices of the user leading to reduces stress levels.

> Apart from these positive influences on the users, certain concerns have been echoed since the genesis of the ADS. One of the essential aspects of ADS development is learning and evolution based on the data acquired from various systems. Such data-driven development provides the user with an opportunity to achieve more efficient use of resources. At the same time, the users' concern regarding privacy and data security cannot be neglected. The vulnerability of systems sharing data continuously and possible ways of circumventing these issues is discussed in the literature [3]. However, one of the primary concerns regarding data privacy was automated surveillance. Any vehicle-embedded ADS would share its information such as location and velocity with the service providers on regular intervals. Thus, automatic ticketing for speeding or entering in the wrong direction could be considered as one of the benign forms of automated surveillance.

The contracts related to data are generally skewed in favor of the entities exploiting data collected from users [4]. Capable regulatory frameworks can respond to and rein in such practices. However, the policy of the European Union (EU) seems too short on this front.

In case of India, currently, the policy architecture has not been altered to allow the use of ADS. The security threats to the ADS and eventually to the user can be classified into three types: one corresponding to sensors and others related to the systems and protocols of the vehicles. These are not limited to the data privacy or security aspects, but are about possible vulnerabilities of ADS against a malevolent party. Hence, from a users' perspective, data privacy and security concerns are twofold: the contractual relationship with the ADS service provider and the external threats.

Another vital concern is overreliance of the user on the ADS and the subsequent skill degradation. This is a direct offshoot of the deep personalization and shared autonomy. These two factors create a sense of complacence in the user. Continuous use of ADS might dull the users' skills and effectively increase the response time. As a result, in a shared system, the user may find it difficult to take over from the ADS to tackle the situation as and when required.

17.4 PSYCHOSOCIAL ASPECTS OF ADS

The psychosocial factors related to ADS were discussed briefly in Sections 11.2 and 11.3. The social aspect involves people and ultimately calls for the psychological involvement of the people. The literature tried to narrate the psychological aspect and decision-making functions [5]. They considered autonomous vehicles as vehicles that could perform a subset of the desired driving task. They identified clumsy automation as the reason for the increased mental workload. The operation of ADS should be considered the evident status of the system and should be intuitive. The decision-making function in ADS may lead to a reduction in driver's awareness of system status and dynamic features of the operating environment. The driver may not be actively engaged in evaluating the information sources leading to decisions if the similar types of decisions are taken and executed due to the repeated use of reference material. The decision-making task during the journey requires the performance of cognitively and visually demanding tasks due to the variability in the environmental conditions, traffic status, and encountered pedestrians. Skill degradation of the driver can be predicted due to increased responsibility for the safe control of the vehicle.

To overcome such challenges, the strategy chosen could have unintended consequences [6]. A strategy could either lead to public outrage if it is self-protective or may scare consumers if it is utilitarian. In both cases, it is tough to manage autonomous ethics. Autonomous ethics can be followed morally or can be prioritized as the lives of passengers' lives. The opaque process of decision making in ADS may result in diminishing trust.

The social acceptance of ADS can also be increased by providing legal certainty to consumers. The vehicles provided should be legally authorized, have appropriate insurance providing compensation for injuries, and more importantly "human drivers" should not be held responsible for actions in automated systems. The automotive industry can utilize vast amounts of data generated from automated vehicles in increasing the social well-being of the users. The data can be used to launch new services to users, make better infrastructure planning decisions, and improve traffic management and asset maintenance. Various decisions related to investment can be enhanced due to the availability of travel information of passengers. Crash investigations can facilitate determination of fault. The road-related revenue at all levels of government can be seen as another aspect under the social impact. The safety improvements in ADS will increase the sale and ultimately, reduction in cost for the consumers. The cost reduction for users can also be achieved due to the efficient use of the current infrastructure of roadways. The revenue of the government for registration and licensing fees can be reduced if the private ownership is reduced. It may also result in lesser parking fees and traffic violation fees.

The time spent on autonomous vehicles should be more productive and less stressful than the usual manual vehicles, and issues such as loss of gesture due to the eye-to-eye contact and acknowledgment; implications for road funding; changes at the individual level and in the workplace relating to taxi, chauffeur, and delivery jobs; changes in skills of driving; physical activity (like exercise); and social activity (like family time) should be addressed. The expected transformations are summarized in Table 17.1.

A case study of Australian traffic and related people have presented their finding in "Social Impacts of Automation in Transport" submitted to the House of Representatives Standing Committee on Industry, Innovation, Science and Resources [7]. The study elaborates the social acceptability of ADS under the umbrella of safety risks, mobility freedom, and cybersecurity issues. Factors contributing to the social acceptability of ADS include the safety of vehicle occupants, other road users, and others near the road environment. The safety risks involved in hardware, software, and the infrastructure pose a challenge. On the hardware front, safety risks include failure of the critical supporting interface and interaction issues between human drivers and automated systems. On the software side, the change in operational parameters, testing decisions taken by the manufacturers, and cybersecurity risks should be considered. The infrastructure angle suggests the difficulties in traffic due to risk-taking on-road profiles. The literature suggests that the ADS will be accepted if it provides mobility freedom to disabled people, older citizens, and children. The social impact can be observed if applied to public transportation. It may result in employment opportunities, education and training, government services, social activities, and reduction in parking space requirements. If the automated vehicles do not generate increased travel on the road, then they will reduce congestion, sustainability, and accessibility leading to increased livability. The biggest threat to ADS can be cyberattacks due to vulnerabilities caused by the extensive use of electronics, sensors, and software

TABLE 17.1   Summary of Systemic Transformations

Transformation in	Dimensions
Experience	Effective utilization of commutation time; mobility and digital communication; sensory dimension on being on the move; strategic test planning; scheduling
Inequalities	Values and preferences of a specific groups of people; quality and quantity of access of different social groups have; organization of urban spaces; types of power that people are subjected to; valuation of human life
Labor	Workforces; transportation employment; labor relations
Systems	Emerging system; drivers of change, citizen participation policies

components. The path of security management can be traced by shared responsibility of government and industry, that is, public and private sectors together.

17.5 AUTHORS' RESEARCH INSIGHTS

The levels of automation in the available ADS literature, generally, address the production side, that is, the vehicle manufacturers and service providers. How can the level of automation regarding the ADS of a society/country/province/region be evaluated? Here, a metric is proposed for determining the level of ADS in a society as the number of highest ADS level commercial vehicles per million ADS commercial vehicles at the second highest level. This metric reflects the level of advancement of that particular society in the field of ADS. It assumes that when the society advances to nth level, the infrastructure and systems to adequately support the $n-1$th level is in place. This metric can easily be used to compare any two societies with respect to ADS development. The levels can be indicated in the format: $LX - Y$, where X represents the highest level and Y represents the number of level X vehicles per million of $X - 1$ vehicles. For example, the number of cars with level 1 ADS features in India in 2015 was about 276,000, and level 0 vehicles was about 28,860,000. Hence, the place of India according to the proposed ADS hierarchy metric would be L1-9665.

REFERENCES

1. Ching-Yao Chan. Advancements, prospects, and impacts of automated driving systems. International Journal of Transportation Science and Technology, 6(3):208–216, 2017.
2. Miltos Kyriakidis, Joost CF de Winter, Neville Stanton, Thierry Bellet, Bart van Arem, Karel Brookhuis, Marieke H Martens, Klaus Bengler, Jan Andersson, Natasha Merat, et al. A human factors perspective on automated driving. Theoretical Issues in Ergonomics Science, 20(3):223–249, 2019.
3. David Eckhoff and Christoph Sommer. Driving for big data? Privacy concerns in vehicular networking. IEEE Security & Privacy, 12(1):77–79, 2014.
4. Philipp Hacker. Personal data, exploitative contracts, and algorithmic fairness: autonomous vehicles meet the internet of things. International Data Privacy Law, 7(4):266–286, 2017.
5. N Reed. Psychology and the automated vehicle. Journal of Psychology & Psychotherapy, 6(4):2161–0487, 2016.
6. Azim Shariff, Jean-Franffcois Bonnefon, and Iyad Rahwan. Psychological road blocks to the adoption of self-driving vehicles. Nature Human Behaviour, 1(10):694–696, 2017.
7. Department of Infrastructure and Regional Development, Australian Government. Social Impacts of Automation in Transport Submission to the House of Representatives Standing Committee on Industry, Innovation, Science and Resources. Technical Report, February 2017.

Anticipating Legal Issues Associated with the Cyber Security and Privacy of Automated Driving Systems in India

Sujata Bali

University of Petroleum and Energy Studies
Dehradun, India

Shamneesh Sharma

Poornima University
Jaipur, India

CONTENTS

DOI: 10.1201/9781003048381-20

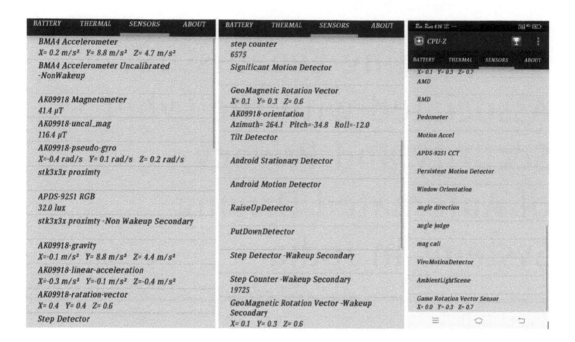

FIGURE 18.1   Smartphone sensor summary (screenshot taken from a VIVO V11 Pro mobile).

18.1 INTRODUCTION

The very-large-scale integration (VLSI) and ultra-large-scale integration (ULSI) technologies have started an era that has brought the sensing techniques into our daily routine with integration techniques on motherboards and fatherboards. The sensors can be in a mobile phone, which senses the data and generates reports. A normal smartphone generally contains 20–30 sensors in it. Figure 18.1 shows various sensors that are deployed to sense and collect data from people's daily routines.

The data collected by the sensors are analyzed by various applications installed on it and then sent to a dedicated server over a distributed or centralized network. If a handy mobile generally contains a minimum of 20 sensor devices in it, a smart vehicle can be imagined with a minimum of 1000 sensors installed on it; the amount of data generated by it will be huge. The science of sensors is applied on a vehicle, and the technology of an autonomous vehicle is introduced to the world where the vehicle could sense the various components of the surrounding environment and operate without any human interventions [1]. Autonomous vehicle technology is dependent on the sensing devices, actuation of mechanical processes, multifarious algorithms, machine learning algorithms, and powerful processing units to execute the software [2].

18.2 VEHICLE AUTOMATION LEVELS

When we talk about the automation process in vehicles, there are six levels that can be implemented:

    1. *No automation:* Vehicles without automation are called manual vehicles. These types of vehicles are fully controlled by the driver and all the tasks like steering control,

braking, and speeding cannot be performed without human intervention. The sensor system is almost negligible in such vehicles.

2. *Driver assistance:* Vehicles with driver assistance are called single-automated system vehicles. A vehicle categorized in this level of automation has a minimum of one advanced driver assistance (ADA) characteristic. Mobility of such vehicles is still supervised by a human, nevertheless for the sake of comfort and convenience, the vehicle has a feature that maintains velocity under some circumstances.

3. *Partial automation:* These vehicles come with a minimum of two advanced driver-assistance systems (ADASs). The features of a successful ADASs are adaptive cruise control, active lane keep assistance, and automatic emergency brakes. Although the vehicles with this level of automation are very comfortable in terms of driving mechanism, the driver will have to be vigorous to observe the progress of the vehicle and be prepared to intercede at any point of time.

4. *Conditional automation:* This vehicle categorized as level 3, and conditional automation can take over full control from the operating system of the vehicle during preferred routes when operating circumstances are encountered. During the selected routes the driver must be attentive and keep concentrating on the road, even when the vehicle is in self-driving mode.

5. *High automation:* This vehicle is categorized as a level 4, and it can complete an excursion deprived of driver involvement, but the vehicle does have some limitations such as being geofenced to the area and forbidden to operate under an assured speed.

6. *Full automation:* The vehicle is well appointed for comprehensive hands-off driving under all conditions. In fully automated vehicles there are self-driving mechanisms and no human interventions during driving. The vehicle has comfortable seats only and there is no steering wheel, pedals, or joysticks (Table 18.1).

TABLE 18.1 Levels in Vehicle Automation and their Brief Description

Automation Level	Automation Type	Examples	Driving Environment Control System
0	No automation	Maruti 800, Alto, 2018 Honda	Human monitors the driving environment
1	Driver assistance	Honda Civic, Honda Accord, Ford Fusion, Kia Stinger GT	
2	Partial automation	Mercedes-Benz Distronic Plus, Nissan ProPilot Assist, Tesla Autopilot	
3	Conditional automation	Audi A8 sedan, Google Test Vehicle (2012)	Automated system monitors the driving environment
4	High automation	Toyota's tested Chauffeur (no vehicles available to customers)	
5	Full automation	Only prototypes are available	

18.3 CYBER ISSUES ASSOCIATED WITH CONNECTED AND SELF-DRIVING AUTONOMOUS VEHICLES

When we talk about connected and self-driving autonomous vehicles, hacking can be considered the most common cyber threat [3]. There have been many cases around the world in which criminals have hacked the cars to keep from parking and ask for ransom [4]. Some of the common cyber-precipitated problems associated with these vehicles are described below:

1. The autonomous transportation system is based on smart technologies and operates by network. Hijacking the system through the network and taking control of the transport system by unwanted users can cause major crashes. The effect on light-detecting and ranging sensors may lead to endless confusion and disaster.

2. There have been cases when logistic companies were delivering their products using autonomous drones, and the hackers attacked the operating system and took control over the delivery. This also can be applied to the operating system of vehicles, and can destroy the vehicle remotely or harm the owner financially.

3. Hacking such a vehicle's information can cause a loss of control over location and routes. With such information someone could hypothetically track the user with an objective to commit burglary or assault. Another course of action may be to redirect the vehicle to a more expedient site.

4. Smart vehicle technology is the technology of connected things. Next, home appliances like the TV, heater, air conditioning, and home gate will be using smart vehicle technology. The access of vehicles may lead to the access of home appliances for the homeowner.

Human development has forced legal development due to social development through the creation of a family/social system in primitive times or technological developments through new inventions/disruptions in present times [5, 6]. Moreover, whenever legislative developments take long to respond, judicial pronouncements fill the gap. Whether it was building a reservoir to water the fields or keeping a dog for protecting property, whenever one's increase in personal convenience has caused loss to others, the law has stepped in to meet the developmental needs of society and their side effects. Looking at ADASs from a legal standpoint [5], we sense the potential technico-legal issues that threaten to stigmatize this technological advancement.

While implementing the system in India, these vehicles can be exposed to various legal aspects like data privacy, motor vehicle actions, cyber security actions, and many more. This chapter is further divided into three parts, related literature, research methodology, and results and discussions, which use hypothetical case studies on the implementation and management of autonomous vehicles.

18.4 RELATED LITERATURE

Thomas P. Novak has worked on the generalized dimensions of a framework of autonomous vehicles [31]. Technologies like artificial intelligence applied to vehicles have created a way to the development of autonomous vehicles. Cunneen Martin, Martin Mullins,

Finbarr Murphy, and Seán Gaines have suggested that framing artificial intelligence onto vehicles is not enough, and applying human intelligence to the moral values is also important [6]. Tripat Gill's research suggested that progress of autonomous vehicles could be successful if a change in the prevailing moral norms happens and governments would promote increased self-interest among the consumers of vehicles [11]. There is a need for proper regulation on the implementations of autonomous vehicles.

A study on the regulations, policies, and liabilities of autonomous vehicles was carried out by Damien A. Riehl [25]. The automotive technology is based on technologies like artificial intelligence, mechatronics, and machine learning. To be integrated with digital technologies, autonomous vehicle technology (AVT) is exposed to cyberattacks. A 2020 study on the attack vectors [27] was done by Christoph Schmittner and coworkers. The implementation of autonomous vehicles in some countries has raised ethical dilemmas and legal issues for all such cases in which autonomous vehicles are involved. One study by Giuseppe Contissa, Francesca Lagioia, and Giovanni Sartor has described that if the technology of artificial intelligence is involved in the production of autonomous vehicles, then there can be certain issues involved in the operating scenarios [5]. The study also focused on three scenarios and their common factors, and reported that in case of such vehicles the chances of harming passengers, pedestrians, or passersby are unavoidable. Smart technology is the future of the upcoming world; the world is full of smart devices like phones, televisions, homes, offices, and now vehicles.

The Government of India has also taken the initiative to make India full of smart cities in a program called Smart Cities Mission. This mission focuses on urban renewal to develop cities to be citizen responsive and sustainable. Malene Freudendal-Pedersen, Sven Kesselring, and Eriketti Servou opine that the smart cities may consist of smart homes and offices, and smart transportation systems are also important aspect of these cities [9]. The smart transportation system consists of smart vehicles, smart parking, and smart traffic systems. The implementation of policies related to smart vehicles is an important factor in India before the production or export of such vehicles.

In 2019, Araz Taeihagh and colleagues published research on governing autonomous vehicles [30]. The research was focused on the safety, liability, privacy, cyber security, and industrial risks that are associated with the autonomous vehicles. The article "Is The Law Ready for Driverless Cars?" by Ryan Calo was published in *Communications of the ACM* in 2018 and stated that the framework for driverless vehicles is ready but the world is not ready with the laws for it [2]. The technical progress has started for autonomous vehicles; one study in New Zealand recommended a major legal change for driverless vehicles [18]. As discussed, the technology is exposed to the cyberattack vectors, but research has been carried out in the direction of making the technology safe for customers. Technologies like face detection [6, 20], driverless braking systems for pedestrians [7], controlled artificial intelligence aspects [8], and ethical guidelines [10] are being enabled into AVT. There are certain legal and ethical challenges related to this integration as highlighted by Vivek K. Singh, Elisabeth Andre, Susanne Boll, Mireille Hildebrandt, David A. Shamma [29].

There are certain challenges to AVT in India. The Indian automobile industry is one of the largest in the world. The major contributors to India's gross domestic product (GDP) are the manufacturing industry. Research carried out in 2019 by Vivek Kumar in respect to driving opportunities in India found that there are 40 lakhs of drivers in India with a shortage of more than 25 lakh drivers [17]. The inculcation of AVT in the Indian automobile market will put the jobs of 1 crore people at stake.

The rules and regulations related to motor vehicles will also be a challenge for AVT. According to the Indian Motor Vehicle Act of 1988, the scope of AVT is almost equivalent to zero [12–14]. In 2019, a California-based company (INTEL) chose India for its automated driving solutions. They started the initial process by gathering the data on traffic patterns, roadside behavior, and transport infrastructure availability for the requirement analysis phase. India is a country in which most of its people are involved in farming and the Indian Government wants to promote farming products [15]. Because of this the autonomous mobility likely will start with the manufacturing of the autonomous tractors. The company, Escorts, which deals with the manufacturing of tractors, has started developing an autonomous tractor with level 2 automation technology [18]. Thus, the upcoming tractors in India may be seen with auto-steer and leverage geofencing features integrated with Global Positioning Systems. Another company, Mahindra and Mahindra, has also created the prototype of a semi-automated tractor and divulged its plans to go for a fully automated tractor [19].

Anoop Thomas et al. has presented a study on the implementation of the autonomous intra-city public transport system in India, where they focused on the smart transportation systems in developing countries and discussed a case study on the current intracity transportation [31]. AVT can enhance safety, reduce road accidents, reduce pollution levels by consuming less fuel, avoid road congestion, and make transportation systems accessible to all [21].

The Indian Government right now is not in favor of implementing fully automated vehicles. Developed countries like the United States, Germany, Singapore, and the Netherlands are at the ranked at the top for supporting fully or semi-automated vehicle technologies, whereas India is at number 24 [22, 23]. The ranking is due to non-supporting behavior, but the automated technology is the need of the hour and one day India will have to start thinking about it too. The researchers at the Indian Institute of Technology, Bombay, carried out an empirical research [24]. The study was based on the analysis of data collected from the students at reputed universities of India and the senior officials of multinational companies. The apprehensions and facts like knowledge about AVT, concerns about and interest in owning an autonomous vehicle were recorded and analyzed in the study [26, 28, 30]. The results of the study were categorized on perceived challenges and potential benefits of AVT in India. The outcomes from this empirical study presented a generalized viewpoint about the user assertiveness toward autonomous vehicles. Organizations like Google, Facebook, and Microsoft want to develop this technology to gain control over the access mechanism of the data. Keshav Kumar and Shamneesh Sharma explain the privacy policies in place for Facebook to collect the user data [16].

18.4.1 Research Gaps

1. AVT is a new field of research and only implemented in a few countries, yet, in India there is a great deal of scope on the implementation of this industry. Limited research has been carried out for setting up this kind of industry in India.

2. There are a few companies working on the prototypes of tractors based on semi-automated or fully automated vehicle technology, so the scope of implementation of this technology in India has started.

3. There is a need to review and reframe the laws on motor vehicles, insurance, information technology, legal procedures, and consumer protection before implementing AVT in India.

18.5 RESEARCH METHODOLOGY

1. The technology of autonomous vehicles is discussed throughout the related literature. Research publications from the last 10 years obtained from distinguished academic and research databases like Web of Science (WoS), Scopus, Springer, and ScienceDirect are considered while analyzing the technical aspects of autonomous vehicles.

2. The cyber-precipitated primary issues related to self-driving vehicles are explored through the studies from the last 10 years.

3. The hypothetical case studies on the implementation and management of autonomous vehicles are discussed. The case studies consist of the technical and legal challenges associated with the management of these vehicles in India.

18.6 RESULTS AND DISCUSSIONS

Based on the research methodology, the researchers have designed hypothetical case studies to elaborate the attack vectors and legal challenges to the AVT in India.

18.6.1 Case Study I: Ultimate Responsibility

The vehicles with an autonomous driving system come with a technology in which driving parameters are controlled by the digital environment, so it is a clear that virtual things are controlling the car. There will be a machine learning algorithm behind the scene, which is driving the car. Let us consider that a person named "Ravi" owns an autonomous vehicle in India and the vehicle was involved in an accident. Now it is necessary to analyze the situation and under which laws this situation will be treated.

The present Motor vehicles Act of 1988 does not permit driving a car without an occupant driver. Section 5 of the Act details that the owner will be legally responsible for ensuring compliance with a driving license and age-limit requirements.

Imagining a future of driverless cars future India, as the current discussion around the world is based on product liability insurance, either the manufacturer or the service provider should be held liable based on the cause of the accident. This will be an entirely new legal approach from the current scenario of the owner's no-fault liability. Presently, the Motor vehicles Act of 1988 under Section 140 makes the owner of a motor vehicle liable to pay compensation in certain cases based on the principle of no fault.

FIGURE 18.2   Correlation between the physical and virtual worlds.

18.6.2 Case Study II: ADS Exposed to Data

AVT lies in between the physical and digital world. The entire technology is based on the actuation based on the data sensed by the sensors (Figure 18.2).

Let us consider a situation in which the data related to ownership, location, routes, and other activities are taken off the server where it is stored, and those data are used to cause a malfunction of the vehicle's operating system. Due to this malfunction, the vehicle jumps the traffic signals. What laws will be applied in this situation?

In India, the detailed rule on traffic laws falls within the domain of both central and state governments. Therefore, as happens in the United States, any further movement in ADASs is possible only with the collaboration of union and state governments. For example, as per Section 112 of the Motor Vehicles Act of 1988, the central government of India has the authority to notify the minimum and maximum speed limits at a national level, whereas a similar power is granted to the state governments or their nominated agency to notify speed limits under their jurisdiction. Assuming this happens, and still on the question of malfunctioning leading to the violation of a traffic signal, who shall be liable to pay the penalty? Looking at the greater role of service provider in such cases rather than the manufacturer, the entity liable to maintain the data will be eventually held liable under the insurance contract, even if initially the penalty is served by the insurance company. The situations will inevitably become more complicated than this simple example, as the conditions of roads and lack of proper maintenance of roads can be further included as mitigating or liability-shifting factors [19].

From the car owner's perspective, such malfunctioning shall give rise to consumer law disputes involving "defect in goods" against the manufacturer and "deficiency in service" against the service provider, depending on the facts of each case. India has recently updated and enforced its "Consumer Protection Act of 2019" to give greater legal emphasis on consumer rights.

18.6.3 Case Study III: Accident Committed by Car Hacked by Someone

The digital world is exposed to cybercrimes like hacking the operating system of a vehicle; for example, the operating system of a vehicle is hacked by person "X," and X uses this vehicle to kidnap a person. How will this situation be treated in the Indian legal system?

The Information Technology Act of 2000, which is termed as the first Indian law to deal with information technology advances, presently covers cybercrimes including hacking. However, in wrongs amounting to crimes under the Indian law, Indian Penal Code 1860 shall also apply. In such situations where traditional definitions of physical crime and cybercrime interplay, it would be better to draft new laws to meet the requirements of new virtual and real-life crimes.

Looking at the comprehensive nature of Indian Penal Code 1860, even if revising the criminal law can be put on hold, there is a glaring need to update the procedural laws and investigators to include the new forms of investigations and evidence.

18.6.4 Case Study IV: Personal Data Protection

Let us consider a situation in which the data related to ownership, location, routes, and other activities are taken from the server where it is stored. This information can be used to attract the user through customized advertisements and suggested routes to prompt certain purchases. Will the law intervene to save the consumer in such cases?

India is on the verge of enacting its first specific data protection law, namely the "Personal Data Protection Bill of 2019." This bill proposes to regulate personal data related to individuals, and the processing, collection, and storage of such data. Under this proposed legislation, Section 13 defines "Data Fiduciary" as a person who determines the purpose and means of processing of personal data. One of the proposed duties of a data fiduciary is to retain personal data only for the purpose for which it is processed and to delete it at the end of processing.

The bill plans to set up a Data Protection Authority. Any individual who is not satisfied with the grievance redressal by the data fiduciary can file a complaint with this Authority. In addition, there are proposed appellate authorities.

18.7 CONCLUSION

On the Gartner Hype Cycle, the technology of autonomous vehicles is in the phase of innovation and soon will enter the stage of "peak of inflated expectations." There is still a long way to go and cover the trough of disillusionment. The technology of autonomous vehicles is based on artificial intelligence and, currently, India has no legal conventions, guidelines, or laws related to the regulation of artificial intelligence technology, but a number of national strategies and road maps related to it were created in 2018.

The Indian Government has taken various national initiatives, such as the report of the Artificial Intelligence Task Force, NITI Aayog discussion paper on a national artificial intelligence strategy, and the Ministry of Electronics and Information Technology Committee reports on artificial intelligence and defense. The semi-automated or fully automated vehicles induction into the Indian transportation industry will create new dimensions, but it can also take away the jobs of 1 million people. The support of the Indian Government is almost zero on autonomous cars as unemployment is a major concern and challenge to the current Indian Government.

However, as has happened in the case of every technological advancement in human history, eventually, due to the benefits of this technology, every country will have to adopt it and India as a developing nation will not be an exception. There are some concerns and challenges to the current transportation industry, but other alternatives to employability may increase the chances of embracing autonomous technology, whereas the technology is new and it will have to become stable in respect to the technical (i.e., cyberattacks), legal (laws changing from country to country and from state to state), and other miscellaneous challenges. This chapter has elaborated on the position of AVT in India and compared it with other parts of the world in respect to its technical and legal aspects. Moreover, before going toward the implementation of AVT, there is a strong need to review the laws on motor vehicle, cyber security, and data privacy.

REFERENCES

1. Grush, B. 2018. The Rise of Autonomous Vehicles: Planning for Deployment and Not Just Development-Research & Development World. [online] Research & Development World. Available at: https://www.rdworldonline.com/the-rise-of-autonomous-vehicles-planning-for-deployment-not-just-development/ [Accessed 8 August 2020].
2. Calo, Ryan. 2018. "Is the Law Ready for Driverless Cars?" *Communications of the ACM* 61 (5): 34–36. https://doi.org/10.1145/3199599
3. Canellas, Marc, and Rachel Haga. 2020. "Viewpoint Unsafe at Any Level." *Communications of the ACM* 63 (3): 31–34. https://doi.org/10.1145/3342102
4. Casey, Anthony J, and Anthony Niblett. 2017. "Self-Driving Contracts." https://ssrn.com/abstract=2927459
5. Contissa, Giuseppe, Francesca Lagioia, and Giovanni Sartor. 2017. "The Ethical Knob: Ethically-Customisable Automated Vehicles and the Law." *Artificial Intelligence and Law* 25 (3): 365–378. https://doi.org/10.1007/s10506-017-9211-z
6. Cunneen, Martin, Martin Mullins, Finbarr Murphy, and Seán Gaines. 2019. "Artificial Driving Intelligence and Moral Agency: Examining the Decision Ontology of Unavoidable Road Traffic Accidents through the Prism of the Trolley Dilemma." *Applied Artificial Intelligence* 33 (3): 267–293. https://doi.org/10.1080/08839514.2018.1560124
7. Finn, E. 2018. "Going Driverless in the City of Cars." *Technology Review* 121 (4): 46–53.
8. Fletcher, Michael A. 2015. "Google, Others Pave Way for Self-Driving Cars." *Technology* 392548 (1): 64–65. http://www.jstor.org/stable/43773229%0Ahttp://about.jstor.org/terms
9. Freudendal-Pedersen, Malene, Sven Kesselring, and Eriketti Servou. 2019. "What Is Smart for the Future City? Mobilities and Automation." *Sustainability (Switzerland)* 11 (1): 1–22. https://doi.org/10.3390/su11010221
10. Gerpott, Torsten J. 2019. "Connected Car." In: Kollman T. (ed.) Handbuch Digitale Wirtschaft. Wiesbaden, Springer Gabler. https://doi.org/10.1007/978-3-658-17345-6_73-1
11. Gill, Tripat. 2020. "Blame It on the Self-Driving Car: How Autonomous Vehicles Can Alter Consumer Morality." *Journal of Consumer Research* 47 (2): 272–291. https://doi.org/10.1093/jcr/ucaa018
12. Hilgendorf, Eric. 2017. "Automated Driving and the Law." *Robotics, Autonomics, and the Law,* 171–94. https://doi.org/10.5771/9783845284651-171
13. Huang, Bert I. 2019. "Law's Halo and the Moral Machine." *Columbia Law Review* 119 (7): 1811–1828.
14. Nishith Desai Associates. 2019. "Preparing for a Driverless Future Preparing for a Driverless Future." http://.www.nishithdesai.com/fileadmin/user_upload/pdfs/Research%20Papers/Preparing_For_a_Driverless_Future.pdf
15. Jana, Arnab, Ahana Sarkar, Jagannath Venkobarao Kallakurchi, and Satish Kumar. 2019. "Autonomous Vehicle as a Future Mode of Transport in India: Analyzing the Perception, Opportunities and Hurdles," *Proceedings of the Eastern Asia Society for Transportation Studies*, 12.
16. Kishore, Keshav, and Shamneesh, Sharma. 2013. "Information Security & Privacy in Real life – Threats & Mitigations: A Review," *International Journal of Computer Science & Technology*, 4 (3): 38–41.

17. Kumar, Vivek. 2019. "Where does India stand in Autonomous Vehicles." https://www.analyticsinsight.net/india-stand-autonomous-vehicles/. (Accessed 24/07/2020).

18. Larkin, John. 2017. "New Laws Needed to Pave the Way for Autonomous Vehicles." *Automotive Industries* 197 (4).

19. Lim, Hazel Si Min, and Araz Taeihagh. 2018. "Autonomous Vehicles for Smart and Sustainable Cities: An in-Depth Exploration of Privacy and Cybersecurity Implications." *Energies* 11 (5): 1062. https://doi.org/10.3390/en11051062

20. Miller, Helena. 2020. "Editor's Note." *Journal of Jewish Education* 86 (1): 1–3. https://doi.org/10.1080/15244113.2020.1711646

21. Walshe, D. G., E. J. Lewis, S. I. Kim, K. O'Sullivan, and B. K. Wiederhold, 2003. "Exploring the Use of Computer Games and Virtual Reality in Exposure Therapy for Fear of Driving Following a Motor Vehicle Accident." *CyberPsychology & Behavior*, 6(3), 329–334.

22. Novak, Thomas P. 2020. "OUP Accepted Manuscript." *Journal of Consumer Research* 47: 292–301. https://doi.org/10.1093/jcr/ucaa024

23. Parsons, J., Mark Shaw, Jeff Rubenstone, Aileen Cho, and Kevin Jost. 2018. "Preparing for a Driverless Future: Autonomous Vehicles Promise to Revolutionize Mobility, but They'll Need the Right Infrastructure to Do It." *ENR: Engineering News-Record*, 24.

24. Pizzi, Peter J. 2017. "Connected Cars and Automated Driving: Privacy Challenges on Wheels." *Defense Counsel Journal* 84 (3): 1–14.

25. Riehl, Damien A. 2016. "Car Minus Driver: Autonomous Vehicles Driving Regulation, Liability and Policy." *Bench & Bar of Minnesota* 35 (October): 20–26.

26. Salmon, Paul M. 2019. "The Horse Has Bolted! Why Human Factors and Ergonomics Has to Catch up with Autonomous Vehicles (and Other Advanced Forms of Automation): Commentary on Hancock (2019) Some Pitfalls in the Promises of Automated and Autonomous Vehicles." *Ergonomics* 62 (4): 502–504. https://doi.org/10.1080/00140139.2018.1563333

27. Schmittner, Christoph, Jrgen Dobaj, Georg Macher, and Eugen Brenner. 2020. "A Preliminary View on Automotive Cyber Security Management Systems." *Proceedings of the 2020 Design, Automation and Test in Europe Conference and Exhibition, DATE 2020*, 1634–1639. https://doi.org/10.23919/DATE48585.2020.9116406

28. Chao, Elaine L. 2017. "Focus On … NHTSA Revises Obama-Era Guidance." 83 (18): 20–23.

29. Singh, Vivek K., Elisabeth Andre, Susanne Boll, Mireille Hildebrandt, and David A. Shamma. 2020. "Legal and Ethical Challenges in Multimedia Research." *IEEE Multimedia* 27 (2): 46–54. https://doi.org/10.1109/MMUL.2020.2994823

30. Taeihagh, Araz, and Hazel Si Min Lim. 2019. "Governing Autonomous Vehicles: Emerging Responses for Safety, Liability, Privacy, Cybersecurity, and Industry Risks." *Transport Reviews* 39 (1): 103–128. https://doi.org/10.1080/01441647.2018.1494640

31. Thomas, Anoop, and Juergen Trost. 2017. "A Study on Implementing Autonomous Intra City Public Transport System in Developing Countries – India," *Procedia Computer Science* 115: 375–382. https://doi.org/10.1016/j.procs.2017.09.093

CHAPTER 19

ADAS Technology

A Review on Challenges, Legal Risk Mitigation and Solutions

Madhusmita Mishra

NIT Rourkela
Rourkela, India

Abhishek Kumar

IIT Jodhpur
Jodhpur, India

CONTENTS

19.1 INTRODUCTION

In this chapter, we have examined the best in innovation behind advanced driver-assistance systems (ADASs) and the mitigation of legal risks associated with it. Significant human errors during driving result from poor attention during driving, increasing speed abnormally, consuming alcohol or drugs, malfunction of vehicle, etc., so all over the world safety features are being added in automobiles. ADASs are these types of features. They help drivers by preventing collisions and guide them during driving and parking. ADASs consist of microcontroller units (MCUs), power semiconductor devices, and electronic control units (ECUs). Examples of ADASs that are integrated in automobiles include tire pressure monitoring system, drowsiness monitoring system, park assist system, adaptive cruise control (ACC) system, blind spot detection system, lane departure warning system, and adaptive front lighting system. Within these, ACC systems are the most popular. They prevent

DOI: 10.1201/9781003048381-21

crashes by changing the speed of the vehicle and maintaining a safe distance from the car in front. Hence all over the world, regulations are formed to make such systems compulsory in automobiles. Examples of such regulation-making authorities are the National Highway Traffic Safety Administration (NHTSA) of the United States and the European Union. These regulations have pushed the demand for more safety features in vehicles, including ADASs. Another reason for the increasing installation rate of ADAS is the rise in the quantity of high-net-worth individuals (HNIs). With the rising demand for ADASs, solution providers are coming up with improved technologies like Continental AG's eHorizon solution, Autoliv's driver-assistance product, and multifunctional sensors. Across the world, China and India are two of the largest automobile producers and buyers in the world, and the road accident and resulting fatality rates in the countries are quite high [1–3]. Both of these factors are forecast to have a combined effect on the popularity of ADASs in the region. This work measures the awareness and acceptance of selected ADASs while considering the influencing factors. This work has reviewed the technical specifications of various features of ADASs, including automatic cruise control, automatic parking, collision avoidance, and lane departure warning. ADASs undertake an autonomous move with all instrumentation and intelligence onboard the automobile. Combining vehicle automation and cooperation by communication technologies lead to a coordinated safety intervention on more than one automobile at the same point in time, but complexity arises with each involved vehicle; hence, significant parameters are needed. This is leading the research toward new development approaches. This work presents ideas for cooperative ADASs through the prototyping stage. In the cooperative approach, the driver gets assistance either from roadways or other vehicles. In this work, we have reviewed some of these assistance systems. Here we have discussed the simulation of some of the modular architecture of ADASs using MATLAB® while considering to embed a vision-based driver-assistance system along with the possible challenges. Here we have given an insight into the work of sensors meant for each assistance system. Implementation of ADASs is limited by the public policy-making rules. In this chapter, we have given insight into the flowchart of policy making for ADAS implementation while taking into consideration regulatory uncertainty associated with the climate change case [4–8].

A recent review states that car buyers are taking an interest in ADAS applications that encourage comfort and economy. The profits of ADAS executions are potentially appreciable because of a substantial reduction in pollution, human suffering, and economical cost. Recent research indicates that user trust is proportional to the number of experiences with ADASs, and facial emotion recognition (FER) may be prognostic of user trust in automation. This section discussed the general technology acceptance models in the context of ADASs.

The rest of this chapter is organized as follows. Section 19.2 discusses various features of ADASs. Section 19.3 highlights acceptance measures and influencing factors along with the integration of blockchain technology with ADASs. Section 19.4 discusses the procedures for cooperative ADAS implementation in MATLAB. Section 19.5 explains the regulatory uncertainty and policy making of ADASs. This chapter concludes with Section 19.6.

19.2 ADAS AND ITS FEATURES

ADASs consist of MCUs, ECUs, and power semiconductor devices. The categories of ADASs are lateral or longitudinal control systems, vision enhancements systems, reversing or parking aids, and intelligent speed adaptation.

Monitoring the sides of the vehicle to prevent collisions, lane warning and keeping, blind spot monitoring, and side-obstacle warning are the functions of lateral control systems. ACC, forward and intersection collision warning and avoidance, "stop and go" system for urban traffic, and pedestrian detection are the functions of longitudinal control systems. Reversing and parking aid mechanisms assist the driver to have a better view of events at the backside of the vehicle while giving a measure of the distance amid the vehicle's bumpers and the nearer obstacles. The driver's capability to tackle sudden potential hazards on roads depends primarily on light and weather conditions. Vision enhancement systems have the facility of night-vision systems, and are generally based on concepts of either near-infrared (IR) images or far-IR video images or both. Intelligent speed adaptation maintains the speed of the vehicle under the critical limit provided by either a navigation system or a communication system. The driver is notified by this limit through screen, sound, or a harder throttle pedal.

The modern automotive system based on ADASs has features like emergency brake system, blind spot detection system, front RADAR for ACC, front-view camera system, and smart rear camera remote park self-parking system.

Generally, ADASs (vision-based) employ at least one camera as a vision sensor. In high-end ADASs, cameras provide both inside and outside vision for the vehicle. The cameras can be monocular or stereo type or IR type. ADASs with monocular cameras have only one lens, so they require less image processing. They can detect obstacles, pedestrians, traffic signs, and lanes outside the vehicle. Inside the vehicle they can detect the driver's face, eye, and head position for analysis purposes. These are not good for distance estimation. ADASs with stereo cameras consist of at least two lenses, each having picture sensors, isolated by a stereo base space. Stereo cameras extract three-dimensional (3D) data from at least two two-dimensional (2D) pictures taken by left and right sensors and estimate the comparative depth of a scene with the use of a disparity map. These have applications in traffic sign identification, obstacles, lanes, and pedestrian sensing as well as estimation of distance with higher accuracy. ADASs can have passive or active IR cameras. The near-IR light source in active IR cameras is built inside the vehicle for illuminating the scene that is not visible to the natural eye and a sensor to captivate the pondered light. The IR sensor in passive IR cameras has every pixel as a temperature sensor, which can capture the thermal radiation emitted by any material. Mainstream night-vision arrangements favors active IR cameras.

ADASs with LIDAR are feasible for collision avoidance, automatic braking, and object detection. LIDAR calculates the distance of an object by evaluating the time taken between firing of a laser beam toward an object and the bounce back of light to the sensor. These provide high-resolution 3D pictures and provide operation at large distances. Being heavy, bulky, highly expensive, and effected by strong effect of atmospheric circumstances (such as fog or rain) on the coverage and precision of these systems limits their uses. The solid-state LIDARs lead to amazing LIDARs that are critically more modest and relatively economical.

RADAR is not impacted by rainy or foggy weather circumstances and is comparatively more inexpensive than LIDAR. ADASs with RADAR can detect longer distance objects.

Ultrasonic sensors utilize sound waves to detect and estimate the length of objects in close proximity of the vehicle. They are placed under the front and rear bumper and provide automatic and parallel parking assist. Photonic mixer device (PMD) cameras have an array of sensors for fast optical sensing. PMDs provide parallel distance measurement without scanning to ensure quicker imaging and prominent lateral resolution [9–11].

Vehicle automation tried by automotive industries (Uber, Google, and Toshiba) have confronted many security, safety, and privacy issues including denial of service (DoS), impersonation, and wormhole attacks. These have given rise to several questions and concerns with respect to the safety of passengers, but most of the solutions are related to the centralized architecture with a single point of failure. So here we have discussed the classification of threat pertaining to autonomous vehicles (AVs). We have given insight into the countermeasures for AV cyberattacks, issues with implementation, and the blockchain approach of overcoming these issues along with open issues and challenges of an AV system based on blockchains, followed by possible future solutions.

19.3 ACCEPTANCE MEASURES AND INFLUENCING FACTORS

Human error plays a major role in traffic accidents. Traffic accidents can be counteracted by (1) behavioral change in humans, (2) vehicle-related measures, and (3) physical road infrastructure-related measures. Each of these make up both passive and active elements. Similarly, passive safety measures are for mitigating the issues of an accident after it is encountered, and active safety measures are for avoiding accidents. Behavioral change in humans belongs to the domain of active safety. Government-initiated action affects the related measures.

For safety measures related to vehicles, there is a distinction between passive components and active components. Critical situation accidents are avoided with electronic stability control (ESC) and anti-lock brake systems, whereas information and communication technology (ICT)-based ADAS applications assist drivers in their driving task continuously, along with increased comfort and efficiency [12].

Measures related to physical road infrastructure are entirely about active safety (includes passive elements also) like "self-explanatory roads," having recognizable road layout with respect to road category and "forgiving roads," having structural layout elements for reducing the post-effects of accidents. The several safety-associated ADAS functions (intersection support, navigation, collision avoidance, speed assistance, and lane keeping) act as substitutes for infrastructure-related measures.

Intelligent decisions of AVs come from communication with road sensors, LIDAR, RADAR, maps, and other AVs. Also, the connectivity and computational complexity of AVs increases with the increment of AVs. A gigantic network of AVs may lead to security and privacy attacks by attackers, causing harm to individuals, AVs themselves, and the property, which leads to failure in driving functions, failure in the vehicle system, data

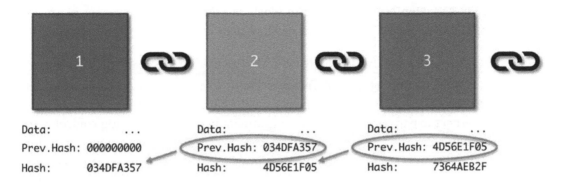

FIGURE 19.1   Blockchain basics.

larceny, vehicle larceny, AV collision, and commercial loss. Data related to decisions during driving and detection of obstacles are obtained from a centralized location (or server) via the wireless communication channel, and this in turn initiates security attacks because, in centralized AV systems, single-point failure may fail the full network and there is limited data control and constrained scalability. Blockchain with smart contracts (SCs) is a technology that can mitigate these challenges and security risks. For years, blockchain technology has been used for security purposes [13, 14] because it is a distributed database system that keeps the deals in a range of blocks. In this technology, there is no server or central authority to keep the records of the full chain, so each member node has duplicate records [9, 15]. Figure 19.1 shows the essential idea of a blockchain. Each block contains a cryptographic hash of the previous block, a time stamp, and transaction data. The decentralized concept of a blockchain is illustrated in Figure 19.2. Immutable property of a blockchain does not allow the record of a block to change after the block is written. AV systems with blockchain technology as a security scheme makes both passengers and drivers secure, safe during the ride, and comfortable. Although solutions made with blockchains enhance the protection of AVs, there are many difficulties in the execution of blockchain-based

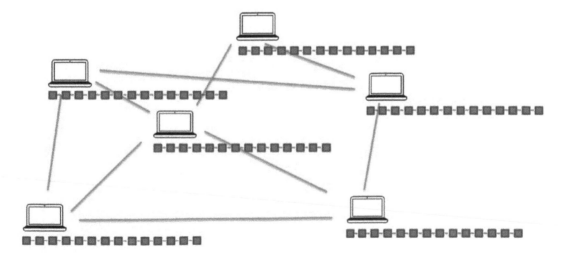

FIGURE 19.2   Decentralized blockchain.

protection for AVs. One of the solutions to block chain challenges is the use of an Low Density Parity Check (LDPC) code to reduce blockchain node memory requirements [16].

19.4 COOPERATIVE ADAS IMPLEMENTATION (MATLAB® APPROACH)

According to the U.S. Department of Transportation, advanced AVs are categorized into five levels by the Society of Automotive Engineers (SAE). The various SAE levels are compared with respect to parameters, such as environment perception, steering control, intelligence, accident responsibility, braking system, throttle pedal, and requirements in safety.

Sensors and actuators are mounted on AVs to provide real-time data for bringing timely efficient decisions. These systems have to work in an unpredictable and dangerous situation by making their own decisions, so there is a real need for deep testing of these kinds of applications. One cannot test the developed applications directly on the road because it is very costly and dangerous during the testing period. Therefore, there is a need to simulate the behavior of the system not only on the road but with a PC-based simulation. MATLAB software tools can be used in this context to develop PC-based simulations.

Taking a "lane keeping system," for example, we can say that to develop this active safety system, we need a multi-domain approach to the solution. This means a part of the arcuate will focus on image processing and the other part will focus on control. The first part of the arcuate will focus on developing MATLAB or C script languages [17]. To do this input will be taken in the form of images, and then it will be analyzed to understand the types of lanes ahead and the vehicle position corresponding to the lanes. The information on the position of the road will be input into the control part of the arcuate. The control part of the arcuate can be modeled by Simulink, and the control part will control the dynamics of the vehicle.

The PC-based simulation is accomplished in the following ways. At first, with respect to different circumstances, videos are recorded. If there are no videos, one can use external tools that are based on Simulink to generate topology of a road from a non-real image. Using this third-party software you can run numerous simulations by taking inputs from sensors (RADAR, LIDAR, etc.) implemented on the vehicle. The recoded videos from both simulations are used to tune the algorithms.

An efficient lane keeping system requires detection of departure of the vehicle from its lane and simultaneously warning the driver for active steering of the vehicle. The algorithmic steps for implementing the lane keeping system in MATLAB is given as follows:

Step 1: Detecting edges to identify the object that will be routed

Step 2: Identification of lanes

Step 3: To identify the position of the vehicle and generate an alarm signal or to organize the system so that the vehicle will steer automatically

The MATLAB software has the following facilities to implement the previously mentioned algorithm:

- After detecting edges, one can use some morphological operations to improve the results, which means closing out gaps. In this way the objects are better defined. Some examples are "imclose," "imfill," etc.

- Then transformation of the edge points obtained into "overhead" view is done by using the function "find."

- Then matrix transformation is used to transform the overhead points to the same kind of points, but they are visualized like one is viewing from a helicopter, and these transformed points are independent of the camera position.

- Then selecting a region of interest (ROI) by taking some reference points, we can find a mathematical description of one line that is passing through the reference points.

The detection of edge is done through the function "edge." This function uses several edge detection algorithms like Sobel, Roberts, LOG, Prewitt, ZeroCross, Canny, etc. By selecting different values for the counter, we can switch between the algorithms.

After developing the algorithm, to test it practically take the "MATLAB code" and generate a "C" code that can be embedded into a microcontroller or DSP toolkit.

19.5 REGULATORY UNCERTAINTY AND POLICY MAKING

Along with solving technical challenges related to control algorithms, ADAS acceptance by customers is also a major issue to manufacturers of automobiles. This is because demonstration of ADASs to customers in real traffic environments is impractical, dangerous, and costly. Hence, a modular structure of a simulation environment for ADAS demonstration must be adopted because it provides virtual prototyping of ADASs and demonstration. Also, novel ADAS models can be planned and appended without substantial user interface changes, and dissimilar ADASs can be incorporated together. The thought-provoking prospects regarding ADAS deployment and public acceptance can be achieved by a flexible test environment. Addressing the driver-vehicle interface concepts ahead of time in evolution phases will ensure that drivers may handle the systems suitably. The random behavior of real traffic scenarios does not permit standardized driving tests. In this context, the modular structure of driving simulators provides a virtual prototyping platform for testing and verifying ADASs by performing the design, testing, and validation in a closed loop along with vehicle components, driver, and environment.

Cost, validity from low-level to high-level, and structural complexity separate driving simulators from each other. Hence, ADAS advancement needs testing environments with different levels of particulars and complexity. The ADAS virtual prototyping framework includes various functional units along with simulation models that were executed with MATLAB/Simulink. The models follow a modular architecture and are developed to communicate in a loosely coupled manner. Minimum effort is required for adding new models of interfaces. Because all models are subjected to real-time applications, the simulations run in real time using the Real-Time Windows Target library from MathWorks.

19.6 CONCLUSION

In this chapter, we have reviewed ADASs along with their advanced features, acceptance measures, and influencing factors. Some solutions to threats in ADASs are highlighted by introducing the concept of blockchain technology and LDPC coding. A systematic algorithm for cooperative ADAS implementation is given in MATLAB along with regulatory uncertainty and policy making. Because every problem cannot be solved by blockchains, future implementation of ADASs must verify that the blockchain technology alone or with LDPC coding is sufficient for solving ADAS security issues.

REFERENCES

1. Aven, Terje, 2016. Risk Assessment and Risk Management Review of Recent Advances on Their Foundation. European Journal of Operational Research, Vol. 253, No. 1, pp: 1–13.
2. Viktorova, Lucie, et al., 2018. Drivers' Acceptance of Advanced Driver Assistance Systems – What to Consider? International Journal for Traffic and Transport Engineering, Vol. 8, pp: 320–333.
3. Hamid, Umar Zakir Abdul, et al., 2016. Current Collision Mitigation Technologies for Advanced Driver Assistance Systems – A Survey. PERINTIS eJournal, Vol. 6, No. 2, pp: 78–90.
4. Brookhuis, Karel A., et al., 2001. Behavioural impacts of Advanced Driver Assistance Systems–An Overview. European Journal of Transport and Infrastructure Research, Vol. 1, pp: 245–253.
5. Massow, Kay, et al., 2018. A Rapid Prototyping Environment for Cooperative Advanced Driver Assistance Systems. Journal of Advanced Transportation, Vol. 2018, No. 2586520, p:32.
6. Abdelgawad, Kareem, et al., 2015. A Modular Architecture of an Interactive Simulation and Training Environment for Advanced Driver Assistance Systems. International Journal on Advances in Software, Vol. 8, pp: 247–261.
7. Velez Gorka, and Otaegui, Oihana, 2016. Embedding vision-based advanced driver assistance systems: a survey. IET Intelligent Transport Systems, Vol. 11, pp: 103–112.
8. Dixon, Liza, Megill, William M., and Nebe, Karsten, 2019. Trust in Automation: An On-Road Study of Trust in Advanced Driver Assistance Systems. The Eighth International Conference on Advances in Vehicular Systems, Technologies and Applications, Rome, Italy.
9. Dugarry, Alexandre, 2004. Advanced Driver Assistance Systems Information Management and Presentation. PhD thesis, Cranfield University, School of Engineering, Applied Mathematics and Computing Group, Bedford, UK.
10. Borhade, Sanket, et al., 2012. Advanced Driver Assistance System. Sixth International Conference on Sensing Technology (ICST), IEEE, pp:718–722.
11. Gupta, Rajesh, et al., 2020. Blockchain-based security attack resilience schemes for autonomous vehicles in industry 4.0: A systematic review. Computers and Electrical Engineering, Vol. 86, p: 15.
12. Lu, Meng, et al., 2005. Technical Feasibility of Advanced Driver Assistance Systems (ADAS) for Road Traffic Safety. Transportation Planning and Technology, Vol. 28, No. 3, pp: 167–187.
13. Bayram, Orkun, 2020. Importance of Blockchain Use in Cross-Border Payments and Evaluation of the Progress in this Area. Doğuş Üniversitesi Dergisi, Vol. 21, pp: 171–189.
14. Coladangelo, Andrea, 2020. A Quantum Money Solution to the Blockchain Scalability Problem. Quantum Vol. 4, p: 297.
15. Ali MS, et al., 2018. Applications of Blockchains in the Internet of Things: A Comprehensive Survey. IEEE Communications Surveys & Tutorials, Vol. 21, No. 2, pp: 676–717.
16. Wu, Huihui, et al., 2020. Distributed Error Correction Coding Scheme for Low Storage Blockchain Systems. IEEE Internet of Things Journal, Vol. 7, No. 8, pp: 1–18.
17. Borhade, Sanket, et al., 2012. Advanced Driver Assistance System. Sixth International Conference on Sensing Technology (ICST), IEEE, pp: 718–722.

III

Autonomous Vehicle Applications

CHAPTER 20

Localization and Mapping for Autonomous Driving

Sridevi M and Sugirtha T

National Institute of Technology
Tiruchirappalli, India

B Ravi Kiran

Navya
France

Senthil Yogamani

Valeo Vision Systems
Galway, Ireland

CONTENTS

DOI: 10.1201/9781003048381-23

20.1 INTRODUCTION

Navigation is one of the fundamental requirements of a driverless car. Currently, vision and range sensors in the car such as camera, RADAR, and Light Detection and Ranging (LiDAR) can help the vehicle to navigate within the field of view (FoV) of respective sensors, but it is hard to get the information about the environment because it is beyond the FoV. These sensors can locate the objects within a range of 300 m with respect to direction and view angle. This FoV range may decrease in dusty weather conditions like snow, fog, and rain, so it is difficult to navigate under these conditions and these sensors may fail in detecting hidden objects. However, it is essential for the ego vehicle to locate itself within the FoV of vision and range sensors to maneuver without human interaction. At any instant, the ego vehicle needs to know its own location, pose, and the location of surrounding objects to reach the destination. Hence, it is crucial to recognize its environment and localize itself with respect to stationary and moving objects like trees, buildings, traffic signs, lane marks, pedestrians, surrounding vehicles, and cyclists. Localization assists the autonomous vehicle to make decisions on various actions like changing lanes, making turns, and to stop driving. Various approaches for localization can be categorized into a Global Positioning System (GPS) based and non-GPS based. GPS-based approaches include Global Navigation Satellite System (GNSS) and inertial measurement unit (IMU). Range sensors and vision sensors are two different types of non-GPS-based approaches. Mapping is the depiction of the environment in which the autonomous vehicle operates. Localization and mapping can be done simultaneously using Simultaneous Localization and Mapping (SLAM). Key steps in SLAM include (1) define the initial pose of the vehicle, (2) generate the map using various sensors and simultaneously compute the pose, and (3) eliminate cumulative errors in pose estimation. Using vision sensors to construct a map is tagged as a visual SLAM. Conventional visual SLAM approaches are laborious to use in real-time applications like autonomous vehicles. But, recently proposed visual SLAM approaches can be easily deployed in autonomous driving systems. This chapter gives a brief introduction to localization and mapping, discusses various use cases and explains different VSLAM approaches.

Over the last three decades, researchers and industries have focused their efforts toward the design of intelligent driver-assistance systems with the goal of reducing road accidents and traffic congestion. Driver-assistance systems have matured over the years, and various deployments are now available in the real world [1]. The Society of Automotive Engineers (SAE) defined six levels of autonomous driving systems (ADS) that range from 0 (no automation) to 5 (fully automated). There still exist many challenges that need to be resolved to achieve full automation. Localization of the vehicles in known or unknown environments is a critical part in achieving true reliable and safe automated driving agents.

To navigate without human intervention, an autonomous vehicle needs to locate itself with respect to a map, at least within a pre-mapped circuit. At any instant, it is necessary for the vehicle to perceive its location with respect to static and dynamic objects like other vehicles, pedestrians, cyclists, trees, buildings, lane marks, curbs, etc., and the location of other objects within an area to reach its destination. This is termed *self-localization* and *remote localization,* respectively. This helps the vehicle to decide on the actions such as stop, drive, change lanes, left turn, or right turn.

Simultaneous localization and mapping (SLAM) is a process by which a system creates a map by perceiving information about its surroundings using different sensors and simultaneously estimates its position. SLAM helps autonomous vehicles to simultaneously build a map and localize itself within the map. It is formulated as a recursive Bayesian estimation problem. Popular algorithms used to solve the Bayes filtering problem include particle filter, extended Kalman filter (EKF), and unscented Kalman filter.

There are two components used to achieve SLAM: (1) sensor signal processing (front-end) and (2) optimization (back-end). Visual SLAM (VSLAM) uses cameras and sensors to acquire images that are preprocessed to extract features for subsequent filtering and optimization steps. Various camera models are available including monocular, fisheye, stereo, and depth. Sensors may be vision or range sensors. This chapter briefly discusses various sensors and maps deployed in VSLAM. It also provides an overview of different VSLAM algorithms and use cases for VSLAM in autonomous driving.

20.2 AUTONOMOUS DRIVING ARCHITECTURE

Figure 20.1 demonstrates the pipeline of the ADS from environment perception using sensors to control actuation. Sensors can be either Global Positioning System (GPS) based or non-GPS based or a combination of both. This will be discussed in detail in Sections 20.3.2.1 and 20.3.2.2. The perception module interprets the sensor input to an intermediate representation, which helps the decision-making system to build the driving policy.

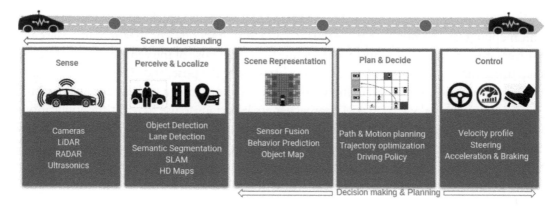

FIGURE 20.1   Modules in a modern autonomous driving vehicle.

This stage includes localization of static and dynamic agents like lane position, state of traffic lights, location of cars and pedestrians, etc. Uncertainties observed in the perception module are also propagated to the remaining ADS modules. Several perception tasks like semantic segmentation [2, 3], depth estimation [4–7], motion estimation [8, 9], soiling detection [10], etc., can be integrated with a multitask model [11–13] to improve the robustness of the ADS.

20.2.1 Scene Interpretation

Mid-level representations that are outputs of the perception module are mapped to high-level abstract representations used to drive decision making. It combines three tasks: scene understanding, decision, and planning. This step fuses information from heterogeneous sensor sources, and renders it independent of the sensor's configuration and calibration procedures [2, 14]. This provides a sensor agnostic state representation of the environment.

20.2.2 Localization and Mapping

Mapping is a static portrayal of the perception module in the automated driving modules [15]. Maps are used prior to evaluate the likelihood of localization of an agent given current observations and the static map representation. One of the early manifestations of automated driving by Google heavily relied on re-localization within pre-mapped areas. Conventional mapping approaches can be improved by semantic object detection for reliable disambiguation. Additionally, high-definition (HD) maps encourage object detection.

20.2.3 Planning and Driving Policy

Trajectory planning is an important component in the ADS pipeline. Route level plans for the driving area are generated by HD maps or GPS-based maps. With this information, the trajectory planning module produces motion level commands to direct the agent. Traditional path planning methods use translations and rotations to transition from source to destination [16]. An agent that can control six degrees of freedom (DoF) is "holonomic," whereas the one with fewer controllable DoFs is "non-holonomic." Conventional algorithms based on Dijkstra's algorithm are not appropriate in non-holonomic cases of automated driving. Instead, rapidly exploring random trees [17] are non-holonomic approaches currently used for motion planning in the ADS pipeline.

20.2.4 Control

The duty of the controller is to define the speed, steering angle, and braking strategy to avoid collisions over every point in the path acquired from a predetermined map like Google maps. Conversely, trajectory tracking performs temporal modeling of vehicle dynamics by considering waypoints sequentially over time. Current vehicle control approaches are based on classical optimal control theory, which formulates the problem as minimizing the cost function defined by $x = f(x(t), u(t))$, where $x(t)$ – set of states and $u(t)$ – control actions. The velocity control is based on two classical closed-loop control methods, proportional integral derivative (PID) controllers and model predictive control (MPC). Although PID controllers aim to minimize a cost function consisting of three terms (current error with proportional term, past errors with integral term, future errors with derivative term), MPC methods help in stabilizing the vehicle behavior during tracking of a specified path [18].

20.3 LOCALIZATION IN AUTONOMOUS DRIVING

In this section, we discuss types of use cases in autonomous driving, types of localization, and map representations.

20.3.1 Use Cases

In the following sections, we discuss various use cases of VSLAM from the perspective of autonomous driving.

20.3.1.1 Parking

Parking needs an accurate map of the neighborhood area surrounding the car while driving at low speed [19]. Different parking scenarios include (1) parking deck, (2) off-street parking area, and (3) parking space at home. Scenarios 1 and 2 are examples of an unknown environment that needs small-scale mapping and home zone is a dedicated application of SLAM. Initially the car learns a trajectory and parallelly records an initial map. When the car enters the home zone again, the home zone park-assist system loads the recorded map, performs relocalization, and the car moves on the learned trajectory. Although both maps discussed in the mapping module are suitable for this use case, two other maps listed below are also applicable:

- *Feature maps:* support park assist system to relocalize

- *Dense point maps:* provide additional information about the environment

20.3.1.2 Highway Driving

Highway driving involves high speed than and two other use cases, which makes it very challenging for the VSLAM approaches to run in real time. It needs a frame rate of 30 frames per second (fps) at least. As the surrounding objects are parallelly arranged, the environment geometry appears to be less complex compared with other use cases. ORB-SLAM [20] achieved high accuracy on the KITTI [24] highway trace. Sparse SLAM techniques have already shown high accuracy for the highway driving scenario, but efficiency can be further improved by a sparse and efficient CNN-based VSLAM approach as highway driving requires a high frame rate [21].

20.3.1.3 Urban Driving

Automated driving in a city is an extremely challenging scenario, particularly for building an extensive data set [22]. Due to the dynamic environment, it is much more complex than highway driving. Urban driving includes more dynamic objects than the parking scenario, which needs to be detected during reconstruction and localization. Although ORB-SLAM [20] achieved high accuracy on the KITTI benchmark suite [23] for highway scene, the results are imprecise on urban scenarios. In contrast, DSO-SLAM [24] provides high performance on a large urban data set. Stereo-DSO [25] ranks higher than LSD-SLAM [26] on the KITTI odometry challenge. Hence, the key strategy is its ability to reassess static points against many dynamic objects. CNNs can be deployed to improve such intelligent tasks, which learn good areas to reconstruct by providing a large-scale data set.

20.3.2 Types of Localization

In this subsection, we discuss two types of localization.

20.3.2.1 Absolute Localization

GPS enables autonomous vehicles to locate themselves in a global coordinate system. This is achieved by utilizing the Global Navigation Satellite System (GNSS) technology, which uses satellite data to locate the car within Earth's coordinate system. Today it is a primary method for navigating cars. GNSS provides sufficient accuracy while determining the position of any object in real time and is cost-effective. Additionally the HD maps discussed earlier can provide absolute localization for pre-mapped areas because they are created by using precise GPS initialization.

20.3.2.2 Relative Localization

ADS require an uninterrupted GPS signal, which is not possible today as many roads are densely populated by tall buildings. Hence, the signal may be lost or degraded. The inertial measurement unit (IMU) incorporates gyroscopes, accelerometers, and magnetometers to measure the orientation and movement without using satellite-based resources like a GPS. Also, it helps to track a vehicle's velocity, position, and altitude by fusing data provided by the IMU with data supplied by other onboard sensors. In this way, IMU ensures accurate positioning and navigation in regions where there is no GPS or in unreliable situations like GPS spoofing. IMU plays a vital role in military applications. Additionally, the modern ADS is equipped with cameras, LiDARs, and RADARs for efficient positioning and navigation.

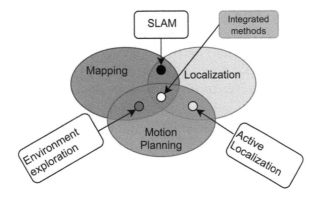

FIGURE 20.2 Different tasks performed by a robot to explore, map, and localize itself in an unknown environment.

20.3.2.3 Active Localization

SLAM conventionally constitutes a mapping step that involves estimating the ego vehicle pose as well as the metric representation of the environment. Active localization is a key domain where, in addition to the conventional mapping step, the algorithm decides the actions of the ego vehicle or robots, thus planning to reduce the uncertainty. Motion control methods are control decisions given to the robot to safely explore and map the environment while increasing the mapping coverage. The seminal paper on active loop closing [27] summarized it in Venn diagram format as shown in Figure 20.2. Active localization achieved various developments in last few years [28].

20.3.3 Sensors

In the following sections we discuss range sensors and vision sensors from the perspective of localization.

20.3.3.1 Range Sensors

A wide variety of range sensors provides driver-assistance functionalities for autonomous vehicles. Most commonly used range sensors are LiDAR and RADAR. LiDAR is a type of laser-based range sensor that emits light beams and collects the reflected light from surrounding objects with a receiver. It determines the distance and posture of an object using the time of arrival of the reflected light beam. LiDAR sensors are available in 2D and 3D. Most 2D and 3D LiDAR sensors use an oscillating mirror and rotating mirror, respectively, to collect the light beam. Most autonomous vehicle industries show promising results by deploying LiDARs in their ADASs. Automotive LiDAR sensors help self-driving cars to avoid collisions by providing excellent field of view (FoV) (360° view) and improve safety. It is expensive compared to other sensors. Recently, solid-state LiDAR systems emerge as less expensive LiDAR sensors.

On the other hand, RADAR sensors use radio waves. They are widely used to detect obstacles. RADAR sensors use time of arrival of the signal to compute the distance to an object. Unlike LiDAR, RADAR helps to determine velocity of the moving objects by considering Doppler shift of the echo. It is less sensitive to weather conditions and can be used for longer distances. They operate at lower frequencies and less expensive than LiDAR sensors. RADAR provides a wider FoV than LiDAR. It is less accurate in determining objects' postures. Hence, RADAR sensors outperform LiDAR in detecting and tracking objects, but fall behind in object recognition. It is difficult to detect very close objects; however, RADAR can detect objects less than a meter and beyond 200 m. Based on this range, RADAR systems can be classified as follows:

- *Short-range RADAR:* below 24 GHz

- *Medium-range RADAR:* between 24 and 77 GHz

- *Long-rang RADAR:* above 77 GHz

20.3.3.2 Vision Sensors

Vision sensors are predominant sensors for autonomous driving application as they facilitate real-time navigation and localization. They are widely preferred because they ensure high accuracy with less computation. Yet, they are more expensive than range sensors. Recent advances in computer vision draws attention to vision sensors for autonomous navigation. They are deployed in a wide variety of autonomous driving tasks like object detection, curb recognition, lane marking, and traffic light and traffic sign detection. Various vision sensors are tabulated in Table 20.1.

As opposed to LiDARs and RADARs, which are called active sensors, cameras are passive sensors. Although they offer high resolution, the data collected are influenced by poor weather conditions like rain, fog, darkness, dust, etc. Hence, computationally expensive deep learning or computer vision algorithms are needed to interpret the camera data, but once interpreted it provides a rich semantic representation of the environment. However, infrared cameras with additional sensing capability perform better in the darkness.

20.3.4 Map Representations

Maps provides a static representation of the environment describing static obstacles and regions obtained during the mapping phase. There are two large representations of maps: graph/topological based or metric based. Topological maps provide adjacency and

TABLE 20.1 Categories of Vision Sensors

Vision Sensors	Advantages
Stereo cameras	Produce distance estimation through 3D construction
Thermal cameras	Improves detection accuracy under challenging weather conditions and at night time
High frame rate cameras	Simplifies detection and tracking of moving objects
Event triggered cameras	Reduced bandwidth for data transmission and low latency reactive path for collision avoidance

connectivity information, whereas metric maps provide geometric and distance-based occupancy information. Finally, maps can be represented by using parametric models for surfaces or structures in the environment. They are continuous and have high resolution. For this reason, they are termed as *vector maps*. Table 20.2 summarizes the different map representations used in autonomous driving.

TABLE 20.2   List of Different Maps Used in Autonomous Driving Infrastructures

Map Category	Description and Utilization
Occupancy grid Maps	An evenly spaced grid is seen in ref. [29], with an estimate of the probability that a location is occupied by an obstacle.
Private small-scale maps	Small-scale maps are obtained from classical semi-dense point cloud maps or landmark-based maps. Customized small-scale maps provide the following advantages. First, they guarantee privacy where it is legally forbidden to map the area (e.g., private residential areas). Second, HD maps cover only a portion of the surrounding area, and finally they detect dynamic structures that differ from global measurements.
Large-scale dense semantic point cloud maps	Google and TomTom adopt the high-precision dense point cloud map with semantic information. These maps are expensive and require large runtime memory to operate. Here mapping serves as an effective cue when compared with live perception. They retrieve static objects like roads, lanes, and traffic signs and from the map and dynamic objects using background extraction methods, given good alignment.
Large-scale landmark-based maps	These maps rely on semantic objects rather than generic 3D point clouds and can be applied to camera data. Mobileye and HERE follow this strategy. They make use of object detection to provide an HD map and improves accuracy by combining observations from different cars.
HD maps	HD maps are considered as the dominant cue and semantic segmentation algorithms refine priors obtained by HD maps. In Figure 20.3, the semantic point cloud alignment provides an accurate semantic segmentation for static objects. Insubstantial objects like the sky are not covered. It needs a good confidence measure like re-projection error for localization accuracy.
PolyMap	PolyMaps are vector-based maps [30] that use line segment primitives. They are used to map an environment with multiple agents.
Hybrid maps	These maps mix two or more representations, for example, feature/landmark-based and vector maps are combined to provide one map [30].

FIGURE 20.3   Example HD map. (Reproduced with permission of TomTom.)

20.4 VISUAL SLAM (VSLAM)

The VSLAM pipeline shown in Figure 20.4 includes various components to deploy SLAM for autonomous driving. This section briefly explains these components.

Figure 20.4 summarizes the perception-based pipeline for ADS. It also illustrates crucial subtasks, such as map creation and ego vehicle pose estimation, within the perception-based pipeline. This is summarized abstractly in the block diagram in Figure 20.5. Formalization of the SLAM problem usually involves an estimate of the conditional probability of the ego vehicle's location and a map of the environment. This can be seen as a maximum a posteriori (MAP) estimation of the posterior distribution of the ego vehicle pose, given a set of sensor measurements and data associations.

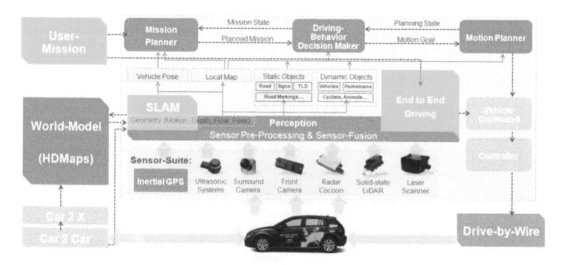

FIGURE 20.4   Perception-based VSLAM pipeline of automated driving.

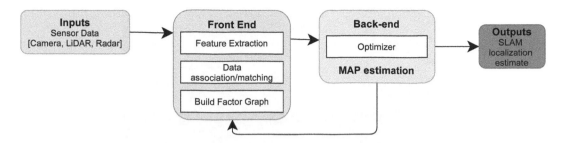

FIGURE 20.5 An abstract representation of key tasks in the SLAM problem.

We summarize various components of VSLAM pipeline below:

- *Initialization:* To start VSLAM in a new environment, it is crucial to estimate the 3D structure of the surroundings and define a coordinate system for camera motion estimation. The global coordinate system builds an initial map by reconstructing part of the environment and estimates the position of the ego vehicle that corresponds to it. The map will be updated iteratively with the sensor data collected over the whole operation.

- *Tracking:* Initialization followed by tracking generates camera trajectory by utilizing consecutive camera images. Most VSLAM approaches widely use keyframes as a primary component for tracking. A new keyframe is created if tracking signifies inadequate overlap between the current frame and the keyframe.

- *Mapping:* This is the process of expanding the initialized map by computing volumetric representation of the environment when the camera captures unexplored regions where mapping has not been carried out. SLAM algorithms are categorized into feature-based and direct methods depending on the map generated. The former generates sparse feature maps, whereas latter yields dense point maps.

- *Global optimization:* Tracking introduces an accumulative drift error into the map in accordance with the camera movement. Global optimization is periodically carried out to reduce the computational complexity caused by the error. Global optimization relies on loop closure detection techniques to suppress the error. Loop closure detects a closed loop if there is a match between the currently observed scene and the one acquired earlier. Loop closure helps to generate a geometrically consistent map. Optimization can be done in two ways: (1) optimizing camera poses (e.g., pose graph optimization) and (2) optimizing both camera poses and the map (e.g., bundle adjustment [BA]). Figure 20.6 illustrates the map generated by the VSLAM pipeline on the monocular fisheye surround view camera.

- *Re-localization:* Tracking may fail occasionally due to various reasons like fast camera motion, motion blurring, etc. SLAM systems do not work if tracking is lost. Thus, re-localization is the ability of the SLAM system to recover from localization failure by recomputing the camera pose corresponding to the map. Several approaches such as matching feature descriptors and bag of words were proposed.

FIGURE 20.6 Simulation results of a map generated by a VSLAM pipeline on monocular fisheye surround view camera.

20.4.1 Classification of SLAM

Based on how the visual measurements obtained from sensors or cameras are processed, VSLAM can be categorized into two types: (1) feature-based (indirect) SLAM and (2) direct SLAM (Table 20.3).

20.4.1.1 Feature-Based SLAM

Feature-based VSLAM algorithms exploit handcrafted feature detectors and descriptors for tracking and depth estimation. MonoSLAM [31] is the first monocular VSLAM approach. It continues to be one of the exclusive methods among all filter-based algorithms. It estimates camera motion and 3D feature points of the surrounding environment using EKF. The computation cost increases with increased feature points for a real-time scenario. PTAM [32] reduced the computation cost of MonoSLAM [31] by executing tracking and

TABLE 20.3 Summary of VSLAM Systems

	Camera Type				Direct/	Map	Loop		
SLAM Methods	Monocular	RGB-D	Stereo	All	Indirect	Density	Closure	Optimization	Year
Mono-SLAM [31]	✓				Indirect	Sparse	×	Optzn using EKF	2007
PTAM [32]	✓				Indirect	Sparse	×	Bundle adjustment optzn	2007
KinectFusion [33]		✓				Dense	×	Data association and point-plane optzn	2011
DTAM [34]		✓					✓	Non-convex optzn	2011
Kintinuous [35]		✓				Dense	✓	Pose graph optzn through iSAM	2012
RGBD-SLAMv2 [36]		✓			Indirect	Dense	✓	Mahalanobis-based g2o graph optzn	2013
LSD-SLAM [26]	✓				Direct	Semi-dense	✓	Gauss Newton-based pose graph optzn	2014
SVO [37]	✓				Direct	–	×	Reprojection error minimization	2014
RTAB-MAP [38]		✓			Indirect	Dense	✓	Graph optzn	2014
Elastic fusion [39]		✓				Dense	✓	Surface loop closure optzn	2015
ORB-SLAM2 [20]				✓	Indirect	Sparse	✓	Levenberg-Marquardt algorithm with g2o optzn	2016
BundleFusion [40]		✓			Indirect	Dense	×	Local to global pose optzn	2017
DSO [24]	✓				Direct	Sparse	×	Nonlinear windowed optzn using Gauss newton	2018
DVSO [41]	✓				Direct	Sparse	✓	Constant-size marginalization	2018
LDSO [42]							✓	Pose graph optzn	2018
VI-DSO [43]	✓				Direct	Sparse	✓	Full bundle adjustment like optzn	2018
Omni-Directional DSO [44]				Fisheye camera	Direct	Sparse	✓	Windowed optzn and marginalization	2018
ProSLAM [45]			✓		Indirect	Sparse	✓	g2o-based pose graph optzn	2018

(Continued)

TABLE 20.3 (*Continued*)   Summary of VSLAM Systems

		VSLAM Systems							
	Camera Type				Direct/	Map	Loop		
SLAM Methods	**Monocular**	**RGB-D**	**Stereo**	**All**	**Indirect**	**Density**	**Closure**	**Optimization**	**Year**
OpenVSLAM [46]				✓	Indirect	Sparse	✓	Pose graph optzn and global bundle adjustment	2019
Uco-SLAM [47]				✓	Direct	Sparse	✓	Local and global map optzn using	2019
D3VO [48]	✓				Direct	Sparse	×	Photometric bundle adjustment optzn	2020

Abbreviation: optzn, optimization.

mapping in separate threads. Due to parallel execution, it can handle many more feature points compared with MonoSLAM [31]. It is the first method to apply BA for optimization of 3D feature points. From the literature reviewed, accuracy of VSLAM increases with an increase in feature points on a map. ORB-SLAM [20] also follows BA-based mapping. It extends PTAM [32] to obtain global map optimization in large environments by including closed-loop detection and global pose graph optimization. It relies on the ORB (FAST and rotated BRIEF) feature descriptor, which makes it robust with low computational cost. ORB-SLAM [20] is the most exhaustive feature-based monocular VSLAM system, which includes the following functionalities: (1) multi-threaded tracking, (2) mapping, and (3) optimization using loop closure detection and BA.

20.4.1.2 Direct SLAM

In contrast to feature-based approaches that rely on handcrafted feature detectors for tracking, direct methods use either all or a portion of pixel intensities of the input image. Dense tracking and mapping (DTAM) [34] is the first complete direct method. It estimates depth information for all pixels using multi-baseline stereo. It initializes the map with stereo measurements and considers space continuity to optimize the map. DTAM measures camera motion by generating a synthetic view from the reconstructed map. LSD-SLAM [26] is another popular method in direct-based approaches. The core idea of LSD-SLAM [26] is from semi-dense VO [49]. It rejects texture-less areas as it is hard to estimate depth information directly from images and improves computational efficiency by considering only the pixels that have a high-intensity gradient. Camera motion estimation of direct methods relies on the reduction of image-level photometric error. Semi-direct VO (SVO) [21] is named as it integrates feature-based tracking and mapping based on sub-pixel feature correspondence that resulted from direct motion estimation. DSO [24], a fully direct method, provides high accuracy on motion estimation, which reduces accumulative error by minimizing both photometric and geometric error factors. It considers both geometric and photometric camera calibrations in the model image formation process.

20.4.2 Extension to Other Types of Cameras

To get dense depth maps of the objects, VSLAM systems deploy RGB-D sensors (e.g., Microsoft Kinect). Also, stereo cameras use point features in estimating camera trajectory and build a map of the environment.

20.4.2.1 RGB-D SLAM

RGB cameras with depth sensors(RGB-D) directly provide 3D structure of the environment along with its texture information. Depth-based VSLAM frameworks widely use the iterative closest point (ICP) algorithm for camera motion estimation. It then reconstructs the 3D structure of the environment by integrating multiple depth maps. Although many approaches were proposed to associate RGB into depth-based VSLAM, we discuss the most popular ones here. KinectFusion [33] represents 3D design of the environment using the truncated signed distance function (TSDF). As TSDF is a volumetric representation, it is configured with two parameters: size and dimension. It combines depth maps acquired in voxel space to reconstruct the 3D map of the surroundings. The 3D map and depth map are given as input to ICP algorithm to estimate camera motion. Kinectfusion [33] has inflexible surface reconstruction that restricts it to work over the area around the initialization point of TSDF. Kintinuous [35] extends KinectFusion [33] with the FOVIS system that maintains TSDF of the unbounded region at any point in time. It deployed a cyclic buffer data structure to incrementally augment the reconstructed surface as the camera rotates. RGB-D SLAMv1 [50] estimates camera motion by taking two RGB-D images as input. It proposed a dense VSLAM method with entropy-based keyframe selection and pose-graph optimization using g2o. RGB-D SLAMv2 [36] framework computes geometric relations from the visual features and associates them with 3D points. The geometric relations and their uncertainties are represented as a pose graph. They employed g2o for graph optimization and the OctoMap [51] approach to generate a 3D occupancy map. RTAB-MAP [38] addresses multi-session mapping with global loop closure detection and proposed a memory management model to update the online map with limited computing resources.

ElasticFusion [39] applies frame-to-model tracking on a surfel-based dense map of the environment. It explicitly handles loop closure with non-rigid deformation of surfels. BundleFusion [40] proposed a real-time global pose alignment framework for 3D reconstruction of the environment. It uses a two-stage hierarchical global pose optimization algorithm. BundleFusion follows a sparse-then-dense alignment strategy of sparse and dense feature correspondences. It generates a high-quality surface and outperforms ElasticFusion [39] with complete scan and improved alignment accuracy.

20.4.2.2 Stereo SLAM

Most popular state-of-the art approaches like ORB-SLAM2 [20] and LSD-SLAM [46], which are widely used in real time, involve high computation cost. ProSLAM [45] aimed to provide a simple stereo-based SLAM system with less computational resources. It generates pose graph-based local maps with four modules, including incremental motion estimation and re-localization.

20.4.2.3 SLAM for All Types of Camera

In ref. [20], the authors proposed ORB-SLAM2, which can operate on monocular, stereo, and RGB-D cameras. Classical VSLAM sub-tasks such as tracking, mapping, and loop closing are achieved in parallel. Ref. [47] proposed UcoSLAM, a robust-tracking method by combining keypoints and fiducial markers. A recent VSLAM framework, OpenVSLAM [46], was proposed to a provide highly usable and extensible SLAM system that can be applied to localize objects captured by any type of camera models like fisheye, equirectangular, and perspective cameras. The motivation behind OpenVSLAM [46] is to overcome the performance drift while using the direct method for rolling shutter cameras.

20.4.2.4 Deep Learning Methods for SLAM

Modern deep neural nets have been used to perform keypoint and feature extraction. The authors of Super-point [52] have demonstrated the use of a VGG-based DNN that outputs robust keypoints and robust features. The goal was to create a synthetic training data set with shapes such as quads, tris, ellipses, cubes, checkerboards, and lines. Training of keypoint extractor and feature extraction task were carried out jointly. The main contribution was performing heavy augmentation over these synthetic training samples, with noise injection that improved the robustness over classical methods and baseline methods such as ORB. Furthermore, the authors propose the use of a self-supervised learning approach, termed as *homographic adaptation*. This constitutes simulating planar camera motion with homographies, while using the synthetically trained keypoint detector to reinforce repeatable keypoint extraction, while removing spurious points.

20.4.3 Semantic SLAM

SLAM methods in the camera or LiDAR modalities generally utilize geometrical features such as lines and corners to extract keypoints to estimate robust correspondences to evaluate the relative pose change for the vehicle or sensor. Semantic information has been used in SLAM frameworks [53] to represent a hierarchy of concepts and relations. For example, a room could contain objects such as chairs and tables, which are obtained based on object detection or semantic segmentation. A review of semantic-slam methods can be found in ref. [54]. During challenging scenarios the semantic information is useful in achieving a better loop closure compared with the feature-based approach as demonstrated in ref. [55]. Ref. [56] proposed joint SLAM mapping and semantic segmentation of images from an RGB-D camera. Tightly coupled semantic-SLAM methodology incorporating visual, inertial, and surround view cameras was proposed in ref. [57]. This provides a semantic map of the parking lot and enables the evaluation of the adjacency of parking slots.

The SUrfel-Mapping Approach (SUMA++) proposed in ref. [58] creates a semantic map using LiDAR scans. Authors utilize range image-based representations to perform scan matching to align the point clouds, while achieving semantic segmentation. The semantic map provides a robust moving object filter and improves the range image-based scan matching by applying semantic constraints.

20.5 HOME PARKING: CASE STUDY

An automated car parking system for urban areas needs to build a map to determine the topology of the building. The system usually stores the trajectories that enable the ego vehicle to drive into the home parking slot in fully automated mode [59]. The sensors robustly detect the landmarks already stored by the system.

Basically the automated parking system has two stages, training and replay, as shown in Figure 20.7. These two phases need to be executed in parallel to get a pleasing result. Features extracted from captured frames are matched and fed to both modules. The training module identifies depth points and calculates vehicle odometry information. It performs map and pose optimization and stores the trained trajectory. The replay module carries out vehicle re-localization by matching the trajectory with the trained trajectory obtained from the training phase. It then generates trajectory replay after processing through vehicle control and the planning unit.

Prior mapping creates a 3D reconstruction along with the trajectory and landmarks from sensor data. A group of key poses surrounded by landmarks spanning the vehicle's trajectory is evaluated. In view of most VSLAM pipelines in the literature, feature-based methods are more suitable for autonomous driving applications as they are memory efficient and less responsive to dynamic objects. A drastic change in intensity value over a region of pixels helps to identify a unique feature in an image. Tracking performs matching of two or more views of the same features to estimate landmarks in the scene. After the vehicle has made an adequate movement, VSLAM captures the next image and performs feature extraction. The real-world position coordinates are obtained by reconstructing matched features.

Both 3D re-projection and VO might introduce drifts. BA-based optimization jointly performs global optimization. Due to computational constraints, optimization can be carried out once in N frames and is termed as *windowed BA*. Global BA is performed at

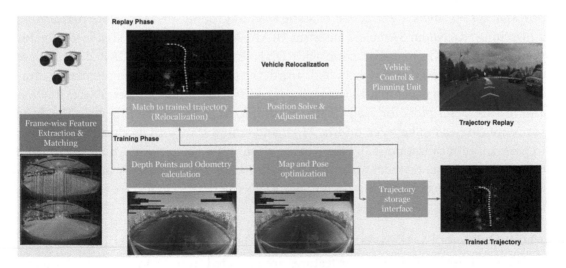

FIGURE 20.7   Block diagram of a VSLAM-based home parking system.

the end of training where all keyframes are optimized to ensure global consistency of the internal VSLAM map.

The final output trajectory is stored as a map in permanent storage and the SLAM algorithms utilize them for re-localization of the vehicle. During re-localization, feature exploration is done on live camera images and is compared with frames from the trained map. If there is a match between live image features and the map, the optimization module estimates current vehicle position with respect to its position during training of the trajectory.

20.6 RANGE SENSOR-BASED SLAM

LiDAR is one of the primary sensors in modern intelligent transport systems [60]. The sensor provides a precise distance estimate of surfaces visible in a 360° FoV around the vehicle, with a restricted vertical FoV. LiDAR-based SLAM methods involves two key steps:

1. Creation of a centimeter-precision 3D map of the environment

2. A matching procedure to estimate the position of the ego vehicle in the environment

Given a sequence of LiDAR clouds during mapping, LiDAR SLAM computes the ego motion of the LiDAR during each sweep and creates a map with point cloud perceived while traversing the environment. This is usually achieved using the ICP, which estimates the transform that minimizes the distance between a reference point set and target point set.

There are many challenges while mapping the environment. First, there are dynamic/moving objects and static objects that appear/disappear between the mapping and driving/re-localization steps. This could potentially interfere in the mapping procedure [61] producing suboptimal matches. Second, the matching step in localization is strongly influenced by the roads or flat surfaces within a map due to a large number of incident points on these structures during mapping as well as re-localization. SLAM preprocessing steps involve extraction of static road or ground surfaces before performing a matching. RANdom SAmple Consensus (RANSAC) methods are a standard now for road extraction. Ground extraction with DNN architectures on LiDAR data achieve real-time prediction performances [62]. Third, the feature extraction is performed aiming to improve the matching. The majority of points will be filtered after road extraction and feature descriptors for each cluster are extracted at the clustering step. Matching scans are carried out between off-line MAP and online scan with its cluster descriptors to perform re-localization [63]. Finally, loop closure is a key problem in SLAM (during the mapping phase) that identifies revisited locations within an already mapped pose in a prior map of the environment. In ref. [64], DNNs were used in feature extraction over range images to achieve precise loop closure.

20.6.1 DNNs for LiDAR SLAM

In ref. [65], linear as well as planar features are extracted from LiDAR data, and features are saved onto a map for future edge-line and plane-surface matching. The matching framework is a parallel pipeline, where LiDAR odometry conduces coarse processing to estimate velocity at a higher frequency, whereas the LiDAR mapping performs fine processing to create maps at a lower frequency. LOAM has been considered to be the state-of-the-art LiDAR motion estimation method without heavy feature extraction.

LO-NET [66] performs LiDAR odometry regression by using two consecutive LiDAR scans in time to learn the 6-DoF pose of the vehicle in an end-to-end learning framework. The scans are first preprocessed to evaluate the normals and represented as a spherical range image that is fed into the DNN to regress the pose. A mask prediction network was also proposed to handle dynamic objects and improve the robustness of the learned features.

A supervised and an unsupervised geometry-aware deep learning-based LiDAR odometry regression framework was proposed in ref. [67]. The framework constitutes feature networks (FeatNet) and a pose network (PoseNet). FeatNets learns features over consecutive LiDAR frames, whereas PoseNet estimates the relative motion between frames with input features. The networks can be trained in both a supervised and unsupervised manner. A differentiable version of ICP as a loss was introduced that needed to be minimized during unsupervised training. In supervised training, when ground-truth motion is given, the predicted motion in Euler form is directly compared with the ground truth. Results were evaluated over the KAIST data set.

20.6.2 RadarSLAM

RADAR is a legacy range-based sensor on automated driving, and ADASs use them to measure the distance, angle, and relative velocity of obstacles. Frequency-modulated continuous-wave RADAR (FMCW RADAR) is the common choice in the ADAS domain. RADAR operates under adverse weather and poor visibility conditions (rain, snow, fog, and dust).

For the task of obstacle detection, various types of RADAR are added to a vehicle based on the proximity of obstacles to be detected:

- *Short-range RADAR(SRR):* for immediate proximity warning and safety in parking assist

- *Medium-range RADAR (MRR):* monitors limits of the vehicle, performs blindspot detection and other-vehicle lane crossover, and avoids side/corner collisions

- *Long-range RADAR (LRR):* are applicable for adaptive cruise control (ACC) and time-to-collision (TTC) estimates

RADAR-based localization has recently been studied. The RADAR sensor provides noisier and lower spatial resolution measurements of keypoints compared with the camera or LiDAR. This makes motion estimation and the SLAM process difficult. RadarSLAM proposed in ref. [68] utilizes RADAR as the mapping sensor and provides a sequence of RADAR scans. It estimates sensor poses and a global consistent map using graph SLAM. Due to the use of RADAR, the method is reported to work better at night, under heavy fog and rain and snowfall, thus performing better than LiDAR and VSLAM methods. Results were evaluated on the Oxford Radar RobotCar Dataset [69].

20.6.3 Prior Map Updates

A cost-intensive component of functional map-based localization systems is required to keep the 3D prior map updated, free from any dynamic objects, and to perform new long-term evolution of the environment. These changes in the environment include facades, vehicles, construction, and vegetation growth. Any functional gain kept for prior maps may be lost due to the frequent recreation of the prior map of the environment. Changing environment is one of the key challenges addressed in refs. [70, 71], in which a model where each ego vehicle independently creates and maintains a set of partial updates over its prior maps is proposed. The confidence of the parametric representation increases with the number of iterations and partial updates performed by each vehicle over the prior map.

20.7 CONCLUSION AND CHALLENGES

In this chapter, we discussed localization and mapping from the perspective of autonomous driving. First, we discussed various components of the autonomous driving architecture to establish the role of localization. Second, various use cases for different driving conditions and categories of localization were discussed. The rest of this chapter demonstrates camera-based VSLAM and range sensor-based SLAM. We discussed different types of VSLAM approaches and cameras deployed with real-time application of home parking as a case study. We hope this chapter helps better understand the usage of localization in autonomous driving for control and path planning.

20.7.1 Deep Learning Methods for SLAM Back-End

There are various sub-tasks in VO and VSLAM pipelines that achieved maturity in the deep learning domain [15]; these are summarized in Figure 20.8. Well-developed deep learning architectures are available for front-end tasks like feature extraction tasks, whereas the back-end tasks such as BAs of the SLAM pipeline remain a challenge. This is mainly due to the variable-sized tensors that are created as output of back-end tasks.

20.7.2 Reinforcement Learning for Active SLAM

Reinforcement learning (RL) is an important domain of machine learning in which a framework to model agent-environment interactions using a set of observations from sensors and agent actions is provided. A scalar reward representing a weak supervisory signal is also provided and is used by the agent as feedback on whether the actions performed were optimal given the sequential history of states and actions. Readers can refer to ref. [72] to better understand this domain. Also, a review on real-world challenges of RL for autonomous driving tasks and applications can be found in ref. [73].

Active localization treats decision making as a problem that conditions the quality of localization and mapping, as already shown in Figure 20.2. One of the key problems is to formulate a good reward function for an active localization problem, where the goal is to perform path planning of the agent to maximize map coverage, reduce uncertainty in the

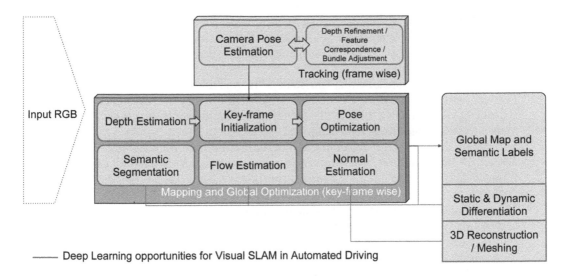

FIGURE 20.8   VSLAM pipeline consists of various geometric and temporal features such as depth regression, optical flow, and motion and pose estimations. Well-established solutions in the domain of deep learning have been achieved for these feature extraction tasks.

localization step, reduce collisions with objects or environment using safe trajectory planning, reduce mapping time or steps, and several other optimality criteria. These problems are addressed in refs. [74–76]. Using deep learning modules for perception and deep RL for path planning algorithms to achieve active localization in an OpenAI-simulated environment were discussed in ref. [77]. Refs. [78, 79] provide a basic study by comparing a sparse, map completion, and information gain rewards using deep RL algorithms. The authors evaluated the performance of agents in a simulated 2D environment.

Another key question addressed in ref. [78] is how to define generalization measures of RL policies in unseen environments. This is one of the key performance metrics of active localization algorithms for autonomous vehicles and robots.

REFERENCES

1. Jonathan Horgan, Ciarán Hughes, John McDonald, and Senthil Yogamani. Vision-based driver assistance systems: Survey, taxonomy and advances. In *2015 IEEE 18th International Conference on Intelligent Transportation Systems*, pages 2032–2039, 2015.
2. Khaled El Madawi, Hazem Rashed, Ahmad El Sallab, Omar Nasr, Hanan Kamel, and Senthil Yogamani. RGB and LiDAR fusion based 3D semantic segmentation for autonomous driving. In *2019 IEEE Intelligent Transportation Systems Conference (ITSC)*, pages 7–12, 2019.
3. Mennatullah Siam, Sara Elkerdawy, Martin Jagersand, and Senthil Yogamani. Deep semantic segmentation for automated driving: Taxonomy, roadmap and challenges. In *2017 IEEE 20th International Conference on Intelligent Transportation Systems (ITSC)*, pages 1–8, 2017.
4. Varun Ravi Kumar, Sandesh Athni Hiremath, Markus Bach, Stefan Milz, Christian Witt, Clément Pinard, Senthil Yogamani, and Patrick Mäder. FisheyeDistanceNet: Self-supervised scale-aware distance estimation using monocular fisheye camera for autonomous driving. In *2020 IEEE International Conference on Robotics and Automation (ICRA)*, pages 574–581, 2020.

5. Varun Ravi Kumar, Marvin Klingner, Senthil Yogamani, Stefan Milz, Tim Fingscheidt, and Patrick Maeder. Syndistnet: Self-supervised monocular fisheye camera distance estimation synergized with semantic segmentation for autonomous driving. *arXiv preprint arXiv:2008.04017*, 2020.

6. Varun Ravi Kumar, Stefan Milz, Christian Witt, Martin Simon, Karl Amende, Johannes Petzold, Senthil Yogamani, and Timo Pech. Monocular fisheye camera depth estimation using sparse LiDAR supervision. In *2018 21st International Conference on Intelligent Transportation Systems (ITSC)*, pages 2853–2858, 2018.

7. Varun Ravi Kumar, Senthil Yogamani, Markus Bach, Christian Witt, Stefan Milz, and Patrick Mader. UnRectDepthNet: Self-supervised monocular depth estimation using a generic framework for handling common camera distortion models. *arXiv preprint arXiv:2007.06676*, 2020.

8. Mennatullah Siam, Heba Mahgoub, Mohamed Zahran, Senthil Yogamani, Martin Jagersand, and Ahmad El-Sallab. MODNet: Motion and appearance based moving object detection network for autonomous driving. In *2018 21st International Conference on Intelligent Transportation Systems (ITSC)*, pages 2859–2864, 2018.

9. Marie Yahiaoui, Hazem Rashed, Letizia Mariotti, Ganesh Sistu, Ian Clancy, Lucie Yahiaoui, Varun Ravi Kumar, and Senthil Yogamani. FisheyeMODNet: Moving object detection on surround-view cameras for autonomous driving. *arXiv preprint arXiv:1908.11789*, 2019.

10. Michal Uřičář, Pavel Křížek, Ganesh Sistu, and Senthil Yogamani. SoilingNet: Soiling detection on automotive surround-view cameras. In *2019 IEEE Intelligent Transportation Systems Conference (ITSC)*, pages 67–72. IEEE, 2019.

11. Sumanth Chennupati, Ganesh Sistu, Senthil Yogamani, and Samir A Rawashdeh. Multinet++: Multi-stream feature aggregation and geometric loss strategy for multi-task learning. In *Proceedings of the IEEE Conference on Computer Vision and Pattern Recognition Workshops*, pages 1–11, 2019.

12. Ganesh Sistu, Isabelle Leang, Sumanth Chennupati, Senthil Yogamani, Ciarán Hughes, Stefan Milz, and Samir Rawashdeh. NeurAll: Towards a unified visual perception model for automated driving. In *2019 IEEE Intelligent Transportation Systems Conference (ITSC)*, pages 796–803, 2019.

13. Senthil Yogamani, Ciarán Hughes, Jonathan Horgan, Ganesh Sistu, Padraig Varley, Derek O'Dea, Michal Uricár, Stefan Milz, Martin Simon, Karl Amende, et al. WoodScape: A multi-task, multi-camera fisheye dataset for autonomous driving. In *Proceedings of the IEEE International Conference on Computer Vision*, pages 9308–9318, 2019.

14. Hazem Rashed, Mohamed Ramzy, Victor Vaquero, Ahmad El Sallab, Ganesh Sistu, and Senthil Yogamani. FuseMODNet: Real-time camera and LiDAR based moving object detection for robust low-light autonomous driving. In *Proceedings of the IEEE International Conference on Computer Vision Workshops*, Seoul, Korea, 2019.

15. Stefan Milz, Georg Arbeiter, Christian Witt, Bassam Abdallah, and Senthil Yogamani. Visual slam for automated driving: Exploring the applications of deep learning. In *Proceedings of the IEEE Conference on Computer Vision and Pattern Recognition Workshops*, pages 247–257, 2018.

16. Steven M LaValle. *Planning Algorithms*. Cambridge University Press, 2006.

17. Steven M LaValle and James J Kuffner Jr. Randomized kinodynamic planning. *International Journal of Robotics Research*, 20(5):378–400, 2001.

18. Brian Paden, Michal Čáp, Sze Zheng Yong, Dmitry Yershov, and Emilio Frazzoli. A survey of motion planning and control techniques for self-driving urban vehicles. *IEEE Transactions on Intelligent Vehicles*, 1(1):33–55, 2016.

19. Markus Heimberger, Jonathan Horgan, Ciarán Hughes, John McDonald, and Senthil Yogamani. Computer vision in automated parking systems: Design, implementation and challenges. *Image and Vision Computing*, 68:88–101, 2017.

20. R. Mur-Artal and J. D. Tardós. ORB-SLAM2: An open-source SLAM system for monocular, stereo, and RGB-D cameras. *IEEE Transactions on Robotics*, 33(5):1255–1262, 2017.
21. Alexandre Briot, Prashanth Viswanath, and Senthil Yogamani. Analysis of efficient CNN design techniques for semantic segmentation. In *Proceedings of the IEEE Conference on Computer Vision and Pattern Recognition Workshops*, pages 663–672, 2018.
22. Michal Uricár, David Hurych, Pavel Krizek, and Senthil Yogamani. Challenges in designing datasets and validation for autonomous driving. *arXiv preprint arXiv:1901.09270*, 2019.
23. A. Geiger, P. Lenz, and R. Urtasun. Are we ready for autonomous driving? the KITTI vision benchmark suite. In *2012 IEEE Conference on Computer Vision and Pattern Recognition*, pages 3354–3361, 2012.
24. J. Engel, V. Koltun, and D. Cremers. Direct sparse odometry. *IEEE Transactions on Pattern Analysis and Machine Intelligence*, 40(3):611–625, 2018.
25. Rui Wang, Martin Schworer, and Daniel Cremers. Stereo DSO: Large-scale direct sparse visual odometry with stereo cameras. In *Proceedings of the IEEE International Conference on Computer Vision (ICCV)*, 2017.
26. Jakob Engel, Thomas Schöps, and Daniel Cremers. LSD-slam: Large-scale direct monocular slam. In *European Conference on Computer Vision*, pages 834–849, 2014.
27. Cyrill Stachniss, Dirk Hähnel, Wolfram Burgard, and Giorgio Grisetti. On actively closing loops in grid-based fastslam. *Advanced Robotics*, 19(10):1059–1079, 2005.
28. Luca Carlone, Jingjing Du, Miguel Kaouk Ng, Basilio Bona, and Marina Indri. Active slam and exploration with particle filters using Kullback-Leibler divergence. *Journal of Intelligent & Robotic Systems*, 75(2):291–311, 2014.
29. Cyrill Stachniss, Giorgio Grisetti, Dirk Hähnel, and Wolfram Burgard. Improved Rao-Blackwellized mapping by adaptive sampling and active loop-closure. In *Proceedings of the Workshop on Self-Organization of AdaptiVE behavior (SOAVE)*, pages 1–15, 2004.
30. Johann Dichtl, Luc Fabresse, Guillaume Lozenguez, and Noury Bouraqadi. Polymap: a 2D polygon-based map format for multi-robot autonomous indoor localization and mapping. In *International Conference on Intelligent Robotics and Applications*, pages 120–131, 2018.
31. A. J. Davison, I. D. Reid, N. D. Molton, and O. Stasse. Monoslam: Real-time single camera slam. *IEEE Transactions on Pattern Analysis and Machine Intelligence*, 29(6):1052–1067, 2007.
32. G. Klein and D. Murray. Parallel tracking and mapping for small AR workspaces. In *2007 6th IEEE and ACM International Symposium on Mixed and Augmented Reality*, pages 225–234, 2007.
33. R. A. Newcombe, S. Izadi, O. Hilliges, D. Molyneaux, D. Kim, A. J. Davison, P. Kohi, J. Shotton, S. Hodges, and A. Fitzgibbon. KinectFusion: Real-time dense surface mapping and tracking. In *2011 10th IEEE International Symposium on Mixed and Augmented Reality*, pages 127–136, 2011.
34. R. A. Newcombe, S. J. Lovegrove, and A. J. Davison. DTAM: Dense tracking and mapping in real-time. In *2011 International Conference on Computer Vision*, pages 2320–2327, 2011.
35. T. Whelan, M. Kaess, M.F. Fallon, H. Johannsson, J.J. Leonard, and J. McDonald. Kintinuous: Spatially extended KinectFusion. In *RSS Workshop on RGB-D: Advanced Reasoning with Depth Cameras*, Sydney, Australia, 2012.
36. F. Endres, J. Hess, J. Sturm, D. Cremers, and W. Burgard. 3-D mapping with an RGB-D camera. *IEEE Transactions on Robotics*, 30(1):177–187, 2014.
37. Christian Forster, Matia Pizzoli, and Davide Scaramuzza. SVO: Fast semi-direct monocular visual odometry. In *2014 IEEE international conference on robotics and automation (ICRA)*, pages 15–22, 2014.
38. Mathieu Labbé and François Michaud. RTAB-map as an open-source LiDAR and visual simultaneous localization and mapping library for large-scale and long-term online operation. *Journal of Field Robotics*, 36(2):416–446, 2019.

39. Thomas Whelan, Renato F. Salas-Moreno, Ben Glocker, Andrew J. Davison, and Stefan Leutenegger. ElasticFusion: Real-time dense slam and light source estimation. *International Journal of Robotics Research*, 35:1697–1716, 2016.

40. Angela Dai, Matthias Nießner, Michael Zollhöfer, Shahram Izadi, and Christian Theobalt. Bundlefusion: Real-time globally consistent 3d reconstruction using on-the-fly surface reintegration. *ACM Transactions on Graphics (ToG)*, 36(4):1, 2017.

41. Nan Yang, Rui Wang, Jorg Stuckler, and Daniel Cremers. Deep virtual stereo odometry: Leveraging deep depth prediction for monocular direct sparse odometry. In *Proceedings of the European Conference on Computer Vision (ECCV)*, 2018.

42. X. Gao, R. Wang, N. Demmel, and D. Cremers. LDSO: Direct sparse odometry with loop closure. In *2018 IEEE/RSJ International Conference on Intelligent Robots and Systems (IROS)*, pages 2198–2204, 2018.

43. Lukas Von Stumberg, Vladyslav Usenko, and Daniel Cremers. Direct sparse visual-inertial odometry using dynamic marginalization. In *2018 IEEE International Conference on Robotics and Automation (ICRA)*, pages 2510–2517, 2018.

44. H. Matsuki, L. von Stumberg, V. Usenko, J. Stückler, and D. Cremers. Omnidirectional DSO: Direct sparse odometry with fisheye cameras. *IEEE Robotics and Automation Letters*, 3(4):3693–3700, 2018.

45. Dominik Schlegel, Mirco Colosi, and Giorgio Grisetti. Proslam: Graph slam from a programmer's perspective. In *2018 IEEE International Conference on Robotics and Automation (ICRA)*, pages 1–9, 2018.

46. Shinya Sumikura, Mikiya Shibuya, and Ken Sakurada. OpenVSLAM: a versatile visual slam framework. In *Proceedings of the 27th ACM International Conference on Multimedia*, pages 2292–2295, 2019.

47. Rafael Muñoz-Salinas and Rafael Medina-Carnicer. UcoSLAM: Simultaneous localization and mapping by fusion of keypoints and squared planar markers. *Pattern Recognition*, 101:107193, 2020.

48. Nan Yang, Lukas von Stumberg, Rui Wang, and Daniel Cremers. D3VO: Deep depth, deep pose and deep uncertainty for monocular visual odometry. In *Proceedings of the IEEE/CVF Conference on Computer Vision and Pattern Recognition (CVPR)*, 2020.

49. Jakob Engel, Jurgen Sturm, and Daniel Cremers. Semi-dense visual odometry for a monocular camera. In *Proceedings of the IEEE International Conference on Computer Vision (ICCV)*, Sydney, NSW, Australia, 2013.

50. C. Kerl, J. Sturm, and D. Cremers. Dense visual slam for RGB-D cameras. In *2013 IEEE/RSJ International Conference on Intelligent Robots and Systems*, pages 2100–2106, 2013.

51. Armin Hornung, Kai M. Wurm, Maren Bennewitz, Cyrill Stachniss, and Wolfram Burgard. OctoMap: An efficient probabilistic 3d mapping framework based on octrees. *Autonomous Robots*, 34:189–206, 2013.

52. Daniel DeTone, Tomasz Malisiewicz, and Andrew Rabinovich. Superpoint: Self-supervised interest point detection and description. In *Proceedings of the IEEE Conference on Computer Vision and Pattern Recognition Workshops*, pages 224–236, 2018.

53. Cipriano Galindo, Alessandro Saffiotti, Silvia Coradeschi, Pär Buschka, Juan-Antonio Fernandez-Madrigal, and Javier González. Multi-hierarchical semantic maps for mobile robotics. In *2005 IEEE/RSJ international conference on intelligent robots and systems*, pages 2278–2283, 2005.

54. Ioannis Kostavelis and Antonios Gasteratos. Semantic mapping for mobile robotics tasks: A survey. *Robotics and Autonomous Systems*, 66:86–103, 2015.

55. Sean L. Bowman, Nikolay Atanasov, Kostas Daniilidis, and George J Pappas. Probabilistic data association for semantic slam. In *2017 IEEE International Conference on Robotics and Automation (ICRA)*, pages 1722–1729, 2017.

56. John McCormac, Ankur Handa, Andrew Davison, and Stefan Leutenegger. SemanticFusion: Dense 3D semantic mapping with convolutional neural networks. In *2017 IEEE International Conference on Robotics and Automation (ICRA)*, pages 4628–4635, 2017.

57. Xuan Shao, Lin Zhang, Tianjun Zhang, Ying Shen, Hongyu Li, and Yicong Zhou. A tightly-coupled semantic slam system with visual, inertial and surround-view sensors for autonomous indoor parking. In *Proceedings of the 28th ACM International Conference on Multimedia*, pages 2691–2699, 2020.

58. Xieyuanli Chen, Andres Milioto, Emanuele Palazzolo, Philippe Giguère, Jens Behley, and Cyrill Stachniss. Suma++: Efficient LiDAR-based semantic slam. In *2019 IEEE/RSJ International Conference on Intelligent Robots and Systems (IROS)*, pages 4530–4537, 2019.

59. Nivedita Tripathi, Ganesh Sistu, and Senthil Yogamani. Trained trajectory based automated parking system using visual slam. *arXiv preprint arXiv:2001.02161*, 2020.

60. Ekim Yurtsever, Jacob Lambert, Alexander Carballo, and Kazuya Takeda. A survey of autonomous driving: Common practices and emerging technologies. *IEEE Access*, 8:58443–58469, 2020.

61. B Ravi Kiran, Luis Roldao, Benat Irastorza, Renzo Verastegui, Sebastian Suss, Senthil Yogamani, Victor Talpaert, Alexandre Lepoutre, and Guillaume Trehard. Real-time dynamic object detection for autonomous driving using prior 3D-maps. In *Proceedings of the European Conference on Computer Vision (ECCV)*, Auckland, New Zealand, 2018.

62. Martin Velas, Michal Spanel, Michal Hradis, and Adam Herout. CNN for very fast ground segmentation in velodyne LiDAR data. In *2018 IEEE International Conference on Autonomous Robot Systems and Competitions (ICARSC)*, pages 97–103, 2018.

63. Renaud Dubé, Daniel Dugas, Elena Stumm, Juan Nieto, Roland Siegwart, and Cesar Cadena. Segmatch: Segment based place recognition in 3d point clouds. In *2017 IEEE International Conference on Robotics and Automation (ICRA)*, pages 5266–5272, 2017.

64. Xieyuanli Chen, Thomas Läbe, Andres Milioto, Timo Röhling, Olga Vysotska, Alexandre Haag, Jens Behley, Cyrill Stachniss, and FKIE Fraunhofer. OverlapNet: Loop closing for LiDAR-based slam. In *Proceedings of Robotics: Science and Systems (RSS)*, Corvalis, Oregon, 2020.

65. Ji Zhang and Sanjiv Singh. LOAM: LiDAR odometry and mapping in real-time. In *Robotics: Science and Systems*, Berkeley, CA, 2014.

66. Qing Li, Shaoyang Chen, Cheng Wang, Xin Li, Chenglu Wen, Ming Cheng, and Jonathan Li. LO-Net: Deep real-time LiDAR odometry. In *Proceedings of the IEEE Conference on Computer Vision and Pattern Recognition*, pages 8473–8482, 2019.

67. Ayoung Kim Younggun Cho, Giseop Kim. Unsupervised geometry-aware deep LiDAR odometry. In *Proceedings of the IEEE International Conference on Robotics and Automation (ICRA)*, Paris, 2020.

68. Ziyang Hong, Yvan Petillot, and Sen Wang. RadarSLAM: RADAR based large-scale slam in all weathers. *arXiv preprint arXiv:2005.02198*, 2020.

69. Dan Barnes, Matthew Gadd, Paul Murcutt, Paul Newman, and Ingmar Posner. The Oxford RADAR Robotcar Dataset: a RADAR extension to the Oxford Robotcar Dataset. In *Proceedings of the IEEE International Conference on Robotics and Automation (ICRA)*, Paris, 2020.

70. Winston Churchill and Paul Newman. Practice makes perfect? managing and leveraging visual experiences for lifelong navigation. In *2012 IEEE International Conference on Robotics and Automation (ICRA)*, pages 4525–4532, 2012.

71. Will Maddern, Geoffrey Pascoe, and Paul Newman. Leveraging experience for large-scale LiDAR localisation in changing cities. In *2015 IEEE International Conference on Robotics and Automation (ICRA)*, pages 1684–1691, 2015.

72. Richard S. Sutton and Andrew G. Barto. *Reinforcement Learning: An Introduction*. MIT Press, 2018.

73. B Ravi Kiran, Ibrahim Sobh, Victor Talpaert, Patrick Mannion, Ahmad A. Al Sallab, Senthil Yogamani, and Patrick Pérez. Deep reinforcement learning for autonomous driving: A survey. *IEEE Transactions on Intelligent Transportation Systems*, 1–18, 2020.

74. Benjamin Charrow, Gregory Kahn, Sachin Patil, Sikang Liu, Ken Goldberg, Pieter Abbeel, Nathan Michael, and Vijay Kumar. Information-theoretic planning with trajectory optimization for dense 3D mapping. *Robotics: Science and Systems*, 11, 2015.

75. Ayoung Kim and Ryan M Eustice. Active visual slam for robotic area coverage: Theory and experiment. *International Journal of Robotics Research*, 34(4–5):457–475, 2015.

76. Thomas Kollar and Nicholas Roy. Trajectory optimization using reinforcement learning for map exploration. *International Journal of Robotics Research*, 27(2):175–196, 2008.

77. Sai Krishna Gottipati, Keehong Seo, Dhaivat Bhatt, Vincent Mai, Krishna Murthy, and Liam Paull. Deep active localization. *IEEE Robotics and Automation Letters*, 4(4):4394–4401, 2019.

78. N. Botteghi, B. Sirmacek, R. Schulte, M. Poel, and C. Brune. Reinforcement learning helps slam: Learning to build maps. *International Archives of the Photogrammetry, Remote Sensing and Spatial Information Sciences*, XLIII-B4-2020:329–335, 2020.

79. Beril Sirmaçek, Nicolò Botteghi, Mustafa Khaled, Stefano Stramigioli, and Mannes Poel. Reinforcement learning and slam based approach for mobile robot navigation in unknown environments. In *ISPRS Workshop Indoor 3D 2019*, June 2019.

CHAPTER 21

GPS-Based Localization of Autonomous Vehicles

Ashwani Kumar Aggarwal

Sant Longowal Institute of Engineering and Technology
Longowal, India

CONTENTS

21.1 INTRODUCTION

Autonomous vehicles are useful for transportation systems, mobile robotics, logistics, etc. GPS is a very convenient way to localize the vehicles in varying environment conditions [1]. The localization of autonomous vehicles in the outdoor environment can be achieved using conventional cameras, depth cameras, mobile networks, communication towers, etc. To augment the localization of such methods or to localize the autonomous vehicles in

DOI: 10.1201/9781003048381-24

which such methods fail to perform, GPS is a very effective tool to localize the vehicles [2]. The main impact of this chapter is to show readers the methods used for localization and the major issues and how these issues are tackled using computer vision techniques. The significance of this work is its applications in mobile robotics for navigation of robotic vehicles in outdoor environments and for intelligent transportation systems for autonomous driving of vehicles.

21.2 LOCALIZATION OF AUTONOMOUS VEHICLES

The localization of autonomous vehicles is a first step for the navigation of autonomous vehicles. The current location of an autonomous vehicle needs to be determined for navigating the vehicle to avoid obstacles in its way. A path-following system using the GPS system has been developed for the transportation of vehicles in real time [3]. A method to capture targets for vehicles has been discussed without using GPS data in ref. [4]. The tactical behavior planning for moving autonomous vehicles in urban cities is discussed in ref. [5]. The estimation of the state of a vehicle using cyber physical methodology is attempted in ref. [6]. The detection of traffic lights using deep learning techniques and the template matching method is done in real time in ref. [7]. An ensemble approach for prediction of obstacles for vehicles has been attempted using deep learning techniques in ref. [8]. The correction in position determination of vehicles using blockchain networks is achieved in ref. [9]. A positioning method for vehicles using low-cost sensors has been described in ref. [10]. The location accuracy of vehicles has been enhanced using the integration of GPS, micro electro mechanical systems (MEMS), and other positioning sensors in ref. [11]. The role of artificial intelligence methods and sensor fusion has been significant in position accuracy enhancement in GPS systems. The use of automatic feature extraction suing artificial intelligence methods and outlier removal is quite beneficial in improving the position accuracy. The sensor fusion of multiple sensors giving complimentary information augments the positioning accuracy improvement. The role of convolutional neural networks (CNNs) for training the model for position accuracy improvement is also quite significant when large data sets of images are given to the CNNs for training tasks and the position of the vehicle is predicted using the trained model.

21.2.1 Need for Localization

The need for precise localization of autonomous vehicles is a necessary step in navigating the vehicle on the road, street, desert terrain, subway, or in a tunnel [12]. Table 21.1 lists the commonly used feature points and feature descriptors for image matching used in localization of autonomous vehicles. Autonomous vehicle speed, direction, acceleration,

TABLE 21.1   Comparison of Features and Descriptors Used in Localization

Feature	Size	Salient Feature	Limitation
SIFT	128	Scale-invariant	Complex
SURF	64	Rotation-invariant	Affine transformation
SUSAN	37	Illumination changes	Scale
MSER-SURF	64	Stability	Illumination changes

and cruise control can be achieved only if the current position of the vehicle is known using vision-based methods, availability of wireless hot spots, or a combination [13]. The accuracy of such methods is not always up to the desired level in varying environmental conditions. The role of GPS in localization of autonomous vehicles has been significant in areas in which the use of mobile networks and computer vision methods fail to precisely localize the autonomous vehicles [14].

21.2.2 Issues and Challenges in Localization

There are several challenges in the precise localization of autonomous vehicles. If the vision-based localization methods are adopted, such methods have limitations such as non-uniform illumination, occlusions, the presence of dynamic obstacles, etc. There are several computer vision-methods that take care of non-uniform illumination by using robust features; however, the effectiveness of such methods depends on many factors like the computational cost of extraction of the features and size of descriptors used to describe the extracted features in the images [15]. The methods to overcome the problems of occlusions and dynamic obstacles in vehicle localization suffer from many drawbacks such as ineffective ways to remove outliers.

Table 21.2 lists the various blocks of GPS satellites with their launch year, number of satellites successfully launched. and number of failures. The GPS satellites are used for localization of autonomous vehicles.

21.2.3 Localization Using GNSS

The GPS consists of a fleet of several satellites orbiting around the earth in space. There are three segments that make up the GPS system, viz. space segment, control segment, and user segment. The space segment of GPS is a set of 24 satellites in orbit around Earth at a distance of approximately 20,200 km. The satellites are launched in such a way that at least four of the satellites are viewable from a given point on the surface of Earth at any time. This allows the user location to be calculated by measuring the time delay in a radio signal received by the GPS receiver and the signal broadcast from each satellite. It uses the speed of propagation to calculate the distance to the satellite (the pseudorange). The signal from one individual satellite needs to be received for each dimension of the position of the GPS user [16] to estimate the position of the GPS user in x, y, and z directions. However, due to

TABLE 21.2   GPS Satellites and Year of Installation

Block	Launch Year	No. of Satellites Successfully Launched	No. of Failures
Block-I	1978	10	1
Block-II	1989	9	0
Block-IIA	1990	19	0
Block-IIR	1997	12	1
Block-IIR-M	2005	8	0
Block-IIF	2010	12	0
Block-III-A	2018	3	0

the mismatch in clock signals of the GPS receiver and that of atomic clocks in satellites, four satellite pseudoranges are required to calculate the four unknowns. The control unit monitors the satellite data and provides controls to the satellites. The user segment is the GPS receiver. Various electronic modules are incorporated in the GPS receivers to mitigate the effects of noise.

The Global Navigation Satellite System (GNSS) is a fleet of many satellites that is used to estimate the location of autonomous vehicles on the ground. The location is given in terms of a coordinate system with latitude and longitude. Each satellite in the GNSS transmits radiofrequency signals giving navigation parameters to the GPS receiver mounted on the top of an autonomous vehicle. The satellites in the GNSS system remain in their orbits and transmit radiofrequency signals. Sometimes there are deviations in the path of satellites from their orbits due to many factors, and many control units are used to bring the satellites back into their orbits. On the GPS satellites, atomic clocks are used that are highly accurate with errors of the order of a few nanoseconds over a period of many years. GNSS was first used for navigation applications in 1973. The first GPS satellite was launched by the U.S. Department of Defense. After that, many GNSS satellites were launched by a number of different countries for numerous applications. Satellite constellations such as GLONASS by the Soviet Union, Compass by China, and the Quasi Zenith Satellite system (QZSS) by Japan have been launched. QZSS augments GPS for estimation of position. The position estimation using GPS in terms of latitude and longitude can be done using at least three satellites. As the clocks used in GPS receivers are not as accurate as atomic clocks in the satellites, it causes a clock offset δt between the atomic clock in the satellite and the clock used in the GPS receiver mounted on the top of the autonomous vehicle. To nullify for the effect of clock offset, radio signals from additional GPS satellites are required. Therefore, it becomes necessary to receive information from at least four satellites for position estimation. The pseudorange (*psr*) is given in Equation (21.1):

$$psr = \delta t \times v = \leq \left(t_{\text{receiver}} - t_{\text{transmitter}} \right) \times v \qquad (21.1)$$

where μ is velocity of light and t_{receiver} and $t_{\text{transmitter}}$ are receiver clock and satellite clock, respectively.

21.2.4 Refinement of GPS Positioning Using Statistical Techniques

The location of autonomous vehicles is estimated using information about the satellite positions and the pseudoranges. The satellites have atomic clocks, whereas clocks in GPS receivers are of low accuracy compared with that of satellite clocks. Because the satellite clocks and the GPS receiver clocks are not synchronized, a constant offset occurs between the satellite clock and the GPS receiver clock. Therefore, signals from at least four satellites are used for estimating the location using a method known as trilateration. If the signal ID is available from more than four satellites, then various optimization techniques are used to obtain the location of the vehicle in the optimal sense. The accuracy of the location estimation is a function of the number of GPS satellites that are visible at that location. Let n_p

be the number of GPS satellites that are visible at a position during a GPS measurement p_i. The position measurement p_i is discarded or is considered in the optimization.

$$P_i = \begin{cases} 1 & ;n_p < N \\ 0 & ;n_p \geq N \end{cases} \tag{21.2}$$

where N is the number of GPS satellites visible.

The number of satellites and their distribution geometry affect the satellite's location accuracy. The term *dilution of precision* (DOP) is used to consider or to discard a GPS measurement for the optimization technique. If the geometry of satellites is collinear and the distribution is not scattered, then the error in location estimation is likely to be high. Therefore, the DOP parameter is used, which quantifies how favorable the geometry of satellites is for accurate location estimation. The location accuracy is dependent on horizontal position accuracy and the accuracy of vertical position estimation. For most of the application of autonomous vehicle localization, the horizontal location accuracy is more relevant than the vertical location accuracy. The horizontal and vertical location accuracy is dependent on the horizontal and vertical DOP, respectively. The horizontal DOP (HDOP) and vertical DOP (VDOP) values can be written by Equation (21.3).

$$HDOP = \sqrt{\sigma_x^2 + \sigma_y^2}$$
$$VDOP = \sqrt{\sigma_z^2} \tag{21.3}$$
$$PDOP = \sqrt{\sigma_x^2 + \sigma_y^2 + \sigma_z^2}$$

where $\sigma_x, \sigma_y, \sigma_z$ are the variances in position estimation in x, y, and z directions.

There are many other types of errors in GPS measurement. When radio signals travel from the satellites to the GPS receiver, these signals pass through various layers of atmosphere. The errors take place due to diffraction and refraction of radio waves in these layers. The main categories of errors are as follows. The ionospheric errors are in the uppermost layer of the atmosphere with an altitude of approximately 50–1200 km from Earth's surface. The speed of radio waves traveling through the ionospheric layer are slowed down. While calculating the GPS location, the speed of radio waves is taken as the speed of light, whereas the actual speed of radio waves is less than that of the speed of light while they travel through the ionosphere. This difference in the speed of radio waves in the ionosphere leads to error in the location estimation. The relationship of decrease in the speed of radio waves in the ionosphere with regards to the frequency of radio waves is given in Equation (21.4).

$$\Delta v = \frac{1}{f^2} \tag{21.4}$$

where f is the frequency of the radio waves. The tropospheric errors in GPS location estimation are caused by the presence of neural atoms, which are present in this layer of the atmosphere. The errors are due to variations in temperature, pressure, humidity, and other atmospheric conditions. The errors due to tropospheric factors are of the order of several meters. Various mathematical models are used to correct for tropospheric errors. The Saastamoinen model is widely used for computing the delay in the traverse of GPS signals in the tropospheric layer.

$$\Delta m = \frac{0.0022768}{\cos z}\left[P_0 + \left(\frac{1255}{T_0} + 0.05\right) \times e_0 - \tan^z\right] \tag{21.5}$$

where P_0 is pressure, z is zenith angle, e_0 is the partial water surface pressure, T_0 is surface temperature, and Δm is the delay in tropospheric layer. The coordinate system for GPS is shown in Figure 21.1.

21.2.5 Geometry-Based Refinement of GPS Positioning

The GPS location accuracy can also be improved using the geometry of the environment. A 3D laser range scanner is used to build a 3D model of the environment in which the GPS receiver receives the GPS signals. As the accuracy of the GPS location depends on the scattering and reflections of the radio signals from the surrounding buildings, the 3D model is useful to identify the signals that are reflected by the walls of surrounding buildings. These signals are excluded from GPS location calculations, hence, improving the accuracy of GPS localization of autonomous vehicles. By considering all the satellite signals, the position is calculated as follows:

$$x - x_1^2 + y - y_1^2 + z - z_1^2 + = r_1^2 \quad \forall \quad x_1, y_1, z_1 \tag{21.6}$$

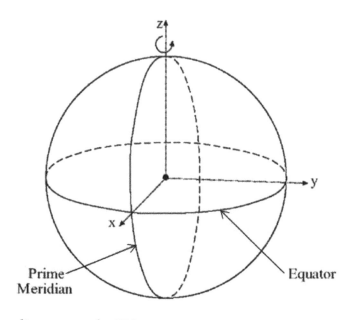

FIGURE 21.1 Coordinate system for GPS.

where x_1, y_1, z_1 are satellite position coordinates. By removing the signals that come after reflections the position is given by

$$x - x_{d1}^2 + y - y_{d1}^2 + z - z_{d1}^2 + = r_1^2 \quad \forall \quad x_{d1}, y_{d1}, z_{d1} \in D \tag{21.7}$$

where D is the set of directly received signals and x_1, y_1, z_1 are satellite position coordinates for directly received signals. It is clear that by revoking the reflected signals, the position accuracy is improved.

21.3 SENSOR FUSION

A single sensor is sometimes not accurate enough for location estimation for an application. Sensor fusion is beneficial when one sensor malfunctions or that sensor is not useful in certain conditions. The sensors that provide complimentary information are useful to fuse together to obtain more accurate location information than the individual sensor location estimates. The fusion of GPS receivers with the inertial navigation system odometry has proved to be an effective way to enhance the localization accuracy of autonomous vehicles.

21.3.1 Inertial Navigation Systems

An inertial navigation system consists of a computer, accelerometers, and gyroscopes. It is also commonly known as the inertial measurement unit (IMU). The accelerometers measure the linear acceleration of the IMU frame. The gyroscopes in the IMU measure the angular velocity of the IMU frame with reference to the inertial reference frame. With the help of the accelerometer and the gyroscope, the linear acceleration and angular velocity information is used to obtain the current position using calculations made by the computer in the IMU. The limitation of the IMU is the drift problem, which causes errors in position calculations.

21.3.2 Wireless Sensor Networks

The wireless sensor networks are used in localization of autonomous vehicles by making use of information from wireless access points. The wireless sensor network-based localization is helpful in cases where GPS signals are not received or are affected by multipath effects. The common techniques used for wireless sensor network-based positioning is the fingerprinting technique. The parameters that are used in this technique are service set identifier (SSID) and media access control (MAC) address [17]. A database of wireless sensor networks that are available in the environment in which the autonomous vehicles move is made and used for localization.

21.3.3 Laser Range Sensors

The use of laser range sensors in obtaining the depth information augments the location information provided by GPS. A laser range sensor uses a laser beam to determine the distance of an object from it. There are various types of laser range sensors for obtaining the depth information. The most common type of laser range sensor is the time of flight

(TOF) type sensor [18]. The principle of working the TOF laser range sensor is measuring the time of traverse of the laser beam to the object, reflected, and then received back by the sensor. The depth information is obtained by multiplying the time of traverse with the speed of light.

21.4 ARTIFICIAL INTELLIGENCE-BASED LOCALIZATION

Localization of autonomous vehicles is done using GPS and vision-based and artificial-based methods. Due to the availability of fast graphic processing units (GPUs) and the development of machine learning algorithms, image data and GPS data are given to artificial intelligence methods to enhance the location accuracy of autonomous vehicles [19].

21.4.1 Computer Vision in Localization

Computer vision-based methods for localization make use of a conventional monochrome camera, stereo camera, red-green-blue (RGB) camera, or a depth camera to obtain the image of the environment in which the autonomous vehicle is moving. The feature points are extracted from the images. The feature points are used for extraction of descriptors, which are used for image-matching methods to estimate the relative position of the camera in one image to another. Various image-matching measures are used for image matching. The Euclidean distance is a widely used image-matching measure for localization of autonomous vehicles. Let I_1 and I_2 be two images and $S_1 \in (u_1,v_1),(u_2,v_2),\cdots,(u_k,v_k)$ and $S_2 \in (p_1,q_1),(p_2,q_2),\cdots,(p_k,q_k)$ be the set of features in these images. The Euclidean distance d_{ij} between two features (u_i,v_i) and (p_j,q_j) is given by Equation (21.8).

$$d_{ij} = \sqrt{(a_1 - b_1)^2 + (a_2 - b_2)^2 + \cdots + +(a_N - b_N)^2} \qquad (21.8)$$

where $(a_1,a_2,\cdots a_N)$ and $(b_1,b_2,\cdots b_N)$ are the descriptors of (u_i,v_i) and (p_j,q_j), respectively. A feature vector (u_i,v_i) in image I_1 is matched to feature (p_j,q_j) in image I_2 if the Euclidean distance is below a threshold value as given in Equation (21.9)

$$s_{ij} = \begin{cases} 1 & \text{if} \quad d_{ij} \leq d_{th} \\ 0 & \text{otherwise} \end{cases} \qquad (21.9)$$

The challenges in image matching due to occlusion, obstacles, and non-uniform illumination are tacked using robust localization methods and machine learning techniques such as k-nearest neighbors, support vector machines, principle component analysis, and deep learning are used. Figure 21.2 show the location of autonomous vehicles using feature points extracted using computer vision techniques.

21.4.2 Kalman Filter-Based Localization

Kalman filter-based localization of autonomous vehicles is an iterative mathematical operation that uses state transitioning. The Kalman filtering combines the uncertainties in the current state of the autonomous vehicle and the uncertainties in the sensor measurements

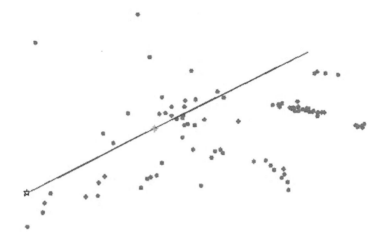

FIGURE 21.2   Location of autonomous vehicle using feature points.

[20]. The uncertainty in the current state as well as uncertainty in the sensor measurements can be described by Gaussian probability distribution. The Kalman filtering for localization works in two steps [21]. The first step is the prediction step in which the Kalman filter gives estimates of the current state and its associated uncertainties. Using the observations, the estimates are updated using weight assignment. As the method is recursive in nature, it is an effective method for real-time applications. The main goal of Klaman filtering is to minimize the loss function in localization. The objective is to estimate the current location of the autonomous vehicle. The difference between the estimate $\hat{x}_k$ and the ground truth x_k is given by Equation (2.10) as:

$$f_1(e_k) = x_k - \hat{x}_k \tag{21.10}$$

A squared error function is given by Equation (21.11) as:

$$f_2(e_k) = (x_k - \hat{x}_k)^2 \tag{21.11}$$

The loss of function F over a period of time is given by Equation (21.12) as:

$$F = E\{f_2(e_k)\} \tag{21.12}$$

where $E\{.\}$ is the expected value of the square error function.

21.4.3 Role of Machine Learning

The machine learning techniques learn from previous explorations of the autonomous vehicle to predict the location estimates. The information about the location of autonomous vehicles is fed to a machine learning framework for the network to learn using explicit feature extraction or using various layers at many abstraction levels. The sensor data obtained from GPS, wireless sensor networks, IMUs, and cameras can be given to a machine learning algorithm to predict the location of the autonomous vehicle. Some of the machine learning methods used for localization are regression methods using support vector machines, linear discriminate analysis, and random forests [22]. The support vector machine divides the two classes using a hyperplane, which can be written as given by Equation (21.13):

$$W.X + b = 0 \tag{21.13}$$

For each vector x_i,

$$\left\{ \begin{array}{ll} W.X_i + b \geq 1 & \text{for} \quad x_i \in \text{class0} \\ W.X_i + b \leq -1 & \text{for} \quad x_i \in \text{class1} \end{array} \right. \tag{21.14}$$

where x_i is the feature vector used for the support vector machine classification.

21.4.4 Use of Convolutional Neural Networks

A CNN is a type of deep neural network that is generally used on images. The images captured by RGB or depth cameras are given to CNNs to learn the environment and predict various classes of obstacles and traffic information providing objects in the scene, such as presence of cars, trees, pedestrians, poles, traffic lights, and sign boards. The detection of such objects is useful for navigating the autonomous vehicles in an environment. The classification of the obstacle is achieved by passing the images through a series of convolutional and max-pooling layers followed by a general artificial neural network. The function of convolutional layers in CNNs is to extract features from the image data at different abstraction levels. The max-pooling layers are useful in noise removal. A set of filters is used in convolutional layers, and max-pooling layers are used with different combinations of strides depending on the likelihood of noise present in the images. Some of the cases in which GPS positioning is not effective are underground pathways, poor lighting conditions, and canyon of trees. In these cases, the GPS is augmented by inertial navigation systems. There are cases where dynamic obstacles, for example, moving trucks, are captured. In such cases, the difference of consecutive frames is taken to eliminate the effect of dynamic obstacles. The vision-based methods suffer from false feature matching points, whereas laser-based and statistical techniques used for improving the positioning of GPS accuracy do not suffer from outliers due to false feature matching points.

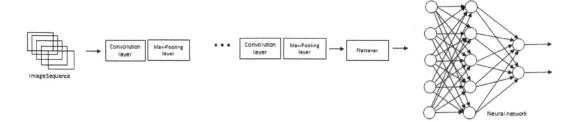

FIGURE 21.3   A convolutional neural network framework.

The strengths of the method are its improvement of position accuracy in case the GPS signal is coming from fewer satellites with many obstructions and multiple reflections. The limitation of the method is that it takes high computational power of the machinery to calculate the correction factors to apply for position accuracy improvement.

21.5 SUMMARY

The localization of autonomous vehicles is the first step toward autonomous navigation. The GPS is a cheap and readily available technique for achieving the localization of autonomous vehicles. However, GPS signal is not always available and if it is available the signals are reflected by buildings, trees, etc., which leads to inaccurate location information. The accuracy of GPS positioning can be enhanced using statistical approaches as well as geometry-based methods. To augment the localization of autonomous vehicles, wireless sensor networks, IMUs, and vision-based methods have proved to be effective tools. The role of machine learning techniques, CNNs. and artificial intelligence methods have been significant in improving on the accuracy of localization. This method performs better than using only the vision-based methods as the issue of false feature point matching is eliminated using laser data and statistical techniques.

FURTHER READING

1. Welch, G., and Bishop, G. (1995). An introduction to the Kalman filter. http://www.cs.unc.edu/~welch/media/pdf/kalman_intro.pdf
2. Krizhevsky, A., Sutskever, I., and Hinton, G. E. (2012). ImageNet Classification with Deep Convolutional Neural Networks. In Advances in Neural Information Processing Systems 25 (NIPS 2012), (pp. 1097–1105).
3. Bulusu, N., Heidemann, J., and Estrin, D. (2000). GPS-Less Low-Cost Outdoor Localization for Very Small Devices. IEEE Personal Communications, 7 (5), 28–34.
4. Stoleru, R., He, T., and Stankovic, J. A. (2004). Walking GPS: A Practical Solution for Localization in Manually Deployed Wireless Sensor Networks. In 29th Annual IEEE International Conference on Local Computer Networks (pp. 480–489).
5. Geiger, A., Moosmann, F., Car, Ö., and Schuster, B. (2012). Automatic camera and range sensor calibration using a single shot. In 2012 IEEE International Conference on Robotics and Automation (pp. 3936–3943).
6. Adorni, G., Cagnoni, S., Enderle, S., Kraetzschmar, G. K., Mordonini, M., Plagge, M., Ritter, M., Sablatnög, S., and Zell, A. (2001). Vision-Based Localization for Mobile Robots. Robotics and Autonomous Systems, 36 (2–3), 103–119.
7. Aggarwal, A. K. (2020). Enhancement of GPS Position Accuracy Using Machine Vision and Deep Learning Techniques. Journal of Computer Science, 16 (5), 651–659.
8. Kumar, A. (2019). Issues and Challenges of Location-Based Services in Cities, National Symposium on Innovations in Geospatial Technology for Sustainable Development with special emphasis on NER, Umiam, Shillong, Meghalaya.
9. Aggarwal, A. K. (2015). On the Use of Artificial Intelligence Techniques in Transportation Systems, International Journal of Soft Computing and Engineering. 5 (5), 21–24.
10. Zhang, H., Berg, A. C., Maire, M., and Malik, J. (2006). SVM-KNN: Discriminative Nearest Neighbor Classification for Visual Category Recognition. In 2006 IEEE Computer Society Conference on Computer Vision and Pattern Recognition (CVPR'06) (vol. 2, pp. 2126–2136).

11. Wan, E. A., and Van Der Merwe, R. (2000). The Unscented Kalman Filter For Nonlinear Estimation. In Proceedings of the IEEE 2000 Adaptive Systems for Signal Processing, Communications, and Control Symposium (pp. 153–158).

12. Sattler, T., Leibe, B., and Kobbelt, L. (2011). Fast Image-Based Localization Using Direct 2D-to-3D Matching. In 2011 International Conference on Computer Vision (pp. 667–674).

13. Maghdid, H. S., Lami, I. A., Ghafoor, K. Z., & Lloret, J. (2016). Seamless Outdoors-Indoors Localization Solutions on SMARTPHONES: Implementation and Challenges. ACM Computing Surveys (CSUR), 48(4), 1–34.

14. De Winter, A., and Baldi, S. (2018). Real-Life Implementation of a GPS-Based Path-Following System for an Autonomous Vehicle. Sensors 18 (11), 3940.

15. Güler, S., and Fidan, B. (2015). Range Based Target Capture and Station Keeping of Nonholonomic Vehicles Without GPS. 2015 European Control Conference (ECC), Linz, Austria (pp. 2970–2975). doi 10.1109ECC.2015.7330989.

16. Sefati, M., Chandiramani, J., Kreiskoether, K., Kampker, A., and Baldi, S. (2017). Towards Tactical Behaviour Planning Under Uncertainties for Automated Vehicles in Urban Scenarios. 2017 IEEE 20th International Conference on Intelligent Transportation Systems (ITSC), Yokohama, Japan (pp. 1–7). doi 10.1109ITSC.2017.8317819.

17. Hashemi, E., Pirani, M., Khajepour, A., Fidan, B., Chen, S., and Litkouhi, B. (2019). Fault Tolerant Consensus for Vehicle State Estimation A Cyber-Physical Approach. IEEE Transactions on Industrial Informatics, 15 (9), 5129–5138. doi:10.1109TII.2019.2898170.

18. John, V., Yoneda, K., Liu, Z., and Mita, S. (2015). Saliency Map Generation by the Convolutional Neural Network for Real-Time Traffic Light Detection Using Template Matching. IEEE Transactions on Computational Imaging, 1 (3), 159–173. doi: 10.1109TCI.2015.2480006.

19. Min, K., Kim, D., Park, J., and Huh, K. (2019). RNN-Based Path Prediction of Obstacle Vehicles With Deep Ensemble. IEEE Transactions on Vehicular Technology, 68 (10), 10252–10256. doi :10.1109TVT.2019.2933232.

20. Li, C., Fu, Y., Yu, F. R., Luan, T. H., and Zhang, Y. (2020). Vehicle Position Correction A Vehicular Blockchain Networks-Based GPS Error Sharing Framework. IEEE Transactions on Intelligent Transportation Systems, 22 (2), 898–912. doi: 10.1109/TITS.2019.2961400.

21. Xu, Q., Li, X., Li, B., Song, X., and Cai, Z. (2016). A Reliable Hybrid Positioning Methodology for Land Vehicles Using Low-Cost Sensors. IEEE Transactions on Intelligent Transportation Systems, 17 (3), 834–847. doi 10.1109TITS.2015.2487518.

22. Xu, Q., Li, X., and Chan, C. (2018). Enhancing Localization Accuracy of MEMS-INSGPSIn-Vehicle Sensors Integration During GPS Outages. IEEE Transactions on Instrumentation and Measurement, 67 (8), 1966–1978. doi 10.1109TIM.2018.2805231.

CHAPTER 22

Video-Based Accident Detection of Cars

Earnest Paul Ijjina

National Institute of Technology Warangal
Warangal, India

CONTENTS

22.1 INTRODUCTION

In the current digital era, technology has become an integral part of daily life. In this decade, the emergence of smart cities and smart transportation emphasizes the need for using technology to monitor humans in their daily activities and to identify the environmental conditions that could be improved. In case of smart cities, intrusion detection, elderly fall detection, fire detection, etc., using video surveillance are becoming the norm. In the transportation sector, technology is used for vehicle speed detection, triple riding detection, automatic payment at toll gates, [1] etc. One of the major necessities of smart transportation is accident detection.

A car is one of the most widely used transportation vehicles, and most modern cars have a dashcam. A dashcam is made up of a camera fitted to record through the front windscreen with an optional rear camera to record the view from the rear windscreen (or) from the rear registration plate. This video stream is stored in a DVR and is used as video evidence in case of vandalism and accidents.

DOI: 10.1201/9781003048381-25

Road accidents are unavoidable as they may occur due to many factors related to the person's car, others vehicles, or even due to environmental/road conditions. An accident should be recognized as soon as possible to provide necessary medical attention, thereby avoiding long-term adverse complications. For vision-based approaches, to detect an accident, a video capturing the car accident is needed to learn the visual cues associated with an accident. The three possible sources of this video are (1) traffic surveillance camera, (2) dashcam video from nearest car, or (3) dashcam video of the car that had the accident. Among these three alternatives, the dashcam video of the vehicle that had the accident is the best for accident detection because of its likely coverage of the accident. Hence, in this work, we aim to design an approach to detect a car accident from its dashcam video. The next section presents the related work.

22.2 RELATED WORK

In the last two decades, the increase in number of automobiles has led to an increase in number of accidents. As a result, there has been an increase in the concern for road safety, and various technologies and policies have been put in place to increase safety. Even with our best efforts, traffic accidents do happen due to bad conditions of the roads, vehicles, weather, and the driver. Hence, due to their unavoidable nature, both industry and academia are exploring new ways and means (like airbags, etc.) to reduce the effects of an accident. Many academic studies were conducted in this area, and some of them are discussed here.

In ref. [2], Selvathi et al. presented a sensor-based monitoring of two-wheel vehicles for detecting drunk driving, helmet-less driving, and accidents. An Arduino-based system monitors the signal from the accelerometer, an alcohol sensor in the helmet and other sensors in the vehicle to identify abnormal reading to detect these events. A crashing switch with an infrared (IR) sensor is used in ref. [3] to detect a crash and the GPS and communication modules are used to send a short messaging service (SMS) to a predefined number. The IR sensor is also used to detect and alert vehicles in close proximity. A de-noising autoencoder is used to learn the spatiotemporal representation of normal traffic, and accidents are recognized from the reconstruction error of the deep learning-based representation in ref. [4]. A weighted extreme learning machine is trained using a self-tuning iterative hard thresholding in ref. [5] to learn the sparse-temporal features in a video for accident detection. A video-based accident recognition approach that detects accidents from the significant change in visual information from the analysis of frame difference was proposed in ref. [6]. A computer vision-based approach to accident recognition based on vehicle tracking was proposed in ref. [7]. This approach detects accidents from the changes in motion dynamics of the vehicles (like the speed and direction of motion) after interaction with other vehicles. An audio-based approach to accident detection was proposed in ref. [8] to detect hazardous events like car skidding and car crashes by using a bag-of-words model on low-level representation of audio. A network of speed sensors placed along the road were used to predict the speed of each vehicle at the next adjacent sensor, and an accident near a sensor is identified from the deviation in the speed of the vehicle from its predicted speed in ref. [9].

A review of the existing approaches to driver fatigue detection, which could lead to accidents, was categorized in ref. [10] based on the features used for detection, like subjective reporting, the biological/physical features of the driver, features from the vehicle during driving, and hybrid features. A drowsiness detection approach utilizing heart rate variability (HRV) analysis was proposed in ref. [11] utilizing multivariate statistical process control on eight HRV features to detect the onset of sleep, which is validated with RR interval fluctuation in the electroencephalogram (EEG) tracing. A deep learning-based distracted driver detection approach was proposed in ref. [12] by extracting ConvNet features from the video of the camera observing the driver's posture, using pretrained deep learning models like VGG-16 [13], AlexNet [14], GoogleNet [15], and ResNet18 [16].

The previous discussion about the existing approaches suggests that the majority of the existing approaches rely on specialized sensors like an accelerometer, speed sensor, crash detector, IR sensor, etc., for detecting accidents. The majority of video-based accident detection approaches use street surveillance camera videos, which can be used to detect the accidents that happen in the camera's field of view only. To overcome the limitations of existing approaches that need specialized sensors, we propose an approach that uses video from the dashcam for accident detection. As the dashcam captures the view in front of the car (as seen from the front windscreen), this video will capture an accident without fail due to its placement within the vehicle of interest. Hence, dashcam video is considered in this study for accident detection due to the certainty of capturing the visual information during an accident. The reminder of this chapter is organized such that Section 22.3 presents the proposed approach, Section 22.4 outlines the experimental study, and the conclusions and future work are discussed in Section 22.5. The details of the proposed approach are discussed in the next section.

22.3 PROPOSED APPROACH

In this work, we propose a deep learning-based approach to accident detection from dashcam video. We consider dashcam video due to its ability to capture the accident, irrespective of the geographical location of the car. In contrast to approaches like those seen in refs. [4, 7] that rely on street camera video (with stationary background) for accident detection, detecting accidents from dashcam video using motion information will be more challenging due to constant motion of the vehicle. Hence, an image-based approach to accident detection is explored in this work.

In the literature, deep learning models were found to be effective for a broad range of computer vision tasks like handwritten digit recognition [17], object classification [18], semantic segmentation [19], etc. In this work, we aim to exploit these models to capture the visual cues in a dashcam video after an accident to recognize a car accident.

There are three potential deep learning approaches to this computer vision task: (1) create and train a new deep neural network (DNN) from the scratch; (2) adapt an existing pretrained DNN model for this domain, i.e., transfer learning; and (3) use a pretrained DNN model for feature extraction and train a classifier on these features for the recognition tasks. As the accidents are rarely recorded, the shortage of observations makes the first two options ineffective, as these approaches need a large number of training samples for

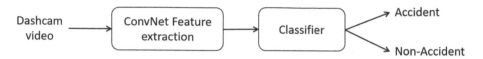

FIGURE 22.1   Proposed approach for detecting car accidents.

effective discrimination. The availability of optimized software/hardware implementations of the existing pretrained models makes the third option suitable for practical real-time applications. Hence, this work explores the use of pretrained models for feature extraction.

The block diagram of the proposed approach is shown in Figure 22.1. The video frames from a dashcam video are given as input to a pretrained DNN model for feature extraction. The extracted features are then used by a classifier for detecting an accident. The details of the experimental study are discussed in the following section.

22.4 EXPERIMENTAL STUDY

As discussed in the previous section, in this work a pretrained deep learning model is used to extract ConvNet features from the frames of a dashcam surveillance video to recognize the accidents. The experimental study was conducted on a dashcam video data set consisting of 60 videos. To identify the optimal DNN model for feature extraction, various pretrained models like AlexNet [14], ResNet18 [16], GoogleNet [15], and VGG-19 [13] were evaluated with traditional classifiers. The details of the data set are discussed in the next section.

22.4.1 Data Set

The data set for this study consists of 60 dashcam videos, out of which the car recoding had the accident in 40 and the rest are non-accident videos. The videos are collected from YouTube and the frame rate is 30 fps with a resolution of 1280 × 720 pixels. The average duration of the videos in this data set is approximately 4 seconds. The first and last frames of some of the accident and non-accident videos in this data set are shown in Figures 22.2 and 22.3, respectively. From these figures, it can be observed that the data set contains accident videos captured under different environmental conditions.

22.4.2 Implementation Details

The experiments were conducted in MATLAB® 2020a (Windows 10) on a HP OMEN Gaming Laptop with CPU @ 2.20 GHz, NVIDIA GTX 1070 GPU, and 16 GB RAM. The pretrained models in MATLAB were used for feature extraction, and 5-fold cross validation was used for experimental evaluation. The extraction of features using deep learning models was carried out in CPU-only mode for comparability of execution time with other CPU-only hardware.

22.4.3 Results

The proposed deep learning approach was evaluated on the data set by extracting features using pretrained convolutional neural network (CNN) models (on the last frame

FIGURE 22.2 Accident videos in the data set. (a) Accident at a road junction, (b) accident during night time, (c) accident on a city road, and (d) accident on a multi-lane city road, with vehicles.

FIGURE 22.3 Non-accident videos in the data set. (a) Dashcam video on a rainy day, (b) dashcam video on city road with vehicles parked on road-side, (c) dashcam video on a snowy day, and (d) dashcam video on a sunny day with direct sunlight on camera.

TABLE 22.1 Performance of the Proposed Approach for Various CNN Model Features and Traditional Classifiers (in Percentage)

Classifier, Model	AlexNet	ResNet18	GoogleNet	VGG-19
Tree	81.7	83.3	81.7	76.7
kNN	90.0	91.7	91.7	91.7
Linear SVM	93.3	**96.7**	90.0	93.3
Quadratic SVM	91.7	**96.7**	91.7	95.0
Cubic SVM	93.3	**96.7**	93.3	93.3
DSS	85.0	90.0	86.7	91.7

Note: The highest values are boldfaced.

Abbreviations: DSS, decision support system; kNN, k-nearest neighbors; SVM, support vector machine.

of the videos) and evaluating traditional classifiers using 5-fold cross validation. The performance for various ConvNet features with traditional classifiers and a rule-based decision support system (DSS) in the proposed approach is given in Table 22.1. From the table, it can be observed that high performance is achieved for ConvNet features extracted by ResNet18 with *support vector machine* (SVM) classifiers, and, irrespective of the model used for ConvNet feature extraction, SVM classifiers achieved better performance.

22.4.4 Analysis

The results in Table 22.1 suggest that the best performance is achieved for ResNet18 features with SVM classifiers. The *linear SVM, quadratic SVM,* and *cubic SVM* achieved the same accuracy. Their respective confusion matrices are shown in Figure 22.4a–c. From these figures, it can be observed that with cubic SVM none of the accidents are misclassified. Because the main objective of this work is to detect accidents, minimizing *false negatives* is preferred over minimizing *false positives.* Because of this, cubic SVM is preferred over linear SVM and quadratic SVM. The receiver operating characteristic (ROC) curve for cubic SVM is shown in Figure 22.4d.

The analysis of the time taken for extracting the ConvNet feature of 30 frames with various pretrained CNN models and the number of observations that can be classified by the best classifier for individual model in 1 second, is given in Table 22.2. The table shows that with the ResNet18 model and cubic SVM, the feature extraction time is 0.036 seconds and prediction time is 0.073 seconds for 30 frames, i.e., an overall prediction time of 0.1 seconds.

TABLE 22.2 Execution Time of the Proposed Approach for Various ConvNet Features and Their Best Classifier

Detail/Model	AlexNet	ResNet18	GoogleNet	VGG-19
Feat. extract (in seconds)	0.024	0.036	0.038	0.037
Best accuracy (in percentage)	93.3	96.7	93.3	95.0
Best SVM classifier	Cubic	Cubic	Cubic	Quadratic
Predicted observations/second	22	410	190	22

Note: Boldfaced terms emphasize the most important details.

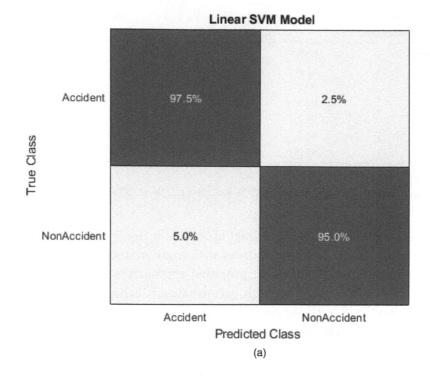

(a)

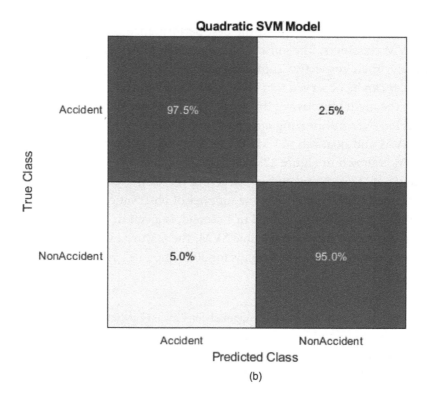

(b)

FIGURE 22.4   Analysis of ResNet18 results with SVM classifiers. (a) Confusion with linear SVM, (b) confusion with quadratic SVM.

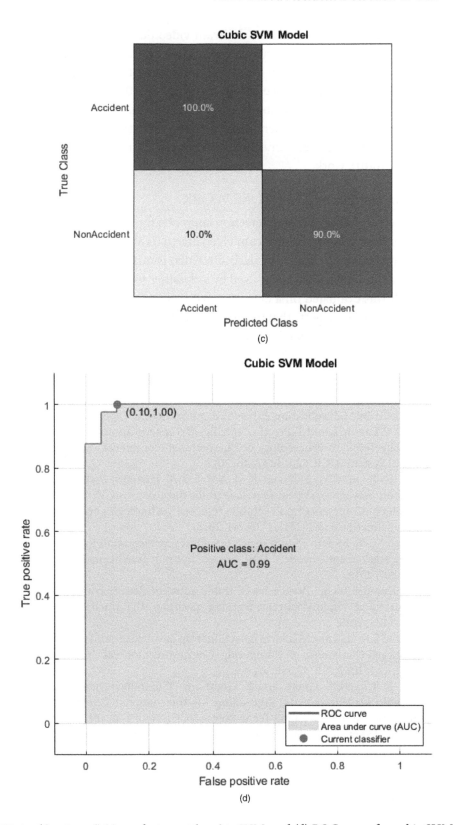

FIGURE 22.4 *(Continued)* (c) confusion with cubic SVM, and (d) ROC curve for cubic SVM.

From the experimental study on the dashcam video data set, it can be concluded that the proposed approach was able to detect accidents in real time without any false negatives. The experimental study conducted with a CPU-only configuration (Section 22.2) suggests that the 30-fps video could be processed in real time, as 30 frames can be processed in 0.1 seconds. This suggests the possibility of an embedded system implementation of the proposed model for real-time accident detection. The robustness of deep learning models could be the reason for the effectiveness of the proposed approach. See the next section for conclusions and future work.

22.5 CONCLUSIONS AND FUTURE WORK

In this work, a video-based accident detection approach for cars was proposed using dashcam video. This work considered dashcam video due to its ability to capture the accident of the vehicle of interest at all times. The dashcam video is utilized by a deep learning model for feature extraction, which in turn is used by a classifier for detecting accidents. The proposed approach was evaluated on a data set consisting of dashcam video of car accidents. The experimental study suggests that the proposed approach recognizes all the accidents in real time. In future, this work can be extended to detect accidents of surrounding vehicles, in addition to the accident of the vehicle with the dashcam.

REFERENCES

1. FASTag. Electronic toll collection. https://fastag.ihmcl.com/. (Accessed: 15 September 2021)
2. D. Selvathi, P. Pavithra, and T. Preethi. "Intelligent transportation system for accident prevention and detection." In Proceedings of International Conference on Intelligent Computing and Control Systems (ICICCS), 442–446, 2017.
3. N.T. S.A. Wadhahi, S.M. Hussain, K.M. Yosof, S.A. Hussain, and A.V. Singh. "Accidents detection and prevention system to reduce traffic hazards using IR sensors." In Proceedings of International Conference on Reliability, Infocom Technologies and Optimization (Trends and Future Directions) (ICRITO), 737–741, 2018.
4. D. Singh, and C.K. Mohan. "Deep spatio-temporal representation for detection of road accidents using stacked autoencoder." IEEE Transactions on Intelligent Transportation Systems, 20(3):879–887, 2019.
5. Y. Yu, M. Xu, and J. Gu. "Vision-based traffic accident detection using sparse spatio-temporal features and weighted extreme learning machine." IET Intelligent Transport Systems, 13(9):1417–1428, 2019.
6. E.P. Ijjina and S.K. Sharma. "Accident detection from dashboard camera video." In Proceedings of International Conference on Computing, Communication and Networking Technologies (ICCCNT), 1–4, 2019.
7. E.P. Ijjina, D. Chand, S. Gupta, and K. Goutham. "Computer vision-based accident detection in traffic surveillance." In Proceedings of International Conference on Computing, Communication and Networking Technologies (ICCCNT), 1–6, 2019.
8. P. Foggia, N. Petkov, A. Saggese, N. Strisciuglio, and M. Vento. "Audio surveillance of roads: a system for detecting anomalous sounds." IEEE Transactions on Intelligent Transportation Systems, 17(1):279–288, 2016.
9. L. Canzian, U. Demiryurek, and M. v. der Schaar. "Collision detection by networked sensors." IEEE Transactions on Signal and Information Processing over Networks, 2(1):1–15, 2016.

10. G. Sikander, and S. Anwar. "Driver fatigue detection systems: a review." IEEE Transactions on Intelligent Transportation Systems, 20(6):2339–2352, 2019.

11. K. Fujiwara, E. Abe, K. Kamata, C. Nakayama, Y. Suzuki, T. Yamakawa, T. Hiraoka, M. Kano, Y. Sumi, F. Masuda, M. Matsuo, and H. Kadotani. "Heart rate variability-based driver drowsiness detection and its validation with EEG." IEEE Transactions on Biomedical Engineering, 66(6):1769–1778, 2019.

12. D. Tran, H. Manh Do, W. Sheng, H. Bai, and G. Chowdhary. "Real-time detection of distracted driving based on deep learning." IET Intelligent Transport Systems, 12(10):1210–1219, 2018.

13. K. Simonyan and A. Zisserman. "Very deep convolutional networks for large-scale image recognition." In Yoshua Bengio and Yann LeCun, editors, In Proceedings of International Conference on Learning Representations (ICLR), 2015. https://dblp.org/rec/journals/corr/SimonyanZ14a.html?view=bibtex

14. A. Krizhevsky, I. Sutskever, and G.E. Hinton. "Imagenet classification with deep convolutional neural networks." In F. Pereira, C.J.C. Burges, L. Bottou, and K.Q. Weinberger, editors, Advances in Neural Information Processing Systems 25, 1097–1105. Curran Associates, Inc., 2012.

15. C. Szegedy, W. Liu, Y. Jia, P. Sermanet, S. Reed, D. Anguelov, D. Erhan, V. Vanhoucke, and A. Rabinovich. "Going deeper with convolutions." In Proceedings of IEEE Conference on Computer Vision and Pattern Recognition (CVPR), 1–9, 2015.

16. K. He, X. Zhang, S. Ren, and J. Sun. "Deep residual learning for image recognition." In Proceedings of IEEE Conference on Computer Vision and Pattern Recognition (CVPR), 770–778, 2016.

17. MNIST handwritten digit database. http://yann.lecun.com/exdb/mnist/

18. ImageNet. ImageNet Large Scale Visual Recognition Competition (ILSVRC). http://www.image-net.org/challenges/LSVRC/

19. V. Badrinarayanan, A. Kendall, and R. Cipolla. SegNet: A deep convolutional encoder-decoder architecture for image segmentation. https://mi.eng.cam.ac.uk/projects/segnet/

CHAPTER 23

ADS and AVS

Its Cyber Security and Privacy Legal Issues

Ravishankar CV

Sambhram Institute of Technology
Bangalore, India

Kavitha KS

Dayananda Sagar College of Engineering
Bangalore, India

CONTENTS

23.1 INTRODUCTION

Providing advanced security, enhanced traveling pleasure, and 24/7 surveillance for individual homes, big establishments, and border areas to observe and record riots or natural disasters is the topmost priority today. In this context, the prominent vehicle systems are unmanned ground vehicles (UGVs) and in particular autonomous driving systems (ADS) and autonomous vehicle systems (AVS), wherein different types of driverless cars and drones of different varieties are available. These are automatic, automated, or autonomous vehicles that operate while in contact with the ground without a human operator [1] or partially with human assistance.

DOI: 10.1201/9781003048381-26

Vehicle automation was conceptualized in 1918, and the first exhibit of an automated vehicle was made by General Motors in 1939 [2]. Driverless vehicles, as they are used by humans, have to be used in places where humans are supposed to coexist like roads, subways, and small streets to highways and city roads. Various legal issues including road traffic signal and road traffic rules, priorities, observations and identification of humans, animals, and road problems, including blockage and dead ends, parking spaces, no parking zones, zebra crossings, as well as atmospheric and environmental conditions all need to be considered.

Today, every system and process is more complex with additional features because of the developments in computer technology. This also affects the development of ADS and AVS, but the usage of these vehicles depends on the efficient functioning of both software and hardware. If an accident happens, resulting in loss of life, there are legal issues in terms of who is responsible, even though logically the owner of the vehicle should be responsible, but was not riding the vehicle at the time. Technically manufacturers could be responsible because of a fault in the software/hardware of the vehicle. Who will be sentenced to jail? Who will initiate the legal case? At the same time, considering the legal issues of various countries, any crime or offense in one country may not be considered a crime in another country, so how to apply universal legal conditions needs to be established and laws regarding the same need to be made.

This chapter first analyzes the issue of cyber security, and in detail discusses the components which contribute to ADS and AVS in terms of cyber security issues and what the best methods are provided as security measures against cyberattacks and hacking. Then, the characteristic features of both ADS and AVS are discussed in the context of humans as well as the legal points related to humans and machines. Then, the present road safety rules and regulations, which are in use now, are analyzed. Also discussed is how it is legally different with respect to driverless vehicle requirements. Based on this suitable comments and opinions were given to establish legal issues and a legal framework.

23.2 IMPORTANCE OF AVS/ADS OVER NON-AUTONOMOUS VEHICLES

Developments in technology have shown how much improvement can be done to motor vehicles in terms of facilities, speed, fuel consumption, driving comfort, communications, seating comfort, ergonomic designs, accident resistance, long distance comfortable journey features, vehicle durability, vehicle shape and aerodynamic design, console design, multiple color combination, braking and wheel movement systems, fuel ignition systems, fuel-efficient new engine designs, optimal efficient engine system, and pollution-free and power- or energy-saving systems. As these features were incorporated into new vehicles, accidents and the death rate of drivers, passengers, and pedestrians (especially men and young people) also increased alarmingly due to rash driving, drunken driving, high speed, drowsiness while driving, skidding, and other reasons. The fatality rates from accidents caused by cars and light and heavy trucks are increasing yearly, leading to the interest in AVS/ADS vehicles. The road safety reports from India, the United States, and the World Health Organization (WHO) clearly suggest that having AVS/ADS features in vehicles would avoid and control fatal death rates due to various types of accidents by cars and

TABLE 23.1 Mortality Details: Between 1988 and 2015 in Different Vehicle Types in the United States

Year	Passenger Cars: Number of Accidents	Trucks (Light and Large): Number of Accidents	Death Passengers (Cars and Light and Large Trucks)	Total Fatality (Not Including Injuries, Drivers, and Other Persons)
1988	307,3000	77,9000	34,114	47,087
1990	283,8000	836,000	32,693	44,599
1995	291,4000	1,108,000	31,991	41,817
2000	239,6000	1,310,000	32,225	41,945
2005	189,3000	1,291,000	31,549	43,510
2010	157,9000	1,111,000	22,273	32,999
2015	178,5000	1,285,000	22,441	35,092

Source: U.S. Department of Transportation–National Highway Traffic Safety Administration Traffic Safety Facts 2015 [3].

light and heavy trucks. The survey report from the U.S. Department of Transportation (USDOT)–National Highway Traffic Safety Administration (NHTSA) discusses various aspects of fatality cases caused by vehicle accidents [3]. Table 23.1 lists general observations extracted from the report.

Table 23.1 clearly shows that year by year the fatality rate is decreasing due to the adoption of new technologies and systems in vehicles, such as anti-accident mechanisms, to ensure safety. Still, the accident rates of both passenger cars and trucks have not decreased much, so more research and related solutions are necessary to reduce the accidents to the lowest possible limit. It is also confirmed that if complete AVS/ADS vehicles are introduced, then the fatality and mortality rate will become almost nil.

The 2019 Road Safety in India: Status Report [4] gives exhaustive details about the mortality rates of passengers, pedestrians, and drivers, wherein 151,417 persons were killed and 469,418 were injured in various road accidents in 2016. It also shows that the average death rate is 10 times greater than the death rate in 1970 with an average compound growth rate of 6%. The expressways in India have a very high mortality rate due to accidents, which is around 1.8 persons per kilometer. A recent study also showed a high pedestrian death rate of approximately 35.1% (76,729 persons) of all deaths. As per the study related to crash patterns, a majority of 68% persons killed are vulnerable road users and 70% of crashes are due to trucks and buses.

In its 2018 Global Status Report on Road Safety [5], the WHO mentioned that the world's eighth leading cause of death is road accidents, claiming approximately 1.35 million people each year and causing injuries to 50 million people. Road accidents are the number one cause of death in the world for children and young adults between 5 and 29 years of age. Table 23.2 lists the road traffic death rates in several countries in 2016.

This gives a broad idea about how vehicle accidents change the socioeconomic status of a society, as a death in a family is a big loss that can change the status of the family and in turn the related village or city also bears the loss. To avoid such a devastating situation, improvement in vehicle safety and road safety measures must be envisaged at the earliest moment; the only possible solution is incorporating and popularizing the AVS/ADS vehicle systems on the road.

TABLE 23.2   Road Traffic Death Rates in the World as Reported by the WHO

Countries	Death Rate Due to Road Accidents per 100,000 Population
Africa	26.6
Southeast Asia	20.7
USA	15.6
Europe	9.3
World	18.3

Source: Global status report on Road Safety 2018. Geneva: World Health Organization; 2018 License: CC BYNC-SA 3.0 IGO [5].

23.3 CYBER SECURITY: BASIC CONCEPTS RELATED TO AUTONOMOUS VEHICLES

The development of electronics, especially in microprocessors and memory devices, leads to drastic developments in the field of computer engineering, especially in hardware and software. This leads to another type of industrial revolution in which the processing industry incorporates computer-controlling mechanisms leading to the production of a large quantity of products with high accuracy, precision quality, and durability. These computers are not only part of the manufacturing industry, they are also used in industries such as defense, pharmaceutical, transportation, communication, medicine, finance, food, agriculture, industry and commerce, share trading, petrochemical and fertilizer.

When computers are introduced in all areas of human life, economic growth is also increased drastically. This leads to the mindset of earning money the easy way, causing criminals to use computer technology in a negative way to hack computers or attack computer systems and networks where a lot of money is involved. It can also lead to attacks on industries, individuals, organizations, or governments causing collateral damage, defamation, and huge financial loss. It is well known that committing a crime in the physical world requires the physical presence of the criminal by himself or with a gang, but cyber-criminals can commit crimes virtually, from some other country. Often this type of attack is not noticed until serious collateral damage is done. This type of criminal act is called cybercrime and those who commit cybercrimes are called cybercriminals or hackers. The activity carried out by these criminals is called a cyberattack or hacking. To overcome cyberattacks the world is investing billions of dollars toward securing computers, computer networks, and computer data against these cyber attackers. This concept is called cyber security.

Generally, all computers and networks can be accessed remotely. Important, confidential, and private data are kept in computers and through the Internet and any transfer of information has to be done securely. If an attack on the client or host computers, or at server computers, or at the transmission stage in the computer network happens, then data modification, data theft, data manipulations, and data corruption will occur. So, a highly advanced end to end point security option is necessary. To achieve these things, data secrecy or information secrecy is achieved by using mathematical modeling or by mathematical means (cryptography), wherein the original information is converted into coded languages (crypto codes). This is carried out by an encryption method, which is used to convert the general data into the coded data, and then these coded data are converted to N number times and into various code levels by using multiple encryption techniques (encryption algorithms). These algorithms have numerous mathematical processes that are used to convert the general text into coded text, and these various methods are used from the basic level of coding by Digital Encryption Standard (DES) to Advanced Encryption Standard (AES) to Rivest–Shamir–Adleman (RSA) Standard algorithms.

To protect and safeguard the encryption process, a new method has been adopted called key generation in which distribution for both sides of the process and the encrypted message are transferred to the receiver end, where it will be converted to a general or original message by the opposite of encryption, or decryption, by using an algorithm that works exactly opposite to the encryption algorithm. To safeguard the interest of both the sending and receiving points, generally passwords, pin numbers, and one-time passwords (OTPs) are used. At the micro level another type of nonlinear code as a key is used. First, there was no key concept and then the single-key technique was used where the same key is used for encryption and decryption. Later, a two-key system was created where one key is used by the sender to send the message and another related key is used by the receiver to receive the message. A three-key concept was then designed in which the sender uses his private key to send the message and similarly the receiver uses the related key of the sender to read the message and again if the receiver is willing to send back the message. The sender uses his private key to send the message now and the sender, once he receives the message back from the receiver, will use the receiver's related key to read the message from the receiver. Various techniques are used to maintain secrecy and safety against the cyberattacks, and various attacks happen from different types of malware phishing attacks, denial of service (DoS) attacks, ransom attacks, virus attacks, zombie attacks, and email attacks.

Today, new technologies are developed because of developments in microcontrollers and memory devices. Battery and lightweight hardware products lead to drones, Internet of Things (IoT) devices, and various credit card and debit card online transactions. This also increases ATM money transactions and online finance transactions, so online fraud is also increasing. Similarly, the public is using Internet and mobile services for all the above. Communication such as social networking and social contacts are widely used, so the number of social web portals is increasing. Online transactions through mobile apps are now very common, so educated and uneducated persons are using them and mobile communication for various transactions without understanding the technology and safety precautions behind all these products. They only know how to use these products to a certain level, but are unaware of the consequences of misuse of these hardware and software items.

Cyber security threats have a heavy cost worldwide. Year by year the loss is increasing, and it is estimated that the total cybercrime loss in 2021 is more than $6 trillion. Cyber threats include activities against the computer and networks as well as behavior shield problems related to suspicious activities, ransomware arsenals, accessing privileged facilities, unauthorized access of critical information and system software, unnecessary intrusive advertisements, emails, unauthorized access of password vaults, cookies, snooping spy-wares, malware, spyware, numerous social media portal attacks like fake codecs, injected threats, bots and botnets, trojans, malware zero day threats, online scams, advanced persistent threats, IoT threats, fake apps, and identity-aware proxies.

Today there are various cyber security threats, for example, deep fakes, synthetic identities, and attacks on social media portals and accounts. Cyber security issues for ADS and AVS are different. Almost all cars and other vehicles are connected to the Internet and Wi-Fi, which leads to the threat of vehicle-based cyberattacks. According to the report by Road Cloud [6], more than 33 million autonomous vehicles are forecast to be sold by 2040. The estimated passenger economy achieved will be $7 trillion by 2050, which reveals the importance given to security issues that come along with these autonomous vehicles. If any attacker, intruder, or cybercriminal is able to access the vehicle's CPU or software/operating system or its application software or collected passwords, then they can steal personal data, technical details, the software of the vehicle music systems to all connectivity mechanisms of the vehicle, General Packet Radio Service (GPRS) and tracking the location of the vehicle, and safety and internal software mechanisms will be under threat. Using these data and information, the cybercriminal can take control of the autonomous vehicle. By taking control, the criminal can stop the car or cause an accident or use if for ransom. If the attack happens to an autonomous truck, the cybercriminal can collect information about starting and destination points, route maps, and whatever items the truck is carrying, and details about the items like type and quantity, and details about the receiver and sender. This information can be used for criminal activities including theft of the vehicle and kidnapping the passengers or the whole vehicle, using the vehicle as a potential bomb, and illegal activities like the shipment of drugs and detonators or to smuggle contraband items and human trafficking. Also possible are terrorist activities like driving the vehicle into a particular target or public place and blowing it up, causing serious damage to the people and property.

23.4 COMPARISON BETWEEN ADS AND AVS

Tracing the history of cart wheels to the bicycle and motorcycle, and scooters, cars, and other heavy vehicles, there has been a constant curiosity and hunger for innovation, which is the predominant trait in all inventors and scientists. Interestingly, the inventors and developers of these types of vehicles and mechanisms are not university graduates in engineering or allied areas; many times they are common people. This demonstrates innovation and invention may come from any person with any background, and at the end of the day, the public wants an easy, comfortable, and safe way to travel. Whether you are a passenger or a driver in a vehicle, satisfaction is always debatable. If you are an owner of the vehicle then driving the vehicle or having a driver is a symbol of prestige, at the same time as an owner of the vehicle if you drive the vehicle yourself there is also prestige and satisfaction. At the same time, relying on technology, especially with family riding in a driverless vehicle, is always questionable and not entirely accepted. Traveling as an individual or with family or with friends on a train or airplane or in a public transportation vehicle, passengers feel they are in the safe hands of experienced drivers, but a driverless vehicle has yet to meet the expectation of individuals. These views and feelings of travelers are a big issue and still have not been thoroughly explored. An advantage of autonomous vehicles is increased accessibility for persons who are currently unable to drive, such as the young or children, elderly persons, sick patients, and persons who are mobility impaired [7]. Earlier autonomous vehicles were too bulky, made too much noise, were more complicated to drive, were less comfortable to drive and ride in, many times did not have a pleasing outlook or color, and created more smoke and consumed more fuel with less mileage. As the years passed various developments in facilities, performance, and ergonomic designs were incorporated, making AVS more important for society and ensuring rapid developments and inventions from 2015 onward.

To develop an end-to-end ADS one must understand the design trade-offs by identifying a few constraints [8], which requires accelerating the algorithms using various accelerator platforms including graphic processing units (GPUs), field programmable gate array (FPGAs), and application specific integrated circuits (ASICs). These drastically reduce the system tail latency by 169×, 10×, and 93×, respectively. Basically the automation level in a car or four-wheeler can be broken down into four stages: stage 1, no automation; stage 2, driver assistance; stage 3, partial automation; and finally, stage 4, full automation.

Stage 1 includes normal cars, which were used by many of us. The stage 2 vehicles use an adaptive cruise control concept, which includes supporting the driver related to identifying driving procedures, drunken driving, sleeping and fatigue identification, and many such practical situations. Stage 3 includes cars in which the driver is assisted by the computer and automation sensors for smooth riding; maneuvering; turning; speed controlling; vehicle parking; toll crossing; traffic analysis; destination location; shortest route finding; emergency message transmission; and finding the nearest emergency hospital, first aid, water, telephone, village, petrol station, hotel, and police station. The fourth stage of car automation is the driverless vehicle movement, which helps the passengers of the car to accomplish driverless car movement from one point to another crossing different roads, junctions, and signals; deciding shortest path and less traffic to reach the destination; stopping the vehicle without causing injuries to the passengers during unexpected situations like immediate entry of animals, people, and vehicles as well as immediate road holes/pits, and humps and road barricades; over speed control; proper usage of gears; petrol/diesel/gasoline refilling; automatic tire re-flattening and proper air pressure maintenance; auto ignition, auto cooling, and temperature maintenance; automatic door opening and closing, automatic window glass or ceiling opening and closing, rear and front windscreen wiper on/off during rain; automatic fuel injection mechanism; automatic video recording; reverse parking assistance; and automatic decision making during probable accident situation.

ADS and AVS look similar and offer a self-driving mechanism or driverless vehicle. The technology is based on radar type sensor technology that uses light instead of radio waves, but there is one small difference, the ADS is a complete mechanism involved in vehicle movement from one point to another point without the aid or assistance of the driver in any manner. The entire system includes vehicle movement, control and driving mechanisms, GPRS, wireless connectivity, and Internet, which were all implemented and utilized for the safe movement of the vehicle. These are called ADS and they handle maneuvering of the vehicle through streets and roads, stopping and going in variable speeds, turning left or right, following traffic signals and other road traffic rules, observing the road humps and pits and zebra crossing lanes, and vehicular movements along the road. These are all done similarly to the human driver but in his or her absence.

AVs have only the vehicle mechanism that contains various resources facilitating the vehicle to move automatically by using automatic engine ignition, fuel injection, and fuel efficiency management; wheel movements; ergonomic design; accident proof or accident prevention mechanisms; automatic windscreen wiping and rain recognition mechanism; fog prevention; skid resistance; gear and brake mechanisms with electronic control mechanisms; vehicle headlight and tail light; and parking assistance and slope resistance. They are also Internet and GPRS ready and have accident response mechanisms.

The basic difference between ADS and AVS is that the ADS has the full mechanism of driverless traveling by the vehicle, whereas the AVS is a vehicle with all the facilities and features to support driverless driving of the vehicle. It is estimated that driverless technologies will add $7 trillion to the global economy and save lakhs of people against vehicle accidents and deaths. At the same time, due to driverless vehicle mechanism implementation, worldwide lakhs of drivers, driving schools and their operations, and government departments that issue driving licenses will lose their jobs. If the vehicle is battery operated or solar energy operated vehicles then again lakhs of petroleum/gasoline stations and their employees will lose their jobs and businesses.

Automated vehicles offers optimized route planning algorithms, which allow the vehicle to avoid known problematic areas and places like schools [9], markets, and other areas. These choices also influence possible decisions about road traffic accident cases. Automated vehicles [10] are basically a combination of cyber-physical systems (CPSs) and IoTs. Such systems require different evaluation strategies to accommodate the complex and hybrid nature of these systems while designing and developing, because a small miscalculation and wrong design drastically alters the situation when AVS are in use. To deal with such situations new suitable standards and parameters have to be established. These standards are not fully available or in a position to be implemented due to various technical and non-technical reasons. Table 23.3 presents a brief comparison between AVS and ADS.

23.5 HOW A MACHINE AND HUMAN DRIVER ARE CONSIDERED LEGALLY: AN ANALYSIS

From various sources, a machine can be defined as an apparatus using mechanical power and having several parts, each with a definite function that together perform a particular task, or a machine (or mechanical device) that is a mechanical structure that uses power to apply forces and control movement to perform an intended action, or a machine is a thing that is created by people to make work easier. It is a tool or invention that multiplies the effect of human effort.

Generally machines convert one form of energy into another form of energy (the fuel power is converted to linear [forward/backward/rotary] motion power) and at the same time a machine can increase the amount of the output force but at the cost of a proportional decrease in the distance moved. The load varies the performance of a machine by equivalent proportion.

TABLE 23.3 Comparison Between AVS and ADS

Features	AVS	ADS
Sensor technology	Based on light rather than radio waves	Based on light rather than radio waves
Driving mechanism	With driver assistance	No driver assistance
Internet ready	Yes	Yes
GPS ready	Yes	Yes
Wireless connectivity	Yes	Yes
Vehicle accidents and deaths	Comparatively less with respect to fully driver-driven vehicles. Insurance and legal issues are similar to driver-driven vehicles.	Almost zero compared with AVS driver-assisted vehicles. Insurance and other legal issues are a problem.
Effect on world driver job market	No loss of job for drivers.	Serious job loss for the drivers will be foreseen.
Traffic congestion problems	No change/very little effect on road traffic congestion.	Drastic reduction in road traffic congestion because the ADS finds the best routes without driving in crowded traffic areas; hence, there is no issue with traffic congestion.
Usage of IoT, 5G, and artificial intelligence (AI) technology	Used to handle fuel control, engine ignition, windscreen wiping, rain recognition, fog prevention, skid resistance, and parking assistance.	These are all found here as basic features along with vehicle maneuvering, following traffic signals and rules, observing road humps and pits, zebra crossings, etc.
Cost	Compared with ADS, it is cheap	Costlier and more expensive than AVS-based vehicles.
Legal issues	Not complicated and applicable similar to fully driver-driven vehicles. Possible to have more universal traffic rules.	More complicated and not possible to have universal traffic rules as each country has its own points of reservation for ADS.
Suitability to all types of vehicles	Suitable for both passenger and goods type vehicles.	Not suitable for all types of vehicles, especially goods vehicles or large transport vehicles.
Vehicle security issues	Moderate and for any cyberattack or system malfunctioning, responsibility and legal binding is to the vehicle driver and owner, depending on the depth of injury or damage.	Serious legal issues will come for vehicle owner, driver, or manufacturer, because throughout the world there are no fully established and universal legal rules and regulations for ADS vehicles. For damage or injury or death, if it happens, the legal issues are not bound by any court of law of that region, instead it can be questioned or argued in any court of the world.
Passenger safety	Good; it is the relationship established between the human driver and passengers to achieve good passenger safety as it involves a human mindset.	Very high; the whole vehicle is under complete machine control so a high quality of safety measures can be achieved.

(Continued)

TABLE 23.3   Comparison Between AVS and ADS   *(Continued)*

Features	AVS	ADS
Latest technological feature implementation and enhancements	Compared with normal vehicles it is highly adoptable.	Impossible to implement all the latest technological features unless extensive trials and testing are done.
Moral obligation	Importance is given to the latest features and passenger comfort.	More importance is given to passenger safety rather than comfort.
Fuel efficiency	Comparatively good with respect to driver-driven vehicles, considering human, machine, weather, and road situations.	Good compared with AVS but depends on the machine, weather, and road situations.
Compatibility with electric/battery driven cars	Good	Good
Compatibility with solar energy driven cars	Not fully tested and implemented due to various technical issues.	Not fully tested and implemented due to various technical issues.
Risk factors	Nonfunctional sensors, malfunction of sensors due to aging and life expectancy, possibility of unexpected glitches in hardware and software.	Nonfunctional sensors, malfunction of sensors due to aging and life expectancy, possibility of unexpected glitches in hardware and software, concern for hacking and cyberattacks.
Mass or public transportation suitability	Comparatively best with respect to driver-driven vehicles.	Not suitable with respect to various risk factors, unforeseen and non-availability of full trail and test experience, and legal issues.
Long distance or short distance traveling suitability	Suitable for both long distance and short distance driving or urban or rural area traveling.	As of now, suitable only for short distance and urban area traveling.
Pollution/emission control	Comparatively good with respect to normal vehicles.	Very high control on pollution and emission as the entire vehicle system works at its maximum efficiency, resulting in reduction in smoke and wastage of fuel and energy.

The same analogy cannot be applied to the human body. Many people have different opinions regarding the human body as a machine, because few accept the human body is a machine. They compare the human body with autonomous machines or vehicles because it is a biological autonomous system and depends on numerous parameters for its independent functioning: it thinks, analyzes, and compares the situation and sequences and guides the body for suitable action with utmost perfection, handling a hair, holding an egg, and making a pot to cutting an onion and even adding salt to the food. Every action is the highest point of artificial intelligence (AI) caliber. Recalling or remembering information that is years old and collecting information with laser accuracy and writing, drawing, or painting, is mind boggling. Also, walking and running as per the body and situation is also commendable; definitely, the brain a is fantastic fuzzy logic system.

Few are arguing this analogy and they think the human body is not a machine, because machines are the product and the outcome of physical and mechanical design; hence, machines have their mechanical complexities but human bodies have organic complexities and occur due to natural selection. Human bodies follow the rules of nature, but machines have to follow the rules of physics and chemistry, and their performances are based on their physical and mathematical modeling.

So, technically, machines are different with respect to human bodies. In the first analysis, the evolution of the human body has greatly changed since its origin. Similarly vehicles or cars have drastically changed since they were first introduced to the world in 1885 by Karl Benz. The first car was fuel powered, but now it is possible to imagine how different cars can be compared with the first vehicle in terms of shape, functionality, appearance, color, mileage, speed, internal and external facilities, driving mechanisms, changes in engine features, door mechanisms, parking mechanisms, accident prevention mechanisms, and wheels and wheel mechanisms. Cars now have become a computer with a passenger sitting inside the car communicating to whole world. Every year new models and features are added, but the same is not possible for the human body, which means nobody can alter the biological features of the human body. So, according to the above analysis, it can be said that machine features cannot be compared with the features of human bodies.

In the second analysis, in which machines are considered to be different from the human body in thinking and analyzing powers, machines cannot think on their own and rely on stored data and logics. The machine's response is entirely different, with respect to human beings, to any incident that happens instantly or accidently, because humans can make decisions that cannot be explained or estimated. Another point is that machines show very similar work in every stage or every time they perform, but humans cannot perform in the same fashion at every stage of the work. Consistency is not dependable in the human body.

Another very important analysis includes the issues pertaining to both machines and human bodies during accidents. If involved in an accident and a machine gets damaged, it can be repaired or new parts can be put in until the case is solved. The vehicle should not be used after the accident or after repair and related services can be used again and expected to perform with the same efficiency. But if humans are in an accident, fatal death or permanent damage to body parts may happen. In some cases, health issues will spoil activities and the performance of the human body. In some cases body limbs or hands or other parts can be replaced by artificial limbs, but it is not possible to expect the human body to perform same as before the accident.

To analyze how a human driver drives the car, after entering the car, one must note if the driver is a single person or with family or with friends; or outside in the rain, heat, or cold; or if he is in an urgent or leisurely situation; or if he is going to the office, or a movie, or to the airport. Often his driving process will vary because the driving process of the human driver depends on his mental status as well as his emotions, situations, and environments. Machines, on the other hand, that are driving the vehicle will not experience these situations; irrespective of the environment and status they will act the same. To emote human behavior machines have to be trained with the help of neural networks and AI, and then the whole car actually becomes a robot. This means that autonomous cars or vehicles are indirectly one type of robot without any human feelings.

For example, there is no system in the world that is foolproof and 100% accurate, so if any untoward accident happens with the vehicle and there is a human driver is inside, only two things will happen. First, the driver will drive away in the vehicle without seeing what happened to the victim or another vehicle or, in the second case, the driver will immediately stop the vehicle and check the health status of the victim and immediately try to save that person by doing first aid or taking the victim in the same vehicle or accompanying in another vehicle to the nearest hospital. What happens in both cases if the vehicle is driverless and autonomous? Such a situation is still not known, and the developers may say that such a situation may not exist. This is unacceptable. Let us assume that a driver immediately slows down the vehicle, parks at the earliest convenience, and runs toward the accident spot and tries to support and help the victims. Can this be expected from driverless vehicles? Because they have not been given these data, they will simply pass the accident.

Let us consider another example. Assume, a buffalo or some animal immediately enters into the path of the driverless vehicle, and the vehicle will automatically suddenly stops due to its internal programmed mechanism. If the vehicle is driven at say 80 km and suddenly halts, what happens to other passengers sitting in the car? How will the driverless car move the vehicle on a slippery road? It is still unknown how the driverless cars will behave. The human mind is complex and very automatic and response is very immediate. Computers or robotic mechanisms have not been developed to that human mind level, so failures are expected.

If legal issues are analyzed, the first and foremost question is, if a fatal accident happens, who will be held responsible, the owner of the vehicle, the dealer, the manufacturing company, or the government authority who issued the license to that vehicle. As everyone is aware, vehicle insurance and individual insurance will still exist, but the legal question is how the insurance company will deal with such cases. Similarly, will the accident victims be willing to ask for compensation in the court against who they feel is responsible? All of these legal issues will come into the picture.

There is another practical case in today's scenarios. Let us imagine the vehicles are used for terrorist activities, kidnapping, hijacking, or such activities as hacking the computer system of driverless vehicles. How the legal actions will be done, and how the offense will be handled by a court of law is still the questionable.

If there was a death due to accidents with driverless car, then the claims as well as punishments will need to be addressed. Sometimes it is the passengers in the car who died in the accidents. How will their cases be handled? Let us assume a passenger in the driverless car had a massive cardiac arrest, and that person is not able to send any messages or call anybody. Imagine the same situation if a human driver is in the car. By seeing the gestures and condition of the passenger, the driver immediately stops the car and tries to give first aid or calls a hospital or for emergency care systems. A driverless car cannot understand this situation, and in reality the passenger will die, even though there is a 100% chance of getting him to best medical treatment. If this is the case, insurance companies will say it is not possible to insure anyone as nobody takes responsibility for the death of the passenger.

There are hundreds of real-time situations like this. It is not possible to use this type of driverless car for very important political leaders like presidents or prime ministers because of the threat of cyberattacks, because no manufacturer can guarantee 100% foolproof systems. We are all aware that recently many top software and hardware industrial giants suffered cyberattacks on their companies, their products, and their company senior employees, including the heads of the organizations.

Above all, every country has their own legal issues and legal rules and procedures, so making a universally acceptable driverless vehicle is quite tough. Even at the basic level of the autonomous vehicle, few countries provide driving mechanisms like steering wheels, gear mechanisms, and brake systems. Although no one can provide100% driverless vehicles, there will be a situation when the human driver will have to drive the vehicle similar to an airplane pilot where the computer in auto mode drives the airplane without driver control. There are some situations when the pilot and copilot overtake the computer control/auto mode and manually pilot the airplane.

In conclusion, the driverless vehicle and human driver-driven vehicle have their own merits and demerits, which should be analyzed and explored even further if only one type of driving mode is chosen. Table 23.4 shows the comparison between normal and AVS/ADS vehicles.

TABLE 23.4 Comparison Between Normal and AVS/ADS Vehicles

Features	Normal Vehicles	AVS/ADS
Weather conditions	These vehicles cannot work efficiently during various weather conditions as the vehicular control is done by the human driver and the mechanism used is not able to efficiently assess the weather conditions and its variations in real time.	These vehicles do not require human driver control. By using various physical parameters the electronic controls made a suitable decision in real time for related weather conditions to use speed, air conditioning, and other such features.
Passenger safety	Depends on the situation and environment; the human driver can make the decision to look after passenger safety by going slow or driving with care.	The passenger safety is completely vested by autonomous systems, from the preset database. The AI looks into passenger preference and acts accordingly. This autonomous system does not recognize if the passengers suffer from serious ailments.
Technology issues and upgradation	There is no much difference if there is a change in technology or new features. The performance and usage of these types of vehicles remain the same.	As technology changes rapidly, especially communication and Internet technology, the cost of renovation or reinstallation of both hardware and software is too high and costly.
Cyberattacks/ hacking	It is not affected much as the features and facilities are lower order hardware and software installations.	As the latest and advanced technology-based hardware and software is installed, the attackers can easily break into the security options of AVS/ADS vehicles compared with conventional non-AVS/ADS vehicles.
Power conversion and fuel efficiency	Not satisfactory; the loss factor is very high with respect to fuel consumption, energy generated, and energy utilized.	Very high and efficient, as AVS/ADS vehicles are based on the latest technologies. The vehicle performs at its maximum efficiency and the loss factor is at the very minimum.
Passenger psychological factor	The passenger will feel tired, disturbed, and uncomfortable both physically and mentally during long distance driving. Restless and sleepless driving or journey leads to fatal accidents and injuries. The passengers cannot be involved in sleeping, recreation, and entertainment as it will disturb the driver.	Whether it is long distance or short distance, the passengers will feel comfortable both physically and mentally as there will be no human interactions for all the technical actions in the vehicle. The passengers can be fully involved in recreation, entertainment, or sleep.

23.6 PRESENT ROAD SAFETY RULES, REGULATIONS FOR THE DRIVERS

Referring to earlier discussed points regarding the legal aspects of driverless vehicles, the present road safety rules are analyzed. Regulations exist in various countries as well as the corresponding punishments related to offenses for breaking road safety rules and accidents. They are entirely different in each country, and many times different states have their own road safety rules compared with their own country depending on the population and natural environments. Some standard norms and procedures are followed by all countries globally, for example, emission and related rules with respect to various policies and standards. The United States follows the California Air Resource Board (CARB) standard; the European Union, the UK, Germany, and other countries follow the Euro-II to Euro-VI standards; China's State Environmental Protection Administration (SEPA) incorporates Euro-IV policies; and Japan follows Heisei 17 standards. India's standards are based on European standards called Bharat Stage Emission Standards (BSES) as the BS-IV standard based on Euro-IV. Now we use the BS-VI standard, and the Government of India has made it compulsory for vehicle manufacturers to manufacture vehicles that comply with the BS-VI standard that were started in April 2020. Various government departments that exist in different countries to handle road traffic and safety rules are as shown in Table 23.5.

Let us briefly go through vehicle rules and regulations that presently exist in the United States and in India for analysis purposes for both existing vehicles and autonomous vehicles. Later in the discussion, AVS- and ADS-related issues in Germany, Republic of Korea, China, and Canada can be analyzed. In the United States, federal laws related to AVS and ADS are entirely different in each state. For general analysis purposes we consider the state of California in the United States.

23.6.1 Vehicle Rules and Regulations in the United States

In the United States, under the USDOT, the road traffic and safety rules were laid down by the NHTSA and they issued Federal Motor Vehicle Safety Standards (FMVSS) that allow

TABLE 23.5 Countries and Their Transport Departments with Vehicle Standards

Countries	Government Departments/Organizations	Standards Followed
India	Transport Department of India	BS-VI
USA	NHTSA under the Department of Transportation.	CARB
China	Ministry of Transport	Euro-IV
Russia	Ministry of Transportation	Euro-VI
Australia	Department of Transport	Euro-VI
Germany	Federal Ministry of Transport & Digital infrastructure (BMVI)	Euro-VI
Canada	Transport Canada	Same as the United States
UK	Department for Transport	Euro-VI
Japan	Ministry of Land, Infrastructure, Transport & Tourism (MLIT).	Heisei-17
Republic of Korea	Ministry of Land Infrastructure and Transport	Fuel economy standards and GHG emission limits

the United States to fulfill the mission to prevent and reduce vehicle crashes and accidents. The rules and regulations for normal vehicles and autonomous vehicles are clearly dealt with in their standards.

Even though the road traffic and safety rules were issued by NHTSA, Texas, Florida, California, Louisiana, and other states have their own vehicle rules and regulations that are slightly altered as per their requirements.

The general vehicles safety rules and considerations [11] are given under various headings like child safety, teen driving, adapted vehicles, pedestrian safety, bicycle safety, older drivers, school bus safety, motorcycle safety, and passenger's vehicle safety. Also, under risky driving headings various types of driving problems associated with accidents were dealt with such as drunk driving, drug-impaired driving, distracted driving, seat belt with/without driving, speeding, drowsy driving, and other such issues. In all these stringent rules and laws the safety of humans is more important. There will be many guides and toolkits provided to implement road safety measures.

The autonomous vehicle-related safety rules and other considerations are given under the technology and innovation part of the NHSTA rules, wherein there exist four section: automated vehicles for safety, vehicle-to-vehicle communication, vehicle cyber security, and vehicle data privacy.

As authors are concentrating on the autonomous vehicle-related issues, especially ADS, the explanation in this chapter discusses autonomous vehicle safety issues. As per the NHTSA, the era of autonomous driving technology has few stages [11]. The stage from 1950 to 2000 wherein safety/conveyance features, cruise controls, seat belt mechanisms, and antilock braking systems are the introduced in vehicle systems. The second stage from 2000 to 2010 is when advanced safety features, electronic stability control, blind spot detection, forward collision warning, and lane departure warning were introduced.

Driverless and autonomous vehicle-related rules and regulations were not yet implemented to their fullest form. The USDOT and White House Office of Science and Technology policy (OSTP) jointly announced public debate and opinions about the automated vehicles and released USDOT Automated Vehicles 2.0 activities in 2017, which is still considered as the cornerstone voluntary guidance document for ADS. It provides complete details and information about the Comprehensive Management Plan for Automated Vehicle Initiatives, automation, accessing resources for learning more about automated vehicles, and data relevant to automation.

Later related policy Automated Vehicles 3.0 was established and effective from October 4, 2018, and Automated Vehicles 4.0 Activities was effective from January 8, 2020. These cover all 38 relevant United States Government (USG) components that have direct or tangential equities in the safe development and integration of AV technologies. AV 4.0 is structured around three main areas: USG automated vehicle principles, administration efforts supporting AV technology growth and leadership, and USG activities and opportunities for collaboration. The latest USDOT policy is seeking public comments on the Automated Vehicles 4.0 by the Federal Register Notice DOT-OST-2019-0179; the comment period closed on April 2, 2020.

23.6.2 Vehicle Rules and Regulations in India

In India various acts, rules, and policies are framed post-independence and are related to all types of vehicles; still, bicycles are given licenses and yearly fees have to be paid to government. The present day motor vehicles act by the Government of India is based on the Motor Vehicles Act of 1988. After this many policies, rules, and regulations were implemented and passed into law. Similarly, the Central Motor Vehicles Act of 1989, the Carriage by Road Act & Rules, and the Central Road Fund Act and Rules are in use in India.

The Motor Vehicles Act of 1988 (59 of 1988) effective from October 14, 1988, is an act to consolidate and amend the law relating to motor vehicles, which basically came from the Motor Vehicles Act of 1939. It is a 233-page document that deals with compensation to be given, driving licenses, permits and permissions, standards for the components and parts of the vehicle, standards for anti-pollution controlling devices and equipment for vehicles, conditions and procedures for issuing fitness certificates, vehicle registration provisions, road safety rules and formalities, punishment in cases of offenses, transporting of hazardous chemicals, flammable and inflammable goods and items, pollution control and standards, and restricting alterations of the vehicles. The Consumer Protection Act of 1986, Information Technology Act of 2000, Geo Spatial Information Regulation Bill of 2016, and Personal Data Protection Bill of 2018 clearly explore all possible safety, protection, and accident-related issues for consumers or passengers of automotive vehicles, but the actual analysis of the effect of automated vehicles on the road and to citizens has not been explored.

Since 1970, the Transport Department of India (please see www.parivahan.gov.in) regional transport offices in all the states who are using Vahan 4.0 and Sarathi 4.0 software issued 10.16 crore driving licenses and registered 25.49 crore vehicles [12]. Various states even implemented standard common acts, rules, and regulations for transport vehicles, and a few new acts, rules, and regulations were in use based on respective state legislation.

No rules and acts exist for driverless or autonomous vehicles in India. The Indian Motor Vehicles Act of 1988 and the related rules that regulate the operation of vehicles in India currently do not allow fully automated systems on the road. A human driver needs to be in control of the vehicle at all times. The Indian Motor Vehicles law does not even permit testing of autonomous vehicles in India. Even though there are no separate laws for self-driving cars and they are treated like any other ordinary car, technological improvements allowed some car models to have partial features of self-driving like starting from cruise control, parking assist, self-parking, lane change assist, automatic emergency braking, 360° viewing, anti-skid mechanisms, advanced engine ignition and fuel-efficient mechanisms, and gearless vehicle transmission.

In 2018, the Indian minister for road transport and highways said at present the Indian Government does not allow autonomous driving and does not support any technology at the cost of jobs. It is a well-known fact that India is one of the biggest automotive industry hubs in the world and contributes around 7.1% of the gross domestic product (GDP) for India. It is estimated that approximately 40 lakhs drivers are in India, and there is a shortage of around 25 lakhs of drivers [13]. If AVS are permitted, gradually there would be a loss of around 1 crore driver jobs [12], which could affect the economy of the people and country. Also, several thousand crores of rupees are invested in the present driver-based vehicle manufacturing industries and thousands of ancillary units and factories are also producing related vehicle engine and hardware parts. Once the driverless vehicles comes into the picture, at first the design and implementation of hardware parts will drastically change. To manufacture all such automobile parts as well as a whole vehicle requires an enormous change in the manufacturing process, which requires a huge money investment. The present world economy is spiraling, especially in the processing industry, which cannot afford such a big change. At the same time, once everything is automated, the employee or worker requirements will also be reduced, which disrupts the job market.

Another important challenge for AVS in India is the bad infrastructure including roads and highways, improper maintenance, unscientifically laid road humps, different dimension of roads, sudden changes from a one-way lane to a two-way lane and vice versa, and no proper zebra crossings and road crossing facilities. Still, in many cases out of 31,846 railway-level crossings 26,903 are unmanned and 4943 are manned. As per the Railway Ministry of India's 2019 budget, they declared there is no manned railway crossing in India [13], which is very positive sign for the AVS. Also, many roads are so narrow that only one vehicle can pass at a time. In this situation AVS make the decision which vehicle moves first.

Now, let us consider various features and issues of AVS and ADS related to testing, certification, and liability frameworks. To have a common compliance factor in this industry, it is assessed or implemented by different countries like the United States, Russia, Canada, Australia, China, the UK, Germany, Republic of Korea, and Singapore. As discussed earlier, the ADS- and AVS-related legal laws and issues were different in different states of the United States, so the authors consider the state of California in the United States for comparison with these countries and the comparison is updated as of May 2020.

The following key elements or parameters were considered for comparison:

- *Acts on permission and restrictions for testing driverless vehicles/autonomous vehicles:* For this, in California, under SB1298, autonomous vehicles with drivers are allowed to be tested on public roads and without drivers under AB 2866. In China the trial permits are considered on a case-by-case basis, whereas in Canada Federal testing is permitted based on the Canadian Motor Vehicle Safety Act (CMVSA). In Germany vehicles operate on public roads as per Section 3 Abs.1 S.1 FZV, but test cars and prototypes require extraordinary permissions. In the Republic of Korea a temporary permission is given from the Minister of Land, Infrastructure and Transport based on the Article 27 Paragraph 1 of the Motor Vehicle Management Act [14].

- *Safety standards to be followed when using autonomous vehicles:* In California, operators are permitted to drive autonomous vehicles by the Department of Motor Vehicles and autonomous vehicles are not permitted to operate on public roads until permission is obtained. In China, the AVS manufacturers and testing organizations follow the regulations on the administration of road testing of autonomous vehicles for trial implementation, which contains many rules and conditions for testing AVS. In Canada Federal, the Canadian Council of Motor Transport Administrators

(CCMTA) maintains the testing guidelines for all the provinces for level 3–5 driving automation systems. In Germany the approval for autonomous vehicles is done by special permission under Section 19 of the German Road Traffic Act and as per the ethical rules for automated and connected vehicular traffic. In emergency situations, the vehicle must autonomously, without human assistance, be entered in safe condition mode. But in the Republic of Korea, the manufacturers and testing agency must get a temporary license from the Minister of Land, Transport and Infrastructure.

- *Condition of providing insurance while testing autonomous vehicles:* In California, the manufacturer or testing agency before testing must provide a bond, surety, and insurance proof of $5 million. In China, the manufacturers must buy liability insurance and provide a letter of guarantee of compensation if any death or accidents happen while testing. In the Republic of Korea, the liability insurance policy and liability mutual agreement under the passenger transport service act must be obtained.

- *Permissions for backup drivers when testing driverless vehicles:* In California, testing AVS driverless vehicles with a backup driver and without a driver is permitted provided various conditions are followed including possessing a valid driver license. In Canada Federal, as per the provincial author and regulations, no permit is necessary for the backup driver for test vehicles [15]. In the Republic of Korea, as per the regulations on safety requirements and testing of AVS in Article 19, having a backup driver is compulsory. In China, the authorized and licensed human driver must accompany the AVS or driverless vehicle [16]. In Germany, as per the report by the Task Force on Ethical Aspects of Connected and Automated Driving, June 2018, the Federal Ministry of Transport and Digital Infrastructure in Serial no.6, Human-Machine Interface, it is clearly mentioned that, if the human driver is not able or willing to resume control when required to do so, it should take appropriate action and the vehicle should warn the driver to perform a minimum risk of vehicle operation.

Basically the hardware components of the autonomous car are considered as analogous to the parts of the human body [17], which allows the user to interact with the stimuli of the outside world. Here the hardware components enable the car to complete tasks such as seeing, communicating, and moving so that the action is very similar to human activities.

Generally, in every vehicle, the steering wheel mechanism, wheel mechanism, engine mechanism, chassis, exhaust mechanism, fuel tank and fuel injection mechanism, braking mechanism, and engine cooling mechanism are common in nature along with suitable interiors for passenger comfort and safety and suitable cabin and body ergonomic designs with suitable colors. The latest technological inventions made ordinary vehicles into sophisticated vehicles with luxury and greater facilities along with various driving mechanisms and features including cruise control, parking assist, self-parking, lane change assist, automatic emergency braking, 360° viewing, anti-skid mechanisms, air condition facilities throughout the cabin, automatic rain-identifying sensor for glass windshield wipers, thermo sensors for good ventilation and environment inside the cabin, air bag provision for the utmost safety for passengers during an accident and emergency, bullet-proof glasses, tough metal construction, punctureless tires, superfast throttle mechanisms, fuel-efficient mechanisms, advanced engine ignition and fuel-efficient mechanisms, gear-less vehicle transmission, highly advanced music systems, provisions for GPS and Internet facility, computers and advanced telecommunication links and facilities, and Wi-Fi and Bluetooth facilities.

Along with this the autonomous vehicle includes additional hardware and software facilities to improve the logical functionality of the autonomous vehicle for driverless driving of the car. Still there is one important aspect of vehicle sensor technology limitation to be considered very seriously. Normally present sensors assess road humps, pits, zebra crossings, and to certain extent water level on the road. It is still unclear how the sensors will analyze the different natural and real-time status of the road in the context of a road filled with mud or sparingly sprayed with mud, or glass, or nails or such harmful items or particles that may not be sensed by the road-sensing mechanisms of the AVS. This could result in serious accidents.

Referring to Indian road accident history, especially on the highways, in many cases vehicles run on the opposite side of the road, due to tire puncture or the driver's fault, or the vehicle gets turned upside down and falls on the opposite road, or sometimes due to brake failure these vehicles at high speed jump the track and land in the opposite lane. Vehicles that run in the opposite direction of an oncoming vehicle can cause serious accidents. In such situations, what will AVS/ADS vehicles do? How will they act in that situation? This has not yet been answered by the manufacturers or designers of AVS/ADS vehicles.

23.7 CYBER SECURITY AND LEGAL ISSUES RELATED TO HARDWARE AND SOFTWARE PARTS OF AUTONOMOUS VEHICLES

Autonomous vehicles have their own priorities related to legal and security issues compared with normal vehicles. Their hardware and software mechanisms change the legal and security paradigm of the worlds' legal systems related to transportation vehicles.

The October 2018 USDOT policy report on preparing for future transportation (Automated Vehicles 3.0) clearly mentions the following six basic principles on which the policy of automated vehicles stand:

1. Prioritizing safety

2. Remain technologically neutral

3. Modernize regulations

4. Encourage consistent regulatory and operational environment

5. Prepare proactively for automation

6. Protect and enhance the freedoms enjoyed by Americans

The general understanding of the autonomous vehicle technical standards are divided into three functional areas. Based on these, the standards and regulations have evolved in those three functional areas and their associated parameters are as follows:

1. *Technology areas:* including software, software engineering, communications, position, navigation and timing, mapping, sensing, infrastructure, and human-machine interface

2. *Functional standards areas:* including definitions and architecture, data, design, maintenance and inspection, functional/performance, protocol, security, testing, and training

3. *Safety areas:* including system safety; operational design domain; object and event detection and response; minimal risk condition; validation methods; human-machine interface; vehicle cyber security; crashworthiness; post-crash behavior; data recording; consumer education and training; federal, state, and local laws; and commercial vehicle inspection

Referring to the above functional areas, cyber security and laws will come under the safety areas, which are very important in terms of legal aspects. It is also expected that, after fully introducing the AVS on roads, the deaths and accidents that are common on roads will be drastically reduced. According to the report [18] out of 39,141 deaths in the United States in all modes of transportation in 2017, the deaths related to motor vehicle crashes totaled 37,133. Similarly, out of all serious motor vehicle accidents 94% involved driver-related faults like impaired driving and distractions. Also, approximately 11,000 deaths are due to drunken driving. Astonishingly two important points related to road deaths in 2017 in the United States include (1) 16% of pedestrians (approximately 5977) died in road accidents through no fault of their own and (2) 10,000 deaths are due to high-speed driving [19]. These accidents ruined many families. Millions of dollars of compensation, jail terms, and loss of vehicles and goods are the by-products of these accidents, which can be fully minimized by proper introduction of AVS on roads.

In AVS, major points of consideration are hardware and software, wherein the hardware includes wheels to mirrors, electronics items, microcontrollers, microprocessors, relays, switches, and indicators and sensors, but legal issues related to the malfunctioning of this software and hardware are not yet ascertained. For example, all hardware, whether it is mechanical or electrical, or electronic items have their own life expectancy and maximum utility time as per the manufacturer. Because of practical usage and road conditions life expectancy may vary and no manufacturer guarantees these items for full functionality and worthiness. Failure of these items causes malfunctioning of software, which leads to serious collapse of vehicle management systems, which in turn causes fatal accidental deaths to pedestrians and vehicle passengers. In such cases, who will be prosecuted? What are the prosecution standards and limitations? It is possible that one country could uphold the responsibility of the manufacturer and another country could uphold the responsibility of the vehicle owner. Is it universally acceptable? Such situations are to be analyzed, and to date no country, including India, has with laws and regulations for autonomous vehicles.

As for the authors' opinions, if autonomous vehicles are to be used worldwide, then a standard policy and legal rules suitable for the whole world should be implemented similar to IEEE standards or IS weight and measure standards.

In the same way, with respect to the AVS, software is even more fatal to pedestrians and vehicle passengers. It could be very dangerous if the software of the vehicle is hacked and controlled by hackers or criminals; for example, the software program used for one vehicle manufacturer is almost the same for all varieties/versions/models of the vehicles with slight changes in advanced or special features, but the basic functionality of the software for driving the vehicle is the same. Even the engines, braking systems, and driving mechanisms are the same in all passenger vehicles, except in additional feature and design aspects, so if any hacker or attacker intruded in or accessed the vehicle software management system or intruded in the servers of the vehicle computer monitoring systems, it is unimaginable what devastation and accidents they could orchestrated. If multiple vehicles are externally controlled and made to collide against other vehicles or crash into people and buildings, or if the same vehicles are purchased and loaded with bombs and grenades with external detonative mechanisms, it is hard to imagine the resulting loss of property and life. The identification of such actions can only be minimized by implementing highly advanced cyber security preventive software and antivirus mechanisms in the vehicle. Wi-Fi is widely used in vehicle monitoring systems and is known to be susceptible to cyberattacks.

Generally, wireless networked systems, like mobile communication, satellite communication, Wi-Fi, wireless network communication, infrared communication, and Bluetooth communication, were all expected to be used by AVS in the near future, but, based on one world cyber security-related survey, 80% of IoT and 71% of mobile applications are not tested for security vulnerabilities. Also, a few wireless vulnerabilities include use of default service set identifiers (SSIDs), default and initial system-generated passwords, access points where tampering may occur, use of the vulnerable Wired Equivalent Privacy (WEP) protocol, Wi-Fi protected access 2 (WPA2) key reinstallation attack (KRACK) vulnerability, and NetSpectre (remote Spectre exploit). These are the loopholes of the wireless networks that are misused by cyber attackers and hackers to attack computer and software systems to wreak havoc using AVS.

At the same time attackers using the previously mentioned vulnerabilities can attack autonomous vehicles by various attacking methods like fake Wi-Fi access points, evil twins, man-in-the-middle attacks, packet sniffing (where there is interception of unencrypted traffic), war-driving (which is a technique to identify and map the vulnerable access points), Warshipping (which is a method of attacking Wi-Fi networks by allowing remote attacks), MAC spoofing, jamming/interference, Bluejacking, Bluesnarfing, IV attack, near-field communication, and replay attack.

Wireless communication, which is also predicted to be used in many aspects of communication systems in autonomous vehicles, uses various security protocols like WEP, WPA, WPA2, and WPA mixed mode protocols. Each protocol has its own drawbacks, application aspects, and security issues. For example, WEP offers a very basic level of security strength and WPA is comparatively stronger than WEP, but WPA2 offers a very high level of security strength.

All software- and hardware-related issues are very serious in AVS. The vulnerabilities should be assessed at the same time as drastic and rapid changes are happening in technology. The present threats may become obsolete in the near future, but at the same time new problems, issues, and threats may appear along with their unimaginable effects and damage. So the departments of justice worldwide have to gear up for the new threats and to work on mitigation of the same and to put various updated laws, rules, and procedures in place. Making these laws universal is a real challenge.

23.8 CONCLUSION

The scenarios of AVS/ADS in the world at present look very bright. Several billions of dollars have been invested in design, development, and manufacture not only by the world's top automobile companies but also from various governments of prominent countries. For example, very recently the U.S. Department of Energy announced funding $60 million to accelerate advanced vehicle technology research [20] and $33 million in funding to support innovative hydrogen and fuel cell research and development (R&D), infrastructure supply chain development and validation, and cost analysis activities [21]. Similarly, Volkswagen has raised its planned investment on digital and electric vehicle technologies to 73 billion euros (65.4 billion pounds), and said it would allocate nearly half its investment budget of 150 billion euros on e-mobility, hybrid cars, a seamless software-based vehicle operating system, and self-driving technologies. As per the 2020 5G report by Aurora Insight, Cisco estimated in its 2020 Internet Report that 5G speeds will be 13 times higher than the average mobile connection by 2023. Also, 5G's technical features like extreme low latency and ultrahigh reliability have great application in autonomous cars and virtual medicine areas [22].

In the future even more players will enter this field not only from automobile manufacturing but also from other sectors like electronics, computer hardware and software companies related to IoT, 5G, blockchain, cloud computing, embedded systems, cyber security, solar power, electrical power, and other related industries by investing large pools of money in AV technologies. Another serious future concern is that petroleum production will reach its lowest level and the entire world must turn to alternate energy or fuel alternatives like solar energy or battery-operated AVS/ADS vehicles, which has its own good and bad outcomes. At the same time replacing all of the petrol/diesel vehicles in the two-wheeler, four-wheeler, and other segment of vehicles is highly impossible; stopping manufacturing and removing those vehicles from the road by not issuing licenses or registration will take several decades. Introducing new universally acceptable vehicle rules and laws will also take several years, because each country and manufacturer requirement is different, along with regulations related to clean energy, green earth, pollution issues, recycling of wastes, carbon emission standards, people safety, passenger safety, vehicle security, cyber security issues, legal issues, pre- and post-accident insurance claims, death and disability issues, punishment and penalty issues, vehicle permits, and registration issues will become very prominent and will be of the utmost importance.

Overall, this chapter looked into various aspects of cyber security, differences between AVS and ADS vehicles, legal issues associated with AVS and ADS vehicles, and threats and security issues in the context of the United States and India. How AVS are legally considered and the advantages of the AVS and ADS over existing driver vehicles were discussed.

It is expected that, in the future, if governments and manufacturers overcome the previously discussed drawbacks, implement suggested alternatives and solutions to the industry problems, and the governments assess in detail the socioeconomic impact of AVS/ADS vehicles to society, the future for AVS and ADS is very bright. We can expect within 10–15 years that it will be very common to see AVS on the roads of every city. In the next 10 years, the present younger generation can see AVS and ADS in remote villages and finally see zero accidents, zero death rate, and zero pollution on the roads.

REFERENCES

1. Roger Bostelman, & Elena Messina, 2019. A-UGV Capabilities – Recommended Guide to Autonomy Levels," International Robot Computing Conference, Naples, Italy.
2. Asif Faisal, Md Kamruzzaman, Tan Yigitcanlar, & Graham Currie, 2019. Understanding autonomous vehicles: A systematic literature review on capability, impact, planning and policy, Journal of Transport and Land Use, 12:1, 45–72.
3. U.S. Department of Transportation, National Highway Traffic Safety Administration, 2015. Traffic Safety Facts 2015. A Compilation of Motor Vehicle Crash Data from the Fatality Analysis Reporting System and the General Estimates System. DOT HS 812 384. NHTSA, Washington DC.
4. Dinesh Mohan, Geetam Tiwari, & Kavi Bhalla, 2020. Road Safety in India: Status Report 2019. Transportation Research & Injury Prevention Programme, Indian Institute of Technology Delhi, New Delhi, India. http://tripp.iitd.ernet.in/assets/publication/Road_Safety_in_India_2019update1.pdf.
5. Global Status Report on Road Safety, 2018. Geneva: World Health Organization. License: CC BYNC-SA 3.0 IGO. https://www.who.int/publications/i/item/9789241565684.
6. Report by Road Cloud, 2019. White Paper: Connected Car data: Improving Autonomous Vehicle Safety at All Levels. www.roadcloud.com.
7. MR Cagney Pty Limited (MRCagney), 2017. Autonomous Vehicles –Research Report. https://www.mrcagney.com/case-studies/research/autonomous-vehicles-research-report/.
8. Shih-Chieh Lin, Yunqi Zhang, Chang-Hong Hsu, Matt Skach, Md E. Haque, Lingjia Tang, & Jason Mars, 2018. The Architectural Implications of Autonomous Driving: Constraints and Acceleration. ASPLOS'18, March 24–28, Williamsburg, VA. htps://doi.org/htps://doi.org/10.1145/3173162.3173191.
9. Martin Cunneen, Martin Mullins, & Finbarr Murphy, 2019. Autonomous Vehicles and Embedded Artificial Intelligence: The Challenges of Framing Machine Driving Decisions, Applied Artificial Intelligence, 33:8, 706–731. DOI: 10.1080/08839514.2019.1600301.
10. National Institute of Standards and Technology, U.S. Department of Commerce, 2019. Consensus Safety Measurement Methodologies for ADS-Equipped Vehicles. https://www.nist.gov/news-events/events/2019/06/consensus-safety-measurement-methodologies-ads-equipped-vehicles.
11. U.S. Department of Transportation, 2020. USDOT Automated Vehicles Activities. https://www.transportation.gov/av.
12. Government of India, Ministry of Road Transport & Highways, 2020. Informational services–Acts, Rules and Policies. https://parivahan.gov.in/parivahan//en/content/act-rules-and-policies.
13. Analytics Insight, 2019. Where Does India Stand in Autonomous Vehicles? https://www.analyticsinsight.net/india-stand-autonomous-vehicles/.

14. Republic of Korea Motor Vehicle Management Act 16101, 2019. National Law Information Centre, Reliable Ministry of Government Legislation. http://www.law.go.kr/eng/engLsSc. do?menuId=1&query=MOTOR%20VEHICLE%20MANAGEMENT%20ACT&x=37&y=23#l iBgcolor0.

15. Jed Chong, 2016. Legal and Social Affairs Division, Parliament of Canada, Automated and Connected Vehicles: Status of the Technology and Key Policy Issues for Canadian Governments. https://lop.parl.ca/sites/PublicWebsite/default/en_CA/ResearchPublications/2 01698E.

16. Articles 10, 12, and 32 of Law of Motor Vehicle Safety, 2016. Laws and Regulations Database of the Republic of China, Ministry of Transportation & Communications. https://law.moj.gov. tw/ENG/LawClass/LawAll.aspx?pcode=K0040065.

17. Sam Huang, 2018. How the Autonomous Car Works: A Technology Overview. https:// medium.com/@thewordofsam/how-the-autonomous-car-works-a-technology overview-5c1ac468606f#.

18. Report Extract on Automated and Connected Driving by Ethics Commission, June 2017. Federal Ministry of Transport & Digital Infrastructure. https://www.bmvi.de/ SharedDocs/EN/publications/report-ethics-commission-automated-and-connected-driving. pdf?__blob=publicationFile.

19. Task Force on Ethical Aspects of Connected and Automated Driving (Ethics Task Force) established by the 2nd High Level Structural Dialogue in Frankfurt/M. on 14 and 15 September 2017, a report in June https://www.bmvi.de/SharedDocs/EN/publications/report-ethics-task-force-automated-driving.pdf?__blob=publicationFile.

20. Office of Energy Efficiency & Renewable Energy, U.S. Department of Energy, 2020. DOE Announces $60 Million to Accelerate Advanced Vehicle Technologies Research. https://www. energy.gov/eere/articles/doe-announces-60-million-accelerate-advanced-vehicle-technologies-research.

21. Office of Energy Efficiency & Renewable energy, US Department of Energy, 2020. Energy Department Announces $33 Million to Advance Hydrogen and Fuel Cell R&D and the H2@Scale Vision. https://www.energy.gov/eere/articles/energy-department-announces-33-million-advance-hydrogen-and-fuel-cell-rd-and-h2scale.

22. Aurora Insight Report, May 2020. 5G Report-Deployments Today for Technologies Tomorrow. https://aurorainsight.com/resource/5g-report-deployments-today-for-technologies-of-tomorrow/.

CHAPTER 24

Open-Pit Mine Autonomous Bot

Apoorva Parashar

Maharshi Dayanand University
Rohtak, India

Anubha Parashar and Vidyadhar Aski

Manipal University Jaipur
Jaipur, India

CONTENTS

24.1 INTRODUCTION

Open-pit mining is mining of an open-cut or a cast that is open. This method is used to extract minerals by removing them from open burrows of the surface of the earth. The project was focused on developing an unmanned ground vehicle for working in the environment of open-pit mines [1–3]. These techniques are distinct from the ones that

DOI: 10.1201/9781003048381-27

require extracting by tunneling the earth. Mines that are open are more useful when ore deposits are closer to the surface of earth [4]. Extracting is done here because the surface structure is thin and material is not suitable for tunneling, for instance, gravel or sand. Underground mining can be useful for searching for the ores that are hard to retrieve because the rock is hard.

Mining in an open-pit is very risky considering its economic viewpoint. One of the starting point of risk is the stability risk. Stabilizing slope comes with many risks in multiple ways, for instance, when we do not have full understanding of geological environments, the harm that mining can cause, and work procedures not able to be executed till completion.

There are two classes of geotechnical perils: moments of slope and falling rock that were not planned [5]. Major consequences of all the geotechnical perils include possible casualties. The probability of all the outcomes must be evaluated very carefully. The risk of falling rocks can lead to casualties and loss in many ways. Production might even halt because of safety issues [6].

The proposed vehicle would easily maneuver along the path of the pit autonomously (Figure 24.1) transporting ore or disposing waste rocks to the dumping ground. Due to the robust localization technique, the vehicle could operate in remote areas without any external help. The objective of the project is to minimize worker hazards and ensure human safety in dangerous places like mining.

Two of the most treacherous postings in mining are transporting goods and their haulage as most of the mishaps and loss happen while carrying out this work. Lately,

FIGURE 24.1 Autonomous driverless car.

due to developments in the automation sector, mining is also on the verge of change; most of the work will be carried out by driverless vehicles, which will reduce the risk factor [7–15].

Vehicles that are driver-less can keep running for a very long time. Such vehicles can run non-stop for a year saving up to 500 hours of work every year. Not only can these vehicles work non-stop, but they also help in solving problems like reduction of fatality and error. Using these vehicles will hugely influence mining in jobs and make them easier (Figure 24.2) [8, 9].

There are few limitations to wall followers, i.e., it is not an intelligent system as the bot is not operational in conditions like landslides and when there are intersections on the path. The bot can easily be misguided into following the wrong path, which could lead it to fall off the edge of the road. The bot is not able to correct itself successfully if it comes too close to the wall. Any attempt to correct its position resulted in the bot moving in a zigzag pattern and thus it failed to follow a straight path as intended. The bot moved with constant speed, which resulted in near collision with the wall in front at turnings, as the ultrasonic sensor in the front of the bot perceived those walls as obstacles so the bot movement was not fluent. Bot movement was inconsistent at turnings in the pit, as distance from the walls at turning is not constant, and the bot tried to maintain a constant distance with the wall.

FIGURE 24.2   Autonomous vehicle architecture.

The following features are incorporated in our final iteration of the bot:

1. The bot can be trained to follow any irregular path, thus making it expendable for any rogue mining environment. Training can be done for as many times as the user wants.

2. Localization of the setup is done using AprilTags, which can identify the live position of the bot in the pit (*X, Y, Z* coordinates along with its yaw, roll, and pitch).

3. AprilTags provide us with an ingenious solution to localization, which can be implemented in any environment and is cost-effective compared with conventional GPS techniques.

   Accuracy of GPS depends on blockage of signal, conditions related to atmosphere, blockage of any signal, and designing or attributes of the receiver. Moreover, precision decreases near trees and bridges. Thus using AprilTags was more logical in this scenario.

4. The training and autonomous drive initiation are done through a user-friendly graphical user interface (GUI) based on Python.

24.2 PROPOSED METHODOLOGY

In this chapter, we have enhanced the working principle according to best articles in recently published research papers. Before reaching to the final build for the bot, several iterations were attempted to drive the vehicle autonomously in the pit. In the following sections we will walk through the same (Figure 24.3).

The pit consists of seven segments of slope stacked together to form a spiral platform of increasing height (Figure 24.4).

A sample dimensional unit of a slope is represented in Figure 24.4. The labeled sides (a–f) are the repeating units of dimensions on each slope and are tabulated for the seven slopes in Table 24.1.

The initial idea was to build a simple wall follower to trace the path of the pit by maintaining a certain distance from the walls on the left side of the pit. To perform it, an ultrasonic sensor is necessary that would require a minimum level of complexity as the bot would have to find the total distance from the wall. We can use an ultrasonic sensor for observing barriers when the robot is in motion as these sensors have a high-level range and a low price [16–24].

The detection mechanism of an ultrasonic sensor is that it discharges bursts of wavelengths in order to listen the echo produced. A short pulse of 40 kHz is released by the sensor when it is controlled by a microcontroller host. The pulse creates advances in the air until it is stopped by any object. After hitting the object surface, the pulse retraces back to the origin point sensor. After the echo is perceived by the sensor, an output signal is generated to request the host to terminate. This is the full timeline for calculating the object distance via returned pulse width [25].

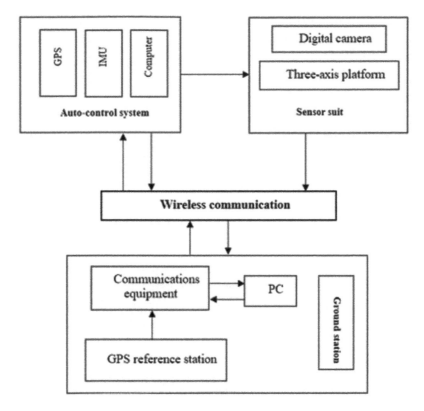

FIGURE 24.3   Proposed methodology.

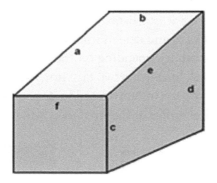

FIGURE 24.4   Slope of the pit.

TABLE 24.1   Pit Dimensions (in Centimeters)

Slope	a	b	c	d	e	f
1	50	27	0	16	40	34
2	40	25	16	23	24	27
3	47	27	23	28	27	25
4	46	26	28	32	25	27
5	47	27	32	37	28	26
6	46	25	37	41	29	27
7	47	31	41	46	57	25

The sensor keeps transmitting waves as the robot walks on the path selected. The distance is computed each time there is an obstacle on the path [26]. If the distance is greater than a threshold the Arduino commands the bot to change the steering angle toward the wall to avoid falling over the edge. The distance between the object and SONAR sensor can be computed by taking the time spent from generation of a wave to the wave retracing back after hitting any object (Figure 24.5).

Echo, Vdd, Trigger, and GND are the four pins found in the HC-SR04 sensor. An ultrasound wave is discharged as a pulse is bid to the Trigger pin. The function of the Echo pin is to transmit the waves detected by the receiver to the controller. The pulse at the Echo pin is directly proportional to the distance between obstacle and the sensor [27].

The following formula is used to calculate distance (units: centimeters):

$$\text{Distance} = 0.5 \times (344 \times \text{reflection time})$$

To reach the closest to the left wall, the robot is instructed to turn left and move forward as soon as the power is turned on. The robot is also instructed to read values from the sensor and to keep moving forward. It rotates its direct current (DC) motor to the right with full speed to take a left turn and does so till it achieves a minimum value. The bot stops as soon as an object approaches its front side.

To overcome the limitations of a wall follower, another solution was to build a line follower that could follow a prescribed pair of lines to keep itself in the middle of the path. A line follower has a direct relation to the light when it comes to its working mechanism. Functions of light on a black and white surface are used here. The light gets consumed when the surface is black and is outright reflected when falling on a white surface. Ground rules for a line-following robot are established on this very principle.

The line-following bot sticks to and detects lines drawn in the area and is autonomous. The lines are drawn black or white depending on the surface color. The robot senses the line (here, we have used a black line) using two proximity sensors mounted vertically parallel at the front of the bot. The servo motor is used to direct the bot along the path [28]. Its rotation angle is 0–180° and mounted at the front side, whereas rear wheels of the bot are

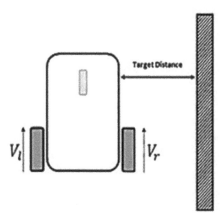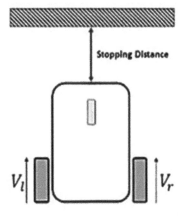

FIGURE 24.5   Proposed operation.

equipped with a 12-V DC motor to move it forward along the path. The bot is also installed with an inertial measurement unit (IMU) sensor. The IMU device has a 6050 MPU plus a digital motion processor (DMP) along with a three-axis accelerometer and gyroscope on a disc of silicon to operate algorithms of the six-axis motion fusion. The IMU values are mapped with the speed of the motor such that the bot's speed increases during inclination and reduces during the downhill climb [29].

The main disadvantage of a line follower is that to follow a path, its color should contrast with the surrounding environment. There are two chief segments of infrared (IR) sensor, the IR transmitter and receiver [30]. The main jobs of this transmitter and receiver are transmitting and receiving the IR waves, respectively. Data are sent to the Vout pin constantly in binary form (0 or 1) via receiver.

The waves from the front of an object are received by the receiver. The sensor gives a binary 0 as an output in this case. When there is no object and the receiver does not get any wave, the output is 1.

Hard objects like doors or a wall, sunlight, fog, smoke, smog, and dust affect the frequencies of an IR signal; therefore, the IR frequencies have difficulty operating efficiently in outdoor conditions, which makes it impossible to use them in open-pit mines. The bot was controlled using keys through the keyboard library of Python. The module can be downloaded using the pip install command on keyboard. The module is used to get full control of the keyboard. The small Python library can hook global events, register hot keys, simulate key presses, and much more. The inbuilt function keyboard.is pressed was used to detect key presses from the user.

Keyboard libraries helps to enter keys, record the keyboard activities, and block the keys until a specified key is entered and simulate the keys. It captures all keys; even onscreen keyboard events are captured. The keyboard module supports complex hot keys. Using this module, we can listen to and send keyboard events. It works on both windows and the Linux operating system [31].

To establish serial communication over a certain port-serial, the serial ('/dev/ttyACM0', 9600) command is used to connect to the ACM0 port of Pi over a 9600-baud rate and the command "readline ()" was used to read a line via serial communication. The limitation of the keyboard library was that it could not be incorporated into Python code for the GUI (explained later) as the keyboard requires the "sudo" command, which is not supported by GUI.

To overcome the shortcomings of the line follower, further attempts were made to apply lane detection through the pi camera. Lane detection is a technique of identifying both the lanes in front of the vehicle and maintaining an average center distance from the lanes.

24.3 LANE DETECTION PROCEDURE

24.3.1 Convert Original Image to Gray Scale

Using the following command any image can be converted to a gray-scaled version.

```
textitcv2.cvtColor(img, cv2.COLOR BGR2GRAY)
```

24.3.2 Apply Slight Gaussian Blur

A Gaussian filter is used to convolute an image in the Gaussian Blur operation rather than the box filter. The image can be smoothed with the help of Gaussian filter as it helps in reducing parts that are of high frequency and is a low-pass filter.

```
cv2.GaussianBlur(img, (5,5), 0)
```

24.3.3 Apply Canny Edge Detector

One of the most admired algorithms for detecting edges is Canny edge detection. John F. Canny generated this algorithm in 1986. This algorithm works well in varied environments. The parameters of this algorithm can be molded according to the edges with various attributes.

The process of this edge detection algorithm can be broken down into five different steps:

1. To remove noise, we smooth the surface with the help of Gaussian filters.

2. Gradients of image intensity are searched.

3. Non-maximum extinction is used to steer clear of fake feedback from edge detection.

4. Threshold of double power is used for regulating the possible edges.

5. Irrationally track the edges: conclude the edge-based detection by subduing weak edges; then there is no connection with the strong ones.

24.3.4 Define Region of Interest

Defining the region of interest helps to weed out unwanted edges detected by the Canny edge detector.

24.3.5 Retrieve Hough Lines

A well-known method for shape detection (of shapes that can be portrayed in a mathematical arrangement) is called the Hough transform. It is a powerful technique that can represent distorted or fragmented shapes. Detecting shapes like ellipses, lines, and circles sometimes becomes problematic with automatic analysis. To acquire pixels or points of an image in a particular curve, preprocessing is done with an edge detector.

At times there are pixels or points missing on the curve or divergence among points on the edge and shapes because of defects in the edge detector. Therefore, grouping of the attributes extracted to their defined shapes (circle, lines, and ellipses) is significant.

The Hough transform helps to make groups of points on edge into candidates of an object. The transform does so by carrying out a direct voting system in a framework of objects.

```
cv2.HoughLinesP(a, 3, np. pi/180, 100, np. array ([]),
        minLine- Length=30, maxLineGap=5)
```

An array of theta and rho values is given in which theta and rho are calculated in radians and pixels, respectively. Before using the Hough transform, an algorithm for detecting edges (Canny edge) or a threshold is implemented so that images are in a binary format. Other criteria for precision are theta and rho. Last variable is threshold; it requires minimal votes to be deemed a line. Consolidate and extrapolate the Hough lines and draw them on an original image extrapolation, which means creating a straight line that is tangential for the data known. Deducting the graph linearly will yield good products when used on a function of linear nature that is not extended tangentially.

To avoid intensive processing on Raspberry Pi, all the processing took place on a PC. To implement that the following changes were made:

1. Establishing camera streaming such that it could be accessed on a PC over the same network was done by creating an mjpg stream from Raspberry Pi.

    Duplicating JPEG frames into output plug-ins is done by an application based on command line streamer-mjpg. This software can be used in converting any JPEG stream on a network based on IP addressing to distinct candidate software that can receive streams in the MJPG format like Cambozola, Chrome, mplayer, VLC, and Firefox.

2. To be able to send commands to Raspberry Pi using a server.

Making a connection for communication with the help of two nodes can be done with the use of socket-based programming. To build an IP connection one vertex takes the input, whereas the other connects to a server. Client extends to the server for instigating a connection.

The Raspberry Pi was used as a server while the client program was run from another computer. The server sends the information regarding controls of the bot to the Arduino through serial communication, while the said data come enters the server.

```
s = socket. Socket (socket.AF INET, socket. SOCK STREAM)
```

An illustration of the node is built and is given two variables (Figure 24.9): a transmission control protocol (TCP) (SOCK STREAM) and ipv4 AF NET. Sockets can either be user data protocol (UDP), i.e., does not make connection, or TCP, i.e., form a connection. For this purpose TCP was preferred.

With the visibility of the lanes the bot tries to drive through the path taking turns as and when required. Whenever the right lane gets out of visibility the bot turns left and vice versa. To take a left turn the PC would send a left command to the server, which would further be relayed to the Arduino using serial communication. The Arduino receives the command and processes it using our previously made program (refer here). The same procedure is followed when taking a right turn.

1. Lane detection using Hough transform is difficult for curves.

2. At times, the lane may not be visible to the camera due to different inclinations of the path.

3. Lane detection using edges of walls and cliffs is difficult due to the uneven surface.

4. At times when there is a car approaching from the opposite direction the lane will not be visible.

5. The paths would be required to be cleared for any obstruction such that edges are clear enough to be distinguished as a lane.

If the lane is not visible to the camera due to a difference in inclination of path, a wide-angle camera can solve the issue. The vehicle can be equipped with actuators to control the facing angle of the camera such that it turns as per the inclination of the path. Through this the path ahead will be constantly visible and, hence, any obstruction can be detected using it.

24.4 IMPLEMENTATION DETAILS

The keypress control of the bot provided a base for the idea to use coordinates of the said path as references to autonomously drive the vehicle once all the points of the path are registered. The coordinates were proposed to be stored in CSV format, which was later accessed to compare with live coordinates detected by using AprilTags placed directly on the top side of the bot. A camera above the pit reads the AprilTags.

The AprilTags detect X-, Y-, and Z-coordinates of the bot along with the roll, yaw, and pitch of the position. While training the bot these coordinates are stored to CSV format on each keypress event along with the steering angle of the bot. AprilTag is a trustworthy system for calibrating the camera and reality based on augmentation and robotics. Exact three-dimensional (3D) location, identity, and direction of camera-related tags can be created with the help of this system.

Theoretically, AprilTags and QR codes are alike as both of them have a bar code in a two-dimensional (2D) format. Nevertheless, they can be detected from a long range as they were built for cyphering payloads of small lengths ranging from 4 to 12 bits. For this research, Tag36h11 is used (Figure 24.6).

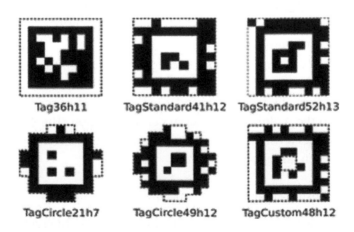

Tag36h11   TagStandard41h12   TagStandard52h13

TagCircle21h7   TagCircle49h12   TagCustom48h12

FIGURE 24.6   AprilTag family.

To calculate the parameters of AprilTags, the following parameters are used:

1. *HAMMING distance:* It is the amount of locations where two distinct symbols are present; thus, it is better to have a high ratio of such symbols. Recognition of distinct tags is a result of a high hamming distance. 36h11 is a family of tags containing a high hamming distance, hence, it is used more.

2. *Family size:* The 36h11 tag family has 586 tag members, thus incorporation of many bots with different IDs is possible in future implementations.

To capture and extract information from AprilTags, the camera needs to be calibrated to account for various distortions.

$$x_{corrected} = x\left(1+k_1 r^2 + k_2 r^4 + k_3 r^6\right)$$
$$y_{corrected} = y\left(1+k_1 r^2 + k_2 r^4 + k_3 r^6\right)$$

Spiral formation makes lines seem as though they are curved. Distortion increases with the increase in distance from the center point of an image. Radial distortion is when a lens that captures the images is not parallel to the plane of imaging, and a tangential formation occurs. It makes a few places appear nearer than presumed. Total distortion via tangents is as follows.

$$x_{corrected} = x + \left[2p_1 xy + p_2\left(r^2 + 2x^2\right)\right]$$
$$y_{corrected} = y + \left[p_1\left(r^2 + 2y^2\right) + 2p_2 xy\right]$$

Five coefficients of distortion are computed. Coefficients of distortion = (k3, p1, k1, p2, k2) and other information like variables of camera are needed. Framework specified to a camera are called intrinsic. Optical centers (cy,cx) and focal length (fy, fx) are intrinsic coefficients. Both of these parameters are used to make a matrix of the camera. The matrix of a camera is particular to each camera; hence, once deduced, it can be used on images captured with a specific camera. Matrix is denoted by a 3 × 3 grid.

The internal coefficient list:

- *Focal length:* This is collected in a 2 × 1 vector of pixels.

- *Principal point:* 2 × 1 vector *cc* is used to depict the coordinates of a main point.

- *Skew coefficient:* *c* is a scalar alpha, which contains an angle between the axis of the pixel in *x,y*.

- *Distortions:* 5 × 1 vector depicts coefficients of image framework.

$$\begin{bmatrix} fc(1) & alpha\_c * fc(1) & cc(1) \\ 0 & fc(2) & cc(2) \\ 0 & 0 & 1 \end{bmatrix}$$

Finding the location of a mobile robot is known as localization. To decide future actions, one of the important things for a bot is to have an idea of its location. To search the location, localization comes into play. Given an AprilTag inside a known (global) location, is it possible to use the relative location and orientation data to extract the bot's absolute global position and orientation.

Upon running the program, the following steps are replicated:

1. *Find tags:* Each tag containing AprilTags in the view of the field is recognized by the camera. To get localization data, it is important to have one tag in the robot's field of view.

2. *Store data:* Pitch, yaw, and roll for all tags that are recognizable are stored inside a structured CSV format when training is done, and the same data are used to drive the bot autonomously when run on test mode.

3. *Obtaining global-tag data for pose:* To acknowledge the localization cycle, the lookup table contains θ, z, y, and x, which are read via segment (Figure 24.7).

There is no requirement for libraries and tools in Flask, and it is a substructure in Python. It is void of a layer of abstraction or other libraries. A server was used to create a host server in which all data from the asset (bot) are collected and displayed for reference. The server can be accessed over the network; hence, its data can be used by any other application. We are using Flask to view the live asset data at our end. It has two components: a debugger and a server of development. Flask shows a unified foundation for testing units. Remits relaxed demands. For sessions for the client, it provides cookies.

FIGURE 24.7   Tag detection.

FIGURE 24.8   Sample Flask server interface.

It is based on one code, requires a great deal of authentication, and is compatible with Google apps (Figure 24.8).

The data from the asset (bot) are stored in a database that can be accessed through the Flask server. Postgre was generated in at the University of California Department of Computer Science. Many ideas were developed by Postgres, which is a database built on enterprise edition of class and can be installed and set up easily. Support for NoSQL and SQL is provided by Postgres. Any problems related to PostgreSQL can be solved with the help of a database system community:

1. A community that is developing fast.

2. Other software for SQL server, DB2, and Oracle.

3. Can work on any operating system.

4. Simultaneously helps users.

5. Provides great performance, indexing is increased.

6. Assists applications like JSON and XML.

7. Contribution of code and skill is given by ANSI SQL.

8. Stores data in a well-organized format, foreign keys are used.

9. Retrieves data, views and Table joins are used.

10. Backup of data is made for replicating and increasing scalability to read.

The bot comes with a few fallback conditions to avoid any major accidents at the pit. Some of the conditions are as follows.

1. The client and server communication are continuously monitored and if this communication breaks for 1 second, a stop signal is passed to the bot.

2. The bot is installed with an ultrasonic sensor on the front, and when it detects any object in front of it (at a range of 10 cm) the bot stops traveling and the user is informed of the object.

3. An ultrasonic sensor is also installed on the left side of the bot that continuously checks if the bot is too near the wall. If it comes too close to the wall, its front wheels turn 170° to the right side. The live coordinates of the bot then correct its path by comparing with the trained model.

The training and testing part is integrated on a GUI using the PyQT library. The PyQT is a library for a cross platform and contains toolkit for widgets and an interface for QT. It is a mix of libraries of QT and Python. This application, which is built on a GUI, is driven by an object rather than executed in sequence like other console-based applications. Events are executed when a user performs any task like mouse selection or clicking. To make an event successful, widgets are used in a building interface for users. To provide a signal response for events, a Qobject class widget is used. The signal does not carry out the operation alone, but a slot connection provides the output.

A GUI was made on PyQT and a brief walkthrough with its elements are mentioned next. The first window a user would get after opening the application is the boot screen. In the background, the app tries to connect with the server (Figure 24.9).

When a successful relationship between a server and a client is built, another screen pops up that tells the user to choose an AprilTag from a set of 36 tags. These tags represent bots, as tags are placed on them (Figure 24.10).

FIGURE 24.9 Boot animation.

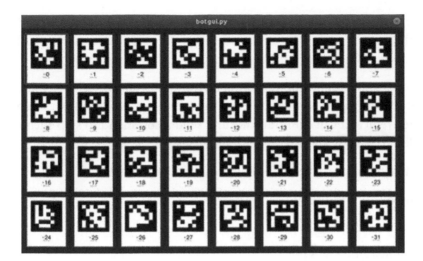

FIGURE 24.10   Menu.

After choosing the tag, the user will be directed to another window where a live feed from the top camera of the pit will be available along with a small picture-in-picture view from the bot's perspective. The window also has buttons to train or test the bot (Figure 24.11a).

Also, if the tag is not in view of the camera, a warning on the screen will be displayed regarding the same.

24.5 RESULTS

24.5.1 Discussion

There are multiple areas in which this model can be used to give better outputs and add more features:

1. The algorithm behind the steer angle prediction can be improved. Right now, it tries to imitate the closest path present on the trained data set. It compares the current coordinate with the stored coordinates in the data set and sets the steer angle accordingly. This can be improved by calculating the angle between the current coordinate and the next coordinate and set the steer angle such that it directs the car to that coordinate.

2. We can implement a better object detection algorithm using the Raspberry Pi camera present on the model.

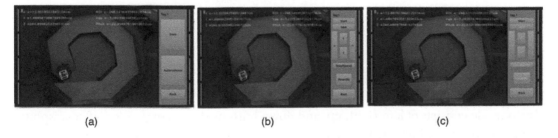

(a)   (b)   (c)

FIGURE 24.11   (a) Test or train mode, (b) train mode, and (c) autonomous mode.

3. The vehicle can be equipped with actuators to control the facing angle of the camera such that it turns as per the inclination of the path. Through this the path ahead will be constantly visible; hence, any obstruction can be detected using it.

4. Machine-to-machine communication can be implemented such that multiple vehicles can be moving in the same path using the same program. If a vehicle is approaching another vehicle it can communicate and send a command to stop such that another vehicle can pass by and later it continues its path.

5. More asset data are to be monitored and stored in a database, such as:

   a. Engine oil pressure:

      i. Unit: PSI

      ii. Low: <15–20 PSI

      iii. High: >80 PSI

   b. Low engine oil:

      i. Unit: L

      ii. Low: <25%

   c. Tire Pressure:

      i. Unit: PSI

      ii. ii. Avg: 55–80 PSI

   d. Thermal Sensor data

   e. Speed monitoring:

      i. Unit: km/hr

      ii. Limit: <25 km/hr

   f. Low battery level indication

   g. Engine vibration

   h. Lubricant oil level sensor

   i. Temperature sensor

24.5.2 Training

24.5.2.1 Train Mode

Train mode consists of left, right, up, and down buttons that change colors if corresponding keys are pressed on the keyboard. It also consists of a save button to register a successful run of the bot and append the data collected to the CSV format. The start button initiates training, whereas the stop button puts the bot in halt. The following are used to train the bot:

1. After installation, run the GUI.

2. The application will now connect to the server. From the tag selection menu, select the tag that is installed on the bot.

3. A new window appears; select the option "train" to navigate to the training window.

4. Make sure the bot is in position and then click on the start button.

5. The up arrow key moves the bot forward and the left arrow key turns the bot to left side by 20° each time the button is pressed. Similarly, the right button turns the bot to right side by 20° each time it is pressed.

6. After a successful run click the save button to store the pit coordinate data into the CSV file format. (This file will be utilized during the autonomous run.) The GUI has the option to record more than one "training Run."

7. When finished with the training, click "Reset" or the "r" button on keyboard to turn the wheels 90° and end the training session.

8. The user can return to another bot for training by navigating back to tag selection or end the session by clicking the close button at the top right corner of the window (Figure 24.11b).

24.5.2.2 Autonomous Mode

In this mode, the user can request the autonomous run of the bot. All other bot controls are disabled (highlighted in white; Figure 24.11c).

24.5.2.2.1 Training Model and Parameters   Place the camera above the pit so that the entire path of the pit is visible. Connect the camera to the user's PC and place the bot at the foot of the path, but make sure the tag of the bot is visible at all times. Run the server program and start the GUI (Figure 24.12).

Run the bot through the path of the pit as many times as is needed until it is trained. Run the GUI file and proceed with the manual for training as discussed earlier or, if already trained, proceed with the autonomous run.

FIGURE 24.12   Training process.

24.6 CONCLUSION

After a few iterations of models and diverse techniques, we were able to create a bot that was able to drive itself autonomously in an open pit. Hence, through this project we learned about many technologies included in a compact self-driving vehicle. We implemented wall follower and line follower initially and went for lane detection. As the challenges faced in those techniques outweighed the success of the objective, we implemented the localization technique through AprilTags and attempted to drive the bot autonomously based on the coordinates received from the position of the bot and training it to drive on those coordinates. Also incorporated were fallback conditions in the program for object detection and wall detection along with a fail-safe condition to stop the bot if the server or client did not respond for a certain period. A Python-based GUI was also created to make the entire process of training and testing the bot easier and user friendly. The sensor data and controls from Raspberry Pi were serially transmitted, and coordinates of the bot were successfully uploaded to a database and rendered using PostgreSQL and the Flask server.

REFERENCES

1. Zhang, J., 2019. End-to-End Learning for Autonomous Driving. PhD dissertation, New York University.
2. Udacity, Inc. 2019. Self-Driving Car Simulator. https://github.com/udacity/self-driving-car-sim. Accessed 5 Feb 2019.
3. Wang, Z., 2018. Self Driving RC Car. https://zhengludwig.wordpress.com/projects/self-driving-rc-car/. Accessed 22 Jan 2019.
4. Desai, S. and Desai, S., 2017. Smart vehicle automation. International Journal of Computer Science and Mobile Computing, 6(9).
5. Hussain, R. and Zeadally, S., 2018. Autonomous cars: research results, issues, and future challenges. IEEE Communications Surveys & Tutorials, 21(2), pp.1275–1313.
6. Rajasekhar, M.V. and Jaswal, A.K., 2015. Autonomous vehicles: the future of automobiles. In 2015 IEEE International Transportation Electrification Conference (ITEC) (pp. 1–6).
7. Rosenzweig, J. and Bartl, M., 2015. A review and analysis of literature on autonomous driving. E-Journal Making-of Innovation, pp. 1–57.
8. Bojarski, M., Del Testa, D., Dworakowski, D., Firner, B., Flepp, B., Goyal, P., Jackel, L.D., Monfort, M., Muller, U., Zhang, J. and Zhang, X., 2016. End to end learning for self-driving cars. arXiv preprint arXiv:1604.07316.
9. Jackel, L.D., Krotkov, E., Perschbacher, M., Pippine, J. and Sullivan, C., 2006. The DARPA LAGR program: Goals, challenges, methodology, and phase I results. Journal of Field Robotics, 23(11–12), pp. 945–973.
10. Lecun, Y., Cosatto, E., Ben, J., Muller, U. and Flepp, B., 2004. Dave: autonomous off-road vehicle control using end-to-end learning. Courant Institute/CBLL, DARPA-IPTO Final Report. http://www.cs.nyu.edu/yann/research/dave/index.html
11. Podpora, M., Korbas, G.P. and Kawala-Janik, A., 2014. YUV vs RGB-choosing a color space for human-machine interaction. FedCSIS Position Papers, 18, pp. 29–34.
12. Pan, Y., Cheng, C.A., Saigol, K., Lee, K., Yan, X., Theodorou, E. and Boots, B., 2017. Agile autonomous driving using end-to-end deep imitation learning. arXiv preprint arXiv:1709.07174.
13. Wang, Z., Lim, E.G., Wang, W., Leach, M. and Man, K.L., 2014. Design of an Arduino-based smart car. In 2014 International SoC Design Conference (ISOCC) (pp. 175–176).

14. Parashar, A., 2019. IoT based automated weather report generation and prediction using machine learning. In Proceedings of the 2019 2nd IEEE International Conference on Intelligent Communication and Computational Techniques (ICCT), Jaipur, India.

15. Parashar A., Parashar A. and Goyal S., 2018 Classifying Gait Data Using Different Machine Learning Techniques and Finding the Optimum Technique of Classification. In: Mishra D., Nayak M., and Joshi A. (eds) Information and Communication Technology for Sustainable Development. Lecture Notes in Networks and Systems, vol 10. Springer, Singapore. https://doi.org/10.1007/978-981-10-3920-1_31

16. National Institute for Occupational Safety and Health (NIOSH), 2018. NIOSH mine and mine worker charts. https://wwwn.cdc.gov/niosh-mining/MMWC#disasters. Accessed 17 July 2018.

17. Bartnitzki, T., 2017. Mining 4.0 – importance of industry 4.0 for the raw materials sector. Mining Report, 153(1), pp.25–31.

18. Yarkan, S., Guzelgoz, S., Arslan, H. and Murphy, R., 2009. Underground Mine Communications: A Survey. IEEE Communications Surveys & Tutorials, 11(3), pp.125–142.

19. Chung, T., 2018. DARPA subterranean challenge aims to revolutionize underground capabilities. https://www.darpa.mil/news-events/2017-12-21.

20. Ferguson, D., Morris, A., Hähnel, D., Baker, C., Omohundro, Z., Reverte, C., Thayer, S., Whittaker, C., Whittaker, W., Burgard, W. and Thrun, S., 2004. An autonomous robotic system for mapping abandoned mines. In proceedings in Advances in Neural Information Processing Systems (vol 16, pp. 587–594).

21. Zlot, R. and Bosse, M., 2014. Efficient Large-Scale 3d Mobile Mapping and Surface Reconstruction of an Underground Mine. In K. Yoshida and S. Tadokoro (eds) Field and Service Robotics, ser. Springer Tracts in Advanced Robotics, vol. 92, pp. 479–493. Springer, Berlin Heidelberg.

22. Grehl, S., Donner, M., Ferber, M., Dietze, A., Mischo, H. and Jung, B., 2015. Mining-rox – mobile robots in underground mining. In Third International Future Mining Conference AUSIMM, (pp. 57–64).

23. Murphy, R., Kravitz, J., Stover, S. and Shoureshi, R., 2009. Mobile robots in mine rescue and recovery. IEEE Robotics & Automation Magazine, 16(2), pp. 91–103.

24. Güth, F., Wolf, F., Grehl, S., Lösch, R., Varga, S., Rezaei, N., Mischo, H., Jung, B., Benndorf, J., Rehkopf, A. and Joseph, Y., 2018. Autonomous robots and the Internet of Things in underground mining. In Conference on Smart Systems Integration, Dresden, Germany (pp. 215–222).

25. Innok Robotics GmbH, 2015. Heros 444 FG – Handbuch. Innok Robotics GmbH, Tech. Rep., Münchsried, Germany.

26. Grehl, S., Sastuba, M., Donner, M., Ferber, M., Schreiter, F., Mischo, H. and Jung, B., Towards virtualization of underground mines using mobile robots – from 3D scans to virtual mines. In International Conference in Mine Planning & Equipment Selection.

27. Quigley, M., Conley, K., Gerkey, B., Faust, J., Foote, T., Leibs, J., Berger, E., Wheeler, R. and Mg, A., 2009. ROS: an open-source robot operating system. In Proceedings of the IEEE Intl. Conf. on Robotics and Automation (ICRA) Workshop on Open Source Robotics.

28. Koenig, N. and Howard, A., 2004. Design and use paradigms for gazebo, an open-source multi-robot simulator. 2004 IEEE/RSJ IROS, vol. 3, IEEE, pp. 2149–2154.

29. Labbe, M. and Michaud, F., 2014. Online global loop closure detection for large-scale multi-session graph-based SLAM. In Proceedings of the IEEE/RSJ International Conference on Intelligent Robots and Systems (pp. 2661–2666).

30. Labbe, M. and Michaud, F., 2013. Appearance-based loop closure detection for online large-scale and long-term operation. IEEE Transactions on Robotics, 29(3), pp. 734–745.

31. Rösmann, C., Hoffmann, F. and Bertram, T., 2015. Planning of multiple robot trajectories in distinctive topologies. In European Conference on Mobile Robots (ECMR) (pp. 1–6).

Index

Note: Locators in *italics* represent figures and **bold** indicate tables in the text.

W

Y